Maneuver and Battle in the Mexican Revolution

Maneuver and Battle in the Mexican Revolution

A Revolution in Military Affairs

JOE LEE JANSSENS

To my family—Diana, Stephanie, Ryan,
and those south of the border.

"The men who devote all their energies to public tranquility thus ensuring progress and, when necessary, who are the first willing to sacrifice their life on the altar of the Fatherland, who by an exemplary record, ... by a perennial sacrifice in honor of others (undeniable altruism), by a force that is not mercenary, and who...are honored with crosses or medals...for courage, study, perseverance, [and] merit, they form what is called nobility; and when merits are rewarded with promotions and ribbons, a braid, gold embroidery or a band, they bring an authority and constitute an honor that sanctions hierarchy; that group of men [made] noble by their own merit and hierarchically superior because of the totality of their duties form—do not be alarmed—an aristocracy of which a Republic can and should boast..."
—Federal General Joaquín Beltrán

"In the preparations for my march south I ran into the difficulties of a lack of funds. Wanting therefore to get commerce moving, since getting commerce going would decrease any obstacles, and seeing moreover how there were mines and individuals that couldn't do anything without currency for trade, I asked Sr. Carranza for ₱5 million in paper for banking operations. But as he could not send me them immediately, I took the measure of printing my own paper money in Chihuahua and in this way I had, going forward, all the centavos that I was needing."
—Constitutionalist General Francisco Villa

Contents

Figures, Maps, and Tables

Preface

This present volume picks up at the beginning of 1913 after the establishment of the Huertista government and continues with the same themes and theses introduced in the prior book, yet it speaks more fully to the concept of military economy. The idea that the revolutionary forces functioned somewhat like businesses do in a market economy came to me as an epiphany. While on a business trip I was reading about Constitutionalist General Francisco Murguía's campaign in northern Coahuila, and I came across the part of his report where he mentioned that his brigade had grown precipitously to over 2,000 men, largely as a result of some 500 ex-Federals defeated in a recent battle who chose to join his brigade, as well as through recruitment. Previously he had never commanded more that about 700 men, and I thought to myself, "his brigade reached the size of a division through acquisitions and organic growth—just like a business does!" After that I began considering all the ways in which the administration and organization of a revolutionary corps, as well as its operating environment, functioned similarly to a business in the marketplace. The parallels came one after another, and they were numerous. Even options theory can be applied to the threat and subsequent use of military force. Suddenly, it became clear why some historians had considered revolutionary generals to be more like businessmen than soldiers, although none had ever articulated the phenomenon in theory or detail.[1] I attempt to fill that lacuna in the historiography herein.

Not included in this book, out of consideration for space, will be a summary of the events that transpired from 1910 to the beginning of 1913 as covered in the first volume, *Maneuver and Battle in the Mexican Revolution: Rise of the Praetorians*. There will be, however, a brief recapitulation of the overthrow of Madero and the subsequent founding of the Constitutionalist movement at the close of the introduction.

As I mentioned in the preface to the first volume, no scholarly military history of the Mexican Revolution has before appeared in English, which is to say that there is no authority on the subject who can provide comment on the tomes that constitute this trilogy. Military historians are uncomfortable commenting about military traditions and a war of which they know nothing, while Latin Americanists contacted by the academic press that I was working with kept trying to force the narrative back into the prevailing historiography, which of course goes off into tangents unrelated to military history. Consequently, without a peer review, small errors of fact may have survived into the final text. So, in order to facilitate and stimulate future discourse, I am providing an email address that readers can use to report any mistakes; or to provide any new insights; to recommend any seminal primary history that I may have overlooked; or, most especially, to alert me to any previously undisclosed source documents (letters, maps, reports, etc.) that they may have in their personal possession that might contribute to a better understanding of the battles and campaigns covered in the text: info@mexicanrevolution.net.

Introduction

At the height of the Cold War military theoreticians began exploring the concept of revolutions in military affairs (RMA): innovations so profound that they permanently changed the very way in which practitioners conducted warfare. The Napoleonic Wars heralded just such a shift. After the devastation of the internecine Thirty Year's War, European powers decided that total war had become too destructive and needed to be limited. For much of the seventeenth and eighteenth centuries, professional armies commanded by noblemen leading soldiers who were "the scum of the earth" characterized conflicts in Europe. The Europeans conducted warfare according to a gentleman's code, shunned fighting battles after going into winter quarters, employed mercenaries, and for the most part tried to minimize the effects of war on civilians. That all changed with Napoleon, and total war returned on a scale never before seen.

Nations mobilized in numbers so great that armies began organizing in combined-arms divisions and corps, and officers' commissions, once the preserve of the nobility and gentry, opened up to the middle classes. Officers ceased buying commissions, receiving them as political patronage, or grudgingly accepting them out of noblesse oblige and genuinely began to embrace the profession of arms. Theoreticians of the art of war such as Clausewitz and Jomini did not just publish their works, but professors also read and lectured on their teachings to cadets, future officers. Once commissioned, they published articles for military journals. In short, officer corps popularized around the beginning of the nineteenth century and by its end they had begun a process of professionalization, not just in Europe but around the world.

To a certain extent the Federal Army kept up with this latter trend, especially with respect to the development of tactical doctrine, but at its core it remained an eighteenth-century-style army. The mass mobilization of 1913 and 1914, unequaled in Mexican history, entailed an RMA for the nation similar to that experienced in Europe a century earlier. It resulted in the annihilation of the Federal Army and with it a permanent change in military culture and the broader civilian society.[1]

The Eighteenth-Century Model

In spite of the many insecurities and inadequacies of the Federal officer corps mentioned in the first volume of this series, in its dealings with outsiders the corps projected a sense of exceptionalism and entitlement almost aristocratic, especially those members who had graduated from the Colegio Militar or ascended to the highest ranks after fighting in the liberal wars. Take, for example, Federal Colonel of Artillery Carlos Chávez, who after many years of retirement in Europe had been recalled to service to fight the Constitutionalists. Described by former Federal Lieutenant (and later newsman and author) Ignacio Muñoz as "tall, of good appearance, [and] brave," he was commissioned in 1914 to guard a section of railroad where he rode in a train of fifteen railcars with two armored gondolas and a caboose that carried his light artillery column. The colonel stayed in the caboose "with refinement to a certain point…And although it was not extraordinary in that Army, it did cause a great impression to see Colonel Chávez all dressed up, uniformed very finely, neat, gloved, showing off the Legion of Honor button on his chest and in the right hand a riding crop with a handle of chiseled gold." He was a gourmet of fine taste who would invite an officer or jefe from time to time to share his table "sprinkled with exquisite wines."[2]

Far from the exception,[3] we are given to understand that Colonel Chávez better represented the rule, and "like the greater part of jefes and officers of his time, belonged to a well-off family, having embraced the profession of arms as a true vocation." Federal Lieutenant Ignacio Muñoz added:

> Thus could be assembled, through several generations, a distinguished officer corps, among whom stand out in stark relief those gentlemen-soldiers who like Rafael Eguía Lis, Felipe Ángeles, Arnoldo Casso López, [José] Refugio Velasco, Rodolfo Casillas, Eduardo Ocaranza, Manuel Tamborrel, Miguel Rodríguez, José ["Gonzalitos"] Herón González, Luis Isunza, Gustavo Garmendia, Gustavo Bazán, Jacinto Treviño, Antonio Monter, Ramón Carmona, and Felipe Alvírez, could serve as an example of *pride and nobility* [emphasis added] in any army of the world.[4]

As elitists, the Federal officers were jealously dismissive of the upstart revolutionaries, whom they did not consider their equals on the battlefield. Colonel José Perdomo typified the hubris of ex-Federals, observing that Constitutionalist General Gabriel Gavira was "not the right one to judge military actions, for not knowing more [about] arms than those of a carpenter," a reference to Gavira's civilian occupation.[5]

Ex-Federals had absolutely no respect for the martial abilities of citizen-soldiers and considered their enterprising approach to campaigning crass, failing to grasp that Constitutionalist jefes placed much more emphasis on the first half of the "citizen-soldier" formula, viewing themselves as politicians and entrepreneurs first and foremost, and military officers second. Nor did the regulars recognize that, as generals without a government sponsor, revolutionaries often had to appropriate from the citizenry what the government freely provided to the Federals. One man's military appropriation is another's thievery, and the Federals soon developed a nickname for the *Constitucionalistas*: *Con-sus-uñas-listas* ("with their claws ready" to steal). This was the dark side of the Constitutionalist Army's ethic, and certainly open to abuse by those of questionable revolutionary scruples.

Yet, unlike the Federal officers, who perpetuated the myth of military exceptionalism and remained secure in their sinecures and shielded from competition by the government's monopoly of violence, Constitutionalists had to hustle to compete for the Three M's (money, men, and materiel). Smug Federal officers derogated "those 'caudillos' who later would make a lucrative profession with the famous 'cannon blast of fifty thousand pesos,'" referencing the aphorism often attributed to Obregón that no general could withstand a cannon blast of fifty thousand pesos, and extolled Federal Army officers who eschewed lucrative pursuits.[6] Similar sentiments prevailed among Europe's nobility, who contemptuously viewed the profit motive as crass and vulgar, and therefore such aristocratic-affecting snobbery in the Federal officer corps should be understood as a deliberate attempt on their part to emulate their British and Continental counterparts.

On the other hand, the men that they led, or rather, drove into combat for the most part represented the dregs of society, for which the army had become little more than an organ for clearing the streets of the republic of vagrants and criminals and sequestering political dissenters. Martinets in the extreme, Federal officers administered summary and frequent corporal, if not capital, punishment on their charges. Muñoz, again, speaks of an unfortunate Norteño corporal named Ignacio Garibay who had become exasperated with a sub-lieutenant, probably a proud eighteen-year old graduate of the Colegio Militar, and fired off a shot to scare the lad into his senses. Other soldiers backed Garibay, and Muñoz had to quickly re-establish order, snatching away Garibay's rifle and forcing the men to fall into formation and then leading them in drill. Thus, "discipline was imposed," Muñoz boasted. "Those [his] men, in the majority our enemies through profound conviction, since they had been consigned to the armed services because of their sympathy for the revolution (Victoriano Huerta always used that procedure to recruit men: those suspected of being revolutionaries were our soldiers), felt the whole weight of severe discipline established in a true army of the line." A few minutes later, after a kangaroo court-martial, Muñoz executed Garibay.[7] One would expect no less excess from an eighteenth-century Prussian officer, likewise used to a soldiery composed almost universally of recalcitrant malcontents. "Hence," in the words of one Constitutionalist, the Federal soldier "needed to feel the saber blow on the back to obey an order."[8]

Thus, on a sociological level the Federal Army very much resembled a European army from the eighteenth century. However, in terms of developing tactical and operational doctrine and logistical regulations (the reader is strongly encouraged to read Appendix A for details on Federal Army doctrine), the army had gone a long way toward joining the twentieth century, notwithstanding the aged officer corps left over from the Liberal-Conservative wars accustomed to decades of life in garrison who occupied the top of the army hierarchy. The latter proved good only for parades, did not keep up with technical training, placed a drag on the army's overall competence and readiness, and clashed with the younger cohort of officers. By the end of the Madero era the modernizing influences upon the officer corps had suffered a serious reversal: a coup by disloyal army officers emulated rather than rejected Madero's surprising endorsement of military activism and brought self-promotion and its attendant suspicions and favoritisms directly home to the Federal Army. In many ways the organization returned to its dysfunctional practices of the previous century, with important implications for the future phase of the conflict.

In the upcoming campaigns some of the most professional officers in the Federal Army who had remained loyal to Madero during the Citadel *cuartelazo* ("barracks coup") were sidelined from important commands, namely, generals Guillermo Rubio Navarrete, Agustín Sanginés, and Joaquín Beltrán. Moreover, there emerged a settling of scores that also had roots in the Citadel cuartelazo in the retaliation against certain groups, specifically the institutional death of the Colegio Militar and the Rural Police Corps. Along these same lines, the careerism (a preoccupation with the Three P's: position, promotion, and pension) manifest in an organization that should have been dominated by a vocational call to serve and a willingness to sacrifice for the greater whole would lead to egoism in the Federal Army that exacerbated suspicions around integrity, which in turn hindered freedom of action by generals in the field and adversely impacted operational effectiveness. Such dysfunction was to be expected. The fundamental problem with praetorian activity in a regular army is analogous to that imposed by guerrilla warfare upon larger society. Ultimately it results in a breakdown of the social and institutional contract that requires decades to repair, time that the Federals did not have.

Just as in Europe in the early nineteenth century, mass mobilization took place at such an accelerated pace that it quickly outran the Federal Army's ability to overcome its many deficiencies and adapt its eighteenth-century model to the new environment. In order to exponentially augment its number of effectives, the Federal Army had to step up recruiting, even subsuming former rebels who accepted amnesty wholesale. On April 1, General Huerta announced to the Congress the adhesion of 84 former insurgent leaders with 6,000 troops, mostly Colorados, to the Huerta government.[9] Next, Huerta transferred the Rural Police Corps from the Ministry of the Interior to War, re-designating them "Scout Corps." The Federals also relied on locally raised paramilitaries such as the Social Defense forces, and near the end of his regime Huerta resorted to the timeworn practice of granting commissions to individuals according to the number of men they could recruit and arm for a Guerrilla.[10] Thus, the skill level of the officer corps became greatly degraded with the avalanche of former rebels, paramilitaries, and novice irregulars being enrolled in the service. In short, in trying to equal the Constitutionalist Army in size, the Federal Army ceased to be regularized and became popularized, sacrificing its very identity in a bid for survival.

The precipitous increase in the scope, scale, and sophistication of operations and the resources mobilized, both human and otherwise, had profound effects in a very short time for both the Federal and Constitutionalist Armies. For the Federals, mass mobilization by a foe meant that it had to respond in kind, and in the act it became popularized, compromised its institutional identity, forfeited any claim to professional exceptionalism, and ultimately suffered defeat. With the defeat of a regular army by citizen-soldiers the nation was well on its way to realizing the end of militarism, a truly social revolution and the signature enduring accomplishment of the revolution. The result for the Constitutionalist Army, which came of age in a burgeoning military economy and then stepped into the place of the defeated Federal Army, was to produce a new kind of officer who evinced more of a business ethos than a warrior's code and complemented society's new anti-militarist convictions.

The Military Economy

The mass mobilization of civilians into conventional military units reaching division and even army corps strength in the North, as well as the Huertista government's continuously escalating response, perforce entailed a redirecting of economic activity and resources away from civilian pursuits and toward the war effort. The totality of the goods and services produced for consumption by armies comprised the "military economy," and on a macro level the fiscal and monetary policies and institutions that a government (or army, in the case of the revolutionaries) adopted to manage and allocate scarce military resources in the prosecution of warfare occurred at the highest level of grand strategy.

For any peacetime army the government simply allocates to the military, but in wartime the army can often look to outside sources of revenues or resources. Sometimes this is done out of logistical expediency, as in the case of foraging, to attenuate the army's overreliance on lengthening and fragile lines of communications. Alternatively, in foreign territory an army may resort to foraging as an act of economic warfare, advancing like a proverbial army of locusts to consume and grow fat on an enemy's resource base and simultaneously deny nourishment to the opposing army. In the Mexican Revolution, where armies had arisen to overthrow the prevailing government and where the establishment of civilian rule anew had been impracticable, they began to reach out into the broader economy for sustenance, taking over customhouses and arrogating other taxation rights in the territory under their control, levying loans on local businesses and wealthy individuals (especially those opposed to the revolution), and confiscating, or rather "intervening" (a term that in revolutionary parlance means to take over and utilize for economic benefit) gambling houses, haciendas, or other businesses in order to operate them for a profit that could be plowed back into the war effort. Logistical needs also forced armies occasionally to commandeer public transportation, most significantly the nation's railroad system. The mobilization of finance, troops, and supplies all belonged to the realm of logistics, but by militarizing the macro-economy as essentially a measure of military economy, or expediency, armies teetered on the edge of economic militarism.

More important for the transformation of society in general and the future of the national defense establishment in particular was the transformation taking place within the major units that would become the Constitutionalist Army, that is, on a micro-economic level where the military functioned much like a business. The operations group concerned itself with destroying the competition in order to dominate the market and increase net worth, in this case by taking booty and prisoners in battle—what Clausewitz called "trophies," supported by functions such as human resources, which included recruitment, promotion, and retention; accounting; purchasing; and payroll.[11] Within the highly competitive market for volunteers, revolutionary leaders had to ensure that their men received pay in a timely fashion at a salary that was comparable to that offered in the broader economy for similar skill levels and offer opportunities for advancement. Jefes hired, fired, promoted, assigned, disciplined, and reassigned subordinates as the situation required. Major unit commands also had financial agencies that secured income, managed finances, and procured supplies to support operations by actively managing those supply chains to acquire quality goods in a timely fashion at the best price available.

BARRIERS TO ENTRY

The Constitutionalists, however, had many obstacles to overcome in order to compete against the Federal Army in this developing environment. Most governments grant a monopoly to the national army to operate in the military economy, and the main goal of the Federal Army officers who overthrew President Madero was to restore peace and destroy the numerous rebels operating throughout the nation, in other words, to reassert that monopoly. In the process of initiating a revolution the Constitutionalists had to confront this legal monopoly and all the attendant barriers to entry, such as geography, access to technical knowledge, and capital. Few monopolies function perfectly, however, and in the case of Mexico, the Rural Police or "Rurales" constituted potential competition for the Mexican Army.[12] In addition to this organization, auxiliary forces (militia) answerable to state governors also limited the Federal Army's monopoly. At the beginning of 1913, the states of Coahuila, Chihuahua, and Sonora had developed the strongest state auxiliaries.

In Sonora, Álvaro Obregón rose to military prominence leading his 4th Irregular Battalion against the Orozquistas in 1912, while Francisco "Pancho" Villa rose to the rank of brevet general serving as a commander, frequently in the vanguard, for General Victoriano Huerta's Division of the North in the campaign from Torreón to Chihuahua. Finally, Pablo González organized his "Auxiliares de Monclova" Corps to fight the Orozquistas in Coahuila, Durango, and Chihuahua. These three commanders would become the greatest army commanders of the war, enjoying a "first mover" advantage in the military economy as well as a tremendous amount of luck—also beneficial to any enterprise. When General Huerta orchestrated his coup d'état, auxiliaries from the states of Sonora, Chihuahua, Coahuila, Durango, and to a lesser extent San Luis Potosí and Zacatecas, along with those Rural Corps with Maderista sympathies, such as Cándido Aguilar's 38th and Orestes

Pereyra's 22nd Rural Corps, formed the core of what would become the Constitutionalist Army.[13] As counterweights to the Federal Army acting in an unconstitutional manner, these paramilitary forces served their purpose by mounting an armed opposition.

Technological

Although many of these units had fought alongside the Federals against Pascual Orozco and had learned the rudiments of campaigning, they still lacked access to technological know-how. The easiest way to overcome this obstacle entailed enlisting those army officers who possessed that knowledge, posing a ticklish proposition for revolutionaries scrupulous to recruit only those officers ideologically suitable to fight for the cause.

The most immediate gap in experience lay in generalship, since at the beginning of the war the sole general to join the Constitutionalists was General Cándido Aguilar, although Villa later accepted Carranza's suzerainty.[14] To acquire more leaders, the First Chief of the Constitutionalist Army, Venustiano Carranza, sought to raid talent from the opposition by sending out a call to all Federal Army officers, with some notable exclusions, to join his army and retain their rank. But despite the broader invitation, the Juarista Carranza displayed a particular predilection for those generals who had participated in the wars of the Reforma, such as Jerónimo Treviño and José María Mier, neither of whom assented to join the revolution, rather than the company men who had achieved prominence under the dictator Porfirio Díaz. Later, when Villa asked for permission to admit captured Federal artillerymen to his ranks, Carranza allowed him to hire all line officers (captains and lieutenants) and enlisted men, but required approval from his office to admit field grade and general officers, that is, middle and senior management. Villa saw Carranza's requirement for permission as a maneuver to ingratiate the Federals of higher rank to Carranza in the competition for senior talent, but that was not the case.[15]

The military marketplace prized artillerymen and their officers most for their technical expertise, since artillery acted as a force multiplier, earning the nickname "king of the battlefield" for its ability (theoretically, although in the Mexican Revolution not so much) to produce a disproportionate number of casualties in battle. Besides the famous artillerist, Felipe Ángeles, Pancho Villa accepted the offers of service and tutelage from others such as Vito Alessio Robles (Engineers), who came over to the cause rather late in April, 1914, and he made sure to fully exploit their talents rather than employ them in the line as infantry or cavalry. At this time Carranza also sent to Villa an aviator and artillerist by the name of Federico Cervantes who had been recruited by Ángeles and later penned biographies of both Villa and Ángeles.[16] Constitutionalist leaders also acquired artillerymen while campaigning, such as when Villa accepted the services of twelve artillerymen captured after the battle of San Andrés. By the time the Constitutionalists entered Torreón in April, 1914, Villa had captured and admitted to his ranks so many ex-Federal officers and their guns that his artillery force made the populace marvel.[17]

The military economy respected infantry skills least, placing them behind the cavalry in importance. Indeed, Ivor Thord-Gray, who trained cavalry officers for Obregón's army corps, confirmed that those unable to cope with the rigors of training to become a cavalry officer petitioned for a transfer to the infantry, which they usually received with an increase in rank as an enticement to get others to step down to a branch with less prestige.[18] Beyond the combat arms, all armies placed a high value on the knowledge of railroads, medical training, telegraphs, and engineering.

In sum, a hierarchy of expertise emerged in the military economy that prized Federal Army officers from the Reforma period over those of the Porfiriato, line officers over field and general grade (unless convincingly revolutionary in sentiment), and artillery and then cavalry over infantry officers.

Legal

To be able to operate in the military economy required access to markets that produced the supplies necessary for waging war, namely weapons and ammunition, which presented legal and logistical hurdles. In the case of the war against Huerta, President Woodrow Wilson did not lift the arms embargo against the Constitutionalists until the beginning of February 1914, almost a full year after the movement had begun, and even then he only abrogated it for a few months.[19] Under such circumstances the Constitutionalists had to resort to hardscrabble measures, such as using industrial workshops to construct cannons or repair those taken from the Federals.[20] More commonly, they used agents to acquire war materiel in the United States and then illegally introduced it into Mexico.

Geographic

By far, possession of towns on the border with the United States offered the best prospect of being able to source arms and ammunition. At the beginning of the war against the Huertistas, the Carrancistas in Coahuila worked hard to extricate the Federals from Piedras Negras, which Carranza achieved by convincing the zone commander, Federal General Mier, to concentrate all his troops in Monterrey. Piedras Negras afforded access to the international arms market, and the conquest of other border towns soon followed.[21] Throughout

1913 and even into 1915, Constitutionalist logistics officers endeavored to acquire more of the .30-30 cartridges used by illegally-obtained and American-made carbines than the 7-mm. rounds for Mausers manufactured overseas, demonstrating the importance of the United States arms markets.[22]

For those revolutionaries operating in states without access to the United States border, geography posed the greatest obstacle to success for two reasons. First, while the Surianos could acquire arms locally by taking them from among the populace, from the police station, from commercial enterprises that might have them on hand to provide for their private security, and, of course, from the Federals, those were not regular and continuous sources of war materiel.[23] Therefore, the scale and sophistication of military activity tended to decrease with distance from the border. Second, and perhaps more importantly, access to foreign markets for the sale of commodities in exchange for hard currency presented another crucial limitation on revolutionary activity imposed by distance. The Norteños experienced little problem selling the precious metals, cotton, cattle, and other goods to the Americans, and later securing debt financing in return for hard currency with which to purchase war materiel. Without access to foreign markets to sell their commodities, the southern states could not hope to raise the capital needed to buy arms even if American foreign policy had permitted, which brings up perhaps the biggest obstacle to any enterprise, access to capital.

Capital

Capital assets in the military economy consisted of artillery pieces, naval ships, airplanes, machine guns, horses and tack, rolling stock, communication gear, and other war materiel. The Rurales, Guerrillas, and state auxiliaries that formed the base of the Constitutionalist Army had carbines, side arms, and machine guns, but not in sufficient numbers, and they obviously lacked the more capital intensive assets among those listed. Getting them required finance capital. Fortunately for the revolutionary cause, the Constitutionalists started out in control of the Coahuila state government, giving them initial funds to start the revolution: ₱48,000 in cash, plus ₱75,000 of the ₱300,000 in loans that the state government authorized Carranza to borrow by decree number 1487 dated February 18, 1913.[24] Villa also received funds to initiate campaigning through the funding of the states of Sonora and Chihuahua; Governor José María Maytorena of Sonora provided Villa with ₱1,000, while Aureliano González, emissary of Chihuahuan Governor Abraham González, gave Villa another ₱1,500. With these funds Villa crossed over into Mexico to begin campaigning.[25]

But for sustained access to financial capital, revolutionary generals had to secure territory in order to gain a tax base and project the power and prospects for success necessary to guarantee currency issued in their name, in other words to implement fiscal and monetary policy. For those groups unable to control territory, trains offered the easiest target for funds because of their mobility, random defenses, and potential value. The Cedillo brothers—Magdeleno, Cleofas, and Saturnino—started out robbing trains and taking some of the money north of the border to buy arms. The first feat of arms of the soon-to-be Constitutionalist Army took place on February 23, 1913, when Carranza ordered Jacinto B. Treviño and Miguel M. Acosta to halt a passenger train on its way to Saltillo and return it to Ramos Arizpe for service in the new army. Ransoming prisoners, a method of raising capital dating back to antiquity, also provided a convenient source of funds early on. Other mobilizations of men with "limited resources at their disposal, were realized on the ground in mixed groups of infantry and cavalry, taking ammunition from the enemy... through formal actions, surprise and ambushes, and those other resources that their audacity and courage advised them," in the words of General Juan Barragán.[26]

GROWTH MODELS

Capital for entry into the military economy took two essential forms, human and financial, both necessary for developing and maintaining armies and equipping them. In the race to command the market for manpower, revolutionary armies could develop several growth strategies. They could opt to grow organically, often a slow method, but one that indicates a popular proposal (or in this case "Plan") for political change when accompanied by robust growth. In 1913 anti-militarism, in general, and anti-praetorianism, in particular, enjoyed wide-spread appeal. Secondly, an army could expand through acquisitions, assimilating large, relatively intact units from the opposing forces. Conversely, leadership may sometimes acquire minor competition in order to idle it and remove it from the marketplace where it might constitute a nuisance rather than a viable threat. At other times, a market participant might negotiate an alliance, temporary or enduring, with potential competitors. Finally, in the event of being unable to overcome a numerical weakness a participant might seek to develop a competitive advantage.

Organic

All initial growth in a revolution must be organic, that is from the bottom up. Many of the various armies that fought in the Constitutionalist revolution, as already demonstrated in the first volume, started out as grassroots efforts, be it as liberal clubs in the North, or in the South according to a tradition of banditry and guerrilla warfare. One difference had been Sonora, which because of its distinct traditions mobilized as a semi-professional army paid for by the national government during the Orozquista Rebellion. In 1913 the Sonoran battalions would provide the most formidable contingent of what would later become the Constitutionalist Army, scoring early victories and securing key border cities. In the process, it would give time for Pancho Villa to mobilize the military colonies of Chihuahua into a fighting force that, joined to those from Durango and the Laguna region, would eclipse in strength and prestige the Sonorans, becoming the first Constitutionalist division to defeat an opposing Federal Army division in the field of combat. The success of Villa's Division of the North on the battlefield extended the territory under its control, enlarged its recruiting base, and gained new adherents, just as successful enterprises attract human capital in non-military endeavors.

Mergers, Acquisitions, and Alliances

Acquisitions via prisoners taken in battle who chose to switch allegiances provided the fastest and easiest avenue for growth. Against Huerta all the revolutionaries had recourse to this strategy in order to gain professional soldiers with technical skills valued in the military economy, although in this regard some revolutionaries proved more discriminating than others. After organic growth and acquisitions, mergers provided the best prospects for swelling one's army and influence quickly, but at the beginning of 1913 no revolutionaries had recourse to this option. However, the government did, effectively folding existing Colorado and other rebel bands still under arms into the Federal Army. Finally, a leadership could form alliances, with the most famous being that which existed between the Yaquis and Mayos and the Sonoran leadership.

Competitive Advantage

As a final strategy in the maximization of human capital, leaders sought to leverage troop strength. They did this mainly through technology and force composition. Achieving the correct mix of combat arms for a given campaign or battle could give a general a competitive advantage. In theory, artillery functioned best as a force multiplier through which a few men with superior technology inflicted asymmetrical casualties upon their enemies. On an operational level, however, cavalry had a mobility that enabled it to engage in multiple locations on the field over a relatively short time frame, acting like a force multiplier vis-à-vis infantry in certain instances. On the other hand, the additional cost of horses, tack, and requisite training far exceeded that of the infantryman's accoutrement and skills. The Constitutionalists tried most often to recruit cowboys, who already knew the rudiments of horseback riding, and trained them hurriedly in garrison or even on the road if necessary. Still, cavalry remained a fairly specialized combat arm that did not suffice in those instances demanding the use of infantry: cavalry that fought dismounted experienced an immediate reduction in firepower on the tactical level because one in four men, per Federal Army regulations, or one in six men, according to "the old custom" observed by the Villistas, had to be assigned to hold the horses.[27] Employing highly skilled cavalry officers and troopers on a firing line amounted to nothing less than a gross misallocation of military resources. In order to maximize one's effectiveness in the military economy, practitioners had to observe proper military economy, here defined as the allocation of scarce military resources.

The Constitutionalist Ethic and Popular Militarism

Operating in the military economy of the Mexican Revolution, citizen-soldiers who brought skills obtained in their civilian careers to the enterprise of initiating, organizing, and leading an armed movement in the field of combat inevitably cultivated an entrepreneurial approach to the business of revolution. Constitutionalist officers who raised battalions and corps sought to maximize the Three M's—men, money, and materiel—under their control and often competed, not always ethically, among their fellow officers for command of these resources. Given the cutthroat nature of the competition, revolutionary commanders, like many Mexican *empresarios*, employed the services of family, either blood relations or kinship achieved through *compadrazgo*, in the most important positions, including key commands and anything related to the custody of assets. In time, the Constitutionalist movement evolved into what became known among some political scientists as the Revolutionary Family. The Federal Army, on the other hand, also had a family feel since many in the officer corps had relatives in the service, but it was a culture based more on a false sense of exceptionalism than a results-oriented meritocracy built on performance and accomplishment.

Quite unlike the supposed elect of the regular army's officer corps, the Constitutionalist generals who replaced the old Federals championed a business-like ethic that recognized only those winners affirmed in the marketplace of violence. Within the context of a revolution in military affairs and the social revolution against militarism that, on the one hand removed the long-held hubris and mystique of exceptionalism perpetuated by army generals and, on the other hand replaced those generals with egalitarian citizen-soldiers, one can cease speaking of "rebels" (as we did in the first volume) and begin referring to "revolutionaries." A transition had begun taking place in 1913 within the Constitutionalist military establishment that jettisoned the eighteenth-century model. Broader society, mobilized to the extent that service in the field became common and ordinary, rejected militarist pretensions to a moral and cultural superiority so promiscuously professed by the academy-trained "sons of the Colegio"—claims that proved as ethereal as their knowledge of the military arts was superficial (See the book written by General Paz of the General Staff, *A Donde Debemos Llegar*, which laments the lack of technical knowledge within the officer corps). Notwithstanding the Federal Army's inability to stand up to the high standards that it professed, and to which it aspired, in the minds of many, citizen-soldiers fighting "a la Mexicana" had drubbed the Federals' "European" army, steeped in "Prussian" behavior and tactics. As Federal General Gustavo Salas allegedly remarked: "*Nosotros, los federales, combatíamos a los constitucionalistas a la prusiana y ellos nos destrozaban a la mexicana.*"[28] Not coincidentally, such observations, once internalized by the masses, contributed greatly to the celebrated renewal, if not discovery, of pride in *la Mexicanidad* growing out of the revolution.

Unfortunately for the Constitutionalist cause, after the cashiering of the Federal Army a new popular militarism began to emerge among the Villista faction that would ultimately result in schism. Yet even as the victors fractured into disparate factions toward the end of 1914, personalities and battlefield/campaign disagreements in many cases continued to be much more significant than political ideology in the realignment of forces for a revolution more social than political.

Themes and Theses

The *Maneuver and Battle in the Mexican Revolution* trilogy poses two over-arching theses: first, that the revolution was not a "small war," but rather the largest war of maneuver ever to occur on the North American continent apart from the U.S. Civil War; and second, that its great success was not political in nature, but rather social—a debunking of the myth of military exceptionalism and with it the end of militarism.[29] A corollary to the latter thesis maintains that ideology, per se, was not an important factor. Rather, combat and operational frictions played a greater role in determining future political allegiances and alliances.

The three main themes: the Defense Establishment; Anti-Americanism; and the Scope, Scale, and Sophistication of military operations grow out of the two theses. In order to eliminate militarism a change had to occur both within the defense establishment as well as in society at large; the progress of that transition needs to be charted and understood. Additionally, the popular misperception of the revolution as a guerrilla affair, borne of a malign neglect arising from a disgust for all things military shared by the academics who dominate the historiography, is rectified by simply narrating the scope, scale, and sophistication of operations so that the revolution's qualities as a war of maneuver executed at the highest levels of grand strategy can be appreciated. Finally, since Marxist historians, confronted with the impossibility of empirically applying Marx's paradigm, had to "pivot" to an exaggerated critique of American imperialism, their anti-American narrative begs to be debunked.[30] Placing the United States of America's involvement in the revolutionary process into proper context and exposing the fabricated pillars of the left's argument goes a long way toward rectifying the historiography.

THE DEFENSE ESTABLISHMENT

In this present volume, which begins shortly after the overthrow and murders of President Francisco Madero and his vice president, José María Pino Suárez, by Federal Army officers, Venustiano Carranza establishes a revolutionary movement based on the twin goals of anti-militarism and the re-establishment of constitutional law. Simple and little-objectionable, these goals altered the character of the conflict from political (anti-reelectionism) to social (anti-militarism). Appealing to the nation's outrage over the praetorian behavior by some in the Federal Army, Carranza soon gathered a widespread following that led to a mass mobilization of citizen-soldiers never seen before or since in Mexico's history.

The crush of citizens joining the Constitutionalist Army had a similar impact on the Federal Army as it did in Europe at the end of the eighteenth century, when the French levée en masse overwhelmed the professional armies of neighboring countries and forced them to adapt to the new normal ushered in by this latest revolution in military affairs. The Federal Army's eighteenth-century model, based on a noble-affecting officer corps, non-commissioned officer disciplinarians, rank-and-file cannon fodder, and the use of mercenaries (Colorados), could not hope to match the numbers, motivation, initiative, and skill of revolutionaries flocking to the Constitutionalist standards. Trying to keep pace with the growing scale of the war led to the admission of more unqualified men into Federal service that only further debased an already depraved system. Increasingly the Federals had to rely on irregulars who, in the best of cases, provided service of incalculable value by bridging the baneful skills gap among the regulars, and in the worst of circumstances, provided a ready and convenient scapegoat.

In-fighting and allegations of treachery, some real but mostly imag-
ined, by and among Federal generals increased as the war progressed, mostly springing from battlefield losses. Such suspicions and hard feelings had
knock-on effects for operational effectiveness, such as General Rubio's recall
from Monterrey and removal from the Matamoros operation and the refusal
to further reinforce Olea at Zacatecas, among others.

Constitutionalists also experienced in-fighting, most notably with
Blanco in Tamaulipas, but in general they remained more open to cooperation and, in some instances even negotiated with each other to
achieve military goals, a phenomenon reflective of their civilian anteced-
ents in business and a culture of less than "regular" discipline. Whereas
Federal officers jockeyed within the Ministry of War to maximize the
"Three Ps" (position, promotion, and pension), Constitutionalist officers
haggled and maneuvered for control over the "Three Ms"—money, men,
and materiel—an indication of their entrepreneurial worldview. In the
Constitutionalist Army, an officer's advancement depended on his ability to recruit men and lead them to victory on the battlefield. Theirs was
a performance-based meritocracy that shunned the career-making professional markers and pedigree rampant in the Federal Army, which in
no small measure resulted in prejudices and rancor between individual
officers.

The Federal Army model could never keep pace with the revolutionaries who mobilized according to regional defense models that have been, and
will be, introduced over the course of the first two volumes of this trilogy:
mestizo-led Indians in Sonora, Suriano guerrillas, the military colonies of
Chihuahua, and agro-industrial elites mobilizing itinerant Laguneros.

AMERICAN INTERVENTIONISM

As the Federal Army marched from defeat to defeat, bickering, division, and
accusations of disloyalty among its officers were but one manifestation of
a general malaise within the organization. Unable to successfully prosecute
warfare in an environment radically changed by the revolution in military
affairs attendant to mass mobilization, Federal Army officers defeated in the
field gave vent to their feelings of the frustration and impotence by conjuring
up all manner of American plots and schemes. Some of the more outlandish
and unsubstantiated claims of U.S. interventionism are that the Americans
trained Constitutionalists aboard U.S. battleships, supplied Obregón with
the intelligence that resulted in his battle plan at Santa María, ferried war materiel to Constitutionalists at Empalme, manned guns for Constitutionalists

at Tampico and Tierra Blanca, and purchased Ciudad Juárez for Villa and then "supplied" him with arms and ammunition.

Sensationalist reporting of secession and filibustering found a receptive audience in an environment of actual heightened American interventionism under President Woodrow Wilson's administration. Wilson applied diplomatic pressure and selective arms embargos against both the revolutionaries and Huerta's government to achieve his ends, ultimately ordering an invasion of the port of Veracruz in April 1914 in order to block a large shipment of arms from reaching the Federal Army. The eighteen months from February 1913 to September 1914 marked the most interventionist period of United States foreign policy during the years of maneuver warfare in the Mexican Revolution and resulted in Huertistas painting the Constitutionalist Army as the cat's paw of Yankee imperialism in an effort to take down the government, facilitate an invasion of the Fatherland, and force concessions from the new revolutionary administration. The Federals continued to make ridiculous claims about the United States aiding the Constitutionalists on a tactical level, but by far the biggest influence that the United States wielded in the outcome of the conflict was on a strategic and operational level.

The threat of invasion in the Northeast had real implications for Federal operational decisions in that theater. The General Staff had always known that a full-scale invasion by the United States would follow the strategy of 1846 and therefore its priorities and distribution of forces (explained later in detail) in Coahuila, Nuevo León, and Tamaulipas reflected this reality.

To the Federal Army's benefit, however, by refusing to recognize the Constitutionalist Army as belligerents and maintaining an arms embargo against the revolutionaries, Washington gave the Federals much-needed time to mobilize, an action that probably resulted in increased casualties by drawing out the war. Not surprisingly, within two months of lifting the arms embargo on February 3, 1914, the Constitutionalist Army Corps of the Northwest and Northeast and Division of the North went fully operational. The arms embargo had bought the Federal Army almost a full year before mass mobilization of the revolutionaries could take place. Six months later, on August 13, 1914, the Federal Army and its eighteenth century model ceased to exist in Mexico, exorcising the demons of Santa Anna and those like him.

The invasion of Veracruz on April 21, 1914, which marked the zenith of American interference in the Revolution, was a colossal blunder in diplomacy that had absolutely no effect on the ultimate outcome of the revolution. After the fall of Huerta, the Americans sought to extricate themselves from the port city in the most responsible manner, and by 1915 U.S. foreign policy toward Mexico had softened to its least interventionist level in the entire course of the revolution as President Wilson waited to see which faction might prevail and restore law and order to the country.

SCOPE, SCALE, SOPHISTICATION OF MILITARY OPERATIONS

During the combat of 1913 to 1914, the scale of military operations continued increasing to entail full army corps executing campaigns of an expanded scope that included states in the East, West, and Center, right up to the doorstep of Mexico City. The ability for major units to range far and wide in significant numbers required a new level of logistical sophistication in the provision of food, fuel, and medical services, among others, and it provided the Federal Army with the opportunity to put its general staff expertise and doctrines into use. With so many new recruits conscripted by the Federal Army, however, and given its atavistic practices and organization model, it proved incapable of educating its soldiers in the highly advanced ternary system that formed the core of its tactical doctrine. Moreover, frequently forced to fight on the defensive, Federal Army commanders often employed the same defective tactics over and over again. Yet they were not alone. In many cases, the Constitutionalists also demonstrated a flawed or pedestrian conception of tactics, with Obregón's troops being the exception. His men evidenced both sound tactics and knowledge of the ternary system.

Early in the campaigning of 1913, Colonel Álvaro Obregón demonstrated a level of operational sophistication by gathering all the state militia in Hermosillo, in the center of state, which subsequently permitted him to exploit interior lines to defeat the Federals in the north first, and then later those in the south. The Federals campaigning in the Northwest also demonstrated a certain degree of sophistication in carrying off an amphibious pincer operation in Sinaloa, albeit on a small scale. In no other theater did a Constitutionalist commander have to factor operations by the Federal Navy into their campaign plans to the extent that Obregón did. To deal with the numerous ports supported by the Federal Navy along his axis of advance, Obregón developed a policy of "island hopping," rendering those forces of the Federal Division of the Yaqui bottled up in Guaymas and Mazatlán sterile.

The most operationally complex theater of 1913 to 1914, however, was in the Northeast, where Pablo González's Constitutionalist Army Corps of the Northeast had to contend with numerous axes of advance, modes of transportation, and an extensive expanse of territory. Villa campaigned in the most simplistic area of operations, essentially along a single axis running from Ciudad Juárez to Chihuahua City and down south to Torreón. Nevertheless, as Villa was battling the Division of the Nazas during the Battle of Fourth Torreón, he had to take measures to deal with a relieving force consisting of at least three columns of troops belonging to the Federal Division of the North and Division of the Bravo, among others. By sending a blocking force to San Pedro in order to give him the space to finish off Torreón, he emerged victorious and, after the Battle of Paredón, precipitated the Federal evacuation of the Northeast.

In spite of the increasing scope and scale of operations, the Federal Army never did formulate or implement a sophisticated or coherent strategy, especially as regards solving the problem of payroll for divisions in the field, mainly because of its model. The General Staff apparently regarded finances as something outside its scope, and the nature of its enlisted component (composed mainly of criminals, political dissenters, and vagrants) did not make abandoning population centers or major arteries advisable. Alternatively, the Constitutionalists under Venustiano Carranza did evidence certain sophistication in the formulation of national strategy involving inter-theater cooperation and in economic policy.

MILITARY ECONOMY

The concept of military economy, as pertains to the acquisition, management, allocation, and control of scarce military resources, and *the* military economy, meaning the marketplace of goods and services produced for and consumed by the military, does not represent a fourth theme, but rather cuts across all three themes: the Scope, Scale, and Sophistication of military operations; the Defense Establishment; and American Interventionism.

As a marketplace, access to the military economy was subject to a governmental and international monopoly granted to the Federal Army. In order for the new Constitutionalist Army to gain entry to the marketplace it had overcome many barriers to entry, not the least of which was this legal one. Many nations officially recognized Huerta's government, and although the United States was not among them, it refused to grant belligerent status to the revolutionaries, and subjected them to an arms embargo. Additionally, American business impacted another hurdle for the Constitutionalists: access to capital. As Constitutionalists "intervened" the haciendas, mills, and other operations belonging to enemies of the revolution, Americans who purchased much of the products had a legitimate responsibility to investigate the provenance of such goods, which Huertistas considered to be stolen. In some instances the Americans scrupulously demanded proof of ownership, for example, when Villa tried to sell cotton taken from Spaniards, and in other cases Federal Army officers complained that Americans simply ignored such details.

Geography posed another crucial barrier to entry for the Constitutionalists. The revolutionaries needed to possess border town entrepôts and seaports, not just to facilitate the entry of war materiel but also to gain access to customs receipts, and in some cases to take control of lucrative vice industries that thrived along the border and provided capital. This geographical limitation may have been the most important since revolutionary intensity of operations decreased exponentially the farther one traveled south, with the Zapatistas having virtually no access to markets in which to sell their goods or purchase war materiel. Military operations designed to acquire crucial towns along the U.S. border initially directed the scope of operations toward these points as Álvaro Obregón marched northward from Hermosillo to the border and Lucio Blanco extended the revolution into Tamaulipas to attack Matamoros. As the revolution progressed, the scope of military operations extended farther southward and brought more territory and diverse assets under the control of the Constitutionalists. The scope of resources expanded from what could be obtained from robbing trains and intervening local haciendas and mills to sell cattle and wheat for arms, to the lucrative garbanzo harvest of the Yaqui Valley, the cotton fields of La Laguna, the petroleum infrastructure and vainillales of the Huasteca, and the henequen plantations of the Yucatán.

Finally, the need to overcome technical barriers to entry had a direct impact upon the new Constitutionalist defense establishment. Francisco Villa placed quite a bit of faith in artillery, and so he had a policy of actively recruiting those ex-Federals who had an expertise in this arm. The enterprising autodidact, Obregón, was not so enamored of artillery and preferred to learn from self-study instead of trying to gain knowledge of the military arts and sciences from ex-Federals, who in many cases were technically deficient anyway.

The growth models adopted by individual commanders directly impacted the culture of the emerging defense establishment that ultimately would replace the Federal Army. Villa proved much more amenable to the acquisition of Federal men, and even entire units, than did Obregón, not just because he desired their technical skills but because he truly respected them as military officers. The admission of so many ex-Federals with questionable revolutionary ideals to the Constitutionalist Division of the North caused concern among the officers of the Constitutionalist Army Corps of the Northeast and that of the Northwest. Both of those commands preferred to grow organically. Of course, there were only so many Federals to begin with and the explosion in the number of men serving in the military economy as the scale of operations skyrocketed could only be explained by organic growth.

As the scale of the revolution progressed, so too the sophistication of campaigns increased and demanded a more artful approach to the acquisition, management, allocation, and control of resources used in military operations—the other definition of military economy. Operationally-speaking virtually all Constitutionalist operations consisted of isolating large Federal garrisons and applying superior numbers to reduce them, in series and parallel, or in other words, properly balancing the principles of Mass and Economy of Force (see the "Tactical and Operational Theory" subheading in Appendix A for a more thorough explanation). Constitutionalists and Federals alike also designed campaigns to acquire for themselves, or deny to the enemy, the benefit of economic resources (for example, cotton, garbanzos, and petroleum). As a matter of course, the Federals destroyed the property of leading Constitutionalists and their backers. Finally, as already mentioned, Obregón factored cost-benefit analysis into deciding whether to attack or leave key ports under a state of siege, essentially economizing his military capital.

On the level of grand strategy, as the scope and scale of the revolution expanded, the Constitutionalists had to attend to the brave new world of monetary and fiscal policy formulation. The developing revolution took on new economic and businesslike dimensions that required a new kind of officer and organization than that of the Federal Army. Competition for the "Three Ms" instead of the "Three Ps" produced an officer more entrepreneurial and attuned to economics, while at the same time the Constitutionalist Army had to develop the institutional rigor necessary for the management of tremendous wealth and resources. Not all major units, however, were the same, and the commercial agency and practices of Villa's Division of the North differed significantly from Obregón and Pablo González's army corps, with profound implications for the campaigns of 1915—the subject of the third trilogy in this series.

Volume Theses

Apart from the two overarching series theses (the success of the revolution was social, not political, and it was not a small war), each volume in the trilogy presents its own thesis and emphasizes a different theme. The attached graphic gives a visual representation of how the overarching theses and themes and individual volume theses intertwine over the course of the years from beginning of 1911 into 1915.

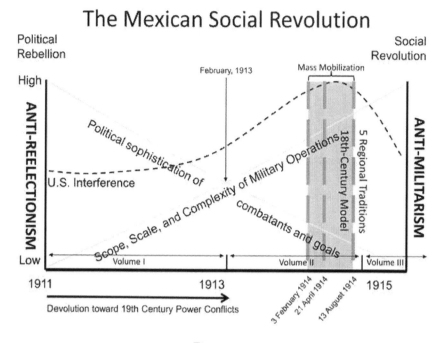

Figure 1.1

The focus of the first volume was on the defense establishment, examining the strengths and weaknesses and hyper-competitiveness in and among the various organizations arising from numerous mobilization regimes and regional traditions. *Maneuver and Battle in the Mexican Revolution: Rise of the Praetorians* demonstrated that Madero's revolution really amounted to little more than a rebellion by a politicized provincial elite with limited goals for change that wound up returning the nation to nineteenth-century anarchy—the periphery against the Center, Liberal militia vs. Conservative regulars, a Suriano guerrilla war, customhouse seizures, and barracks uprisings—and ultimately climaxed in a praetorian palace coup. The growing popularization of the forces mobilized during the Madero years carried with it an attendant drop in political sophistication.

Whereas the first volume dealt fundamentally with the defense establishment, the text in this current volume overwhelmingly concentrates on the scope, scale, and sophistication of military operations, which is to say, tactics, operations, strategy, and combat narrative, and to a much lesser extent on how American interventionism impacted these. Military Economy, while an important concept does not stand on its own but rather, as previously stated, cuts across the three main themes. The reader is encouraged to be cognizant of those instances where intersections occur.

Maneuver and Battle in the Mexican Revolution: A Revolution in Military Affairs poses the multi-pronged thesis that: although the Federal Army manifested evidence of professionalization, culturally it maintained an eighteenth-century model that could not compete in an environment of mass mobilization; in trying to match the avalanche of citizens joining the Constitutionalist Army the Federal Army expanded beyond its means to ensure quality and its officer corps became adulterated, degraded, and lost all pretense to exceptionalism; by defeating a professional army identified with the European tradition, Mexicans embraced pride in Mexicanidad and banished the militarists' mythical concept of *don de mando* ("gift of command") from the collective popular psyche; service in the ranks became common, facilitating the removal of any mystique attached to the army; and in order to compete in an expanding and vibrant military economy and manage the human and material capital entailed in mass mobilization a new brand of enterprising army officer emerged to replace the old.

Unfortunately for the nation, the demise of the Federal Army occasioned a new-style, popular militarism and the climactic round of battles and campaigns of 1915. The third volume in this trilogy will explore the issues and concepts of popular militarism, the increasing numbers and ideological indifference of citizens entering the military economy, *indigenismo*, grand strategy, sectional rivalries, and the death of the military-agricultural complex in Mexico.

*   *   *

In the first volume we saw that on February 18, 1913, Federal General Victoriano Huerta and his fellow praetorians removed President Francisco Madero and his Vice President José María Pino Suárez from office and advised the nation of his assumption of power. In Saltillo, the capital of Coahuila State, Governor Venustiano Carranza refused recognition of Huerta's government on constitutional grounds, since the national senate did not possess the authority to vest Huerta with executive power. Additionally, although the inauguration proceedings technically followed legal succession guidelines (that is, oaths of office and appointments, followed quickly by resignations), Congress had never ratified the cabinet positions that the Huertistas juggled in order to effect the transition of power. Coahuila's state legislature supported

Carranza's position and approved decree number 1421 on February 19, refusing to recognize Huerta, granting Carranza special powers to organize armed forces, and encouraging other states to follow suit.

After a series of clashes with federal forces, Coahuila's state forces retired northward to Hacienda de Guadalupe where on March 26, 1913, Carranza dictated a document to his private secretary, the militia captain Alfredo Breceda, which became known as the Plan de Guadalupe. The plan disavowed Huerta as the president of the republic and refused to recognize the national Congress, tribunal, or any state government loyal to him. It also served as the organic charter of the Constitutionalist Army, which was established to defend the constitution of 1857 and to oppose the illegal Huertista government that had violated it; all revolutionaries submitting to this plan became known as Constitutionalists. Endorsed mainly by irregular officers, the plan contained no social agenda and only two political objectives, purposefully designed to arouse the least number of objections from potential supporters: reestablish constitutional government and end militarism under a "First Chief," Venustiano Carranza.[31]

Independent of the state government in Coahuila, the leaders in Sonora reached a similar decision not to ratify Huerta's government, but they did so under a different legal standing. After Huerta's palace coup, Governor José María Maytorena gave in to Colonel Álvaro Obregón's request to fire the jefe de las armas of Hermosillo, Heriberto Rivera, a Federal officer of dubious allegiance, and to concentrate the state's paramilitaries in the state capital, a noticeable movement of troops that the zone chief, Federal General Miguel Gil, did nothing to counter. The Federal general did, however, intercept and impound in Empalme Station a remittance of two hundred .30-30 carbines and 45,000 cartridges sent by Maytorena to the municipal president of Navojoa, suggesting that the shipment seemed very suspicious since in that part of the state there was no insurrection to fight, even though rebellious Yaquis had been committing outrages down there for years. This rather unwise act, which occurred on February 23 (and others by Federal officers), did not appreciably alter the military situation except to give the Sonora legislature a legal basis to revolt under the allegation that the federal government had violated the state's sovereignty. Maytorena was not present when the state government conducted its vote on March 4 because he had requested six-months leave "for health reasons," withdrawn ₱12,000 from the state treasury as an advance in salary and expenses, appointed Ignacio L. Pesqueira as the interim governor, and abandoned the country.

To many, the contents of Governor Pesqueira's telegram notifying the national government of its decision to deny recognition of Huerta as president and its proposal to "enter again in cordial relations with the Center as soon as it might so legally designate another president" read like a withdrawal from the "federal pact." Such actions excited and renewed historical antagonisms between the North and the Center that had existed since Santa Anna tried to quash the powerful state militias in Zacatecas and Texas in the early years of nationhood. Fears of Norteños seceding from the rest of Mexico were long-standing and well-founded, reflecting Mexico's continued insecurities after losing half of its national territory in the 1830s and 1840s and subsequent secessionist conspiracies under Servando Canales, José María Carbajal, and most recently, Orozco. Federal Army soldiers, overwhelmingly from the Center, expressed their disgust for the Norteño revolutionaries hailing from those desert lands of the North known as the Grand Chichimec by referring to them as *chichimecas*, or '*mecos* for short, a pre-Columbian term used by the Mexica for the northern tribes that translates as "sons of dogs."

In Chihuahua, Federal officers escorting Governor Abraham González to Mexico City stopped the train forty kilometers south of the state capital, ordered him to step down, and then shot him like a dog, burying him in a shallow grave. González had been under arrest in the state capital since February 22 for the "crime" of authorizing Chihuahua's state auxiliaries to buy arms and ammunition. By murdering him, the praetorians sought to cut off the head of the political opposition in the state, but numerous Maderista leaders throughout Chihuahua and in Durango and Zacatecas had already taken up arms and later joined the Constitutionalist cause. These leaders included Pancho Villa, who crossed over the international border into Chihuahua with eight followers to begin his campaign against Huerta around the same time as González's murder.

As soon as the state forces of Sonora and Coahuila were able to secure towns on the international border, the revolutionaries communicated with each other via the United States, and civilian representatives from these two states met in El Paso and San Antonio, Texas, where they decided to formalize a union of forces. On April 18, 1913, at the railway station in Monclova, Coahuila, with Dr. Samuel Navarro representing the Chihuahua Constitutionalist junta, revolutionary officials drafted the Monclova Accords. Under the agreement all three states endorsed the Plan de Guadalupe and approved Roberto V. Pesqueira to go to Washington D.C. and obtain formal recognition as a belligerent from the government of the United States. Up to this moment, the Plan de Guadalupe existed only as a document signed by the militia officers of Coahuila, but with the weight of Chihuahua and Sonora behind the document, the legislature of Coahuila ratified the Plan in decree number 1498 the day after the signing of the Monclova Accords.

Four months later, on August 18, Sonora's legislature also ratified the Plan de Guadalupe, forming one army with its Norteño sister states under the First Chief.

That is where volume one ended and this volume picks up: in the midst of an armed response to a praetorian regime that would trigger a revolution in military affairs in Mexico. In general, RMAs are defined by developments in technology, doctrine, and/or organization that profoundly and irrevocably change how war is prosecuted. Although historians do not always agree on when these turning points occur, many point to the Gunpowder Revolution of early modern Europe, the Mass Armies of the Napoleonic era, and the Industrial Revolution as three such events. The Mexican Revolution occurred at the intersection of the latter two, anticipating World War I in both the application of many new inventions in transportation, communications, and weapon systems to the prosecution of warfare and in full mobilization for total war.

Never before or since has Mexico experienced a mobilization of the masses, also referred to as the "democratization" of warfare, such as it experienced during the revolution. During the years of 1913 and 1914 the scope, scale, and sophistication of combat operations expanded greatly. Constitutionalist divisions grew into army corps as the scale of battles increased, and for the first time maneuver operations advanced right up to the doorstep of Mexico City. The war took on a truly national scope, progressing from single-theater maneuver operations across several states during the Orozco rebellion to multiple theaters simultaneously engaged in maneuver warfare. The need to carry out military operations on a grander level necessarily entailed the use of more economic resources, and in turn, increasingly complex methods of acquiring and managing the requisite assets. Revolutionaries began to engage not only in direct taxation for the sustenance of their armies but also in the engineering of taxation regimes, that is, crafting fiscal policy. They issued their own scrip, vouchers, bonds, and currency, meaning they formulated monetary policy as regards the value, denominations, and timing of issuances.

Confronted with a foe that brought such bountiful resources to bear in the war effort, the Federal Army had to respond in kind, trying to match the copious number of men that the Constitutionalists placed into the field of operations in an attempt to bring "the obstinate rebelliousness of the northern border" to heel. However, its eighteenth-century model army of privilege-seeking, European-affecting, metropolitan types dressed in gaudy uniforms who were accustomed to commanding political dissenters and disengaged campesinos, Indians, vagrants, and jailhouse rabble in defense of an ill-defined concept of Patria was ill-suited to mass mobilization. Yet Federal

General Guillermo Rubio Navarrete, apparently oblivious to history, blamed President Madero for the need to resort to the *levée en masse* and send untrained conscripts north to fight the revolutionaries. In his mind, had Madero only allowed the army to recruit to its full complement in 1912, it would not have had to resort to such measures, even though it had always been so for Mexico's regular army. Still, fellow Colegio Militar graduate General Federico Cervantes echoed Rubio's line of reasoning, saying the "leva" explained why competent officers with good European arms and ammunition could not "withstand the onslaught of the revolutionary troops."[32] The sons of the Colegio Militar held too high an opinion of themselves and their abilities, which paled in comparison to the skills, knowledge, and competencies of the citizen-soldiers organized according to regional martial traditions and fighting a *la Mexicana*.

As the Federal Army tried to mobilize to meet the Constitutionalist challenge two significant developments occurred: one within the organization and another within society at large. As more and more men entered into Federal service, an adulteration of competency and degradation of skills took place that removed all pretense to military exceptionalism. For society, in general, service in the military became commonplace, removing any mystique associated with the profession of arms. With the defeat of the Federal Army a social revolution was born that erased any notions of a singular "gift of command" that privileged generals over civilian leaders in times of crisis. Citizen-soldiers handily beat the regulars, and in later years *constantly* reminded them that they could always do so again. Thus, the root cause of militarism—the belief in the supremacy of army officers over civilians not only in warfare but in a leadership style that could be applied to governance and economics—was forever obliterated in Mexico. In 1914 the Norteños would conquer Mexico City, annihilate the Federal Army, and eventually bring the era of barracks uprisings and palace coups to a permanent conclusion.

One

Northern Sonora

Colonel Álvaro Obregón wasted no time in loading his 4th Irregular Battalion on trains and making for the international border on March 6, a mere two days after the state legislature's no confidence vote for Huerta. Fresh on the heels of the young colonel's successful campaign against the Colorados, Interim Governor Pesqueira had appointed Obregón to the post of Chief of the War Section with Juan Cabral as the chief of the northern sector. Obregón's mission was to join those revolutionaries already operating in the region against the Federals in order to secure the state's northern border and gain access to arms and ammunition from the United States, get control over customs duties collected at ports of entry and tax receipts from U.S. mining concerns operating in the area, and ensure the flow of exports necessary to sustain the economy. Joining Obregón in the undertaking would be Aniceto Campos in

Fronteras, who had been the first to rebel in the region on February 23 by disarming the local garrison and gathering supporters to his side; Manuel Diéguez, the Municipal President of Cananea who had recruited about 300 men; and Plutarco Elías Calles who, with Pedro Bracamontes from Nacozari, had 500 followers outside Agua Prieta. These revolutionaries faced approximately 500 Federals under General Pedro Ojeda in Agua Prieta, Federal Colonel José Ramón Morenos with 600 in Cananea, and another 300 or so Federals in Nogales under Colonels Emilio Kosterlitzky and Manuel Reyes. The rest of the Sonoran state militia was concentrated in the center of the state around the capital, Hermosillo, where they were well-positioned to work on interior lines of communication and defeat the Federals in detail, first in the north and then those in the south under Federal General Miguel Gil. Gil, the zone commander, had begun concentrating his area forces around Empalme at the outset of hostilities, forming an effective force of 1,200 Federals ready to strike north toward Hermosillo with the port city of Guaymas as a base of operations. He also had a holding force of some six hundred men in Torín, headquarters of the 1st Military Zone, to keep the Yaqui tribe at bay.[1]

THE TAKING OF NOGALES, MARCH 13

Colonel Obregón's first major stop on the trip north was at Magdalena, where Colonel Juan G. Cabral joined Obregón. Colonel Cabral, at just twenty-eight years of age, possessed an average intelligence, spoke English, and had no vices, but he was not known for being very sociable. The revolution had found him working as a second-class clerk in the mining town of Cananea, a position which he abandoned in 1910 to join the fight. Up to that time Cabral had observed a conduct beyond reproach, but by 1913 he had become inexplicably wealthy. Augmented by Cabral and his twenty-five soldiers, along with elements of the 47th and 48th Rural Corps, Obregón's column again got underway on March 10, reaching as far as Los Alizos Canyon where it had to halt due to the condition of the tracks. Obregón could not afford any delay because Federal General Pedro Ojeda threatened to reinforce Nogales, his first campaign objective, so the column struck out on foot. Around 5 p.m. the column stopped for the night and set up security service under the inclemency of driving snow and rain, resuming the march the following morning and reaching Lomas shortly after noon. Adhering to a formulaic way of proceeding, Colonel Obregón sent a commission to ask the garrison under Colonel Kosterlitzky to surrender the plaza.[2] Kosterlitzky wisely refused to meet in private with the emissaries, and a conference took place in the Mexican consulate of Nogales, Arizona, with Obregón's emissaries, Kosterlitzky, Federal Lieutenant Colonel Manuel Reyes, the Customs Administrator E. Alonso, and Mexican Consul Ángel Aguilar in attendance. The revolutionaries showed up and presented their credentials and stated that they wished to avoid bloodshed and the risk of an international incident with the United States. The Federals, however, refused to surrender the plaza; Kosterlitzky stated that his intention was to defend the plaza until "firing the last cartridge and spilling the last drop of blood," as Obregón put it. Twice the conference was interrupted by Reyes' aide, first to announce the continuing approach of the revolutionaries and then later that the enemy was surrounding one of the trenches. Since the revolutionaries made no specific proposals, according to the two Federal leaders, the conference ended.[3]

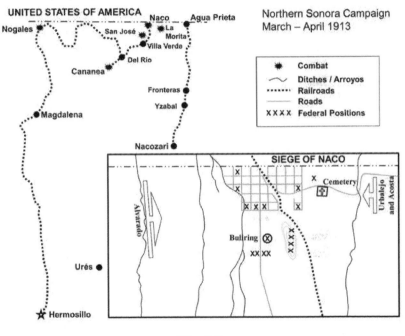

Map 1.1

At some point during the movement north, revolutionary Colonel Jesús Chávez Camacho with two hundred men of the 5th Irregular Battalion of Sonora and fifty-eight more from the Voluntarios de Hermosillo Corps under Captain Fernando S. Betancourt also joined Obregón, bringing the total to about 900 revolutionaries, comprised mostly of Yaqui, Mayo, and Pima Indians, some wearing khaki uniforms and carrying Mausers, and others still in breechclout with bows and arrows. They faced Lieutenant Colonel Manuel Reyes with eighty-eight men from one company of the 5th Infantry Battalion, and approximately 180 Fiscal Gendarmes (employees of the Treasury) under Kosterlitzky; some of the latter, however, had been recruited by Juan Cabral, who had become a leader in Fiscal Gendarmes after the success of the 1910 insurgency, and so they could not be counted on to lend faithful service.[4] That explains why Kosterlitzky interspersed them with the regulars.

The Federal defenses for Nogales consisted of trenches prepared on the hills to the east and west of the town. At the summit of Los Locos Hill, on the east side and closest to the border, commanded by Second Sergeant Manuel Hernández, Reyes placed a corporal and seven soldiers of the 5th Battalion and twelve gendarmes led by Corporal Leonardo Manzaneda. Continuing clockwise, on Mendoza Hill just south of Los Locos, he placed Sub-lieutenant Florentino Cuatle with a corporal, a private first class, and seven men of the 5th Battalion, and twelve gendarmes all under Lieutenant José I. Galoz; due south of that, at post number 3 on Ojeda Hill on the southeastern edge of the town under Captain Miguel del Valle, he assigned two corporals, a sergeant, and seven men of the 5th, and twelve gendarmes led by Corporal Agustín Duarte. Opposite that post, on the southwest corner, Captain Justino Mendieta commanded two corporals, a sergeant, two privates first class and six soldiers of the 5th along with twelve gendarmes under Corporal Miguel Reyes on the hill called Depósito de Agua with trenches running north and south. Continuing back to the north, on the high El Ranchito Hill, the Federal post number 5 was commanded by Sergeant Juan Flores with a corporal, two privates first class, and five soldiers of the 5th, and twelve gendarmes under Corporal Rodrigo de la Mora. Post number six was on Panteón Hill and consisted of two corporals, a private first class, five men of the 5th, and twelve gendarmes commanded by Corporal Graciano Viniegra. A corporal, one private first class, and four soldiers of the 5th, along with twelve gendarmes under Corporal Florentino Llamas, manned El Cuartel (or District) Hill closest to the international boundary, with Second Sergeant Teodoro Rodríguez in charge. Finally, Reyes established a firing line due south of town running from Ojeda Hill to Depósito del Agua and manned by twenty-four infantrymen from the 5th led by Sub-lieutenant Jesús Molina and thirty gendarmes under Corporal Rolando Quiroz, with an outpost of another twenty-five gendarmes under Paymaster ("*habilitado*") Corporal Pedro González situated 500 meters ahead to give news of the enemy's approach. The firing line remained dug in from 6 p.m. on the night of March 12 until the start of the battle at 5 a.m. on the thirteenth. Kosterlitzky had no reserves.[5]

Obregón planned for two columns to attack at 1 a.m. on March 13. The first was composed of 150 men from the 4th Irregular Battalion of Sonora under Major Antonio A. Guerrero against the trenches on the east side of the plaza, parallel to the international boundary line to avoid rounds landing in the United States. The second group of 150 men from the 5th Irregular Battalion of Sonora under First Captain Gonzalo A. Escobar was to assault the trenches on the west side while Obregón and Cabral distracted the Federals with a frontal feint carried out by fifteen of Cabral's dragoons.[6]

Obregón's plan of attack did not go according to plan. At 12:30 a.m. on March 13 he had left with Cabral to take up position for the feint, but by two o'clock the east and west pincer groups—each having to make wide berths to get into place—still had not opened fire, so he returned to his camp. At 4 a.m. he again moved into position south of town and sent a message to both his flanking commanders not to open fire if they were not ready to attack before daybreak. The Federals inside the plaza had no idea whether the revolutionaries would attack during the night, since it was very dark and exceedingly rainy and cold, obscuring observation. Precisely at dawn when the Federal bugles blew reveille, fire erupted to the east and south— the runners carrying Obregón's revised orders had reached the attack column leaders too late. But as soon as Escobar and Guerrero received the new directives, they broke contact, except for a group of Escobar's men under the command of Captain José María Acosta, who had advanced too far to safely retreat. Federal Captain del Valle had been killed in the initial exchange, and Reyes ordered thirty men from the southern firing line to his position, while he himself rushed to Ojeda Hill. Obregón immediately ordered all units to resume fire and sent a detachment of the 5th Sonoran to reinforce Acosta; at 10 a.m. he sent even more men, this time from Betancourt's Voluntarios de Hermosillo.[7]

Combat continued all through the morning at close range in different places without the volleys ceasing for a moment. No attack occurred on Panteón Hill precisely because that assault force wandered too far north and entered U.S. territory, whereupon American soldiers disarmed the revolutionaries and took them into custody. Numerous patrols of U.S. soldiers guarded the international dividing line, as rounds fell on American territory from every direction, shattering windows, splintering wood, and exploding in the stone walls of the town. The Americans had already made it known that they would return fire on whichever Mexican force endangered Americans, potentially making for a three-way battle. Inside the plaza sometime after noon, Kosterlitzky put in a call to apprise the Mexican consul of the dire situation; although the revolutionaries had not taken any trenches, he was running out of ammunition and would not have enough to last the night, especially since, as he reported, the enemy had received six hundred more reinforcements. Colonel Reyes, meanwhile, went up and down the lines unceasingly to encourage his soldiers. The customs administrator, who had moved the money and most of the archives into the consulate on the U.S. side, remained in his office dictating orders to his supervisors and employees to the last moment.[8] Around this time the revolutionary Acosta initiated a vigorous attack against the Federal trenches, and Obregón ordered Colonel Chávez to send Captain Reyes N. Gutiérrez with a detachment of twenty-two men from the 5th Sonoran and fifteen from the 47th Rurales to take the hills to the west in preparation for a night assault.[9]

When a stray bullet happened to hit a U.S. soldier standing only a few paces from the Mexican consulate, the Americans sprang into action. A bugler blew "to arms," and Major Daniel C. Tate, who had arrived with 300 troops to reinforce Captain Cornelius Smith's two hundred men, rushed to the international line along with the majority of the soldiers. The alarm caused Kosterlitzky, Reyes, the custom administrator, and the consul to do the same on the Mexican side. Upon coming together, the American major informed the Mexican consul that if the shooting did not cease presently, then he would be forced to respond energetically. But the consul was obviously in no condition to control events, and just then the bad news arrived that the ammunition was insufficient to keep up the fight much longer. Fearing an invasion by the Americans that "seemed imminent, to judge by the excitement of the [American] troops," the consul resolved to withdraw the government forces to the borderline. Seeing Reyes and Kosterlitzky on horseback there at the line, the revolutionaries unleashed a volley that sent the consul and customs administrator hastening back to the consulate and the two jefes back into the Mexican city of Nogales.[10]

Immediately the consul communicated the government's decision to abandon the fight and turn over their weapons to the Americans, to which Major Tate not only agreed but even ordered his own bugler to sound the Mexican retreat call. The troops received orders to concentrate in the customhouse while the consul and customs administrator searched fruitlessly for vehicles in which to deposit the weapons. Unilaterally pulling out of a battle is no easy feat. Coming together once again at the borderline, with Major Tate standing on the U.S. side and Kosterlitzky on the Mexican side, the American officer demanded an immediate cessation of shooting. Kosterlitzky said he would give the order as soon as the revolutionaries did so, and he suggested that Tate so inform the revolutionaries of the agreement. But Tate said none of his men could cross over into Mexican territory, and a certain Pedro Torres then said he would deliver the news under white flag in an automobile, which he did. When Obregón received the message from the American consul saying that rounds were landing on the United States' side of the border, he ordered a cease-fire in expectation of resuming the attack under cover of night. However, before the order could take effect, Gutiérrez and Acosta made such a solid push that the Federals opposite them, running short of ammunition and most likely expecting a night attack, began to abandon their positions and pass over into the United States.[11]

Fighting continued for nearly an hour between Colonel Reyes' outposts and Obregon's men west of the city, but as soon as word could reach the Federals about the agreement with the Americans, they too ceased firing and assembled on the city plaza and then marched to the American side of the line and surrendered to Colonel Wilbur E. Wilder of the U.S. 5th Cavalry.[12] Consul Aguilar confirmed that the government forces withdrew in an orderly fashion in spite of the shooting, which continued for some time later, and handed over their weapons at the borderline: the majority of "soldiers of the line as well as the fiscal gendarmes gathered, passed the borderline tranquilly, and came to American territory." Just such an occurrence had been expected and perhaps even anticipated. One day Kosterlitzky had invited then-Captain Cornelius C. Smith to his headquarters in Sonora for lunch even before the battle had begun and told the American that he preferred to pass over into the United States and surrender to the U.S. Army rather than to Obregón. A place was designated for them to deposit their weapons and equipment and another for their horses.[13]

Hundreds of U.S. citizens came to greet Colonels Kosterlitzky and Reyes as they entered onto American soil and congratulate them for the brave stand they had made against overwhelming odds, extending them every courtesy. In order to completely spare the Americans and their property any harm, Kosterlitzky would have had to march out of the city and fight the Constitutionalists in the open field, which probably would have entailed annihilation. As it was, the Colonel did extend the defenses as far out from the border as the number of his effectives would allow. After the Federals had marched across the border, turned over their weapons, and disbanded, Obregón and Cabral assembled their men and took possession of the city at 8 a.m. the next morning.[14]

At seven o'clock that evening a U.S. colonel sent a message to the Sonorans saying that he was withdrawing his troops from the line since order had been restored on the Mexican side. The Federals had fought twelve hours without food or water, and their ammunition was almost exhausted. Officially, Obregón confirmed losing six dead and nine wounded against the Federal losses of one officer and three men dead, seven wounded, with twenty taken prisoner, including one officer; but the local Red Cross reported that twenty-seven wounded soldiers, mostly Constitutionalists, had been take to the Sisters Hospital from the battle. Colonel Kosterlitzky's trumpeter was also killed and his orderly wounded when the revolutionaries made a rush on the Federal trenches. Private Allen A. Umfleet of the U.S. 5th Cavalry, the American shot while doing police duty on International Street, had a wound from a bullet that entered through the nose and face and came out the back of his neck. Miraculously he survived and returned to duty sometime later. The victory at Nogales constituted a major political and military victory, giving the revolution a base of operations to introduce all necessary elements and equipment into the country.[15]

Obregón credited the Federals, not the skill of his own forces, with the loss of Nogales. The latter had spent six long days traveling north through the freezing snow and rain, repairing and ultimately having to abandon the railroads. If the federal government had truly wanted to save Nogales, he reasoned, it had plenty of time to send reinforcements. On March 6 Kosterlitzky had told his superior, General Ojeda, who was in Agua Prieta, "I know that in Hermosillo they are preparing to disavow the central government; better said, they have already done so. Their first act will be to attack Nogales," and therefore he urged an "immediate concentration of our forces." Ojeda, seemingly more worried about rumors of Pancho Villa meeting in Tucson with Governor Maytorena than Obregón marching northward with hundreds of men, and without any sense of irony, chastised Kosterlitzky for exaggerating facts. Three days later Kosterlitzky reported that people arriving in Nogales from Magdalena informed him that Álvaro Obregón with eight hundred men had reached the latter plaza on the night of March 7. Kosterlitzky received no reply, and so he sent the same message again, this time in code, hoping to receive an answer. Then Ojeda responded telling the colonel to pay no mind to hearsay, saying he was coming to Nogales with three thousand men and that there was another Federal column headed to Hermosillo that was four thousand men strong. Ojeda only reacted with a sense of urgency once he received the final plea for help from Federal Lieutenant Colonel Reyes in Nogales on March 11 informing him that Obregón had left Magdalena the day before with an estimated twelve hundred men and an unspecified number of machine guns. That same day Ojeda wired Kosterlitzky that he was leaving Agua Prieta immediately headed for Nogales. He lied, and it was too late anyway.[16]

Pedro Ojeda, of less than medium height with a pronounced bulk and slow gait, had a ruddy, round face that shone behind hazel blue eyes and under white, short-cropped hair; the wide nostrils of his nose protruded over a straight, bushy moustache. He was born in Oaxaca, same as his parents, in the barrio of la Merced and attended the school of Don Pancho Barranco, a disciplinarian famous for handling the cane. Ojeda followed his father, who had fought the French in Oaxaca and Puebla, into the army and by nineteen was a lieutenant, seconding Porfirio Díaz's Plan de Tuxtepec in 1876 that overthrew civilian President Sebastian Lerdo de Tejada. His baptism of fire, at San Juan Epatlán, pointed to his bravery. In that battle, at the head of a small Guerrilla, he mixed with the enemy, fighting with machete blows. Upon the success of the revolt, he was confirmed as lieutenant and entered into the Supreme Powers Battalion. After twenty-two years he was discharged from that unit as a major and joined the 25th, and later the 9th, which he left as a colonel to take charge of the 14th, all infantry battalions. During his career, understanding that a soldier does not receive a formal education while in the service, he dedicated himself to self-study, with a special interest in fortifications.[17]

Ojeda had been sent to Sonora during Madero's 1910 rebellion by the Secretary of War and he participated in the actions at San Rafael, Sahuaripa, and La Colorada. But he had had his greatest success with a string of victories in the territory of Tepic. The Huertista chronicler of the Federal efforts in Sonora, Rómulo Velasco Ceballos, wrote of him:

> Ojeda is the idol of his troops. He is, because he never leaves them for any reason, not in the field, at leisure time, and much less in combat, in which he loses the notion of hierarchy, since he puts himself on the line of fire; he does [so], in order to make himself inexorably obeyed by his soldiers; he also shows paternal care for his [men]—of course, in the dry manner of his character—and he is the idol of his troops, finally, because he does not exploit them in the least; just the opposite. Alluding to the scarcity of funds, this leader stated, 'I am poor, because I do not want to be anything more than a soldier; my field is not business...'[18]

Ceballos' claims to the contrary, the historical record does not support the image of Ojeda as a paternalistic figure who stuck by his men through thick and thin. Rather, he was the typical career military bureaucrat, a martinet and a praetorian, whose rejection of lucrative pursuits and resignation to poverty aspired to an unpossessed nobility.

The forces that Ojeda had in his command, known as the "Sonoran Column," could be divided into two cohorts: one comprised of Federals, or soldiers "of the line," and another made up of paramilitaries. The first group consisted of small units belonging to the 5th, 10th, 27th and 28th infantry battalions, two 80-mm. Mondragón mortars, and a machine-gun section, for a total of 350 men. The irregular contingent consisted of the Voluntarios del Norte Corps and some guards from the 48th Rural Corps that together formed a total of two hundred riders. At the outset of hostilities the Sonoran Column had been distributed to four places somewhat distant from Agua Prieta, the column headquarters. Ojeda called in his detachments (or they straggled in after being beaten and chased out of the plazas they were garrisoning) and on March 12 got started on the road to Naco, which, like Agua Prieta, was on the border. He had with him 450 men, only thirty mounted, because he had left behind thirty men to maintain order in Agua Prieta and the mounted Voluntarios del Norte had deserted with their weapons.[19]

After Ojeda left Agua Prieta, Lieutenant Colonel Plutarco Elías Calles and about six hundred revolutionaries rolled in from Yzabal in a freight train to take possession of the town. Most of the thirty men that Ojeda had left behind joined the revolution, but a half dozen chose to cross over into the United States instead. Inside the plaza Calles' men found a cache of weapons and some 18,000 rounds of ammunition left behind by Ojeda because, the Huertistas swore, he was not able, nor did he consider it prudent, to take with him the numerous Remington and Winchester carbines of various calibers that were in the plaza "in excess." So, Ojeda had arranged with the Mexican consul in Douglas, Arizona, across the border from Agua Prieta, to have them placed in a boxcar and taken over to the American side in order to keep them from falling into the hands of the revolutionaries. According to the conspiracist Ceballos, however, the "American authorities fulfilled their commitment in such a way that" Calles gained possession of them.[20] This entirely unsubstantiated charge against the American authorities poses a multitude of questions: Why phrase what the American authorities allegedly did in such vague and cryptic terms? Who were the rightful owners of the weapons? Why is it up to local government in the United States to solve matters of national consequence to Mexico? And finally, what proof is there that this ever even happened?

On March 13 at 2 p.m. Ojeda arrived in Naco and decided to spend the night there after learning that at least three bridges had been destroyed between Naco and Del Río Station, where Constitutionalist Colonel Manuel M. Diéguez had four hundred men blocking the Federal path. Additionally, he learned that night of the fall of Nogales, which meant he no longer had an urgent reason to get to Nogales, and by the next day he was already under a loose siege in Naco, with revolutionaries commanded by Calles lining the hills south of town as well as those of La Morita, some eight kilometers from the plaza on the Agua Prieta side.[21]

Plutarco Elías Calles was an illegitimate member of the prominent Elías family of cattlemen in Sonora's northeast, who went by the surname of his stepfather. He had a checkered record in several middle class occupations and had played host to meetings of the liberal clubs while he lived in Guaymas before the revolution, but by 1910 he was back on the border at work in northeast Sonora with the family business in Fronteras. Upon the Maderista victory, Governor Maytorena had appointed Calles the *comisario* ("magistrate") of Agua Prieta, a post he had resigned after the Citadel coup in order to fight the Huertista regime. Immediately afterward, Calles had been in Douglas, Arizona, raising funds and troops and now he had around six hundred men, with key subordinates Pedro Bracamontes, Miguel Samaniego, Cruz Gálvez, Arnulfo R. Gómez, Escajeda, and others.[22]

Before he had departed Agua Prieta, Calles phoned Colonel Obregón in Nogales and left a message informing his superior of his intention to attack Ojeda. But Obregón knew Ojeda's mettle because his 4th Irregular Battalion had been a part of Ojeda's column previously, and so he wanted Calles to wait to attack until their forces could unite and be assured of a victory, since a loss there would be a setback for the revolutionaries. Immediately Obregón ordered Major Carlos Félix with the 47th Rural Corps to start repairs on the rail line between Nogales and Cananea in order to attack both the latter mining town and Naco. Then he tried to phone Calles and have him suspend the attack on Naco so they could face Ojeda together. He left the message with the Commercial Agency, now called the "Revolutionary Agency," of Roberto V. Pesqueira in Douglas. Congressman Adolfo de la Huerta, who had abandoned Mexico City after the coup, agreed to carry the message to Calles, but he did not arrive in time to stop Calles from marching on Naco.[23]

Combat at La Morita (or Papalote), March 15

Upon arriving at the outskirts of Naco, Calles made a cursory reconnaissance of the plaza and retired to the hills located eight kilometers south and east of town, a place called La Morita, also known as Lomas de Papalote. Ojeda's confidence in his men and his own abilities did not permit him to remain besieged, even though he may have been outnumbered. On March 15 Ojeda joined his men in their very meager breakfast and then, exhibiting the presumed martial spirit of all Federal officers, Ojeda took the initiative. At seven o'clock, little by little, his men began marching out of the plaza to present formal combat. Fifty men remained behind in the plaza as a rearguard.[24]

Approximately halfway on the road from Naco to La Morita, the commander of Auxiliary forces, Francisco Escandón, with his thirty riders carried out a reconnaissance of the Constitutionalist positions. Calles, with Pedro Bracamontes as his second in command, had distributed the revolutionaries as best they could in the hills overlooking the plain where Naco lies when the two forces began to exchange fire for nearly twenty minutes, which was long enough for the Federal scouts to ascertain their enemies' positions with precision. Escandón reported back, "The enemy is dug in on the six summits of La Morita, general."[25]

The column continued advancing and, when the hills pointed out by Escandón came into view, the troops, without any orders, began to pick up the pace. Their officers tried to slow them, but they were filled with excitement. Once within rifle range, General Ojeda's combat veterans deployed with rapid and precise movements into three lines in front of the Constitutionalists with the mortar section situated in the center to the rear. On the Federal southern wing were men from the 5th and 27th Infantry Battalions along with a section of Madsen light machine guns, while on the northern wing Ojeda had those of the Federal Auxiliary Corps who had remained loyal to the national government along with his Colt machine guns. He held one hundred men of the 10th Infantry Battalion and a detachment from the 48th Rural Corps, who had likewise declined to join the revolutionaries, in reserve. Then the general harangued his men: "No one has beaten [down] the soldiers of the Federation; we have always been on top of everyone. Let's show it, muchachos! ¡Viva the Supreme Government! ¡Viva the 5th! ¡Viva the 10th, viva the 27th, viva the 28th Battalion. At them!"[26]

The rifle fire heated up, and the Federals directed their aim at the first hill closest to the border, mounting an exemplary attack with machine gun cover and steady advances. The artillery went into action hurling both impact and shrapnel shells. The crews watched each shot bounce off the rocks of the makeshift fieldworks erected by the revolutionaries and with each impact exclaimed, "Spot on!" The Constitutionalists fought bravely, but by 12:30 Ojeda's Federals had pushed Calles' men from their line of fire on the first three hills, forcing them to retreat to a second set of hills to their rear. Then Federal Comandante Rafael Villaseñor, with the one hundred men held in reserve, marched through the left flank to cut off the revolutionaries' most probable route of retreat; at the same time, Escandón flanked them on the right side.[27]

The revolutionaries hotly contested possession of the fourth hill and at one point the Federals could not remain standing because the fire coming at them "was burning." "Face down," ordered Ojeda, who was with this group of soldiers. And only he, with his short, chubby figure, remained firm, until a short while later the artillery handled by Captain Jesús Cordero landed another "Exact" hit, at which time the general yelled, "Up and at them!" Then spying one soldier hiding behind a bush, Ojeda walked toward him thundering: "Forward!" Shortly thereafter the bugle sounded victory for the fourth time. The revolutionaries could not hold out any longer and after six hours of continuous combat beat a hasty retreat back to Agua Prieta.[28]

During the pursuit, Villaseñor's Rurales shot some fleeing revolutionaries in the back and took twenty-six prisoners. Upon returning to report to Ojeda, the comandante smoothed his curly beard, beaming with pride: his previously dismounted guards had been turned into cavalry, having captured 353 horses and mules as well as ammunition, arms, and food taken as booty from the revolutionaries. The Federals reported three killed in action and twenty-two wounded, including one officer, but counted ninety-three dead revolutionaries in addition to the prisoners captured. Calles and Bracamontes, the revolutionary leaders, had learned a lesson the hard way. By 3 p.m. the Federal column was returning to Naco under arms while keeping their eyes on the revolutionaries occupying the hills south of town, who had made no attempt against the short garrison left behind to guard the plaza while Ojeda defeated their comrades at La Morita. No history of this encounter exists in the Constitutionalist literature.[29]

Next it was Obregón's turn to try to crack the Naco nut. Still in Nogales on March 16, Obregón officially appointed Juan Cabral as his second-in-command. Three days later the column finally left for Naco after having been reinforced by Colonel Salvador Alvarado and his command, part of the Federal Auxiliary Corps that had opted to join the revolution. Reaching Agua Verde in the evening of the next day, Cabral wrote a note to Ojeda exhorting him to exit Naco and fight in the open in order to avoid an international incident, since that plaza, like Agua Prieta and Nogales, shared a border with the United States. Ojeda wisely refused; the revolutionaries totaled more than three thousand men. Obregón attacked with only two hundred men in an attempt to trick Ojeda into coming out of his fortifications to beat the much smaller force, but Ojeda recognized the stratagem. So after a brief exchange of fire, Obregón gathered his officers and revealed his plan to attack Cananea and force Ojeda to abandon Naco and come to the aid of his fellow Federals.[30] It made better sense anyway to attack Cananea and thus clear a sizable Federal force to their rear, and the mining town offered the prospect of more money and access to many recruits, since it had always been sympathetic to the revolution. Additionally, since they already possessed customs at Nogales and Agua Prieta, the Constitutionalists had access to money and of course arms and ammunition and therefore had no pressing need to capture Naco, which was a third-rate port of entry.[31]

BATTLE OF CANANEA, MARCH 24-26

Obregón's column joined Colonel Diéguez, the recent Municipal President of Cananea, at Del Río Station on the twenty-third, where the latter had been since the opening of hostilities in order to prevent the Federals in Cananea from making for the border. Trying to avoid bloodshed, Obregón sent a message to the Cananea garrison commander, Federal Colonel José Ramón Moreno of the 5th Infantry Battalion, asking for his surrender and fixing 6 a.m. the next day as the deadline for a reply; Moreno declined, saying he had orders to defend the plaza.[32]

Cananea was the site of the most famous mining strike leading up to the revolution, where numerous future leaders of the Constitutionalist Army Corps of the Northwest became politicized and militarized: Salvador Alvarado, Juan G. Cabral, Esteban Baca Calderón, and Manuel Diéguez. Of the latter, Ceballos dismissively opined that in polite company Diéguez would not pass for much, but in comparison to his Constitutionalist colleagues he became exceptional. His ambition knew no bounds, nor did he restrain himself from any means to achieve his aims. A socialist trending toward anarchist, he proved the most accomplished of agitators since it was he who initiated, organized, and carried off the famous 1906 strike in Cananea that cost so many lives and that almost provoked a fight with the United States. For this the government tried and remanded him to the castle prison of San Juan de Ulúa along with his acolyte, a man utterly devoid of any personality of his own, Esteban Baca Calderón.[33] Diéguez and Calderón had been released from prison, along with many other political prisoners, after the overthrow of Porfirio Díaz.

Obregón wanted to perform a detailed recon of the place, but there was no time to lose so he accepted the plan proposed by his principal lieutenants: Diéguez with about 500 men of the Voluntarios de Cananea Corps would attack the barracks from the north through the Las Tinacos mine; Colonel Alvarado with his corps of 450 men was to assault through the town from the east, virtually unopposed; and Obregón with Cabral would attack from the south, through the Luz Cananea mine (about 1,400 meters from the Federal barracks) with about 450 men from parts of the 5th Irregular Infantry of Sonora, the 47th Rural Corps, and the Voluntarios de Hermosillo. Major Aniceto Campos approached the west side with 200 or so men, while Colonel Chávez Camacho was to remain in Lechería (about six kilometers northeast of the plaza) with parts of the 4th Irregular Infantry, 48th Rural Police Corps, and the Voluntarios de Hermosillo and Voluntarios de Magdalena corps, totaling about four hundred men, to watch over the rail line from Naco and provide protection for the rear of Alvarado's assault. Obregón distributed his

four machine guns: one to Diéguez, another with Cabral, and two with
Alvarado.[34]

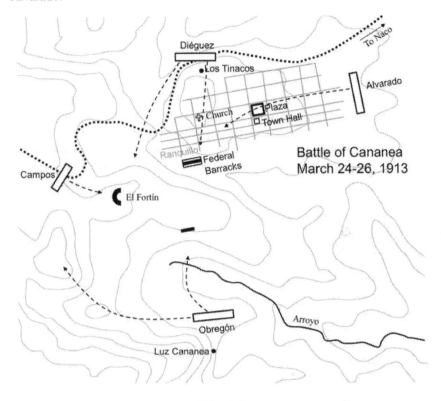

Map 1.2

The Constitutionalists approached by rail in a great convoy that stopped
five kilometers from the plaza. Upon catching sight of the revolutionaries
between four and five o'clock in the afternoon of March 23, Federal Colonel
Moreno made his dispositions to defend the town. With the exception of First
Captain Pablo C. García and about 100 men of the 28th Infantry Battalion
at the meat packing facility outside of town in the direction of Naco, and a
section of troops with one machine gun in a small lunette fort on El Fortín
Hill about one thousand meters west of the barracks, all four hundred or so of
Moreno's Federals from the 5th, 14th, and 28th Infantry Battalions, were all
holed up in their barracks on the southwest corner of town and some nearby
houses facing south to Luz Cananea. Moreno had not constructed defensive
works of any sort, even around the barracks, and he left most of the town
completely undefended.[35]

March 24

During the night, Moreno increased Captain García's contingent with forty-five men and then ordered him back to the barracks as the revolutionaries penetrated the plaza occupying the best positions available for a sustained attack, such as the church, the Alexandria Hotel, the town hall, the rail line on a high steep slope, Luz Cananea, and even the upscale Ranquillo District. The Huertistas claimed that this latter district had been declared neutral territory by both opposing forces (unlikely since it covered the vulnerable rear of the Federal barracks) owing to the fact that it was very elegant with property owned by important interests, meaning the Constitutionalists had reneged on the agreement. Obregón reached his area of responsibility at 1 a.m. and began to deploy his force, sending some men under Captain Escobar to scale the hills on his left that offered some advantage. Then at daybreak he personally emplaced his machine gun in front of the telephone office of Luz Cananea. At six o'clock Obregón opened fire on an adobe house occupied by Federals on the rooftop who were in the midst of receiving a reinforcing platoon of comrades running from the barracks to give aid. West of town, Diéguez opened fire on El Fortín from a hill near some tanks and supported by an old cannon under the direction of revolutionary Major Aniceto C. Campos. Alvarado also engaged the enemy around 8 a.m. and the shooting around town became generalized.[36]

From February 21, when hostile demonstrations against Huerta began inside the town, until March 23, Colonel Moreno had not made one single defensive work in the plaza. It was not until the evening of the twenty-third when his men began stacking some rocks and filling bags with sand. Therefore, in order to seek out the enemy, who were perfectly hidden, the Federals had to leave their barracks and cross open ground without the smallest bush for concealment or the least undulation for cover. And so they sacrificed their lives, as officers bravely stood in the midst of combat even as enlisted men fighting from prone positions were killed. In no time there were dozens of dead and wounded outside the barracks.[37]

Shortly after noon, Obregón made a detailed reconnaissance and decided that El Fortín provided the key to the Federal defenses. So, he ordered a night assault on that position, to be aided by enfilading fire at the Federal trenches from two machine guns personally directed by Colonel Diéguez. The fighting lasted the rest of the day, but ceased around ten o'clock at night. The attack under Lieutenant Tiburcio Morales had succeeded in dislodging the Federals from their works, but upon hearing that the fort was mined and that the Federals were just waiting for the revolutionaries to occupy it so they could blow it, Morales had withdrawn to the rail cut. Obregón immediately ordered Morales to reoccupy El Fortín, but it was too late—the Federals had already moved back in. They opened up with machine-gun fire on Morales, who tried to fulfill his orders in vain. In the moonlight he and his men presented easy targets and he had to withdraw.[38]

March 25

Fighting renewed in the morning of the following day until mid-afternoon when Moreno spoke with Salvador Alvarado by phone. Moments later Alvarado (possibly attended by an American consul named Riket) showed up at the barracks; Moreno went away with them and returned a short while later announcing to his officers that, incredibly, Alvarado had signed a truce scheduled to last until noon the next day. Obregón was livid but he had to honor the truce because the local populace had learned about it and had resumed daily activities, and to renew fighting would have resulted in unacceptable collateral damage. During the truce the Federals removed the dead and wounded, and notwithstanding the fact that it violated the terms of the cease-fire, they established loopholes all around the barracks, made new interior lines since the patio riddled with bullets proved its unsuitability for communication, and constructed three emplacements to provide cover for the machine guns. The armistice was not long enough to permit the collecting of all the dead and wounded, so it was extended another two hours at the request of the Constitutionalists. At 2 p.m. combat resumed.[39]

That night a large number of Yaquis, who often made use of the dark in battle, assaulted the barracks. In order to do so, they had to go up a wide and pronounced slope, in close combat. The defenders allowed them to reach just beyond the halfway mark and then opened up with lively volleys that sounded like the ripping of a large piece of fabric. Then the Yaquis began to beat their drums, quickly, ardently, and continuously, those famous war drums that fire them up in the fight and whose sound no one should have to hear. "Forward, at them" sounded the drums, and they kept coming. When only fifty meters separated the attackers from the defenders, Federal Captain García, with an improvised sling, hurled a great petard at them whose detonation shook the barracks. The attackers vacillated for a moment witnessing the holes in their ranks. The war drum beat furiously, but another bomb, as well as the Mauser fire, heaped fear upon the attackers. Under the cover of night they retreated to their original positions not knowing that those two bombs, which García had made during some down time, were the only ones he had.[40]

March 26

The next morning, after three days of fighting, the Federal troops began to flag in spirits and weaken in body from thirst and hunger, since the Constitutionalists had cut the water to the barracks and Moreno had not stockpiled water or ammunition. In the evening some soldiers, mainly from the 5th, abandoned their positions on the line and said that they did not want to fight any longer. Moreno tried to get them to fight for one more day, but they refused, raising their weapons, beating the slings, and yelling "¡Viva la Libertad!" Moreno had no choice but to go to the telephone and call Alvarado, saying: "Señor general [sic], I surrender unconditionally. For greater security, I am leaving the machine guns on El Fortín." The move was fortuitous for the Constitutionalists because late that afternoon of March 26, Obregón received news that Ojeda had left Naco to come to the aid of the embattled garrison of Cananea; Obregón had already begun readying his forces and Alvarado's to meet the train from Naco while Diéguez prepared to make a new night assault on the Federal works when Moreno surrendered.[41]

The battle ended with six killed and two officers and fifteen soldiers wounded for the Constitutionalists, numbers undoubtedly understated by Obregón given the higher casualties reported by the defenders. They collected booty amounting to three machine guns, five hundred Mausers, 30,000 rounds, horses, mules, and other equipment. The Federals lost one officer and twenty-eight men killed, five officers and fifty-two men wounded, and eight officers, including Moreno, taken prisoner and sent to the Hermosillo Penitentiary. Around two hundred or more Federals, no officers, joined the Constitutionalist ranks. Some of Moreno's officers managed to escape under cover of night. They had wanted to keep fighting, since only Moreno's own "Golden" 5th Infantry Battalion, the major component of his force, had refused to fight, but Moreno would not listen. Those officers opted to flee, choosing to brave the danger of the elements and the possibility of being captured as active combatants over the risk of surrendering.[42]

Federal Captain Pablo C. García; Lieutenants Carlos L. Miranda and Joaquín Domínguez; and Sub-lieutenants Víctor Corral, Cándido Gómez, Secundino Anda, and Antonio Rodríguez; and others escaped, heading for Luz Cananea Hill and the fast-flowing arroyo beside it. Along this terrain feature they could make out the revolutionaries getting ready to attack General Ojeda. Considering it impossible to continue on ahead without being discovered, they went into the arroyo, although the water was up to their waists and thus continued on their way. At eight o'clock that night they carried on, encountering groups of revolutionaries here and there, so close to the river that it could be said that they brushed up against their enemy. The Federals had to eat dinner in the water, whose temperature only added to the already cold March weather. They continued on until 3 a.m. when they were able to leave the water and ascend the hills of Los Ajos, which was no easy feat. They spent twenty-four hours in those rocks: cold, starving, and on the lookout for Constitutionalists. On March 28 they reached a ranch near San José Canyon where they were forced to butcher a cow for sustenance since the owners refused to help them. They finally reached Naco at 9 p.m. and reported to General Ojeda without further delay.[43]

Analysis

The Federals blamed the defeat on the hated gringos and the Federal commander, Moreno. At the Colegio Militar Moreno had received the nickname "the little lamb" ("*El Borreguito*"), and with his white hair and courtly demeanor he continued to personify the appellation, being the prototype of fineness and courtesy. He always kept his cool, never showing any anger and never raising his voice, so as not to offend someone. It was said of him that if someone were to step on his foot, bruising it, he would remove his hat and ask to be excused for having had his foot underneath the other person's. In short, he guarded his honor too tightly and behaved too gentlemanly for war, according to some.[44]

The Huertistas levelled four specific charges against Moreno. On February 28 Moreno witnessed a demonstration in town against Huerta, where the citizens hurled insults against the army and fifty Nacionales took control of four hundred rifles and ammunition from the town hall and joined the revolution with Diéguez. Moreno was aware of all of this and became responsible for his own defeat because he: 1.) did not bring the fifty Nacionales into line; 2.) did not use force to make the soldiers respected, permitting civilians to come right up to the barracks doors and hurl insults; 3.) did not order one single defensive work erected when he had a month to do so, mostly because he was on tenterhooks and did not want to provoke the townsfolk; and 4.) did not order his weapons destroyed before surrendering.[45] One could also add to this already damning list that he had failed to stockpile resources for a siege.

Huertistas, continuing their vilification of the dread Yankees, also claimed that the latter recruited fifty filibusters exclusively for the defense of the Banco de Cananea, which promptly sent them to join the revolutionaries. "With maternal diligence" and in plain sight of everyone, without trying to hide their actions since they deemed Cananea to be American, not Mexican, soil, the gringos drove automobiles loaded with food and ammunition out to the Constitutionalists upon their approach to the town.[46] Why American capitalists would be enthusiastic to lend material aid to the Constitutionalists, many of whose leaders had caused them so much anguish only a short seven years earlier in the strike and riots, received no explanation.

BATTLE OF SAN JOSÉ, MARCH 28

Ever since leaving Agua Prieta, Ojeda had been trying to link up with Moreno in Cananea; only Calles' revolutionaries on the hills south of town threatening to attack at any moment had kept him from realizing that mission. That impediment started to clear on March 22 when the revolutionaries, taking the greatest precautions to hide their movements, began withdrawing from the hills to attack Cananea. Still their activity did not escape the notice of General Ojeda, who guessed that either this was an attempt to draw him out of the plaza in order to defeat him on more favorable ground, or, quite correctly, that they were leaving to attack Cananea. In the first case, given the few men in his command, he did not want to risk an open field battle. In the second case, based on conversations held daily with Colonel Moreno by telegraph (either out of ignorance or negligence, the revolutionaries did not destroy all the telegraph lines), his rapid advance was far from imperative because, assuming that Moreno had properly prepared for its defense, Cananea could have held out for quite a while. Equally significant, Ojeda had made no effort to procure the carts and hitches, which he did not have, necessary for such a march.[47]

Notwithstanding the foregoing, and since his scouts confirmed that attacking Cananea was indeed the reason for the withdrawal of the revolutionaries, by March 26 General Ojeda was ready to march and departed without delay. After a few hours on the road the Federals ran into the forces of Bracamontes and Calles, who did not put up any resistance but rather fled precipitously, causing Ojeda quicken his pace. He spent the night in El Papalote and very early in the morning continued the advance, soon learning of the fall of the plaza from Major Alfonso Parra and Captain Leovigildo Lozano, who had escaped the siege. Parra and Lozano also informed Ojeda that, according to what they had learned in Cananea, Calles and Bracamontes had planned to hit the Sonoran Column in the rearguard while another force left Cananea to attack its front. This information proved correct: Obregón readied his troops in order to engage Ojeda's Federals somewhere between Villa Verde and Mesa Station (just beyond Del Río) based on information about Ojeda's whereabouts from two Americans whom the Constitutionalist jefe had encountered. Colonel Alvarado's command had already left in the vanguard, and Obregón sent orders to Calles and Bracamontes to follow Ojeda closely and attack his forces from the rear as soon as they heard Alvarado's forces engage the Federal column to the front. Thus informed, Ojeda halted the march at Villa Verde, only an hour away from Cananea, and spent the entire night continually scanning the horizon toward the lights of Cananea. Then in the early morning his column began returning to Naco, having first destroyed some railroad bridges to slow Obregón's progress.[48]

Obregón raced after Ojeda until he reached the first burnt bridge at Villa Verde, at which point he gave up the chase and returned to Cananea so that his men might enjoy a well-deserved rest. Not mentioned by either Obregón or Calles was the ensuing battle on March 28 at San José Canyon, confirmed by news accounts and Ojeda's service record, between the Federals and the forces of Colonel Calles and Bracamontes, in which the latter tried to block the former's return to Naco.[49]

Around 10:30 a.m. Ojeda's Federals spotted about six hundred Constitutionalists occupying the hills that form the canyon of San José, elevated, rocky, uneven, and with numerous cliffs, off to the west. The column continued to advance and then deployed into three fronts: one to attack and flank the Constitutionalists on the right side, a second one to try to take possession of the entrance into the sierra and clear both heights, and the rest charged with attacking and flanking the Constitutionalists on the left while threatening their rearguard at the same time. One of the 80-mm. mortars supported the advance of the left wing, while also firing on the Constitutionalist positions in the center; the other supported the right wing, clearing the Constitutionalist left. The machine-gun section set up so it could protect the Federals ascending in the center up through the canyon; finally, fifty men remained in reserve. The Constitutionalists formed a large semi-circle with the canyon in the center.[50]

Thus deployed, the Federals attacked, with the assault being vigorous and the Constitutionalist defense stiff, especially by those in the center who occupied an important and high position. The Federal artillery thundered and the battle had not even finished the first phase when a trail of dust could be seen far off in the distance coming from Cananea, indicating the approach of Obregón's column by rail, since in the bright light of day the engine could be seen belching a horizontal plume of smoke. So, the Federals had to finish the battle quickly.[51]

Thirty Federal horsemen and the mortar crew then received orders from Ojeda to initiate the advance, and understanding the urgency of triumphing as soon as possible, the soldiers gave an extraordinary push. One soldier yelled, "You...gringo sell-outs!" and the rest yelled, "Sell-outs!" and enthusiastically delivered the assault. The Constitutionalists on the receiving end of the charge concentrated their fire on this group, which continued to advance without returning fire in a desperate struggle with the enemy to the front.

The Federal right took advantage of these events and advanced relatively easily, but the Constitutionalists held their ground. A quarter hour, then a half-
hour, passed and still the Federals did not conquer the heights.[52]

General Ojeda and Captain Cordero, the commander of the artillery,
were on a small eminence, a target favored by the Constitutionalists. Cordero
heard the dry crack that bullets make upon ricocheting against rocks, looked
around, and saw on a smooth rock a few centimeters from his commanding
general, a multitude of metal rings that the projectiles left after hitting. "They
are shooting at you, general," he said, trying to get him to displace. "Shoot at,
but do not hit," Ojeda replied without moving, with his habitual calmness,
and continued looking through his field glasses at the battle.[53]

"Throw a bomb at them, they are bothering those poor [men]," Ojeda
said to a gunner, pointing to a group of Federals starting to gain the heights.
Finally, those revolutionaries on the Constitutionalist left, measuring the resolve with which the Federal artillery and infantry maneuvering jointly came
at them as well as those entering the canyon in the center who stopped at
nothing, started to retreat. That left their Constitutionalist compañeros on
the right exposed to a flanking attack. It was a propitious turn of events for
Ojeda, and his artillery redoubled its fire, working with the infantry that
secured the heights. The Constitutionalists could not hold out any longer
and started to retreat, first precipitously, and then in good order. Since the
terrain was not conducive to a cavalry pursuit, the Federals used artillery, lobbing shells at the retreating Constitutionalists as the Federal bugles resounded
with *diana*. "Rally," General Ojeda ordered, and in a few minutes the column
had reformed and was ready for the march, making haste to escape the view
of Alvarado's Constitutionalists approaching by rail. The Sonoran Column
entered Naco on March 28 at 9 p.m., triumphant against Calles for a second
time.[54]

BATTLE OF NACO

When Ojeda's Sonoran Column re-entered Naco, he found the place virtually
abandoned with the exception of some one hundred Chinese remaining behind to guard their small businesses. Upon entering the building of the magistrate, they found the cadaver of Lieutenant Agustín Rodríguez, who had
fought under Colonel Moreno at Cananea. Rodríguez, it was later learned,
had entered the town without taking the necessary precautions and some
individuals with revolutionary sympathies had seized and killed him.[55]

As he waited for the Constitutionalist attack that he knew was coming,
Ojeda gave day-to-day, personal instruction to his troops. He had already
noticed some subversive ideas spreading among them, so one morning as his

troops formed up to drill Ojeda harangued them, especially addressing those of the "Golden" 5th Battalion, whose comrades had mutinied in Cananea. He basically told them that the Constitutionalists were going to attack soon, there was no way to deny it—anyone could see that they were very great in numbers and it would take an enormous effort to repulse them, but Ojeda had confidence that they had it in them. Then he said, "I want a solemn display that you are ready to go to the end. One step forward everyone who is resolved to [give it] all!" The ranks moved forward uniformly, except one soldier from the 5th. "Front and Center!" he yelled at the soldier. Glaring with rage at the soldier who was now standing in front of him he said, "We are not in Cananea here! Here we do our duty! Shoot this man!" Minutes later, the discharge sounded.[56] This vignette of the soldier's death comes to us not as a denunciation by an outraged Constitutionalist, but rather by way of an admirer of the Federal Army and its methods. Other stories about how Ojeda tortured to death those prisoners taken from the two battles with Calles and even innocent civilians (perhaps as revenge for the murder of Rodríguez) who sympathized with the Constitutionalists, got back to Obregón, who generally tried to respect the lives of captured Federals, sending the officers to the penitentiary in Hermosillo instead of summarily executing them as others did.[57] In this respect Obregón held the moral high ground.

Obregón's Constitutionalists left Cananea on March 31, pressing north to Naco and arriving at El Papalote the next day where the commanding officer met and conferred with Calles and Alvarado. Naco was adjacent to the U.S.-Mexico border and could only be assaulted from the east and west, since a southern attack might result in rounds from the attackers landing in U.S. territory, so the Constitutionalists decided to try to draw Ojeda out of town one more time using a stratagem. Alvarado would march with the column to La Noria, where Ojeda knew that Calles was all alone, while Obregón headed for Nogales with the empty trains spreading the rumor throughout the border that his column was headed for Hermosillo to attack Federal General Gil. But after several days during which Ojeda made no move to advance, Obregón returned to the east to try to figure out how to attack and take the town.[58] For Ojeda's part, he could not figure out why the Constitutionalists limited themselves to harassing fire for eight days, concluding that perhaps their intention had been to exhaust the defenders by forcing them to remain always alert, or maybe they were trying to get them to squander their ammunition.[59]

In the meantime, General Ojeda continued to improve his defenses with barricades of stone and sandbags placed at the entrance of all streets around the perimeter of the town, using the windows of the perimeter buildings as loopholes. On top one of these buildings he placed his machine guns to cover his front (that is, elevated and in defilade). He also placed his two 80-mm. pieces in the bullring protected by barricades of stone and adobe and with infantry support. On the roof of the police station, chosen as the headquarters, he placed twenty-five men who, supplied with a machine gun and a telemeter, improvised a defense using sandbags; another building situated across from the headquarters held twenty-five soldiers and two machine guns. Finally, he established two advance positions, one covering the road to Agua Prieta and another on the mound that overlooked the east side, and piled up boards and railroad crossties that he intended to set on fire and light up the fields of fire in case of a night attack. Obregón placed the bulk of his men to the west of the plaza on the undulating ground there, and the rest on the hills to the south and the flatlands to the east on the other side of the railroad.[60] (See Map 1.1)

Tactical Command	Major Unit organic to	J	O	T	Total
Federals:					
Parra, Alfonso (Major)	5th Infantry Battalion	1	20	152	173
Figueroa, Edmundo (1st CPT)	10th Infantry Battalion		4	100	104
Méndez, Raúl A. (2nd CPT)	27th Infantry Battalion		1	30	31
Villaseñor, Rafael (Comandante)	47th & 48th Rural Corps	1	4	80	85
Amarillas, Tiburcio (2nd Officer)	Federal Auxiliary Corps		2	60	62
Escandón, Francisco (Colonel)	Agua Prieta Fed Aux Corps	1	6	80	87
Cordero, Jesús (2nd CPT)	Section of 80-mm. Mortars		2	20	22
Cadena, Rafael A. (LT)	Section of Machine Guns		2	30	32
					596
Constitutionalists (estimated):					
Alvarado, Salvador (Colonel)	Federal Auxiliary Corps				434
Manríquez, Federico (Major)	3rd Irr. Infantry Battalion of Sonora				317
Guerrero, Antonio A. (LTC)	4th Irr. Infantry Battalion of Sonora				433
Chávez Camacho, Jesús (Colonel)	5th Irr. Infantry Battalion of Sonora				436
Félix, Carlos (Major)	47th Federal Rural Corps				125
Acosta, José M. (1st CPT)	48th Rural Corps				74
Diéguez, Manuel M. (Colonel)	Voluntarios de Cananea				400
Betancourt, Fernando	Voluntarios de Hermosillo				61
Ramírez, Manuel (1st CPT)	Voluntarios de Horcasitas				58
Kloss, Maximiliano (1st CPT)	Section of Machine Guns				42
Calles, Plutarco Elías (LTC)					300
Bracamontes, Pedro (LTC)					400
	Voluntarios de Magdalena				35
					3,115

Table 1.1 Battle of Naco Troop Strengths

April 8

Because the Federals had clear fields of fire extending out several hundred meters, Colonel Obregón decided to employ an "Emissary of Peace," a train filled with explosives designed to enter Naco, explode, and sow panic amongst the defenders. Colonel Alvarado's men, situated some eight hundred meters to the west of Naco, would attack when the train exploded, joined by Calles and Bracamontes' men attacking from the east. Since Bracamontes was to prepare the train, Calles retained command of the east flank. Diéguez's men remained behind Alvarado's, in reserve. On the night of April 7 Obregón kept his promise to inform the American authorities of any assault on Naco so they could evacuate the U.S. side and went to Agua Prieta to report that the assault would take place the next day. But the American colonel who was to receive the message had gone to Naco, so Obregón returned to Calles' camp at 10:00 and sent a message to the American from there. At 11:30 p.m. Colonel John Guilfoyle arrived and Obregón conferred with him for about a half-hour. Afterward Obregón went to kilometer 9 on the railroad; he had to take the long way around through La Morita and El Papalote and did not arrive until 2 a.m. There he learned that Alvarado had changed the plan of attack at the insistence of Bracamontes. Instead of using the train, Bracamontes went on foot with a cart loaded with dynamite, some cables, wires, etc., that he planned to explode. Obregón sent Bracamontes a note to inform him that he would be held responsible for the outcome of the battle if he contravened Obregón's instructions, and he also sent a message to Alvarado informing him of what he had told Bracamontes. Obregón thought that would be the end of the matter, since he had categorically commanded that no one should attack before the explosion, and therefore Bracamontes would be forced to go with the original plan.[61]

But at 4 a.m. the Federals discovered the presence of Alvarado's men and there was a thunderous volley from the rolling terrain to the west. The bullring and those positions closest to it returned fire; from that moment on the hissing of bullets was incessant. After about an hour the besiegers, disregarding the Federal artillery, started to come down from the heights in an assault that served no other purpose than to thin their ranks, forcing them back to their original positions, but without being discouraged. On the contrary, the Constitutionalists seemed to draw strength from the Federal bugle calls of *diana*. They reorganized and charged again, and again, for three hours.[62]

Suddenly the furious yelps of a yapping puppy in a very close ditch drew the attention of some defenders in the bullring. "What is that?" Federal Captain Luis G. Mendoza inquired. Then answering himself, he said, "It must be those wretches" (although he actually used a harsher word). And with that he loaded a Marten Hale rifle grenade and fired it in the direction of the suspicious noise, to good effect. Suddenly fire became generalized from that direction, no farther than sixty meters away. Approaching with serpentine stealth and feline cunning, the Yaquis had succeeded in taking possession of a ditch, evading the Federal watch established there. Undoubtedly, they had positioned themselves there to cooperate at the opportune moment in the assault with their compañeros to the Federal rear. The defenders realized the tactical advantage held by the Yaquis and they saw very clearly that the only effective measure for clearing them from there would be an assault. There was no other way.[63]

Colonel Escandón proposed the assault, and soon the word passed up and down the various positions on the line—"Assault, assault." Calling Captain Mendoza by his nickname, he said, "You, Comodino, fall on the right flank to beat them right in that position, and we will hit them in the front...At my command everyone, hurl themselves [forward]." For a moment the shooting stopped, substituted by the clanking of bayonets fixing on Mausers. Then a few words of encouragement from the officers, and suddenly: "Assault!" The Federals cleared their trenches, racing like crazy for the enemy. Arriving at the edge of the ditch, they fired their weapons, point blank, and fell upon the Constitutionalists using their bayonets. The Yaquis recoiled against the opposite walls of the arroyo and shot their weapons in a last effort. Others, without thinking of the dangers to their own comrades, and with only the desire to kill, lit their hand bombs. Meanwhile the other positions fell silent, awaiting the outcome of that magnificent and bloody struggle. The revolutionaries began to flee, leaving some behind lying in their pools of blood. The Constitutionalists to the west then withdrew without firing another shot to the hills to the south.[64]

When those who had participated in the assault entered the plaza for their meal, General Ojeda was at the door of the headquarters cheering them, and they returned the cheer, "Viva our General Ojeda!" General Ojeda personally doled out the food to his men. He had barely finished when the joking started as they cleaned their weapons, some finding them jammed by blood that had run from the bayonet all the way to the bolt, even plugging the muzzle. News of the counterattack caught the attention of President Huerta who had Ojeda promoted to general of brigade.[65]

That night, according to the Huertista anti-American rant, the Constitutionalists entered U.S. soil and constructed four lines of fighting positions to better dominate and flank the Federals. The foxholes started from near the rolling terrain about a thousand meters to the west from Naco and went a good distance inside the United States, all under the watchful eyes of the men of the U.S. 9th Cavalry Regiment, which was patrolling inside its own territory the places contiguous to the theater of combat. The American authorities even allowed the Constitutionalists to emplace a machine gun right next to the landmark that served as the dividing line between the two countries whence they could hit the Federal positions inside the houses, protect the advance of their attack force, and keep the streets clear. What is more, patrols of the U.S. 9th allegedly used automobiles to deliver as much food as the Constitutionalists desired right to their foxholes, making sure to turn off their headlights at nighttime. Around 6 p.m. a train arrived bringing the Constitutionalists combat gear and collecting the wounded. The Federals, listening to the bellowing winds, remained alert in their positions. The Constitutionalists spent the next couple of days preparing for a night assault.[66]

April 10

At 3 a.m. on April 10 the Constitutionalists used a train to push the "Emissary" to kilometer 7 in the direction of Naco and then waited for an explosion that never came. Since Alvarado's men never heard anything, and since they had received categorical instructions not to attack without hearing the detonation, they did not enter into action. But around 4 a.m. some Constitutionalists attacked the bullring trying to take possession of the artillery there. Captain Cordero, in command of the pieces, recognized their intent, and let them come into range and then swept them with grapeshot, aided by rifle fire from the infantry support. Around seven in the morning the Federals noticed the "máquina loca" that threatened not just the whole town, but the U.S. side as well. The platform car loaded with five boxes of dynamite and powder had rolled to a stop somewhere between kilometer 5 and 6 where it was later collected by the Constitutionalists and returned to the original departure point.[67]

Thus, nothing of much importance happened during the day until around 6 p.m. when about two hundred Federals on the east side entered into action, extending themselves through the plain to clear those revolutionaries barricaded in the arroyo and the cemetery. From inside the plaza reinforcements rushed to join them and together, impelled by the energy of the push and in the heat of the moment, they threw back the Constitutionalists after about an hour. After that, night settled in and a dead calm reigned until around 10:30 p.m.[68]

Whistling among the Yaquis announced to the Federals that the revolutionaries were communicating orders to each other. The defenders did no more than straighten up to take a look when in an instant an enormous and moving serpent of light formed by rifle fire interrupted the shadows. The Constitutionalists, impetuous as ever, launched a furious attack on the plaza. Naco exploded with rifle fire, yells, howls, commands, the crackling of machine guns, and the report of shells and grenades. The carnage lasted an hour and a half, resulting in a new victory for the defenders who forced the attackers back to their original positions.[69]

While still dark Federal Captain Mendoza, who was quite corpulent, asked Ojeda for permission to take twenty men to see if he could capture the machine gun located near the marker on the international border from the *mecos* ("chichimeca"). Ojeda refused, initially, but after repeated requests he relented. Mendoza, wrapped in a wide and long black cape, took the lead in front of twenty men and Sub-lieutenant Secundino Anda as they made their way along the border, using the terrain to conceal themselves, until they arrived about two hundred meters away from the machine gun. Then he ordered everyone down as he prepared his Marten Hale grenade when, from the other side, there came a sudden discharge; Mendoza dropped the weapon, opened his arms, and fell. Then, according to the Federals, the Constitutionalists charged from their foxholes on U.S. territory and forced the rest of Mendoza's overwhelmed small force to flee.[70]

At some point the sub-lieutenant stopped his fellow Federals in their flight, shouting "the Federation does not flee!" and the detachment turned to defend itself. Then something quite tragi-comic happened. The sub-lieutenant, a diminutive figure, tried to carry the corpulent Captain Mendoza, seriously wounded and moribund, in the midst of the firefight. He eventually saved the captain from falling into enemy hands, but at times they had to roll him and at others four men had to carry him, until they got him back to safety. Despite their efforts he died shortly thereafter. All day and night the shooting did not stop. The garrison was now at four days without sleep, and because of the small number of Federal defenders, there was no opportunity for men to take shifts resting.[71]

April 11

After the failed Emissary of the previous day the Constitutionalists agreed that they would make one more attempt, but if the detonation failed to occur this time, then they would attack anyway. Additionally, at 3:30 a.m. Obregón had personally pushed the Emissary all the way to kilometer 4 and then waited once again for an explosion that never happened. After the obligatory time for the Emissary to deliver the message had passed, Obregón then waited for the assault to occur. And he waited, and waited. Nothing…all he could hear was the rifle and artillery fire of the Federals, no return from the Constitutionalists, so he went with his staff to the major staging area of his forces and found no one there. Next, he marched off to Calles' camp. From there he scheduled a meeting to be held the following day at noon at headquarters for all the Constitutionalist commanders.[72]

April 12

Back at headquarters Obregón received a report from Colonel Alvarado about the previous day's failed assault. Alvarado had arrived at the appointed assault position at 2:45 a.m., and when the signal of attack had been given Majors Carlos Félix and Luis Bule left with their men to deliver the assault. Alvarado followed behind with the Voluntarios de Magdalena Corps. Only ten minutes had passed when Félix came back to report that the Emissary had slowed down and stopped short of Naco. Félix returned to his men to continue the advance, but he was unable to proceed because his men refused to enter into battle, demoralized by the Federal artillery exploding around them amid the chaparral. Almost at the same time Major Bule appeared before Alvarado declaring that his men also refused to go forward and had begun dispersing in small groups, so Alvarado and the two majors decided to spend the rest of the hours of darkness collecting up the dispersed so that upon daybreak the Federal machine guns would not cut them to pieces. Meanwhile, a Captain López de Mendoza, who was to bring the 5th Irregular into position, got lost in the night and could not bring that contingent into place. At the same time, Obregón noticed that on the east side the forces of Bracamontes, Calles, José María Acosta, and Arnulfo R. Gómez only fired a few rounds and then retreated under the pressure of Federal artillery fire.[73]

After reading Alvarado's report, Obregón started to prepare for the meeting with his principal jefes when the first of them, Pedro Bracamontes, arrived with some armed men and threatened to kill Obregón, saying that he had betrayed them and they needed to get him out of the way. Obregón managed to impose his will on Bracamontes and his supporters without having to resort to force, which he could have done by appealing to his own men in the surrounding camps, but from then on the two men would be hard and fast enemies. A little while later the rest of the commanders arrived and began speaking of the difficulties that they had encountered; the demoralization that some jefes, officers, and men had begun to experience; and the need to take Naco as soon as possible. Alvarado specifically mentioned the formidable Federal defensive works and that his men were not used to attacking such fortifications, as the previous night's action had proved. Bracamontes said that his men had always been used as cannon fodder and therefore did not trust higher command, while Major Bule also said his men refused to enter into combat. But Majors Francisco Urbalejo, Félix, Acosta, and Captain Gómez backed Obregón's plan of assault and indicated their willingness to enter into action and do their duty, asking only that the hour of attack be changed to 3 a.m. Obregón agreed to this slight modification, judging it reasonable. Then the other officers agreed to lead their men into the combat, and Diéguez, whose men had been held in reserve, offered to lead his command in the assault the following day were the upcoming attack to fail.[74]

The new plan of attack proposed that Colonel Alvarado's Federal Auxiliary Corps deploy on the west side along a ditch about eight hundred meters from the town and continue harassing the besieged Federals. There would be two columns of attack. Constitutionalist Major Félix commanded one column composed of two hundred men from the 47th Rural Corps, the 5th Irregular Battalion of Sonora, and the Voluntarios de Horcasitas Corp that would attack from the west, departing from the ditch containing Alvarado's men, with Diéguez's men in reserve behind them. A second assault column under Major Acosta to the east with 150 men of the 48th Rural Corps, the 3rd Irregular Battalion of Sonora (Arnulfo R. Gómez), was supported by Calles' and Bracamontes' men in reserve.[75] The requirements of international diplomacy and the need to attenuate as much as possible any projectiles landing on the U.S. side of the line account for this unusual east-west order of battle, which exposed the Constitutionalists to friendly fire as they charged against a common point of convergence from opposite directions.

At 5 p.m. Obregón ordered those who were going to take part in the attack to begin taking their places, first delivering a speech that extolled the worthiness of their cause. The excitement built up to such a degree that Second Captain Tiburcio Morales and four soldiers who were ill left the railcar serving as a field hospital and requested permission to take part in the attack, which Obregón allowed. Obregón marched with Major Félix to the ditch eight hundred meters distant from the town where Alvarado's men were busy harassing the Federals as Félix's men tried to get some sleep so that they would be fresh for the early morning assault.[76]

Inside the town Ojeda became taciturn. Sometimes he broke his silence, and even joked, but he could not avoid the obvious. There was no more ammunition but what the men had in their cartridge belts, the Marten Hale grenades had been reduced to twenty-five, and the mortars only had three shells. But then he received a message: The Secretary of War told him that in a short while he would receive an abundant shipment of ammunition. The United States had agreed to allow passage of ammunition to the defenders of Naco. On the other side, a long convoy brought reinforcements to the Constitutionalists in the afternoon. The shooting was slow, but continuous. The Americans spread out a great number of armored cars along the international line, and then someone told Captain Cordero that the attack would be at 3 a.m. "How do you know?" he asked. The answer: because the Constitutionalist cars covered their headlights three times, and then the cars on U.S. side did the same, confirming the message received.[77]

April 13

At midnight Félix's men began to get ready for the attack and then started moving into position as Majors Urbalejo and Acosta and their men did the same on the east side. Around 1 a.m. one volley was heard, followed by many more, and soon the shooting became generalized. Constitutionalists to the west opened fire and began to advance on the town under the cover of darkness. One of the Federal mortars ran out of ammunition and its crew immediately disabled the weapon. The Federals inside the town observed the muzzle flashes of the Constitutionalists and quickly deduced a flanking maneuver intending to cut the Federals off from the U.S., so General Ojeda immediately ordered the heights closest to the borderline occupied. The besiegers had to attack the positions of the 10th Battalion, commanded by Captain Edmundo Figueroa, effectively assisted by Captain Adolfo Martínez working a machine gun. The assault was not long in coming. It had an ardor so crazy, so sanguinary, that Figueroa and Martínez were almost left without any people, but the attackers turned back. The two Federal officers requested reinforcements that arrived in a timely fashion, but so too did the second attack. A terrible fight resumed until the Constitutionalists, with horrible losses, retreated.[78]

Ojeda lit the woodpiles, which perfectly illuminated the fields of fire—but then the smoke began to obscure the battlefield and revolutionaries and Federals became mixed in the first line of trenches such that the defenders' machine guns and cannon only tore up unoccupied terrain. Obregón wanted to send in Alvarado's men, but they refused to attack in the dark.[79] Ojeda ordered the remaining mortar placed a short distance from the border, because he was convinced that the Yankees were allowing the revolutionaries to use their territory, later declaring that his suspicions had been confirmed. With Figueroa and Martínez reinforced by the mortar, as alleged by the Federals, the Constitutionalists knew they could not roll up the defenses. So they entered from the United States' side, charging en masse through the street closest to the international line. But Cordero was there and received them with grapeshot. Decimated, they retreated. Comandante Villaseñor, on the east side, tried to cut off the Constitutionalist escape. He would have done it, but the thirty-six Yaquis in his command turned their guns on him, and joining their brethren, penetrated the plaza. That left no Federal positions remaining except those of the "Cubillas Hermanos" commercial house, the hotel, the South edge, the bullring, and the cemetery on the east side.[80] Throughout the revolution, the Federal defenders of plazas occupied the local cemeteries because they were located on high ground and offered potential cover, meaning that they possessed tactical significance and could not just be left to the enemy, but because they were also located on the outskirts of town, occupying them tended to stretch the lines of defense for garrisons typically already undermanned.

At daybreak, 5:30 a.m., Obregón sent in two hundred of Alvarado's men under Major Bule to reinforce those Constitutionalists attacking on the west side. From the east the men of Captains Miguel M. Antúnez and Escajeda joined the fight, followed quickly by all of Calles' and Bracamontes' men. As the Federals began to run out of ammunition, they abandoned their positions to cross the international line, until Ojeda remained with only about one hundred men covering the bullring, the hotel, and the "Cubillas" house.[81] The lack of ammunition in the bullring and immediate positions ultimately reduced Ojeda to occupying "Cubillas," situated at the end of Internacional Street just a short distance from U.S. territory, and the hotel. There he holed up with the few men left who had ammunition. It was only because of the presence of these few men, fifty at most, that he could keep Calles with his people and those Yaquis who had just defected from cutting off the retreat of the defenders. When Calles appeared opposite "Cubillas," the mortar crew blocking Internacional Street barely had time to shoot at him and escape to "Cubillas." Ojeda asked sub-lieutenants José Ramírez and Francisco González how many shells they had left. One was the answer. "Lob it at them." Choosing two men to accompany them, they ran back outside the building to the piece, fired off the round, disabled the weapon by removing the breechblock, and escaped across the border. The round was a direct hit on the houses occupied by Calles' men, causing them to smoke and burn.[82]

After that the combat died down a little. But there were still those Federals who wanted to leave nothing to the Constitutionalists, so they went about collecting any ammunition from the cadavers of their compañeros. Suddenly, there were shots coming from the Hotel, not far from the Federal position. "Go see what that is," General Ojeda commanded. It was Captain Cordero, shooting the Federals' livestock so that they would not fall into the hands of the Constitutionalists. He saved the last round for his beloved horse; caressing it, he spoke its name and then shot it in the head.[83]

The shooting picked up again, and then the Federals in the hotel who had expended all their ammunition ran to join Ojeda. "General, we have no ammunition." The general turned red, yelling "Ammunition, ammunition, I have no ammunition!" His officers were overwhelmed at seeing him lose his composure. The ammunition was just across the border, but the Yankees were withholding it from him. When Ojeda's Yaquis began to abandon the eastern defenses immediate to the border around mid-morning, he destroyed his machine guns and other materiel the best he could, set fire to his magazine, and sent his men across the border, telling them to leave their weapons and try not to get hit.[84]

One of the general's aides, the short, seventeen-year-old Sub-lieutenant Alfredo Serret, refused to surrender. In a foolhardy move, he left cover to shoot at the revolutionaries and got himself killed. A fellow sub-lieutenant retrieved his lifeless comrade, but the soldier trying to carry him over the border only took a few steps outside the "Cubillas" house when he was felled with a bullet to the face. Burly Sergeant Romero of the 5th Battalion stepped forward saying, "I will carry him myself and return," which he did to the applause of Americans on the other side. Finally, Ojeda was only left with about six men, including Colonel Escandón, whom he ordered to burn the remaining rifles. He crossed over to the other side where he was congratulated by the commander of the U.S. 9th. Moments later, with "Cubillas" housing the armament in flames, Escandón crossed with three soldiers. The Federals were taken to the Opera House and detained.[85]

By noon all scattered resistance had ended. The Federals suffered seventy-nine killed and twenty-three wounded, with two officers and eighty men taken prisoner. The Constitutionalists mourned the loss of two officers and fifteen troops killed and forty men wounded, including four officers, figures that were surely understated. The actual number of casualties probably approached two hundred. Obregón claimed as booty the two 80-mm. mortars, 104 Mausers, 30,000 rounds, horses, mules, and other equipment, although the Federals claimed that the guns had been disabled and the Mausers burned.[86] The Constitutionalists had complete control of northern Sonora.

Southern Sonora

In the southern part of the state, numerous local officials also declared their rejection of the new Huertista government and began recruiting and organizing troops, starting with state legislator Carlos Planck in La Colorada, who recruited about two hundred middling-armed men in early March, and then followed by Rosario García in Sahuaripa District. In Alamos District, José J. Obregón (Colonel Álvaro Obregón's brother), Fermín Carpio, and Severiano (son of Don Severiano) Talamantes, Jr., who raised about six hundred Mayo Indians, mostly armed with bows and arrows but a few with firearms, also recruited men to the cause. Since Colonel Benjamín Hill had been appointed by the interim governor as the chief of operations in the south, he left Hermosillo at the beginning of March with an escort of about one hundred men from the 5th Irregular Battalion of Sonora and headed for La Colorada, just thirty kilometers

southeast of the state capital to meet with Planck. From there he continued on to La Cuesta and Tecoripa to interview Anacleto Girón, a Maderista
leader from the mining region of La Concentración and La Dura who
promised to raise a sizeable contingent of volunteers for the revolution.
Hill conferred upon him the rank of lieutenant colonel and left Tecoripa
for La Concentración on March 17.[87]

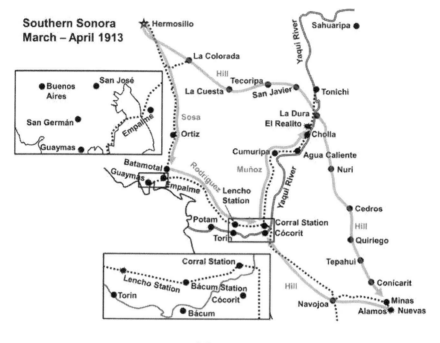

Map 1.3

The Federal commander in charge of maintaining order in southern
Sonora was Colonel Jesús P. Díaz, who had taken over as Jefe de las Armas of
Torín after General Gil left for Empalme. Given that most of the inhabitants
in the region were against the Federals and he only had about six hundred
men, his mission left him spread quite thin. For now his Federals retained
control of the Southern Pacific Railroad from Empalme as far south as
Lencho Station, which was only 3.5 kilometers north of the town of Torín,
headquarters of the 1st Military Zone and located on the Yaqui River. But
when brothers Pedro and Ignacio Quiroz took up arms in Cócorit, just south
of Corral Station, and Anacleto Girón with three hundred men reinforced
the Municipal President of La Dura, who had already taken up arms against
the government, the Federals divined the intentions of the revolutionaries to

take possession of the railroad line from Tonichi to Corral Station, and then march on Guaymas. Therefore, General Gil ordered Díaz to send a column to attack La Dura.[88]

LA DURA AND LA CONCENTRACIÓN, MARCH 18-19

Federal Lieutenant Colonel Eleazar C. Muñoz departed Torín on March 17 with Captain Roberto Montaño de la Llave and nine men of the 10th Battalion and one machine gun and marched north to Lencho Station to meet up with the rest of his command, four officers and 150 men of the 28th Battalion commanded by First Captain Salvador Flores. Obeying orders received from the Zone Chief, Muñoz loaded his men on a train and headed to Corral Station where he picked up another fifty men and two officers of the 28th under Second Captain Pablo R. Moreno and continued north toward La Dura, some 116 kilometers away. Due to the imprudence of Hill and the Quiroz brothers, who remained unaware of the Federal column's approach, Muñoz was able to advance as far as Agua Caliente, where he detrained due to some burnt bridges, and continued on foot. The first day's march ended in Cholla, only twelve kilometers from La Dura, where the Federals spent the night. They had barely begun the second day's march when they encountered the advance forces of the Constitutionalists.[89]

Around 9 a.m. they reached El Realito where the townsfolk told them that the people of La Concentración and La Dura had joined forces under Anacleto Girón and had fortified the latter town in order to be able to repulse the Federals. From then on, Muñoz took extreme precautions, sending a section from the 10th in the vanguard. At that point the Federals had to go through one of the rockiest canyons in the region, formed by mountainous and steep walls, through which the Yaqui River flows. The Constitutionalists placed their forces in a choice location about three kilometers from La Dura at an unfordable bend in the river where they could place men on heights to the north, east, and west. Entering the area Federal Captain Montaño started to take fire. Muñoz immediately deployed his force to conquer the heights, keeping Montaño's men deployed on a firing line supported by the railroad embankment where he had his machine gun and sending Captain Flores to scale and clear the revolutionaries from the hills on the west side.[90]

Around 3 p.m. Flores had achieved his objective and forced the Constitutionalists to flee to the north when he was attacked from the direction of San Javier, which must have been Colonel Hill. Hill's men could not push Flores' Federals off their positions and fell back to a nearby hill in order to continue the fight. To the east, Muñoz decided to send Captain Moreno with fifty men to enter the woods and try to surprise the Constitutionalists at the summit of that hill. The Constitutionalists on that side did not notice Moreno's Federals until too late and retreated back toward La Dura, permitting Moreno to advance to within two kilometers of the town. At that point he had to stop and hold his position as night closed in. The next morning the fighting resumed, with the Federals still unable to put the Constitutionalists to flight and take possession of the towns, so Muñoz decided to break contact and withdraw.[91]

After two days of combat his Federals were very hungry; zone headquarters had not provided any food, and the soldiers had not eaten anything since a small breakfast two days earlier. Additionally, the Constitutionalists maintained control of a third commanding hill, and the Federals had run exceedingly low on ammunition. They had only been issued one hundred rounds per man and that surely was not enough to accomplish their mission. Muñoz had his men improvise some makeshift litters to transport the wounded, and at 3 a.m. on March 20 they retreated under the concealment of darkness, covered by a Sub-lieutenant Ramos in the rearguard. The following day Muñoz gave his report from Cumuripa to General Gil; he had lost two killed, four wounded, and four missing, but he claimed to have recovered twelve dead revolutionaries on the field of combat. Gil ordered Muñoz's command to return to Corral Station.[92]

The fight at La Dura once again demonstrated how deficiencies in the Federal Army's logistical practices could lead to defeat. The Huertista chronicler Ceballos drew comparisons between the Federal Army and Santa Anna's that had been defeated by the Americans over half a century before, complaining that little had changed since lieutenant colonel of artillery Manuel Balbontín wrote: "As far as the feeding of the troops on campaign, the Government worries itself little. Any force put on the march, whoever has command takes care of feeding it with whatever resources might be found on the way. It never brings along a quartermaster, and even if there were one, means of transportation would be lacking." The Federal Army's logistical inadequacies were painfully obvious to all observers, civilian and military alike. Moreover, this oversight did not just occur in Sonora but in all parts of the country where the Federal soldiers earned the well-deserved nickname *bocas de palo*, "for having lost the custom of eating," just like the veterans of Mexico's Army of the North in 1847.[93] Employing the same methods as practiced by Santa Anna against the Texans and Americans would only produce a similar ignominious defeat.

ALAMOS, APRIL 5-17

After La Dura, Benjamín Hill headed south for Alamos, essentially taking the same route that the invading Colorados had taken the year before: Nuri, Cedros, Quiriego, Tepahui, and Conícarit. On April 5 Hill took the bulk of his forces to Minas Nuevas on the road between Navojoa and Alamos where he intended to cut the rails and establish his headquarters in order to threaten the latter plaza.[94] The Constitutionalists wanted to take Alamos for two reasons: 1.) to keep any government elements in the southern part of the state and Alamos from uniting with the main Federal concentration, and 2.) to take control of the annual garbanzo harvest that yielded annually about five million pesos, although getting the product past Empalme, which was occupied by General Gil's soldiers, to foreign markets still posed a problem for the Constitutionalists.[95]

As Hill's advance forces moved into Minas Nuevas they ran into about seventy Huertistas from Alamos, and a heated firefight erupted that lasted about a half-hour. Afterward the Huertistas fled back to Alamos leaving behind four dead, including Alfredo Santini. The jefe de las armas of Alamos, Pánfilo Santini, commanded the garrison with the assistance of Adrián Marcor, the jefe político of the district who had so ably defended the plaza against the Colorados the year before. Apparently, the garrison only consisted of about two hundred volunteers raised in the town. First Captain (EME) Flavio S. Palomares, who happened to be in the plaza on unlimited leave, helped direct the construction of some defensive works. They mostly consisted of a series of lunettes on Campana Hill and another on Guadalupe Hill about three hundred meters from the edge of town on the road to Minas Nuevas. Hill's spies, rather mistakenly, reported that the garrison consisted of more than five hundred men with abundant ammunition, and that the Huertistas had constructed fortifications all around the town and planted mines in those places that the Constitutionalists would have to penetrate in an attack.[96]

Based on these reports, Hill decided to orchestrate a series of feints against the town and force the defenders to exhaust their ammunition. The tactic produced the desired results since every time Hill's men approached the defenders overreacted with copious fire. After eleven such faked assaults the Constitutionalists prepared to deliver the real thing since the defenders' morale and ammunition both had diminished sufficiently. Thus, on the day of April 16 Lieutenant Colonel José Díaz López with the volunteer force that he had raised in Chínipas set up on the hills of Agua Escondida in order to attack the plaza from the west, while Hill with about two hundred men approached through the Capilla de Zapopan to the north. The opposing forces battled each other all day and Hill succeeded in reaching as far as La Esmeralda, some two kilometers from Alamos, and ordered an attack on the Huertista fort just four hundred meters away. The fighting continued throughout the night and Constitutionalist Colonel Alejandro Gandarilla arrived after a forced march with thirty more men to participate in the attack.[97]

At 1 a.m. the Huertistas raised the white flag of parlay, but as it was subsequently revealed that they were not yet prepared to surrender the plaza, the battle renewed with more intensity than before. The Huertistas occupying Campana Hill opposite the railroad station posed a particular problem for the Constitutionalists, and so Colonel Hill sent a group under Colonel Juan Antonio García with Major Juan Cruz to clear it, which they accomplished around 1 p.m. Two hours later the Huertistas surrendered unconditionally. Since Hill's men were in the worst need of food and equipment he paroled his prisoners, mostly wealthy civilians, levying upon them stiff fines. With these funds Hill could afford to outfit his men; provide funds to expeditionary troops from Sinaloa, as well as Díaz's Guerrilla from Chínipas; and start to repair the railway to Cruz de Piedra, due east of the port of Guaymas. Of course, one soldier's military economy is another's thievery. In no time the Huertista propaganda machine reported how, with a rifle in hand, Hill succeeded in settling some mortgages that he had in Alamos and then deposited $160,000 in a bank in Nogales, Arizona.[98] Small arms and ammunition are the working capital of revolutionaries, however, and one must have money to procure them.

The day after Hill took Alamos, representatives of the State of Sonora arrived in Coahuila. After meeting with First Chief Carranza they signed the Monclova Accords, later ratified by the Sonoran legislature, which committed the army of Sonora to the Constitutionalist cause, although the Sonorans had been called "Constitutionalists" weeks before these formal acts of signing. At this point, the Sonoran soldiers turned their attentions to the remaining Federal concentrations at Empalme and Torín. Obregón left Alvarado and Calles to safeguard the U.S. border while he went to Hermosillo only to learn, on April 19, that Constitutionalist Colonel Ramón V. Sosa had just been defeated in combat at San Germán the day before. In order to lift the spirits of Sosa's men, as well as to begin operations in the southern part of the state, he left for Batamotal Station (only twelve kilometers north of Guaymas) where Sosa had his camp.[99]

Sosa had departed Hermosillo headed south on the same day as Obregón had gone north, March 6. Governor Pesqueira had given Sosa command of the remnants of the 2nd Irregular Cavalry Corps under the leadership of Major Jesús Trujillo (described by Ceballos as a highwayman and cattle rustler being sought for his crimes) with just five officers and about 150 men. Their mission was to go to the Guaymas Valley, tear up the railroad track between Ortiz and Empalme, recruit people to the cause, and keep an eye on the Federals around Guaymas and Torín who might try to make a move against Hermosillo. Sosa did such an impressive job of accomplishing his assignments that by mid-April he had taken up track, established his headquarters at Batamotal Station, and so effectively recruited that his force now reached about eight hundred men, rivaling the number of Federals stationed in and around Guaymas.[100]

Federal General Gil, during Hill's siege of Alamos and under the threat of Sosa in Batamotal Station, had decided to give priority to protecting the Yaqui River from Torín to Potam and, most of all, the area around the city and port of Guaymas. Therefore, he sent the Voluntarios del Mayo Corps to Potam, left the 10th Battalion and parts of the 2nd Rural Corps and 21st Irregular Cavalry Corps in Torín, and brought the 14th Battalion to Guaymas. Around Guaymas he had the 27th Infantry Battalion in Empalme to cover the rail line from there to Lencho Station; the 28th Infantry Battalion in the Rancho de San José de Guaymas in order to watch over the road from Aranjuez and La Pasión Canyon; and in the tannery of San Germán, the 50th Auxiliary Battalion. The remainder of his forces he kept inside the city of Guaymas, all total about eight hundred men.[101]

Nevertheless, Constitutionalist Colonel Sosa retained the initiative and operational supremacy over the Federals to such an extent that on April 5 he sent his mounted forces as far south as Bácum where they destroyed a section of Federals belonging to the 10th Battalion commanded by Lieutenant Adolfo Martínez. Federal Colonel Díaz had sent Martínez to collect up some arms at the nearby Hacienda de Esperanza when they ran into the Constitutionalists. After a two hour firefight the revolutionaries dispersed or captured all those Federals whom they did not kill or wound.[102] In the meantime, those Federals inside Guaymas started to suffer from demoralization since General Gil maintained a defensive posture and the federal government appeared to have abandoned them to their own devices as they confronted, arguably, the forces of the most dangerous state in the country, given Sonora's proximity to the United States and the number, quality, organization, and equipment of her troops. Things started to look up a bit on the same April 5, when Federal Captain Alfonso Martínez Perdomo arrived in Guaymas aboard the *General I. Pesqueira* (of the Compañía Naviera del Pacífico) with four power type artillery pieces, six machine guns, and four officers and sixty-one men.[103]

Alternatively, the meager reinforcements proved notable on three levels: 1. their small numbers increased the discouragement among Gil's soldiers, who had been expecting many more according to scuttlebutt; 2. the over-whelmingly pro-Constitutionalist inhabitants of Guaymas were confirmed in their beliefs that the Federals had no hopes of defeating the Sonorans; and 3. the news of the arrivals actually lifted the spirits of the Constitutionalists, who judged the Federal government weak given such a tepid response. Moreover, on April 18, a second "wave" of Federal reinforcements arrived: twenty officers fresh out of school with an accompanying twenty-nine soldiers. That same day Colonel Sosa learned of Obregón's victory at Naco and, most likely out of a pique of jealousy, decided to attack San Germán to begin a play for Guaymas.[104]

SAN GERMÁN, APRIL 18

General Gil had withdrawn the 27th Infantry Battalion from Empalme to Guaymas on April 15 when he learned that the Constitutionalists were coming down the old Hermosillo road, and the next day he sent Lieutenant Ariza Pérez of the 14th Infantry with eight hand-picked men to burn some crossties on the bridge connecting Guaymas to Empalme, although with unknown effect. Then, at about 3 p.m. on April 18, Gil received word from Lieutenant Colonel Antonio Flores, commander of the 28th Battalion, that he was under attack by about sixty mounted men who approached shouting and firing off their weapons; the Federals took up position and began returning fire. The Federal general ordered Flores to hold his ground and told him that the 50th was coming up the Camino Real from the San Germán tannery to reinforce and support the 28th.[105]

The 50th was commanded by Lieutenant Colonel Ignacio Gómez, who had previously commanded the Federal Auxiliary Corps before it defected virtually wholesale to the Constitutionalists under now-Colonel Salvador Alvarado. As Gómez moved to the northeast, keeping an eye toward the hills of Aranjuez as Gil had instructed him, he noticed that the Constitutionalists had arrived at the pass between Buenos Aires and La Carbonera, and so on his own initiative he halted his progress toward San José to the northeast and deployed his one hundred men on line between the enemy and San Germán, with twenty men on the summit of La Carbonera on the enemy's flank. In effect the sixty revolutionaries attacking San José—an obvious diversion—had broken contact after about fifteen minutes and moved off to the west to join the rest of the group. Now Gómez faced all of Sosa's seven hundred Constitutionalists.[106]

General Gil in San Germán with the 14th Battalion and the artillery sent orders to Gómez to hold his position until the 14th could arrive. This battalion left one section behind as support for the artillery that was in the tannery and marched through a pass of small hills to the west on the Constitutionalist right. The appearance of this force of about 250 men threatening to envelop his whole command forced Sosa to beat a retreat in complete disorder around 5:30 p.m. Since Gil had no cavalry he could not arrange a pursuit. A relatively minor affair, tactically speaking, the Federals only fired off 14,500 Mauser cartridges, did not engage their artillery at all, and recorded only six men wounded (only one seriously), while they recovered twenty-seven dead Constitutionalists, took one prisoner, and later received news of eighty-seven enemy wounded.[107]

Lencho Station, April 24

Reflecting upon Sosa's failed attempt on Guaymas, Obregón realized that he could not conquer the port in a coup de main, especially since his forces had been reduced to only about forty rounds per man, on average. So, he decided to wait for more supplies and to send a Lieutenant Colonel (first name unknown) Rodríguez south with about three hundred mounted men to operate in the Yaqui River region, try to make contact with Colonel Hill, and then attack Federal Army zone headquarters at Torín. The Constitutionalists believed the town to be defended by six hundred Federals, including those led by the irregular jefe José Tiburcio Otero.[108]

After taking Alamos Colonel Hill had begun repairing the rails to Navojoa and then toward Empalme, according to orders received from Obregón. By April 23 Hill was in Cócorit, just less than thirty kilometers from Torín with an advance force in Bácum, when he linked up with Rodríguez's force sent by Obregón. Together the two had around seven hundred men to attack a Federal force estimated at six hundred.[109]

The Federals, meanwhile, had reports that a Constitutionalist military train had just left with three hundred infantrymen to repair the railroad between Navojoa and the camp at Batamotal in order to assist the advance of Colonel Hill's column, which counted Fermín Carpio, Severiano Talamantes Jr., and Ignacio Quiroz among its chief lieutenants. Once the Constitutionalists from north and south of the state linked up, it was believed that they would have an effective fighting force of five thousand men with which to attack Guaymas.[110]

Lencho Station, which was surrounded by a thicket where the wild thistle called "cholla" abounded, offered the best place to stop the Constitutionalists advancing up from the south. Federal Colonel Jesús P. Díaz ordered the commander of the detachment at Lencho, Lieutenant Emilio Maupomé, to take out some sections of rail in Lencho Station and destroy four railroad bridges to the north and seven to the south. On the morning of April 24

Maupomé called Díaz to report dust clouds announcing the approach of a Constitutionalist column coming up from Bataconcita comprised of cavalry and infantry, but as soon as they passed El Tabaco canal, they had split into two with the larger force of infantry heading up the canal to Lencho Station and the smaller mounted contingent continuing on to Torín. Ostensibly the second group sought to keep the Federal garrison from coming to the aid of those at Lencho. Díaz told the lieutenant, who commanded two officers and seventy-three men of the 10th Infantry and a Guerrilla of ten mounted volunteers from Bácum, to retreat if outnumbered, but to destroy the buildings there first. However, by the time he issued these orders the Constitutionalists had already occupied the hills surrounding the station and opened fire. It was 8 a.m. Then, the Constitutionalists downed a telephone pole to cut off communications to the station.[111]

The Yaquis penetrated the thicket, as only they can do, and thus got to within eighty meters of the defending Federals. The Federal positions included nineteen men in a building called the "casa blanca" with Maupomé on a corner of the rooftop personally directing the fire of the only machine gun they had, protected by an improvised parapet of adobe bricks; in another house that functioned as the barracks were another thirty-five men plus the ten volunteers, and in a third house another twenty-nine under the leadership of a Sergeant López. The Constitutionalists attacked tenaciously, but were pushed back by the machine gun that fired at them as soon as they exited the brush. They attacked from the east and then tested the north and finally the west.[112]

Colonel Díaz tried to reinforce the beleaguered force at Lencho Station by sending the commander of the Voluntarios del Mayo Corps, José Tiburcio Otero, with thirty-eight men: ten from his own unit and twenty-five men and three officers of the 10th Battalion. This reinforcing contingent, upon arriving at the Tabaco Canal, was surprised by the mounted Constitutionalists who ambushed them resulting in a much compromised situation for the Federals. So to give effective aid to his comrades, at 8:30 Díaz sent a second force commanded by First Captain Julián J. Arellano with another fifty men of his own 10th Battalion that arrived a half-hour later. However, even these reinforcements could not force the Constitutionalists to yield passage. So Díaz sent a third force under Sub-lieutenant Salvador Méndez with a machine gun and also forwarded Second Captain Roberto Montaño de la Llave with a 70-mm. gun to fire a few shells at the enemy, who finally fled to the north to rejoin the other Constitutionalists. The Federal relief force followed after them, and once it reached Lencho the combat surrounding the station grew in intensity.[113]

The issue was still undecided around 11:30 a.m., so Díaz finally sent a fourth force commanded by First Captain Mariano Sandoval of the 10th with fifty soldiers, two officers and eighteen men of the Voluntarios del Mayo, and two of the 1st Military Zone's guides, which arrived at the station about an hour and a half later. At that point the Federals succeeded in turning the tide and putting the revolutionaries to flight; the Constitutionalists withdrew to Bácum Station, Bataconcita, and then Bácum. Maupomé gave pursuit, but his men could only do so much since they were on foot and the 27th Rural Corps, the Federals' closest sizeable mounted group, was seventy-seven kilometers away in Potam. The Federals lost three dead and nine wounded and reported nineteen dead and more than ten wounded Constitutionalists. They captured nine horses, 39 Winchester carbines, three .30 special rifles, 147 Mausers, 1,135 rounds, four hand bombs, and two first aid kits.[114]

The Anti-gringo Screed

One book that is of incalculable worth for this time frame is *La Infamia Yanqui* ("The Yankee Infamy") by Rómulo Velasco Ceballos, which is notable on two accounts. First, the Federal officers who campaigned in Sonora obviously had the ear of Ceballos, whom they regaled with their war stories, provided with pictures, assisted in drawing maps, and so forth. On that score, the stories he tells in his book either jibe with the official reports that the officers filed with the Secretary of Defense or they fill a lacuna left by the absence of such reports, such as the Battle of Santa Rosa, for which no official report is extant. In other instances, Ceballos served as an eyewitness to events of importance for military history. Second, as the title would imply, Ceballos provides us with a plethora of rants typical of the Huertista hysteria that accused Americans of colluding with the separatist Constitutionalists in order to destabilize the country and then annex parts of Mexican territory.

According to this line of reasoning, the United States was happy to see Mexico again in internal upheaval, "because our weakness meant for it possibilities of absorption and the sureness of greater domination of our natural riches…Therefore, we insist, it is worthy of anathema the current movement of the North and of every other movement that, like it, counts on Yankee money, arms, territory and even government. To ally themselves to the Americans in a similar way [as in 1847] is to authorize them to wound us with the knife that they have never let drop from their hand."[115]

The list of Ceballos's accusations was long: First, Yankees provided fifty filibusters and drove automobiles loaded with food and ammunition out to the Constitutionalists upon their approach to Cananea. Second, the American authorities in Douglas, Arizona, allowed weaponry from Agua Prieta to fall into

Constitutionalist hands. Third, at Naco the Constitutionalists communicated with the U.S. Army, and the Americans permitted the Constitutionalists to dig foxholes a good distance inside their territory to get enfilading fire on the Federals, while the 9th U.S. Cavalry allegedly used cars to deliver food right to the Constitutionalist foxholes, making sure to turn off their headlights at nighttime. Fourth, the night of the attack on San Germán, April 18, the U.S.S. *California* sent launches to Empalme against the prohibition of the Huertista Governor of Sonora, Colonel Francisco H. García, and General Gil in order to carry news of Federal troop movements to the Constitutionalists; in effect, U.S. sailors provided spy service for the Constitutionalists, walking the streets of the port during the day and reporting what they had seen by night. The U.S.S. *California* even changed its mooring to the Isla de Pájaros to serve as a communications center for the Constitutionalists, and when General Gil moved his forces up to San José de Guaymas in an attempt to cut off the Constitutionalists at Empalme after the battle of San Germán, U.S. Admiral W. C. Cowles sent a launch from the U.S.S. *Pittsburgh* to Empalme on the eve of the maneuver and the next day the Constitutionalists abandoned the plaza escaping the Federal pincer (the implication being that the Americans learned of the Federal operation ahead of time and warned the Constitutionalists to get out of Empalme). Fifth, the American Southern Pacific Railroad, alleging financial exigency that Ceballos (obviously not an accountant) challenged, began running the line between Nogales and Empalme without approval from Mexico City, providing money and an expanded range of operations to the Constitutionalists. Also, an American citizen with the last name of Lawton who was a general agent of freight and passengers for Southern Pacific was always talking about an upcoming U.S. intervention. And finally, sixth, Huerta's government had to deport L. H. Morrison, an American employee of the Richardson Company (one of the richest in the republic and accused of using its automobiles to traffic weapons to the revolutionaries), for the crime of traveling with "lots of copies of documents," among them copies of telegrams with news of the fall of Naco, which were plastered all over Sonora in public places, begging the question, so what?[116]

Of all logical fallacies, the appeal from ignorance is perhaps the most insidious. Señor Ceballos freely proffered the most fantastical allegations, such as U.S. Army soldiers delivering chow like so much room service (this claim may be grounded in racism since the troopers of the 9th were African-Americans) to Constitutionalists in the field at Naco and the Americans allowing the revolutionaries to set up a firing line on U.S. territory, or the U.S. Navy offloading war materiel and providing intelligence services to the Constitutionalists; these reports privileged the ability of Americans to acquire and disseminate military information over that of the Constitutionalists' own intelligence service and news easily obtainable in the public domain. Ceballos not only provided absolutely no proof for the baseless and unsubstantiated accusations that he expected his readership to accept at face value but also rejected out of hand any logical explanations.

It is entirely conceivable that the Constitutionalist foxholes at Naco only appeared to be on U.S. territory, especially when one considers the lack of physical barrier separating the two countries in the area and remembers the Constitutionalists at Nogales who accidentally wandered north of the border and were captured and disarmed by American soldiers. (Significantly, Ceballos had nothing to say about the American misdeeds during the attack on Nogales, where there was a local independent press and many U.S. Army soldiers and civilian witnesses.) Additionally, Obregón admitted to communications with the Americans, even meeting with the American colonel at his own headquarters on Mexican soil, but there was nothing either untoward, suspect, or even unprecedented about this meeting; the intent behind the meeting was to exchange information about the upcoming battle in order to avoid unanticipated events and reactions by the U.S. Army and to permit Americans on the northern side to seek shelter.

Entirely missing from the Huertista narrative are any qualms that Ojeda might have experienced about backing himself up to the U.S. border to economize his force (that is, eliminate 180° of his perimeter) and compel the Constitutionalists to attack in an ill-advised east-west direction, as previously mentioned, all the while arranging an escape hatch at the expense of putting American lives and property in harm's way.

Most perplexing, and perhaps offensive, was Ceballos' expectation that the United States government, military, citizens, and companies behave as loyal Huertistas. If indeed Huerta's Secretary of War sent ammunition to Ojeda at Naco, what obligation did the United States have to expedite its clearance through customs? Why did the Federals have to drag U.S. authorities into their war? One must remember that the United States Government, like most Mexicans then and now, did not recognize the legitimacy of Huerta's government. If the American Southern Pacific Railroad continued to run its business without prejudice and the employees of the Richardson Company kept the company of members of prominent revolutionary families in the area, then where is the crime?

*　　*　　*

With a ready state defense establishment paid for by the government in Mexico City, ironically, the Sonorans were well equipped to provide the swiftest and most successful military response to the Citadel cuartelazo and subsequent palace coup. And even at this early stage, the Constitutionalists were exhibiting their enterprising spirit with the conversion of Roberto V. Pesqueira's Commercial Agency of Douglas into the "Revolutionary Agency." Joined by former congressman Adolfo de la Huerta and later many others, this group became what one historian has called the "border brokers," with a commercial network penetrating deep into the United States utilized in the acquisition of war materiel. The money that supplied these commercial agents came from military victories already achieved in these opening first two months. The first money came from securing northern Sonora and its access to tax receipts from local industry, customs levies, and of course, markets. A short time later, in southern Sonora, Benjamín Hill took Alamos then levied loans on the wealthy Huertistas to outfit his men; provide funds to expeditionary troops farther south and east in Sinaloa and Chínipas, Chihuahua; and to begin repairing the railway to Cruz de Piedra, due east of the port of Guaymas.

The entrepreneurial nature of the Constitutionalists stood in stark contrast to the martinets of the Federal Army, such as Pedro Ojeda who snuffed out a possible mutiny, such as that endured at Cananea, by summarily executing a soldier from the Golden 5th. Confronted with a similar challenge to his authority from Pedro Bracamontes that included a threat on his very life, Obregón responded with reason and conviction to get his subordinates to lead their men in a successful assault on Naco. Without regular discipline, instances of insubordination and dissention, almost always over military considerations and never over political ideology, occurred not too infrequently among the Constitutionalists, and revolutionaries in the field often had recourse to persuasion and negotiation to defuse tense situations.

Notwithstanding the lack of regular discipline, on a tactical level the revolutionaries in several instances outperformed the professionals of the Federal Army. Colonel Obregón at both Naco and Cananea placed his machine guns in enfilade and on the ground for effective grazing fire, while Federal General Ojeda placed his up high and in defilade at Naco. Similarly, Federal Lieutenant Maupomé at Lencho Station placed his machine gun on a rooftop and Federal Colonel Díaz sent one single cannon into combat that was used in a direct fire role, even though doctrine dictated using artillery massed and in an indirect fire capacity. (See Appendix A for more information on the placement of machine guns) Federal Colonel Moreno also received a sharp rebuke for his defective leadership in the defense of Cananea; not preparing defenses; not destroying his weapons before surrendering; and not stockpiling provisions, water, or ammunition. A lack of food and ammunition likewise forced

Colonel Eleazar C. Muñoz to turn back at La Dura, once again highlighting the Federal Army's inefficient logistical system, especially as regards operations into revolutionary-held territory. Finally, one observes how an irregular jefe, Otero, was entrusted to lead regulars in the effort to relieve the Federals under attack at Lencho Station. On the other hand, the Constitutionalist defeat at San Germán demonstrated how professionals could disconcert new practitioners in the military arts through maneuver.

On a strategic level, the chess-like moves to control the exceedingly important garbanzo harvest at this early stage of the conflict are astounding: Colonel Hill took Alamos and Federal Gil pushed out from Guaymas to Empalme in an attempt to block the export and monetization of the legumes. But Gil could not stop the Constitutionalists from gathering in the center of the state in order to work on interior lines and defeat the Federals in detail. Ojeda played into his enemy's hands by not coming to the rescue of Kosterlitzky, and then going to the rescue of Moreno too late. Obregón next showed an inclination toward the "indirect method" (discussed in the third volume) to pull Ojeda out of Naco so that he might be caught in a pincer and defeated, but he failed to capitalize on the maneuver, and Calles suffered a defeat at San José. As a result of the Federal Army's monopoly on violence in Mexico and the U.S. arms embargo against the revolutionaries, Ojeda had fire superiority (machine guns, mortars, Marten Hale rifle grenades) in both his victories over Calles and later at Naco, which some might consider an unfair advantage. Ojeda also used the border to his advantage at Naco, economizing his forces and inducing the Constitutionalists to adopt a faulty order of battle (east-west flanks facing each other) out of concerns over rounds landing in the United States. Geopolitical interactions with the United States presented benefits and disadvantages to commanders on both sides, Federal and Constitutionalist, and factored into their decision-making. They operated in a complex diplomatic milieu that did not unilaterally favor one side over the other, but as long as the Constitutionalists kept on winning, their own complaints against the Americans remained somewhat muted. The Huertistas, on the other hand, cranked up the propaganda machine by alleging every kind of transgression. As long as the list of offenses committed by Americans proffered by Señor Ceballos had been so far, he would have much more to say about Americans interfering in the upcoming battles of the Guaymas Valley campaign and immediately thereafter.

Two

Mobilization: March–May, 1913

Three Routes of Advance—Strategic Importance of the Northeast—Axes of Operations in the Northeaster—Cándido Aguilar—Constitutionalist Soldiers—Bookworms and Bookkeepers—Engineer-cum-Artilleryman Carlos Prieto—Arming the Revolutionaries—Intelligence and Troops from the South—Lucio Blanco, Jesús Agustín Castro, and the 21st to Tamaulipas—First Battle of Ciudad Victoria—Carranza's Commanders—General Trucy Aubert in Nuevo León—Ricardo Peña Marches on Monclova—Federal Army Mobilization Measures and Woes and Carranza's Counter Decrees—Chihuahua's Environment—Villa's Return—Military Colonies Mobilize—Charcos—Ojo Caliente—Santa Bárbara—Conchos—Jiménez—Camargo—Federals Abandon Parral—Carranza Puts Villa in Command—Conchos Station—Matías Pazuengo—Durango's 1910 Rebels Return to Service—Cuencamé—El Rodeo—Luis Anaya's Federal Column—Rancho Picardías and Santa Gabriel—First Battle of Durango City and the Federal Pursuit

While the events in Sonora during Huerta's first two months in office were certainly cause for alarm, it did not fill the administration with panic simply because the Northwest did not carry the same strategic weight as other regions of the country. From the perspective of the federal government, with its base of operations secure along the Mexico

City-Veracruz pipeline for the moment, the revolutionaries in the North could invade the Center along three lines of advance: the first from the border towns of the Northeast—Nuevo Laredo, Matamoros, and Piedras Negras—through Monterrey and Saltillo and continuing to San Luis Potosí and points south; the second from Ciudad Juárez in Chihuahua and driving southward to Torreón, Zacatecas, and Aguascalientes; and the third from Sonora to Culiacán, Tepic, and Guadalajara. Federal Army planners deemed this last line of invasion through the Pacific practically impossible because of its great length, because it did not have railroad connections all the way into the Central Plateau, and it required Constitutionalist mastery of the seas since Federals could disembark at numerous points along the coast to cut the Constitutionalist lines of communication. The line of invasion through the heartland from Chihuahua posed a greater threat to the government than the Pacific approach, but still less so than the Northeastern route because it was longer, had only one railroad which possessed great engineering works (meaning bridges) that would be difficult to reconstruct if destroyed by retreating Federals, and south of Torreón the route from the Northeast was much more favorable for the Constitutionalists.[1]

The Northeast

Indeed, the Northeast received the most attention from Federal Army planners for a multitude of vital reasons, not the least being 1.) that it possessed the shortest routes from the North to Mexico City; 2.) its close proximity to the United States railroad centers; 3.) its absolute lack of physical obstacles and geographic broken ground (mountain ranges) perpendicular to the line; 4.) its immediate command of Monterrey, the most important industrial city of the republic, and the ease with which it could be converted into a great base of operations by virtue of its railroad links with Nuevo Laredo, Matamoros, and Piedras Negras; 5.) its control of the coal mines of Coahuila; 6.) its accessibility by Federal follow-on troops disembarking in Tampico; 7.) its numerous railroads whose total destruction was impossible owing to their relatively few engineering works; and 8.) its domination of the theater of operations on the plateau starting from Monterrey, east of the Sierra Madres Oriental.[2]

Map 1.4

In sum, and as opposed to other sectors of the nation, the Northeast possessed progressive state capitals, numerous border towns, and seaports, and they were all connected by railroads and waterways that provided entrepôts for war materiel and multiple axes of operations: 1.) Torreón-Saltillo-Monterrey, 2.) San Luis Potosí-Saltillo-Piedras Negras, 3.) Monterrey-Nuevo Laredo, 4.) Monterrey-Ciudad Victoria-Tampico, 5.) San Luis Potosí-Tampico, 6.) Matamoros-Nuevo Laredo-Piedras Negras, 7.) Lampazos-Monclova-Cuatro Ciénagas-Sierra Mojada, and 8.) Matamoros-Monterrey. The competing armies plotted moves and countermoves designed to secure these strategic points and, once possessed, to keep the lines of communication open between them. Most important were the border towns through which revolutionaries could export cattle and other agricultural products in exchange for war materiel.[3] But while Carranza and his Constitutionalists in the Northeast had been able to take possession of Piedras Negras through diplomacy, they were in no condition to begin offensive operations.

ORIGINS OF THE DIVISION OF THE NORTHEAST

After the failed attack on Saltillo and signing the Plan de Guadalupe in the last week of March, the Constitutionalists continued north to the city of Monclova. The First Chief established his headquarters there in order to coordinate with and receive the new adherents to his movement, where one of the first men to join him was General Cándido Aguilar, the only general in the Constitutionalist ranks at that time. General Aguilar and his *jarochos* of the 38th Rural Corps had been in Durango State at the end of 1912 fighting against the Orozquistas from their base at San Juan de Guadalupe. In December Aguilar had led his Rurales and some local citizens in a surprise attack against the plaza of Chalchihuites, Zacatecas, a strategic halfway point between the Durango and Zacatecas state capitals on the Central Railroad that the rebels Benjamín Argumedo, Cheché Campos, and Indiano Mariano had occupied. Aguilar and his men expelled the Colorados from the town after an hour's combat, but the rebels regrouped and retook the town, with Aguilar's men having to spend the night on a nearby hill. At 5 a.m. the next morning Aguilar again assaulted the plaza, and after three hours of heated fighting, sometimes in close quarters combat employing the blade, the government forces emerged victorious and then turned to recapture Huejuquilla, Jalisco, on December 18, 1912. For his actions of December 6 at Chalchihuites, the Jefe de las Armas of Zacatecas, Juan de Dios Arzamendi, recommended Aguilar for the Military Merit Cross, Third Class, which was to be presented on February 5.[4]

But General Aguilar never received the commendation, because after a few more engagements in December, he became ill with pneumonia and requested leave to recuperate in Córdoba, Veracruz. He was still there when the Citadel cuartelazo took place, and he immediately reported to President Madero in Mexico City to offer his services. A week later Aguilar escaped out the back of the National Palace when the praetorians seized Madero and he returned to Córdoba. From there he made his way to Guatemala, Panama, the United States, and was one of the first to show up in Monclova to offer his services to Carranza.[5] Aguilar had been under arms since Madero's rebellion in 1910 and had participated in campaigns against the Zapatistas, Felicistas, and Orozquistas. Now he would fight the Huertistas.

The rank and file who flocked to the Constitutionalist colors in Coahuila included miners, ranchers from the Rio Grande area, some Kickapoos from Múzquiz, railroad employees, old revolutionaries from the time of José María Garza Galán or supporters of the Flores Magón from Viezca or Las Vacas (Ciudad Acuña), and others from the state's pueblos and countryside.[6] However, according to then-Captain Manuel W. González,

"Almost all…were campesinos of little, or better said no, education, but noble and brave, who instinctively felt the Revolutionary Ideal, and fought for it with the hope of vindicating their rights and the rights of the people."[7] The Constitutionalist Army men, officers, and jefes were young, healthy in body and spirits, hardened by the fatigues of their earlier work in the fields, full of enthusiasm, and above all, volunteers; there was no need to inspect the troops, since all were ready to march or fight at any hour of the day or night.[8]

González likewise boasted of his fellow revolutionaries' lack of military credentials and proclivities:

> a group of poorly armed patriots, almost totally with .30-30s, without military instruction, since although it is true that there were a few of us who had belonged to the army of the line, like [Francisco] Urquizo, Benjamín Bouchez, Agustín Maciel, and two or three more, the rest of us were composed of office workers, railroad men, telegraphers, farmers, and cowboys, who neither knew nor wanted to know of 'marches,' or 'flanks,' or 'half-turns,' nor did we give three peanuts for military discipline.[9]

Urquizo concurred saying, "That of 'whoever be a man, follow me,' was the only command that our jefes knew, and it was very far from being an order, since it left each person to choose whether to follow or not." And in combat, as though more for self-preservation, everyone would yell at different times and tones: "Open up! Open up!" in order to fashion some form of a firing line. The Constitutionalist soldier did not fight just because his jefe so ordered it, but rather to help his compañeros in this or that feat of arms, as though they were somehow obligated to follow orders that did not apply to his own person. Similarly, in the very beginning the revolutionary groupings did not constitute proper military units with typical organizational names but rather went by the name of the jefe that commanded them or figured at the head of them; for example, the force that Colonel Sixto Ugalde commanded came to be "Don Sixto's people," and that of Orestes Pereyra, "those of Don Orestes."[10]

The jefe of each armed group placed his trust in his "secretary," who generally speaking was the biggest bookworm of the group and in charge of drafting the few letters that were necessary, as well as writing the speeches that were delivered sparingly. Another important person in each group, a kind of third boss, held a position something akin to the "Jefe del Detall"

in the army, but at that time among the revolutionaries it was simply designated the "bookkeeper." Many who came to occupy those positions had
previously been clerks for haciendas, converted into bookkeepers by the
vicissitudes of history and because the responsibilities of the military and
civilian positions closely matched one another. They even kept the same
notebooks that before had been used for paying peons and a shabby cash
book, in which they kept track of things such as fodder for the horses, *la
pastura* as it was called; the beeves sacrificed for the sustenance of the force;
and other expenses.[11]

The original artillery consisted of home-made pieces created in the
railroad workshops of Piedras Negras by Carlos Prieto, an engineer who
joined the Constitutionalist Army. Weaponry was hard to come by even
in the border town of Piedras Negras because of the U.S. government's
embargo. The Constitutionalists were only able to restock after the failed
battle of Saltillo in late March owing to the sympathies of individuals
residing in Texas and other places all along the border, having to resort
to non-military grade .30-30 carbines, which had shorter effective ranges
than the Federals' Mausers. Still, the U.S. government captured and jailed
Constitutionalist agents in the United States trying to purchase war materiel, resulting in a continual, but small trickle of smuggled arms and
ammunition that managed to evade the notice of authorities. Many of the
revolutionaries went without weapons, expecting to get them from the
Federals, and the ranchers among them sometimes rode right up to the
Federal firing line in battle, roped the enemy's machine guns, and then
returned to their camp with them.[12]

Lacking sufficient elements of war, and still in the throes of mobilization, the Constitutionalists destroyed the railroad and other communications in order to inhibit the intelligence about their organizing efforts
that might be available to the Federals.[13] Conversely, Carranza obtained
crucial intelligence from his adherents in the nation's capital. After pro-
claiming his Plan de Guadalupe the First Chieftaincy began receiving the
Secretary of War's "Weekly Statements of the Distributions of the Federal
Forces in the National Territory" report from Captain Mariano Vázquez
Shiafino of the Federal General Staff with regularity. Alberto Pani, who
had worked in the Madero administration and went on to provide valu-
able service to the Constitutionalist movement, later wrote of the weekly
Federal Army distribution report, "The fact that, on occasion, such valu-
able documents arrived at my office before the Presidency [Huerta] of the
Republic shows the efficacy of our collaboration with [some inside] the

Secretary of War." Continuing on, he concluded, "In sum, that was how, as revolutionaries living in Mexico City we put ourselves at the service of the good cause; we lived a life of anguishing uncertainty and constant dangers, greater perhaps than those in the places where the fight was unfolding."[14]

Northeasterners already under arms in the South also rallied to the Constitutionalist cause. On March 25, the 2nd Carabineros de Coahuila Corps jumped its barracks in Mexico City, journeying south to operate with Genevevo de la O's Zapatistas, who had been in rebellion against the Madero government. The uprising of these intrepid soldiers steeled the resolve in other Maderistas, such as Comandante Gertrudis G. Sánchez of the 28th Rural Corps who seconded Carranza from Guerrero State with 450 men on March 31 and made his way to Michoacán to campaign; José Rentería Luviano's 41st Rural Corps; and the 21st Rural Corps in Tlalnepantla, Mexico State, headed by Jesús Agustín Castro, which traveled north to Tamaulipas to join Carranza's efforts.[15]

TAMAULIPAS

In one of the most momentous decisions to date, First Chief Carranza sent Colonel Lucio Blanco to secure the vital rail and port city of Matamoros in the first days of April. Blanco's movement into the Tamaulipas area of operations coincided with the arrival of Jesús Agustín Castro's 21st Rural Corps, which had earlier escaped from Tlalnepantla to make its way north and join the Constitutionalist cause.[16] After Huerta's palace coup in February Castro's 21st remained in Mexico City until mid-March when it was ordered back to its barracks in Tlalnepantla. Afterward, some officers of decidedly Porfirista affiliation were then assigned to the corps, not to mention that all the officers of the 14th Rural Corps who also garrisoned the town were of that same political persuasion. After consultations that Castro conducted with his subordinate officers, including his cousin Miguel M. Navarrete, Emiliano P. Nafarrate, and Juan Jiménez Méndez, they all decided to rebel after the paymasters had arrived with the monthly payroll. They would then disarm the 14th Rural Corps, relieving them of all their war materiel, and invite the detachments of the 39th and 50th to share in the 21st Rural Corps' "movement" against the Huertista regime.[17]

At 8 p.m. on March 29, while standing in the Tlalnepantla railroad station, Castro turned over command of the 21st to First Officer Navarrete, leaving him with orders to march to Villa del Carbón the next day and collect all the detachments, since those officers already had their orders, and continue to Tamaulipas State. Castro then got on a train headed north to meet with Carranza, the only leader of a revolution that he recognized, who the Metropolitan press said had crossed over into the U.S. with some followers to get war materiel. Castro passed through San Luis Potosí headed for Tampico where he arrived on March 30, traveling on free passes that the government had given to him previously, since without these he probably would not have been able to make the trip with his limited resources. But the use of these passes also made him more vulnerable to capture by the Huertistas.[18]

From Tampico he went to Monterrey on March 31 and immediately left there the next day at 7 a.m. in order to arrive in Matamoros by 3 p.m. and cross over into Brownsville. After two days in Brownsville, he departed on April 3 for San Antonio at 2 a.m. and arrived at 8 p.m., his primary purpose for stopping there being to meet with Emilio Madero and arrange for some war materiel. But Don Emilio had had enough of revolutions and obviously still grieving over the loss of his brothers, Francisco and Gustavo, supposedly told Castro, "I am not going to get into affairs again; the Mexican people are miserable wretches." But he did give Castro fifteen dollars so that he could get to Eagle Pass, where he arrived at 5 p.m. The next day Castro interviewed with Don Venustiano at his headquarters in the customhouse at Piedras Negras, but the First Chief could not help him because the revolutionary movement was just getting started and everyone was coming to Carranza for material assistance. He did, however, give Castro instructions that carried faculties for naming jefes and officers in the Constitutionalist Army, organizing troops, and doing whatever he thought might benefit the Revolution in the states of San Luis Potosí and Tamaulipas.[19]

On April 8 Carranza and Castro left for Monclova Station where the latter was introduced to Colonels Jesús Carranza and Pablo González, who had just arrived from Lampazos and the vicinity of Nuevo Laredo. The First Chief then ordered Major Francisco Aguirre de León with thirty or thirty-five poorly armed men who were even worse for ammunition to escort Castro on his trip to reunite with his command. With this escort, one hundred dynamite bombs, and ₱250, Castro left by train for Baján, departing the next day, April 11, to find his Rural Police corps and fulfill the First Chief's instructions. Upon approaching Morales Station in the evening of April 16 Castro and his escort destroyed several kilometers of railway and telegraphs and four or five insignificant small wooden bridges. They then headed for Hacienda Mamulique, spent the next day in Sombreretillo, and continued to Cerralvo where they arrived on April 21.[20]

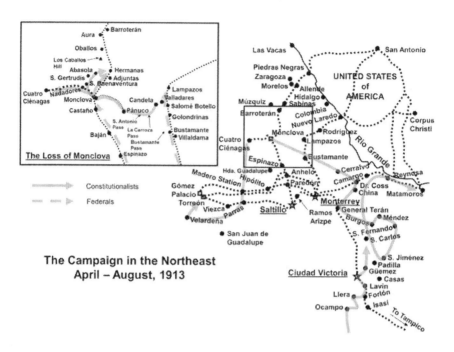

Map 1.5

Here, Castro ran into some rather bad luck, since as it happened, Colonel Lucio Blanco had just passed through the area a short while before, fighting brief engagements against the Federals in Cerralvo and Alhaja, Nuevo León, on April 10 and 12, respectively. On orders from Federal General José María Mier, General Fernando Trucy Aubert sent a small column of Federals consisting of about 160 men from the 8th, 12th, and 32nd (Auxiliary) Cavalry Regiments commanded by Lieutenant Colonel Amado Pérez Gil to clear out the revolutionaries marauding in the area of Sabinas Hidalgo and Cerralvo. The Federals left Lampazos on April 19. Five days later, on April 24 as Castro was getting ready to continue the march, he was surprised in Cerralvo by Pérez Gil, whose men captured one of Castro's pickets. Major Aguirre managed to escape with Castro and the bugler following closely on his heels. The Constitutionalists lost the one hundred bombs and another forty or so remounts being led by their halters, including a horse that Carranza had given to Castro as a gift. The Huertistas lost four killed, including a machine gun officer who was shot while trying to set up his weapon, and another three who pursued too closely, while Castro lamented three killed and two taken prisoner. By this time, Blanco had already entered Tamaulipas State and was long gone from Nuevo León.[21]

Lucio Blanco had left Monclova headed for Matamoros with 250 men, counting among his most prominent subalterns Lieutenant Colonels Andrés Saucedo and Cesáreo Castro, and First Captains Gustavo A. Elizondo, Francisco J. Múgica, and Alejo G. González. After passing through Cerralvo and Alhaja, Blanco's column made its way through Dr. Coss and China to enter Tamaulipas state through the pueblo of General Terán, where it again sustained brief combat, taking possession of Burgos on April 22. As Blanco invaded the northern part of the state from the east, Castro's 21st Rural Corps under the command of Miguel M. Navarrete coming up from the south caught the Federals in Tamaulipas State in a squeeze, attacking the state capital, Ciudad Victoria (also simply referred to as "Victoria") on the same day that Blanco occupied Burgos.[22]

It had been over three weeks since Castro had left his 21st Corps behind in Tlalnepantla; the day after his departure thirty-nine members of the 21st Rural Corps voted to second the Plan de Guadalupe on March 30, and then at 9 p.m. that night, under the leadership of Miguel Navarrete, they took the officers of the 14th Rural Corps prisoner and confiscated all their materiel.[23] Immediately afterward they departed for San Gerónimo on the Monte Albano Railroad, traveling through Colmena, Tlilán, and Progreso to arrive at the Hacienda de San Gerónimo. They collected up detachments as they went along until they totaled more than one hundred men, not counting the fifty Rurales of the 39th Corps commanded by First Captain Macario M. Hernández who also joined them; because of the circumstances of their revolt all the members of the 21st Rural Corps had not able to go north. While at the hacienda the group reorganized, gave promotions, and distributed payroll. This act set a dangerous precedent for the 21st whereby loyalty, rather than martial ability, was rewarded with increases in rank, and would later engender an imbroglio with the First Chief comparable to that involving Lucio Blanco, discussed in Chapter 7.[24]

Continuing forward under Navarrete's leadership, the 21st passed through Villa de Carbón and Jilotepec where, after a short firefight that sent the small garrison in flight, Lieutenant Rosalío Quiñones with another fifty men coming from Toluca joined the column. On April 2 they again got underway for San Francisco Soyaniquilpan, running into Federal forces of three arms twice as large as theirs and occupying good positions. Captain Navarrete at the front of the column ordered his men to charge the church from where the Federals were pouring in copious fire. Fifteen minutes later Captain Gumersindo Hernández had taken the church, and Navarrete left the captain there with sixteen men and continued to press the fight. But since the Constitutionalists could not gain any advantage, they withdrew to the hills. In this combat Navarrete lost six soldiers killed and one corporal and four soldiers taken prisoner. The Federals also had several casualties. At 10 p.m. the revolutionaries abandoned the field and continued to Zarco Arroyo. By the time the column entered Hidalgo State, Navarrete commanded two hundred men.[25]

The column passed through Barranca Seca and reached Pacula on April 5, crossed the Moctezuma River two days later, and marching toward Landa, Querétaro, reached Hacienda de Hongas just before midnight. The men unsaddled their mounts and took a break. Lieutenant Quiñones and three compañeros went to a local dance that night where they were apprehended by the authorities. Quiñones' aide Luis Villa got away and made it back to the camp in the early morning hours to report the incident, but by then about two hundred Huertistas were already attacking, shooting at the hacienda from the fences. Initially, the Constitutionalist jefes thought that the noise was just celebratory rockets and did not realize the true situation until Lieutenant Francisco M. Viramontes sounded the alarm to repel the enemy. The 21st took to the high ground and repulsed the attack, but Villa was killed in the maneuver.[26]

Continuing on through San Luis Potosí, the 21st arrived at Llera, Tamaulipas, on the morning of April 18. Captain Emiliano Nafarrate headed for the offices of Telephones and Treasury, but the lines were cut, and there was no money since the treasurer had fled with the other officials and all the funds upon the approach of the Constitutionalists. The Constitutionalists were joined there by twenty-six men recruited by Eladio Castro on his ranch, ten more recruited from the town, and Filiberto Sánchez. At 3 p.m. on April 20 the 21st left Llera for Hacienda Forlón. Along the way Captain Nafarrate detached an advance party of forty men to verify how well the trains were keeping up with their schedules; these men succeeded in capturing the telegrapher at Forlón Station before he could notify the Federals of the 21st's presence. The rest of the column arrived at Hacienda Forlón to a warm reception only two hours after leaving Llera. That same afternoon Eladio Castro received orders to march to the station and cut the rails. At the same time Captain Miguel Navarrete, commander of the column, sent another advance force to the road from Isasi Station because he had learned of a detachment of the 10th Rurales coming from about forty kilometers south of Forlón to attack the Constitutionalists.[27]

In effect, upon learning that troops of the 21st were approaching Ciudad Victoria along the railway, the 10th tried to race ahead of Captain Navarrete and his Constitutionalists, skirting the east side of the Sierra of Tamaulipas and passing through Lavín Station around 5 a.m. on April 21. Twelve hours later the 21st arrived at that latter point, delayed by attending to the work of destroying the rails and burning bridges. After a quick meal in El Capulín, Navarrete's Constitutionalists continued on to the outskirts of Ciudad Victoria, arriving at 5:30 a.m. on April 22, and straightaway attacked.[28]

Battle of Ciudad Victoria, April 22

On the south side Constitutionalist Captain Gumersindo Hernández with Lieutenant Jiménez Méndez conquered the Sanctuary of Guadalupe and a seventeen man outpost; at the cemetery on the east side of town, Captain Macario Hernández with Lieutenant Blas Corral and another fifty men repulsed the Federal advanced forces, numbering about eighty, who came out to meet them (see map in Chapter 7 for layout of city). After all of the Constitutionalists attacking from the east had reached the first streets on the cemetery side, Captain Hernández ordered them to follow down el Camino Real, and they steadily pushed back the Huertistas for two blocks. Then they received a counter order from Captain Navarrete to send back a few men to oppose the Federals trying to outflank them to the north. As Eladio Castro was one of those advancing down el Camino Real and heard the command, he returned with some compañeros and passing through the cemetery where Lieutenant Corral was guarding the horses, he joined with Navarrete and others to head for Las Vírgenes heights where the Constitutionalists continued to repulse the mounted charges being made against them.[29]

As Navarrete saw that those Federals trying to outflank the 21st to the right of the line of fire were beginning to disperse, he headed down Mercado Street toward the market, constantly repulsing the Federal mounted charges with the timely arrival and assistance of Filiberto Sánchez and others. Together they succeeded in scattering the Federals throughout the city streets. By 10:30 a.m. Captain Navarrete and Sánchez had taken the market, but in the process the 21st Brigade had lost four men killed up this point, including the bugler, Lucio Sarellano. Navarrete and Sánchez quickly ate and headed for the main park to remove the Federals occupying the tower there. But the tower was protected by the Federals in the commercial houses, the city hall, and the jail, making it impossible to conquer the point, so the Constitutionalists returned to the market. It was during this attack that a bullet destroyed Captain Navarrete's field glasses, grazing his left chest; the binoculars gave the captain an extra twelve months to live. Also noteworthy was the courageous soldadera Victoria Becerra who braved the exchange of gunfire to deliver coffee to Navarrete and Sánchez.[30]

Around 2 p.m. the Constitutionalists withdrew from the market to their previous positions in the cemetery, leaving behind four dead and the wounded Tereso Gómez and F. Hernández, who were later collected by the Red Cross. Captain Macario Hernández and others who were wounded continued to resist in the cemetery until 3 p.m. when the Federals' superior numbers and heavy fire forced them to withdraw, regretfully leaving behind the wounded Lieutenant Conrado Gallardo, who was later stoned to death by the guards of the 10th Rural Corps. The eighty or so Constitutionalists who had been laying down fire from the Sanctuary of Guadalupe were completely exhausted when they faced a spirited attack by a column of Federals. Not being able to resist the greater numbers they had to retreat, succeeding in saving the greater part of the horses. But, since they did not know that Navarrete had already abandoned the cemetery, they headed for that location. Lieutenant Jiménez Méndez and Captain Gumersindo Hernández led these troops coming from the sanctuary. The latter was in the lead when he noticed that the Federals had taken possession of the cemetery, and not knowing where Navarrete had gone, he took a course for the northeast staying to the side of the road until reaching about one kilometer from Güemez.[31] The attack on Ciudad Victoria had been a failure.

The Federals in Ciudad Victoria did not give pursuit because they feared a second attack. Moreover, to the north Colonel Lucio Blanco took the plaza of Méndez on April 23, and then turned south, taking San Fernando the next day and Santander Jiménez on April 27. His movements forced the Federals to fall back to defend Ciudad Victoria.[32] Captain Hernández of the 21st, still separated from Captain Navarrete after the failed attack on the state capital, received reports that Blanco was in Burgos with 250 well-armed and equipped men and went to join with him. Since this was the first that anyone from the 21st had heard of another revolutionary party since leaving Tlalnepantla, their excitement was so tremendous that after only just having arrived they left San Carlos at 1 a.m. for Burgos. In Burgos, of course, they learned that Blanco had already left. They finally caught up to Blanco at Santander Jiménez on April 28.[33]

Two days later Captains Navarrete and Nafarrate also joined Blanco, whereupon Blanco wheeled to the north for an attack on Matamoros. Blanco's activity had forced the Federals to concentrate in Matamoros and Ciudad Victoria, and with the number of men that he now had Blanco judged it the right time for a coup de main on the vital entrepôt of Matamoros. Upon reaching Hacienda Encinal (twenty-three kilometers northeast of Santander Jiménez) on May 3, however, the combined forces received a message from General Jesús Agustín Castro to await his arrival there; the linkup took place in the early morning hours of May 4. Blanco invited Castro to join with him in attacking Matamoros, but Castro thought that the venture would fail and declined to participate, instead marching off the next day with his men back south to Santander Jiménez.[34]

Straightaway Castro ratified the following appointments: Miguel M. Navarrete to Colonel; Macario Hernández to lieutenant colonel; Corral, Jiménez Méndez, Gumersindo Hernández, and Viramontes to major; and some old soldiers to officers. He also divided his "brigade" into two regiments, "Leales de Tlalnepantla" and "Dragones de Tamaulipas," commanded by Jiménez Méndez and Corral, with Navarrete as chief of staff. Luis Caballero also received the rank of major and began to organize his forces, and ten men of Castro's command, most notably Emiliano P. Nafarrate, applied to switch to Caballero's command, which Castro permitted. Once he had agreed on the organization of his brigade, which only topped 150 men, Castro marched to Padilla and then Casas. Shortly thereafter, on May 13, because of "intrigues," according to the official historian of the brigade, Lieutenant Colonel Aguirre de León along with Lieutenant Colonel Macario Hernández and Major Gumersindo Hernández separated with forty men from the brigade and headed for Ocampo. It is equally likely that Macario Hernández, who belonged to the 39th Corps, and Aguirre, who had completed the mission given him by the First Chief, simply realized that the 21st under Castro was more interested in promotions and riches than in fighting and decided to separate from that command. For the next three months Castro's "brigade" traveled around southern Tamaulipas and northeastern San Luis Potosí interdicting rail traffic and engaging in small skirmishes.[35]

In the meantime, undeterred by Castro's pessimism, Blanco continued to carry out his plans for the capture of Matamoros. To keep any Federal reinforcements from plazas along the rail lines from reaching Matamoros, Blanco began to destroy the line between Camargo and Reynosa, taking the latter plaza, defended by Federal Colonel Víctor Peña and the 27th Auxiliary Cavalry Regiment, on May 10.[36] A few more weeks would pass before he was ready to attack Matamoros.

Coahuila-Nuevo León

As First Chief of the Constitutionalist Army, Carranza quickly transformed himself into the nerve center of commanders in the Northeast, dispersing some, such as Lucio Blanco and Jesús Agustín Castro, to spread the revolution, while simultaneously accepted the allegiance and coordinating the efforts of new supporters. Among the more significant were the brothers Luis and Eulalio Gutiérrez, who operated in the border area of southern Coahuila, northern Zacatecas, and San Luis Potosí from their base of operations in Concepción del Oro, Zacatecas; they were mainly limited to disrupting rail traffic between Saltillo and San Luis Potosí. Colonels Jesús Dávila Sánchez and Ernesto Santos Coy covered roughly the same area, but independently of the Gutiérrez brothers, while Francisco Coss remained in the Sierra de Arteaga (just east of Saltillo), Coahuila, where he enjoyed wide popularity, attacking rail traffic between Saltillo and Monterrey. Carranza's main maneuver force commanders were his brother Jesús Carranza, based in far eastern Coahuila at Candela, who attacked and took Lampazos on March 28, and Pablo González in Monclova. For the time being, the condition of the rail lines stymied any Federal advance from Saltillo against Monclova and González's men posted there.[37]

Instead, on April 1 Federal General Trucy Aubert left Saltillo bound for Lampazos with a combined arms column of around 1,000 men from the 1st and 9th Infantry Battalions; the 5th, 8th, 12th, 13th, and 32nd (Auxiliary) Cavalry Regiments; two field pieces of the 5th Artillery Regiment; and a section of machine guns, intending to avenge the Constitutionalist victory of March 28. On that previous date, Colonel Pablo González, leaving a reduced garrison in Monclova of two hundred men, met up with Colonel Carranza at his Candela headquarters and then marched northward toward Lampazos from the direction of Monterrey, tearing up the railroad as they advanced. Defended by just over two hundred Federals belonging to the 6th, 19th Auxiliary, and 27th Auxiliary Cavalry Regiments; the Fiscal Gendarmes; and some irregulars under Auxiliary Lieutenant Colonel Nemesio Chávez Martínez, the government forces had no chance in the face of overwhelming numbers of revolutionaries and retreated back to Monterrey. In the engagement they lost one officer and thirty men killed, including nine executed by the Constitutionalists, with five wounded. The loss of that militarily important town cost the commanding general of the 3rd Military Zone, Emiliano Lojero, his job. Pending the arrival of his replacement, General of Brigade Fernando González (son of the former President of the Republic), Secretary of War Mondragón personally gave Trucy Aubert his orders to retake Lampazos.[38]

On April 4 in Bustamante Canyon, González and Carranza tried to ambush Trucy Aubert, who responded by attempting to envelop the opposing forces. The resulting encounter amounted to little as the Constitutionalists suffered only eighteen dead while the Federals reported only one killed and the Federals continued on their way. Trucy Aubert received orders to go all the way to Nuevo Laredo, which had been attacked by revolutionaries on March 18 without success, and Carranza returned with his men to his base at Candela, and González with his men to Monclova.[39]

Two weeks later, on April 19, the commander in Saltillo, General Arnoldo Casso López sent Colonel Ricardo Peña with one 75-mm. artillery piece and a column of 850 men to finish off Pablo González in Monclova. Composed mainly of Rurales freshly raised down south, most of Peña's men had only recently arrived on March 24 under escort by Colonel Luis Medina Barrón. González's command blocked the Federal advance along the rail line leading to Piedras Negras, where the First Chief had moved his headquarters. The condition of the railroad slowed Peña's column considerably, but on the twenty-second he learned of an advance force of 150 Constitutionalists under the command of Lieutenant Colonel Francisco Coss at Hacienda La Perla. Taking about four hundred men from the 42nd Auxiliary Battalion, 6th Cavalry Regiment, 8th Rural Corps, the Federal Rural Corps of Guanajuato, the Auxiliary Corps of Guanajuato, and a section of machine guns, Peña struck out overland for the hacienda. As La Perla came into sight at 9 a.m., the Federals began taking fire from the Constitutionalists aligned along the railroad embankment. Peña pressed the attack, with his infantry in the center, the 8th Rural Corps as left flanking guards, and the two Guanajuato Corps as right flanking guards, with the machine-gun section between the 42nd and Guanajuato units. The Constitutionalists withdrew to the main house of La Perla and then to Hacienda Espinazo, ten kilometers to the north, and even farther. Some of the fleeing Carrancistas tried to scale Espinazo ridge, which was occupied by their comrades, but due to the steepness of the hill they remained stuck and were cut down by the Federals. In this lengthy engagement, the Federals lost three men and the Constitutionalists fourteen.[40]

Peña fell back toward Reata, sixteen kilometers south of Espinazo, and rested on the twenty-third, but the next day he again made contact with the revolutionaries at La Perla. They fired on him from the west ridge of the Sierra de Espinazo de Ambrosio, with most of the Constitutionalists to the north. Deploying his infantry on a firing line, he sent his Rurales to disperse the revolutionaries, who slipped back down the east side of the ridge and escaped. Advancing farther he ran into more Constitutionalists firing on him, this time from the eastern side of the Sierra Azul to the west of the railroad. Again Peña sent his Rurales to force the revolutionaries from the field toward Espinazo Station where their main force awaited; the Constitutionalists loaded on trains and retreated north with their cavalry following along the rail line. The Federals recovered thirty dead and five wounded Constitutionalists while incurring three of their own killed and two wounded.[41]

In neighboring Nuevo León, while in Lampazos with the bulk of his brigade, Trucy Aubert learned on May 3 that the short garrison of eighty-four men from the 6th and 9th Cavalry Regiments that he had left in Villaldama under Colonel Antonio Villanueva had been annihilated and his lines of communication with Monterrey cut in a surprise attack by Colonel Carranza commanding six hundred men. Only Colonel Villanueva and ten troopers from his unfortunate command succeeded in reaching Monterrey. For the defeat at Villaldama, Huerta fired Trucy Aubert and replaced him with General of Brigade Joaquín Téllez who arrived in Monterrey on May 8 accompanied by General Fernando González. They each assumed their new commands the next day, Téllez of Trucy Aubert's operations column, and González of the Division of the Bravo.[42]

Finally, on May 14, Peña's Federals and González's Constitutionalists again fought at Baján Station, a mere forty-five kilometers from La Perla, such was the Federal's pace toward Monclova. Attacked from north, east, and west, the Federals managed to repel the Constitutionalist-initiated attack. Given the complete "systematic" destruction of the rails ahead of him, and following orders from Casso López, Peña left a strong detachment at Espinazo Station and returned to Saltillo at the end of May.[43] No other major action or offensive occurred in Coahuila during the spring. As important as the conquest of the Northeast was to the Federal Army, it still needed time to mobilize.

Huerta had waited more than a month after assuming the presidency to issue Decree 435, which he signed on April 1. That decree "suppressed" the military zones, converting each of those peacetime commands into operational divisions.[44] (See Zone-Division Area of Operations Cross-reference Table) Another decree followed on April 24 shortening the time-in-grade requirement for promotion, not including battlefield promotions and those deemed necessary to be able to campaign properly (meaning out of necessity), to two years for company-grade officers and three for jefes and generals, assuming a vacancy existed.[45] He increased extra pay ("*sobresueldo*") and abolished Decree 387 of December 1908 to make the "school" (training program) of the soldier "rudimentary," which probably entailed basic customs and courtesies and how to march and load and fire, but not aim, a weapon.[46]

1913 FEDERAL ZONE/DIVISION CROSS-REFERENCE AND AREAS OF OPERATIONS			
1913 Divisions	State	Capital	1910 Zone
Division of the Yaqui, HQ in Hermosillo, Sonora	Baja California	La Paz	1
	Sinaloa	Culiacán	1
	Sonora	Hermosillo	1
Division of the North, HQ in Chihuahua, Chihuahua	Chihuahua	Chihuahua	2
Division of the Bravo, HQ in Monterrey, Nuevo León	Coahuila a.)	Saltillo	3
a.) sans Parras & Viezca districts of Coahuila	Nuevo León	Monterrey	3
	Tamaulipas	Ciudad Victoria	3
Division of the Nazas, HQ in Torreón, Coahuila	Aguascalientes	Aguascalientes	5
b.) only Parras & Viezca districts of Coahuila	Coahuila b.)	Saltillo	3
	Durango	Durango	2
	Zacatecas	Zacatecas	5
Division of the West, HQ in Guadalajara, Jalisco	Colima	Colima	4
	Jalisco	Guadalajara	4
	Tepic	Tepic	Jefatura-Navy
Division of the Center, HQ in Celaya, Guanajuato	Guanajuato	Guanajuato	6
	Querétaro	Querétaro	6
	San Luis Potosí	San Luis Potosí	5
	Michoacán	Morelia	6
Division of the Federal District, HQ in Mexico, Federal District	Hidalgo	Pachuca	DF Comandancia
	Mexico	Toluca	DF Comandancia
c.) only Ozuluama, Tantoyuca, Chicontepec, and Tuxpan districts of Veracruz	Federal District	Mexico City	DF Comandancia
	Vera Cruz c.)	Jalapa	VC Comandancia
Division of the East, HQ in Puebla, Puebla	Puebla	Puebla	7
d.) sans Tehuantepec and Juchitán districts of Oaxaca	Tlaxcala	Tlaxcala	7
and Ozuluama, Tantoyuca, Chicontepec and Tuxpan	Oaxaca d.)	Oaxaca	8
Districts of Veracruz	Veracruz d.)	Jalapa	VC Comandancia
e.) plus Minatitlán & Acayucan Districts of Veracruz	Veracruz e.)	Jalapa	9
Division of the South, HQ in Iguala, Guerrero	Guerrero	Chilpancingo	7
	Morelos	Cuernavaca	DF Comandancia
Division of the Peninsula, HQ in Mérida, Yucatán	Campeche	Campeche	10
f.) only Tehuantepec and Juchitán districts of Oaxaca	Chiapas	Tuxtla Gutiérrez	9
	Tabasco	Villahermosa	10
	Yucatán	Mérida	10
	Quintana Roo	Chetumal	10
	Oaxaca f.)	Oaxaca	9

Table 1.2

But for whatever reason he did not address the system of recruitment until more than three months after assuming the presidency, with Decree 437. Signed by Huerta at the end of May, it did not take effect until June 1, 1913, abrogating the law of May 28, 1869, which had instituted the lottery and volunteer system of recruitment, in favor of a Law of Obligatory Military Service. The decree ruled that all men over eighteen and less than forty-five years of age who were not heads of household or the sole source of support for a family and made more than a soldier's pay must serve, with no substitutes allowed. Those not serving still had to receive instruction; from then on Mexico under Huerta would increasingly undergo a process of militarization that in the end would reach ridiculous proportions.[47]

Practically speaking, and in the words of the prolific chronicler of the revolution, General Francisco Urquizo, the Federal troops were "Sad Indians, gloomy, indifferent, who did not care if they died or killed," and other citizens who were forced, taken preferably from the jails, delinquents, then, or consigned to the armed services by jefe políticos, who always obeyed the orders of the hacendados or town bosses. Cannon fodder, 'soldier Juan' of every age, from His Serene Highness, the ill-fated Don Antonio López de Santa Anna, down through the Porfiriato. Poorly fed on atole, chile, and beans; [they were] black meat, weak and sad, who went off to kill people without knowing why, and who were forced to enter into combat with saber blows; who could just as easily die from bullets of the enemy to the front as by rifles of their comrades, [standing] before any wall; people who constantly heard from their corporals or sergeants the penal laws as daily litanies: 'commit this or that crime and...penalty of death, penalty of death, penalty of death!'[48]

The Federal soldier's condition was common knowledge according to Constitutionalist Alfredo Aragón, who like Urquizo fought in Coahuila during the spring of 1913: "The spectacle was public; soldiers remained in their barracks for six days, and on Sunday, which they used to have free, they went out to take a stroll, but never alone, [rather] in small groups that were watched over by corporals, sergeants, and officers of the company." He continued, "If we used to see this in peacetime, what could be expected in a future war?" More than any other reason, Aragón believed that the Federal Army's peculiar tradition of securing recruits explained the Federals' inability to dislodge and disperse the limited number of Constitutionalists operating along the Monclova-Piedras Negras line, since "If custody were necessary for a simple stroll, it was undoubtable that in a civil war the troops would not want to fight. For this reason, Federal mobilization was always slow [and] full of difficulties, since lacking the will of the soldier, which might have had a positive effect, a negative one was had."[49] Thus, three hundred Constitutionalists managed to keep Federal combat units marching in the direction of Monclova at bay until July.[50]

Meanwhile, safe in his headquarters in Piedras Negras the First Chief countered Huerta's decrees with several of his own designed to organize, support, and provide legal bases for the Revolution. He began with recalling all Maderista generals, jefes, and officers to duty, at their previous rank. He also gave Federal officers the same opportunity for thirty days, starting on April 20, with the exception of those who had participated in Félix Díaz's uprising of the previous October in Veracruz and/or the shameful Citadel cuartelazo and subsequent palace coup; only a handful of Federal officers accepted the offer. Six days later Carranza authorized the printing of Constitutionalist money to fund his army, since "it is the duty of all Mexicans to contribute in a proportional part for the expenses of the Army and to the reestablishment of Constitutional Order," and "the best means of providing these needs without causing direct and material harm to the inhabitants of the Country is the creation of paper money." Then he took a step toward ensuring the neutrality of the United States by agreeing to indemnify all foreign property that might be harmed by the revolution. Finally, as the deadline for Federal officers to switch sides approached, he revived Benito Juárez's Law of January 25, 1862, also known as the "Juárez Law," fixing the penalty of death upon all collaborators who upheld Huerta's government.[51] Federal Army officers blamed "the Juárez Law" for the conflict's devolution into a savage, internecine struggle of no quarter, but Carranza defended the severity of the penalty based on the egregiousness of the army's crimes against Mexico's institutions.[52]

Precisely because it lacked moral authority, the Federal Army simply could not match the Constitutionalists operating in the North in quality or numbers, which continued to grow, although Huerta tried. Decree 438 issued on May 30 raised the army to a permanent level of 80,000 men, and a few days later, in a Napoleonesque move intended to motivate men to join up and perform heroically in combat, Huerta issued Accord Number 130549, notifying commands that those countrymen who "lend interesting service, distinguishing themselves specifically in acts of war, will be deserving of the Cross of Military Merit."[53] But increasing the size of the Federal Army in an attempt to outnumber the prolific revolutionary forces only exacerbated the problems of incompetence, authoritarianism, and demotivation, and simply offering medals for valorous service could not remedy structural deficiencies when "command in the Federal Army was regularly held by mature men, and at times not just mature but old," who often lacked the martial spirit required of officers to actively seek out and destroy the enemy. In contrast, the enlisted men, according to Urquizo, "had to be always watched over in order to avoid, as much as possible, incessant desertions. The officers and noncoms were true jailers," making it "dangerous to disperse" to conduct operations, virtually precluding any offensive maneuvers and committing units to defending towns, railroads, haciendas, mines, and other high value targets.[54]

Map 1.6 Railroads in the Mexican Revolution

Perhaps recognizing that his army was good for little more than custody and defense of the national patrimony—the Federal Army's de facto primary mission—and to respond to the crush of revolutionary activity, the Interim President of the Republic, General Huerta, instituted a system of military trains on May 15 to "ensure to the extent possible, expeditious communication for military operations, passenger traffic, and cargo trains." The routes covered by the military train system, and presumably most strategically significant, were: 1. Mexico City-Veracruz, Mexican Railroad; 2. Mexico City-Veracruz, Interoceanic Railroad; 3. Mexico City-Torreón, Central Railroad; 4. Mexico City-Torreón, branch and National Railroad; 5. San Luís Potosí-Tampico; 6. Saltillo-Matamoros; 7. Monterrey-Nuevo Laredo; 8. Monterrey-Torreón, International Railroad; 8. Reata-Ciudad Porfirio Díaz [Piedras Negras]; 9. Torreón-Durango; 10. Torreón-Chihuahua City; 11. Chihuahua City-Ciudad Juárez; 12. Irapuato-Colima; 13. Mexico-Ixtla; and 14. Mexico City-Zacatecas. Each train comprised one locomotive and two or three railcars containing fifty Federal regulars or loyal militia, and as added insurance, the Federals some- times loaded the families of prominent revolutionaries aboard to discourage attacks.[55] Such tactics only added to the regime's aura of illegality and drove recruits into the revolution, ultimately proving counterproductive.

Chihuahua

Those who decided to take up arms against the new Huertista regime in Chihuahua faced a host of obstacles in getting operations started that was unique to the state. Francisco Ontiveros, the administrative chief of the González Ortega Brigade and Colonel Toribio Ortegas' private secretary and biographer, set forth the best description of difficulties facing would-be revolutionaries in those early days of 1913 in Chihuahua. First and foremost, on March 7 the Federals unceremoniously executed the governor of the state, Abraham González, leaving the state without a leader or even a figurehead. Whereas Coahuila had a strong governor and Sonora an activist legislature, each backed by a military leader with a command: Pablo González and Álvaro Obregón, respectively, Chihuahua lacked both political leadership and military unity of command, since the state's highest ranking revolutionary, General Francisco "Pancho" Villa, only reentered the state the day before González's murder and "still did not know anything for certain."[56]

From an economic standpoint, two colossal rebellions over the course of two years had almost exhausted the state's sources of riches, leaving it with very few resources and even less promise for a vibrant challenge to the new regime. Add to this the frightful desolation of the countryside, its paralyzed industries, its stagnated commerce, and the immense, uncultivated fields:[57]

> Everywhere, burned out haciendas, fields empty from a lack of labor, since the peaceful inhabitants had fled terrorized before the barbarity of the Reds [Colorados], and solitary regions where before there was a populace full of life and animation…The scarcity was terrible, without harvesting crops, since no one wanted to sow; torn apart and alone the cattle raisers were at the complete disposal of gangs of bandits who lived from rustling. One could say the horse herds were no more, since the twelve or fifteen thousand of Orozco's men had provided themselves with the horses of the state.…In such conditions Constitutionalism entered our native state.[58]

Another legacy bequeathed to Chihuahua as the cradle of the ill-fated Orozquista Rebellion had been the Federal Division of the North, arguably the largest and best division in the Federal Army, which occupied the state with the majority of its forces and rendered revolutionaries almost impotent to second the Constitutionalist movement. The Federals also had taken the precaution of breaking up the volunteer corps and assigning them to the jefes de las armas in all the most important towns of the state, with each one having spies to watch over the citizen-soldiers and the least of their activities. The commander of the division, the famous Antonio Rábago, resided in the state capital; in Ciudad Juárez, Colonel Juan J. Vázquez; in Casas Grandes, Major Manuel M. Bridat; in Ciudad Guerrero, Colonel (probably Fernando J.) Zarate; in Santa Rosalía de Camargo ("Camargo"), Colonel Manuel Pueblita; in Ojinaga, Captain Alberto Ortiz; in Jiménez, Lieutenant Colonel Adolfo Rivera; in Parral, Colonel Salvador Mercado; and in Escalón, Captain Julio Cejudo. Six field artillery batteries, some mountain gun batteries, and about twenty machine guns commanded by Lieutenant Colonels Lauro Cejudo and Miguel Barrios and Majors José María Aldana, Alberto Rodríguez, and others made up the division artillery.[59]

Still and all, the state of Chihuahua was one of the first to answer Carranza's call to arms, notwithstanding the fact that on the one hand the praetorians controlled of all the important plazas in the state with strong garrisons, and on the other, as Ontiveros so eloquently put it, the "Red Brigandage had allied itself with praetorianism, and the capital being the cradle of that opprobrious party, had prepared an enormous contingent for the usurpers."[60] Just as it had done during Madero's rebellion in 1910, Chihuahua would play a commanding role in the Constitutionalist revolution.

VILLA'S RETURN

After escaping from prison in Mexico City in December, Villa passed through Guaymas and Nogales, stopped in Tucson for a few days, and then arrived in El Paso in early January 1913. Villa contacted Abraham González to place himself at the government's service, should it need him, and warn the governor of the upcoming cuartelazo; he knew about it because the plotters had offered to free him from prison if he seconded the coup. Don Abraham responded to Villa by telling him to remain in the United States. Sensing that the Maderistas did not understand the urgency of the situation, Villa begged to meet personally with González. Instead, Don Abraham sent Licenciado Aureliano González to meet with Villa. After hearing him out the licenciado offered to pay Villa a salary according to his rank if he were to remain in El Paso. Instead, Villa asked for a loan of ₱1,500, which he received. After Villa learned of the Citadel cuartelazo he began using those funds to buy rifles, ammunition, horses, and saddles. When news of Abraham González's murder reached him, Villa went to see Governor Maytorena, who had just arrived in Tucson, and got from the Sonoran ₱1,000 that he used to buy some skinny horses.[61]

Then sometime around March 8 Villa crossed over into national territory with eight companions and headed for San Andrés with the intention of organizing a force. After about a week of traveling backroads and even footpaths to avoid the main arteries and towns, he arrived in San Andrés where his wife lived and interviewed the municipal president, who promised to raise some forces and join Villa later. Next, Villa headed for Chavarría and collected his brothers Antonio and Hipólito, Andrés Rivera, and four other men. Continuing on to Santa Isabel he sent Federal General Rábago a telegram to taunt him that read: "Knowing that the government that you represent is going to request my extradition I have resolved to come here and remove the bother, since you now have me in Mexico, proposed to fight the tyranny that you represent, or rather that of Huerta, Mondragón, and [their] henchmen. Pancho Villa."[62]

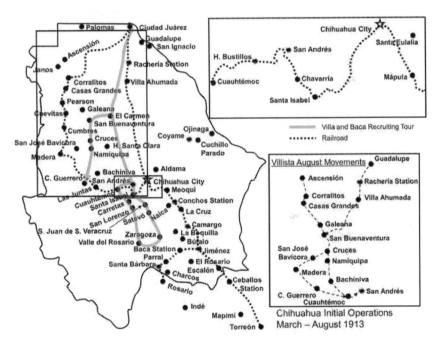

Map 1.7

From there, Villa toured all over central Chihuahua, going to San Juan de Santa Veracruz where he gathered sixty men from nearby Ciénaga de Ortiz and area ranches, and then to Satevó where he summoned his buddy Fidel Ávila. Villa told him to gather recruits from San José and Santa Juana de las Cuevas, while he moved on to Pilar de Conchos (Valle de Zaragoza) and Valle del Rosario. Later, parties of revolutionaries began coming to join him, among them Major Félix Rivero from San José de las Cuevas with sixty men, and then Captain Benito Artalejo with more men. Both Rivero and Artalejo had been with Colonel Rosalío Hernández at Ceballos Station back in February before separating from him with the intention of joining Villa, with whom they had served back in 1910. Everywhere Villa went people of the fields showed up to enlist in his force. Visiting the surrounding areas, especially large haciendas owned by the Terrazas, he executed administrators, opened granaries to the poor, and with similar populist activities succeeded in recruiting a group of 250 armed men by the time he returned to meet up with Ávila, who had another 160 men.[63]

Villa instructed Ávila to remain in the area and continue to see how many more men he could gather while Villa turned north toward San Nicolás de Carretas and San Lorenzo to continue recruiting on his roundabout way back to San Andrés.[64] Upon passing through San Antonio de los Arenales (today Cuauhtémoc), Villa learned of an approaching enemy column. Since Villa's group only numbered a couple hundred men, and considering Villa's prestige as a warrior, General Rábago had decided to send Major Jesús M. Yáñez to pursue and defeat him before his command reached critical mass. Yáñez had been the second-in-command of General José de la Luz Soto, whom Villa had relieved of command in Parral back in 1912 when Soto tried to pass over to the Colorados; sent to Mexico City under guard, Soto was later executed. Villa defeated Yáñez in a small but heated engagement, and the latter returned to Chihuahua City to inform Rábago that capturing Villa was not going to be so easy as supposed.[65]

Shortly thereafter, on April 10, Villa experienced success by judiciously attacking a soft and potentially lucrative target chosen by many revolutionaries at the start of a campaign, a passenger train traveling between Santa Isabel and Chavarría. On that train he had the good fortune of finding 122 silver bars worth $75,000. Riding the train back into San Andrés he found himself fighting Huertistas since the municipal president, far from raising men to join Villa, had armed some of the local populace with weapons received from Rábago and started to shoot up Villa's men, killing seven. As night began to fall Villa began to fear that more Federals might come and possibly recapture the silver, so he gave each of his men one bar, since it was the only way to transport such weight, and slipped away. They escaped to Mount Sonoloapa and from there they made their way to Bachíniva, where they had to bury one of those men wounded in the San Andrés fight. Before departing the locale Villa ordered his men to do the same with the silver, choosing a good hiding place. He continued to recruit throughout the military colonies in western

Chihuahua, traveling up through the Valley of San Buenaventura where the people turned out to receive him with great affection.[66]

The Military Colonies Mobilize

Many in the military colonies had known the quiet man they called "*el Güero*" since the turn of the century when he used to hide out there whenever "things got hot" with the Porfirian authorities. Villa frequently appeared in the area with three other men whose acquaintance he had made in the La Silla region south of Satevó: Manuel Baca, Andrés Luján, and Telesforo Terrazas. These three men came from the area of Cruces and Namiquipa and introduced Villa to others who developed a fondness for the man who spoke with a command voice, never suspecting that he was the famous Pancho Villa.[67] And Villa felt quite at home there in western Chihuahua.

Villa's compañero Manuel Baca had prepared the way for his arrival. Baca had met up with Villa shortly after he entered national territory and traveled with him as far south as Hacienda del Carmen (today Flores Magón) where he commissioned Baca to go with Jesús Acosta and visit Guerrero district and Namiquipa to begin organizing support. Baca stopped in Namiquipa on March 18 on his way to Ciudad Guerrero and met with Andrés U. Vargas, Eligio Hernández, and José de la Luz Nevárez at Candelario Cervantes' ranch, "El Oso," to deliver the news that Pancho Villa had returned to Chihuahua and that Major Isaac Arroyo from Ciudad Juárez had already joined him. On April 3 Colonel Andrés U. Vargas began recruiting volunteers at his ranch "Los Cerritos" east of Namiquipa, as did others in the mountain region of western Chihuahua. Villa also ordered Colonel Vargas to "intervene" the Hacienda Santa Clara in Namiquipa municipality, later appointing Colonel Telesforo Terrazas as the administrator. He would follow this act with other haciendas to provide food and mounts for the cowboys who became his troopers, as well as for their families, in the upcoming campaign. In no time Villa's network had come alive with his key lieutenants recruiting all over western Chihuahua. The original military colonies: Namiquipa, Galeana, Cruces, and surrounding areas provided significant support to Villa, especially Namiquipa.[68] Unlike the many commanders of Guerrillas, Auxiliaries, and Rurales who simply marched off to fight Huerta, Villa had to raise his brigade from the ground up. The military colonies afforded the most prolific recruiting ground for just such an endeavor.

The militancy of western Chihuahua could be traced to a phenomenon with roots in colonial administration. The Spanish crown founded five military colonies in Chihuahua—Namiquipa, Galeana, Casas Grandes, Janos, and Cruces—along a route adjacent to the eastern edge of the western Sierra Madre Mountains that Apaches took to raid from present-day Arizona and New Mexico into the Mexican interior. Strategically placed amid the timber and mining interests of western Chihuahua, soldier-farmers populated the military colonies to not only hinder Apache raiding parties but also supply the communities that grew up around the extractive industries with provisions. The *vecinos*, or citizens, accepted an obligation to bear arms in service to the crown and in return received political autonomy, small plots of land that each settler received to work as his own, and large land grants held in common that all could use for pasturing their livestock.[69]

Later, in the national period, the federal government founded additional military colonies in the aftermath of the war with the United States and again after the French Intervention, such as Cuchillo Parado. With Chihuahua pacified in the 1880's and the vecinos constructively demobilized, the Terrazas-Creel clan began an aggressive legal campaign to strip the military colonies of their hard-won lands.[70] Using the law of *terrenos baldíos* ("idle lands"), outsiders confiscated the common lands of the military colonies by "denouncing" them as idle, and thus available for purchase from the federal government. When Enrique Creel, the son-in-law of Luis Terrazas and heir apparent to the Terrazas-Creel clan, took over the governorship of the state from his father-in-law, he initiated a 1905 law that afforded even more effective confiscation of lands from the military colonies. Within the year many colonists were paying rent to the usurpers of their patrimony, making them psychologically party to a great travesty and ripe for revolution.[71] Decades and even centuries of payment in blood for their rights meant that Chihuahua's military colonists would not readily surrender them.[72] Villa's recruiting activities continued to keep him busy for at least another month during which time the other revolutionaries fought the Federals for control of the state.

SOUTHERN AND CENTRAL OPERATIONS

After the failed attempt by Manuel Chao to take Parral at the beginning of March (see the first volume), Federal Brigadier Salvador R. Mercado sent the section of 75-mm. guns back to Chihuahua City and ordered Lieutenant Colonel Adolfo Ramírez to take a company from the 9th Battalion and garrison Jiménez. Federal Colonel Manuel Landa, with about four hundred men belonging to the 7th Cavalry Regiment and the Lavalle y Bassó Corps with two 70-mm. mountain guns and two machine guns, pursued Chao into Durango State without ever catching the revolutionaries because they separated into several groups with Cuevas designated as the rally point. During the march back to Parral two groups of revolutionaries attacked Landa's column at Rancho de Charcos (about sixteen kilometers north of Ocampo) on March 14. Although Landa estimated the total of the two groups at twice his own number, realistically they probably did not number more than three hundred men, with one of the groups commanded by Román Arreola, a subordinate of Tomás Urbina, and an unnamed leader in charge of the other.[73]

The revolutionaries hit at 9 a.m., and Landa placed his men in a disposition of combat with the troopers of the 7th Cavalry in a line of shooters, protected on the left and right (east and west) by flank guards and centered two kilometers behind the firing line, that is, in perfect defilade, he placed his artillery and machine guns—a defective placement for the machine guns. After three hours of combat the revolutionaries fled leaving behind eighteen dead. The Federals had two killed and twelve wounded, including one jefe, four officers, and seven enlisted. Landa continued on to Parral arriving the next day. Chao, for his part, regrouped at Cuevas and then crossed back into Chihuahua to link up with Maclovio and Luis Herrera at Santa Bárbara on March 20.[74]

Farther to the north, the Federal commander of the Camargo garrison, Colonel Manuel García Pueblita (the son of a famous general of division killed in Uruapan, Michoacán on June 23, 1865 fighting the French) also tried to finish off Rosalío Hernández's Constitutionalists, who had been operating in the area since February. Pueblita had permitted Hernández to remain in the vicinity, essentially trying to recruit him and keep the townsfolk mollified since the revolution had many sympathizers in Camargo. Nonetheless, on March 21 Federal First Captain Ramón Carreón Hernández, leading two hundred men, surprised Hernández, who did not maintain proper security, at his headquarters in Ojo Caliente only two kilometers west of Camargo. The Federals had already taken possession of some nearby hills and opened fire when the revolutionaries came running out of their barracks to take up position on a hill next to the pueblo. After a two hour firefight, Hernández's men retreated in an easterly direction. They lost only two men, believed to have been taken prisoner, and two wounded. The Federals likewise had light casualties with only one irregular first captain wounded.[75]

Santa Bárbara March 23

In Chihuahua the only remaining action worthy of note in the month occurred on March 23 with the force that General Mercado sent against Chao and the Herreras in Santa Bárbara. Two hundred irregular dragoons of the Flores Alatorre and Rangel Corps made their way overland from Parral to dislodge the seven hundred revolutionaries located there. Another force under First Captain Eudaldo Fernández Traconis, adjutant of the 23rd Infantry

Battalion, followed by rail with 118 infantrymen and gunners of the 6th and 23rd battalions, one 80-mm. cannon, and one machine gun. Finally, Mercado sent another 160 mounted men belonging to the irregular cavalry Lavalle y Bassó Corps. After taking some time to repair rails, Traconis reached Adrián Station where his infantry detrained and then moved forward to join the irregulars of the Flores Alatorre and Rangel Corps who had already been battling the enemy for some time. Gradually, the men of Chao and Herrera had pushed the Colorados back, taking ground, and killing Hermenegildo Rangel, commander of his eponymous corps. Traconis threw his infantrymen into the fight. Under covering fire provided by the cannon "El Niño" and the one machine gun they dislodged the revolutionaries from the hills to the north of town. The Federals then turned their efforts on the town proper. Outnumbered and outgunned the revolutionaries once again had to yield. Traconis reestablished the civilian authorities and then withdrew to Parral, which Chao continued to harass and isolate by cutting the telegraph and destroying the railroad to Jiménez.[76]

Conchos Station April 2

The next major action occurred on April 2, when part of the 6th Battalion commanded by Federal Major Cirilo Ortiz attacked Colonel Hernández's force as it crossed the railway at Conchos Station, initiating a firefight that lasted about an hour starting around 10 a.m. Hernández had orders not to attack and was shooting in retreat to a hill called Los Picachos where he learned that Maclovio Herrera was in Naica and making a forced march to reinforce him. At about 3 p.m. the two forces united and then left for Conchos Station where they again joined battle with Ortiz's Federals about an hour later. Herrera sent a group to burn a bridge to the Federal rear in order to impede any retreat and then attacked on the left side of the railway with such impetus that he forced the Federals back to the station. By 6:30 p.m. the Federals had been trounced and were fleeing at full steam back to the north. The detachment sent by Herrera did not arrive in time to burn the bridge, but the damage inflicted was palpable nonetheless: the Federals lost about twenty killed, thirteen prisoners, and a considerable number of wounded. Colonel Herrera received credit for the victory.[77]

Two days later, on April 4, Herrera received orders from General Villa to report with his men to Zaragoza while Hernández remained along the railway interrupting Federal lines of communication, although it is not clear if Herrera heeded those orders. Hernández fought another action just a few days later when a Federal train coming from La Cruz attacked him at Hacienda del Corraleño (just south of La Cruz on the railroad), and soon another Federal train coming from Camargo brought more reinforcements to a fight that lasted until nightfall; the next day the Constitutionalists found one Federal officer and three soldiers dead on the field of combat, while the revolutionaries likewise lost one officer and one enlisted killed. Subsequently Hernández won another small skirmish in San Pablo de Meoqui, and he was still there when the Battle of Camargo (see below) took place.[78] In the meantime Villa moved to Pilar de Conchos (Zaragoza) where he received a communication from Colonel Hernández placing himself at the general's service, since at that time Villa had not formally joined the Constitutionalist movement and therefore only exercised referent authority. Villa then sent Captains Manuel Ochoa and Miguel Saavedra to transmit orders and confer with Hernández over next moves.[79]

Jiménez April 13

Around this time Colonel Tomás Urbina entered Chihuahua from northern Durango to campaign. Initially, Urbina had taken up arms against the government in Indé, Durango, and began operations on March 30. That day he and his eight hundred men defeated the 130 Federals of the 21st Infantry Battalion and Voluntarios del Potosí Corps under Federal Lieutenant Colonel Félix López who were defending the mining town of Mapimí, Durango, only seventy-five kilometers west of Torreón. Urbina remained in that plaza until the approach of the fearsome Irregular Brigadier Jesús José "Cheché" Campos forced him to evacuate on April 12 and take the same northerly route into Chihuahua territory through Villa López, some twenty-one kilometers from Jiménez, as General Trucy Aubert had the year before. With six hundred Constitutionalists, Urbina attacked Jiménez on the following day, coming at the plaza from all directions. Overwhelmed, the leader of the one hundred Federals of the 9th Infantry Battalion garrisoning that plaza, Lieutenant Colonel Ramírez, rushed to the telegraph office to request immediate reinforcements from Camargo, to the north, and Parral, to the west.[80]

The Constitutionalists entered the town through El Molino and El Santuario on the west side, and by around 6 a.m. they already had possession of that side of the city. The Federals held the streets downtown and the principal buildings of the plaza, including the church and jail, extending through Libertad Street to Zaragoza Street, across from the Calzada del Río where they had their most advance positions. The fighting lasted all day and by 3 p.m. the Constitutionalists had penetrated as far as downtown, where the fighting became especially heated. The Federals started to flag, and it was expected that by nightfall the Constitutionalists would possess the town, but then Colonel Urbina got wind of Federal reinforcements coming up from

Escalón to give aid to the besieged. So, he pulled back his forces and allowed the Federals to enter so he could then attack the combined force. The reinforcements consisting of about one hundred men commanded by Second Captain Julio Cejudo entered the town during the night without any obstacle, and the next day the Constitutionalists resumed their attack.[81]

The revolutionaries delivered an assault so ferocious that the Federals soon become demoralized and confusion entered into their ranks. When Lieutenant Colonel Ramírez passed by a tailor shop on Hidalgo Street in the company of several officers, one of the townsfolk came out with pistol in hand and shot the colonel dead. The accompanying Federal officers riddled the pistolero with bullets, but after learning of the death of the Jefe de las Armas, panic spread throughout the Federal ranks, and the Constitutionalists redoubled their efforts, taking the plaza and dealing the Federals a new disaster. The Federals dispersed in complete disorder to the nearest large towns of Camargo, Parral, and Torreón without presenting any further opposition. Only a few of the two hundred Federals succeeded in escaping and the Constitutionalists executed the few officers they captured. Urbina remained in possession of the town for several days until learning of the approach of a Federal column on the way from Parral.[82]

General Mercado responded immediately to Ramírez's telegraphic appeal by sending a force commanded by First Captain Traconis consisting of three hundred men from the 6th and 23rd Infantry Battalions, machine guns, and an 80-mm. gun (probably "El Niño") from Parral by train, along with 120 mounted Colorados under Colonel José Flores Alatorre and Lieutenant Colonel Casimiro Michel, who had taken over command of the Rangel Corps after the death of its leader in the attack on Santa Bárbara. Along the way Traconis fought Chao's men at Gomera Station (two kilometers west of Parral), and on April 14 he fought the men of Cástulo Herrera, who operated at that time around Camargo in cooperation with Rosalío Hernández. Traconis had to make some repairs to the railway as he went along, slowing his progress. Finally, on the fifteenth Traconis reached Jiménez and dislodged Urbina from that location after three hours of combat, collecting booty of 100 weapons, 300 dynamite bombs, and 107 horses; Urbina had decided to abandon the town in order to spare it the horrors of a bombardment.[83]

The next day Traconis began to gather in some Federals dispersed from Ramirez's command. Following orders from Mercado, the captain started to make his way back to Parral on April 20, but after traveling scarcely fifty kilometers he encountered a group of Constitutionalists at Baca Station and killed thirty-seven of them and wounded several others. In Baca he learned that Urbina, along with Chao, Herrera, and Hernández, some fifteen hundred men total, planned to attack Camargo, so he halted his return to Parral and decided instead to try to go to the aid of his fellow Federals there.[84]

Camargo April 23

The combined forces of Colonels Chao and Herrera left El Rosario for Camargo district in order to attack the seat of government, Santa Rosalía de Camargo. Near Troya Station (seven kilometers west of Baca Station) Chao and Herrera ran into a Federal military train with artillery and, boldly attacking it, forced the Federals to return toward Parral. After that brief encounter the Constitutionalists went into camp at Hacienda de Búfalo and agreed on a plan of attack. Federal Colonel Manuel Pueblita with one company of the 6th Infantry Battalion and three squadrons of his own 3rd Cavalry Regiment, a total of 350 men, garrisoned the town. The night before the attack he and his officers had gotten drunk. Partying turned out to be a problem for the Federals, since the night before the attack on Jiménez the officers had gone to a dance, pointing to a general inattention to proper security.[85]

Colonel Pueblita well knew his vulnerable position, and he had been requesting reinforcements ever since the attack on Jiménez of April 13 when he had sent a squadron commanded by First Captain Ismael Pozos to answer the call from Colonel Ramírez for reinforcements. Ostensibly Pozos' squadron had been wiped out, or at least dispersed because it was never heard from again. On the same day, April 13, Pueblita also sent a repair train escorted by a section of the 3rd Regiment under Lieutenant Fernando Solares toward Chihuahua City in order to keep the railroad link open to the north. Revolutionaries attacked the train, killed the lieutenant and seven of his charges, and strung up their corpses. No reinforcements would be forthcoming.[86]

The Federal defenses for Camargo consisted of an outer perimeter with nine combat positions defended by eight men each, three on the east along the railroad (in the station, on the bridge over the Conchos, and on a hill covering the road to Boquilla del Rey) and six on the west side taking advantage of the natural obstacle created by the Conchos River (one covering the road to La Cruz, another over the road to Ojo Caliente, a third south of the latter some three hundred meters away, a fourth covering the road and railway to San Francisco de Conchos, the fifth south of town between the two railroads, and the sixth covering the road to Enramada and Jiménez). The interior perimeter made use of the prominent buildings in the town: the church, where the Federals installed their two Madsen machine guns; another where they had stabled the horses; the third at the flour mill; and the last at the children's school. Pueblita had his headquarters in the main plaza, the location of his barracks.[87]

The Constitutionalists attacked on April 23 from three directions. They started at 4:30 a.m. from the southwest through a point known as El Gato Negro; from the north in the direction of the railroad bridge; and from the east on the side of the station. At the beginning of combat the Federals experienced a great confusion, but they soon collected themselves and put up an admirable defense. Pueblita had to reinforce the exterior positions, since they had too few defenders, but his men fought like furies. The battle reached its zenith with the opposing forces shooting at each other at point blank range inside the town at street intersections. As the sun came up the battle was going the Constitutionalists' way, since Maclovio Herrera's men had taken the school house and the bullring from the Federals and reduced them to their positions downtown, the tower of the church, the public jail, the town hall, the clock tower, and the civilian hospital.[88]

Notwithstanding the precariousness of the Federals' situation, the fight dragged on with numerous casualties on both sides. Upon leaving his house through Lerdo de Tejada Street a group of Constitutionalists caught up to Colonel Pueblita around 10 a.m. and killed him, leaving him laid out in the middle of the street. The Jefe Político Casimiro Carbajal, "a recalcitrant Porfirista," experienced the same fate. Colonel Maclovio Herrera, his brother Luis, and another Constitutionalist jefe had been lightly wounded. Similar to the battle of Jiménez, the loss of the Federal commander once again sowed panic, and Federal Major Lamberto Marín abandoned the barracks in the middle of the plaza and made for the Civil Hospital. By noon almost the entire city, except the hospital occupied by about 100 perfectly armed Federals, had fallen into Constitutionalist hands. Said hospital was on the outskirts of town in a direct line from González Ortega Street but completely apart from surrounding houses with clear fields of fire for five hundred meters in all directions. The Constitutionalists made several attempts to attack it, but lost too many men and so decided to wait until nightfall.[89]

When Rosalío Hernández learned that the attack on Camargo had begun, however, he abruptly left San Pablo de Meoqui to bring aid. He arrived around 2 p.m., and after conferring with Herrera and Chao, he agreed that his people would attack the hospital forthwith. An hour later Hernández, seconded by officers Enrique Portillo and Roque Gándara, assaulted the "impregnable fortification," as Ontiveros called it, with his corps. Hopping over the mud wall of the corral the Constitutionalists penetrated the defenses. As one Federal leveled his weapon to shoot Lieutenant Gándara in the back, Hernández shot him dead. After a brief firefight the Federals surrendered. The Constitutionalists shot all the officers they captured, including First Captain Carreón; very few escaped, among them Major Marín, who slipped away in a scout train. Major Luis G. García, the commander of the company from the 6th Infantry was killed in action.[90]

The next day Captain Traconis and his relief force reached kilometer 1441 on the Central and, upon learning of the disaster at Camargo, turned around and headed south for Torreón. His glacial rate of advance, which the federal captain blamed on the condition of the railroad tracks, had been responsible for his inability to reinforce Camargo. He reached Torreón on April 25 and his column was joined to the Division of the Nazas and took on the unit designation "Force Traconis."[91]

In the battle for Camargo, Pueblita committed several errors common to Federal commanders, such as trying to defend too much terrain for the size of his force and placing his two Madsen machine guns in a central position (as opposed to on the flanks) and up high, in the church.

The Federals lost many men, with the 3rd Cavalry Regiment being obliterated, but the Constitutionalists captured the majority of the enlisted and spared their lives. After having them take about 150 of their deceased comrades outside the city for burial, Herrera delivered a speech to the Federal enlisted men offering to accept into his ranks anyone who wanted to voluntarily join the Constitutionalists and to find work for those who did not. He wound up sending about one hundred to the dam on the Conchos River at La Boquilla to work, and he installed Constitutionalist civilian authorities in the town.[92]

The loss of Jiménez and Camargo left the Federal garrison of eight hundred men at Parral isolated and exposed; so on May 6 General Mercado abandoned the town with the families of the town's científicos in tow as he retreated northward to Chihuahua City. Mercado enumerated various reasons for abandoning the town, including a lack of ammunition, provisions, and funds to pay his men and a force insufficient in numbers to mount a proper defense of the plaza. Moreover, he distrusted the loyalty of his irregulars as well as the local populace. From that point on, the Federal Division of the North remained cut off from Torreón and relegated to operating along the Ciudad Juárez-Chihuahua City line, since Toribio Ortega's revolutionaries had occupied Ojinaga almost two months earlier.[93]

With Parral open, Colonel Chao moved in to occupy the town on May 20, three days after Mercado reached the state capital, and General Francisco Villa came down south from western Chihuahua; according to some reports, Villa and Mercado crossed paths on the way and even fought a brief engagement. As he made his triumphal entry into Camargo the town turned out to greet Pancho Villa, to cheer him on, and to throw floral bouquets at his feet. His first act was to confiscate the warehouses of the firm Sordo y Blanco, owned by Spaniards who had been engaged, so it was alleged, in unscrupulous business practices with the local populace. Goods were distributed to the troops and sold to the people at very low prices.[94]

At this juncture, the First Chief sent Lieutenant Colonel Eleuterio Hermosillo and Doctor Samuel Navarro, of the Chihuahuan Revolutionary Junta, to Camargo to interview Villa and offer to recognize his rank of brigadier within the Constitutionalist Army, which Villa accepted on May 26. Officially, Huerta had only made Villa a brevet ("*honorario*") brigadier in 1912, but no matter. The permanent brigadier's commission conferred upon Villa by Carranza made him the highest ranking revolutionary in the state with seniority over Colonels Urbina, Herrera, Chao, Ortega, and Hernández. Up to that point none of the other revolutionaries in the state had accepted his leadership, except Hernández, because they thought they had done just fine defeating the Federals without him and they commanded more troops than he did.[95] A few days later Villa directed his first battle as a commanding general.

When advance forces in Ortiz notified Villa of the approach of a Federal column, he sent Colonel Hernández and Major Félix Romero to counter the Federal movement. The Federals in Chihuahua City could not permit the Constitutionalists to sit astride their lines of communications to Torreón, and so this Federal column had come down to clear the Constitutionalists from the Camargo region. The opposing forces finally met in battle at Saucillo Station (about five kilometers north of Conchos Station), but due to the overwhelming numerical superiority of the Federals the Constitutionalists had to retreat to Conchos Station. Afterward, Constitutionalist Major Mucio Uranga and his staff, who were in some cars near Saucillo Station, entered that locale thinking that it was still held by Constitutionalists. The Federals there captured and shot Uranga and his aides, nailing him in the stomach with a bayonet.[96]

Conchos Station May 30

In response Villa ordered Maclovio Herrera with six hundred men to Saucillo to reinforce Hernández and hold up the Federal column, which the Constitutionalists estimated to number one thousand men with eight cannons commanded by a Colonel (probably Cayetano) Romero. Of course, Hernández was not in Saucillo, but six kilometers due south at Conchos Station where Herrera joined him. Villa followed on May 30 to take charge of the total force. Observing the approaching Federals in the morning hours he deployed his infantry on a broad front supported by cavalry; then his infantry charged at an attack step, opening fire. The Federal artillery responded intermittently spewing forth shrapnel at the Constitutionalists who, deployed along an extensive line, began gaining some ground. The Federals then attempted a flanking movement that the Constitutionalists repulsed. Still, the Federals continued to hold their positions and fight tenaciously, convinced that they would emerge victorious once General Antonio Rojas arrived with his three hundred Colorados to reinforce them. As soon as Rojas joined the battle the Federals regained their spirits and renewed the push against the Constitutionalists, who numbered about two thousand combatants.[97]

But the Constitutionalists refused to yield the field and at length succeeded in repulsing the Federals, sending them back to their trains that first just pulled back toward Saucillo and then later all the way to Chihuahua City. Executing an enveloping movement, some Constitutionalists managed to get to the Federals' lead train and capture some provisions, but they could not advance fast and far enough to cut off the rest of the Federal convoy because they were dismounted and exhausted by the fighting and the merciless sun, which caused a frightful thirst. Nevertheless, they recovered a considerable amount of booty, 200 Mausers, 40,000 rounds, and eight boxes of 80-mm. shells, although the Federals got away with their guns. The Constitutionalists suffered sixty wounded, including Major Benito Artalejo wounded in an arm, and many dead, but calculated the losses as being even worse for the Federals, who lost 100 men killed, many dispersed, and 116 taken prisoner, those officers captured being shot immediately. This was the first in a chain of battlefield successes for General Villa, and afterward his men withdrew to La Cruz to rest, subsequently pulling back to Camargo.[98]

Durango

When news of the overthrow, imprisonment, and deaths of Señores Madero and Pino Suárez reached Durango, the rich people threw parties and drank champagne while the principal public employees as well as those of the commercial houses gathered in the popular cantinas to celebrate. The governor of the state, Carlos Patoni, who had close ties to the wealthy class, could be seen speaking frequently with Federal Army jefes in the statehouse and on the streets. These encounters led the numerous mobilizing revolutionaries to suspect that he was a clandestine-Porfirista and fully attuned to the projects and plans of the revelers, who later would form the Social Defense and take up arms against the revolution. One individual who had joined Madero's rebellion in 1910 and reached the rank of major, Matías Pazuengo, however, did not just suspect Patoni of being anti-Maderista, he was convinced of it. In September of the previous year (1912) Emilio Madero had told him that "when Patoni had entered into office he requested of the Central

Government, that all the garrisons be of Federals," as opposed to Maderista paramilitaries. Eventually, fearing for his life, the governor would take a leave of absence and turn over office to his friend, Jesús Perea.[99]

Meanwhile, Major Pazuengo and others, such as the Arrieta brothers, Domingo and Mariano, began getting in touch with their men from the 1910 rebellion and preparing for the upcoming fight. As this was going on, the Jefe Político, Engineer, and Maderista, Pastor Rouaix, called Pazuengo and told him to get out of the state capital because the orders for his arrest were expected to come down at any moment. Rouaix also told him that while he would resign before serving the warrants, the gentleman whom he suspected would be chosen to replace him, Licenciado Ángel del Palacio, would have no qualms about complying with the orders. Pazuengo and the leading Maderistas held a meeting to discuss the issue, but they thought that the state executive and legislature would stand up to the new regime. They were wrong.[100]

It was soon learned that Interim Governor Perea, the state legislature, and those in government were in agreement with the Federal Jefe de las Armas and working to grant recognition to Huerta's usurper government. Not only did they start arresting leading Maderistas but also anyone suspected of sympathizing with the revolutionaries, including Pazuengo who was arrested on April 1, 1913. Through the efforts of others, namely Licenciado Juan Santa Marina and Emiliano G. Saravia, Pazuengo gained his freedom after about a week of incarceration.[101] Upon his release, Pazuengo sought out his old soldiers, who had already taken up arms; since he knew where they were "marauding" it took him no more than one day to find them. They put themselves under his command, and then the group left for Labor de Guadalupe where Calixto Contreras and Orestes Pereyra already had assembled about one thousand armed and mounted revolutionaries, with rosy prospects for recruiting additional men very quickly since more and more were arriving daily.[102]

THE 1910 REVOLUTIONARIES

The leading revolutionaries from Durango in 1913 had all participated in Madero's 1910 rebellion. Domingo Arrieta, who was born on August 4, 1874 at Rancho de Vascongil, Canelas district, never attended primary school, and from his youth worked as a teamster and miner; he had witnessed the injustices inflicted upon workers by their employers, became a fervent Anti-Reelectionist, and on November 20, 1910 took up arms in his hometown with his brothers Mariano and Eduardo against the Porfirian government. Major Pazuengo's career had similar beginnings. In 1910 he had been in a mining camp called Río Verde, District of San Dimas, Durango, almost on the border with Sinaloa state when he read in the newspapers of Madero's rebellion and how every day more and more events were developing in favor of the "holy cause." Approaching the operators who worked for him, Pazuengo began exposing them to the agreeability of seconding the movement and then led his followers into rebellion.[103]

Two other important leaders came from the area around Cuencamé in the east, the Tarahumara Indian Calixto Contreras who was described as "thin, short, with a large forehead, brave and humble," and future general Severiano Ceniceros. They had become activists even before 1910 because of the great tyranny that the owners of Hacienda de Sombreretillos perpetrated against the indigenous residents of the pueblo of Ocuila (about five kilometers due south of Cuencamé), which made them disposed to back the revolution in later years. Said owners of Sombreretillos finished off the pueblo and consigned Calixto Contreras with two of his nephews to the ranks of the Federal Army for several years; at the same time they had Severiano Ceniceros, who possessed the Indians' power of attorney, put in jail. For this reason in the year 1910 Calixto Contreras took part in the juntas of Torreón and rebelled in Cuencamé on November 20. Ever since, Calixto Contreras, accompanied by Severiano Ceniceros, had directed the revolutionary efforts in the districts of Cuencamé, Nazas, and part of San Juan del Río.[104]

Another leader who operated in Lagunera region, who had not only commanded men, but actually fought during Madero's rebellion against the Orozquistas and now against Huerta's government, was Orestes Pereyra.[105]

Although in the aftermath of Madero's rebellion Domingo Arrieta, Calixto Contreras, Orestes Pereyra, and Jesús Agustín Castro had been confirmed in rank as comandantes and commanded of a corps of Rurales, as a result of budgetary cutbacks by the end of 1912 only the Zacatecan Martín Triana in San Juan de Guadalupe and Pereyra in Pedriceña commanded Rural Police corps inside the state: the 22nd and 44th, respectively. Nevertheless, the numerous Rural Police comandantes within the state "in depot" (including Tomás Urbina in the northern districts of Indé y El Oro) still commanded the allegiance of many men with access to arms, who were ready, willing, and able to take them up again, as demonstrated.[106]

A NEW FIGHT AGAINST THE FEDERALS

The revolutionary effort in the eastern part of the state got started in March 1913 under Calixto Contreras with principal subordinates Severiano Ceniceros and Orestes Pereyra and about seven hundred men interdicting Federal communications between Torreón and Durango City. Brothers Mariano and Domingo Arrieta also began recruiting troops for the revolution in their hometown of Canelas in western Durango immediately following the

Mexico City coup, eventually equaling Contreras in the number of soldiers. To combat these revolutionaries and Tomás Urbinas' Auxiliaries to the north, Federal Brigadier Eutiquio Munguía, had about two thousand men spread out over the states of Durango and Zacatecas. But in early March Colorado General Benjamín Argumedo (now working for Huerta's government) arrived in Gómez Palacio with nine hundred mounted irregulars from Monterrey, and eight hundred men of the Federal 1st Cavalry Regiment under Federal Brigadier Luis G. Anaya (newly promoted for his role in the Citadel uprising) also reported to Torreón.[107]

**Durango State Operations
March – June 1913**

Map 1.8

The destruction of the rails between Torreón and Durango City put the garrison of the state's capital in a very precarious situation. Consequently the jefe de las armas, Federal Colonel Justiniano Gómez, sent a repair train and escort commanded by First Captain Francisco Gálvez with about one hundred soldiers to begin repairing the destruction caused by Pereyra and Contreras. The train left on March 13 and arrived the next day at a place of destruction between Pasaje and Centro (five kilometers to the north of Pasaje) stations when Pereyra's men attacked. The Federals fought back for about five hours and then the repair train pushed its way through to Pedriceña. When General Munguía learned that Gálvez was under attack he sent Lieutenant Colonel Esteban Barrios of the 15th Cavalry Regiment with two hundred men by train to reinforce him. Barrios arrived at Pedriceña at 4:30 p.m. and linked up with Captain Gálvez who told him that Pereyra had withdrawn to Cuencamé. Barrios figured that he had a sufficiently large force to beat the revolutionaries, and his Federals detrained to continue on foot, arriving at Cuencamé around 10:00 p.m. The Federals penetrated the town and surprised the guards of the 22nd, but quickly recovering the Rurales returned fire from rooftops, doorways, and around corners. Colonel Barrios was killed in the opening minutes of combat and First Captain Jesús V. García of the 1st Regiment assumed command. Noticing that he was greatly outnumbered and surrounded, the captain retreated after two hours of combat, arriving back at Pedriceña at 5 a.m. to report one dead, six wounded, and twenty-four of his men dispersed. The revolutionaries recovered good weapons, ample ammunition, and experienced an overall improvement in morale. Gálvez's train arrived in Torreón the same day.[108]

After that victory the forces of Pereyra and Contreras abandoned Cuencamé for Nazas, and then fell upon the Federal garrison of El Rodeo where many of the irregulars there, including the commander, decided to join the revolution without putting up a fight. Next, Contreras sent a column of two hundred men to attack San Juan del Río, and when the Federal garrison commander there, Irregular Lieutenant Colonel Serafín R. Hernández, found out about the force headed his way from a sub-lieutenant who had fled El Rodeo, he sent an urgent appeal to the 11th Military Zone headquarters for reinforcements. As soon as Contreras' men appeared before the town on March 23, Hernández abandoned the plaza. Some of his men defected to the revolution, and the rest followed him to Canatlán with the revolutionaries harassing the Huertistas for a good stretch of the way. Hernández's command finally reached Canatlán and then Durango City where he received the happy news that he had been promoted to full colonel of infantry.[109]

Pereyra and Contreras pursued Hernández to Canatlán and then simulated a northern movement to unite with Domingo and Mariano Arrieta, whose Guadalupe Victoria Brigade was threatening to take Santiago Papasquiaro. Since the commander of Durango City, Colonel Gómez, did not have enough men to garrison Santiago Papasquiaro, he answered the jefe político's request to send troops by increasing Colonel Hernández's command with another eighty men so that he now had two hundred and sent him back to Canatlán, with orders to continue on to Santiago Papasquiaro. After passing from Canatlán, which had already been abandoned by Contreras and Pereyra, he continued on; however, after having gone only a short distance he learned that about one thousand revolutionaries in the sierra waited to attack him down the road, so he returned to Canatlán.[110] Meanwhile, Pereyra and Contreras had already started back for Cuencamé, on a collision course with Federal General Anaya's column.

After the revolutionaries killed Colonel Barrios in Cuencamé, General Munguía ordered General Anaya with a combined arms team of five hundred men from the 20th and 24th Infantry Battalions; the 1st, 15th, 22nd Auxiliary, 30th Auxiliary, and 32nd Auxiliary Cavalry Regiments; and two 80-mm. guns from the 1st Artillery Regiment, to attack the revolutionaries headquartered in Cuencamé. Anaya reported not finding any rebels in Cuencamé upon his arrival on March 20, which resulted in new orders to march on San Juan del Río, but he also received news that Contreras and Pereyra were threatening Santiago Papasquiaro, so Anaya figured that they had skipped San Juan del Río and therefore he headed straight for Santiago Papasquiaro in western Durango. In reality it was the Arrietas who stood on the doorstep of the latter town. Anaya reached Durango City by rail on March 25, learning en route of a group of revolutionaries at San Gabriel Station (today Villa Madero), and so he detached about seventy infantry and 120 irregular cavalry under Irregular Major Aurelio G. García to backtrack to that location while he continued on to Canatlán with the rest of the men. García arrived at San Gabriel Station without incident and spent the night at the station. When García learned that the revolutionaries had been sighted at La Tapona the major requested orders from Durango City and Colonel Gómez told him to attack.[111]

The following day, March 26, the major loaded his infantry in carts and with his cavalry headed for Hacienda La Tapona (today Guadalupe Victoria), the reported location of the revolutionaries, where he learned that Contreras' men had doubled back to San Gabriel Station. Racing back toward the station he arrived at night. The next morning his infantry commanded by Second Captain Salvador Dayo spotted some seven hundred revolutionaries about twelve kilometers north of the station at Rancho Picardías. The revolutionaries did an about face to present a front to the Federals. Major García deployed his infantry and even some of his cavalry on line to extend his own front, employing the rest of his cavalry in an attempt to outflank the revolutionaries, but since Contreras' force so greatly outnumbered García's, it was the revolutionaries who succeed in executing an enveloping maneuver, forcing the Federals to attempt a retreat. The Federals fled north, pursued all the way, to Catalina Station (today Ignacio Allende) where García took a head count and realized that he had lost all of his infantry and 54 cavalrymen, or about 125 of his original 190 men.[112]

Anaya had tried to come to the rescue of his subordinate when he learned that Contreras and Pereyra were at Santa Gabriel Station, leaving Colonel Hernández behind in Canatlán, but he arrived at Santa Gabriel late in the day after García had already left the area. The revolutionaries, however, were still there, and Anaya engaged them in a battle that lasted into the next day when, aided by his artillery, which fired more than two hundred shells, and the arrival of an additional one hundred Durango state troopers, his condition improved a bit. But at around 10 a.m. the revolutionaries again executed a large enveloping maneuver to reach Chorro Station, some twelve kilometers south of San Gabriel Station, where Anaya had left his convoy. The revolutionaries took possession of Anaya's trains, sacked them, and then burned them to prevent the Federals from using them for a retreat. Around noon Anaya realized that his situation only continued to go from bad to worse, since he was beginning to run low on ammunition, so he began retreating to Hacienda del Refugio in echelon making use of a large dust cloud. From there he changed into a column of march and reached Durango City on March 29. García made it Torreón two days later with the remnants of his command to report his disaster.[113]

The many victories that Contreras and Pereyra enjoyed over the Federals increased their prestige and caused many fence-riders in Durango to declare for the Constitutionalists. In equal measure the frustration grew in Mexico City as Huerta transformed the 11th Military Zone into the Division of the Nazas on April 1 and recalled General of Division Ignacio A. Bravo from retirement to replace Brigadier Eutiquio Munguía as commander of the new unit. He also replaced Colonel Gómez as the Jefe de las Armas with Colonel Ignacio Morelos Zaragoza, who in turn was almost immediately replaced by Brigadier Antonio M. Escudero, commander of the 14th Cavalry Regiment. As the ranking officer, Escudero already should have been in command. It was a thankless task for all Federal officers concerned because, as more citizens joined the ranks of the Constitutionalists, their commanders felt sufficiently strong to attack the state capital and had already begun tearing up railroad track between Torreón and Durango City in preparation for just such an attack.[114]

In response to the destruction of the rails, Munguía sent strong detachments to Pedriceña and Velardeña along with a repair train and Federal escort to maintain order in the two mining towns and reestablish communications to Durango City, which had the effect of bringing some five hundred Federal soldiers into the area. On April 1 the Zone Chief found out that Contreras had begun tearing up track between Pedriceña and Pasaje Station and sent Comandante Moisés Zamora with a regiment of about three hundred irregulars belonging to General Jesús José "Cheché" Campos' brigade from Torreón to reinforce Pedriceña, and also ordered the repair train into the area. The regiment of irregulars arrived the next day. On April 3 a general action took place that began with Contreras' fifteen hundred men attacking the repair train, and then drawing the garrisons of Pedriceña and Velardeña into a fray that, despite the distances covered and the number of troops involved, only resulted in the Federals losing two killed, five wounded, and thirteen dispersed against an estimated of forty to fifty casualties for the revolutionaries. The next day Comandante Zamora returned to Torreón and the repair train continued its fool's errand, since it never did succeed in repairing the rails faster than the Constitutionalists could return to destroy them.[115]

In early April Constitutionalist General Contreras agreed to a proposal put forth by Domingo and Mariano Arrieta and Matías and Sergio Pazuengo to attack Durango City. Contreras and Pereyra arrived just outside of Durango City and established their headquarters at Hacienda de la Labor de Guadalupe (to the northeast), joining the Pazuengos who were already there, and awaited the forces of Arrieta in order to formulate a plan of attack. In mid-April the Arrietas arrived to the north of the city, and by April 20 they had their men quartered at the Hacienda de Tapias (east of the plaza) and other locations in the vicinity, bringing the estimated total number of revolutionaries to three thousand. With the city effectively cut off from Torreón, the Constitutionalists reached an agreement at Rancho San Ignacio, just outside the city, to deliver the assault on April 24 in the early morning hours, with General Contreras and Pereyra attacking in the north, another group from Pereyra's column on the east, and the whole eight hundred man column of Generals Mariano and Domingo Arrieta on the west.[116]

To defend the plaza, Brigadier Escudero had some six hundred men of the 24th and 36th (Auxiliary) Infantry Battalions; the 1st, 14th, and 15th Cavalry Regiments; and two Saint Chamond Mondragón 75-mm. cannons from the 1st Artillery Regiment. Additionally, 120 local citizens agreed to serve in the "Social Defense Volunteer Corps" at the orders of Cavalry Major Rafael Vega y Roca. Escudero copied the same plan that the Federals had used to successfully defend the plaza in May 1911, placing small detachments around the outskirts of town at seven key points (Ojo de Agua, el Sanctuary of Guadalupe, the extreme end of Leyva Street, Rancho de Zataráin, Rancho de Granados, the sentry box at Analco, and Los Remedios Hill), and in the interior of the town his men occupied the solid buildings of the cathedral and the sanctuary and church of Santa Ana, whose towers served perfectly as points of observation.[117] (See Durango City map in Chapter 4)

FIRST BATTLE OF DURANGO CITY APRIL 23-26

Around 3 p.m. on April 23 the revolutionaries initiated an attack against the railroad station and the Sanctuary of Guadalupe on the north side of the town, but since they were too far away very few of their rounds reached the sanctuary over the two hours that the shooting lasted. During the night the Constitutionalists proceeded to surround the town completely. About 3:30 a.m. they simultaneously attacked all points of the Federal defense, trying to locate a weak spot. After four hours the Constitutionalists succeeded in conquering the little fort at Rancho de Zataráin, because of the large number of attackers and also because of support from civilian sympathizers on the interior of the town firing from rooftops and other hidden places into the rear of the Federal defenses. But Escudero had his reserve, a group from the 14th Cavalry Regiment, counterattack, and supported by the two cannons, they succeeded in retaking Rancho de Zataráin by nine o'clock the next morning.[118]

As the assault was not very uniform across the sectors, the plaza still had not fallen by ten in the morning, since for reasons unknown General Contreras' men had not budged an inch from the side of Mercado Hill, while Pereyra's assault force (which included Pazuengo's command) had penetrated as far as the state penitentiary. But since Contreras' men refused to attack, and a Federal detachment began pushing back the Constitutionalists in the cemetery and threatening to surround Pereyra's column, orders were given to fall back to Rancho San Ignacio, while the Arrietas fought off-and-on in the direction of Remedios Hill. It must be said here that unlike the vast majority of Constitutionalists, those from Durango State, in general, and Contreras' in particular, quickly gained a well-deserved reputation for lacking discipline. As might be expected, the retreat emboldened Federal Lieutenant Colonel Ignacio Morelos Zaragoza's Huertista volunteers as well as General Escudero's Federals, who then put up an even greater resistance. So around 4 p.m. Contreras and Pereyra agreed to break off the attack and try again after nightfall, but the Arrietas vacillated, and did not respond to the new plan of attack, mainly because their men needed a rest. When 10 p.m. came and went without the signal for the assault coming from the Arrietas, Generals

Pereyra and Contreras decided to do nothing, which turned out to be a good thing, since without all the forces engaged the assault probably would have failed and only resulted in a waste of ammunition.[119]

In the early morning hours of the next day the Constitutionalists made a determined push from Mercado Hill on the north side and against the Sanctuary of Guadalupe and the small fort at the Ojo de Agua located on the city's northwest corner. The Federals repulsed this attack, again, thanks to artillery located on the east side of the city and the propitious arrival of the intrepid Irregular General "Cheché" Campos with 350 mounted Colorados.[120] A little sleepless because of the worries of their commands, the principal Constitutionalist commanders on the east side, that is, José Carrillo, Pazuengo, and Pereyra, had imprudently forgotten about the Huertista forces advancing from Torreón to Durango that had been getting closer and closer. A surprised small security force very close to Rancho San Ignacio to the north in the direction of Rancho La Calera suddenly returned fire from Campos' Colorados, and Major Pazuengo reported that "the most complete disorder and confusion" reigned there. Some Constitutionalists fled bareback, others with saddles but not saddle blankets, and others however they could, since otherwise "we would have been surrounded to the rear if the movement had not been made as quickly as it was to Mercado Hill, where the forces of General Contreras were located." The Colorados pursued the Constitutionalists to Mercado Hill, but were there repulsed by the Constitutionalists who held the high ground; at one point, the citizens of the town came out to fight the Colorados, thinking that they were Constitutionalists until through communications and signals "the jefe de las armas recognized his own." This firefight lasted from 10 a.m. until nightfall. The Constitutionalists did not suffer many losses from Campos' grand entrance, according to Pazuengos, but the campesinos and peons of the haciendas that the Colorados had encountered on their journey suffered greatly, since the Colorados, judging them to be Maderistas "did carnage to the poor defenseless peons of the haciendas."[121]

In view of the condition of their men and the Federal relief force, the Constitutionalist leaders decided that Durango would be much harder to conquer than previously thought. After one final feeble assault on the twenty-sixth they scattered. The Pazuengos brothers retired north toward Pánuco and sent word to the Arrietas to reunite with them in Canatlán; Contreras and Pereyra returned to Cuencamé; and others dispersed to Cañitas de Felipe Pescador in Zacatecas. The Federals lamented sixteen of their own dead and nine wounded, while finding sixty-two Constitutionalist corpses. In the successful defense of the city, the Federals properly employed artillery and cavalry for shock effect and benefited from Contreras' notoriously unruly and undisciplined troops.[122]

Against seemingly impossible odds, General Campos wasted no time in forming five columns to pursue the retreating Constitutionalists, who overwhelmingly outnumbered his own forces. Those Colorados sent against Canatlán attacked the Constitutionalists, who possessed the best positions to repulse any attempts at envelopment, on May 1. Colorado jefe Luis Escajeda dared to present battle with only four hundred mounted men, most probably because he had received intelligence that the Constitutionalists were short of ammunition. So assured of triumphing were the Colorados that they did not take due care with either their vanguard or rearguard. The Constitutionalist jefe José Carrillo, seeing this, suggested that all the Constitutionalist commanders order their men to hold their fire until the Colorados arrived at the water inlet on the edge of town. Once they did, all opened fire; the fierce firefight lasted thirty minutes. Caught in a crossfire, the Colorados did an about-face and raced off as fast as they had come, leaving behind many dead and wounded, but especially horses.[123]

Those Colorados sent after the Arrietas fought them on two more occasions in the first half of May at Canatlán without being able to defeat them and so returned to Durango City, arriving on May 22. General Campos chased after the revolutionary parties that retreated toward the southeast and then experienced some skirmishes fighting to keep the road open to Cañitas. Contreras and Pereyra returned to their base at Cuencamé without incident, began tearing up track again, and on May 5 attacked the 230 or so men of the combined arms team under Federal Major Eufrasio Radillo that garrisoned Pedriceña in an attempt to keep the lines between Durango and Torreón open. Completely overwhelmed and running short of ammunition at 6 p.m. on May 6, the Federals disabled their one 70-mm. mountain piece, loaded up on trains, and headed for Torreón. At Huarichic Canyon the main body of Contreras' brigade forced Radillo to detrain and fight his way to division headquarters. One group headed for Picardías to pick up the Central Railroad and the other continued along the Durango-Torreón railway; only about 125 of Radillo's men made it back to Torreón, with the rest being killed, captured, or dispersed.[124]

Thereafter, General Bravo could not afford to send more troops to garrison Pedriceña-Velardeña because around this same time Comandante Martín Triana and Gregorio García with four hundred Constitutionalists carried off a surprise attack against the fifty-man Federal garrison of Matamoros (twenty-four kilometers east of Torreón), annihilating it and threatening to cut off the

Division of the Nazas from Saltillo. In response, Bravo sent Colorado General Marcelo Caraveo with his brigade of about 250 men and some detachments from the 18th and 20th infantry battalions by train; they retook Matamoros that same day, sending Triana back to San Juan de Guadalupe.[125]

Constitutionalists and Federals continued to fight over the rail lines for the rest of May and into June. Comandante Triana, operating from his base in San Juan de Guadalupe in far east Durango, disrupted the rail traffic between Torreón and Zacatecas, while Colorado General Campos, following orders from Federal General Aurelio Blanquet to go out and defeat the revolutionaries in detail, led a campaign against Contreras and Pereyra that resulted in a few minor engagements on May 24 and 25. Around this time, the Arrieta brothers invited Tomás Urbina, who had departed from Chihuahua on April 23 and had been marauding in the north of Durango ever since, to lead a new coordinated attack on Durango City. They believed that with all the forces of the state united under the single command of the tough and well-equipped Urbina they could conquer Durango.[126] Future events would prove them right.

*   *   *

The Constitutionalists in the Northeast mobilized quickly, not only because they had a nucleus of Auxiliary and Rural Police corps to coalesce around but also because officers quickly adapted their civilian expertise to military applications and motivated citizens flocked to the revolutionary standards. Additionally, Maderista commanders of insurgent outfits that had been mustered out of service in 1911 and 1912, namely in Durango, quickly rounded up their men and returned to campaigning. Only Villa had to recruit his brigade from the ground up, principally from among Chihuahua's military colonies, and he did not appreciably participate in combat during the first three months, only accepting a Constitutionalist commission at the end of May. In the meantime, he captured silver bullion from a train, intervened haciendas, and raided warehouses of Spaniards to supply his brigade, while Carranza gained access to resources by authorizing the printing of paper money, an expedient necessary for fielding his army, although he still had to contend with an arms embargo leveled against his movement.

Conversely, while the poorly-armed and largely untrained and undisciplined (especially in Durango) Constitutionalists rapidly mobilized and massed for operations, the Federals got off to a slow start. Even though

Huerta "suppressed" the military zones fairly quickly, by April 1, he had waited months to change the legal means of recruitment and increase the authorized size of the army. Yet, the Federal Army continued to have the same problems recruiting quality soldiers in necessary numbers as always, and resorted to the same tried-and-failed schemes that had been in practice going back to Santa Anna's time: dragooning recalcitrant political opponents, criminals,[127] vagrants, and disengaged Indians to fill out the ranks, and with the same results. Mobilization was slow, training rudimentary, and effectiveness in the field tragic. Cannon fodder could not prosecute modern warfare, in general, nor function appropriate to the ternary system, in particular. Under such circumstances the Federals' primary mission, perforce, devolved from offensive operations to safeguarding the nation's patrimony and projecting government control along the numerous arteries, especially railroads, and inside countless towns, haciendas, mines, and other high value targets. In so doing, however, their detachments and flying columns were isolated and/or annihilated: Lampazos and Villaldama in Nuevo León; Jiménez, Santa Rosalía de Camargo, and Conchos Station in Chihuahua; and Cuencamé, El Rodeo, Rancho Picardías, and Santa Gabriel in Durango. Only Cheché Campos' flying column of Colorados achieved any degree of success, although it also gained notoriety for committing atrocities. By the end of May the Federals were stalled in Coahuila, relegated to the state capital and periphery in Tamaulipas, and reduced to the Ciudad Juárez-Chihuahua City and Torreón-Durango City lines in Chihuahua and Durango, respectively.

Given such woeful results, suspicions about the loyalties and competence of Federal officers resulted in the sacking of several key leaders: Fernando Trucy Aubert and Emiliano Lojero in the Division of the Bravo and Eutiquio Munguía and Justiniano Gómez in the Division of the Nazas. These were just the beginning; the rotation of officers through leadership positions would continue right up until the demise of the Federal Army, as officers fired from one command would show up to take charge of another whose leader had been removed for cause, for the simple reason that there were only so many Federal generals to choose from and most were aged and unschooled. Their subordinates were no better, as the initial engagements revealed at least two common tactical deficiencies that became prevalent among Federal officers, placing machine guns up high and/or in defilade and pushing out a perimeter defense too large for the number of available troops to man it. The errors committed by Federal officers in terms of strategy, tactics, and logistics would result in numerous calamities in the coming months, as the operating environment became ever more complex. For the first time, the federal government had a revolution on its hands, a revolution that threatened Mexico City from along numerous axes of advance, most notably from the Northeast, which not only comprised the most strategically important region, but also the most complex environment for military operations.

Three

Luis Medina Barrón's Relief Column—General Miguel Gil Relieved—Medina Barrón Takes Over—Battle of Santa Rosa—Charge of the 8th Rurales—Federal Artillery Savaged—The Sierra Juárez Auxiliary Battalion of Oaxaca—Comparisons to His Excellency Santa Anna—Obregón's Generalship—Governor Pesqueira Promoted—Ojeda Arrives in Guaymas—Díaz abandons Torín and Southern Sonora—The "American" biplane—General Miguel Girón Killed—Battle of San Alejandro—Yaqui versus Zapotec—Battle of Santa María—Alvarado's Ternary Disposition—The Federals Escape Annihilation—A Cost-Benefit Analysis—The Siege of Guaymas—More Anti-American Hysteria

Guaymas Valley

On May 1, almost two full months after Obregón had begun campaigning a flotilla of five ships arrived in the port of Guaymas and disgorged 1,500,000 7-mm. cartridges, five artillery pieces, two machine guns, and Federal Brigadier Luis Medina Barrón with reinforcements for the Division of the Yaqui. Medina Barrón's column left Mexico City by rail on April 22, and then embarked on April 25 and set sail from Manzanillo. His column was but one of many military columns that would sally forth from the metropolis to attempt to bring the defiant provincials to heel. And what a column it was. An estimated 1,000 of the 1,200 men had never before put on a uniform, much less handled a Mauser, before disembarking.[1] The Huertista Rómulo Velasco Ceballos, remarked of these paladins of the Fatherland:

In the main from the jails of México [City], showing traces of inebriation from pulque on their countenance and in the whole of their organism a lamentable lack of vigor. Used to the delightful climate of the Valley of Mexico, were such men going to have the spirit and courage to fight under the furnace of these fields, where the Fahrenheit thermometer reaches the 119 degree mark? Habituated to the asphalt streets of the Metropolis, would it be easy for them to climb steep and uneven hills, carrying on their back their weapon, clothes, ammunition, their supplies, and all this [while] suffering a frightful thirst because the burning deserts of Sonora refuse even one drop of water? On what would they establish the enthusiasm to transform their weakness into strength? On their political opinions? ... If they do not have them! And if they do, they are reduced to the simple cry of: ¡Viva Madero! or ¡Viva Zapata![2]

Ceballos bemoaned the lopsidedness of the upcoming contest, since the revolutionaries were sons of Sonora, accustomed to the incredible variations of the climate, and battle-hardened because everyone had been fighting rebel Indians for thirty years; they were men of a stout and robust type with little need of creature comforts and "they had the very important assistance of the Yaqui, a truly military type, a warrior race [known] for its bravery, obedience, and somberness."[3]

From the Constitutionalist point of view, however, they could only observe with dismay the spectacle of Federal gunboats arriving and the offloading of artillery, materiel, and numerous men. Obregón grossly overestimated the reinforcements at 3,000 and knew that the "Federals in Guaymas were making every kind of preparation to undertake their advance on Hermosillo."[4] If the Federals seemed unfit for the task before them to their Huertista supporters, the Constitutionalists felt overwhelmed. Effectively, with these latest reinforcements General Miguel Gil had 2,100 Federals in the Guaymas Valley against the estimated 3,000 Constitutionalists in the area who possessed no artillery. The Federal general finally believed that he had the upper hand in numbers, firepower, and materiel, and therefore did not need to call in Colonel Díaz's men from down south, who would have provided an additional estimated force of 600 men, before beginning his march to retake the state capital.[5]

BATTLE OF SANTA ROSA

On May 2, after a reconnaissance made using its spotlights the night before, the Federal transport *General Guerrero* bombarded the Constitutionalist advance positions in Empalme, which accomplished two objectives: clearing the revolutionaries from the station and keeping them from uniting with the Constitutionalist cavalry forces from the south. That same day, just hours after the bombardment, the Federals got underway leaving behind only the 27th Infantry under Colonel Miguel Girón with three hundred men to secure the port and collecting the 14th, 28th, and 50th (Auxiliary) Battalions in San José de Guaymas, where the column spent the first night.[6]

The second day the main force reached Empalme and went into camp with a small advance force in the direction of Batamotal, which engaged in a light firefight with the Constitutionalist rearguard and forced the revolutionaries to hurriedly fall back on Maytorena Station. The following day, May 4, the Federal vanguard continued northward toward Maytorena Station and again engaged some Constitutionalists, killing ten. In return, they lost one killed and two wounded by a machine gun emplaced in the caboose of the retreating Constitutionalist convoy.[7]

At this point in the advance General Gil had an estimated 1,600 men in the column of march (in rough numbers and estimates): Colonel Luis F. Eguiluz's 400 men of the 28th Infantry; crews for six machine guns; First Captain Alfonso Martínez's artillery with 160 men; 300 of the 53rd Auxiliary Infantry Battalion under Francisco Cota; the 50th Auxiliary Infantry Battalion under Lieutenant Colonel Ignacio Gómez with 275 infantrymen; 130 guards of the 8th Rural Corps under Lieutenant Colonel Juan N. de la Vega; Major Nicolás González's Auxiliary Corps of Guanajuato with 120 mounted riders (these last two units apparently having come with General Medina Barrón from Coahuila); and possibly men from the 25th Infantry Battalion.[8]

As the Federals advanced farther inland Obregón intended to oblige them by withdrawing to the north, forcing them to stretch their lines of communication, use up what supplies they carried with them, and detach security details that would diminish their effective combat strength. Compelling opponents to exhaust their materiel and decrease their numbers before attacking them would become a signature tactic for Obregón and a clear sign of his understanding of the principles of war. As Gil advanced on Hermosillo and distanced himself from his base of operations at Guaymas, the plan seemed to be working with an estimated 600 Federals already left behind at Guaymas and Empalme to guard his lines of communication against a possible coup de main.[9]

After the brief firefight the day before at Maytorena Station, Gil deemed that contact had been made, and on May 5 the Federals sent the 50th Battalion, the Auxiliary Corps of Guanajuato, Voluntarios de Xico (53rd Battalion), and a battery of artillery to Santa María. The rest of the column advanced to San

Antonio de Arriba (just south of Maytorena Station), for two reasons: so Gil could ascertain the intentions of the Constitutionalists and to get water, since that of Maytorena Station did not suffice. Those who went to San Antonio advanced the next day to join the group at Santa María. And finally, on May 7, the whole column returned to Maytorena Station where it had sent the 50th Battalion the day before. In effect, Gil remained moving around Maytorena Station for three days, unmolested by the Constitutionalists, with no evidence of any overarching plan. That same day he received orders from the Secretary of War to hand over command to General Medina Barrón who would be the interim commander until General Pedro Ojeda could make his way back from the United States to assume command of the Division of the Yaqui.[10]

Medina Barrón

Much better qualified for the upcoming campaign than his charges was the new Federal commander, General Medina Barrón, who had made his bones prosecuting a competent campaign against the Yaqui Indians between 1902 and 1911, and therefore knew the geography of Sonora. Forty-one years old and ambitious, he had been born in Jerez, a district seat in Zacatecas State, to Licenciado Urbano Medina, and Doña Josefa Barrón, the daughter of a general who fought the Americans in 1847. At sixteen he had been forced to abandon his studies due to financial circumstances and join the army as a private, soon rising to the rank of sub-lieutenant in the 4th Infantry Battalion, which he left as a First Captain to join the 11th Infantry Battalion. A short time later, while still in the army, he took command of the 11th Rural Police Corps and then went to Sonora where he began to gain fame as capable and brave in an army where very few officers stood out. In dealing with subordinates, Medina Barrón was even-tempered and firm without being abusive or offensive. Having only recently been a first captain, he soon commanded a brigade, since in addition to the 11th the government gave him command of the Federal Auxiliary Corps and the Sonoran National Guard. By 1913 he had participated in more than fifteen "battles" and around forty firefights, succeeding in pacifying part of the Yaqui tribe and establishing personal relationships with his Yaqui counterparts in the process. Most famously he received recognition for bringing about the surrender and pacification of Luis Bule, who now served under Obregón.[11]

General Medina Barrón was not one to just sit and wait until Ojeda could arrive, and so the eager new commander immediately resumed the march on May 8, sending the 28th Infantry Battalion under Colonel Eguiluz ahead to reinforce the vanguard and advance to Santa Rosa Station (nine kilometers north of Maytorena Station), where a few hours later the 53rd joined them. During this displacement the Federals engaged the Constitutionalist rear-guard under Major Jesús Trujillo in a brief firefight. Upon arriving at Santa Rosa, the 28th established security, placing seven observation posts to the west, near the sierra, and two to the north, one of which was over a ditch hidden among the trees. The 53rd took up position on the right where the dominant terrain feature was a house, referred to as the Santa Rosa de Arriba House, situated about a kilometer and a half to the east of the station and hidden in the densest part of a thicket. The retreating Obregón reached Ortiz Station, at which point, obeying a command from Governor Pesqueira not to retreat any farther, Obregón countermarched and finally, after four days of delay and retreat, prepared to do battle.[12]

Taking Colonel Cabral, his chief of staff Major Nicolás Díaz de León, Major Carlos Félix, and Captain Benjamín Chaparro with him, Obregón reconnoitered a hill a little less than a kilometer from the enemy where he devised the following disposition. In the center he decided to have Colonel Cabral lead a force of about five hundred men from the 4th Irregular Battalion, ex-Insurgents Corps and the State National Guard, and part of the 3rd Irregular Battalion with principal subalterns Major Francisco R. Manzo, Major Francisco G. Manríquez, and First Captain Arnulfo R. Gómez. On his left (east) wing he planned for Colonel Ramón V. Sosa to attack with about twelve hundred men from parts of the 47th and 48th Rural Corps; State National Guard; 5th Irregular Battalion; Voluntarios de Río de Sonora, Guaymas, Mátape, and Hermosillo; the ex-Insurgents Corps; and the Fieles de Huiribis Battalion, with principal leaders Majors José María Acosta, Carlos Félix, Jesús Trujillo, Aurelio Amavisca, and First Captain Lino Morales. And finally, on the right (west) under Colonel Manuel M. Diéguez he sent about one thousand men of Voluntarios de Cananea and de Arizpe, and the Federal Auxiliary Corps under Majors Francisco Contreras, Luis Bule, and Francisco Urbalejo, along with some other minor volunteer units. After victories at Cananea and Naco, Obregón's four machine guns had grown in number to fourteen, which he apportioned accordingly: two 7-mm. Colts to First Captain Lino Morales and two more to First Captain J. Gonzalo Escobar on the left; two with Diéguez and one with Bule on the right; and two with Major Manzo in the center, retaining five in reserve.[13] This battle, along with Cananea and the action at San Joaquín that marked Obregón's ascent, demonstrated the growing predilection that the caudillo from Huatabampo had for machine guns, not just because of the demonstrated efficacy of these weapons but perhaps also owing to his fascination with all things mechanical.

Tactical Command	Major Unit organic to	J	O	T	Total
Center					
Cabral, Juan G. (Colonel)	Column Commander	1	2		3
Gómez, Arnulfo R. (1st CPT)	3rd Irr Infantry Battalion of Sonora		4	100	104
Manzo, Francisco R. (Major)	4th Irr Infantry Battalion of Sonora	1	21	200	222
Gutiérrez, Reyes N. (1st CPT)	5th Irr Infantry Battalion of Sonora		4	50	54
Manríquez, Francisco (Major)	Ex-Insurgents and National Guard	1	5	60	66
Ramírez, Miguel (1st CPT)	Voluntarios de Horcasitas		4	55	59
Right (West) flank					
Diéguez, Manuel M. (Colonel)	Column Commander	1	1		2
Quiroga, Pablo (1st CPT)	Voluntarios de Cananea		5	150	155
Contreras, Francisco (Major)	Voluntarios de Arizpe	1	12	200	213
Alvarado, Salvador (Colonel)	Column Commander	1	2		3
Bule/Urbalejo (Majors)	Federal Auxiliary Corps	2	21	441	464
Various	Volunteers*	3	11	202	216
Left (East) flank					
Sosa, Ramón V. (Colonel)	Column Commander	1	2		3
Gutiérrez/Acosta (Majors)	48th Rural Corps and National Guard	2	19	200	221
Félix, Carlos (Major)	47th Rural Corp & 5th Irr Infantry Battalion of Sonora	1	9	235	245
Amavisca, Aurelio (Major)	Voluntarios de Río de Sonora, Guaymas, Hermosillo	1	26	215	242
Trujillo, Jesús (Major)	2nd Irr Cavalry ("Ex-Insurgents") Corps of Sonora	1	5	100	106
Morales, Lino (1st CPT)	Fieles de Huiribis Battalion		22	300	322
Pesqueira, Jesús (2nd CPT)	Voluntarios de Mátape		6	40	46
Reserve					
Rivero, Tiburcio (1st CPT)	Voluntarios de Cananea		10	350	360
Kloss, Maximiliano (1st CPT)	14 Machine Guns		5	40	45
					3,151

* Voluntarios de "Benito Juárez," "Zaragoza," "Bacerac," "Pilares de Nacozari," and "Magdalena."

Table 1.3 Battle of Santa Rosa Constitutionalist Estimated Troop Strength

In the afternoon, the Constitutionalists moved forward in small groups to occupy the heights to the north of the Federals while their trains approached to about five kilometers from the Federal positions. A considerable concentration of forces took place throughout the night.[14]

May 9

Very early in the morning, about 3:30 a.m., the Constitutionalists hurled themselves against the advance Federal positions to the north and the west, and without much effort and in short order succeeded in enveloping them. Federal Major Marciano Mora Quirarte with a part of the 3rd Company of the 28th and a Lieutenant Torres, who carried a machine gun, left on the double to lend assistance. They understood that the Federal situation was extremely compromised, and without hesitation they engaged the Constitutionalists at a few meters distance; return fire hit them from the north, east, and west as they defended themselves from those directions. In some places the lines became mixed and fighting was hand to hand. The number of Federals compared to revolutionaries was too unfavorable, and within minutes Federal Lieutenant Torres, another named Aldana, and a Sub-lieutenant Ramos fell, the first wounded, the latter two dead.[15]

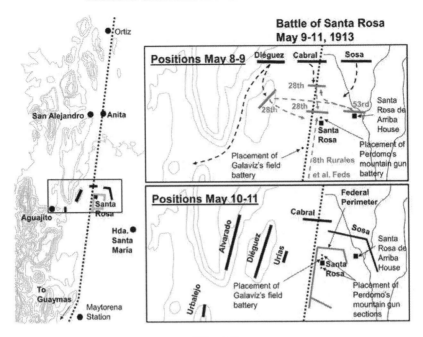

Map 1.9

Constitutionalist Major Manzo fought bravely and Majors Bule and Urbalejo tightened the circle, fighting like lions at the front of their men. Major Contreras covering their rear itched to enter into the fight, and Colonel Diéguez, with his signature calm, carried out his movements boldly and opportunely. The Constitutionalist forces in the center inflicted tremendous casualties on the Federals and in the first encounter killed one jefe, five officers, and more than fifty soldiers as Manzo's men captured another forty. In the most heated moment of battle Obregón sent his aide, Captain Chaparro, to give an order to Major Manzo. Passing through fire Chaparro noticed two Constitutionalists taken prisoner by Federals and with intrepidness freed them, one being Lieutenant Manuel Mendoza.[16]

Similar acts of heroism occurred on the Constitutionalist left. In the first moments Major Jesús Gutiérrez was killed and Captain Escobar wounded. Gutiérrez had been much beloved, and his loss stoked the ardor of Majors Acosta, Trujillo, and Félix, who redoubled their efforts. The right was no less tenacious, and Major Bule, one of the most prestigious of the Yaquis, had just fallen dead there from a bullet to the head. (One theory behind his death is that the Constitutionalists murdered Bule because he was a compadre of Medina Barrón and refused to fight against him.)[17] Bule's *mansos* passed to the command of Major José María Acosta. Under the weight of the attack, no option remained for the Federals but to fall back on the Santa Rosa Station and the surrounding houses. Then the jefe of the point, Colonel Eguiluz, made the 53rd advance to lend aid to his 28th, but moving this unit exposed it to fire on the flanks and to the rear. The battalion's men could not stop to return fire because the need to advance quickly was too pressing. The battalion moved with such celerity that there was not even time to attend to the soldiers' women-folk, who had been left to the rear and were captured by the Yaquis. In the maneuver Federal Sub-lieutenant Daniel Gándara ended up wounded immediately upon making contact, forcing him to take up a defensive position where he proved most effective.[18]

During the displacement the 53rd divided into two groups: one headed for the hills in defense of the 28th and the other, following along the railway, opposed the enveloping movement that the Constitutionalists initiated along a ditch. This was one of the fiercest and most dangerous moments of the action, but there almost by chance were Federal Colonel Heriberto Rivera and Major Cota, adding luster to the warrior legends of Sonora, and Captain José Riva Palacio, a grandson of Vicente Guerrero and nephew of the famous general and writer of the same last name. At one point all three had to resort to firing their pistols.[19]

As this was happening, a soldier perched atop a pole inside the combat zone swept by fire communicated with Federal headquarters by telephone, saying that the fire was copious, the Constitutionalists were trying to envelop them, and that the 53rd had already been repulsed. The man was head of the guards, Baldomero Jiménez. The Federal camp back in Maytorena awoke to the sounds of bugles, trumpets, and horns blowing "enemy to the front," "enemy on the right." There was no need to roll up bedrolls, or strike tents, since the soldiers had neither. Everyone got up to the informal command of "¡Arriba, muchachos!" But the train engines had yet to get up steam. At 5:30, that is, two hours after receiving the alarm, the first convoy with two machine guns on the top of the railcars left transporting the 50th Auxiliary Battalion and the 25th Battalion into action. Cheerful yells in anticipation of victory from those departing and those remaining behind echoed in the station.[20] Just before 8 a.m. Obregón saw the smoke on the horizon announcing the approach of the main body of Federals from Maytorena Station. Slowly the convoy got closer. Obregón could measure the length of the force from van-guard to rear covering an extension of seventy-eight telephone posts, which gave him some indication of the size of the force. According to prisoners interrogated, Obregón knew that the Federals had fifteen hundred between infantry and artillery and another three hundred dragoons, with twelve machine guns and eight large caliber cannons.[21]

The Federals detrained opposite Aguajito, and the two corps combined to form a firing line along the rails that extended past the station house of Santa Rosa and tied off with the extreme vanguard. In order to achieve the disposition they had to use the blade, rolling up the Constitutionalists there and freeing some prisoners the Constitutionalists had taken from the 28th. Medina Barrón had already sent the 8th Rural Corps (and probably the Auxiliary Corps of Guanajuato) ahead to reinforce the vanguard. These unadvisedly entered into combat mounted, providing fodder for the Constitutionalist machine guns. Within an hour they had been reduced from their original three hundred to about sixty or seventy men who fled in complete dispersion in every direction, some not stopping until reaching Guaymas. Already the battlefield was littered with corpses as Brigadier Medina Barrón was arriving at Santa Rosa. The general went up and down the firing line directing encouraging words at his soldiers, who were in the prone position defending the rail line, or as it might be better stated, using the embankment for protection. As soon as possible, and after surveying the battlefield, Medina Barrón exchanged words with Colonel Eguiluz, asking him: "Those hills to the front are ours?" "Yes, General, my battalion has them." Being versed in combat ("combat," that is, skirmishes being the operative word), the general stated "We are good." Then, Captain Riva Palacio stepped up addressing Colonel Eguiluz and rectifying him said, "Sir, those hills that the general is asking about, the enemy has..."[22]

No sooner had Riva Palacio finished speaking when the brigadier's leg weakened and he began rubbing it. "Well, that changes things." "Did they wound you, general?" "Yes," he said pausing, "Let's see: reinforce the lines on the berm to the front, the railway, and the bridge," and turning to Riva Palacio he said, "captain, communicate to General Gil that it is necessary to advance the artillery." Colonel Eguiluz, situated a few meters away to dictate orders, received two bullets almost at the same time, one going in the back of the head and coming out his mouth, destroying his jaw. That was at about 9:30, and already the rail station had turned into a charnel house filled with wounded soldiers.[23]

The mountain battery that marched at a trot at the head of the rest of the column stopped two kilometers before Santa Rosa and fired at the Constitutionalists occupying the house of Santa Rosa de Arriba, previously occupied by the 53rd, in an attempt to clear the enemy from there. The captain of those pieces, Alfonso Martínez Perdomo, received orders to advance to where General Medina Barrón was. The general ordered the guns to go into battery immediately in front of the houses around the station. By now the combat had become generalized. The battery had barely set up when it began to suffer the effects of Constitutionalist rifle fire. First, several draft mules, then artillerymen, enlisted as well as officers were hit. A slaughter in every way, as the Constitutionalists, expert shots and safely ensconced in the rocks on hills six hundred meters away, picked them off.[24]

First Captain Martínez Perdomo, nevertheless, opened fire, first trying to clear the Constitutionalists to the west, then to the north, and lastly to the east, achieving some success, since he pushed them back from their most advance positions. Captain Martínez Perdomo had barely just made some corrections to his fire when he went happily from piece to piece to offer encouragement. Stopping at Lieutenant Enrique Tenopala's gun he looked on with particular satisfaction. As a *chucha cuerera*, which is to say, already experienced in combat and brave, Tenopala was calmly firing away, making magnificent shots. The captain was congratulating this officer when Tenopala dropped to his knees. Trying to get up, he again fell down, wounded in both legs. "Take heart, Lieutenant. It is nothing!" and without moving to take cover he had the lieutenant carried inside the Santa Rosa station house.[25]

Constitutionalist bullets continued to bounce off the wheels and firing mechanisms of the Federals' guns. Second Sergeant Leonides Martínez fell dead, then gunner Trinidad García, followed later by another Second Sergeant, Pascual Hernández; and they kept falling. Captain Martínez Perdomo, eager to search out the farthest points of the Constitutionalist positions and shred them, climbed a small embankment where he was standing out above the rest of the artillerymen and raised up his field glasses to look intently at the field when he felt an impact in his chest. From there, still looking through his glasses, he yelled with enthusiasm at the effects of a salvo: "Very good ... very good!" When he came down he tried to hide his wound by using a handker-chief to plug the hole, but his pale features gave him away. A corporal asked, "Are you wounded, captain?" "No. What wound?" "Yes, Captain." The word soon spread among the battery, but he insisted that it was nothing and that he would remain at his post, "as long as I can, with you." The general invited the captain to retire, but he refused. Lieutenant Tenopala stuck his head out of the door of the house and gave his men words of encouragement, "don't flag, boys, get tough" (*no se agüiten, duro, duro, muchachos*).[26]

Martínez Perdomo's battery continued firing and soon Feliciano Martínez and Gabino Acevedo added their names to the dead. Among the untouched was Corporal Fernando Oseguera, who was carrying ammunition, mov-ing pieces, then watching the effects of the shots. "Oseguera!" the captain yelled at the corporal, who turned and snapped to attention, "At your orders, captain." "No craziness." "No worries, captain." Corporal Oseguera loaded a gun, took one last look in the sight, and awaited the command to fire when a bullet hit him in the head, making him tumble. "Now it happened!" Martínez Perdomo yelled angrily at the corporal, who must have heard the order he had been awaiting because he pulled the lanyard, the shot fired, and he fell dead.[27]

The elevated sierra to the west appeared completely covered with Constitutionalists behind every rock. To the north Captain Morlet, who occupied the most forward and dangerous position in that direction, alternatively resisted and forced back the avalanche of revolutionaries who tried to push their way forward, as well as opposing a vast line of Yaquis not disposed to yield the Santa Rosa de Arriba house to the east. Upon the arrival of the rest of the column, the Federals reinforced the line along the railroad that was about a half a kilometer in length, as well as the two ditches that ran nearly perpendicular to the rails and extended a great distance to the east. These two lines of defense were closed by a third ditch only partially occupied by the Federals—that part closest to the Santa Rosa de Arriba.[28] From Obregón's vantage point the Federals were deployed in a right angle stretching from the houses of Santa Rosa to the railroad and then down the length of the railroad about one kilometer. Most probably he could not see the complete enemy disposition because of the brush, but he was correct in one respect: the Federals could not advance.[29]

At about 11 a.m. Constitutionalist Colonel Salvador Alvarado arrived from Nogales with twenty-four officers and 434 men belonging to the Federal Auxiliary Corps (some members of this unit had been engaged in combat since the beginning of the battle) and Voluntarios de Benito Juárez, Zaragoza, Bacerac, Pilares de Nacozari, and Magdalena to reinforce the Constitutionalist right (west) flank, where the action was fiercest. Major Urbalejo covered one of the most important points, Aguajito, against several attempts by the Federals to take possession of it. The two forces remained relatively stationary, with the Constitutionalists trying to force the Federals to break and run, while the latter tried to dislodge Obregón's forces and continue northward.[30]

The house of Santa Rosa de Arriba became the sight of some of the most heated fighting shortly after the arrival of the rest of the Federal column. In order to recuperate it, the 3rd Company of the 14th Battalion was detached under the protective fire of Captain Miguel S. Ramos' section (Ramón Galaviz's battery) next to the railroad, across from Aguajito. From the first moments that the Yaquis occupied the house it was christened by the Federals with the name "the mysterious house," because it was hidden in the thicket and murderous and copious rifle fire poured from it without any of the occupants providing a target. Yet, the 3rd Company led by Captain Celso Sandoval charged against the mysterious house with the bravery and serenity that had made the 14th Battalion famous. It cost many lives, but the Federals finally dislodged the Yaquis from the house. The joy experienced by the new occupants did not last long. Soon the Yaquis reformed and returned to assault in greater numbers, determined to avenge the attack. To the beat of war drums they rushed into combat, impetuous and uncontainable, forcing the Federals to abandon the field and the house.[31]

The men of the 14th could not return with news of defeat, so they again courageously charged, with bayonets fixed, against the coveted position. During the most intense moments of the assault a corporal tried to take three Yaquis prisoner, one of whom at the command of "Surrender!" approached the corporal and with the butt of a rifle split his head open, and then, in one bound and clutching his weapon, jumped down a deep well. The Federals retook the mysterious house, but it fell to the Yaquis one more time before the Federals captured it a third time and held on to it for the rest of the day.[32]

May 10

The shooting did not cease throughout the night, but it did slow a little around dawn. Taking advantage of this respite, General Medina Barrón brought the field battery that had been opposite Aguajito up to the main house at Santa Rosa Station, duly covering its trajectory, and placed the guns in between the two sections of Captain Martínez Perdomo's battery.[33] Upon getting into position the field artillery began to take punishing rifle fire, just as the two mountain sections had, which made it necessary to return fire with shell bursts. For the Federals it was of paramount importance to take possession of the heights situated to the west of the station, because of the devastation being inflicted on them from those locations. With this in mind, the commanding general assigned the objective to Captain José Martínez del Río. Taking 150 men, the captain raced to the position pointed out to him, rushing forward without stopping. Covering him were Captain Galaviz's guns, accurately aimed at the hills. On the side of the low hills, under fire almost perpendicular to the Constitutionalist center, he did not cease his efforts until the bugle call *diana* sounded throughout the camp announcing mission accomplished—the Constitutionalists no longer possessed those heights. Then the harder work followed for the artillery: to clear the Constitutionalists from the heights behind those just conquered that towered over Martínez del Río and his men.[34]

But the Constitutionalists did not take this reversal lying down. The Federals had emplaced a machine gun on the hill and were protected by artillery about 350 meters to the east. Lieutenant Enrique Urías of the 4th Irregular Battalion of Sonora took about twenty men from his unit and with another fifteen of Diéguez's men fell furiously upon Martínez del Río and his Federals occupying the heights below. A half-hour later the two groups could be seen battling for the hill, with Urías and his Constitutionalists possessing one half of the hill and the Federals the other, engaged in fierce combat. Eventually the Constitutionalists emerged victorious, whereupon they blew *diana*. Immediately afterward the Federal artillery opened up, firing about seventy shells that left the hill covered in smoke. The Constitutionalists ignored these effects and continued to dig in.[35]

Martínez del Río once again assaulted the hill, leading his men against the heights. Even though they were engaged in the fight, all the Federals along the railroad fixed their eyes on the captain. Fully cognizant of their attention, he held his arm aloft and pointing toward the summit. The discharge of rifle fire and pounding of the guns protected the captain's command as it retook the heights to the shouts of his fellow Federals: "¡Viva the Army!" "¡Viva Supreme Government!" "¡Viva Martínez del Río!" Then, the Constitutionalists returned like furies, forcing the Federal captain to have to yield the heights as the afternoon wound down: his Federals had begun to suffer from a lack of water, food, and sufficient ammunition amid the overwhelming push of revolutionaries starting to close in and around.[36]

The sun going down put the sierra in relief against the sky. A great shadow fell on the plains below, and then night closed in. The shooting that had continued without ceasing redoubled in intensity around 8 p.m. Suddenly, under the mesmerizing Yaqui war drums, a torrent of Constitutionalists rushed to assault all the Federal positions. Not one single point was safe from the possibility of succumbing to the weight of the Constitutionalist onslaught. Thousands of muzzle flashes lit up the darkness and reflected against the thicket. Shouts, yells, curses, and commands created a horrible confusion. Only the implacable war drums succeeded in dominating all the sounds with their crazy, obstinate, and crude drum roll. The Federals began to falter and in some places the Constitutionalists even penetrated the Federal positions.[37]

Then, the column's commander, General Medina Barrón, advanced to the firing line. With a thunderous voice he cursed the Constitutionalists and harangued his men, announcing at the end, "Here we have more than a half million rounds to hit the backsides of those wretches! At them! Viva the Army!" And with that the Federals began to surge forward as though desiring to meet the enemy on their own terms instead of awaiting death at the bottom of a trench, and forced them back to the foothills. Then the "cease fire" bugle calls began to ring out all over from the Federal side. But the men kept shooting just the same, ignoring them, until the bugles began to blow *diana* and then the troops returned to their positions and in unison yelled "¡Viva the Army!" as the night fell silent under the dull moonlight.[38]

In the darkness some Federal draftees began filtering back toward Guaymas, like frightened sheep, spreading rumors of defeat and an unparalleled disaster. Many remaining on the firing line had not eaten for thirty-six hours and were hungry. Those who had food ate. Others, on their own initiative, began to bury the dead men and horses in order to attenuate the stench. Men began to look upon any compañeros who had water with envy. Then, in the middle of the night, another attack, this one possibly more vicious than the first, began. Word had already spread that if there were another attack then the men should wait until the enemy got close to open fire. Therefore, they waited until the Constitutionalists were eighty to one hundred meters away and then opened up with a volley that, combined with the grapeshot fired by the cannons, wreaked havoc in their ranks forcing them to retreat. The attack continued for another two hours. At the conclusion the Federals again blew *diana*. Ever since withstanding the first assault, the greenhorns had been gaining in confidence.[39]

In total three back and forth assaults took place during the night.[40] Everywhere there were disconcerting scenes of battle, but one place surpassed all others in its horror: the station house that served a triple purpose as headquarters, hospital, and ammunition storeroom. During letups in combat the artillery officers took refuge there among their wounded comrades who had been shot up by the expert Constitutionalist marksmen. In those moments when the fight was fiercest, terror, anguish, and anxiety reflected in the eyes of the wounded, and even some of those who were not. Captain Miguel S. "Chueco" Ramos, intelligent, modest, and respected for his quiet demeanor and serenity in the fray, began to sing the songs most in vogue at the time (*Valentina, Magdalena*) in order to lift everyone's spirits, forcing others to play the part of the chorus.[41]

May 11

From the positions that they had held since the first day the Constitutionalists continued the fight, especially making use of their machine guns, with Federal artillerymen being their favorite targets. With Lieutenant Tenopala wounded, Sub-lieutenants Salvador Torres and Luis D. Rojas had to take charge of the pieces. Both officers had just left the Escuela de Aspirantes and exhibited the blind courage and bordering-on-festive enthusiasm that attends one's first combat. Rojas was the most gung-ho; barely eighteen years old, he rushed to the most dangerous places, drawing the attention of all. His father, "already an old man, had told Captain Martínez Perdomo in Mexico City, before leaving: 'I recommend my son to you, Señor Captain; see that he does not acquire any vices. That is what worries me. If he dies, that is the soldier's lot ... he will know how to do it with dignity.' And as though he had a premonition, the poor old man shed abundant tears."[42]

Martínez Perdomo had to reprove his charge against needlessly exposing himself to so much fire. On the second day of combat the captain had noticed Rojas on the high water tower next to the station observing a shot and yelled: "Get down; they are going to see you!" "They aren't going to do anything to me, captain," he replied. And just then a bullet knocked the safari hat, worn by Federal artillerymen, off his head, singeing his hair. Then bullets started to ping against the sheet metal of the water tower, and Rojas jumped down to the edge of the tank. As he started to descend the ladder, impacting bullets marked his trajectory. Upon reaching bottom he said, "You see, Captain, they aren't going to do anything to me." Martínez Perdomo responded, "Bullets [may] respect the brave, like you; but don't put your faith in it."[43]

Around 4 p.m. on May 11 Obregón made a reconnaissance of the battlefield and determined that the Federals could not move from their current positions, but he also learned that his own ammunition was running short. About that same time Colonel Diéguez had managed to take some of his men and move to within about one hundred meters of the Federal batteries. Obregón wanted Colonel Sosa to support the maneuver, but he refused, complaining of a lack of ammunition.[44]

As night closed in, after three days of combat, the Constitutionalist machine guns were so well-aimed at the artillery pieces that it was impossible for the Federal gunners to remain in position. Not even the bravest soldiers dared to do it. So great was the danger, or rather the assuredness, of dying there that the commander himself authorized them to pull back a few paces during a lull. Rojas remained until the end, alone, fired a shot, and then retreated. Nonetheless, the functioning of artillery was indispensable to the Federal position, and then General Medina Barrón pointed to the enemy position that needed to be cleared. "It is raining [bullets] on my piece, general!" Rojas exclaimed. The brigadier stood looking surprised at Rojas' objection and in an affectionate voice said: "What? Now you are afraid, sub-lieutenant?" "No, general," Rojas replied, saluting and then dashing off to his gun. He aimed it, loaded it, and made one shot, whose report could still be heard echoing when the soldiers yelled in fear, "They killed the sub-lieutenant!" Rojas fell on the cannon, with a head wound. He must have retained some consciousness, because days later, just when he was about to succumb to his injuries, he squeezed the hand of Señorita Beatriz Bringas, who had attended to him in his death agony, never leaving his side.[45] His father's fears had been realized.

A little while after the wounding of Rojas, the Constitutionalist shooting began to diminish. Thinking that they were retreating, Medina Barrón's Chief of Staff, Colonel Francisco A. Salido, suggested that with one final push they could probably take the heights, but after seventy hours of combat, no food, and thirsty, the spirits of the Federal soldiers weighed on the commanding general's mind. So under cover of night, the Federals prepared to retire to Maytorena Station. They had no trains, because on the first day of combat they had been removed to Guaymas by a cowardly Federal officer. He was supposed to pull the trains back out of danger, but upon seeing a burning bridge he feared that trains might be cut off and so he took them all the way back to the port where they remained.[46]

At 11 p.m., in perfect order, the "parade" began, with the Auxiliary Corps of Guanajuato in the vanguard, followed by the artillery, next the cars and impedimenta, and finally the infantry; the wounded, ammunition, and provisions were placed in carts and pulled by hand, crossing without incident over the same burned bridge that had so concerned the unnamed jefe. General Medina Barrón remained in the rearguard with Colonel Salido; Lieutenant Colonel Edmundo Dávalos; Major Mora Quirarte; Captain Riva Palacio; and Lieutenants Octavio de la Fuente, Francisco C. Yáñez and Raymundo Urcid, who with a machine gun and one hundred men fired the last shots in the Battle of Santa Rosa, one of the bloodiest and most hotly contested of the battles waged since 1910. The next morning after Obregón received the resupply of ammunition that he had been awaiting, he sent Major Trujillo with 150 Constitutionalists to pursue the Federals who already had a three kilometer head start. The distance was so great that any shots fired were wholly inaccurate, and the Federals did not even bother to return fire.[47]

Obregón lost forty-two men and officers and counted 422 dead Federals. He gained a tremendous amount of booty, including six machine guns and seven crates with 2,500 cartridges for same, one box of tools, 26 artillery shells, one limber, 200 Mausers, 30,000 (a number that appears with suspicious frequency in his reports) 7-mm. cartridges, rolling stock, 230 saddles, 40 horses, 25 mules, three boxcars with food, three passenger cars, two field telephones, a range finder, and 180 prisoners.[48] The Federals admitted to casualties in excess of one thousand men, but also made the spurious claim that the Constitutionalists lost even more. Federal General Guillermo Rubio Navarrete labeled the battle "indecisive," but since the Constitutionalists held the field, the victory belonged to them.[49]

Analysis

In 1908 the Mexican General Staff published a Spanish translation of A. S. Martynov's account of the Russian-Japanese War of 1905. Much of what the book contained verified the appropriateness of Mexican tactical doctrine, and any officer who had bothered to read the three pages on the latest realities of warfare would have been instantly up to date on what to expect on the modern battlefield, especially with respect to artillery. However, instead of massing their batteries in hidden positions in order to saturate zones with indirect fire from kilometers away, the Federals piecemealed their batteries, first here and then there, and then placed them quite literally on the firing line, employing them in direct fire missions. The results? From an offensive perspective the Federal artillery effectiveness could not have been less salutary. Obregón—who had no artillery—marveled at Lieutenant Urías' ability to get to within 350 meters of the Federals' guns, withstand a barrage of about seventy shells, and still hold his position. In effect, as evidenced by the lack of any urgent appeals to his superiors to acquire artillery as soon as possible in order to match the Federals in firepower, he remained largely unimpressed by the efficacy of artillery. From a defensive point of view the Federal artillery tactics proved downright tragic. The Federal gunners and artillery officers endured terrifying sniper and punishing machine-gun fire at combat range (three to six hundred meters) such that they could barely stick their heads up to spot their rounds, much less man their pieces. From even this early stage in his career, Obregón was beginning to understand the efficacy of infantry and machine guns over artillery and cavalry, having observed the disastrous mounted charge of the 8th Rural Corps. Just as significantly, the Yaquis and Mayos, so terrified of Federal cannons encountered in the low-intensity combat of previous wars, were becoming inured to the effects of multiple batteries in formal battle.

Also factoring in the Federal defeat had been the hastiness with which General Gil left Guaymas to begin his advance on Hermosillo. As of April 30, the 510 *serranos* ("mountaineers") of the Sierra Juárez Auxiliary Battalion of Oaxaca were on the way. With four jefes, ten officers, and 268 horses they would have been of exceeding utility to the Federal column. Escorted by Federal General Gustavo Adolfo Maass, the battalion entered the Bay of Guaymas at 10:15 a.m. on May 11, that is, twelve hours before the retreat from Santa Rosa. There was time then to disembark them, arm them, give them ammunition, put them on trains, and send them to Santa Rosa, which was no more than twenty-seven kilometers away. And while one might argue that the serranos were worn out from the trip, then one can also affirm that these were not recruits, but rather veterans who had been fighting President

Madero's administration and had accepted Huerta's offer of amnesty in exchange for serving alongside the Federals. The jefe who had removed the trains and spread the story about the burnt bridge cutting off the column at Santa Rosa, however, along with the fugitive recruits steaming into Guaymas with exaggerated news of a hair-raising disaster, most likely factored into the decision, whoever made it, not to send the serranos into the battle.[50]

Viewed from a historical perspective, once again comparisons between Federal Army generalship and the inept Santa Anna reemerge, beginning with emptying the jails of criminals and the streets of vagrants to fill out the ranks of the army. Other tactical blunders at Santa Rosa parallel those of Santa Anna's defeat at the Battle of Angostura against the Americans: at Angostura Santa Anna retreated because the troops had no food, while in Santa Rosa it was because of a lack of food and water; at Angostura because the army had become very fatigued and could not fight the next day, just as at Santa Rosa; at Angostura Santa Anna thought that if the force remained on the field of battle many of his soldiers would disband, while at Santa Rosa they had already begun to slip away during the second night. At Angostura he took no measures to collect up the dispersed, same as at Santa Rosa. Even Obregón was rumored to have observed about the Federal failure: "When will we learn the lessons of history?"[51]

Alternatively, Obregón burst with pride about his own men, who reflected a new Mexican way of war, saying in his report, "I feel proud to command a column such as this. I had nothing to order Colonels Cabral, Alvarado and Diéguez, Sosa and Camacho; they operated with true initiative and opportunity," a latitude diametrically opposed to the command style of Federal Army officers, steeped in rigid control and highly suspicious of peers and subordinates. Obregón, amazingly, seemed to have matured as a field general almost overnight. From this battle on, he never micro-managed; he simply explained in broad strokes how he expected the battle to develop and let his subordinates use their own judgment and initiative as to the timing of movements and countermoves to check the opposing force. For his victory Obregón received a promotion to brigadier, and a few days later Alvarado received the same.[52]

First Chief Carranza also conferred upon the interim governor of Sonora, Pesqueira, the rank of general of brigade with effect on May 17. Obregón said that he received the rank because of the purely military nature of many of his activities in acquiring and distributing war materiel. The historian Hector Aguilar Camín, on the other hand, opined that the First Chief promoted Pesqueira so he would have seniority over Obregón and others who had been promoted to brigadier after the Battle of Santa Rosa, in order to privilege the political over the military.[53] Regardless, the Constitutionalist brigades and divisions that would emanate from Sonora maintained the most rationalized number of generals to jefes to officers to enlisted men of any other ground force during the revolution, most especially in comparison to the Federal Army.

BATTLE OF SAN ALEJANDRO

It took almost a month for General Pedro Ojeda to get back to again command forces in the field after having passed over to the United States during the Battle of Naco on April 13. Because of the spirited defense of Naco that he had mounted, the Federal government named Ojeda as the new commander of the Division of the Yaqui. Released on his own recognizance by U.S. authorities, along with other Federal jefes and officers, he traveled to Los Angeles hoping to get transportation back to Mexican soil, but authorities temporarily detained him. After a few more days he managed to make his way to Ensenada, Baja California, and thence to Mazatlán from which he again set sail for Guaymas.[54] The news of Ojeda's appointment and his subsequent arrival at Guaymas on May 13, especially within the context of the defeat at Santa Rosa and concomitant to Medina Barrón pulling back to Empalme from Maytorena Station, sparked great enthusiasm in the port. All the Federal jefes, officers, and—most of all—the enlisted expressed good cheer at the announcement. The 14th Infantry, Ojeda's old battalion, seemed especially joyous to have its former colonel back.[55]

When the ship bringing Ojeda arrived in Guaymas, General Gil sent a representative to greet him. After the courtesies de rigueur, Ojeda asked: "Where are those '*mecos*?" "To the south, near Cruz de Piedra, general; to the North—from Tres Gitos onward," was the answer. "And have you blasted them?" "No, general." "Well, blast them. That is why I came, to blast them." After a minute of silence he continued, "Where did you say the 'mecos are?" "To the south, near ..." "And you haven't blasted them?" "No, general." "Now you all will see. I come to blast them. To avenge myself. In Naco they blasted me, because of the [lack of] ammunition ... Ahhh ... but now I am coming!" And thusly the new commanding general and his reception committee passed the time traveling from the ship to the dock, inquiring about the 'mecos, where they might be, and the promise he had made to blast them, to avenge himself.[56]

Displaying a great amount of energy and initiative, upon arrival Ojeda avoided all the pomp and circumstance usually attendant to a change in command in order to get right down to work, to blast the 'mecos. At once and for the first time he organized the division's battalions into brigades and then resupplied his troops in order to lift their morale. He also ordered the machine shops in Empalme to create "armored gondolas" and mounted two 80-mm. guns on platform rail cars, likewise armored.[57] Then he ordered the advance positions to the north and south to push forward and gain more ground. With Ojeda at the helm public opinion began to diverge. Some said that with a capable jefe like him in charge he should start operations as soon as possible. Others, thinking of the *Morelos*, which was in Manzanillo ready to embark seasoned troops, said no; he should wait for the arrival of more veteran troops. But when the *Morelos* returned to Guaymas on May 20 it only brought a measly five officers. That very day, Ojeda scouted northward to very close to Maytorena Station in an armored gondola with an 80-mm. gun.[58] It would not be much longer.

Finally, on May 22, Colonel Jesús P. Díaz, jefe de las armas of Torín, who had been incommunicado with Guaymas since the Battle at Lencho Station and could no longer maintain his position after the Federal defeat at Santa Rosa, fell back on Empalme to join with the main Federal concentration. That left Colonel Benjamín Hill's column in full control of the wealthy Yaqui Valley and able to advance to Cruz de Piedra where it could cooperate with the rest of the Constitutionalist forces in the state gathering around Moreno Station.[59]

The Federal Advance

Six days later, May 28, Ojeda began his march on Hermosillo, taking with him about 2,600 men of his total division strength in Sonora of 3,600, eight of his twelve machine guns, and seven of his ten artillery pieces, leaving the rest in Guaymas and Empalme to serve as a depot and safe zone in case of a defeat. Ojeda brought along most of the elements from his 1st Brigade, commanded by Brigadier Luis Medina Barrón. From the 2nd Brigade he had all its mounted units and a company from the 28th Infantry Battalion under that brigade's commanding officer, General Miguel Girón, as well as artillery from the 1st and 5th Artillery Regiments. Their numbers made quite an impression on Obregón, who calculated the total Federals facing him at 6,000 men, with sixteen large caliber cannons and twenty machine guns, or almost double the figures per Federal Army records. To oppose them Obregón had essentially the same 3,000 or so men as during the Battle of Santa Rosa under his direct command, Colonel Hill with his seven hundred men repairing the railroad down south, and one final column of unknown strength commanded by Colonel José María Ochoa that consisted of elements from the 4th Irregular Battalion of Sonora, the Voluntarios de Arizpe Corps, and the 31st and 47th Rural Corps, probably about four hundred men who most likely had remained in Hermosillo during the previous battle as a security force.[60]

Tactical Command	Major Unit organic to	G	J	O	I	Total
Medina Barrón, Luis (Brigadier)	1st Brigade	1				1
Díaz, Jesús P. (Colonel)	10th Infantry Battalion		2	19	469	490
Santibáñez, Manuel F. (Colonel)	14th Infantry Battalion		3	15	312	330
	(with one Machine-gun Section)					
Gómez, Ignacio (LTC)	50th Auxiliary Infantry Battalion		2	14	210	226
Cota, Francisco (Major)	53rd Auxiliary Infantry Battalion		1	9	236	246
León, Pedro (Colonel)	Sierra Juárez (Oaxaca) Auxiliary Battalion		3	9	150	162
Girón, Miguel (Brigadier)	2nd Brigade	1				1
Flores, Antonio (LTC)	28th Infantry Battalion (1 Company)		1	10	109	120
De la Vega, Juan N. (LTC)	8th Rural Corps (reinforced after Santa Rosa)		1	8	107	116
Tapia, Higinio (Major)	21st Irregular Cavalry Corps		2	10	187	199
Unknown	27th Rural Corps				50	50
Tiburcio Otero, José (Colonel)	Voluntarios del Mayo Corps		2	26	174	202
González, Nicolás (Major)	Auxiliary Corps of Guanajuato		1	6	129	136
Sámano, Alberto (Colonel)	Sámano Irregular Corps		1	5	187	193
Unknown	Voluntarios de Bacum			1	7	8
	Artillery					
Ramos, Miguel S. (1st CPT)	1st Artillery Regiment			3	60	63
	(three 75-mm. Mondragóns)					
Martínez Perdomo, Alfonso (1st CPT)	5th Artillery Regiment			4	79	83
	(two 70-mm. Grusson and two 75-mm. Mondragóns)					
Cruz, Raymundo (LT)	Machine Guns (8)			2	18	20
						2,646

Table 1.4 Battle of Santa María Federal Troop Strength

In his mind, Obregón divided the approaching combat as played out into two distinct phases, the first he called the Siege of Ortiz, in which he destroyed the rail lines behind the Federal column, harassed its rear, and cut off its supply of water. The second he called the Battle of Santa María, a hammer and anvil operation in which retreating Federals attempting to reach water sources at Santa María ran into Benjamín Hill's column, only to be smashed in the rear by Obregón, a maneuver labeled "Napoleonic" by the historian, General Miguel Sánchez Lamego.[61] The Federals, by contrast, referred to the first phase as the Battle of San Alejandro and the second as the Battle of Santa Maria.

The two or three replacement units that had joined the Federal division since the last battle were much better in quality than those lost in the previous outing, but the column still suffered from low morale, something that having the hero of Naco at the helm could not counterbalance. The confidence gained in his previous successful battles at La Morita and San José against Calles, the desire to respond in the shortest time to the honor of being appointed to lead the division, and his thirst for personal vengeance compelled Ojeda to begin the march to conquer Hermosillo, committing many of the same mistakes as Gil had.[62]

The Federal column left the Guaymas area undertaking all the usual prescriptions: scouts, a vanguard, flank guards, a support, and reserve. The support had four locomotives and sixteen boxcars, the only rolling stock that the revolutionaries had left behind at Empalme, which the Federals gave preference to transporting ammunition, provisions, and fodder over men. At the head of the column the Sierra Juárez Battalion under the leadership of Colonel Francisco Chiapa, a Norteño who was as impressed with his Indians as anyone, led the way. While generally a good idea to employ irregulars familiar with the terrain as scouts and in the vanguard, the irregulars of the Sierra Juárez Battalion hailed from Oaxaca. On the plus side, however, the sierras of Sonora were nothing compared to the cliffs and precipices of the mountains in their home state.[63]

The Federals made good time reaching Batamotal on the first day and engaged Colonel Diéguez's Constitutionalists, who had the mission of maintaining contact while the rest of the Constitutionalists countermarched back toward the north. Obregón sought to maintain a separation between the two armies of at least twenty kilometers so that the Federals would be blind to his intentions.[64] On the second day of the Federal movement, May 29, an airplane appeared flying over the valley floor where the Oaxacans were. This may have been the first time that a vehicle of this type had been used in warfare in Mexico and, sadly for the Federals, it was not the government who employed it. At first the Federals became excited at seeing the "birdie," but once they realized that it belonged to the Constitutionalists, and considering Obregón's prior victory at Santa Rosa, the draftees could not help but feel the impact of the strength and sophistication of the revolution. This airplane had been acquired in the United States and subsequently impounded as war contraband, but a few hours later it was stolen. This made the official confiscation nothing more than a fig leaf of neutrality in the eyes of the Federals, who also claimed to have caught an American dynamiting the railroad during their movement.[65]

The Federals continued to advance with two hundred mounted soldiers in the extreme vanguard. The rest of the vanguard was one kilometer back and consisted of the Sierra Juárez Battalion, an armored flatbed railcar with two 75-mm. cannons, some two hundred infantrymen with two machine guns for artillery support, and two mounted groups of about two hundred riders each about two kilometers distant from the rail on each flank. Another four kilometers back was the main body of troops followed by another small body of cavalry trailing one kilometer behind to bring up the rear. The column advanced with the cannons of the vanguard platform car engaged in reconnaissance by fire, shooting at points suspected of possibly hiding Constitutionalists. At night the train and most of the cavalry rejoined the main body, while the infantry of the vanguard dug foxholes on the hills and lit large bonfires, supported by the remainder of the cavalry. The Federals continued in this manner for several days, varying their pace of advance with the extent of destruction to the rail line and availability of materials to make repairs and pulling in all troops to the camp at night except a small extreme vanguard. Several encounters with Colonel Diéguez took place, but none very serious because the Constitutionalists continued to fall back as the Federals advanced, drawing them farther north.[66]

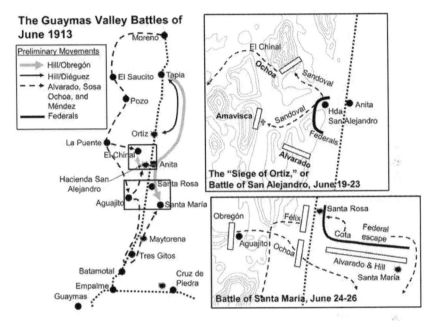

Map 1.10

At Ortiz Station Obregón ordered Diéguez's column off the line and replaced it with Alvarado's, instructing the latter commander to continue harassing the Federals. He sent Diéguez's column to Tapia Station (fourteen kilometers north of Ortiz) and gave orders for Colonel Hill in Cruz de Piedra to join the main body at Moreno Station (twenty-five kilometers north of Ortiz). During his displacement, Hill made contact early on with some Federals commanded by Federal General Miguel Girón, commander of the 2nd Brigade, Division of the Yaqui.[67]

At 7.30 a.m. on June 12 General Girón had left Empalme and headed east to begin repairing the rails, taking along one company of the 14th Battalion with about one hundred men, about as many more belonging to the 25th Rural Corps commanded by Comandante Rafael Villaseñor y Villaseñor and, once again demonstrating an ignorance of the arm, one 80-mm. gun and its ten man crew: one cannon was useless for anything except as a potential gift for the Revolution. Upon reaching kilometer marker 19, very close to Cruz de Piedra, the repair team halted. As a precaution, Girón ordered Villaseñor to disembark his men and horses and scout out about five hundred meters to the front. When the Rurales returned to report nothing suspicious, General Girón ordered the crews to begin the repair job. Just as the work was getting started, Hill's men attacked the Federals from the north, south, and east; they had been using the brush to conceal their movements. The Federals fled back toward the train, abandoning the armored gondola carrying the 80-mm. gun in the process. Girón ordered the Rurales to charge the Constitutionalists and push them back so that the locomotive could hook up the gondola. In that moment, Girón was gravely wounded, spreading demoralization in the troops. Villaseñor took charge of the situation and succeeded in driving back Hill's men so that the gondola and its field piece could be rescued, whereupon the Federal train returned immediately to Empalme and Villaseñor's Rurales broke contact, following behind. A relatively minor affair, only Girón, one of Villaseñor's officers, and one soldier were killed; an additional five enlisted men received wounds. Colonel Heriberto Rivera, the former commander of the Hermosillo plaza, replaced Girón as the brigade commander.[68]

At Ortiz Station the Federal column halted on June 9 in order to repair a fairly expansive bridge seventy meters long and seven meters high, which the Federals estimated would take more than fifteen days to repair because of a lack of materials. While inspecting the area Federal Sub-lieutenant Rafael Valenzuela discovered forty boxes of dynamite set to blow, just like others that the Constitutionalists had planted at points along the railway where they thought the Federal column might stop to camp. Valenzuela was promoted on the spot. The Constitutionalists did not just destroy bridges and rails but also plugged wells to deprive the Federals of water. At those places where the Constitutionalists could not disable the pumps of wells, they poisoned them with potassium cyanide. Hence, Ojeda's column advanced slowly and painstakingly.[69]

On the other side, the Constitutionalists fell back to Moreno Station and the hills to the east, whence they constantly harassed the Federal column, which often counterattacked, pushing the Constitutionalists off their ground. But the momentary triumph of these encounters (such as at El Pozo where the Oaxacans killed several Constitutionalists, took some prisoners, and captured some weapons and horses) came at the cost of weakening the Federal rearguard. Since the Federals never knew which of these skirmishes might develop into a full-blown battle, they had to decrease the number of men committed to security service in order to remain massed. The Huertista Governor of Sonora, Colonel Francisco H. García, became very alarmed at Ojeda's vulnerable position and called him to express his fears that the Constitutionalists from the south might take the port of Guaymas, or that Ojeda's column might be surrounded and cut off. Ojeda replied, "If the rebels [sic] enter Guaymas ... then I'll get them out ... In two hours I'll get them out!"[70]

Obregón now drafted his battle orders. Colonel Jesús Chávez Camacho would take ample supplies and the Voluntarios de Bacerac, Pilares de Nacozari, and Magdalena to Cruz de Piedra in order to "sustain the siege through the[Federal] rearguard"; Alvarado with his column, less those assigned to Colonel Chávez Camacho, along with Sosa's column with three machine guns would depart Moreno Station on June 16 taking a far western route through El Represo, El Saucito, and La Puente to arrive at Aguajito by the morning of June 19 and deny the Federals any water from that location. Colonel Ochoa's column (except Major Fructuoso Méndez and his men) would follow along with Alvarado, breaking off at La Puente to travel east to El Chinal, some four kilometers south of Ortiz; he would have four machine guns. Méndez would continue past Aguajito to destroy the rail line between Tres Gitos and Batamotal, south of Maytorena Station, before the morning of June 19 and then proceed to link up with Colonel Hill at Santa María. Diéguez's column with two machine guns was to depart from Tapia on the afternoon of June 18 and with Hill simulate a flanking attack from the east in the vicinity of Ortiz. After this combined attack, Hill and Diéguez would countermarch to Tapia. At nightfall Hill's men would then return making a wide semi-circle to arrive at the Anita switch and begin cutting the rails and telegraph as he moved south. Finally they would go into camp at Santa María to deny the water source there to the Federals. The remaining five machine guns would remain in Moreno Station as a reserve while Obregón and his staff and escort commanded by Captain Juan Cruz accompanied Hill as far as Anita and then continued on to El Chinal where he set up his command post. All movements were to take place at night so that the Federals might have no idea of the Constitutionalist dispositions.[71]

June 19

These chess-like maneuvers had the simple purpose of placing Alvarado to the Federals' far left rear, Hill to their far right rear, Ochoa on their left, and Diéguez to their front. Amazingly, these intricate movements came off without a hitch, and by the morning of June 19 all Constitutionalist commanders were at their appointed positions. Obregón arrived at El Chinal at 4 a.m., and he could hear Hill's men starting to blow up the rails with dynamite. Constitutionalist Major Méndez likewise accomplished his mission of cutting the Federal lines of communication between Batamotal and Tres Gitos.[72]

As a consequence of the disrupted lines, the Federals sent Captain Fernando Curiel south from Ortiz Station with a repair train containing an armored gondola and two Gruson 57-mm. pieces to investigate. About one hundred riders of the Voluntarios del Mayo Corps ("Los Colorados") provided mounted escort, with Major Rafael A. Toledo on the left flank with fifty men and Captain Pablo Matus on the right against the sierra with sixty. Upon arriving at Anita the repair train encountered the destruction inflicted by Hill's men during their trajectory to Santa María, the infantry support dismounted, and the crews began the repair work. General Medina Barrón ordered scouting to continue to the south, but now only with Toledo's men, as Matus' Colorados had to take the hills near San Alejandro with all celerity and dig in there, which they accomplished, engaging some Constitutionalists along the way. Meanwhile Toledo, with the section of two Gruson cannons unloaded from the train upon arriving at the high berm at Santa Rosa, reconnoitered all the way to Maytorena Station, skirmishing with small parties of Constitutionalists and forcing them back.[73]

About one kilometer before Maytorena Station Toledo received news from a dispersed Federal who had been part of an advance force. His contingent had been destroyed with some of his comrades taken prisoner by the Constitutionalists who, in overwhelming numbers, now occupied the best points to the Federal rear, where they surely expected to engage Ojeda. Toledo received an order to countermarch, and upon trying to effect it, Alvarado's Constitutionalists attacked him spiritedly. The Federals pulled back from the south toward Hacienda San Alejandro, and around 8:30 p.m., after the shooting had dropped off a bit, withdrew back to Ortiz. The Constitutionalists occupied the whole sierra parallel to the railway, extending from the Anita switch southward to Santa Rosa Station.[74]

June 20

In the early morning hours Second Officer Francisco Escudero with about twenty men of the 2nd Rural Corps guarding Maytorena Station noticed that communications had been cut to the north as well as to the south. Then around 8:30 Constitutionalist Major Méndez, acting on his own initiative, attacked Escudero's small Federal picket. It was a lopsided affair. The Federals had lost one officer and six men when Escudero abandoned his post and fled with his remaining men to avoid being taken prisoner, making his way to Empalme. Major Méndez, following his orders, left behind a detachment under First Captain Eleazar Amavisca and then went to Santa María to meet up with Hill. Federal Colonel Rivera with the 2nd Brigade in Empalme, meanwhile, had sent a repair train guarded by First Captain Heliodoro López de

Nava and sixty men of the 47th north toward Maytorena in an attempt to reestablish lines of communication. After finishing the repairs to the railroad and reaching Maytorena he noticed the Constitutionalists occupying it, and a firefight erupted as he tried to dislodge them. He soon became convinced that he was outnumbered and retreated back to Empalme, reporting four killed and eighteen missing, whom Amavisca had taken prisoner, without any casualties among the Constitutionalists.[75]

Farther north, General Ojeda still needed to reestablish his lines of communications so he sent a train south to resume the repair work. Around 9 a.m. a much larger column than the day before consisting of five hundred Federals from the 50th Auxiliary Infantry Battalion, a company of the 14th of the same arm, and the 8th Rurales commanded by Federal Lieutenant Colonel Ignacio Gómez departed Ortiz. Taking the same precautions as regards formation and methods of movement as the previous day, the column dismounted before Anita to reconnoiter. In view of the fact that the repair crews could not fix even one single rail because of the Constitutionalists' harassing fire, the Federal commander made the decision to occupy the hacienda and heights of San Alejandro in order to provide protection to the crews.[76] Gómez formulated the following maneuver: Captains José Flores and Eligio Sombra and Sub-lieutenant Prudencio Méndez with fifty men would take the meseta of San Alejandro, passing through the right side of the estate of that name. Captain Samuel H. Gutiérrez and Sub-lieutenants Dolores Matus and Librado C. García, with fifty men, were assigned the same objective, but were to pass through the center of the hacienda, where Captain Juan Meneses with Sub-lieutenants Jorge Tirán, Tranquilino González, and Juan Pérez leading a force equal in number would take possession of the main house. Captain Pablo Matus and his Colorados protected the Federal left.[77]

The main house of Hacienda San Alejandro had a masonry construction with a room arrangement very favorable for defense, somewhat akin to a fortress. Located in a desolate area that for years had been devastated by Yaqui incursions, it had been purposefully designed. With respect to its topographical position, the house did not offer any advantage since it was on a slope in the bend of the low meseta that extended to the south until it turned into the heights of Santa Rosa. To the west and north the heights of the mountain range known as Sierra Libre dominated, while expansive plains extended to the east, cut by the railroad approximately eight hundred meters away from the estate.[78] Alvarado's Constitutionalists occupied the heights on the Federal left and center, as well as the middle part of the meseta. Upon noticing the maneuvers of Lieutenant Colonel Gómez's men, they started to oppose them, first opening up with machine-gun fire and later with all their rifles around noon. The Federals took the hacienda, but could advance no further. Combat was fierce, with both groups holding firm in their positions. Alvarado threw more and more men into the fight and Gómez requested reinforcements.[79]

Ojeda upped the ante almost immediately by sending another five hundred men from the 10th Infantry, Major Toledo's Colorados, and mounted troops of the 8th and 27th Rural Corps and 21st Irregular Cavalry and five more artillery pieces commanded by General Medina Barrón, who arrived promptly. On General Ojeda's orders Medina Barrón assumed tactical command and the fighting heated up.[80] Since the most forward Constitutionalists were a very short distance from the Federals in the direction of El Chinal, impeding them from reaching the San Alejandro watering hole, Medina Barrón knew that he had to clear them from their positions. So he ordered the batteries of Captains Miguel S. Ramos and Martínez Perdomo, emplaced at the railway, to begin firing on them. All the cannon shots that afternoon were very accurate, but one especially lifted the Federals' spirits. One of the well-concealed Constitutionalist machine guns was engaged in a duel with Federal Sub-lieutenant Tirán's machine gun. Suddenly an artillery corporal became enraged, cursing and making gestures at the revolutionaries and then turning to his battery captain very respectfully and humbly asked: "Do you want me to silence it, captain?" "Let's see what you do. Aim it." As the corporal went to work, his compañeros looked on smiling. Finally, he pulled the lanyard and the machine gun position with its crew exploded. The Federals, full of glee, satisfied themselves in the false belief that the "filibuster" Maximiliano Kloss had been among those blown up. "Take this," General Medina Barrón said, handing the corporal a peso, "it is not your reward; soon you will be given what you deserve."[81]

Notwithstanding the good play of their artillery, the Federals were unable to dislodge the Constitutionalists to the west just below the heights of El Chinal, who were covering the approach to the watering hole of San Alejandro with three machine guns. Since Medina Barrón could not escape the realization that without access to water there would be no way for the Federals to prevail, he decided to put together a night assault. He ordered First Captain Mariano Sandoval of the 10th Infantry Battalion to leave thirty men of his company in the advance position that he was watching over and attack through the right flank. Sandoval, carrying out the extremely difficult assignment, entered into the narrow pass formed by two enormous hills through which he had to cross before beginning to ascend the heights of El Chinal held by the enemy. Surreptitiously making their way over open terrain, his Federals began to climb up. No one, until he so ordered, was to fire a shot. And only when he was a few meters from the Constitutionalists did his Federals fall upon them, with the cry of "¡Viva!" to the Army and Ojeda.[82]

Constitutionalist Colonel Ochoa commanded the position at El Chinal with elements from the 4th Irregular Battalion, the Voluntarios de Altar Corps, the 31st and 47th Rural Corps, forces commanded by Captain Francisco Beltrán, and a machine gun section under Major Kloss. In effect, the one hundred men from the Voluntarios de Arizpe Corps at the foot of El Chinal assigned to provide security to Ochoa's column failed in their mission. At 9:30 p.m. the Federals opened fire on Ochoa's camp. Obregón ordered Ochoa to abandon his position without returning fire and move his column to Aguajito in order to avoid a prolonged engagement on the left wing "that might separate us from the general plan that had been adopted." Obregón, likewise, transferred his headquarters to that latter position.[83]

June 21

The next day the Federals extended their radius of action: the column already occupied the meseta of Ortiz and the three eminences to the south of town when Ojedo sent the Sierra Juárez Auxiliary Battalion into the fight at San Alejandro. The Constitutionalists held the high sierra to the west, as well as all along the railway from Santa Rosa to the south. Never, throughout the whole campaign, did the Yaquis display their courage like at San Alejandro. Coming down from the hills with reckless abandon, they attacked the Federal positions. The 50th held one of the positions most important to the defense, the key actually. After having been roughly attacked, the first and second companies of the Sierra Juárez Auxiliary Battalion under the leadership of officers Jiménez Figueroa and Martínez Carrasco charged to reinforce the 50th. The Oaxacans did not wait for orders. As soon as they arrived, they simply surveyed the situation and promptly started to come down off the hill to counterattack the Yaquis, but Lieutenant Colonel Ignacio Gómez yelled at them not to advance beyond the firing line. Obeying his command they halted and Gómez could be heard saying: "These, I like these ... but restrain yourselves a bit."[84]

The arrival of the serranos only spurred on the Yaquis, who began to make the roughest play for the Federal hill but accomplished nothing except to sap the morale of the defenders. During a Constitutionalist assault Lieutenant Colonel Gómez was shouting encouragement to his men when a bullet hit and killed him at exactly the most heated moment of attack, around 2 p.m. Upon receiving the news of the death of Gómez, whom all respected for his bravery, Medina Barrón swallowed any anguish he might have felt and made a casual statement of pity.[85] At the foot of some poplars at the main house of Hacienda San Alejandro, not far from where Luis Bule had been buried, four Federal soldiers carried the cadaver of Gómez on their shoulders, after which jefes, officers, and enlisted filed past, all with their heads down in deep sorrow. The solemnity of the event did not keep the revolutionaries from launching a hail of projectiles at the Federal retinue. But the pain of the loss was worse than the danger, as the men paid little attention to the bullets. Placing the coffin on the earth Medina Barrón pronounced some trembling words of praise for the jefe. The sounds of battle continued to resound against the sierra. Some soldiers cried. And the Constitutionalist bullets continued to kick up dust around the gravesite. Captain Ramos, *el Chueco*, returned to his pieces and showered the hill possessed by the revolutionaries with magnificent bursts of shrapnel.[86]

The Federals somewhat recovered their spirits, but the Yaquis continued to taunt them yelling "Viva Sierra Juárez!" The Oaxacans responded, "Viva!" "Come on in. Here is Oaxaca! Here is Sierra Juárez!" The two brave groups of Indians, one from the North, one from the South, fought through the night as the Yaquis dodged from boulder to boulder to reach the Federal trenches at the summit. *Noo dee*? ("Who goes there?") the Zapotecs asked. And if the answer *Dictaa*! ("Mexico") did not come back immediately, then the serranos killed another Yaqui. And so it went on throughout the night. Only at first light did the fighting stop.[87] By fighting the Federals the entire day and into the night General Alvarado's Constitutionalists gave Colonel Ochoa's men the opportunity to rest up.[88]

June 22

In the morning, after the *pinole* had been distributed to the 53rd Battalion, which covered the line farthest to the north of Ortiz, General Ojeda decided to play a joke on Captain Riva Palacio. "Now you have your pinole, let's see if they run." It was only a joke since the 53rd had always acquitted itself well in battle, but Riva Palacio took it as an offense. So, a few hours later he asked as many jefes as necessary for permission to attack the enemy. No one would listen, thinking such a display useless and even counterproductive, until at the very last he asked the commanding general: "Go, go." Ojeda said, without any hesitation.[89]

Full of joy, Riva Palacio handpicked the best men from his battalion and the most promising of officers: Captains Manuel Sánchez Hidalgo and Jesús Cordero; Lieutenants Miguel Guerrero, known as the "Tiger of Tijuana," Raymundo Urcid, and Álvaro Tajonar y Bordas; and Sub-lieutenants Jorge

Olimón, Luis V. Barronta, José Ibarra, and Gustavo Arévalo, all young men from eighteen to twenty-five, at the most.[90] They intended to attack Diéguez at Tapia Station to the north with six hundred men of the 10th Infantry Battalion, the 53rd Auxiliary Battalion, and the Rural Corps of Guanajuato.[91]

The force left Ortiz at 3 p.m., stopped at a destroyed bridge, detrained, and rushed forward. Guerrero and Urcid took the hill on the left to provide protection to the small force that was going to contest possession of two separate elevations. The Constitutionalists, hidden among the broken ground covered in briers and brambles, opened fire on the Federals. Then the powerful 80-mm. cannon handled by Cordero opened fire to provide cover to Riva Palacio, who advanced under its protection and was also supported by his compañeros on the left. The young officers entered the fray full of enthusiasm and eager to prove themselves. Upon reaching the foot of the first hill occupied by the Constitutionalists, they attempted to dress their ranks and enter into combat as though they were on parade down the Paseo de la Reforma. The Constitutionalists turned tail and fled. Continuing on, Lieutenant "Tigre" Guerrero tried to flank the other enemy position accompanied by "Chato" Urcid while Riva Palacio and Tajonar attacked the front, once again forcing the Constitutionalists to abandon their positions. When the light of day began to fade, around seven o'clock, the group of Federals returned to their original positions around Ortiz, the officers pleased with their little demonstration. When they ran into the Colorados that Ojeda had sent to protect their rearguard, they unleashed the greatest hullabaloo. "¡Vivan los Colorados!" they yelled, answered with "¡Viva la 53rd!" followed by more rounds of "vivas" to the army, the officers, and so on.[92]

June 23

Combat continued around San Alejandro but without any change in the situation. In addition to the hill that Captain Sandoval had conquered three days earlier, there was another hill occupied by the Constitutionalists of Major Aurelio Amavisca to the west of the low ridge of San Alejandro that Medina Barrón had to take under control. Once again Medina Barrón turned to Sandoval to accomplish the mission of striking the revolutionaries, but this attempt was not as successful as the first encounter. Sandoval's Federals attacked the Constitutionalists well into the night catching them by surprise, but the Constitutionalists quickly recovered and did not yield their position. When Sandoval tried to lead his men in an effort to roll up the position in a daring maneuver the captain was killed just a few steps from the Constitutionalist lines. No matter how many times his men tried, they simply could not recover his corpse. Only one sergeant even succeeded in reaching him. He removed his wallet, which contained the company's pay, and delivered it to command without so much as one peso missing.[93]

June 24

As the Federal pressure on San Alejandro started to decrease it was agreed among the Constitutionalist leaders to give some of General Alvarado's men a well-deserved rest so that they might be ready and able to reinforce without delay any direction in which the Federals might attempt a breakout. Those units taken off the line were Lieutenant Colonel Urbalejo's Federal Auxiliary Corps; Major Amavisca's Voluntarios de Río de Sonora, Voluntarios de Guaymas, and Voluntarios de Zaragoza; forty men from the Benito Juárez Company; and forty more from the Special Guard. Lieutenant Colonel Urbalejo and Major Lino Morales had distinguished themselves in all the attacks that the Federals attempted against them. They had not only repulsed them, but had sometimes even taken ground from the Federals, keeping them confined to the vicinity of the main house at San Alejandro.[94]

In the Federal camp General Ojeda finally reached the conclusion that he could not continue on to Hermosillo, and instead had to retreat. The greater portion of his men had been fighting day and night without rest for six days with the impossibility of repairing the railroad, under the blazing sun with no shade whatsoever, and with water starting to running low: the watering hole at San Alejandro had gone dry and the supply from Ortiz was insufficient for the column's needs. By that time the Federals had only consumed a little more than 100,000 7-mm. and 30,000 .30-30 cartridges and 480 75-mm. and 800 70-mm. shells. The distance at which the two forces engaged each other most likely explained the large number of artillery shells and decreased number of small arms and machine-gun rounds expended.[95]

BATTLE OF SANTA MARÍA

June 25

On orders from Ojeda, Medina Barrón commanded the Federal combatants on the hills of San Alejandro to fall back on the main house of Hacienda San Alejandro and then rejoin the rest of the column at Anita whence they undertook the march to Guaymas. Major Toledo with fifty mounted men and one hundred infantrymen had already scouted and repaired the national road from Ortiz to Santa María. It was necessary to hit on that latter place since there was a water well there that could satisfy the thirsty troops. The movement began at 3 a.m. as the Federals broke contact without being sensed by the Constitutionalists, abandoning San Alejandro for Anita Station where they joined the rest of the Federal column coming from Ortiz. The Federals did not feel bad about losing, only exhausted. For a whole month they had spent some startling hours in the elements, over the scorching earth of Sonora. The commanding general suffered like everyone. His bed, whenever he happened to sleep, was a hard bench in the caboose of his train.[96]

The Federal order of march, ostensibly, consisted of the 50th Infantry, one section of Gruson guns, and the Sámano Irregular Corps of cavalry, commanded by the irregular Colonel Francisco Chiapa, who was very knowledgeable about the region, in the vanguard; the 14th and 10th Infantry, a company from the 28th Infantry, and the Sierra Juárez Battalion in the main body; followed by the artillery and impedimenta with the 53rd Battalion in the rearguard. The Voluntarios del Mayo and the Auxiliary Corps of Guanajuato provided security on the right flank, that is, closest to the sierra, with the 8th Rural Corps, the 21st Irregular Cavalry Corps, and part of the 27th Rural Corps providing flank guards on the left, to the east.[97]

About four kilometers from San Alejandro the Federals stopped to allow the ammunition car, which was lagging, to catch up. A little farther on the column again halted for several hours in order to attend to the heavy impedimenta, consisting of nineteen carts pulled by mules and horses, ill-fed due to the lack of pasture and also exhausted by thirst. After ditching everyone's baggage and luggage, the Federal retreat continued on until 6 a.m. There was not a house or tree in sight, just a wasteland everywhere one looked as officers yelled, "onward, onward, no reason to stop." The sandy road that traversed numerous gulches, in spite of the repairs made by Toledo, was the principal obstacle to their progress. As Ojeda complained, "The awful state of the road that we were covering, totally sandy, crossed by deep arroyos, and covered on the left and right by thick mounds, forced us to make frequent and prolonged stops since the carts, mainly those carrying ammunition, were passed through those arroyos with very great difficulty." Thus, the Constitutionalists had plenty of time to divine the Federals' intentions.[98]

About one hour later, around 7 a.m., Constitutionalist Captain Beltrán, who was occupying the highest hills opposite San Alejandro, reported that the Federals were marching through the valley, east of the railroad. Obregón immediately left to take up position on the hill in front of Aguajito in order to fully investigate what he had been told. General Alvarado and a few officers from his staff accompanied him. From that position he could plainly see that the Federals were headed for the water at Santa María. Obregón sent an emergency dispatch to Hill to get his men ready to receive the Federals; he ordered Diéguez to move south and occupy Ortiz Station, which Diéguez had already done on his own initiative, and to begin repairing the rails under the expert supervision of Major J. L. Gutiérrez, the jefe of trains. Alvarado took the rested troops, numbering about 650 men, and immediately got underway to reinforce Hill. Ochoa and the rest of Alvarado's men began moving into position to attack the Federal rear.[99]

By 9 a.m. the heat was already unbearable. Even the best prepared Federals no longer had one drop of water. One of the women, a vendor who had a great number of trinkets in her inventory, fell from heat stroke. Later, soldiers began falling from the same malady. They tried to encourage one another: "Cheer up; in the Santa María you can drink water. To Santa María." The men continued on, sweaty, unhappy, with their head down to shield their eyes from the blazing sun, but encouraged by the thought of water. When the Federals noticed some enemy movement in Santa Rosa their artillery went into action trying to clear the small group of houses.[100]

Finally, Major Toledo and his fifty Colorados in the vanguard reported spotting the enemy at the hacienda. When the bugles began to announce an upcoming fight, the electricity that had lit up the eyes of the soldiers before had gone out of them, replaced with a sense of resignation.[101] Santa María lies between Santa Rosa and Maytorena Station on completely level ground opposite the railroad from the sierra, and because of its many square plots and berms, resembled a giant chess board. The berms made of earth more than a meter thick offered a great defense, since apart from protecting the whole shooter's body the berms also nullified the effects of artillery. Against a mass of loose earth projectiles do nothing more than throw up dust clouds. Add to this the fact that the well was only a few meters from the main house of the hacienda, itself built like a fort, and that the berms served as obstacles to the Federals, impeding their progress while affording the Constitutionalists already at the hacienda plenty of time to receive reinforcements.[102]

The Federal 14th and 50th battalions with three companies of the Oaxacans advanced first with the artillery of Captain Ramos covering their deployment. The Constitutionalists were about three hundred meters to the north of the main house of the hacienda where Hill had placed his men on a firing line, taking advantage of the berms and ditches; there were also Constitutionalists behind dirt walls and in the small houses that surrounded the main house of the hacienda. The astuteness of the revolutionaries once again showed through in the first contact.[103]

They allowed the Federals in the center to approach, feigning a hasty retreat that appeared to force them to abandon some arms and horses that the emboldened Oaxacans rushed forward to collect up. The Constitutionalists then began taunting the Federals with water, letting them see the precious liquid whose absence made them so desperate. Then the Federals charged forward so precipitously that they forced the advance Constitutionalists to fall back on the main body, and that is when the combat began in earnest. The Federals reorganized and then tried to clear the enemy from berm to berm, something akin to the hedgerows of Normandy, along an extension of two kilometers. The artillery peppered the group of small surrounding houses with shrapnel, forcing the Constitutionalists back to the main house.[104]

With the battle cries, "To the well!" "To drink water!" the Federals, driven more by self-preservation than courage, made a desperate push forward, clearing the Constitutionalists from their positions one by one. The fight became surreal as the Federals captured a watermelon field and began to engorge themselves, ignoring the fact that hundreds of carbines might riddle their body. Right there in the middle of the field, because their thirst was so great and furious that it did not permit delay, they cut open the enormous fruits in one slash and sank their jaws into the pulp, enjoying a brief reprieve from maddening thirst until shots poured in, putting an anguished and painful end to the scene.[105]

The sunstroke victims were everywhere, and not just among the enlisted, but among the officers as well. Staff officers, like Lieutenant Octavio de la Fuente, had the worst lot. As aides they had to communicate the wishes of the commander, delivering ammunition here, telling the Oaxacans not to get too far ahead there, delivering other communications, and collapsing from heat exhaustion and sunstroke. Enlisted men also fell out from the less severe heat exhaustion, and whenever a jefe or officer tried to raise them up to enter into combat, they only groaned and shrank to receive the blows from their superiors. It was then that Ojeda covered the whole field, delivering hits, kicks, and slaps until his hands began to bleed. His blows had no more effect than to produce lamentations from his charges, many of whom were nothing more than recruits dressed up like soldiers. Ojeda had never had to fight with men such as these before. The others, the veterans, the thousand veterans, were at the front fighting.[106]

At 12:30 p.m. Alvarado arrived at Santa María with his men to reinforce Hill's brigade, already engaging the Federals who were making unheard of attempts to reach the water. Alvarado began dictating orders, sending the 1st and 3rd companies of the Federal Auxiliary Corps and forty men of the Voluntarios de Benito Juárez to the center; to the right Lieutenant Colonel Trujillo's and Major Rivera Domínguez's men and the 4th company of the Federal Auxiliary Corps; and to the left the 2nd company of the Federal Auxiliary Corps, the Voluntarios de Río de Sonora, Guaymas, and Zaragoza, and Major Méndez's men. He placed Major Belisario García's men as support and Captain Francisco D. Quiroz's men in reserve: a proper disposition according to the ternary system.[107]

By 2:30 combat had already become generalized with the Federals pouring in very copious rifle and artillery fire. They first tried a frontal assault and were repulsed. Then they tested the Constitutionalist right, but Colonel Trujillo putting up stiff resistance turned back that attack as well. The Federals persisted in their attempts to take some of the Constitutionalist positions, but always without success.[108]

By 4 p.m. Ochoa's column had finally reached Aguajito, and Obregón ordered him to march down to the railroad immediately to attack the Federals on their right flank. Originally, as previously mentioned, he had intended for Ochoa to hit the Federals in the rear, but as their column stretched all the way back to beyond Santa Rosa, by circling around to their rear Ochoa would have left open the path to Aguajito and its water source. When Ochoa reached the railroad Obregón once again changed his mind. The Federals continued to attack Alvarado in the center, so Obregón ordered Ochoa to take four hundred men and four machine guns to reinforce Alvarado so that that jefe might better utilize those forces to protect the Constitutionalist right (east) flank around which the Federals might attempt to escape. Ochoa got started at about 5:30 p.m.[109]

A half hour later Obregón ordered an attack from the railroad against the Federal right. At that time the Federal bugles sounded "enemy to the rear" announcing that Ojeda's column was about to be surrounded. In response the jefe of the 53rd Battalion, Major Francisco Cota, divided a force into three groups under lieutenants Guerrero, Urcid, and Tajonar and commanded by Captain Riva Palacio. These officers from the beginning decided not to simply resist but rather to attack back toward Santa Rosa, and thus succeeded in repulsing the Constitutionalists, even taking some prisoners. The Federal guns, in support, bombarded the hills near Aguajito, confirming in Obregón's mind their intention to take that vital water source. Nevertheless, about an hour later the situation had turned desperate for the Federals. Even the veterans had become highly fatigued, as they executed one final and decisive effort to get to the water. Obregón ordered Diéguez to come down from Ortiz to guard San Alejandro with all haste and had Lieutenant Colonel Félix with the remainder of Ochoa's column cover from Maytorena all the way back toward Santa Úrsula Canyon, the entrance to Aguajito. Obregón returned to Aguajito, and with the forces remaining there (including his escort and staff), covered the area hills to be able to defend against any attempt on Aguajito.[110]

Back in front of Santa María, General Medina Barrón notified the various unit commanders that there would be one final assault to reach the water once every preparatory measure had been taken, including moving the artillery to cover the assault. "To the water!" the jefes and officers yelled, leading their men in the attack. There were some who, crazy from thirst, cleared the last berm and lunged at their foes without any regard to the one thousand Constitutionalist muzzles surrounding the water well; many of them died with their hands cupped trying to deliver the liquid to their lips. But those were only the impetuous, daring, and brave. The more reticent Federals remained behind, firing randomly and putting their resolute comrades in danger. Unfortunately for the Federals, courage, unlike fear, is not so contagious and the assault failed. Medina Barrón's command retreated after being decimated.[111]

Ojeda stopped distributing punches to his men long enough to reorganize them for a new assault. Once again their eagerness to reach the water inspired a desperate charge that only produced a prodigious number of casualties. Lieutenant Colonel Eduardo López of the 10th Battalion, who had been performing gallantly, with Major Agustín Estrada, Second Captain E. Ángeles, and Sub-lieutenants Josefat Plata and Felipe Ramírez of the 14th Battalion fell upon clearing the Constitutionalist berm, without any colleagues to attend to their wounds, since Medina Barrón had to beat a retreat with less than one hundred men.[112]

Captain Riva Palacio then collapsed from the heat at the foot of Medina Barrón's horse, only to later recover and return to the fight, where he fell again, refusing to listen to the advice to rest a while. Riva Palacio had a reputation for being brave, but he maintained that it was not bravery but rather a healthy sense of shame and a fear of dishonoring his parents. He was later killed at Los Mochis, Sinaloa, along with Chato Urcid.[113]

At 6:30 p.m. Federal buglers blew calls of "enemy to the front!" "enemy to the right!" "enemy to the left!" and "enemy to the rear!" They were completely surrounded. The artillery fired off all its remaining ammunition and then Chueco Ramos and Martínez Perdomo disabled their pieces. One hour later, the column began preparing for a breakout; the signal came at 10:30 p.m. when Ojeda ordered the bugle calls of "enemy to the right" and "enemy to the left" blown. The Federals disengaged, abandoned the artillery and ammunition wagons, and with the mounted troops in one group and the infantry and artillerymen led by Colonel Jesús P. Díaz in another, the Federals skirted around the right flank of the Constitutionalists toward the Sierra de Bacatete, and made their way as best they could to Guaymas and Empalme, the main body arriving at that later location around 6 a.m.[114]

Not all heard the bugle calls. The Oaxacans and the 53rd Battalion kept right on fighting until about 11 p.m., when Major Cota realized the scale of the calamity and disengaged to begin the long march home. He had time to collect up a few other obedient men who had remained glued to their positions. Despite their late withdrawal, perfect knowledge of the terrain permitted this jefe to exfiltrate without event. No unit had more men reach the safety of Empalme.[115]

June 25-26

Once again the Federals had slipped away during the night without the Constitutionalists being aware. Around 3 a.m. Obregón ordered those troops stretching from Maytorena Hill to Aguajito to advance simultaneously toward the railroad, a maneuver that took until 5:30 to complete. Lieutenant Colonel Félix captured thirteen Federals who spoke of the Federal plan of dispersal to the east. Moments later Obregón received a confirmation from General Alvarado that Ochoa had not fulfilled his mission to take up position on the Constitutionalist right flank where he would have been in a position to contain the Federals: no one knew where he had gone. Obregón ordered a pursuit toward Empalme, but it was too late. General Alvarado sent Lieutenant Colonel Trujillo and Major Antúnez's cavalry toward Cruz de Piedra to search the eastern part of the valley for stragglers.[116]

The scene on the way to Guaymas was painful for the Federals who were on the receiving end of every outrage. Colonel Francisco Chiapa lovingly led his wife, recently up and about after giving birth, and a young lady on the way back. They took turns riding a donkey, slow as one might imagine, and eventually they were captured, along with a Lieutenant Moreno accompanying them. Chiapa knew what that meant, since he had been punishing rebels in Sonora since 1910. Ignoring the tears of the women and the children about to be made fatherless Constitutionalist Colonel Eduardo Hay led the two officers back to Santa María where they were shot.[117]

According to Federal reports, Ojeda lost two jefes, seven officers, and 76 troops killed; two jefes, nine officers, and 75 troops wounded; and one jefe, nine officers, and 451 dispersed, a casualty rate of about 25 percent. Obregón's number of killed to wounded matched the near symmetry of the Federals: two officers and 25 troops killed and two officers and 28 men wounded. His report also confirmed that 300 corpses had already been incinerated as of the night of June 27 and that he had taken 728 Federals prisoner, many of the officers being shot depending on when they were captured, and by whom. Neither commander probably knew the exact figures, but one can reckon that the campaign was an utter disaster for the Federals and a great victory for the Constitutionalists, especially in terms of booty: nine cannons with 2,000 shells; 530 rifles; five machine guns; 190,000 cartridges; and 25 transport cars containing materiel such as typewriters, rangefinders, field telephones, field glasses, and four strongboxes with 40,000 pesos in cash as well as important documents. The Constitutionalists later returned the cannons to use, although not in perfect condition, with the help of the facilities and personnel of The Cananea Consolidated Copper Company.[118]

Analysis

Ojeda's mission was a fool's errand since the Federals did not have enough men to hold both Guaymas and Hermosillo and no one in their right military mind would consider pressing on to Hermosillo and exchanging the port for the state capital as a base of operations. Aside from that, Ojeda should have been charged with seeking out and destroying Obregón's brigade, but he did not have enough cavalry or people intimate with the terrain to provide any semblance of situational awareness and over half his force consisted of raw recruits, soldiers in name only, and hardly able to maneuver over the rough ground and prevail against the elements. Therefore, while about half his force battled the majority of Obregón's, the rest sat idle in Ortiz. Forced to own up to his failure, the Federal commander did what all losers did—he blamed the Americans: "an American piloting a biplane" in the service of the Constitutionalists discovered that the Federals had "no troops between Maytorena station and Santa Rosa, that is, that they had their line of communications unprotected, [and] surely that was when the idea of making a maneuver around the rearguard of their adversaries germinated in his [Obregón's] brain."[119] Actually, a Frenchman by the name of Didier Masson piloted the aircraft, although an American named Reuben Hopkins helped him to smuggle in the plane, for which he received a captaincy from the revolutionaries and condemnation from the U.S. government.[120] Ojeda simply could not bring himself to admit the truth: the Federal Army was an unworthy adversary.

During the campaign, while Obregón was in Moreno Station, he received a letter from Federal Lieutenant Colonel Eleazar C. Muñoz with whom he had developed a cordial relationship, first as a member of Sanginés' column in 1912 and later operating under General Gil. Muñoz relayed Ojeda's offer to recognize Obregón's rank, among other concessions, if he would separate from the revolution and join the Federal Army. In his scathing letter of rejection, the Constitutionalist commander took the opportunity to personally insult Ojeda:

> I am not one who would fight in defense of a criminal government, [but rather] one who has been disposed to sacrifice his life defending

the national dignity; but if, by some monstrosity I were to lower myself to such degradation, I would not put myself under the orders of
a man who, without any military knowledge, has always led his men
to disaster and shame, to then leave them abandoned in the hour
of danger and whom I only know by his back from wherever I have
defeated him, and I am sure to defeat him [again].[121]

Even though Obregón may have respected Ojeda's combativeness, as evidenced back in March when he warned Calles against attempting to attack
Ojeda at Naco without reinforcements, Ojeda remained a typical Federal
Army general to the core: a praetorian ignorant of the military arts and sciences (in spite of his claims of self-study) and largely uninterested in the
welfare of his men, all of which Obregón referenced.

In contrast, the Battle of Santa María, waged from June 18 to 26, revealed Obregón as one of the most talented developing officers in the
Constitutionalist Army. He mastered the principle of maneuver early in his
career, rarely fighting a battle in a location that was not of his choosing and
always maintaining his freedom of action. He always dictated the terms of
battle, and thus never lost. But he also revealed a penchant for overly-compli-
cated and interdependent battle plans that would follow him throughout his
career, possibly as a result of his background in mechanics and his fascination
with multiple moving parts. Worse, he displayed a surprising reluctance to
alter those plans and adapt to the changing battlefield.

Governor Maytorena, who later wrote a cynical account of Obregón's performance, pointed out Obregón's numerous advantages over the Federals in
troop strength, materiel, knowledge of the terrain, and battle-hardened warriors acclimatized to the hot North versus a bunch of draftees from temperate
zones who were exhausted from the long march, and among whom numbered even a few dragooned Zapatistas. Maytorena also insulted Obregón's
moral courage, alleging that during the confusion of the battle he wanted
to retreat but Colonel Manuel Diéguez convinced him to continue fighting.
Maytorena gave all the glory to Obregón's subordinates, and there may have
been a kernel of truth in what Maytorena had to say. But it was all based on
hearsay, because during the battle he was cowering in the United States.[122]

Siege of Guaymas

After the Battle of Santa María, the Constitutionalists possessed all of Sonora
except Guaymas, which they invested on June 28. Given the terrain around
the port, General Ojeda ordered the 10th, 14th, 27th, 28th, 50th, and 53rd
battalions to establish a defensive firing line extending from the railroad

bridge that crosses over to Empalme to the road that connects Guaymas with San Germán, crossing over all the crests of the hills without any gaps. (See Battle of Empalme Station map in Chapter 8 for area terrain) He likewise ordered some advance positions placed in a range of hills to the north to protect the radiotelegraph of Bacochibampo located there. And finally, to make the most effective defense of the main entrance into the port, that is, on the north side between the hills called Bacochibampo and Roca Fuerte, he ordered those positions occupied with interlocking fields of fire. The line of defense extended twelve kilometers, with the defenders completely exposed on hills utterly devoid of vegetation. These dispositions were effected on June 26, the day after Santa María.[123]

Obregón had wanted to follow up on the success of Santa María immediately because he thought that the Federals were in such a weakened state that the Constitutionalists could take the port, but when he polled his column commanders they impressed upon him the very fatigued state of their men. Guaymas would have to wait. As commander, Obregón took full responsibility for the decision. Instead of pursuing Guaymas, Obregón recalled Colonel Ochoa, who after failing to block the Federal escape on the Constitutionalist right during the battle, for reasons never revealed, had taken it upon himself (and without informing headquarters) to give pursuit single-handedly with just his column. He also ordered Diéguez, at San Alejandro, to continue moving to the south leaving some forces behind to help Major Gutiérrez repair the rails. On the morning of the twenty-seventh the Voluntarios de Cananea Corps under the direction of Gutiérrez had finished the repairs as far as Maytorena Station, where Colonel Diéguez had the rest of his men camped. Obregón arrived at 8 a.m. and gave Diéguez orders to move his column to Hacienda El Pardo, northeast of Guaymas. He also arranged to finish cleaning up the battlefield while he took his staff, escort, and some of Colonel Hill's cavalry and headed for Tres Gitos and Batamotal. He then detached Hill's cavalry to Empalme, which the Federals had abandoned, and headed with his escort and staff to San José de Guaymas, northeast of Guaymas and very near Hacienda El Pardo.[124]

In San José de Guaymas Obregón ran into an advance force belonging to Colonel Trujillo commanded by a First Captain Antonio Loustaunau whom he straightaway ordered to occupy the hill opposite the town known as the old Vigía. The Captain accomplished this mission at 2 a.m. on June 28, killing four Federals and taking twelve prisoners without incurring any casualties. Other Constitutionalist units also moved up, with Ochoa's column and part of Diéguez's reaching El Pardo at midnight and General Alvarado arriving at San José de Guaymas a short while later with part of his column.[125]

In the morning, Obregón took his staff and with two companies of the 4th Battalion went to reinforce Captain Loustaunau and to take a look at the Federal defenses. Grasping the importance of another hill to the left, Batuecas, Obregón sent Major Fructuoso Méndez with 150 men to occupy it, which they accomplished at 7 p.m. The Federals of the 10th Battalion and parts of the 27th and 28th positioned on the Rincón del Burro tried to send a force to cover the hill, but either because of the energy of the revolutionaries, or because the Federals still had not recovered from the week's combat, Méndez's Constitutionalists were able to force the Federals to abandon their positions and fall back on secondary positions, which were anchored on Tortuga Hill on the right and then continued to Punta Arena and El Cabezón hills and finally tied in with the "July 13" redoubt.[126]

The next day Obregón went to see Méndez on Batuecas Hill in order to make a detailed reconnaissance of the Federal positions. At that moment Méndez's men got into a fierce firefight, and even though the Federals returned rifle and machine-gun fire and opened up with field and naval artillery as well, Obregón got the distinct impression that he could easily push back the Federals. Nevertheless, he ordered Méndez to hold his present position and conserve his ammunition because he wanted to inspect the Federal left in order to effect a combined simultaneous attack. Obregón intended to do that the next day, but he returned to San José de Guaymas a victim of heat stroke and was bedridden for five days, during which time he left Diéguez and Ochoa in charge of the west, on the San Germán side, trying to narrow the siege lines.[127]

By the time Obregón recovered, Colonel Ochoa had taken Bacochibampo Hill to the north; Colonel Diéguez had taken the hills of El Tunel, the location of the freshwater supply for the town; and General Alvarado and Major Méndez held the cordillera in front of San José de Guaymas all the way to Tortuga Hill, across from Empalme. In short, they controlled the high ground all around Guaymas. The Federals continued to pour in naval and field artillery fire, but without effect, as the Constitutionalists returned fire. The Constitutionalists had strict orders to confine themselves to their positions until a general plan of attack had been formulated, and it was during this time that the famous Chief Ignacio Mori, who commanded the bronco faction of Yaquis, decided to declare his allegiance to Carranza.[128]

As the Constitutionalists continued skirmishing around the port city Obregón started to despair of the situation and his low ammunition—he was consuming about 15,000 rounds per day—and he appealed to Governor Pesqueira's rationalism. He proposed three courses of action: attack by previously selected sectors in succession; an all-out general assault; and lastly, a blockade. In every instance he considered the cost-benefit ratio of men lost and ammunition consumed to the possibility of capturing the Federal garrison and its military materiel. An advance by sectors had a good possibility of success, with few casualties, but with a good chance of the Federals escaping, at a cost of one million rounds consumed. Meanwhile, a general assault would have only a 50 percent chance of success, a small probability of capturing the garrison intact, and use up about four million rounds. Unlike Pancho Villa and Pablo González, Obregón appreciated the dangers and destructiveness of frontal assaults early in his formation. Finally, a blockade would free up half the besieging force and require only a paltry consumption of rounds. When another 1,136 Federals disembarked in Guaymas with twelve artillery pieces and a great amount of ammunition on July 11, the Constitutionalists opted to blockade the port city and continue south to Sinaloa, pulling back the next day to Cruz de Piedra (Hill), Maytorena Station (Alvarado and Diéguez), and Santa María (Ochoa), with advance detachments in Tres Gitos, Batamotal, and Empalme.[129] As Miguel Alessio Robles cogently remarked, "Obregón's strategy [sic] in battles was notable, but more notable still was his extraordinary quality of knowing how to care for his men so that they were not uselessly sacrificed in a fight."[130]

Once the threat of attack had passed, General Ojeda published congratulations to the citizens and defenders of Guaymas, especially, Lieutenant Colonel Eleazar C. Muñoz, Major Francisco Cota, First Captain Pablo A. Flores, and the officers of the staff that had defended the most attacked points. After this, Ojeda received the baton of a divisionary, with promotion effective July 14, and Medina Barrón was promoted to the rank of general of brigade.[131]

More Conspiracies

The disastrous battles of June provoked another round of ludicrous conspiracies involving Americans trying to help the Constitutionalists secede from Mexico. Specifically, during the campaign, American Admiral W. C. Cowles from offshore Guaymas interfered with the radiotelegraphs in Bacochibampo and Empalme (the latter belonging to the American Southern Pacific Railroad), in order to hold Ojeda's column and Guaymas incommunicado with Mexico City in contravention of the Berlin Convention, which gave the Mexican government a right to priority in service; moreover, the American ships in the Pacific did the same at other ports, most importantly Mazatlán. The U.S. Navy also provided instruction to Constitutionalists aboard their battleships, it was alleged, and detained every Mexican ship, commercial or naval, to learn its departure point, destination, and any other information of interest to the Constitutionalists and spread rumors unfavorable to Huerta's government, including news that Huerta was going to resign soon.[132]

The baseless accusations continued. After the Battle of Santa María the Federals could not possibly conceive of any explanation why the Constitutionalists did not press home the victory and take Guaymas, except that they had to consult first with their Yankee allies, the American consul in Hermosillo and the management of the Southern Pacific Railroad, who provided maps of the port. Moreover, one night even before the siege had begun, spotlights from Yankee naval vessels lit up the coast in order to help the Constitutionalists overcome the darkness, "the greatest obstacle" to their effort, in an unsuccessful attempt against the Federal detachment positioned at Pleamar. Upset over the incident the Huertista governor threatened the American superintendent of the Southern Pacific Railroad and demanded an explanation from Admiral Cowles, which he received but apparently not to his satisfaction. Then on the night of July 6 "when the fight [for Guaymas] reached one of the most anguishing and fierce moments the searchlight of the *Pittsburgh* bathed the hills of the defense in light, from trench to trench, blinding the defenders to thus deliver them up, dazzled, indefensible and evident to the enemy." The next day Ojeda registered an official complaint with Admiral W. C. Cowles who offered regrets for the unintentional illumination of the previous night, explaining that the lights of the ship were directed at the beach on the west side of the ship where there was a small camp of refugees and that any rays that fell upon the Federal positions was by coincidence. Thereafter, the Americans, "tormented by the desire for the arrival of the moment of Sonora's separation!" continued to travel to Empalme on their launches, in spite of the Federal's strict prohibition against doing so, taking "food, ammunition, and arms to the 'Constitutionalists.'" Cowles explained that he was on the boats fishing for tarpon and Governor García then wrote a letter to Cowles prohibiting him from the crime of fishing for tarpon, but Cowles kept right on fishing tarpon. On July 14, thirty sailors of the Mexican gunboat *Tampico* went ashore at Empalme to view the effects of their gunfire on the railroad. As soon as they landed, whistles from the shops of the Southern Pacific began to blow as a warning to some Constitutionalists still left behind who then fled the station under the fire from the Federal sailors. Finally, after the Federals lost southern Sonora, "a ship that, although sailing under the flag of a European country represents Yankee interests, turned filibuster in order for that product [garbanzos] to leave through Topolobampo, and to realize every type of commerce, including of arms and ammunition, with the rebels [sic]."[133]

The Huertista Ceballos, who lodged these accusations of meddling against the Americans, ridiculed Admiral Cowles' explanation that he was "fishing tarpon" on the launches in favor of the much more outrageously illogical explanation that the launches were delivering war materiel to the Constitutionalists; and again, he provided no evidence. Likewise, Ceballos sarcastically characterized the one time when the U.S. Navy's searchlights accidentally lit up the Federal trenches as a "coincidence," precisely because it never happened again. The Federals simply refused to acknowledge that the Navy had to tend to its own nighttime security and apparently could not apprehend that Cowles' mission was to protect the lives and interests of foreign citizens, including the many people who had fled the port for the safety of area islands and beaches in the darkness. Moreover, any argument about the U.S. Navy ignoring mandates from the Huertista government regarding maintaining contact with those citizens, be they in Guaymas or the surrounding islands or coastline, or with foreign interests, be it the Southern Pacific Railroad at Empalme or the Richardson Company, were without legal standing since the United States government did not acknowledge the legitimacy of the Huertista government. The Federal Army had a job to do and so did the U.S. Navy.

Finally, if an American-owned, European-flagged ship traded garbanzos for arms and ammunition with the Constitutionalists, then that was in contravention of the U.S. embargo against the Constitutionalists. However, from a purely military standpoint, the Constitutionalists won the battle for the valley and those were the spoils of war. Huerta had no right to demand that the United States fight his war for him. And if the U.S. Navy's radiotelegraphs interfered with the Federals' transmissions because the latter had weak equipment, then why is that the fault of the Americans? Strong transmissions from Japanese warships likewise overpowered the wireless transmissions of the various belligerents in the course of the revolution at different points and times.

Huertistas manufactured all manner of lies, exaggerations, and half-truths in a bid to mobilize support for the illegal government, and Federal Army officers defeated in battle indulged them in a feeble attempt to explain away their failures. But conspiracy theories did not detour the course of the war and could not rescue the careers of Federal Army officers.

*　　*　　*

The Guaymas Valley Campaign involved full divisions operating with an amphibious dimension, engaged in watchmaker-like maneuvers over open terrain where the use of geography factored prominently in military outcomes, and once again exposed the deficiencies inherent in the Federal Army's way of war: subpar specimens for combat forced to don a uniform and sent into battle without any training, led by courageous officers who exhibited little knowledge of the art or science of warfare, only somewhat counterbalanced by motivated irregulars (Major Toledo's Colorados and the Oaxacans) who performed the most dangerous and crucial missions for a column relegated to operating along a single axis of advance along the railroad, forced to safeguard towns and infrastructure, utterly predictable, and lacking all imagination. The regulars gave no indications of indoctrination in the ternary system of combat, and employed their artillery in direct fire missions that proved ineffective, on the one hand, and exposed the artillerymen to lethal enemy fire, on the other.

The Constitutionalists could not have been more different from their foes. Their soldiers consisted of the sons of Sonora, battle-hardened, knowledgeable of the terrain, and acclimatized to the harsh natural elements. They had little trouble living off the land, maintained absolute freedom of action in the face of the plodding Federal movements, developed and executed a superior campaign plan redolent of the indirect method by using water instead of frontal assaults to defeat an enemy compelled to assume the tactical offense and deliver suicidal assaults, and employed the ternary system at Santa María with a firing line, support, and reserve. While preparing to assault Guaymas, Obregón measured his chances of success with a keen appreciation for military economy and convinced Governor Pesqueira to leave the port in a permanent state of investment, with the shortage of ammunition caused by the U.S.-imposed embargo factoring into the equation.

Federal General Ojeda could not abide being defeated in combat by novice irregulars and blamed the United States for his defeat: the biplane it provided to Obregón gave him the idea for his battle plan at Santa María; the U.S. Navy lit up the hills surrounding Guaymas for a Constitutionalist attack, ferried supplies onshore to the Constitutionalists, provided them training on their battleships, and interrupted Huertista communications with Mexico City; unknown American civilians dynamited the railroads, furnished maps to the Constitutionalists, gave them warnings about Federal Army movements, and traded in arms and ammunition for garbanzo beans. The problem with these accusations is that all are unsubstantiated, preposterous, inconsequential, or inaccurate. Obregón was already maturing into a very capable field commander and needed no biplane to formulate his plan. The lighting up of the Federal trenches occurred one time, was not in concert with an all-out assault on the port, resulted in little harm, and received a due explanation and apology. The allegations of training sessions on American battleships does not merit any comment. Finally, simply because Surianos did not have close personal and professional ties to the Americans like the Sonorans had with their counterparts in Arizona does not mean that either of those two parties should have to apologize for their relationships. The Huertista propagandists maligned the Sonorans calling them "separatists" and damned the Americans, "tormented by the desire for the arrival of the moment of Sonora's separation!" But one hundred years after these events Sonora continues as a proud member of the United States of Mexico, and the nation did not lose one inch of ground in the whole course of the Revolution. Indeed, if one includes the sub-soil, then one could persuasively argue that Mexico gained territory, first de jure in 1917 and then de facto in 1938. The entire "Constitutionalism as the Cat's Paw of American Imperialism" argument lacks all credibility.

There can be no mistake. The Federals in 1913 Sonora lost to General Obregón and his Constitutionalists for numerous reasons far more weighty than what might be labeled the "foreign factor." Many have proclaimed Obregón to be a military genius, but no one has ever said the same about one single Federal general, except maybe Felipe Ángeles. The Federal Army was so deficient in every aspect and every theater, in fact, that by the time the Guaymas Valley Campaign had ended in late June, some believe that Huerta had already lost the war.

Four

A War Lost: June, 1913

Pánfilo Natera—Fresnillo—Battle of Zacatecas—Battle of Matamoros—Secretary of War Mondragón Fired—Revolutionaries Mass for Unity of Command in Durango—Planting for Upcoming Campaign Season—The Social Defense—Battle of Durango City—Forced Loans—Sacking of Durango City—Popular Militarism—Villa turns North—Federal General Rábago replaced by Mercado—Bustillos—Santa Eulalia—Federal Captain Margarito Gómez defects with Machine Guns—Aldama—Chihuahua City under Siege and Ciudad Juárez Threatened—Casas Grandes—The Colorado Pipeline—Villa barters for War Materiel—Máximo Castillo—Juan N. Medina—Toribio Ortega and Ojinaga—Federals Lose War in less than Six Months

I n addition to the virtual loss of Sonora, by the end of June the Federal government had lost other states, capitals, key ports of entry, or had been relegated to operating along restricted corridors in Chihuahua, Durango, Zacatecas, and Tamaulipas. Indeed, even at this early stage in the Constitutionalist revolution the Federal hold on the North had become so tenuous that historian General Miguel Sánchez Lamego deemed the war already lost. We will return to Sánchez Lamego's thesis at the end of this chapter.

Zacatecas

The figurehead of the revolution in Zacatecas, a large state in central Mexico just north of the Bajío region, was Second Officer Pánfilo Natera of the 26th Rural Police Corps. With the support of sixty men, he had taken up arms against the government in Nieves, Zacatecas, on April 10, and soon other important revolutionaries joined him: Second Officer Santos Bañuelos, J. Trinidad Cervantes, and former Second Officer Pedro Caloca, who convinced another fifty men from the 26th Rural Corps to recognize him as their leader. With other defecting Federals and state Auxiliaries, Natera soon had a force of four hundred poorly armed men against the nine hundred state and federal forces, part of the new Federal Division of the Center, that Brigadier Jesús Aréchiga had scattered in garrisons around the state. On May 8, Natera orchestrated his first successful battle when he stormed and took Fresnillo, a major town in central Zacatecas defended at the time by ninety men of the 31st Auxiliary Cavalry Regiment, the 48th Rural Corps, and the 1st Zacatecan Auxiliary Corps under Jefe del Detall Natividad del Toro. In the midst of combat a group of del Toro's men accepted offers to defect to the Constitutionalists, but del Toro continued to fight on and, holed up in the church tower, decided to commit suicide before surrendering. The Constitutionalists retained possession of the plaza until mid-May when a Federal relief column under General Pascual Orozco, Jr., making its way from Mexico City to Chihuahua City, passed through the region and forced the Constitutionalists to move off to the west and into northern Jalisco state.[1]

BATTLE OF ZACATECAS, JUNE 5-6, 1913

After Orozco had passed, the Zacatecans resolved to take the state capital and began destroying the rail and telegraph lines south of Zacatecas to inhibit Federal reinforcements arriving from Aguascalientes. Federal Colonel Miguel Rivera, who had replaced Aréchiga on May 19, anticipated an attack and therefore prepared two lines of defense for the plaza (for a general outlay see map in Chapter 15) with a perimeter of about 100 men: thirty on La Bufa and twenty on El Grillo hills, fifteen at the sentry house on the road to Jerez and fifteen guarding the road to Guadalupe, and ten at the rail station. In the interior of the small Carretas plaza he placed ten men, thirty in the headquarters, ten at the Presbyterian church, ten in the cathedral, and another thirty in the churches of Santo Domingo, San Juan de Oro, and Guadalupe. Other men were also located in the Cobre and Moneda barracks and the Citadel.

For the battle, Rivera could count on about four hundred troops from the 1st, 20th, and 21st Infantry Battalions; the 24th and 31st Auxiliary Cavalry Regiments; and about sixty state troops. He faced an estimated twelve hundred Constitutionalists.[2]

At 4:30 a.m. on the morning of June 5, the revolutionaries attacked from the south, east, and west. Natera had set up his command post in the train station and attempted to take La Bufa Hill in a rather disorderly manner, which the Federals repulsed after being reinforced by troops from inside the plaza. By the morning of the next day, the Constitutionalists had occupied houses on the outskirts of town and turned their attention to taking El Grillo Hill, which they succeeded in doing around 11 a.m. Next, they turned to pounce on Las Peñitas neighborhood and the Cobre barracks, although the latter held out as the defenders from the perimeter pulled back to the interior of the town, the Citadel barracks, and La Bufa Hill. Around 6 p.m., with his ammunition running low, Colonel Rivera began to concentrate all his forces on La Bufa, so that within three hours most of his troops were on the hill. At that time he decided to make his way to Hacienda de Troncoso and ultimately Aguascalientes. But in the darkness, the broken terrain made for a very disorderly retreat, as small isolated groups did their best to put distance between themselves and the revolutionaries. As of June 10, only 155 men from the Zacatecas garrison had managed to reach Aguascalientes.[3]

In military terms, the Battle of Zacatecas was a minor tactical affair, but strategically the loss of Zacatecas opened up Mexico City to attack from the North and politically and diplomatically it was the first major plaza lost to date in the heartland.[4] Additionally, it was preceded only days before by the loss of Matamoros.

BATTLE OF MATAMOROS JUNE 3

The reader will remember that the First Chief had sent Constitutionalist Colonel Lucio Blanco from Monclova to attack Matamoros in the early days of April. After destroying the railroads and other communications to isolate Matamoros from reinforcements, Blanco set up camp at Hacienda de Río Bravo and began to prepare for his assault on Matamoros. Soon he was joined by Luis Caballero and his small group from San Fernando and other important revolutionaries, such as Francisco Cosío Robelo and Fortunato Zuazua, some of whom were returning from the United States. Alternatively, Jesús Agustín Castro abandoned Blanco, as previously mentioned, because he judged any attempt on Matamoros too risky and turned southward with all of his, now renamed, 21st Brigade, except for a small group of ten men under Major Emiliano P. Nafarrate, who began recruiting for his new "21st Regiment."[5]

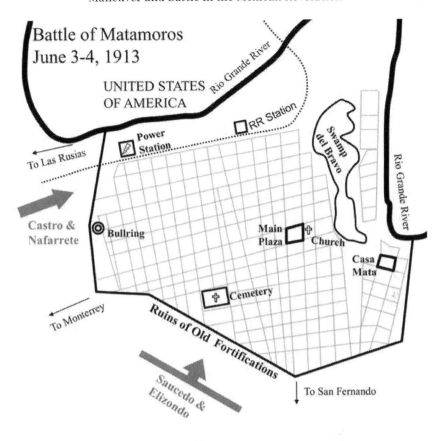

**Battle of Matamoros
June 3-4, 1913**

UNITED STATES
OF AMERICA

Rio Grande River

RR Station

Power
Station

Swamp
del Bravo

To Las Rusias

Rio Grande River

Castro &
Nafarrete

Bullring

Main
Plaza

Church

Casa
Mata

To Monterrey

Ruins of Old Fortifications

Cemetery

Saucedo &
Elizondo

To San Fernando

Map 1.11

Inside Matamoros the jefe de las armas, Federal Major Esteban Ramos, commanded men belonging to the 6th Cavalry Regiment, 10th Rural Corps, 37th Auxiliary Infantry Battalion, the Fiscal Gendarmes, Municipal Police, and volunteers of the Social Defense. In total they numbered roughly half as many as Blanco's Constitutionalists. Major Ramos established a defensive line on the outskirts of town covering the west, east, and south sides of the city, that is, the sides not touching the United States, using a continuous slit trench with various strong points such as from east to west, the Casa Mata, San Fernando Gate ("*Garita*"), the cemetery, the power plant, and the rail station. This line was reinforced by an electric wire connected to the power plant. In the interior the commander established a second defensive perimeter around the main plaza, barricading the street entrances with sandbags, stones, and other materials. The jefatura de las armas building in the plaza functioned as the command center. Ramos placed the "Félix Díaz" and "Antonio Echazarreta"

Volunteer Corps, some 110 men, in the eastern sector, from the Rio Grande to the San Fernando Gate, under the command of Comandante Hilario Echazarreta. He placed the western sector under Jefe del Detall Crispín Carlos Medina, covering the line from the San Fernando Gate to the Rail Station, with Captain Alberto Jones (who had retired as of November 5, 1906, but had been recalled to service by Huerta's government) and the 37th at the Monterrey Gate; the Fiscal Gendarmes at the power station; and the rest of his forces he distributed along the perimeter. Ramos also placed one old smooth-bore cannon on a platform at the rail station inside the city. With barely enough men to cover the trench, he had no reserve to speak of.[6]

Tactical Command	Major Unit organic to	J	O	T	Total
Federals:					
Cerón, Luis (1st CPT)	6th Cavalry Regiment (mainly musicians)		1	35	36
Jones, Alberto (1st CPT)	37th Irregular Infantry Corps		1	49	50
Medina, Crispín C. (Jefe del Detall)	10th Rural Corps	1	3	60	64
Echegaray, (LT)	Gendarmería Fiscal		1	60	61
Reyna, Manuel (Comandante)	Municipal Police		1	29	30
Echazarreta, Hilario (Comandante)	"Félix Díaz" Volunteer Corps	2	11	76	89
Echazarreta, Antonio (Comandante)	"Antonio Echazarreta" Volunteer Corps	1	5	30	36
López, Lorenzo (Comandante)	"Exploradores del Bravo" Volunteer Corps	1	2	30	33
Cuéllar, Eugenio (1st CPT)	Guerrilla "Cuéllar"		3	35	38
Ochoa, Daniel (LT)	Special Corps		1	25	26
Cervantes, Severiano (LT)	27th Auxiliary Cavalry Regiment		1	8	9
					472
Constitutionalists (estimated):					
Castro, Cesáreo (Colonel)	Regionales de Coahuila				200
Nafarrete, Emiliano P. (Major)	21st Regiment				10
Saucedo, Andrés (LTC)	2nd Carabineros de San Luis Potosí				200
Elizondo, Gustavo A. (Major)	Libres del Norte				150
González, Porfirio G. (LTC)	Carabineros de Nuevo León				150
Caballero, Luis (LTC)	Patriotas de Tamaulipas				200
					910

Table 1.5 Battle of Matamoros Troop Strengths

On June 2 Colonel Blanco concentrated his forces at Las Rusias, three to four kilometers upriver. The next morning he divided his forces into three columns and started for Matamoros: Colonel Cesáreo Castro with the Regionales de Coahuila Corps and the men from the 21st Regiment under Nafarrate, some 200 men, were to attack the west and take control of the power plant, which Blanco deemed the most important point; Lieutenant Colonel Andrés Saucedo with his 2nd Carabineros de San Luis Potosí (recruited mostly from the states of Nuevo León and Tamaulipas in spite of the name) and Major Gustavo Elizondo's Libres del Norte Corps formed the second column under Blanco's immediate command attacking the south side with about 350 men, between the gates to San Fernando and

Monterrey; Lieutenant Colonel Porfirio González's Carabineros de Nuevo León and Luis Caballero's (newly raised and mostly unarmed) Patriotas de Tamaulipas Corps formed the third column with about 350 men that Blanco held in reserve. At 9 a.m. on June 3, the Constitutionalists, supplied with dynamite bombs, opened fire and attacked across the open terrain. Channeling his attack on the power plant, Castro succeeded in disabling the perimeter's electrical wire by blowing it with dynamite, and then the Federals' smoothbore cannon exploded after just a few shots. By noon Castro's men had taken possession of the bullring and the power plant, making the Federal positions in the rest of the western sector untenable. Many of those Federals fled to the United States along with Major Ramos, who had a wounded hand (possibly self-inflicted), while the eastern sector continued to fight on. Unaware of Ramos' whereabouts, Federal Lieutenant Colonel Marcial Garza Rivas took over command at about 4 p.m. and ordered a concentration of forces around the second line of defense, which the forces of the eastern sector began to carry out, maintaining contact with the Constitutionalists.[7]

Completely surrounded, the Federals' situation proved unsustainable, and by 5:30 the following morning the last of the government's resistance had ended. The majority of defenders fled across the border to the United States; others tried to slip through the Constitutionalist lines, with most being mopped up, but Garza Rivas managed to reach Monterrey with about twenty men. Major Nafarrate rounded up prisoners, many of them volunteer youths from Matamoros, and with Captain Otilio Falcón began personally executing them, until Blanco and the other jefes found out and stopped the carnage.[8]

Blanco's casualties amounted to twenty-seven wounded, four seriously, and eighteen dead, with two officers figuring among the wounded. The Federals lost more than one hundred men killed, the actual number being difficult to specify due to the speed which with the victors incinerated the corpses, and twenty-seven prisoners; the Constitutionalists set free the enlisted men, but summarily executed jefe Antonio Echazarreta, whom they captured two days later at El Pedernal about fifteen kilometers southeast of Matamoros. The booty captured on this occasion amounted to about 30,000 rounds, 200 carbines, and 150 horses with saddles, which paled in comparison to the plaza's strategic worth as a resupply and refit depot for the Constitutionalists. Soon flying columns were operating out of Matamoros, and war materiel received there enabled units in the center of the country, as far away as the Huasteca, to take the fight to the Huertista regime.[9] The Federals never again possessed Matamoros.

The loss of Matamoros, described by Federal General Guillermo Rubio Navarrete as "inexplicable," provoked a great deal of consternation within the Federal Army. An expert plan for the port's defense had been presented to Huerta, but he dithered and the plaza fell. The problem for the Federals, in spite of sufficient time for the government to respond, had been not reinforcing the plaza, perhaps owing to an underestimation of the Constitutionalists' capabilities or, more likely, the inability to raise enough soldiers to mobilize a relief column. The plaza's defenses had too few men, with too many irregulars and volunteers, covering too large a perimeter. Perhaps more cogently, and considering the ample time allowed, a more youthful and vigorous commanding officer might have better prepared for defense. Ramos had held the rank of major since 1878. General Lauro Villar, as the commander of the 3rd Zone, had written in Ramos' evaluation of 1910: "He makes an effort to perform details entrusted to him satisfactorily, although his age does not help. He has little training and only knows the regulations from his time."[10]

Now, the Constitutionalists possessed two of the three largest border towns in the Northeast, Matamoros and Piedras Negras, and Jesús Carranza, operating in far western Coahuila and northern Nuevo León, threatened the third, Nuevo Laredo. The Mexican consul in Laredo, Texas, echoed the town's fears that "the rebel [sic] element … infatuated with the results achieved in Matamoros" might attack Nuevo Laredo at any moment during June. The Federal Army, however, still was not yet ready to begin actively campaigning in the Northeast.[11] Regardless, something had to be done.

In the June 13 council of war ("Junta de Generales"), Huerta and his generals huddled to discuss a major two-pronged offensive planned for the Northeast. Huerta's nephew, General Joaquín Maass, Jr., would depart from Saltillo moving up the rail line toward Piedras Negras with twenty-five hundred men, while simultaneously General Rubio Navarrete advanced from Monterrey toward Matamoros with eighteen hundred men furnished with 5 million cartridges. Also during this pivotal meeting, Secretary of War Manuel Mondragón, one of the ringleaders of the Citadel cuartelazo, tendered his resignation over the loss of Zacatecas. Huerta accepted Mondragón's offer and appointed General of Division Aurelio Blanquet to replace him. The loss of Zacatecas forced the Federals to reduce Maass' force to fifteen hundred men in order to reallocate one thousand troops to General of Brigade José Delgado, who received the mission to retake Zacatecas. For this reason the losses of Matamoros and Zacatecas, although more than six hundred kilometers apart, need to be considered within the same context. Delgado united with Irregular General Emilio Campa, whose group was already in transit, in Aguascalientes and collected Colonel Rivera and the remnants of his dispersed command to enter Zacatecas on June 16. Natera's Constitutionalists engaged Delgado's Federals briefly in Guadalupe the day before, but then abandoned Zacatecas bound for the north.[12] A few days later, the Federals experienced the loss of another major plaza—Durango City—that carried with it the loss of an entire state.

Durango

THE INVITATION

After the first failed attack on Durango City in April, the Constitutionalists had no intentions other than to return and attack the capital city once they thought that they had enough men, which they knew would not take long. Their forces grew daily as, according to Major Matías Pazuengo, "armed campesinos in groups of one hundred, two hundred, twenty, ten, and five showed up daily," increasing not only their numbers but also their spirits. They also knew that General Tomás Urbina had conquered Mapimí District, Durango, and Jiménez, Chihuahua, and was headed to Parral, so they sent a commission under Colonel Enrique Natera to wherever Urbina might be and entice him to participate in the taking of Durango.[13]

Urbina sent a message back suggesting that they should take care to organizing themselves as well as possible and that "if upon arrival he saw us organized he would be moved to return [with his men], because he had his forces entirely organized and disciplined and he also notified us that if for the taking of Durango we did not have an agreement to give command to one General, the one who inspired the most confidence, then neither would he accept to add his people to a muddle. With this frankness he spoke to us in his communication and as everything that he suggested to us was naturally fair," the jefes Pereyra, Arrieta, Contreras, and Pazuengo all decided to abide by his conditions. They sent a letter back to Urbina in Nieves, his home base, and said that they agreed to his terms. Then they began concentrating around Canatlán, because at that time their forces were scattered about with Contreras in Pedriceña; Pereyra and Pazuengos at Hacienda de Cuatimapé; and General Arrietas' troops all over, from Patos Station, Hacienda de la Magdalena, and the mining town Tejámen (all three in the same general vicinity) to Santiago Papasquiaro and Tepehuanes.[14]

The Arrietas had around two thousand men, General Pereyra no less than one thousand perfectly armed and mounted, and with the men of Urbina and of Contreras the Constitutionalist commanders of Durango had the complete assurance of taking the state capital. From mid-May to June 10 the Constitutionalists did nothing but organize their forces, fatten up the horses, and since they knew that they would emerge victorious, they saw to plantings on all the haciendas, distributing plots of land to campesinos together with mules or oxen and sufficient seed for the agricultural year.[15]

At the same time a new armed faction composed of capitalists, hacendados, businessmen, industrialists, miners, and all their dependents called the "Social Defense" started to form in Durango City. The Constitutionalists estimated this force at between seven hundred and one thousand men, although in reality they only amounted to half of the lower estimate. News of this new group quickly reached the ears of the Constitutionalists in Canatlán, not more than fifty kilometers from the state capital. According to reports, this organization had very diverse political views. Pazuengos seemed to consider them quite innocent and even innocuous, saying that some joined just to defend their homes and families, while others played soldier, carrying out military exercises in the streets and sporting fancy uniforms with all the trimmings of high-ranking officers. Little by little the jefe de las armas looked upon these men with satisfaction and began assigning them to forts on the outskirts of town as advance forces, creating quite a spectacle of the many volunteers. But Juan Barragán saw something much more sinister in the Social Defense, describing the reign of terror that it carried out against known and suspected Maderistas inside the city as revenge for losses suffered in the first attack on Durango, and how the archbishop used the power of the confessional to force young men to join the organization, ostensibly making absolution contingent upon their participation.[16] The truth was probably somewhere in between the two extremes.

SECOND BATTLE OF DURANGO CITY, JUNE 17-18

The Constitutionalists began converging on Durango City from Canatlán to set the siege, together with General Contreras approaching from the northeast. Once the city had been surrounded the Constitutionalists met at Hacienda de Navacoyan and swore to submit to the general-in-chief whom they would elect, which resulted in the appointment of General Urbina, and to agree on the date of the attack, for which they selected the afternoon of June 17, 1913.[17] The Pereyra Brigade covered the hippodrome on the east side of the city, threatening the fortifications from the cemetery to Rancho de Granados with close to one thousand men; to the south and west were the forces of General Urbina and the Arrietas with more than two thousand of the best-prepared revolutionaries (the ones who took Los Remedios Hill in the previous battle for Durango) who tied off with Calixto Contreras' people on the side of Ojo de Agua; Contreras contributed the biggest contingent with forces topping three thousand men.[18]

Tactical Command	Major Unit organic to	J	O	T	Total
Federals (estimated):					
Euzástiga, Rutilo (2nd CPT)	1st Cavalry Regiment		3	80	83
Rodríguez, Carlos (Major)	14th Cavalry Regiment	1	5	185	191
Olague, Rafael (Major)	15th Cavalry Regiment	1	6	150	157
	16th Rural Corps	1	6	150	157
	24th Infantry Battalion			90	90
Hernández, Serafín R. (Colonel)	36th Auxiliary Infantry Battalion	1	6	200	207
Torres, Esteban (1st CPT)	1st Artillery Regiment		3	28	31
	(two 75-mm. Saint Chamond Mondragóns)				
	Victoria Battalion			75	75
	Volunteers of Santiago Papasquiaro			50	50
Vega Roca, Rafael (Major)	Social Defense	1		250	251
					1,292
Constitutionalists (estimated):					
Pereyra Sr., Orestes	Pereyra Brigade				1,000
Arrieta, Mariano (Colonel)	Guadalupe Victoria Brigade				1,000
Urbina, Tomás (Colonel)	Morelos Brigade				1,000
Contreras, Calixto (Colonel)	Juárez of Durango Brigade				3,000
					6,000

Table 1.6 Second Battle of Durango City Troop Strengths

Inside the city Brigadier Antonio M. Escudero had at his disposal an estimated 900 Federals as well as another 375 men of the state forces, in round numbers. Not present were Cheché Campos and his Colorados, who had not been well-received in Durango City and therefore returned to Torreón. Escudero placed his men in sixteen strong points around the perimeter of the city: 150 men and two Madsen light machine guns at the sanctuary and hill of Guadalupe, 130 men on San Diego hill, 108 men in the slaughterhouse and Rancho de Zataráin, 140 men at Rancho de Granados /cemetery/hippodrome, 190 men in the south (the artillery and an infantry support of 100 men in Rancho de la Ciénaga), 142 on Los Remedios Hill (which overlooks and dominates the plaza), 120 men spread along the Ojo de Agua-Fortín Olague-Hospital line, and thirty-five men in the workshops of San José. The remaining Federals he placed in reserve while the state troops occupied the more solid buildings inside the city: the Santa Ana and San José churches, the statehouse, city hall, the penitentiary, and the cathedral.[19]

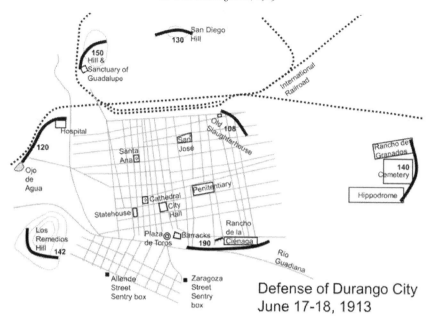

Defense of Durango City
June 17-18, 1913

Map 1.12

Although it was quite atypical for the battles of the Mexican Revolution, this one did resemble a mob attack, lacking military discipline and knowledge of tactics and featuring little coordinated effort. The Constitutionalist leaders departed Hacienda de Navacoyan to rejoin their commands and led them to their jump-off positions as dictated by the chief of operations (Urbina) during the afternoon, alerting the Federals to their locations in the process. The attack was to start at 11 p.m. with the agreed-upon signal being one illumination rocket. In order not to confuse each other with the Huertistas, the Constitutionalists rolled up their right pant leg. Not even one minute past the appointed time the general gave the signal and the Constitutionalists opened fire and began to converge downtown.[20]

From the moment that the shooting started it was obvious that the fighting was more heated to the south and west than to the north and east, owing to the fact that Los Remedios Hill on the southwest side was the position most heavily defended by the Federals. Also from the start of the battle a fifth column went into action inside the city, shooting the Federal defenders in the back, and attacking the town hall and penitentiary, at which point Major Rafael Vega y Roca took eighty Social Defense troops to attempt to restore order. Riding out in the open, he presented an opportune target, and he was shot dead off his horse; his terrified troops immediately dispersed. All through the night and into the morning light the fighting continued with the shooting of cannons, the explosions of dynamite bombs that the Constitutionalists had in enormous quantities, the crack of rifle fire, and the shouting of men everywhere; slowly the Constitutionalists began advancing, closing in. Then the Constitutionalists began to threaten the south, attempting to capture the artillery there, which forced Escudero to commit his remaining reserve to that area. By the morning of the eighteenth the attack intensified, with the Constitutionalists taking Los Remedios Hill around 9 a.m.; the forts at Ojo de Agua and Olague on the northwest side fell to a rear attack by the townsfolk a short time later, and inside the city the citizens began sacking the commercial enterprises.[21]

Around ten in the morning it was noticed that the Federals were no longer returning fire from this or that position and they were only still putting up a resistance on the Sanctuary of Guadalupe side. While the Social Defense continued to hold firm in many positions, principally those on the north and east side, the Federals had rallied to their barracks. With his ammunition nearing exhaustion Escudero had decided to abandon the city and save what men he could; he ordered his Federals to immediately organize to evacuate the plaza. When some Social Defense jefes came to ask what was going on with these arrangements he simply told them to return to their posts and hold back the enemy, evading the question while he abandoned the plaza with his Federals. Others said he confessed that he was going to evacuate the plaza and told the volunteers to get away as best they could, basically declaring every man for himself. Further resistance was useless and some volunteers decided to accompany General Escudero and the Federals, while other factions quickly exited the city through the side of the railroad that leads to the large plains to the east, and still others remained behind to test their luck.[22]

Major Pazuengo was there on the east side, where the Federals chose to attempt their breakout. For a while the fighting grew fierce, since they proposed to break the siege lines at all cost. The Federals also surprised Pereyra's men at Hacienda de Dolores and San Juan de Avila, which resulted in a desperate, open-field struggle from 12:30 to 4 p.m., when the Constitutionalists physically could no longer fight because their exhausted horses had begun falling dead from exposure to the sun. It goes without saying that cadavers, as many Federal as Constitutionalist and members of the Social Defense, sowed the fields on the east side between Hacienda de San Martín Navacoyan and Rancho Tepetate and the surrounding area. Two prominent hacendados from Durango City, Don Emilio Bracho and Miguel Lozaya, perished there adding to their number, but Escudero finally succeeded in breaking out.[23]

Inside the city the archbishop personally proposed to guarantee Urbina's safety by inviting him to get into his automobile and accompany him into the plaza. Urbina accepted and was followed by his staff and the rest of the forces. Upon arriving downtown, however, they took fire from the rooftops and balconies of the main houses of the wealthy, which put the archbishop in danger with Urbina's forces since they surmised the whole affair to be a trick. Upon arriving at the statehouse Urbina ordered the archbishop taken to the penitentiary while he investigated. In reality, many Federals did not even know that Escudero had quit the town, and they continued fighting from rooftops and church towers until after nightfall, when the Constitutionalists finally subdued them.[24]

Many members of the Social Defense were apprehended. Others turned themselves in voluntarily, and since they had fought even harder than the Federals many Constitutionalists wanted them shot. Yet only two prisoners were executed, and that took place inside the penitentiary three days after the taking of the city: Federal Irregular Colonel Serafín Hernández, who allegedly had been cruel and murderous while campaigning throughout the state; and the Commander of Rurales in the state, Felipe Muñoz, who had been in charge of rounding up and arresting the Maderistas in the city for the "Usurper" Huerta. The Constitutionalists also sought out one of the principal defenders of Huertismo, Colonel Ignacio Morelos Zaragoza, but failed to locate him. They later learned that he had hidden in the Colegio Marista before escaping.[25]

Instead of executing the Social Defense members, Urbina pardoned them and imposed upon them hefty fines, which were allocated according to what each could pay based on information that the prisoners themselves provided. Urbina also imposed a forced loan on the banks based on what they had on hand and posted guards to prevent the Social Defense prisoners from withdrawing any money to pay their fines.[26] Why? Because Urbina wanted all the cash in the banks and denying the prisoners access to their bank accounts forced them to cough up whatever they had squirreled away in their homes for a rainy day. Urbina collected one million pesos from the banks, commercial houses, and the cathedral for use in his upcoming campaigns, not to mention the prisoners' fines.[27]

Those Huertistas who escaped capture scattered in several directions. General Escudero's defeated column, traveling with ousted Governor Jesús Perea, sought to reach the Central Railroad (since the Durango-Torreón Railroad was destroyed for long stretches), taking a course for San Miguel del Mezquital. A few days later after a tortuous march they entered into the district of San Juan de Guadalupe and then Mancha Station on the Central Railroad. There Escudero reported in to General Bravo who ordered him to embark on a train for Torreón. Another column of the Huertista escapees, composed of the members of the Social Defense, continued on to Zacatecas over the Rancho Grande road, but they committed the imprudence of sending notice to the area ranches to have food ready for them. When the news reached Constitutionalist General Pánfilo Natera in Abrego, he sent a force to intercept them. Catching them in Dos Hermanas, the Constitutionalists killed some and took others prisoner, including a hacendado named Ávila, while the rest escaped to Zacatecas and from there headed for Mexico City. Some Federal cavalry commanded by Major Carlos Rodríguez also managed to reach Torreón by taking backroads and detours, and still other Huertistas fled to Mazatlán, Sinaloa. With such a large number of the Federals defeated at Durango City arriving in Torreón the public soon learned of the enormous disaster suffered by the government and "formed a thousand conjectures, granting the Constitutionalists a numerical magnitude far from" reality, according to one local journalist. In Mexico City the leading Huertistas of Durango also contributed to the wild speculation. They blamed General Escudero for the loss of the plaza for not having executed Maderista civilians and then selling the plaza to the revolutionaries for unspecified thousands of pesos, charges for which he had to stand trial. Had he not been a close friend of Secretary of War Blanquet, Escudero opined, they might have succeeded in having him shot. What no one can deny is that the Federal casualties had indeed been staggering, exceeding 50 percent, while Constitutionalist casualties have never been recorded. The explanation for the Federal defeat was simple: too few men defending a widened perimeter, especially in the dark at the battle's opening.[28]

The Federals never again occupied Durango City.

SACKING AND BURNING

After taking possession of the Federals' barracks and resting the horses, Major Pazuengo headed for downtown where he saw the best clothing and food stores sacked and set ablaze. The soldiers from the various brigades were mixed in together, and even though they all knew who Pazuengo was, and would have recognized the other jefes, too, "it was almost impossible for the jefes to restore order" among the rioting citizens, and none dared to try. Pazuengo went looking for the top commanders and ran into General Domingo Arrieta on San Juan de Dios Street where he told him about what he had seen going on downtown. Arrieta replied: "it is best that you go home, they just

wounded Colonel Arriola and I also escaped being shot up by my own compañeros, so let us leave things in this condition; let us see in the morning
at a very good hour with a few of your best people and others to whom I
will appeal if we can firmly bring to order this people of Durango, who are
the ones bringing shame on us."[29] Arrieta added, "take good notice that our
soldiers are not the ones doing the sacking, and all it would take is to stroll
through the barracks and tell them to collect all the articles that the looters
passing by are carrying on orders from high command, but do not take them
prisoner because we will not find a place to lock up so many people." Taking
this as an order, Pazuengo took a tour through some barracks and enlisted the
aid of the soldiers there. By the following day most of the soldiers billeted in
the barracks had accumulated great quantities of merchandise, of every kind,
some of which was returned to the owners who claimed their property while
the troops kept the rest.[30]

One theory of events that quickly gained currency maintained that
the commercial houses of Castillo, Daessele, "La Suiza," and "La Francia
Maritima" had not been burned down by revolutionaries, or even the townsfolk, but rather by the owners or their clerks, who had intentionally set the
stores ablaze in order to collect an indemnification. In a similar manner, the
Constitutionalists blamed the sackings on the town's citizens, who capitalized
on the disorder created by the various columns taking the city by fire and
sword.[31]

EMERGENCE OF A POPULAR MILITARISM

After the battle, Urbina headed for Torreón to try to capture that town along
with Contreras and Pereyra. Mariano Arrieta went back to western Durango
and then crossed over the Sierra Madre Occidental into Sinaloa with one
thousand men to operate with Constitutionalists in that state, while Domingo
Arrieta garrisoned the state capital with about five hundred men, assuming
the position of Military Commander of the Plaza.[32] Engineer Pastor Rouaix
became the governor of Durango, an appointment that Major Pazuengo
opposed, although not because he had anything against Rouaix personally;
rather, he reflected the growing popular militarism of yet one more future
Conventionist: "Thus the Government was settled, but I want to make clear
that I am not a supporter in times of revolution of appointing civilian authorities that cannot make themselves respected and it is preferable to just
appoint military chiefs who take charge of the situation and respond without
hindrances or formulas of any kind to keep the order and dictate the measures
that the needs of the moment demand."[33]

Chihuahua

At the beginning of June, Villa decided to move into Northwest Chihuahua in order to more easily obtain supplies from the Constitutionalist jefes in Sonora for the outfitting of his brigade, with the ultimate goal of attacking and capturing Ciudad Juárez. Additionally, since all the other major commanders had locked up their own area of operations Villa wanted to go where he could recruit without any competition among the military colonies where he had connections and where there were no other leading former Maderistas in the area. Accordingly, on June 5 he abandoned Camargo and ordered Maclovio Herrera, Manuel Chao, and Trinidad Rodríguez to harass the Federals in the south; Hernández was to interdict the rails between Escalón and Ortiz in order to block traffic south of Chihuahua City, where General Mercado had received command of the Federal Division of the North. General Rábago had been fired for having the twin defects, in Huerta's opinion, of being too soft and having ties to Félix Díaz to boot. Villa's trajectory took him first to Naica (forty kilometers distant), Hacienda Santa Gertrudis (about halfway between Naico and Satevó), Satevó where they rested a day, and then Santa Isabel, and finally San Andrés. On June 11 his budding brigade left for Bustillos (twenty-five kilometers west of San Andrés), which it occupied for a few days with the horses stabled in the slaughterhouse of the hacienda and the jefes and officers staying in the rooms of the main house.[34] The next day Villa ordered Colonel Toribio Ortega to begin mobilizing from his base of operations at Ojinaga toward Ciudad Juárez in order to cooperate in the taking of that important border city.[35]

BUSTILLOS JUNE 13

With his brigade still encamped at Hacienda Bustillos, at 3 p.m. on June 13 the Villista bugles suddenly started blowing "boots and saddles." Those with horses mounted up and in combination with the infantry formed a line perpendicular to the railroad running from the rails to Hacienda Bustillos. A train appeared coming from the west and began to disgorge Federals of the 33rd Infantry Battalion and Orozquista volunteers commanded by "the old man," Colonel Jesús Mancilla, who deployed on a firing line opposite the Constitutionalists. About fifteen hundred meters from the hacienda the Federals opened fire on some of Villa's men who were mounted, and shortly thereafter the combat became generalized. Villa then ordered his men to take up positions behind the low stone walls on either side of the railroad, and the Federals similarly took cover behind some adobe structures and placed a machine gun next to the station and their trains. Then a train that Villa had sent to burn railroad bridges beyond Santa Isabel returned bringing another fifty revolutionaries; Villa ordered the returning train hurled at the lead Federal locomotive to disable it. The amount of fire from both sides was intense. Another Federal train then appeared from the west and unloaded more soldiers, who quickly deployed on line. By now the Federals had about five hundred men in the fight, but it was not enough, and they began to yield ground. Finally, they gathered up their wounded, loaded on the trains, and retreated back to their post at Cusihuiriáchic, leaving behind a train engine, an express car, and fifty-four dead, with the wounded being carried off aboard the retreating trains. The battle probably had developed as a meeting engagement while Mancilla was in the process of moving his command to Chihuahua City. Villa suffered one dead and seven wounded. The battle report for Bustillos was the first one that Villa submitted to the First Chief as a Constitutionalist general. For this inconclusive action Mancilla received a promotion to general.[36]

Chihuahua City

After Villa left to head north, the remaining Constitutionalists in the south decided to increase the pressure on Chihuahua City. Colonel Maclovio Herrera's people mobilized from Jiménez and Parral while Hernández's came up from Camargo, for a total of thirteen hundred men. Herrera's men went to Mápula and thence to Los Charcos while Hernández headed to Aldama. The Constitutionalists approached the Federals' positions in those locations and exchanged fire, but did not assault because they did not have enough men. Instead, they wanted to wait for the return of Villa with Ortega. But one day the Federals surprised a Constitutionalist detachment in Santa Eulalia commanded by one of Herrera's officers. Some escaped while the rest were captured and executed.[37]

Meanwhile in Aldama, Hernández with the three hundred men of his column experienced a pleasant surprise. Federal Second Captain Margarito Gómez defected to the Constitutionalists in Aldama with two Rexers, 18,000 rounds, and personnel trained to use them. In response, on July 5 the Federal commander of the Division of the North sent Colonel Manuel Landa with about seven hundred troops composed of men from the colonel's own 7th Regiment and some Colorado irregulars to dislodge the Constitutionalists from Aldama. Hernández learned of the column's approach and prepared to receive them, positioning his people in the nearby sierra. The next day Hernández's men began exchanging fire with the Federal advance forces and then later the battle became generalized. The Federals tried to gain the defilade just in front of Aldama, but were repulsed with great losses, many being victims of Gómez's Rexers. Twice the Federals tried to deliver a cavalry charge to capture the guns but had to retreat in the face of overwhelming firepower. Seeing the impossibility of prevailing, the Federals began to abandon the field and the Constitutionalists counterattacked, taking two machine guns and a good number of prisoners.[38]

Unable to defeat even the most minor of Constitutionalist commands, the Federals in Chihuahua City soon found themselves in a loose siege, cut off from the rest of the nation. The state capital quickly began to run short of foodstuffs causing the Federals to declare martial law, institute an 8 p.m. curfew, and forbid citizens to leave the city.[39] As Landa left to attack Hernández on July 5, General Mercado sent a message full of anguish to the Secretary of War:

> I am honored to communicate to you that the enemy, numbering at least 3,500, is located immediate to this plaza. On a daily basis I am receiving the strangest demands from the most advanced posts, which I have made known to the defense; but if this situation is prolonged indefinitely it will be made unbearable, since the most basic necessities have been already consumed; I have pay up to the 10th of this month, that [money] existing in the banks and the State Treasury having been exhausted. I urgently need any force from the south to advance overland, since the railroad is ineffective. The bandit Villa near Ciudad Juárez with 2,000 men. At the moment they all unite to attack Ciudad Juárez it will find itself in a difficult situation. Very respectfully, General in Chief, Salvador R. Mercado.[40]

The Secretary of War responded to Mercado's appeal by informing him that Pascual Orozco, Jr., was on the way with his column of Colorados from Torreón.[41]

VILLA'S MOVEMENT NORTH

Villa's column left Bustillos with his wounded aboard two trains and the rest of his troops following mounted in two columns, one on either side of the rails, to arrive at San Antonio de los Arenales and camp at Casa Colorada. Early on June 16 the brigade continued to Los Pedernales, passing through the notorious Malpaso Canyon to stop in Hacienda del Rosario (La Junta), where it gained possession of three more trains. With five trains total the brigade transported more than one thousand men to Madera Station. On June

18 the trains left for the mountains, passing through the long tunnel at Las Cumbres to stop in Cuevitas Station, where they held up because of a burnt bridge. The next day they arrived at Pearson.[42] On the same day Francisco Villa entered Namiquipa to the shouts of "¡Viva Villa!" as everyone turned out to witness the great warrior.[43]

Casas Grandes

Having collected the forces that his agents had recruited from Namiquipa, who would become a core group of the Villa Brigade, General Villa continued north. By June 20, he stood with his men before Casas Grandes, occupied by forces belonging to Colorado General José Inés Salazar. Far Northwest Chihuahua—Ascensión and Casas Grandes—had always been Orozquista in sympathies, and many Orozquista generals came from or operated in the region: Emilio P. Campa, the Quevedos, Jerónimo R. Azcárate, José Inés Salazar, and others. As Villa himself remarked, "those people were pure Colorado." No matter, he needed to occupy the region as a point of transit for war materiel along the Colorado contraband pipeline between Columbus, New Mexico, and Palomas, Chihuahua.[44]

As he approached Casas Grandes General Villa learned that brothers Silvestre and Arturo Quevedo were in command of the garrison there, so he ordered his men to deploy in open order and advance on the town. At that point he received a communication from the town's garrison saying that they would hand over the plaza without resistance. Villa knew it could be a stratagem and told his men to be prepared. As expected, at about 11 a.m. when the Constitutionalists had advanced to about forty meters from the town, the plaza erupted with rifle fire and all the Constitutionalists hit the dirt, since they were out in the open across flat terrain and made perfect targets. The Orozquistas were ensconced in two solid defensive positions, one behind adobe, stone, and sand, and the other in the barracks with firing positions on the rooftop. Shooting lasted all the rest of the day as the Constitutionalists prepared to make a night assault.[45]

The night was frightfully stormy and, except for occasional lightning, which the Constitutionalists made use of to charge the Colorado positions, pitch black. At 9 p.m. Major Santiago Ramírez led the assault against the first position and using dynamite bombs dislodged the Colorados from that position as the sound of thunder and explosions echoed into the night. Meanwhile, others attacked in different directions, the yells of pain from the wounded and the cries of enthusiasm from the attackers mixing with the howling wind and the thunder. The Colorados exited their trenches and the corrals shooting and yelling. They put up the stiffest resistance in the station, where Villa believed that his men had killed Colonel Jerónimo R. Azcárate and his captain son. The confusion of the combatants in the shadows was terrific as the soldiers ran through the streets yelling, ""Who goes there?" only to be answered with "Villa!" Many Orozquistas saved their lives in this manner.[46]

After two hours of combat the Colorados, having lost forty killed and sixty men taken prisoner, yielded the plaza to the Constitutionalists. Villa had all the prisoners, "two times a traitor," (first under Orozco in 1912 and now under Huerta) executed by lining them up in groups of three and shooting with one round passing through each group in order to conserve ammunition. Ontiveros confirmed that in the light of day "the sight was frightful. In the streets, plazas, and fortifications there were bodies mutilated by bombs, skulls burst to pieces, gray matter incrusted in the walls where the shootings had taken place, and everywhere blood trails … Death with all its horrors and consequences." Silvestre Quevedo, whom Ontiveros described as a man "of all political hues, Magonista, Maderista, Vazquista, Orozquista, and Huertista, had unfortunately come out only wounded" and along with Major (not Colonel) Jerónimo R. Azcárate, his first captain son Jerónimo Jr., and the remaining Colorado survivors succeeded in escaping to Ciudad Juárez where they reported the outcome of the battle in all its gory detail.[47]

On June 24 Villa's column continued north through the Mormon settlement Colonia Dublán (two kilometers north of Nuevo Casas Grandes) and Corralitos to arrive in Ascensión where Villa then sent Juan Dozal to Palomas (opposite Columbus, New Mexico) to pick up the trains to Agua Prieta and propose a cattle-for-ammunition deal to Constitutionalist Colonel Plutarco Elías Calles. He also wanted Dozal to ask the Sonorans to lend him one thousand men so that he could take Ciudad Juárez. Once out of Chihuahua, however, Dozal abandoned the revolution and so Calles had to send the 35,000 rounds under escort by Porfirio Talamantes.[48]

With the ammunition from Sonora Villa could moderately supply his men, but shortly thereafter he had to send Majors Santiago Ramírez and Porfirio Talamantes with about three hundred men on a mission down to Casas Grandes to surprise the forces of Colonel Máximo Castillo. According to the historian General Sánchez Lamego, Colonel Máximo Castillo had led Villa's displacement northward with a vanguard of 200 men and, making contact with ninety-one men of the Salazar Brigade at Pearson Station (forty kilometers south of Nuevo Casas Grandes), had fought a short battle on June 11 that resulted in the deaths of fifteen Colorados, including their commander, a colonel by the name of Rojas, and another twenty wounded, while Castillo only lost two killed.[49] But Ontiveros said nothing of the sort happened; he maintained that Castillo had been part of Salazar's brigade until the Colorados joined with Huerta. At that point he separated from them to operate on his own account, but his men began deserting him until he only had about one hundred left, and now he had taken up residence in Casas Grandes. Ramírez and Talamantes attacked the town and easily defeated Castillo's men and captured a Colonel (possibly Juan) Parra, whom they shot. They pardoned the rest of their prisoners.[50]

Villa made use of his time in Ascención to also begin training his men, accepting the services of Juan N. Medina, who had come from Ojinaga with thirty men. A former Federal sub-lieutenant of cavalry, Medina had served a decade earlier during the Yaqui wars, but repulsed by the barbarity unleashed on the indigenes during those campaigns, he resigned his commission for humanitarian reasons. His social consciousness resembled that of another ex-Federal soon to join Villa, Felipe Ángeles.[51] Villa valued the martial skills and grit of his Federal adversaries who "exceeded many revolutionary men in courage; or rather, they not only knew how to organize armies for battles, but they also knew how to expose their life in a fight for the people's cause." Previously he had praised General Juan J. Navarro's conduct in the 1911 Battle of Ciudad Juárez, marveling at the Federal general's coolness and ability to maintain his men's morale and composure in a hopeless situation, calling him the "undeniably brave defender of the plaza." Now, whenever Medina was the officer of the day, he told his men, "tonight we can sleep with our shoes off," in an attempt to get his men to emulate the ex-Federal officer's observance of the "services of campaign" (that is, procedures), especially with regard to security. Medina served as a kind of Baron Von Steuben for Villa's nascent brigade for the month and a half that it remained in Ascención, with many services of campaign starting to be observed after his arrival.[52]

Villa also tended to diplomatic matters in Ascención, receiving envoys Juan Sánchez Azcona and Alfredo Breceda sent by the First Chief of the Revolution, Venustiano Carranza. Villa had harbored reservations about extending recognition to Carranza, and felt pangs of regret even more strongly when he found out that the First Chief had it in mind to make him a subordinate of Obregón. Villa believed the revolutionaries of each state operated of their own accord and therefore trying to arrange a military hierarchy that presupposed overall coordination amounted to nonsense, which at this point in the war was true. However, he had willingly accepted a commission in Carranza's Constitutionalist Army in May, and he was starting to realize the military benefits of cooperating with Carranza and the Sonorans. Therefore, he agreed to second the Plan de Guadalupe and recognize the First Chief, conditional on the continued patriotic posture of the latter, of course. He also asked Carranza's representatives for one additional favor. In his opinion the revolutionaries in Sonora did not know how to employ artillery in their campaigns, so if there were any guns not being used he asked to please have them forwarded to his command.[53]

After a month and half in Ascensión, deep in Colorado territory, the Villa Brigade was finally ready to begin operations, but its commander had given up his hopes of attacking Ciudad Juárez and instead ordered Ortega to move in a southwesterly direction with his regiment and rendezvous with the rest of the brigade.

Toribio Ortega and Northern Operations

Maderista Colonel Toribio Ortega had been operating on his own account in northeastern Chihuahua ever since the beginning of Huerta's coup. At that time Ortega left Cuchillo Parado to go interview with the Federal jefe de las armas in Ojinaga, a first captain of artillery by the name of Alberto Ortiz who asked Ortega if he was prepared to recognize the new government. Ortega said that he would never side with murder and returned to Cuchillo Parado to assemble his men, determined to attack Ojinaga. Captain Ortiz also tried to get irregular Colonel José de la Cruz Sánchez to support Huerta, but that colonel remained noncommittal. In the meantime, Sánchez's second-in-command, Lieutenant Colonel José Licón, assembled the two hundred irregulars in the plaza and told all who intended not to recognize Huerta's government to take one step forward. As if on command, all moved forward. Apprised of this display, Sánchez ordered all the rifles collected, and he turned them into the Mexican consul in Marfa, Texas, and retired to private life. Sánchez had always been an inept operator who lacked martial vigor, and in light of events it was probably all he could do; he would not fight for or against Huerta, but his actions had virtually handed the first entrepôt over to the revolution.[54]

When Ortega returned with his men to Ojinaga he found the place devoid of any opposing force, since Captain Ortiz wisely had crossed over into Presidio, Texas. The possession of this minor border town provided the Constitutionalists with a point of entry for arms and war materiel, and an early source of funds from duties charged on cattle exported to the United States. Ortega began raising funds to buy war materiel and made contact with the First Chief, who told him to reach out to Villa and place himself at the general's orders. Straightaway Ortega sent a courier to request orders from Villa.[55]

On April 30 Ortega received a report from Cuchillo Parado that the Huertista Eduardo Armendáriz had appeared in Coyame, some twenty-one kilometers away from the former town. Ortega knew that Lieutenant

Colonel Eleuterio Hermosillo was headed in that direction sent by Villa so he ordered Major Crispín Juárez to take ten men and catch up with Colonel Hermosillo and agree on a plan to attack Coyame. On May 1 at 6 a.m. the Constitutionalists delivered the assault, attacking the hills Ciénaga Chica, El Centinela, and La Cal. They fought all day without being able to dislodge the Huertistas, but then the next day at 8 o'clock a definitive push resulted in the capture of the town, forcing the Huertistas to flee in disbandment and leaving behind some dead, wounded, six prisoners, rifles, ammunition, and mounts.[56]

Ortega then got busy trying to get arms and ammunition for his command. He bought two Colt machine guns and fifty rifles from the United States, but Lieutenant Colonel Porfirio Ornelas, who was sent to get the materiel across the border, was only able to smuggle one Colt across. Around this same time Colonel Ortega crossed into Presidio, Texas, where Huertista spies denounced him for breaking neutrality laws and got him arrested by American soldiers and sent to jail in Marfa, Texas. Eight days later he was released on bail set at $7,000. The day after he arrived back in Ojinaga, which would have been in mid-June, orders came down from Villa to mobilize to Guadalupe, some sixty-five kilometers away from Ciudad Juárez.[57]

Ortega led a column of 350 men to go meet up with Villa and eventually attack Ciudad Juárez, crossing the most desolate and punishing desert, utterly devoid of vegetation. They passed through several small ghost hamlets where the only evidence of previous life was red adobe hovels. The distance from Ojinaga to Guadalupe was about 260 kilometers. The last day of June, the column arrived in the vicinity of Guadalupe, and Ortega ordered First Captain Celso Rayos with 100 men to lead an attack on San Ignacio while the rest of the forces hit Guadalupe. The next day, July 1, Ortega's Constitutionalists took both towns, wiping out the whole Federal picket in San Ignacio and quite nearly doing the same in Guadalupe, taking some prisoners there.[58]

In Ascensión Villa bought ammunition from the United States that he had delivered to Ortega in Guadalupe. One delivery of 50,000 rounds fell into Salazar's hands in Rancho Zaragoza because of some miscommunication between the escorts of the ammunition and Ortega's men sent to collect it, but all the other deliveries, including one for 150,000 cartridges, arrived without incident.[59] Ortega remained there outside Ciudad Juárez until called by Villa to turn south at the beginning of August.

Huerta Loses the War in Less than Six Months

By the end of June the Constitutionalists had control of the whole border, except Ciudad Juárez and Nuevo Laredo, and the only offensives that the

Federal Army had undertaken had either stalled, in Coahuila and Chihuahua; ended in disaster, in Sonora; or had failed to even mobilize, in Tamaulipas. As previously stated, General Sánchez Lamego thought that at this point in time the Federals had already lost the war, and several systemic deficiencies in the Federal Army's war machine and situation support his thesis. The Federal Army: had low troop levels in proportion to extent of country; lacked military cartography that would have permitted a logical strategy in the face of rapidly developing local uprisings and the Federal Army's ignorance of the geography in the North; and needed to garrison key towns and provincial capitals to confirm the government's control and thus legitimacy. This last point contained the most pertinent reason for Huerta's defeat. The imperative to project the illusion of normalcy on the international stage for an illegitimate government under heavy attack by dissenting forces within the country prevented the Federal Army from going fully operational, and therefore further impeded the forging of a coherent strategy. Fighting revolutionaries in straight-up conventional warfare amounts to tacitly admitting them as equals, militarily and politically; such an admission validates the insurgents' cause and results in political defeat. For example, while many historians believe that the Tet Offensive in Vietnam was operationally a military victory for the United States, it was a political, and hence strategic, loss.[60]

In order to effectively campaign in the environment of revolutionary Mexico, one needed to be able to take advantage of mobility afforded by trains and horses, the former providing speed and the latter flexibility. Indeed the Mexican Revolution has been referred to as the War of Horses and Trains. Yet for the Federals the nation's railroad system proved both a blessing and a curse. Porfirio Díaz's cabal, the "railroaders," brought the iron horses to Mexico in great numbers in the nineteenth century. Railroads and telegraphs extended the reach of central government, providing formidable assets for expeditious responses to local uprisings. However, the railroad system also represented a highly visible sector of state patrimony and military value that had to be protected. The two combat arms—artillery and infantry—most dependent upon the new mode of transportation and most capable of efficiently defending the trains came to dominate in the Federal Army, to the neglect of the more expensive and versatile cavalry. Thus, the bulk of the Huerta's soldiers remained in garrison and tied to the rails precisely when they should have been massing to maneuver.[61]

As an example, Federal General Rubio confirmed that the Federal Division of the North had five thousand infantrymen, five batteries of artillery, six batteries of machine guns, and a small portion of cavalry with pathetic mounts, which he blamed on Madero's refusal to provide remounts. As a result of its very organization, the Federal Division of the North remained ineffective in Chihuahua owing to the extent and geography of the state: a great quantity of artillery made it inappropriate to maneuver in the region, and the lack of cavalry made it very vulnerable to revolutionary dragoons. But one Constitutionalist blamed the sorry state of the Federal cavalry not on Madero, but on the malfeasance of cavalry officers, saying "that the horses of these corps were generally incomplete [with respect to authorized numbers] or in atrocious conditions because the jefes used to eat more straw than the beasts, a notorious fact which never was remedied."[62]

Federal Cavalry Major Juan Torrea offered a more general condemnation of the Federal Army's cavalry department: "In the higher ranks, generals and jefes without any vocation or fondness [for the army], who knew little or nothing about the arm had led the Department of Cavalry, and this lack of knowledge did not stop there at the Secretary of War, but went [down] to the upper commands of units organized for maneuver or to march off to campaigns who in the great majority did not know—when the time arrived—how to utilize the cavalry, and most of the time limited themselves to moving it in the mistaken concept of a mounted infantry with special arms and instructions." Problems continued with company-grade officers. Many captains had spent years and years in the role of adjutant or commander of squadrons without the least aspirations for promotion. They were very happy to occupy their post, convinced that they would not advance any further in their career because they might have performed poorly at a lower rank. There was no law of elimination and, because of neglect by the departments of the various arms, those who did not perform in their positions continued to keep them. Subpar officers just collected their paychecks, stood in front of their horses at inspection, performed poorly, and evaded whenever possible the routine duties of garrison life.[63]

The garrisoning of soldiers at various points along the rails and in the hinterlands gave rise to at least two more problems. The constant cycle of detaching to garrison duty, recollecting for short-term operations, and then detaching again broke down unit cohesion. Battalion-size combat teams, or "columns" in the vernacular, of Federals often comprised a patchwork of elements from five to ten different battalions, regiments, or corps with a predictable result: the atomization of organic units prevented the formation of any esprit de corps. Almost as bad, on those occasions where an irregular jefe, as the highest ranking officer present, took charge over regular army officers, professional resentments and jealousies surfaced. Finally, infantry scattered throughout the country that could be loaded onto trains and rushed to hotspots during periodic disturbances became isolated and annihilated during the general mobilization of revolutionaries in 1913. On campaign, fear of being cut off from supplies and reinforcements turned railroads into both a spatial and temporal vulnerability, since their constant repair delayed the Federal rates of advance, especially during the spring and summer 1913 offensive in Coahuila.

The Federals curiously embraced the rails even as they bemoaned the impropriety of a force composition so lacking in horses. Instead of mounting their own infantry, they recruited mounted irregulars, overwhelmingly Colorados, with the result that Federals became dependent on their erstwhile enemies to take the fight to their present foes. Constitutionalist General Juan Barragán Rodríguez observed that the Federals, "no matter how powerful their columns might be, never operated outside of the rail lines, while the leaders of revolutionary origin, even those like Argumedo and Orozco ... undertook real campaigns, realizing deeds of great significance, without mattering to them the distance from their base of operations."[64] Generals Caraveo, Benjamín Argumedo, and Juan Andrew Almazán all agreed that the Federal regulars left "the most difficult and dangerous tasks" to the irregulars, and Argumedo, in particular, developed a knack for arriving just in the nick of time to save the Federals. Imperious Federals willing to risk the lives of their irregular allies caused friction in the heat of battle, and no doubt decreased the combat effectiveness of the whole.[65] In contrast, the Constitutionalists raised ample units of dragoons (only Sonora had significant infantry) to enhance cross-country mobility, initiative, and on limited occasions to deliver a powerful thrust to strike moral terror in the enemy when employed in mounted charges.[66]

On those occasions when Huerta did authorize offensive operations he compounded his relative lack of troops by insisting on taking the offensive in multiple military zones simultaneously. Often the Federal columns were inferior in number to the revolutionaries, a disadvantage that he overlooked possibly because he thought his regulars superior in quality—which they were not. The Federal Army that Huerta inherited from Porfirio Díaz reflected the ossification of the former regime. With many officers over fifty years of age, it proved excessively aged at the highest levels for vigorous campaigning and much too accustomed to garrison life and ingrained in regulations, but often not up to date in the latest tactics, especially as regards the ubiquitous auxiliary and irregular officers. Meanwhile, the revolutionary officer corps consisted of energetic country boys, generally younger than forty years of age. As the Federal losses mounted with divisions destroyed or pushed into the United States where the authorities disarmed and confined them, the Constitutionalists actually started to experience an edge in battle experience over the hastily formed replacement units of the Federal Army. Highly motivated and operating on home territory with all that implies as far as public sympathy, knowledge of the terrain, and intelligence, the Constitutionalists bested Huerta's regulars.

If indeed Sánchez Lamego's thesis was correct, then Pancho Villa played a rather limited role in the Constitutionalist victory. By the end of June, 1913, he had only directed one general action, at Conchos Station, with a majority of his troops being those that the First Chief had placed under his command. Removing prestige from Villa may have been just what Sánchez Lamego had in mind, however, since he came up in the post-revolutionary army of the 1920s and 1930s and clearly identified with the professionals of the Federal Army who suffered their most ignominious defeats at the hands of the Centaur of the North.

* * *

The fight for north central Mexico in the short time frame of March to June is notable for several reasons. First, on an operational level, the combat in those initial months did not resemble conventional maneuver warfare so much as a struggle for local predominance. Leaders defected with their Rurales or state Auxiliaries and fought Federals for towns and the main arteries. They made attempts against state capitals and key points on the railroad that stretched from the Center to Ciudad Juárez, delivering the lifeblood of Federal Army divisions in the North. As Federals sought to hold onto these points and clung to the rails, continuing in a constabulary mission instead of massing to carry out operations in the field, they allowed their meager forces to be spread thin, cut off, and annihilated in detail, dangled before the Constitutionalists like so much fruit ripe for the picking. In contrast, the Constitutionalists maintained absolute freedom of action and raised large numbers, especially in Durango, of enthusiastic and capable fighters, albeit undisciplined ones, with youthful and energetic leaders who massed their forces and achieved unity of command.

Constitutionalist commanders also looked to the economic side of warfare, with revolutionaries in Durango seeing to the planting of crops for upcoming campaigns and resorting to forced loans. In Chihuahua Villa broached a cattle-for-ammunition deal with his counterparts in Sonora. Still, Americans put a crimp on the Constitutionalists' importation of arms and ammunition, even arresting Colonel Toribio Ortega and necessitating measures of military economy such as the shooting of three Colorados at a time to conserve ammunition.

By the end of June 1913 the Constitutionalists held all the major north-ern ports of entry with the exception of Nuevo Laredo and Ciudad Juárez, having captured Ojinaga without firing a shot and taking Matamoros just days before the humiliating losses by the Federals of Durango City and Zacatecas. Federal casualties in the latter three battles had been staggering, mainly, it would appear, because the commanders had not agreed on signals or established communications in spite of the fact that Federal Army doctrine specifically called attention to this singular vulnerability associated with the defense of, and retreat from, plazas. Other key reasons for their reversals had been a shortage of Federals available to defend the nation's numerous strategic plazas; the fact that they continually set a defensive perimeter far too long for the number of available troops; the lack of unit cohesion as indicated by the hodge-podge of unit designations in even the smallest of forces; and because they had no cavalry to speak of, local commanders had to rely overwhelm-ingly on mounted irregulars and, more especially, on undependable and un-trained Social Defense volunteers. Moreover, commanders, such as Ramos at Matamoros and Bravo in Torreón, were excessively aged for active cam-paigning and/or unreliable, such as Federal Captain Margarito Gómez who defected to the Constitutionalists with machine guns, and the commanding general of the Federal Division of the North, General Rábago, whom Huerta dismissed for his questionable loyalties. The leading citizens of Durango like-wise harbored suspicions about General Escudero's allegiances, making public their allegations that he had sold the capital city to revolutionaries for untold thousands of pesos. In Escudero's opinion, only the timely appointment of his friend, General Aurelio Blanquet, to the position of secretary of war had spared him from a firing squad for losing Durango City.

In reality, an incoherent national strategy, lack of operational mobili-zation, and tactical ignorance, had been responsible for the Federals losing Durango and northern Zacatecas permanently, and they were reduced to op-erating along the Ciudad Juárez-Chihuahua City line in Chihuahua by June 30. Yet in July they would begin a coordinated campaign to capture Coahuila and Nuevo León and achieve some success, an indication that although the war may have been lost, it was far from over.

Five

The Federals Strike Back:
July–September, 1913

A Revamped Federal Officer Corps—Rural Police Corps Terminated—Changes to the Federal Tables of Organization—Generals Maass and Rubio Strike at Eastern Coahuila—Battles of Candela—Battle of Monclova—Federals Destroy Property of Constitutionalists—First Chief Heads for La Laguna—Cándido Aguilar and the Constitutionalist Division of the Center—Battle of Torreón—Constitutionalist Leaders Return to their Area of Operations—Aguilar Takes a Course for the Huasteca—First Chief to Sonora—Cheché Campos Executed—Rubio Accomplishes Mission—Battle of Las Hermanas—González Abandons Coahuila—Orozco's Column Departs Torreón—Jiménez—Díaz Station—Camargo—Toribio Ortega and Ranchería Station—Silvestre Juárez's Cause—San Andrés—Wounded to and Ammunition from Sonora—Onward to Torreón

Reorganization in the Federal Army

In July and August, Huerta once again turned to writing decrees designed to mobilize his army and give it an edge. He had experienced some success with the pen early in his career when Porfirio Díaz had selected his outline for the organization of the General Staff in 1879, an honor which won the young graduate of the Colegio Militar a promotion to captain.[1] Perhaps he thought he could write his way to victory. He had already decreed an increase in the size of the army to 80,000 men and now he needed to provide it with leadership. Decree 442 dated July 3, 1913, facilitated the formation of new officers. Corps, battalion, and regimental commanders could make "cadets" of promising men over eighteen years of age and pay them two-thirds the salary of sub-lieutenants. Cadets were to train in "Garrison Schools," abbreviated training that embraced in summary form the same program of instruction imparted in the schools that churned out sub-lieutenants. Upon reaching the proper level of preparation, the colonels or jefes of the corps were to examine the cadets and, if they passed, recommend them to their commanding division general to commission them as sub-lieutenants. The Escuela Nacional de Aspirantes was no longer necessary and Article 3 of the decree eliminated it.[2]

The Colegio Militar also was impacted. Article 4 of Decree 442 abolished the Colegio Militar and replaced it with three institutions: the Preparatory Military School, the Professional Military School, and the Superior Military School. The preparatory curriculum was to last three years and provide for the "essentially practical" formation of sub-lieutenants for the three combat arms and engineers. The professional school, also three years in duration, would enroll officers who had already served one year in field command, exhibited a martial spirit, and had completed the preparatory program—either in the Preparatory Military School or in Garrison Schools. The Superior School offered a three-year program to educate officers for service on the General Staff, with first captain being the minimum rank accepted, and two years of field command and completion of professional and preparatory schools as prerequisites.[3]

As a short-term expedient, the decree provided for a transitory disposition: First, the students in the Escuela Nacional de Aspirantes were to report to the field, to the units that they had belonged to as cadets. Second, current students in the Colegio Militar were to continue there until September 15, taking the courses prescribed by regulation, with monthly grades replacing exams. The Seventh Year cadets were to go immediately to the field to finish their studies; the Third to Sixth Year cadets were to go into the field for a year with the rank of sub-lieutenant and then return to the Professional School later. Those cadets in their first and second years were directed to engage in the practical course from September 16 to December, then take a one month vacation, and then return in January, 1914, to the Preparatory School to complete the new program. Thus, Huerta pushed the Tacticals in their final year of study and all the Technicals from the Colegio Militar along with the students from the Escuela Nacional de Aspirantes into the field, with adverse consequences. Ill-prepared, immature, and bursting with the pretensions attendant to sons of the Colegio Militar, many officers ranging in age from sixteen to twenty years old would be leading men into combat for the first time, and they could not be counted on to render good service.[4]

The alumni of the Colegio Militar considered its replacement by the Preparatory Military School to be the highest act of betrayal by Huerta against his alma mater and punishment for its cadets remaining loyal to Madero during the Citadel cuartelazo. After September, it consisted of only 233 students, 166 of the first year and 67 of the second. The twenty-five student lieutenants and ninety Year 3-7 cadets comprised the Professional Military School until their graduation in September—they were not replaced and the school went dormant, although the faculty remained. The Superior Military School was a dead letter; it never came into existence.[5]

The most significant changes, however, applied directly to the combat arms. In the interest of "unity of command and action in military operations," on July 31 Huerta transferred all Rural Police Corps from the Secretary of Interior to the Secretary of War, upholding their "volunteer" status, and renaming them "Scout Corps" (*Cuerpos Exploradores*), each with a newly authorized strength of five hundred men; said transfer officially took effect on August 15.[6]

With Decree 449, Huerta again made the larger regiment, instead of the battalion, the main maneuver unit for the infantry, in order to accommodate a larger army. The battalion with its full complement of officers and staff had been Mexico's answer for an expansible army. Now each regiment would have one colonel, a lieutenant colonel, two majors (each in charge of one of the regiment's two battalions), and a staff of almost forty men along with forty more in the regimental band. On a peace footing each battalion would have four companies, each with three sections composed of six five-man squads commanded by a corporal. On a war footing, which Huerta placed the Army, the five-man squads doubled to ten men, raising the infantry regiment's total authorized strength to a whopping 1,840 men.[7] This new structure greatly reduced the officer-to-enlisted ratio for the new regiments, which somewhat attenuated the urgency for more officers, but it weighed heavily on non-commissioned officers, a perennial weakness in Mexican armies.

| 1913 Regulation Infantry Regiment (War Footing) | | | | | |
Unit	Commander	2nd in Command	Highest Enlisted	Men- Full Strength	Composed of
Regiment	Colonel	Lieutenant Colonel		1,840	2 Battalions and Staff*
Battalion	Major			864	4 Companies and Staff
Company	1st Captain	2nd Captain	1st Sergeant	216	Officers & 3 Sections
Section	Lieutenant	Sub-Lieutenant	2nd Sergeant	71	Officers & 2 Platoons
Platoon	2nd Sergeant			34	Platoon Chief & 3 Squads
Squad	Corporal			11	1 Corporal & 10 Riflemen

*Also includes Musicians, Regimental Reserve Company, two Machine Gun Sections, one Mounted Squad, and Staff, but does not include the "Depot" Company

| 1913 Regulation Cavalry Regiment (War Footing) | | | | | |
Unit	Commander	2nd in Command	Highest Enlisted	Men- Full Strength	Composed of
Regiment	Colonel	Lieutenant Colonel		739	5 Squadrons and Staff*
Squadron	1st Captain	2nd Captain	1st Sergeant	129	Officers, Staff & 2 Sections**
Section	Lieutenant	Sub-Lieutenant	2nd Sergeant	60	Officers & 3 Platoons
Platoon	2nd Sergeant			19	Platoon Chief & 2 Squads
Squad	Corporal			9	1 Corporal & 8 Troopers

*Also includes Regimental Musicians, Regimental Reserve Squadron, one Madsen Machine Gun Section, one Squad of Mounted Sappers, and Staff

**Includes two Assistants and four Musicians

Table 1.7

The cavalry underwent a less radical transformation, with the regiment being increased to about 565 men, mainly through the addition of musicians, a Madsen light-machine gun section, mounted sappers, staff, and a fifth short ("*en cuadro*"), squadron commanded by supernumerary "depot" officers. Huerta set the cavalry squad at six men, commanded by a corporal. But on a war footing the squad size increased to nine men and the fifth squadron expanded to normal strength to serve as the regiment's reserve, raising the authorized strength of each cavalry regiment to almost 750 men.[8] Additionally, he added one more squadron of Army Gendarmes; an additional Sapper Battalion, to be named the 2nd Sapper Battalion; and increased the size of the Invalid Corps in expectation of casualties from upcoming campaigning.[9] Also with an eye to impending offensives, Huerta created the "Valor y Abnegación" medal for anyone who fought a battle and did not otherwise receive recognition and the "Valor y Abnegación" Cross, which was gold for jefes and generals, silver for officers, and bronze for the troops.[10]

One final momentous change came with the issuing of Irregular Commissions, in addition to the Permanent and Auxiliary patents. At the beginning of the Huertista regime it was possible to speak officially of "irregular auxiliary" units, however, as more and more Irregular officers and units entered the service it would appear that there was an increasing effort to create a distinction between Auxiliary and Irregular units. The main difference between the two was in the level of discipline, with Auxiliaries possessing "regular discipline," whereas irregulars had "scant discipline."[11] In general terms, cavalry "regiments" raised after the 18th were Auxiliaries; the newer Irregular cavalry "corps" started over in numbering with the establishment of the 1st Irregular Cavalry Corps. Similarly, Auxiliary infantry was organized in battalions, whereas Irregular Infantry units were designated "corps"; unlike with the cavalry, Irregular infantry corps numbers were both high and low, beginning with the 1st Irregular Infantry Corps but with others apparently continuing the Auxiliary numbering scheme, such as the 52nd Irregular Infantry Corps. As stated above, according to decree number 449 of August 25, 1913, the Permanent and Auxiliary infantry units were re-designated "regiments," although in many cases they continued to be called "battalions," probably owing to customary usage and the fact that few grew to true regimental size. Finally, those jefes and officers who had belonged to the Rural Police Corps retained the ranking system of that organization (Comandante, Jefe del Detall, etc.) and were listed in the Federal Army Escalafón under the heading "Jefes and Officers belonging to the Scout Corps," although one still encounters references to army officers holding other patents assigned to "Rural Corps."

(In order to be consistent and avoid any confusion that might arise from referring to the same unit by different names, the formula "irregular auxiliary" will not be used in the text even though that might have been the unit name in the official reports. Every effort has been made to cull the various units according to their official status as Permanent and Auxiliary Regiments (Cavalry) and Battalions (Infantry), and Irregular (Cavalry and Infantry) and Rural/Scout Corps. Finally, although the Colorado generals had been granted Permanent commissions by the beginning of 1914, throughout the text these men and their units will continue to be regarded as "irregulars" according to their true nature.)

As these policy initiatives were being formulated and finalized in the summer, the Federal Army finally reached a point of preparedness to launch three columns into the North: General Pascual Orozco's to Chihuahua, Joaquín Maass' into Coahuila, and General Guillermo Rubio Navarrete's marching through Nuevo León.

The Federal Coahuila Campaign

As Federal Generals Maass and Rubio left Mexico City headed for Monterrey, Federal General Joaquín Téllez, who had replaced Trucy Aubert on the Monterrey-Laredo rail line, sent troops to clear revolutionaries out of Hacienda Mamulique and Bustamante in order to assure his lines of communication with Monterrey and then headed north to operate out of Nuevo Laredo.[12] General Maass planned to attack northward from Saltillo toward Monclova in order to secure the Saltillo-Piedras Negras line, and Rubio, instead of trying to recapture Matamoros as originally planned in Huerta's June war council, would secure and consolidate possession of the Monterrey-Laredo line. Maass' column took priority, since it had the mission to destroy the Constitutionalist forces in Monclova, but the belief by leading Constitutionalists that the two Federal columns intended to cooperate seems incorrect, at least initially, since Huerta made no such reference in his telegram to Rubio changing his mission. Huerta seemed to view the two columns as independent of each other and likewise separate from General Fernando González's Division of the Bravo since both columns reported directly to the Secretary of War, with the only exception being to obey "every order from division headquarters that redounds to the benefit of general service." Moreover, it seems clear that he deemed the reestablishment of traffic a higher priority than offensive operations, as future events would suggest.[13]

The two operations got off to a slow start as General Maass' column consisting of cavalry, irregular infantry, machine guns, and cannons, all told about 1,750 men, maintained a dilatory pace of advance from San Luis Potosí to Saltillo. That caused the Secretary of War to keep General Rubio's Federals from leaving Monterrey, just in case they might be needed to go to the aid of Saltillo in the event that it was attacked by the large party of revolutionaries rumored to be in the area. Rubio reported the adverse impact on morale caused by the large contingent of revolutionaries operating with impunity in northern Coahuila and swore that if allowed to advance he could take Monclova in three days. Ignoring him, on June 25 War told General Rubio he could begin operations toward Nuevo Laredo; his column wasted no time advancing rapidly northward to arrive in Golondrinas only two days later. The whole way Rubio begged for more men, especially from the Division of the Bravo whom he thought should garrison the railroad, and for permission to attack the revolutionaries in Candela.[14]

In June 1913, the Constitutionalists still had no battalions or brigades in Candela, just three corps commanded by lieutenant colonels Francisco Murguía, Teodoro Elizondo, and Alfredo Ricaut, reporting to Jesús Carranza. These corps had a total strength of three hundred men who possessed good mounts, but were short of ammunition and poorly armed, mostly with

.30-30s. Numerous future generals figured among the group, including Fortunato Maycotte, Fortunato Zuazua, Pablo González, Jr. (not a son of Colonel Pablo González), Heliodoro Pérez, José Santos, José V. Elizondo, Agustín Millán, and others. Carranza's men operated out of Candela over an extended radius of action, northwest to Lampazos, east to Salomé Botello, and southeast to Bustamante.[15] Exasperated with the revolutionaries after a firefight in Salomé Botello on July 2, General Rubio left the 17th Cavalry Regiment and 9th Irregular Cavalry Corps in Golondrinas on the rail line and, taking his cannons and machine guns, of which the revolutionaries had neither, pursued the Constitutionalists in the direction of Candela, to the west.[16]

BATTLES FOR CANDELA JULY 2 AND 8

In a column of three arms Rubio and his Federals attacked through Salomé Botello and Valladares, where they ran into the advance guard of Colonel Jesús Carranza's brigade, just northeast of Candela. The Federals pushed through Valladares and continued on toward Candela, a town located off the Monterrey-Nuevo Laredo rail line, just over the state line inside Coahuila (twenty-five kilometers southwest of Lampazos). As the sound of battle erupted a trail of refugees began to stream from the town. Facing impossible odds, since they were outnumbered and had no machine guns to use against the Federals, who did, Carranza realized his obligation to fight a delaying action so that the local populace, well-known for its revolutionary sympathies and fearful of reprisals by the Federals, could escape. The Constitutionalists contested every inch of ground on the outskirts of town and then into Candela proper until Carranza judged sufficient time had been gained to abandon it. He then ordered his men to begin retreating as best they could, since they did not know the appropriate tactics for such a maneuver. Carranza's men fled westward toward the town of Pánuco where they hoped to reach the eastern terminus of the Montaña Pánuco-Monclova branch line, ride the rails to Monclova, and link up with Colonel Pablo González. The Constitutionalists suffered eighty killed, according to General Rubio, and the Federals twelve, with about as many wounded.[17]

The following day, General Rubio again requested permission to continue pushing west to conquer Monclova:

> This operation destroys the most important concentration of Carrancistas and puts the State of Nuevo León safe from a new invasion. My mission is to repair the railway; I think that the most

efficacious way to protect it is to severely punish the concentrations [of Constitutionalists] that might be near it and are the ones who constantly destroy it. For this reason I undertook the operation yesterday, the results of which I now communicate. Now I hope the C. President designates this brigade to take Monclova.[18]

The Secretary of War denied Rubio's request, so he remained in Nuevo León and left an observation detachment under Lieutenant Colonel José Alessio Robles at Candela. Maass still had not left Saltillo.[19]

Meanwhile, Carranza's Constitutionalists remained in San Antonio Canyon with advance forces at La Carroza Pass (immediate to Candela), while Carranza and staff went to the Gloria de Pánuco Station of the Montaña Pánuco-Monclova line, a "less than narrow" gauge railway. Catching a train, Carranza continued on to Monclova where he met with Colonel Pablo González, and the two then held a conference by telegraph with Don Venustiano, who was in Piedras Negras. The First Chief ordered them to leave with González's men and immediately retake Candela, "the key to our operations in the east of Coahuila, and whence we constantly threatened the Mexican Railroad line to Laredo."[20] These very words from Constitutionalist staff officer Manuel W. González vindicated General Rubio's thinking about the importance of Candela and Monclova, but the First Chief's imprudence would ultimately lead to the loss of the Saltillo-Piedras Negras line, result in the abandonment of any plans to dominate the Monterrey-Nuevo Laredo line, and force the First Chief to seek refuge in Sonora.

The following day the First Chief left Piedras Negras for Monclova, along with the artillery and the Constitutionalist Sapper Battalion that he had earlier ordered Francisco L. Urquizo to organize. The artillery consisted of two batteries: one heavy caliber with three 80-mm. guns manufactured from locomotive axles in the railroad workshops of Piedras Negras by the engineer and Major Carlos Prieto and Captain Manuel Pérez Treviño with the assistance of mechanic Patricio de León, and the second "battery" commanded by Lieutenant Alberto Salinas consisting of one small cannon, affectionately nicknamed "El Rorro." At the same time the cavalry commanded by Majors Ildefonso "Poncho" Vázquez, Samuel G. Vázquez, Jesús Soto, Pedro Vázquez, and Lieutenant Colonel Francisco Sánchez Herrera, among others, also left the border town and headed for San Antonio Canyon, the staging area. Leaving behind 150 men under Lieutenant Colonel Emilio Salinas to garrison Monclova, Colonels

Carranza and González returned to Candela retracing the same route of egress that Jesús Carranza had taken earlier from Candela. They left Monclova on July 4 and passed through Gloria, where they spent a day. By this time, the revolutionaries were already practicing the "services of campaign" like veterans.[21]

The day before the next battle, the Constitutionalists threw a motivational gala of speech and song, and even Sonoran Governor José María Maytorena showed up to briefly confer with the First Chief who had come to direct the battle. On the night of July 7, the men under Pablo González and Jesús Carranza, this time with machine guns commanded by Bruno Gloria and Daniel Díaz Couder, moved through San Antonio Canyon, wondering why no Federals were in their path, then to Rancho San Pedro and La Carroza Canyon. At 11 p.m., while passing through Candela Pass, Poncho Vázquez's men received the challenge "who goes there" and responded with rifle fire. After a firefight of about one half hour, they pushed through to Candela. Outside the town, the First Chief called a halt and gave orders to attack in the early morning.[22]

In the early hours of July 8 the Constitutionalist infantry crossed a small bridge about one kilometer south of town and deployed on line before the town, with the cavalry on the flanks. Irrespective of the firefight the previous evening, the Federals seemed to suspect that the closest large enemy force was in Monclova and therefore had not paid attention to proper security: they had not posted sentries or sent out scout patrols. One sapper officer, Primitivo González, became separated from his battalion and had even entered a house inside the town by mistake. After greeting the female owner and requesting some food he lit up a cigarette and nonchalantly asked the name of the town. Upon learning that it was Candela, the Constitutionalist officer raced out of there without so much as thanking the woman.[23]

Major Prieto placed his cannons behind some trees, south of town, and Lieutenant Colonel Jacinto Treviño, Don Venustiano's chief of staff, led the machine guns under Bruno Gloria and Urquizo's sappers in the center; on the left (west) wing was Pablo González with subalterns Poncho Vázquez, Francisco Sánchez Herrera, Jesús Soto, Samuel Vázquez, Federico Silva, and others; to the east, in the direction of Golondrinas and Carrizal, Jesús Carranza attacked with Francisco Murguía, Teodoro Elizondo, Alfredo Ricaut, Fortunato Maycotte, José Santos, Pablo González, Jr., Heliodoro Pérez, Fortunato Zuazua, Jesús González Morín, Aniceto Farías, José V. "El Colorado" Elizondo, and others. They faced José Alessio Robles' three hundred Federals. At this point, the Constitutionalists were inexperienced enough that the staffs of González and Carranza actually took places on the firing line with the normal "Juans," although at that time officers did not call their men "Juans" or "soldiers" but rather *"muchachos."*[24]

Figure 1.2 "El Marqués," the Artillery Dog that transmitted orders in the Monclova-area battles of Candela and Las Hermanas, taking them through the streets still under the Federals' control. Leonor Villegas de Magnón Papers, Special Collections, University of Houston Libraries, http://digital.lib.uh.edu/collection/ville/item/26/show/24

As the Federals slumbered, Lieutenant Colonel Jacinto Treviño took charge of the infantry (sappers) and advanced in an extended firing line until they ran into a small group of Federals. The battle opened at 5 a.m. Colonel González had positioned himself on a small hill near the pueblo and ordered an all-out assault of infantry and cavalry with the battle cry "¡Viva Carranza!", because in México armed supporters always invoke the name of whoever personifies their faction. The cavalry on the flanks closed the circle, but they left open the road to Lampazos on the north side as a route of egress for the Federals. The Constitutionalists with nine hundred men attacked a force they estimated to total five hundred men consisting of one cavalry regiment and a machine-gun section, but in actuality the numbers approached closer to three hundred from the 1st Cavalry Regiment and 9th Irregular Corps, with their horses tied up in a row for a quick retreat; one section of machine guns; and another of Rexers. The Federals immediately awoke and sought vantage points in the highest spots of the pueblo to place their crew-served weapons, like the belfry in the church tower, and sent their men onto the rooftops of high houses and barracks. According to the Constitutionalist Alfredo Aragón, the Federal officers then withdrew the ladders so that it was impossible for their men to come down, such that "they were [made] prisoners of their own [people]." The Vázquez squadron to the north charged forward to the firing line. After tying up their horses they went at the defenders who, kneeling fired volleys that almost annihilated the squadron, according to Aragón, who was hit in the head and passed out. His aide pulled him to safety and leaned him against a wall where, semi-conscious, he struggled to grasp the events unfolding.[25]

With the phone lines cut, the Federal commander Alessio Robles had to send Captain Rodolfo Díaz de la Vega by automobile to Lampazos to report the attack. The Constitutionalists deployed their cannon, training "El Rorro" on the church tower, and stormed the cemetery on the northeast side, capturing it and a crew-served weapon from the Federals, while mounted revolutionaries pushed into the houses of the town and cleared the Federals from the upper levels. The Constitutionalist infantry advanced slowly through the south and took possession of a mill and a wide bridge and there assumed the prone position and continued to shoot. To the east a company advanced with grenades, throwing them everywhere to penetrate the city. The Federal machine guns (called *bailarinas* by some Constitutionalists) in the towers began to fire in bursts. The shooting was copious, and soon dead and wounded Constitutionalists were being carried from the field on litters and pushcarts. The Federals who stepped in amongst some oak trees to shoot began falling dead, and then began fleeing, some so hastily that they left their greatcoats behind. Captain Alberto Salinas, only nineteen years old, placed the two Constitutionalist machine guns on the hills in front of the town at the entrance to the main street. He managed to quiet the Federal machine guns and shoot at the Federals on the rooftops, who returned fire. The Constitutionalists inside the town engaged in close quarters combat.[26]

After two hours of fierce combat the church bells rang out with victory, the bugles blew *diana*, and the Federals fled, their enlisted men dying as those few in the church who fought on until they ran out of ammunition covered the officers' escape to Lampazos. The Constitutionalists executed those captured Federals who did not agree to join the revolutionaries, as well as the local priest, whom they allegedly found with a hot weapon in his hands amid a mountain of empty shell casings. The Federals lost twenty-eight killed, including one officer, and seventy-seven wounded, including Colonel Alessio Robles, as well as thirty-two dispersed. In equipment they lost two Hotchkiss machine guns, 200 Mauser rifles, 167 horses (used to transform Urquizo's sappers into mounted infantry), sixteen mules, and some ammunition.[27] After Candela some Constitutionalists took to calling General Guillermo Rubio Navarrete "the quartermaster of the Revolution" because he began "leaving magnificent elements as war booty every time that we defeated him, such as ammunition, arms, horses, saddles, machine guns, and even clothing and victuals."[28]

There is no account of Constitutionalist casualties. After passing out from his head wound, Aragón woke up two hours later to find himself face to face with the First Chief, who offered him a cup of broth that he had personally prepared. All the wounded received the same, making them feel "respect, veneration by the man who was leading us to victory and accompanied us in [our] suffering."[29] The First Chief promoted his brother and Colonel González to the rank of brigadier for their part in the successful battle.

The Constitutionalists had no time to enjoy their victory because the next day, July 9, Constitutionalist Lieutenant Colonel Emilio Salinas, Jefe de las Armas of Monclova, sent a message to say that Maass was advancing on the city.[30] Additionally, they had to worry about General Rubio's reaction to the loss. When Federal Captain de la Vega had arrived in Lampazos General Rubio immediately embarked 110 men commanded by Captain Joaquín de la Peña, Chief of Automobiles, in the brigade's ten cars and set out with them, issuing orders for the mounted forces of the brigade, consisting of an artillery battery and a mounted machine gun battery, to follow with the greatest speed along with all the brigade's infantry. Rubio left behind only a small force in Lampazos to guard the repair trains. By the time Rubio arrived with reinforcements the Constitutionalists had already started back for Monclova to protect the city from the Maass column. Rubio's entire brigade concentrated in Candela, but the cavalry of Alessio Robles, which had returned after taking a triangular route of escape from Candela to Salomé Botello, Lampazos, and back to Candela, arrived too exhausted to be able to undertake pursuit operations. Rubio once more requested permission to lead his brigade against Monclova only to be told that the Maass column was already marching in that direction.[31]

BATTLE OF MONCLOVA JULY 10

The victory at Candela put the Constitutionalists in a precarious situation. To carry off his coup de main, González had taken all available forces in the area except a garrison of about one hundred in Monclova and a squadron of cavalrymen watching over the Federal advance position at Espinazo, where the lead Federals had been since the engagement near Baján Station in May, about a month earlier. In order to reach Monclova González's Constitutionalist cavalry would have to make a forced march over two and half days, and the infantry would have a two-day march to reach the railhead at Gloria de Pánuco and then make the last leg by train. Moreover, Rubio Navarrete reported the concentration of Constitutionalists in Candela to Maass, spurring the Federal onward.[32]

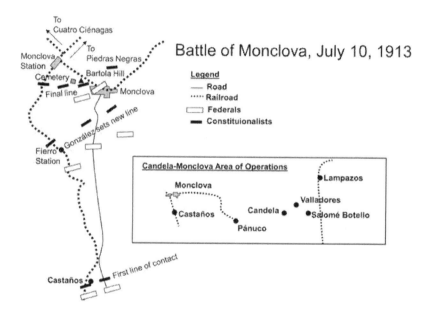

Map 1.13

Maass abandoned the rails, leaving behind about two hundred foot soldiers of the Federal District Security Infantry Regiment, a section of 80-mm. cannons of the 3rd Artillery Regiment, and Engineers to provide aid and security for the rail repair crew. He undertook the march north to Monclova with the rest of his column on July 7. His attack force comprised about fifteen hundred men.[33]

Tactical Command	Major Unit organic to	J	O	T	Total
Federals:					
Limón, Hernando (LTC)	Federal District Security Infantry Regiment	1	9	556	566
Navarro, Miguel (1st CPT)	13th Cavalry Regiment		4	60	64
Escoto, Antonio (Major)	1st Regiment of Gendarmes (Mounted)	1	17	228	246
Alvarez, Arturo A. (Colonel)	42nd Auxiliary Infantry Battalion	1	12	450	463
Ballesteros, Manuel (LTC)	47th Auxiliary Infantry Battalion	1	3	147	151
Castillo, Timoteo A. (1st CPT)	Guerrero Battalion		5	93	98
Jiménez, Luis (1st CPT)	Machine Gun Regiment		2	29	31
	Section of Rexers		1	18	19
	1st Artillery Regiment (Section of 37-mm. Hotchkiss)	1	22		23
Izunza, Agustín (1st CPT)	2nd Artillery Regiment (Battery of 75-mm. Mondragóns)		5	71	76
Flores Betancourt, Enrique (2nd CPT)	3rd Artillery Regiment (Section 80-mm. guns)		2	25	27
	Engineer Park			40	40
					1,804
Constitutionalists (estimated):					
Carranza, Jesús (Colonel)		3	15	300	318
González, Pablo (Colonel)	Staff and Escort	3	21	60	84
Suárez Gamboa, Ricardo (Major)	Medical Service	1	1	8	10
Urquizo, Francisco (1st CPT)	Sappers		20	300	320
Sánchez Herrera, Francisco (LTC)	2nd Regiment Libres del Norte	1	16	200	217
Vázquez, Ildefonso (Major)	Vázquez Squadron	1	8	100	109
Gloria, Bruno (1st CPT)	Machine Gun Battery (two 37-mm. Hotchkiss)		3	15	18
Prieto, Carlos (Major)	Artillery Battery (two 80-mm., one 70-mm.)	1	6	50	57
Salinas, Emilio (LTC)					150
Other Constitutionalists in the area					
Cárdenas, Manuel (Major)					100
Carranza, Sebastián (LTC)					100
					1,483

Table 1.8 Battle of Monclova Troop Strengths

The Federal order of march had the mounted Gendarmes leading the extreme vanguard, with the 42nd Auxiliaries in the vanguard, then the main column, and a mounted contingent of the 42nd for the rearguard. The Federals first made contact with the advance Constitutionalists in Bocatoche, four kilometers south of Castaño where the water pumps that supply Monclova station are located, and immediately forced them back. Constitutionalist Lieutenant Colonel Salinas, commander of Monclova, telegraphed Candela asking for immediate reinforcements and went out to join the fight. The First Chief responded by ordering Pablo González to race ahead of the main force with the Sapper Battalion. González left at 3 a.m. on July 9, arriving at Monclova seventeen hours later where he found the town quiet; many civilians had left the town and Colonel Salinas had already gathered up all available forces and displaced to Castaños where the battle raged. At 6:30 a.m. the next morning González left with the sappers by train for Castaños to join the fight, but he stopped at Fierro Station upon running into Constitutionalist cavalry retreating in disorder. González ordered his men to dismount from the train and form a firing line perpendicular to the railroad. Advancing in good order they made contact with the Federals under the watchful eye of González, who remained on the train. Inexplicably the bombs sowed along the road and in Bocatoche Station had failed to detonate and hinder the Federal advance.[34]

The Constitutionalist infantry engaged the Federals and took up position in a creek as the Federal artillery pounded nearby hills in the mistaken belief that Constitutionalists might be there and aimed at the train that had brought them, forcing the train to constantly move. A short time later, a bugle call informed the Constitutionalists of Federal forces in strength on the right, prompting the Constitutionalists to try to reinforce that wing. Then, the Federals divided their force, leaving a group to hold down the Constitutionalists while a larger force made for Monclova around the eastern flank. González backed up to Monclova, contesting the ground all the way, in order to link up with his cavalry, which would be arriving in piecemeal fashion from Candela, and organize them to meet the Federals.[35]

Jesús Carranza's column saddled up at 2 a.m. on July 10 and continued the march to Monclova, arriving from the east through the España barrio in a hail of gunfire around 10 a.m. just as the triumphant Federals were sounding the parish bells in town. They made their way to the train station on the west side where General Carranza met up with the First Chief. Surrounded by officers, the two brothers conferred and sent dispatches to González who was still in the fight along the rails to the south. The First Chief's staff and Jesús Carranza's brigade then began departing for Nadadores, as the Federals occupied La Bartola Hill (about halfway between the plaza and the train station) and began training artillery fire on the landmark Hotel Internacional and the station. A whistling artillery round sailed high over the First Chief and his officers, and Colonel Treviño remarked that this was only the first of three rounds that gunners call the "pitchfork," wherein the first cannon of a battery fired one shot far, then the second short, and the third right on target. The First Chief said that Treviño was only speculating until the third landed a mere ten meters away, causing Carranza to confess, "This time it seems you are correct." Against the backdrop of impacting Federal artillery shells, the First Chief exchanged dispatches with General González and arranged for the evacuation of the hospital with the doctors, nurses, and the wounded to Piedras Negras. The plaza was lost. Only after the First Chief received confirmation from González that he would continue covering the Constitutionalist retreat and then withdraw to Las Hermanas did Don Venustiano depart for Cuatro Ciénagas, his hometown.[36]

The Constitutionalist infantry continued to withdraw northward, suffering heavy casualties, including some being taken prisoner, but maintaining contact with the enemy; they arrived at the station around 2 p.m., just in time to catch the last train north. The Constitutionalist cavalry continued to engage the Federals, with the shooting remaining generalized for about another hour, before opposing forces in overwhelming numbers forced González's men to retire in disorganization toward Las Hermanas, farther still to the north. Lieutenant Colonels Jesús Ramírez Quintanilla and Alfredo Ricaut arrived from Candela too late to make it to the station, and went straight to Las Hermanas. Murguía retreated through San Buenaventura and turned at Borregas Pass to reach Las Hermanas. Some of the Constitutionalist cavalry headed west with the First Chief to Cuatro Ciénagas, pursued by the Federals.[37]

In the Battle of Monclova, the Federals lost 13 killed, including one officer; a jefe, one officer, and 22 wounded; plus 15 missing, and calculated the Constitutionalist losses at 130 killed and 200 wounded. They recovered three cannons, seventy-five rifles, and one of the machine guns taken from Alessio Robles earlier at Candela. In the running battle the Federals had consumed 200,000 cartridges, 498 75-mm. shells, and 710 37-mm. projectiles.[38] Had Huerta allowed General Rubio Navarrete to pursue González and Carranza from Candela, the two Federal brigades might have annihilated the Carrancistas, but instead Huerta ordered Rubio Navarrete to return to Lampazos, perhaps—as Barragán averred—so that his nephew, General Maass, could claim all the glory.[39] Nevertheless, Rubio seemed satisfied with the outcome, saying: "A few days later I found out that the group that withdrew from Candela was defeated by said [Maass'] column—the maneuver thus had been a great success."[40]

The loss of Monclova forced Venustiano Carranza to flee westward, escaping the Federal columns of Maass and Rubio Navarrete. At Nadadores he ran into a commission of thirty troops from the Laguna region under Major Alberto Cuevas and Víctor Elizondo sent to invite the First Chief to place himself at the head of the Constitutionalists preparing to attack Torreón. The Federals also caught up to Carranza at Nadadores and reported an engagement in which they inflicted some casualties on the revolutionaries. As they passed through the heartland of the leading revolutionaries from the state, the Huertistas vented their anger on property belonging to friends and relatives of the Constitutionalists, firebombing the El Carmen and El Fuente mills. Pablo González had been the director and administrator of the former mill, which was owned by his father-in-law, Federico Miller, since before the Maderista Revolution. Fernando and Emilio Miller had also joined the Constitutionalists, with the former having already died in action. One can only speculate as to how many citizens joined their family members already serving in the revolutionary ranks just to avoid persecution by the advancing Huertistas. The Federals continued to chase Carranza and his escort, now headed for Torreón, through the El Carmen Pass and into the Sacramento Valley.[41]

Torreón was a key crossroads in north central Mexico; here the railroad from Chihuahua in the north intersected with those heading south to the capitals of Durango and Zacatecas states. Three railroads also connected Torreón to Saltillo and Monterrey to the east and Monclova and Piedras Negras to the north. A major population center with lucrative cotton production and manufacturing concerns (including dynamite factories), it possessed political, economic, and military value, so the First Chief readily accepted the invitation to go oversee the attack. Just getting there, however, would entail risks. The Lagunero chiefs, such as Calixto Contreras, Orestes Pereyra, and others, knew that Federal Irregular General Benjamín Argumedo intended to intercept the First Chief at Madero Station, a point of forced passage, and so they sent an additional escort to provide security.[42]

Since Carranza no longer intended to reunite with González in Las Hermanas, once he reached Cuatro Ciénagas he ordered Pablo González to delay the Federal Army's advance to the north as long as possible in order to take pressure off of La Laguna and Sonora. By tying up the columns of Maass and Rubio Navarrete and Téllez's Division of the Bravo, General González gave much needed time and relief to other revolutionary forces, although it would be a stretch to say that in doing so he had won the revolution.[43] The First Chief's party left Cuatro Ciénagas on July 15 and met up with the Lagunero escort of three hundred Constitutionalists under Colonel Gregorio García and Lieutenant Colonel Roberto Rivas at Australia. Colonel García managed to defeat Argumedo and clear the way to Parras, Velardeña, and Torreón for the First Chief's party, but he lost his life fighting the Colorados in the encounter at Madero Station.[44]

BATTLE OF FIRST TORREÓN

After entering the capital of Durango in June, the Constitutionalists replenished their supplies of arms and other elements, recruited new adherents, and reorganized; at the beginning of July they had a total of 9,000 men (a stated but probably inaccurate figure) when they decided to attack Torreón. Contreras' men stopped in Cuencamé and spent about four days there while their general attended to some personal business in his nearby hometown of Ocuila. In the meantime, General Urbina continued moving toward Pedriceña Station together with General Pereyra's brigade. Once there, they made a reconnaissance toward Torreón, since that was where the Federals who threatened to advance on Durango City were located.[45]

According to Constitutionalist Colonel Matías Pazuengo, many of the individuals who had belonged to the Social Defense of Durango City, "forgetting the benevolence with which they were treated by the revolutionaries and the offerings that they made to never again get involved against the revolution," began seeking to "avenge the outrages of which they had been the subject on behalf of the revolutionaries" as soon as they arrived in Mexico City. Working with the Secretary of War through the influence of a certain Licenciado Manuel Garza Aldape, and in connivance with the Duranguense reactionaries settled in the nation's capital, they succeeded in getting an expeditionary column formed under the command of General Felipe Alvírez that some of them joined. They arrived with Alvírez and his Sapper Battalion on July 11, constituting the base force of a column being formed in Torreón to retake Durango City, but the advance of the Constitutionalists from Pedriceña had put Alvírez's Durango City campaign on hold.[46]

Also among the Federal forces inside Torreón were about eight hundred mounted irregulars belonging to Generals Benjamín Argumedo and Emilio P. Campa who had been en route to Monterrey after spending the months of April and May in Aguascalientes organizing; however, they had been stopped from reaching their appointed destination and redirected because the Constitutionalists had cut the railroad to the east at Madero Station.[47] In effect, the garrison at Torreón had become almost completely cut off from the rest of the republic in every direction except south to Zacatecas, and the Constitutionalists were working on that.

At the beginning of July, before abandoning Monclova, the First Chief sent General Cándido Aguilar south to Zacatecas to confer with General Pánfilo Natera in Río Grande. Since the Central Railroad had not been destroyed in a systematic manner, Aguilar ordered General Natera and Colonel Pedro Caloca to tend to these duties. They destroyed the rails from Cañitas to Simón, and even engaged in combat on July 14 between La Mancha and Calvo (ten kilometers north of La Mancha) stations against Lieutenant Colonel Eugenio Escobar Tavera's Huertistas from Torreón while tearing up the tracks. In San Juan de Guadalupe Aguilar gathered Colonels Eugenio Aguirre Benavides, Martín Triana, José Isabel Robles, Gregorio E. García, and General Natera in an attempt to impose some order on a movement that had become stalled because of personal enmities and rancor. Aguilar formed a "Local War Junta" that permitted the forces to mobilize in a coordinated fashion and to attend to the needs of the troops. Between the five commands they totaled four thousand men and assumed the designation of the Division of the Center, with General Aguilar commanding.[48]

Tactical Command	Major Unit organic to	G	J	O	T	Total
Alvírez, Felipe (Brigadier)	Sapper Battalion	1		16	350	367
	2nd Infantry Battalion			4	162	166
Torres, Isidro (1st CPT)	4th Infantry Battalion			5	138	143
Solórzano, Esteban (1st CPT)	6th Infantry Battalion			5	45	50
Arellano, Adrián (Major)	9th Infantry Battalion			2	64	66
Rojas, Miguel (1st CPT)	17th Infantry Battalion			3	45	48
Gallardo, Antonio (LTC)	18th Infantry Battalion			8	200	208
Escudero, Leocadio (2nd CPT)	20th Infantry Battalion			3	19	22
Campero, Francisco A. (LT)	21st Infantry Battalion			1	34	35
Santamaría, Ignacio (LT)	23rd Infantry Battalion			1	27	28
Fernández Traconis, Eudaldo (Major)	Traconis Force (from Parral)		1	23	212	236
Anaya, Luis G. (Brigadier)	1st Cavalry Regiment	1	2	15	156	174
Carrillo, Ignacio B. (LTC)	2nd Cavalry Regiment		1	5	109	115
Escobar Tavera, Eugenio (LTC)	3rd Cavalry Regiment		1	4	35	40
Munguía, Eutiquio (Brigadier)	5th Cavalry Regiment	1	1	12	250	264
Sardaneta, Enrique (Colonel)	14th Cavalry Regiment		1	11	102	114
Ayala, Ramón (Major)	15th Cavalry Regiment		1	12	52	65
García, Aurelio C. (LTC)	22nd Auxiliary Cavalry Regiment		1	8	164	173
Loreto Howell, Jesús (1st CPT)	32nd Auxiliary Cavalry Regiment			18	246	264
González, Pedro (1st Officer)	1st Rural Corps			6	68	74
Villanueva, Manuel (Jefe del Detall)	3rd Rural Corps			12	204	216
Galavíz, José G. (1st CPT)	3rd Artillery Regiment			3	50	53
Tapia, José (Major)	4th Artillery Regiment		1	2	47	50
Núñez, Luis F. (1st CPT)	5th Artillery Regiment			2	42	44
Morales, Félix S. (2nd CPT)	Machine Gun Regiment			1	13	14
Macías, Blas U. (2nd CPT)	"El Niño" Cannon			2	12	14
Argumedo, Benjamín (Brigadier)	Argumedo Brigade	1			500	501
Campa, Emilio P. (Brigadier)	Campa Brigade	1			300	301
Domínguez, Luciano (Major)	Cazadores del Nazas Corps		1	12	89	102
						3,947

Table 1.9 Battle of First Torreón Federal Estimated Troop Strength

Thus the Federal Division of the Nazas commanded by General of Division Ignacio A. Bravo faced a possible total of 9,000 Constitutionalists, although in the initial phase of the attack on Torreón probably only about 5,000 men under Urbina, Contreras, and Pereyra took part. To defend the city General Bravo could count on about 1,400 infantrymen, some 1,100 regular cavalry and Rurales, another 1,300 mounted irregulars, and 200 artillerymen. Among other notables inside the city were the praetorian General Luis G. Anaya, Brigadier Eutiquio Munguía, and Major Eudaldo Fernández Traconis, who had had to flee to Torreón when Constitutionalists Manuel Chao and Maclovio Herrera took Camargo, Chihuahua, back in April.[49]

July 20

The Constitutionalists decided that General Pereyra's brigade accompanied by a regiment from Contreras' should be in the vanguard to make contact with the lead Federals.[50] General Bravo, instead of preparing Torreón for a defense, had sent out a force of 440 men under General Eutiquio Munguía to locate and engage the enemy. This column, represented by elements of the 18th Infantry

Battalion; the 5th (with two Madsen light machine guns), 15th, 22nd Auxiliary, and 32nd Auxiliary Cavalry Regiments; a section of machine guns; the 80-mm. "El Niño" cannon and crew; and a section of two mountain guns, moved westward toward Avilés about eighteen kilometers from Torreón leaving around 1 a.m. on July 20. The infantry traveled by train and the rest were mounted. As parties from the 18th Battalion and 32nd Regiment proceeded to set up security in the hills about eight hundred meters west of Hacienda de Avilés, they ran into the Constitutionalist vanguard at 6:00 a.m. Munguía immediately sent the rest of the 32nd and his mountain guns to reinforce the advance forces and ordered Lieutenant Colonel Antonio Gallardo, in command of those lead elements, to push the Constitutionalists from their positions. About this time the revolutionaries to the south of this initial zone of combat attacked Hacienda de Avilés, where Federals of the 18th Battalion and 5th Cavalry Regiment put up a stubborn defense. Munguía reinforced Gallardo further with some men from the 15th and 22nd Cavalry Regiments, and with these he managed to push the Constitutionalists off the hills, but as they too received reinforcements, the battle continued to rage until about 5 p.m. That afternoon Munguía requested reinforcements from General Bravo, who sent him another five hundred men, including four 75-mm. Schneider Canet guns. Given that Munguía had reported the Constitutionalist strength at two thousand, almost double the reinforced Federal strength, Bravo appeared to have placed a good portion of his artillery in jeopardy of capture by the revolutionaries.[51]

July 21

During the night the Constitutionalists continued reinforcing the line, and in the morning they retook the hills from Gallardo. Munguía sent detachments from the 1st and 3rd Rural Corps that he had received from Torreón to Gallardo and ordered him at 6:30 a.m. to retake the hills, which he did but with heavy losses. With the 18th and 21st Battalion and one hundred Sappers (these last two groups were part of the reinforcements from Torreón) Munguía ordered an attack and sent the 5th Regiment on an enveloping maneuver around the north flank, all under the support of a heavy cannonade. But the attack crashed against stiff Constitutionalist resistance and the revolutionaries then counterattacked by hurling themselves at the Federals, overwhelming them with their numbers, and forcing Munguía to order a withdrawal to Torreón.[52]

Soon the Federals were fleeing in headlong retreat followed by the Constitutionalists who raced after them with such abandon that units became disorganized, with some men headed for Torreón while most went to Lerdo. The main group of Constitutionalists made contact with the Lerdo garrison's advance forces at around 5 p.m. on July 21, along the banks of the Nazas River, and hit with such momentum that they immediately pushed the Huertistas back to the edge of town. Joined to the rest of the Federal garrison commanded by General Emilio Campa and Colonel Federico Reyna the government forces fought for more than four hours before pulling back. Meantime, the jefe político Roberto Cesor transferred the prisoners from the public jail and requested that the Electric Train Company make a few railcars available to transport those civilians who wanted to flee to Torreón. Many had already fled, so there were few who left the city at this time.[53]

Those Constitutionalists who had chased the Federals into Torreón, some four hundred men, believed that the city's capitulation was imminent and succeeded in reaching as far as midway into the city limits. But then some disorganization entered into the ranks of the Constitutionalists as they realized that they were engaged in heated combat with a much greater number of Federal troops, and before the Constitutionalist generals could capitalize on the situation, the Federals had already repulsed the much smaller group from Torreón. Constitutionalist headquarters issued orders for their troops to rally to El Huarache on the outskirts of Torreón, but not all units complied with the orders. While some regiments and squadrons did obey forthwith, for others it was nearly impossible to get them out of the cities of Lerdo and Gómez Palacio, probably because they were still engaged in combat.[54]

The Federals inside Lerdo retreated to Gómez Palacio just minutes before 9 p.m. making use of the cover of darkness to effect their movement. They had no intentions of holding Gómez Palacio and sent their wounded straight to the Red Cross military hospital in Torreón. The Constitutionalists followed closely on their heels, appearing on the edge of Gómez Palacio an hour later, with Contreras' men in the center traveling up the main road connecting the two towns, Pereyra's men to the south on the old factory road, and Urbina and Arrieta's to the north toward La Pila Hill. They only engaged the extreme Federal rearguard commanded by First Captain José Loreto Howel while the rest of Campa and Reyna's men obeyed orders to pull back to Torreón.[55]

July 22

When Munguía's troops had come straggling into Torreón in the afternoon of July 21, General Bravo called in the garrison from nearby San Pedro de las Colonias under Lieutenant Colonel Ignacio Mateos of the 1st Cavalry Regiment. Mateos left San Pedro de las Colonias the next morning accompanied by the municipal gendarmes from San Pedro de las Colonias who were conducting prisoners from that city's jail. Upon the convoy arriving at the railyard of the National Railroad on Gómez Palacio's east side, Mateos heard the sound of rifle fire and realized that the barracks of his 1st Regiment was under attack. Inside was a detachment commanded by a Federal lieutenant who most likely had not received the word to evacuate the city the night before. Mateos immediately ordered his column into the fray, sending the 17th Battalion and 1st Regiment in the center supported by his machine guns, while Argumedo's irregulars went around to the left and right; all these troops had previously made up the garrison of San Pedro. With this disposition Mateos managed to force the Constitutionalists back to La Pila Hill north of town, and then dislodged them from that location as well. The military trains then got underway for Torreón taking fire all the while as a few of Argumedo's men covered the rear of the column. Once inside Torreón, Argumedo's men occupied their barracks and awaited their next orders.[56]

They did not have long to wait, because that same day General Bravo sent Argumedo and his brigade to Viezca to clear that town of a small force of 150 poorly armed Constitutionalists commanded by Lieutenant Colonel J. Salomé Rivera. Argumedo had a reputation as a fearsome warrior. He used to pace up and down the lines of his men with a large machete encouraging them to hold their ground, and many times he had come to the rescue of regulars in trouble. With three of his squadrons totaling about 275 men as well as another 100 under Lieutenant Colonel Espiridión Rodríguez that he picked up in Matamoros Laguna (twenty-four kilometers west of Torreón) along the way, he easily defeated Rivera's Constitutionalists, mortally wounding the commander and sending the rest fleeing. Argumedo counted thirty-one dead revolutionaries upon cleaning up the battlefield and returned to Torreón, arriving on the twenty-sixth and taking up the southeast corner of the defenses.[57]

General Bravo had divided Torreón into four defensive sectors, each corresponding to the four cardinal directions, assigning low probabilities of attack to the northern, eastern, and southern sectors because of the clear fields of fire, and a high degree to the western sector. Bravo gave command of these last two sectors to General Munguía and put at his disposal about seven hundred men, essentially consisting of the same force he had fought with at Avilés, from the 6th, 9th, 18th (these last three under Gallardo), and 20th Infantry Battalions; the 5th, 15th, and 32nd (Auxiliary) Cavalry Regiments; and the section of 70-mm. mountain guns.[58]

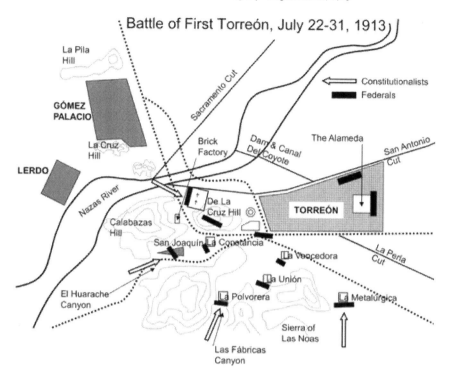

Map 1.14

The western avenue of approach to Torreón went through El Huarache Canyon, which opened up into the barrio of San Joaquín, and then La Constancia factory, before facing the railroad embankment with De la Cruz Hill behind it and the town immediately to the east of this. Munguía had advance troops in San Joaquín, La Constancia, and the cemetery, which was located on the north side (right flank) of the western sector next to De la Cruz Hill. He placed one hundred infantrymen from the 4th, 6th, and 20th Battalions with one of his mountain guns under Major Adrián Arellano on De la Cruz Hill, the main geographical point on this west side, where there already was a battery of 75-mm. Schneider Canets. The other mountain piece he placed at the intersection of the railroads, where it was also supported by infantrymen of the 18th, and he placed two of his Madsen light machine guns supported by troopers of the 5th Cavalry close by. The intersection delimited the western sector from the southern, which consisted of the railroad embankment running east in the direction of Saltillo; placing machine guns here gave good enfilading fire for both sectors. Finally, Munguía placed his third Madsen in the Molino (mill) de la Alianza, which served as his headquarters.[59]

Previously Bravo had formed two brigades, one called the "interim mixed" Brigade and the other the "reserve brigade." The former consisted of about 250 infantrymen, 450 cavalrymen, and 50 artillerymen of the 17th, 20th, 21st, and 23rd Infantry Battalions; the 1st, 14th, and 22nd (Auxiliary) Cavalry Regiments; Force "Traconis"; and the 4th Artillery Regiment (four 80-mm. cannons) under the command of Brigadier Luis G. Anaya, whom Bravo assigned to cover the northern sector. But since the Nazas River and associated cuts and ditches (Tlahualilo, Sacramento, San Antonio) covered the north, these troops remained bivouacked in Falcón and Treviño streets. The reserve brigade under Brigadier Eduardo Ocaranza (who had been trying to return to Mexico City before the siege occurred) remained encamped along the alameda, covering the eastern section and comprised elements from the 2nd and 4th Infantry Battalions and 1st and 3rd Rural Corps—essentially the same forces that had reinforced Munguía at Avilés. Under his own command, as reserves, Bravo held the un-brigaded units of the Sapper Battalion, the Cazadores del Nazas Corps, the 2nd and 3rd Cavalry Regiments, and the rest of his artillery.[60]

As the Constitutionalists closed in for a siege of Torreón, the merchants inside the city posted a sharp increase in prices, and people rushed to stock up on food for what might be a protracted siege. At first it seemed as though the Constitutionalists would desist in the attempt on Torreón, but then at 1:15 p.m. one of the guns on De La Cruz Hill began firing. Citizens on the streets began scurrying for cover with a look of terror on their faces as merchants hurried to close shop. The mostly-unarmed Social Defense, numbering a mere forty-seven men, immediately turned out. The jefe político ordered the local police to assist them in arming themselves with weapons collected from citizens, and then the Social Defense force took up position guarding town hall.[61]

The battery on De la Cruz Hill continued firing on the Constitutionalists who moved into position to close the ring around Torreón and around nightfall shooting of varying intensity could be heard coming from the direction of Huarache Canyon and San Joaquín. The Constitutionalists were making a push to gain the small La Constancia Hill, east of San Joaquín and south of the railroad intersection, where they came under fire from the guns on De la Cruz Hill. At this time Munguía sent three different groups of infantry to different points in Las Fábricas Canyon, the other main avenue of approach just south of town and east of El Huarache: one under First Captain Esteban Solórzano of the 6th he sent into the canyon, another under First Captain Manuel Báez of the 18th he sent to reconnoiter La Union factory located at the north end of canyon, and the last under Lieutenant Colonel Gallardo he sent to La Vencedora factory, which came under heavy attack. Fortunately for Gallardo, Captain Báez was able to come to his aid and together they repulsed the Constitutionalists. In the same area, Sub-lieutenant Moisés M. Rojas of the 18th received orders to take the crest called "Torreón Azul." He was also attacked, but he held his position.[62]

July 23

Around 1 a.m. on the twenty-third, the Constitutionalists attacking from the south got to within 150 meters of the Casa Redonda and engaged the Cazadores del Nazas defending the place. Major Enríquez received credit for the successful defense, because he had ordered small fortifications built. At 2 a.m. the Constitutionalists again made an attempt on La Constancia Hill but were repulsed by the artillery and machine guns at the railway intersection and from De la Cruz Hill; that is when the shooting reached is highest pitch. To the south in the Las Fábricas Canyon area, Captain Solórzano reinforced Sub-lieutenant Rojas on Torreón Azul with forty men of the 4th and 18th at 5 a.m. and General Bravo ordered some fifty-five sappers under Lieutenant Zeferino Mendoza to reinforce De la Cruz as the shooting trailed off.[63]

The morning broke cloudy and cool, threatening rain. The Constitutionalists on Calabazas and Ladrillera Hills were shooting only sporadically, perhaps in an effort to conserve ammunition or to wait for reinforcements, those inside the city surmised. Confronted with the Constitutionalists on the hills to their front, the Federals formed a firing line along the rail embankment in front of De la Cruz Hill, with Gallardo and Báez and men of the 18th Infantry and 32nd Auxiliary cavalry on the right, the section of the Madsen machine guns commanded by Second Captain Manuel Romero A. and supported by troopers of the 5th under Lieutenant Francisco Aguiar Béjar in the center, and Major Ramón Ayala of the 15th Regiment on the left extending as far as the intersection of the rails.[64]

Very few civilians could be seen on the streets, which had been occupied for blocks by cavalry regiments in bivouac, while ambulances transporting wounded from the previous night's fighting crisscrossed the city ceaselessly. Some of the inhabitants had been accused of shooting at Federals from their windows and rooftops and the Social Defense served search warrants on those private residences.[65]

According to the local newspaper, at 9 a.m. Gallardo and the 32nd attacked through Huarache Canyon as the Cazadores del Nazas moved from the south side of the plaza into new positions near the river. Exasperated with the shooting coming from the direction of El Huarache Canyon, General Bravo, had ordered his men to put the barrio of San Joaquín to the torch. The Constitutionalists counterattacked and threw Gallardo and his Federals back as the Cazadores del Nazas covered their retreat. Thereafter shooting trailed off and only isolated shots could be heard throughout the rest of the day.[66]

July 24

After a lull in the fighting of a few hours, the revolutionaries began another assault, this one perhaps more formidable than that of the night before. They attacked La Constancia factory and the south side of De la Cruz in the early morning hours, but the Federal firing line turned them back. The Constitutionalists next tried to attack through the cemetery on the Federal right. An avalanche of Constitutionalists rapidly assaulted the northwest side of De la Cruz Hill employing dynamite bombs and forcing the defenders to retreat toward De la Cruz with the attackers on their heels. The Federal guns opened fire throwing shrapnel on the first wave of revolutionaries, tearing them to pieces, as another group just as numerous as the first assaulted with the same intentions of taking the guns. They, too, failed. Bravo immediately reinforced the hill with one hundred sappers under First Captain Rafael Díaz, thereby enabling the position commander, Major Arellano, to withstand several more assaults and finally repulse the enemy and even retake the cemetery. Around 4 a.m. the shooting stopped. Both sides had suffered many casualties.[67]

The morning remained quite calm after the carnage of the night before. From the heights inside the city, the Federals watched as Constitutionalists constructed fortifications on La Metalúrgica Hill under the direction of an engineer. At 11 a.m., on orders from headquarters, some civilians were executed by firing squad, presumably members of the fifth column who had been firing on the Federals from within the city.[68] Also at that hour, General Bravo ordered Colonel Julio Ibáñez, a staff officer, to take a force of sappers and counterattack some revolutionaries, who had taken up position west of La Constancia factory, which must have been directly to the front of De la Cruz to the southwest. Covering fire from the railway intersection and Báez on his left and Solórzano on the right flank provided support for the assault. Ibáñez accomplished his mission, but suffered a mortal wound in the process. Around 2 p.m. the revolutionaries again attacked through La Constancia; this time Lieutenant Colonel Ignacio B. Carrillo of the 2nd Regiment led the counterattack, supported by the battery of 75-mm. Schneider Canets that had relocated to the rail intersection in support. The Federal assault failed as the Constitutionalists sought cover in what remained of the houses there and delivered a punishing hail of fire that caused Carrillo many casualties.[69]

Observing Carrillo's retreat, General Bravo ordered Brigadier Felipe Alvírez to take the remaining sappers not already employed in combat, about one hundred, plus thirty more from the 15th Regiment to attack the houses around La Constancia and dislodge the enemy. Earlier that very day, Bravo had appointed Alvírez as Munguía's second-in-command and attached the sappers and four 75-mm. guns of the 3rd Artillery Regiment under First Captain José G. Galaviz to the western sector. Alvírez succeeded, after hard fighting, in retaking the area and that night he leveled the few remaining houses, continuing to exchange fire with the revolutionaries on Calabazas Hill.[70]

July 25

Inside the city rumors circulated that another horrifying assault would again take place, and in fact at midnight the guns on De la Cruz Hill firing away again tore the night's air as the Constitutionalists launched an attack on the cemetery from Calabazas Hill that lasted three hours. The combat was bloody and vicious, as the Constitutionalists on the southwest side pushed back the Huertistas from several positions and forced them into the city. Around 1:30 a.m. on the twenty-fifth the Constitutionalists penetrated the barrios of La Fe and La Unión and, it was reported, for a short span of about ten minutes even took possession of some Federal caissons as tough hand-to-hand fighting took place next to the guns. The Federals moved "El Niño" loaded on its platform from one end of town to the other along the rails, firing at the Constitutionalists. Both sides suffered incalculable casualties in the fighting that lasted about five and a half hours, after which the Federals had retaken those positions previously given up.[71]

In the morning, General Bravo finally realized that he needed to raise some defenses, and so while his men were still taking fire he ordered that sandbags be placed on the railroad embankment eight hundred meters north of the brick factory, covering the approach to Gómez Palacio; in front of the remaining positions at the railroad intersection; at the crest of Torreón Azul; and on the observation post 150 meters from the latter. He also commanded that boxcars be moved into place to protect the left flank facing El Huarache Canyon, on which he placed the 5th Regiment's Madsens with two loopholes facing forward and two on the left, protected by twenty-one infantry men of the 23rd Battalion, seventy-five sappers, and eighty troopers from the 5th Regiment.[72]

For the fourth straight night, the Constitutionalists again attacked the Federal positions all along the line, although this time a little bit earlier, starting at 11 p.m. The rifle fire continued without letup, punctuated by the report of the Federal guns and from time to time by the explosion of dynamite tossed by the revolutionaries at the Schneider Canets at the intersection but accomplishing little.[73]

July 26-28

The night of July 26 passed with little happening. Only random exchanges of gunfire took place and the next morning rumors again began to circulate that the Constitutionalists were awaiting reinforcements from Chihuahua and Durango to resume the attack. Since no attack had happened the night before, in the morning the local populace began crowding at the doors of stores. It was believed that the Constitutionalists might be retreating because large plumes of smoke coming from trains in Gómez Palacio could be seen rising from the station.[74] Bravo reported using the respite to improve his defenses by increasing the height and depth of the barricades located eight hundred meters from the brick factory, and placing rail cars on the track to protect against the possible approach of a "*máquina loca*" from the direction of either Gómez Palacio or El Huarache Canyon. On the night of the twenty-eighth the Federals employed coal-burning spotlights to light up the fields of fire, supposedly with good results, and only small firefights took place in the daylight hours of the next day.[75]

July 29

In the early morning hours of July 29 General Argumedo and the mobile reserve created by Bravo under the command of Lieutenant Colonel Escobar Tavera and consisting of elements of the 9th, 18th and 21st Infantry Battalion, attacked the Constitutionalists at La Metalúrgica, on the far southeast outskirts of town.[76] Thinking that the Constitutionalists might use Metalúrgica Canyon to attack the south and east sides of the city, General Bravo ordered Argumedo's Irregulars and part of Colonel Federico Reyna's command to reinforce the extreme advance positions. They made contact at 8:30 a.m. with a light exchange of gunfire after which the Constitutionalists made a strong push to take the Metalúrgica district. The ensuing combat lasted for two and a half hours, at the end of which the Constitutionalists pulled back to their positions on Metalúrgica Hill. But Argumedo was not content to let the Constitutionalists remain there, and with eighty of his men assaulted the hill and after a half hour he succeeded in dislodging them from there. Meanwhile, at 11:30 a.m. a column of Irregulars and cavalry led by the Municipal Jefe J. A. Villanueva returned from Viesca with provisions (wheat, beans, and corn), entering from the east side of the plaza, which was the only side not covered by the Constitutionalists. Some shooting, hardly worthy of mention, took place in the afternoon.[77]

The First Chief's Visit

Toward the end of July the Constitutionalists besieging Torreón received news that the First Chief was approaching from Monclova on the Viezca side and had entered the district of San Juan de Guadalupe, Durango. Carranza gave General Aguilar orders on July 27 to participate in the attack on Torreón. So, leaving General Natera with five hundred men on the Central Railroad to prevent Federal reinforcements from arriving from the south while Colonel Trinidad Cervantes and two hundred men continued to destroy the rails, Aguilar left with Colonels Triana, Benavides, and Robles for Torreón.[78]

From San Juan de Guadalupe the First Chief headed for Velardeña and afterwards took a train to visit the forces camped in El Huarache. Colonel Pazuengo recorded the great disappointment that his appearance created: "it was hoped that said First Chief would bring lots of people and a great quantity of ammunition, but caused disillusionment when he was seen arriving with only a few hundred men between Jefes, Officers, and guards, and that he was bringing no war materiel."[79] The day after his arrival the First Chief held a meeting of his military leaders in his railcar; in it they agreed to renew the general attack on Torreón, although with little hope for success since they had been fighting for nine days and ammunition was running short. But no one wanted to disappoint the First Chief, who wanted to take the plaza and establish his headquarters there.[80]

In the early morning hours of July 30 another massive attack began, starting between 12:30 and 1 a.m. with an infernal explosion that rocked the city and infused panic in its citizens. The Constitutionalists had launched a máquina loca loaded with a great quantity of explosives to crash into the scout train in the station of the National Railroad, but the Federal gunners on De la Cruz Hill and those manning the platform railcar carrying El Niño noticed the movement and began firing on the train and one of the shells had made a direct hit precisely as it entered Huarache Canyon. The signal had been given, and a monstrous assault began in all its fury and intensity as the revolutionaries launched attacks all along the Federal line across open ground. They charged against the north end of the Federal line from the direction of Gómez Palacio where Gallardo's defenders kept them confined to the surrounding hills. Finally, they assaulted through Las Fábricas (also called La Polvorera) Canyon toward Torreón Azul and against La Metalúrgica Company. Huerta's men, tired, decimated, and famished made every effort to repulse the attack from behind their fortifications. The Federals suffered such enormous casualties that a provisional cemetery founded just days earlier had been almost completely filled. Nevertheless, they succeed in turning back the Constitutionalists.[81]

Shortly after noon, the Constitutionalists began to withdraw to Avilés, Gómez Palacio, and Lerdo. A disgusted First Chief said that the Duranguenses did not know how to fight and prepared to leave. The Federals lost two jefes, seven officers, and 102 soldiers killed; one jefe, fourteen officers, and 140 men wounded; and fifty-five troops dispersed. They had consumed around 400,000 cartridges over about five days of heavy combat.[82]

The Apprehension of Cheché Campos

On the night of the same day that Don Venustiano had arrived, news spread of the apprehension of the famous Cheché Campos, who was denounced to Urbinas' forces in Gómez Palacio. Campos had had a falling out with the Federal commander, General Bravo, and escaped execution, but his officers were not so lucky. Bravo had heard that Campos' men and some railroad employees in Gómez Palacio were plotting to turn on their Federal allies as the Constitutionalists approached to attack. The assassination of the city's jefe político would signal the start of the mutiny. Therefore, when Jefe Político Marcos Hernández turned up dead, Bravo immediately ordered General Munguía to take the 5th Regiment and a section of artillery and besiege the barracks of the Irregulars, apprehend those implicated in the plot, and execute them. Munguía executed all those with the rank of first captain on up, including Generals Pablo Lavín and Luis Caro, the latter believed to have been the one who ordered the murder of Hernández. One railroad employee who had been involved in the plot and succeeded in escaping north to join the Constitutionalists was none other than Rodolfo Fierro, who would become one of Villa's most trusted lieutenants. That the main Constitutionalist thrust came through Lerdo and Gómez Palacio possibly validated General Bravo's suspicions about the Gómez Palacio garrison. He later remembered the whole affair proudly as a clear example of how Federal Army officers were to instill discipline in potentially unruly soldiers, apparently without any regard to the effect that summary executions of officers might have on morale.[83]

Campos may have been fortunate to escape the clutches of Bravo but his luck only went so far. The Constitutionalist generals agreed to form a court-martial which Licenciado Emiliano G. Saravia mediated. Campos was condemned to death for, among other things, having burned more than one hundred haciendas, which was proved. Before dying he asked to speak to Generals Urbina and Contreras in order to request, as a final grace, that the revolution not take away the four *reales* (probably referring to plots of land, or small mines) that he was leaving to his wife and daughter to live off, so that he might die happy. The generals so agreed, endeavoring to see that these small interests remained untouched.[84]

Before the execution Colonel Pazuengo went to see Cheché Campos to ask him why the Orozquistas recognized Huerta's government when the rest of the nation did not, and why they had not renounced it as the Zapatista faction had. Campos answered, smoking, that at first the Orozquistas did not recognized Huerta, but only asked for guarantees to go to Mexico City. Once there, however, "they painted things so beautifully for them and they were told that the Government had so many arms and so many soldiers [ready] to fight" that he decided right then and there to join the government in order to pacify the country, "but that now he was perfectly convinced, in spite of the fact that they were going to shoot him, that no government against the Maderista sentiment could ever be established in Mexico."[85]

Analysis

The Constitutionalists failed in the attack on Torreón principally because they did not have enough men in the fight; were undisciplined, that is, inattentive to orders from command, either because they did not want to participate in the battle or because they did not trust in their ability to prevail; and because the push was not uniform, which resulted in ammunition being frittered away while the Federals had plenty of ammunition as well as reinforcements that arrived opportunely. The nominal General in Chief, Tomás R. Urbina, made a great sacrifice of his forces in trying to raise his men's spirits with repeated assaults, all in vain. General Pereyra's brigade performed best, but it was also the smallest. The largest brigade in the fight was General Contreras', which exceeded 3,000 men, but this brigade also manifested the least interest in taking Torreón, even though its brigade commander displayed loyalty and great personal courage. Upon there retreat toward Durango City the Federals attacked the Constitutionalists in San Carlos and made a play for the military train occupied by the valiant General Contreras, his staff, escort, and a few others. About to be surrounded, they put up a tenacious fight and frustrated the Federals' attempted enveloping maneuver. General Contreras was seriously wounded in this encounter, and his troops managed to get out and head for Velardeña where they enjoyed a good rest, convinced that they could never take Torreón.[86]

General Bravo also performed poorly. He did not prepare any defenses, deployed his artillery on line with the infantry where a surge by the Constitutionalists might have captured the pieces, and he did not use his interior lines to refresh his men, with the result that some Federals hardly fired one single shot.[87]

The Jefes Retreat to Reorganize

As the Nazas at that time was fully flowing, many Constitutionalists simply pulled back to Gómez Palacio and Lerdo, with the result that separated by the river neither the Federals nor Constitutionalists could dislodge one or the other for forty-eight days. Finally, on August 5, General Munguía pushed the Constitutionalists out of the neighboring two cities (although the Constitutionalists took them back within two weeks).[88] For the successful defense of Torreón, Huerta promoted Brigadiers Felipe Alvírez, Eduardo Ocaranza, and Eutiquio Munguía to the rank of general of brigade. He gave the latter command of the Division of the Nazas, permitting the seventy-six year old Bravo to remain on hand as an adviser and attend to his ill health, although that may have just been a cover story, as will be seen after the next battle for Torreón.[89]

For Carranza, Torreón seemed to be just the last in a string of defeats after his botched tactics at Saltillo and the Monclova debacle, both of his own making; he would prove to be a much better strategist than tactician, although to be fair, in the Battle of First Torreón Carranza had to surmount the twin problems of a notorious lack of military discipline amongst the troops as well as the absence of a unified command. After the battle he ordered all his commanders in the Laguna region to keep the Chihuahua, Torreón, and Zacatecas garrisons incommunicado, with two exceptions. He gave General Cándido Aguilar a small force and sent him to his native state of Veracruz as the Military Commander and Chief of Operations in order to capture the Huasteca, an important petroleum region. And he told Eulalio Gutiérrez to return to Concepción del Oro, Zacatecas, to operate in northern San Luis Potosí. General Urbina took a course for Mapimí to the District of El Oro and Indé, his men's hometowns. General Contreras remained in Velardeña blocking the Federals from advancing on Durango City. General Pereyra went to Lerdo and from there headed to Mapimí. Meanwhile, General Arrieta with his brigade, which continued to increase in size from day to day, remained the Military Commander of the Plaza of Durango City. Arrieta's forces had not taken any part in the combat for Torreón and gave a sense of reassurance to those whose brigades had been weakened by the fighting.[90] Two months would pass before the lagunero chiefs would again invite an outsider to lead the attack on Gómez Palacio and Torreón, with decidedly different results.

In the meantime, the First Chief continued on to Durango City to meet with Generals Mariano and Domingo Arrieta and thence to Parral to consult with Manuel Chao and Maclovio Herrera. He finally reached Chinabampo, Sinaloa on September 12 where the constitutionally elected Governor Felipe Riveros received him; two days later General Obregón came to greet him at El Fuerte. Because of the relative stability of Sonora in comparison to the Northeast, Carranza established his headquarters and government in that state in order to be in a position to exert his authority across all regions. But back in the Metropolis, Carranza's tour stirred rumors in the press of a Northwest secessionist movement to found the new Sochiloa Republic formed of the states of Sonora, Chihuahua, and Sinaloa.[91]

BATTLE OF LAS HERMANAS AUGUST 16

After the loss of Monclova, General Pablo González arrived first at Las Hermanas with only his staff. Later, other commands began to drift in: Francisco Urquizo with his mounted Sappers, Elías Uribe with his Laguneros, Alfredo Ricaut and "Poncho" Vázquez, the bold Carlos Osuna and Martín Salinas, Lieutenant Colonel and Licenciado Pablo A. de la Garza (González's Chief of Staff), José E. Santos, José María Castilla (Municipal President of Abasolo), Samuel G. Vázquez, Major Jesús Ramírez Quintanilla with his people, Carlos Prieto with his cannons, Bruno Gloria and Daniel Díaz Couder with the machine guns, Juan C. Zertuche, Eloy Carranza, Captain Hayashi (a nationalized Japanese), Tránsito G. Galarza (a railroader), and others.[92] Among those reporting in with Francisco Murguía from San Buenaventura were Benjamín Garza, Heliodoro Pérez, and Fortunato Maycotte. Returning from Cuatro Ciénagas with Jesús Carranza were Francisco Sánchez Herrera, Jesús Novoa, Ramón Sánchez Herrera, Sebastián Carranza, and Ricardo González V. All of these men either reached the rank of general or played an important role in the Revolution. Antonio I. Villarreal, who had been a Maderista diplomat in Spain, returned from overseas and also joined the revolutionaries at Las Hermanas. He was confirmed in the rank of colonel and given command of the newly formed 1st Brigade, with José E. Santos as his chief of staff and regimental commanders Ildefonso "Poncho" Vázquez, Jesús Ramírez Quintanilla, Elías Uribe, and Juan N. Vela. Aside from Villarreal's brigade, there were two others: Jesús Carranza's with regimental commanders Teodoro Elizondo, Alfredo Ricaut, and Atilano Barrera (with subalterns Reynaldo Garza, F. Sánchez Herrera, and Erbey González Díaz), and Murguía's brigade with subalterns Fortunato Maycotte, Benjamín Garza, Bruno Neira, Carlos and Arcadio Osuna, and Martín Salinas.[93]

    González established his headquarters at Hacienda Las Hermanas and began to reorganize and resupply his forces from his base of operations in Piedras Negras. His advance cavalry guarded against any attack by Maass from the south or Rubio Navarrete from the east. Over the next few months Maass' Federals would resume a slow and cautionary rate of advance, taking care to make sure that the rails and the lines of communications remained intact and open to the south. The Constitutionalist cavalry was billeted at area haciendas and small towns; the artillery at Hermanas Station; and the machine guns, headquarters, staff escort, and impedimenta at Hacienda Las Hermanas. Future Constitutionalist General Francisco Urquizo remembered those summer days fondly. A warehouse with a large patio in Sabinas owned by the coal company served as his Sapper battalion's barracks, while the officers stayed in a local schoolhouse. After breakfast there was training in the morning, but the men had the afternoons free. The local *cervecería* supplied unlimited beer, although Urquizo could not remember any incidence of drunkenness, and the two cathouses that served the miners found themselves a new clientele.[94]

To the east, General Rubio's forces proudly proclaimed on July 24 that rail traffic between Monterrey and Laredo had been reestablished, an event of importance because, as General Téllez had stated earlier, it was "of an enormous effect on morale overseas and especially of urgency for the treasury since more than 80 trains contribute collections greater than 100,000 pesos each month, and besides which it would demoralize the rebels [sic] greatly."[95] For this accomplishment Rubio received a promotion, but after two months of patrolling, guarding, and repairing the lines north to Nuevo Laredo and even to the south between Monterrey and Tampico he had grown weary of being able to develop only the smallest of offensive operations.[96] With the accomplishment of his mission General Rubio and his brigade now came under the direct orders of General Téllez, who took over command of the Division of the Bravo from General Fernando González at the end of July. Rubio lost half his command, with three hundred men sent to Ciudad Victoria and another two hundred and an artillery section attached to the Maass column.[97] He could not even carry off a planned four-day "offensive reconnaissance" to clear the Constitutionalists from the Hidalgo and Colombia area (on the Rio Grande about half-way between Piedras Negras and Nuevo Laredo) without either requesting reinforcements from another brigade to increase the garrison at Lampazos or suspending all repair works on the railway, since the demands of that detail required three permanent repair escorts "plus the repair train that in fact goes out every day."[98] Less than a week later he appealed directly to the President for a more active role in the war effort, requesting of Huerta that "another offensive mission be given us, [to recapture] Matamoros or [fight in] Sonora, there being no enemy in the zone in which [my] Brigade operates."[99] Rubio never got over being removed from his initial mission to attack and capture Matamoros; for as long as he was in the Northeast his gaze remained fixed on that port city.

From July 14 to August 10, reports filtered in daily to Constitutionalist headquarters at Las Hermanas of fighting around Monclova and even to the outskirts of the city as Murguía, Sánchez Herrera, Ramírez Quintanilla, and Poncho Vázquez clashed with the Federals at San Buenaventura, El Carmen Pass, Las Adjuntas, and haciendas de la Cruz and Luisiana. Lieutenant Colonel Teodoro Elizondo guarded San Antonio Pass, keeping the Federals in Monclova incommunicado with Candela and Lampazos, while Jesús Soto watched over Bustamante Pass, even making incursions to threaten the Monterrey-Laredo Railroad. The Federals responded by bringing in more artillery.[100] In turn, the Constitutionalists used dynamite procured in Lampazos to compensate for the lack of carbine and machine-gun ammunition in combat. But the dynamite did not always explode when it was supposed to. At other times it detonated too early, killing the revolutionaries, although Captain Manuel "W" González said, "[w]e had good dynamiters because the people from the coal mines knew how to handle explosives well and Juan Hernández García, the Maycottes, the Maltos, Cayetano Santoyo and others lent magnificent service."[101] Perhaps too good, because on July 15 Huerta abrogated Madero's Decree 429 of May 4, 1912, once again outlawing the importation of arms, ammunition, or any related materiel, as well as dynamite, caps, or any other explosives for industrial use without express permission from the Secretary of War.[102]

After a month of training and organization González's men were raring for a fight. On August 13, after a patriotic harangue from Licenciado Isidro Fabela they moved south to attack Monclova, the infantry by train and the cavalry and artillery by horse and mule. Upon reaching and concentrating their forces at Rancho de las Adjuntas in the evening, the Constitutionalists learned that a combined-arms column of Federals had already resumed the initiative, advancing to Abasolo Viejo. The Federals had taken most of their troops northward leaving Monclova wide open for the taking, but in their position at Abasolo they threatened to move into Las Hermanas and cut the Constitutionalists off from their base of supply at Piedras Negras. Immediately González retraced his trajectory to Las Hermanas. He occupied the small hills to the south of the rail station to await the Federals who would have to attack over flat, exposed terrain to dislodge them. On the morning of August 14 he sent his cousin, Colonel Antonio I. Villarreal, to take two squadrons and feel out the enemy at Abasolo Viejo.[103]

Villarreal fell into an ambush crossing a field of maize just before dusk and fought desperately until the early morning hours of the next day. His whole command was dispersed or lost, his Constitutionalists making their way back to Las Hermanas as best they could. González's staff placed the main body of his command in an L-shaped defense to protect the rail station with the Vázquez, Ramírez Quintanilla, and Ricaut squadrons in an arroyo south of the station lined up perpendicular to the rail line and Elías Uribe's Zaragoza Regiment along the rail line shielded by the rail embankment. The Constitutionalists placed "El Rorro" cannon on a small hill also south of the station that was dubbed "artillery" hill, protected by a section of sappers and the headquarters escort. There was also a section of 80-mm. guns on the ridges of the small hills opposite the station, protected by the rest of the sapper battalion and the machine gun battery on the heights of these hills. González had about 1,000 men. The next day the Federals appeared coming up the road from Abasolo Viejo. Shortly before noon they took up position about four kilometers south of the Constitutionalist disposition. The Federals formed a square of infantry and cavalry as their artillery went into battery and loosed a barrage targeted at the rail line and hills south of the station that lasted until dark. The inferior Constitutionalist artillery did not return fire because the Federals remained out of range.[104]

The next morning the Federals again opened up with a barrage, this time aiming for the station itself, which forced the Constitutionalists to move their trains farther north to safety. By 7:30 the battle had begun with the two Constitutionalist lines (North-South and East-West) advancing forward as the Federal infantry began to form up in attack columns of single companies. On this occasion the Constitutionalist artillery opened fire, causing at least two Federal cavalry charges to retreat until some of the pieces broke down (in one instance the ejector failed, so Prieto had to open the breechblock and shoot through the muzzle with his pistol to force the shell out), forcing them to be withdrawn from battle, which must have adversely affected the morale of the Constitutionalist cavalry because it then initiated an orderly retreat. José Santos' horse was shot dead, and he had to run back to retrieve his saddle under fire. But he also may have gone just to get his bottle of mescal, which he called "ignorance"; every time he took a swig he used to tell his compañeros that he was finishing off ignorance. At this point the Federal infantry attacked and the contest for the hill occupied by the Constitutionalist sappers and machine guns became very active until the Constitutionalists had exhausted almost all their ammunition and began to withdraw in echelon around 4 p.m. First the train with the wounded departed and then, after all the trains were away, González ordered the rails destroyed and headed for Oballos. As the Constitutionalists retreated, the Federal artillery continued to shoot, but almost immediately after Jesús Carranza removed the black leather hat from his head the Federal bugles, as though on cue, sounded the cease-fire.[105]

The Constitutionalists reported few losses: maybe a dozen killed and about the same number wounded, including Lieutenant Daniel Díaz Couder's freakish head wound. Thanks to the work of Major Doctor Ricardo Suárez Gamboa and the medical staff, the lieutenant reported 100 percent ready for duty after about fifteen days none the worse for wear and sporting only a small scar on his nose and neck, the location of the entry and exit wounds, respectively. During recovery, however, he was so sensitive that he could not even bear to wear a shirt. If so much as a fly landed on his body, he would burst out screaming in pain.[106]

In spite of losing the battle, the good order displayed by the revolutionaries reassured them of their abilities. The Constitutionalists halted in Oballos and burned the mine at Lampacitos to deprive the Federals of the coal there. González established his headquarters at Aura Station and began to collect his men, except for Murguía and his group, who remained around Santa Gertrudis (near San Buenaventura).[107]

Huerta now gave up any hopes of catching the Constitutionalists between Maass' and Rubio Navarrete's columns, and he instructed General Téllez, commander of the Division of the Bravo that "all Federal forces were to advance simultaneously on Hermanas, Sabinas, and [Piedras Negras]… with the object of making the rebels [sic] withdraw to the desert [of western Coahuila] where it will be difficult for them reorganize."[108] But Téllez's orders to General Rubio seemed to lack the same sense of urgency. He waited until two days after Maass' Federals had battled González between Monclova and Hermanas before telling Rubio to "please prepare long scouting missions to the north with competent effectives and artillery… to cut off any rebels [sic] who might be able to march from Colombia or Hidalgo to protect the rebel forces." He estimated the Constitutionalist relief force departing from Colombia to number only between two and three hundred men. But his next two sentences sounded at once cautious and decisive: "The movement should be without leaving Lampazos unattended. The time has arrived to employ our elements with all speed."[109] Rubio confidently replied that a great desert separated Lampazos from Guadalupe, where he believed the Constitutionalists to be, and therefore to come east the Constitutionalists would be forced to follow the Rio Grande, in which case their movement would be sensed.[110] As it would turn out, he was wrong.

Between August 18 and 26, Villarreal's men waged combat in Abasolo and Rodríguez, while Murguía fought in San Buenaventura and Ricaut's men in Hermanas, taking the towns and then giving them up once the Federals received reinforcements, in hit-and-run fashion. The greatest challenge, however, came from Federal irregulars fighting under the capable and intelligent Luis Alberto Guajardo, a very practical warrior who was the commander who had virtually destroyed the Colorado invasion of Coahuila by Marcelo Caraveo the year before and was intimately familiar with the region and greatly respected by the Constitutionalists.[111]

On September 4, Murguía waged a fierce battle at El Carmen Pass. Villarreal, who had spent the night in Santa Gertrudis, four kilometers distant from San Buenaventura, attacked the latter town on September 5 at 6 a.m., penetrating as far as the main plaza. But since they did not cut the lines of communication between Monclova and Nadadores, Federal reinforcements arrived around 2 p.m. and drove the Constitutionalists back to Borregas Pass where the revolutionaries went into camp and mourned their losses. First Captain José María Vargas and Lieutenant Pedro Riojas had been killed and Lieutenant Colonel Poncho Vázquez, Second Captain Gonzalo de la Garza, Jesús B. Rodríguez, Rafael Lara, Lieutenant Alfredo López Prado, and twenty-five troops were wounded. Vázquez's wounds were bad enough that he had to turn over command of his regiment to Francisco Silva and go to the military hospital in Piedras Negras.[112] From mid-August to the end of September González delayed Maass' advance by destroying the railway to the Federal's rear, forcing him to constantly waste time reestablishing his lines of communication to Saltillo.[113]

Around this time, Constitutionalist Lieutenant Colonel Elías Uribe asked for and received permission to go fight in La Laguna, where he was from. He left with a small escort, turning over command of his regiment to Major Rafael Saldaña Galván. On September 21, the Constitutionalists mobilized to stop the Federals trying to advance on Constitutionalist headquarters at Aura Station along the rail line. Villarreal with the majority of his men attacked the Federals at Abasolo, on the Federal left, while González and Carranza attacked Hermanas with the forces of Ricaut, Juan N. Vela, Eduardo Castro, and others. Saldaña Galván died in the attack, gut shot at the beginning of the attack on Abasolo where he rode at the front of Villarreal's column. The Federals forced González and Carranza back to Aura. Villarreal had to give up Abasolo Viejo, but he remained in possession of Abasolo Nuevo and La Libertad. When he learned that the Federals had captured Las Hermanas, however, he feared for his vulnerable left flank and retreated to Aura Station through Los Caballos Hill.[114]

A week later, two strong columns of Federals attacked Aura and after six hours of combat forced the Constitutionalists back to Barroterán, the last position of defense on the International Railroad and where the last action in the Coahuila campaign took place. Constitutionalist Colonels Villarreal, Murguía, Ricaut, and Atilano Barrera were arrayed along the hills at Barroterán with González and Carranza in the middle, close to the trains that they still had. The battle began with a tremendous Federal barrage by the Betancourt and Leniza batteries. General Joaquín Maass commanded the Federals with principal subordinates, Colonels Wilfrido Massieu and Arturo A. Alvarez with the 42nd and 47th Auxiliary Infantry Battalions, the Guerrero Battalion, the Security Regiment, the Gendarmes of the Army, the 13th Cavalry Regiment, and the irregulars commanded by Colonel Luis Alberto Guajardo, around 1,500 men total. González and Murguía tried to contain their men, who began to retreat, and finally the two had to follow, keeping up with the trains at a gallop. González had already ordered all the forces in Coahuila to abandon Múzquiz, Sabinas, and the coal mines and for the forces in Piedras Negras, Zaragoza, and Morelos to concentrate in Allende in preparation of leaving to campaign in Nuevo León State.[115]

The Constitutionalists withdrew to Sabinas, destroying the track behind them. In the rail station at Sabinas, González and Carranza held a conference with their jefes and discussed abandoning Coahuila to undertake a campaign along the National Railroad, a decision that would ultimately lead them to victory at Ciudad Victoria. The mounted forces continued to gather in Allende, while the trains continued toward Piedras Negras tearing up track. The railroaders then went to Hidalgo, where they were armed and given mounts in order to participate in the campaign along the National Railroad in Nuevo Leon. The hospital and nurses under General Pedro Martínez Pérez escaped to Eagle Pass, Texas, while the doctors left to accompany the soldiers on campaign.[116] On the afternoon of October 7 the Federals finally marched into Piedras Negras, previously vacated by the Constitutionalists.[117]

ANALYSIS

The Federal pincer strategy designed to destroy the Constitutionalists in Coahuila and drive them into the desert had been frustrated by constant delays in trying to keep open their own lines of communication, improper coordination of their field forces, internal politics, and the drain of near daily skirmishing. What is more, the campaign's political objective had backfired, since it resulted in the First Chief leaving Coahuila to begin a tour of major revolutionary commands, further legitimizing his leadership and unifying the movement. The Federals had conquered Coahuila, but the revolution in the Northeast continued to metastasize, spilling over into Nuevo León and Tamaulipas under the command of General Pablo González who had just been appointed command of the Constitutionalist Army Corps of the Northeast.[118]

Chihuahua

PASCUAL OROZCO'S COLUMN

The idea for Pascual Orozco Jr.'s column started with a handshake, or rather a hug. Since none of his former enemies in the North made a bid for his support, Orozco accepted the only forthcoming offer for his services—from Huerta. The two struck a deal based largely on money and Orozco's reinstatement in the Rural Police Corps, but in order to provide the thinnest veneer of respectability Orozco got the government to commit (however sincerely) to enact land reform, the supposed goal behind Orozco's rebellion of the previous year. They sealed the agreement with an awkward embrace captured forever in the infamous and widely-disseminated photograph taken in the Hotel Lascuráin. After accepting Huerta's amnesty and agreeing to fight for the Federal Army in a marriage of convenience, Orozco and his Colorados had marched up from Mexico City through Zacatecas. Like Villa, they were only now in the summer of 1913 prepared to begin campaigning in earnest.[119]

Orozco and his men departed Torreón in the evening of July 1 headed northward to reinforce General Salvador Mercado and his besieged Federals in Chihuahua City. The Federals could only send highly-motivated irregulars on a cross-country campaign through enemy territory with insecure lines of communication and not lose a significant number of men to desertion. Spending the night in Bermejillo, the Orozquistas stayed there for two days to finish organizing the column. The Orozco Brigade, as it was called, contained 15 jefes, 194 officers, and 943 men along with two 70-mm. mountain pieces, apportioned among three battalions, one corps, and five regiments, all extremely under strength and top-heavy in officers, which was probably indicative of their hope of recruiting more soldiers once on their native soil in Chihuahua. On July 4 the column again got underway. It passed through Conejos the next day, and then on July 6 Orozco's advance scouts ran into a party of about eighty Constitutionalists escorting food and fodder in the vicinity of Hacienda Jaral Grande. A rather intense firefight broke out and the Colorados wound up killing six of the Constitutionalists and capturing their provisions. The column set up camp in Yermo and then continued on the road, making nighttime stops in Ceballos, Escalón, Rellano, and finally, on July 10, Dolores Station.[120]

Upon setting camp around Dolores Station, Orozco received news about the proximity of some Constitutionalists and immediately ordered a few regiments of cavalry, probably about two hundred men, to go and clear them out. At kilometer 1364 on the Central Railroad (about eight kilometers south of Jiménez) his Colorados ran into the Constitutionalists and defeated the opposing force, killing eighteen and taking four prisoners, "of whom were made an exemplary punishment," meaning he had them killed. The column then broke camp and continued on with a nighttime march. A Constitutionalist colonel named González (probably Miguel), who had been in charge of the small garrison in Jiménez, fell back to Camargo. Orozco wanted to hurry up and occupy the town while it was empty; his men entered the plaza on July 11 at 3 p.m. Before the Constitutionalists abandoned Jiménez they sent word to Colonel Maclovio Herrera that Orozco was coming up from Torreón with a column of one thousand men, most of whom were reported to be infantry recruited according to the Federal style, meaning through the draft, although this information was probably inaccurate. Immediately Herrera ordered his men to head south. By the time they reached Camargo, however, Orozco had already occupied Jiménez, and so Herrera headed to Hacienda San Isidro, just two kilometers from the railway, where he set camp and awaited the bulk of his force coming down under the command of Lieutenant Colonel Trinidad Rodríguez. In Jiménez, Orozco sent a telegram in Herrera's name to Constitutionalist General Manuel Chao in Parral requesting reinforcements. Sensing a trap, instead of reinforcements Chao sent a passenger train that the Colorados shot up and captured upon its arrival three hours later. With his trap foiled, Orozco ordered Marcelo Caraveo to load all the infantry aboard the train and had them continue moving to the north toward Díaz Station (halfway between Jiménez and Camargo) as Orozco followed with the cavalry.[121]

Díaz Station July 12

In the early morning hours of July 12, upon arrival at Díaz Station, Orozco's men caught sight of the Constitutionalist trains and surmised that they were unaware of the presence of Orozco's Colorados because they were running with their lights on. So, taking advantage of the darkness, Orozco deployed his men for a 4:30 a.m. assault. He detached his various units in several directions for the purpose of cutting off a Constitutionalist retreat. In the morning a Constitutionalist train heading southward from Camargo noticed the Colorados at Díaz Station and stopped as the Constitutionalists poured out of the train. Colonel Herrera marched his men off to confront the Colorados, who were lined up behind the railroad embankment. Herrera opened fire from the hills opposite the train station and led his men into battle with his usual bravado, from the front. But given the evenness of the terrain and the Colorados' well-chosen positions he knew that it would be near impossible to move them. The rifle fire grew intense as Herrera had his horse shot out from underneath him and received a wound to the foot. A relief train arrived from the north to reinforce Herrera but because of the Orozquista rifle fire, both copious and accurate, not one individual was able to get off and eventually the train had to pull back toward the north. At some point confusion entered the Constitutionalist ranks, probably because they sensed that Orozco had outflanked them, and they broke and ran in utter disorder, some headed down the Parral River to La Boquilla and others back to Camargo. Constitutionalist Colonel Trinidad Rodríguez marshaled the various minor units, collected up the stragglers as best he could, and returned to Camargo to await the "red vandals."[122]

The whole affair lasted a short six hours. Cleaning up the battlefield, the Colorados found thirty-six dead Constitutionalists, took nine prisoners, and collected weapons and twenty-five horses and ten mules. Orozco suspected that there might have been even more Constitutionalists killed because he did not have the time to dedicate to a detailed inspection of the field of combat. Orozco lost twenty killed as well as two officers and thirty-two soldiers wounded. After the cavalry returned from the pursuit, Orozco again got underway headed for Santa Rosalía de Camargo on July 14, attending to the proper services of campaign as relate to security.[123]

Camargo July 14

Orozco's column arrived at Camargo around noon. After receiving reports from all his commanders that the city had been abandoned by enemy forces, he ordered a detailed reconnaissance of the hills surrounding the plaza. The scouts reported seeing Constitutionalists making use of the broken ground to conceal themselves and so Orozco dictated his disposition. He placed artillery at a point called "the Citadel," across from the train station, sending considerable detachments to cover all the prominent points to the north of the city, such that his men achieved interlocking fields of fire, and readying a strong column of mounted infantry extending from north to south to protect the flank; the mounted infantry made use of the irrigation ditch there as a natural parapet with the trees for concealment.[124]

Colonel Trinidad Rodríguez placed his Constitutionalists around the city and attacked the Colorados. The action began on the wings of Orozco's men deployed in a line of shooters parallel to the north, and on the east side of the city. Then Orozco's outposts to the southeast reported another group of revolutionaries coming from the south trying to hit the Colorado rearguard and outflank his men along the natural parapet provided by the irrigation ditch. He immediately threw in his cavalry reserve to protect his left flank and rear, which arrived opportunely. Within just a few moments the Constitutionalists on the Ojo Caliente side, that is, to the west, withdrew leaving the rest of the line compromised. The combat became generalized to the north, northeast, and southeast. Then Orozco sent an infantry force to make use of the natural cover and concealment to execute a quick and hidden movement to outflank the Constitutionalist line of fire parallel to the north side of the town. This force caught the Constitutionalists in enfilading fire, even a little to their rear, forcing a group to flee to the west side of the town where they sought refuge in some houses. But the Colorado artillery soon dislodged them and forced them back toward the northeast. Discouraged, the Constitutionalists began to quit the fight. After seven hours of combat they undertook a full retreat to the protection of the hills to the west and northwest.[125]

An hour later Orozco observed reinforcements for the revolutionaries arriving from the north, and then the Constitutionalists delivered another assault, attacking on all sides in an effort to breach the perimeter. Rodríguez demonstrated exceptional valor, and with incredible audacity penetrated to the center of the city and there personally fired on the enemy, who possessed the high points inside the town and had recourse to a Rexer. The defenders began pouring in return machine-gun fire on the Constitutionalists that hit Colonel González's horse; the colonel barely escaped with his life. Finally after two more hours of combat the Constitutionalists again retreated, pursued by Orozco's cavalry reserve. Upon reaching the safety of Conchos Station, they sent a request for more ammunition to the Revolutionary Junta in El Paso and then departed for Naica.[126]

The Colorados recovered seventy-three dead Constitutionalists, took eighteen prisoners, and captured 160 mounts, including a prized horse belonging to Chao's second-in-command, Eulogio Ortiz, along with some other equipment of U.S. manufacture. They lost twenty-five of their own killed (including three officers) and fifty-one troops wounded in the battle waged against an estimated fifteen hundred Constitutionalists belonging to Rodríguez, Herrera, Chao, and Hernández. Orozco's column finally arrived in Chihuahua City on July 22.[127] Once in Chihuahua, however, Orozco never again led men in the field. One explanation for this abrupt change in zeal may have been Huerta's refusal to appoint Orozco to governor, in spite of Mercado's recommendation that he do so.[128] As much as Huerta distrusted his own Federal generals, the chances that he would promote a caudillo like Orozco to governor were slim.

VILLA'S RETURN SOUTH

For various reasons Villa decided to postpone the attack on Ciudad Juárez so that he could march south and mass his forces. Perhaps the Federal column that General Mercado had sent under Colonel Francisco Castro to Ciudad Juárez at the beginning of July factored foremost into his decision. Castro brought with him the 23rd Infantry Battalion, raising the total number of defenders inside Ciudad Juárez to some eleven hundred men, including additional regulars from the 15th battalion, four hundred irregulars, and another forty artillerymen manning four cannons and four machine guns. In addition Villa realized that, after a month in Guadalupe, Ortega's position had become quite compromised: he was isolated from the other Constitutionalists and facing opposing forces greater in number and resources inside Ciudad Juárez. So, on July 26 Villa sent Major Santiago Ramírez with three hundred men to Guadalupe for the purpose of reinforcing Ortega and escorting his troops and the ammunition that they had been stockpiling. Ramírez brought a letter for Ortega containing instructions to report to Casas Grandes with his regiment and join the rest of the Villa Brigade.[129]

Ranchería Station August 5

Two days after Ramírez's arrival the 650-man column was ready to depart and meet up with the rest of the Villa Brigade at San Buenaventura, the designated rendezvous point. Once underway they received word of a train with a great amount of money, arms, and provisions leaving Ciudad Juárez for Chihuahua City. In effect, with the capital city garrison cut off from the nearest concentration of Federals at Torreón, General Mercado had sent General Jesús Mancilla to Ciudad Juárez to buy foodstuffs for his division as well as for the town, which was suffering from a scarcity of staples. The train was making its return run. Ortega and Ramírez decided to attack the convoy and made a forced march to Ranchería Station (ninety-four kilometers south of Ciudad Juárez), leaving their impedimenta with a 100-man guard detail at a ranch called Los Charcos. At 4 a.m., when the column arrived, Colonel Ortega ordered Major Ramírez to take possession of the railway about a kilometer south of the station, with categorical orders to hold his fire until the first train had passed. Ortega's González Ortega Regiment took up position on some hills to the east of the railway just opposite the station, and the colonel emplaced a machine gun on a small hill that had a cross that was a bit closer to the station. The plan was for Ramírez to open fire making a southerly movement while Ortega assaulted the trains to the rear and side. The men slept in their positions and then the next day saw the first train and then more: nine trains in total.[130]

The Federal convoy escort consisted of General Mancilla commanding the 15th and 33rd Battalion, Alberto Terrazas' Social Defense forces, and José Inés Salazar's Colorados under the immediate command of Colonel Carlos Martínez and closely matched the Constitutionalists in numbers. As soon as Major Ramírez grasped the enormity of the Federal convoy, fear overcame him and he sounded the retreat call just as Ortega's machine guns opened fire. Thereafter the major could not regain control of his men and had to flee to the west, pursued by Federals of the 15th Battalion and a picket of cavalry. Ortega, meanwhile, experienced some success, his machine gun tearing up the Huertista infantrymen as they attempted to detrain, soon leaving the embankment full of corpses. The Federal infantry tried to organize in columns and attack the Constitutionalists, but again the machine gun stopped them cold, and they began to flee in disorder, leaving behind two trains.[131]

Ortega only had 250 men with him to the east of the railway. The Huertistas launched the 33rd Battalion and Social Defense volunteers against Ortega under the protection of two cannons and four machine guns supported by four hundred horsemen under irregular Colonel Carlos Martínez, making a flanking movement behind the hills. The carnage was horrible, as Ortega's single machine gun was put out of commission by a piece of shrapnel; the entire machine-gun crew died at their post. Twice the Huertistas tried to ascend to Ortega's positions, but they were repulsed with tremendous losses, leaving the hills littered with dead. Then, gathering all the infantry, they made one last push reaching the summit and engaged Ortega's men in hand-to-hand combat.[132]

The Constitutionalist defense was nothing short of heroic. It was, however, impossible to hold their ground, virtually surrounded as they were, and the Constitutionalists had to beat a retreat under a shower of bullets. Colonel Ortega was the last to leave the field, covering the retreat of his men; Colorado Colonel Martínez gave pursuit for about two kilometers and then returned to the trains. According to the prisoners taken, whom the Constitutionalists immediately executed after interrogation, the Huertista losses totaled 150 dead and 200 wounded, unbelievably high numbers. The Constitutionalists lost the machine gun, which was put out of service, and an "express" with ammunition that fell into the hands of the Huertistas, both of which were regrettable, but not as much as the losses in personnel: twenty wounded, among them Lieutenant Colonel Isaac Arroyo and Captains Pedro and Cruz Jasso and Indalecio Varela, as well as the death of thirteen soldiers, Major Manuel Benavides, and the nonagenarian First Captain Silvestre Juárez, who fought like a man seventy years his junior.[133]

Silvestre Juárez had joined Ortega in 1910 and had lost one son fighting in Madero's rebellion and then another in Orozco's. Being from Coyame, a hotbed of Porfiristas, he responded to a Huertista recruiter's offer of land for those who would fight for the usurper with: "We don't fight for recompense, or to acquire anything, but for the Cause, because we are patriots," making a revolution simply for the purpose of acquiring land sound crass. One can only guess at the "Cause" he was referring to: rule of law, constitutionalist observance, respect for life and the "Supreme Powers" (that is, the federal-level executive, legislative, and judiciary), or anti-militarism, but he and his sons had been prepared to die for those beliefs. And now Captain Juárez was alone in the world and fully expected to die on campaign. The day of the fight at Ranchería he was shot in the leg and could not ride, so he remained in his position until the arrival of the Huertistas, shooting a Huertista officer dead and another behind him when still others came up behind him and coldcocked him with the butt of a rifle. When he came to they asked who he was, and he said, "I am Silvestre Juárez, First Captain of Ortega's forces. Shoot me." And so they did, leaving him there next to the stone that he had been using for cover.[134]

The next day Ortega and Ramírez again joined forces heading for Villa Ahumada and then undertook the march to San Buenaventura, where they awaited the arrival of General Villa. On August 13 Villa's men left Ascención headed first to Corralitos and then to Nueva Casas Grande where they remained for three days. Continuing on through Galeana the brigade arrived on August 18 at San Buenaventura, a beautiful little pueblo in a fertile valley with most of the buildings surrounded by orchards and gardens that presented a very picturesque scene. Ortega had been waiting for Villa about six days when he received notice that Villa was about to arrive and went out with his whole force to meet him. Ortega introduced his officers to the general.[135]

Once united, the brigade proceeded to Cruces where Villa found out that Colorados had occupied Madera and shot the mayor appointed by Villa, so Villa sent Major Porfirio Talamantes to take a course through San José Bavícora and defeat those Colorados. The rest of the brigade continued on to Namiquipa where it stayed for two days and Villa appointed Toribio Ortega to be his second-in-command, with immediate command of the González Ortega Regiment passing to Lieutenant Colonel Porfirio Ornelas and Lieutenant Colonel Eleuterio Hermosillo becoming the brigade chief of staff. While in Namiquipa, Villa received dispatches informing him of a combined

Federal and Colorado force at San Andrés sent by Federal General Mercado to intercept his Constitutionalists, and he decided to attack it. Heading for Bachíniva the brigade crossed through a beautiful land of picturesque mountains covered with pines, cedars, evergreen oaks, and immense potato fields to arrive at Hacienda del Rubio (today Colonia Álvaro Obregón on the west side of Cuauhtémoc). On August 23 Major Talamantes caught up to the main body at Hacienda del Rubio after completing his mission to clear the Colorados out of Madera. Resolved to attack San Andrés, the Villa Brigade passed through San Antonio de los Arenales (today Cuauhtémoc) so that the Huertistas would not sense their approach, and then turned easterly toward Bustillos. They arrived near San Andrés around midnight.[136]

San Andrés August 26

Colorado General Félix Terrazas' force at San Andrés consisted mostly of Orozquistas and a few Federals; he had a total of 980 men armed with Mausers according to Villa, although other sources put the figure lower, at between 400 and 600. Villa's brigade had 1,025 men at this point.[137] The Constitutionalists approached unnoticed by the Colorados until one sentry fired a shot around 5:30 a.m. that alerted the rest to take up position and begin pouring in heavy fire. The shooting continued into the morning as the Constitutionalists tried to occupy favorable ground and Villa ordered his men to keep up a "partial" fire, since they lacked an abundance of ammunition, in order to ascertain the exact disposition of the opposing force. In the daylight they could take measure of the opposing force's positions on a mesa next to the town that thoroughly dominated the terrain. There were four hundred Colorados there, with more on the edge of town and all along where the trains were. In the daylight their two cannons went into action, firing rapidly.[138]

Villa placed the town under siege and slowly began tightening the circle for the purpose of being in position to deliver a night assault. The González Ortega Regiment attacked the mesa and the town as the 1st, 2nd, and 3rd Squadrons of the 1st Regiment and the 2nd Regiment with other small units assaulted the other positions and the trains where the Federal artillery was located. The shooting went on all day. First Captain Celso Rayos took a few of his men and tried to dislodge the "reds" from the mesa. But as he approached the top the shooting from the fortifications increased so much in intensity that the captain fell never to rise again, while Second Captain Antonio Moreno was wounded. Respected for his knowledge of the art of war, Rayos had such humility and courage that he astonished others. Major Félix Rivero also died in the assault; descended from Indians and of stone-cold courage he was a serious man of few words who fought with characteristic serenity, was always ready to do his duty, and had been one of the first people to join Villa upon his return from the United States.[139]

As night began to fall the Colorados had abandoned the mesa for the town, where the González Ortega Regiment had penetrated to the first houses on the outskirts. Those attacking the trains were getting closer, too. Villa knew the enemy guns had to be silenced and asked Juan N. Medina, his chief advisor, for his thoughts on the matter. Medina agreed with Villa that the guns had to be taken out, and once night had fallen, Major Benito Artalejo executed Medina's plan of attack, lobbing dynamite at the two 75-mm. Mondragón field pieces and finally conquering the position and capturing its personnel. At that point the Federals broke and ran, and Terrazas escaped with an escort numbering anywhere from thirty to sixty men. The Constitutionalists captured the Federals' trains, reducing the Colorados to impotence. As morning broke, the fighting had concluded.[140]

The battlefield offered stunning images of bodies and puddles of blood everywhere. During the night one of the Constitutionalists had tried to wake up a buddy to relieve him from his watch, but his compañero would not budge. So, he tried to shake him and then removed his hat to discover that his face had been blown apart by a bullet. Giant pyres of dead were heaped up, topped with firewood, and set ablaze; the next day they presented a Dantesque and macabre scene, with rigid and contracted hands raised to the heavens, as if in a gesture of desperation, craniums with eyes popped out of their sockets, scorched skin, half-burned intestines protruding from bellies, and torsos without heads.[141] General Caraveo said that Villa "permitted his men to cruelly burn alive all the wounded and shoot en masse those who remained standing."[142] But this is not believable: Villa had no problem killing, but no other sources mention him engaging in torture.

The Constitutionalists collected seventy-two dead; four wounded, whom they sent to the hospital; and another 237 Colorados taken prisoner, whom they led away in groups and shot according to the Juárez Law, including three colonels, two lieutenant colonels, several majors, and a multitude of officers of lesser rank. No one was spared, not even the enlisted men, who knew what they were doing upon volunteering and thus were guilty of their crimes in the eyes of the Constitutionalists. The lone exception was twelve Federal artillerymen, who were prized for their technical knowledge and permitted to join the brigade. Villa reported his own losses at five officers and sixteen men killed and two jefes, two officers, and twenty-seven men wounded, including his good friend, Lieutenant Colonel Eleuterio Hermosillo. The booty amounted to 421 7-mm. rifles, 20,000 rounds, and seven trains with unimportant miscellaneous contents.[143]

Villa sent his wounded under the escort of Major Julio Acosta and 150 soldiers to go by train to Madera and thence to Agua Prieta, Sonora. Due to a lack of pasture area Villa had to leave San Andrés for Hacienda Bustillos where he learned of a second force sent to attack him from Chihuahua City composed of eight hundred men, with five hundred commanded by Generals Caraveo and Mancilla approaching by rail. Villa had First Captain Andrés Rivera take ten men on a scouting and delay mission to blow up the rails at a place close to the tunnels, an order he successfully executed, forcing the train carrying five hundred men to derail and even firing a few shots at the Federals at said location. Rivera's actions held up the Federal column for eight days, during which time an argument ensued over what to do next. Toribio Ortega suggested that they lie in wait for the enemy, while Villa wanted to take the fight to the enemy, even though they did not have enough ammunition for another engagement on the scale of San Andrés. Medina did not want to wait, because the infantry support necessary to defend the artillery pieces in combat would require 150 men alone, decreasing the numbers available for the firing line. In response Ortega said that they should dump the pieces. Villa, incredulous, rebuked his friend Ortega's shortsightedness, along with all hack revolutionaries who thought themselves soldiers, and instead took Medina's advice to avoid battle until he could increase his numbers.[144] Having observed the Federal guns in the field during the Orozco campaign of 1912, Villa had a greater appreciation for the artillery arm than did his counterpart Pablo González or even Obregón, who tended to favor infantry and machine guns over artillery and cavalry in battles.

So Villa decided to evade the Federals. From Bustillos he went to San Antonio de los Arenales where Lieutenant Colonel (probably Julián) Granados and Major Carlos Carranza, the First Chief's nephew, joined Villa with three hundred men, and then continued on a westward course through Malpaso, to Pedernales, where he remained for two days. He then ordered the rails lifted from Rosario and left for Bachíniva where Colonel Fidel Ávila, whom Villa had sent to Sonora before leaving Ascensión, arrived with a column bringing ammunition. In Las Chepas (about five kilometers due south of Bachíniva) Villa distributed 200,000 cartridges and made the forty-kilometer trek back to Hacienda del Rubio and then Bustillos to set up camp. By making the circular trip Villa threw the Huertistas off his trail; they instead followed the trains conducting Villa's wounded to Agua Prieta.[145]

At this point there is some confusion about what happened next. General Juan Barragán, soon to be the First Chief's chief of staff, suggested that after having dodged the Huertistas, Villa was making preparations to lay siege to Chihuahua City when he received a commission from the revolutionary jefes of Durango and the Laguna region to come help them attack Torreón, similar to the commission that had invited the First Chief to do the same back in July. Villa's supporters, in contrast, maintain that Villa had planned all along to go to Camargo and unite with the forces of Herrera, Hernández, and Chao. Once there he learned of the Constitutionalists' failed attack on Torreón, and how, emboldened by their victory, the Federals in Torreón had tried to invade Chihuahua on two separate occasions, although they were turned back by Herrera at Santa Clara both times. Right then and there, General Villa decided to attack Torreón. No matter how Torreón as an objective came to his attention, the logic for attacking it remained the same: a.) Villa had cannons captured from San Andrés that he could use in the assault, b.) Chihuahua City was too strong, having just received Orozco and his reinforcements, c.) Chihuahua City posed no real threat to his rear, d.) he needed the extra men from the commands in the lagunera region to increase his scale of operations, and e.) Torreón presented a much bigger prize, militarily, than Chihuahua City.[146]

Villa left Bustillos with his brigade and then crossed through San Nicolás de Carretas where it was raining profusely and the town was holding a festival. Villa decided to halt and try out a campaign tent taken from the Colorados at San Andrés. Some of his men began to get drunk on sotol, and Villa responded by having all the alcohol confiscated and poured in the river. Then the men started gulping down river water, so he lit it afire with a match. The story, whether true or apocryphal, exemplifies Villa's intolerance for soldiers drinking while on campaign. The following day the brigade went to Satevó and Santa Gertrudis (about twenty-five kilometers southwest of Naica), and then the next day they marched eighty kilometers to Ojo Caliente near La Boquilla dam on the Conchos River to arrive at Santa Rosalío Camargo on September 15. Hernandez's men gave the Villa Brigade a warm reception. At a conference held in the Hotel Hidalgo the jefes resolved to go to Jiménez to collect Urbina and his brigade and then join with Contreras for the attack on Torreón.[147] On the last day of summer in 1913, Villa would be directing the battle for Torreón, his first major battle ever, over seven months after the Citadel cuartelazo.

*   *   *

Nowhere are the disadvantages of the legal and capital barriers to entry and the American arms embargo more evident than in González's forces in the Northeast. The Constitutionalists fighting in the region were poorly armed, mostly with .30-30s, homemade cannons, and a few machine guns. Short of ammunition, they had to use dynamite to compensate for their lack of firepower, at great danger to their persons. At Candela on July 2 Constitutionalists had no machine guns, although the Federals did, and at Las Hermanas their homemade cannons did not have the range to hit the Federals, who did possess effective guns. Without artillery, the Constitutionalists had to resort to planting bombs that they hoped the Federals would detonate, but on the road to Monclova and at Bocatoche Station they failed to explode. The Federals at Torreón had the use of spotlights to light up the fields of fire at night while the Constitutionalist received the great disappointment of seeing the First Chief arrive without any war materiel, much less additional people. Huerta sought to clamp down even further on what the Constitutionalists could get their hands on by rescinding Madero's Decree Number 429 of May 4, 1912, making permission from War necessary to import any industrial material, such as dynamite, that might be repurposed for war.

The application of the military arts and sciences on display in the North by both Federals and Constitutionalists revealed both abilities and limitations. At Las Hermanas the Federals inexplicably formed up in an infantry square, which in spite of what some historians have said, did not adhere to Federal Army tactical doctrine. And yet once again, at Candela, they allowed themselves to be surprised because they did not maintain proper security. At Torreón, Federal General Bravo also performed poorly, deploying his artillery on the firing line, not preparing defenses, and not utilizing his interior lines of communication to keep fresh troops in the fight. On the other side, Jesús Carranza's Constitutionalists at Candela admitted to an ignorance of appropriate tactics for retreating, and Constitutionalist staff officers occupied the firing line, because they did not know any better. The Constitutionalists who attacked Torreón lacked discipline and a true unity of command and carried off assaults in an uncoordinated fashion. On the plus side, despite their defeat at Las Hermanas, the good fighting and orderly retreat gave González's Constitutionalists some reassurance in their abilities. After Las Hermanas, González kept Federal columns at bay for almost two months by hitting the communications and minor towns to their rear.

Because of its eighteenth-century practices for filling out the ranks, the Federal Army could only count on irregulars like Orozco's Colorados to travel cross-country without secure lines of communications and not lose people to desertion. On the other hand, Huerta's unwillingness to trust his generals, most especially in refusing to make Orozco the military governor of Chihuahua, led to that general disengaging from combat operations and others, such as Rubio, being sidelined. War took away Rubio's mission to recapture Matamoros and refused to give him permission to attack toward Monclova, possibly based on favoritism for Huerta's nephew, General Maass. But Rubio's subsequent recall to Mexico City (discussed in chapter 7) reveals that perhaps Huerta did not fully trust Rubio. Refusal of permission by War for Rubio to advance on Monclova resulted in his holding force at Candela being defeated and probably quashed any possibility of catching González's forces in a pincer and annihilating them. But in forcing the Constitutionalists to retake Candela, War's refusal resulted in the Constitutionalists losing all of Coahuila, a rare win for the Federal Army and a demonstration of the steep learning curve experienced by citizen-soldiers seeking to master the operational arts. Unfortunately for Huerta, though, by forcing the First Chief out of Coahuila he compelled Carranza to embark on an odyssey through the North, solidifying his leadership of the pan-Norteño movement.

The Constitutionalist Army also fell prey to internal politics and discord, such as that experienced by General Aguilar among the leaders of the developing Division of the Center, which would become a matter of concern later, although for now it did not seem to hinder effective operations.

In this time frame, the government's defense establishment continued to experience great change. The first casualty of the revolution was the Rural Police Corps, which after August of 1913, ceased to exist as an organization. It appeared for several years later that the Colegio Militar would suffer the same fate, as both were dissolved by Huerta, not the Jacobin Constitutionalists as one might have predicted. In order to provide officers for the greatly expanded army, Huerta crafted policy changes that both attenuated their requisite numbers, and provided for an initial tranche of those officers. The new Federal tables of organization and equipment somewhat ameliorated the urgency for new officers by reducing the officer-to-men ratio, but it placed a heavy burden on the noncommissioned officer corps. The newest officers consisted of those youngsters ushered out of the Escuela Nacional and the Colegio Militar (Preparatory Military School). Huerta's decrees also formalized a special kind of on-the-job training in the field for "cadets," essentially doing to the officer corps what he had done to the enlisted men with Decree number 436 of May 1, where he made the School of the Soldier "rudimentary." The new category of cadet degraded the Federal Officer Corps by injecting it with an up-and-coming group possessing no more expertise than the revolutionaries, whose newest officers despite their lack of schooling likewise had recourse to Federal Army doctrine and a hands-on combat education. In this respect, the Federals fared much worse, because the youths from the military institutions failed miserably with regards to horsemanship and other field know-how when compared to that possessed by the Norteño officers with rural roots, and more especially with respect to leadership attributes. The Federal artillery offered the only true technical edge over the Constitutionalists, as Villa demonstrated by sparing the lives of the artillerymen at San Andrés—the genesis of his favored artillery and cavalry force composition. Villa's upcoming victory at Torreón would greatly expand and solidify his artillery contingent.

Six

Villa Secures Chihuahua:
September–November, 1913

Fierro, Chao, and the First Chief—La Laguna—The Scout Train—
Villa's Division of the North—Avilés—Felipe Alvírez—Second
Torreón—Huerta's Second Coup—U.S. Arms Embargo—Plana
Mayor Expanded—Riches of Torreón—A Rough Return to
Chihuahua—Colorados Lead the Way at La Cruz and Camargo—
Regimentation of Villa's Division—Battle of Chihuahua City—Dr.
Samuel Navarro's Death—A Trojan Horse—Ciudad Juárez—Tierra
Blanca—Mercado Abandons Chihuahua City—Villa Tends to Civil
Administration

The Villa Brigade began arriving at Jiménez on September 18 to find Constitutionalist General Tomás Urbina and his men waiting and gambling recklessly with gold coins from the pillaging of Durango City. Here Villa met for the first time Rodolfo "the butcher" (not his civilian occupation) Fierro, a member of Urbina's brigade who would become one of his most loyal and trusted lieutenants. Villa took advantage of the time there to organize his forces and, even at this early stage, began complaining about the discord sown by the First Chief, who had preceded his arrival by a month, among the principal revolutionaries in the area. Most likely Villa was referring to Colonel Manuel Chao, whom Carranza apparently had promised the position of governor of Chihuahua, and his refusal to join the campaign for Torreón. Chao still wanted to be the commander of all Constitutionalist forces in Chihuahua, and he had certainly earned the post by being the first to take up arms in the state and encouraging others to do so, but he was only a colonel and Villa was a general, by order of Carranza. Villa must have made his displeasure well known because Urbina asked him if he had done the right thing in supplying the mendicant First Chief with sixty pesos and a worn-out horse to continue his trip to Sonora, giving Villa a good laugh.[1]

At the Jiménez station, the two thousand men who formed the Villa Brigade began embarking on four trains and headed for Bermejillo, Durango. General Herrera with his Juárez Brigade of eight hundred men was already down south, having recently turned back the Federals twice at Santa Clara.[2]

La Laguna Mobilizes

The region known as La Laguna (also known as the Comarca Lagunera, or the lagunera region) was a relatively new political and economic area with a history of development more emblematic of the Wild West in the United States than the rest of northern Mexico. La Laguna straddled the border of Coahuila and Durango states, and for centuries it had been abandoned by all but a few indigenous people and great landholders. In 1880 the Madero family, inspired by its Civil War-era wealth accumulated in trafficking contraband Confederate cotton, spearheaded a move into the region to found a cotton empire. The region prospered and boomtowns, American-style, sprouted in typical frontier fashion. The railroads came to serve the plantations and subsequently revitalized the region's moribund mining sector by reducing transportation costs. Mining and cotton, in turn, attracted smelters and soap and dynamite (made from cottonseed) factories. In time the region became the scene of a gold rush-like industry based on guayule, a plant with rubber properties that grew wild in the Coahuilan desert. The people attracted to the region's quick riches, high pay, and transient work were similarly wild and erratic, tendencies that were exacerbated by the unpredictable flow of the area's lifeblood: water.[3]

The very nature of the region's laborers and their work created a fertile breeding ground for rebels. Unlike the other parts of Mexico, especially in the South, there were no pueblos with roots stretching back centuries where campesinos engaged in subsistence farming; the agricultural workers made their living as wage earners and migrants, a sizable portion of whom rotated between La Laguna and the United States according to crop seasons. Their travels gave them a worldly outlook alien to many of their Mexican peon counterparts and exposed them to radical ideals and the concepts of fair treatment and pay espoused by the concept of a moral economy. Many of the region's miners and railroaders likewise had worked in the United States where they, too, had received an education in ideas on class war and collective bargaining. Furthermore, their work as cotton pickers had accustomed them to mobilizing quickly in order to harvest the cotton as it matured. These groups supplied the revolution with leaders such as Calixto Contreras, Orestes Pereyra, and Sixto Ugalde.[4]

Centered on the plazas of Gómez-Palacio and Torreón at the confluence of national railroads, the region had immense operational and strategic importance aside from the wealth that could sustain armies there. Its inhabitants had participated meaningfully in the Madero and Orozco rebellions, and now they came into the full orbit of conventional warfare.

Battle of Second Torreón

At the beginning of September the War ministry ordered Federal Brigadier Eutiquio Munguía to assume command of the Division of the Nazas from the infirm General Bravo, who continued to reside in Torreón in an advisory capacity. General Munguía also received instructions to assume an offensive posture, since after the Battle of First Torreón the Constitutionalists still maintained control of Gómez Palacio, Lerdo, and San Pedro de las Colonias, keeping the Federals under a loose state of siege with telegraph and railroad communications cut. No ammunition or additional men had been able to get through to the embattled division, which had been forced to economize its ammunition, at times compelling its troops to merely deploy in a menacing manner to present battle without firing a shot. A 1,000-man relief column under Federal General Fernando Trucy Aubert bringing 500,000 rifle cartridges and thousands of artillery shells had not been able to advance any farther than Letona Station (218 kilometers east of Torreón) due to the conditions of the rails. The Secretary of War had also instructed Colonel Antonio Delgadillo's 1,000-man column in Zacatecas to head north to Torreón if any threat of attack on that former plaza had passed, although General Natera had been able to block Delgadillo's passage during the first battle for Torreón. Surrounded and increasingly short of ammunition due to a lack of resupply, General Munguía nevertheless ordered Brigadier Eduardo Ocaranza to retake Gómez Palacio, which he did after a tough fight on September 6. Colorado Generals Argumedo and Campa retook Lerdo on the next day. Subsequently, Munguía left General Campa in Lerdo to garrison the town with about four hundred men, and had General Anaya garrison Gómez Palacio with as many more. A week later Argumedo dislodged the Constitutionalists from San Pedro de las Colonias.[5]

Villa's entry into La Laguna spurred the Federals to greater activity. General Ocaranza again headed north to attack the advance force of Villistas with about three hundred men of the "Scout Train" (armed with the cannon "El Niño" and one machine gun), the idea of a flying column or rapid reaction force for the Federals, who rarely departed from the rails. Ocaranza made contact with the Constitutionalists at Vergel Station, pushing them back to around Bermejillo, where he fought for over two days beginning September 15. The fighting was most fierce at Hacienda Santa Clara, near Noe Station, but the growing weight of arriving Constitutionalists finally forced the scout train to retire to Gómez Palacio. On September 21 General Ocaranza again took the Scout Train out, this time to the east in an attempt to repair the rails and link up with General Trucy Aubert's column. Ocaranza's men began fixing the rails at Tizoc Station (171 kilometers east of Torreón), but the Constitutionalists tore up the track to the west, essentially cutting them off, and then attacked the Scout Train. Ocaranza's column successfully fended off the assault, but he had to continue east toward General Trucy Aubert in order to complete the link up, which he did on September 28 when he filed a telegraphic report to the Secretary of War. According to his estimates, War needed to send two thousand men immediately to reinforce the embattled Division of the Nazas and rescue it, as well as keep the great prize from falling into the hands of the Constitutionalists: millions of pesos worth of cotton.[6]

The Constitutionalists continued to concentrate north of Gómez Palacio and give time for those troops traveling on horseback to arrive. Locals, who had been anxiously awaiting the revolutionaries, joined the Constitutionalists in droves, allowing officers to raise squadrons and regiments in a matter of days.[7] Early on September 22 the rest of the Constitutionalists arrived, and at noon the first report of the Federal guns in Torreón could be heard. Villa came with the sixth train and ordered his artillery pieces tested, but received poor results since the revolutionaries still had to train gunners in how to handle them.[8] From Bermejillo, the Constitutionalists departed for Mapimí, where they spent the night. They left the next day for Hacienda de La Goma, crossing the Nazas under a swift current to then turn back north and spend the night at said hacienda on September 25. With two men from his staff, Villa next took an automobile south to Velardeña to invite Calixto Contreras and his men to participate in the attack on Torreón. Two days later Contreras' forces arrived under the command of General Severiano Ceniceros along with five hundred men belonging to General Domingo Arrieta. At this point eight to nine thousand men made up the total Constitutionalist expeditionary division.[9]

In response to these developments, General Munguía ordered General Felipe Alvírez to attack the Constitutionalists on the south side of the river. He also called in General Benjamín Argumedo and his Colorados from San Pedro de Las Colonias to form another column with General Emilio P. Campa's brigade and attack from Lerdo, on the north side of the river, protecting Alvírez's flank. Although Villa suspected that the total of the three Federal commands amounted to two thousand men, the true number was probably a little more than half that size.[10]

The Nazas River separated the cities of Gómez Palacio and Lerdo on the north side from Torreón to the south. For the most part, Torreón was unassailable from the north and east where it opened out into flat terrain that afforded any defender fantastic fields of fire. The hills and broken terrain to the south and west, however, presented a more favorable or at least neutral proposition. Attackers could find some cover and relief from rapid-fire weapons, even if artillery located on the elevations could extend their range. Here, the canyons of El Huarache and Las Fábricas, formed by the hills of Calabazas, Polvorera, and the Sierra of Las Noas, provided precarious avenues of approach; once past these, an aggressor need only negotiate De la Cruz Hill and then the plaza itself. Likewise, La Pila Hill stood like a sentinel north of Gómez Palacio and Lerdo, while La Cruz Hill overlooked the two smaller plazas from the south, close by the river.

SEPTEMBER 29

At Hacienda La Loma, south of the Nazas, Villa's and Urbina's brigades began to take fire from the Federals under General Alvírez to the front, and Argumedo and Campa's irregulars from the north side of the river. Villa convened a hasty council of war.[11] Aside from Villa's brigade, which numbered 2,000 men, the revolutionary forces were commanded by Calixto Contreras (3,000), Maclovio Herrera (500), Tomás Urbina (1,000), Eugenio Aguirre Benavides (500), Domingo B. Yuriar (500), Juan E. García (500), and others. Recognizing that the various brigades should be formed into one division, Villa suggested that he, Calixto Contreras, or Tomás Urbina be elected as the general in charge. Then Juan Medina stood up and spoke as an authority on military matters, echoing the need to organize as a division and establish unity of command. The group elected Villa, and on September 29, 1913, Villa's storied Division of the North (not to be confused with its Federal counterpart bearing the same name) came into existence.[12]

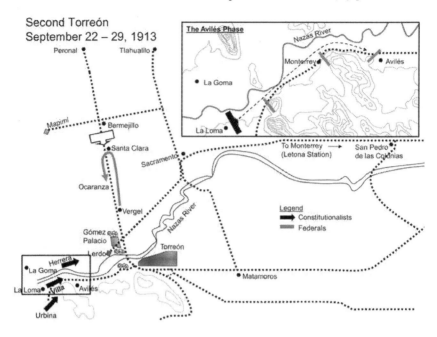

Map 1.15

As the Constitutionalist generals met in their council of war, Campa's cannon began to fire on their troops and Villa wasted no time in preparing his orders. The Villa Brigade would attack from La Loma toward Avilés on the south side of the Nazas. Herrera's Benito Juárez Brigade, still located on the north side of the Nazas, he ordered to continue toward Lerdo and attack Emilio Campa's brigade, which was attempting to outflank the Constitutionalists, while Urbina's Morelos Brigade took up position on Villa's right flank. The general axis of attack came from Torreón's southwest side, just like the failed attack in July, so as to take advantage of the broken terrain there and avoid the plains and their clear fields of fire to the north and east. The same Federal units that had defended the city two months earlier still remained, except for General Ocaranza's Brigade (the 2nd and 4th Infantry Battalions and the 1st and 3rd Rural Police Corps), which had been cut off from Torreón while on its mission to repair the railway toward Saltillo, leaving approximately 3,500 Federals for the defense of the city. General Trucy Aubert's relief column, underway since the end of August and approaching from the east, would not arrive in time for the battle.[13]

At about 1 p.m., seeing that the Federal general made no attempt to advance past Avilés with his main body of troops and with all of Villa's forces mounted in the fields stretching out in front of Hacienda La Loma, the Villistas began to cannonade a hill about two kilometers away. Villa gave the order to advance immediately. The Díaz and González Ortega regiments raced forward at a full gallop against the advance Federal positions, engaging in combat shortly thereafter. After two hours of fighting the Constitutionalists dislodged the defenders from the first hills. Then the order was given to advance the artillery commanded by Constitutionalist Major Margarito Gómez. The Huertistas occupied a position on the hills next to a ranch called Monterrey, three kilometers west of Avilés. There, the battle resumed with rifle fire and an artillery duel. Major Gómez, in command of the artillery, was wounded in the arm by shrapnel, while Major Enrique Portillo took a bullet to the leg.[14]

The battle continued, seemingly without end, until the Constitutionalists forced the Federals back from Rancho Monterrey to Avilés, where they dug in. Colonel Toribio Ortega advanced with the Villa Brigade against the town while General Urbina left with the cavalry to appear in their rear and cut off any retreat. While the fighting was still going on, the Constitutionalists shot fifty prisoners captured during the running battle from La Loma to Avilés on the side of a small hill just before the town. Meanwhile, the battle continued to develop around Avilés with the Federals completely besieged in the chapel and a two-story house. "Our families," as Major Francisco Ontiveros put it, attacked spiritedly. They conquered the last positions around 5 p.m. as the Federals began to flee their fieldworks in confusion.[15]

The Villistas had succeeded in taking Avilés "by fire and sword." The Federals suffered tremendously in the battle, losing about half their men (467 dead), including many of their officers, the courageous General Alvírez, and his entire staff. Those lucky few who managed to escape the trenches fled to Torreón. Entering Avilés, Villa gazed upon the naked corpse of the Federal general, lifeless in a building entryway, stripped of all his worldly possessions. Many versions of how he died circulated, with some saying he committed suicide while others maintained that he had died in combat. There was no shortage of those who swore that they had seen him killed. According to Colonel Matías Pazuengo it was a combination of the two stories. The general had been surrounded with some of his principal subordinates in the main house of the hacienda where he had taken refuge. Some revolutionaries eventually penetrated the premises and "it is said that one of them fired on General Alvírez who was there without his jacket or kepi and just in his [uniform] pants with a stripe [and] that upon seeing himself in such conditions Gen. Alvírez committed suicide."[16]

Similar to Custer's Last Stand, this engagement soon gained the appellation *"el desastre de Avilés"* among Federals. Constitutionalist Majors Rodolfo

Fierro and Pablo C. Seáñez executed nineteen Colorados and Federal officers according to the Benito Juárez Law, among them several Duranguenses, probably of the Social Defense who had escaped to Mexico City after the Battle of Second Durango City and then returned to Durango with Alvírez. Villa's Chief of Staff, Colonel Juan Medina, spared the artillery gunners in exchange for their promise to operate the two pieces captured. In this preparatory engagement Villa had lost thirty-eight killed and seventy-one wounded. The booty collected totaled two Schneider Canet guns, 360 shells, 532 7-mm. Mausers, and 150,000 rounds to be used in the taking of Torreón itself. To the north, Herrera and Colonel Juan E. García likewise defeated Campa's men in a fight that was waged with equal proportions and numbers of men and armament on both sides. Herrera relieved the Colorados of one 75-mm. cannon, took some prisoners, and forced the rest to flee toward Torreón.[17]

To help rescue the doomed forward command, General Munguía ordered General Luis Anaya to take a battery and some men to go reinforce General Alvírez. However, after traveling only two kilometers past Huarache Canyon he began to run into the Federals dispersed from Avilés who informed him that Alvírez's column had been virtually wiped out. In view of this news, Anaya held up, ordered his artillery to go into battery, and sent a courier back to Munguía to ask if he should still continue forward. Munguía considered the battery exposed, and he did not want those men fleeing from Avilés spreading demoralizing rumors among the rest of his troops. He told Anaya to round them up and not permit them past Huarache Canyon and the Barracks of the 5th Regiment, which was on the road to Avilés, but it was too late. The survivors entered the city from many different directions and began to spread the news about the disaster.[18]

Following the example of his predecessor, General Bravo, General Munguía had not prepared any defensive works for the cities prior to receiving the Constitutionalist onslaught. He arranged for two lines of defense: one exterior, to keep the Constitutionalist artillery out of range of his main defenses, and an interior line, with his reserve assembled in the Alameda.[19] The exterior line consisted of two hundred infantrymen and Rurales from the 18th Infantry Battalion and 1st and 3rd Rural Corps under Major Manuel Villanueva on Calabazas Hill (the most important hill), another one hundred men on La Polvorera Hill to the south on the other side of El Huarache Canyon, and finally, fifty men on La Unión Hill. For an interior line Munguía had two hundred men in a firing line along the railroad embankment that ran in front of De la Cruz Hill commanded by the capable Lieutenant Colonel Antonio Gallardo, and immediately behind them another two hundred men and one artillery piece on the hill proper with Major Adrián Arellano commanding. He also dispatched some small detachments to cover the Metalúrgica factory on the southeast side of the city and a small detachment of Argumedo's brigade at La Unión factory, also to the southeast, close to La Unión Hill. The reserve in the Alameda consisted of elements of the 5th Cavalry regiment, the Voluntarios de Mapimí, and some local citizens of the Social Defense under staff officer Lieutenant Colonel José E. Castaños. Campa's irregulars covered the north side of the city.[20]

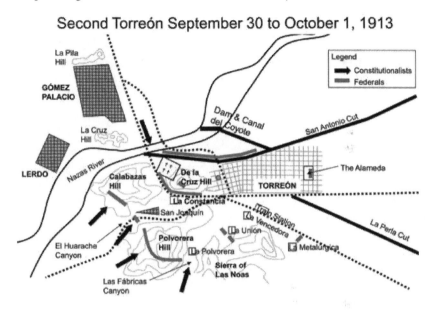

Second Torreón September 30 to October 1, 1913

Map 1.16

SEPTEMBER 30

Mid-afternoon the following day, Villa left Avilés to conduct a reconnaissance en force, aided by his Guide Corps ("*Cuerpo de Guías*") and accompanied by Colonels Toribio Ortega, José Rodríguez, and Juan Medina. They made contact with the Federals after riding about an hour and then fought almost up to the foot of Calabazas Hill. By 5 p.m. the shooting became generalized and the revolutionaries pushed the Federal advance forces back through Huarache Canyon aided by Alvírez's turncoat Federal artillerymen, who directed suppressive fire against their former comrades who were manning the guns covering the entrance to the canyon. A larger force composed of the brigades of Herrera, García, and Contreras pushed the Colorados under Campa back through Lerdo and Gómez Palacio to the San Antonio cut, north of Torreón, as the Constitutionalists slowly tightened the noose. On Villa's right, General

Eugenio Aguirre Benavides' Zaragoza Brigade dismounted, one soldier holding the horses for six men as per the old custom, and attacked through Las Fábricas (sometimes called La Polvorera) Canyon accompanied by Yuriar's men. In the early morning hours, making use of the cover of darkness in a favorite tactic of Villa's that gave added benefit to an advantage in numbers, Villa's dismounted dragoons scaled the hills on the west side, slowly taking positions away from the Federals.[21]

OCTOBER 1

Around midnight the Constitutionalists took La Polvorera Hill and pushed the defenders in El Huarache Canyon back to their trenches at San Joaquín. When General Munguía found out about these developments he ordered one hundred men from the 18th Infantry Battalion and 1st Cavalry Regiment to counterattack and retake La Polvorera Hill at around 3 a.m., but they failed to accomplish the mission. At daybreak, the Constitutionalists succeeded in outflanking the Federals on Calabazas and finally took the hill, forcing the defenders under Major Manuel Villanueva, who was killed, to flee (First Captain Esteban Solórzano was seriously wounded). Almost all the positions had been taken from the Federals, leaving only De la Cruz Hill and the fortifications inside the town in Federal possession. The Constitutionalists then placed machine guns on Calabazas and lit up De la Cruz Hill. Their columns penetrated through El Huarache Canyon and right up to the railroad in savage fighting. All day long the two opposing forces' artillery thundered away at each other in an incessant duel. Mounted on his horse, pistol in hand, Villa inspected the lines, giving orders and encouraging the men. Throughout the day the Constitutionalists maintained their positions, repulsing all attempts by the Federals to throw them back, including another attack against La Polvorera Hill at 9 a.m. by two hundred Colorados supported by two machine guns and divided into two columns; one led personally by General Argumedo and the other by Colonel Narciso Martínez, the latter dying in the attempt. The Constitutionalists interpreted these efforts as attempts to make space for a break out, not to push back their lines.[22]

As the Constitutionalists began to descend from Calabazas Hill they encountered the Federals under Lieutenant Colonel Antonio Gallardo of the 18th Battalion arrayed along the railroad embankment in an attempt to hold back the tide of revolutionaries. Around 11:00 a.m. General Munguía had to personally reinforce Gallardo with a squadron of the Voluntarios de Mapimí when the colonel's men all but abandoned him to eat lunch, somewhat validating those Federal officers who refused to feed their men during combat because they thought that it took their mind off the task at hand. Some of the volunteers did not want to take up position, forcing Munguía to person-ally place them on the line. In contrast, Sub-lieutenant Braulio Torres, who commanded two Rexers supporting Gallardo, had been wounded twice, but still remained in the fight. The Federals' situation continued to deteriorate and at noon, fearing a defeat, Munguía ordered two thousand brand new Mausers stored in a warehouse burned in order to keep them from falling into enemy hands. At 3:30 the Federals on De la Cruz Hill phoned to announce a column of Constitutionalist cavalry penetrating through Huarache Canyon. Munguía, who was standing next to an artillery piece commanded by a Captain Mañón, ordered him to take his gun, find the column, and open fire on it. But Mañón ran out of ammunition and the dismounted revolutionar-ies scaled the sides of the hill and, making use of the broken terrain, began to pour in fire. Around 5:30 p.m. the Constitutionalists made another push through Huarache Canyon in successive waves. Just as the fighting reached its highest pitch, Maclovio Herrera's Constitutionalists, having accomplished their objective to take Lerdo and Gómez Palacio, showed up to the northwest attacking against the river and the cuts. By 6 p.m. Federal soldiers, weary of fighting and hungry, "entered into a period of indifference such that the of-ficers could hardly succeed in making themselves obeyed," as Munguía later stated.[23]

Around this time there came a lull in the fighting, and Villa walked the lines, overseeing the resupply of ammunition, lifting his men's spirits, and preparing for one final dismounted assault. His men were dressed in civilian clothes but had rolled up their right sleeves and removed their hats to identify themselves as revolutionaries. Villa also commissioned Colonel Medina to review the revolutionaries' dispositions, ensuring that appropriate measures and precautions had been taken, and then at 8 p.m., shortly after nightfall, the Villistas made one large "enveloping" push from the north and west and southwest. The Constitutionalists took De la Cruz Hill, the last commanding position held by the Federals and the point from which Munguía was observ-ing events. The Constitutionalists chased the Federals down the hill and into the city as Federals all along the line began to abandon their posts and flee through the streets to the east. Spanish citizens, fearful of possible Villista atrocities directed against them, also began to exit, sweeping along many of the Federals with them. The final collapse of the Federal defenses only took about thirty minutes.[24]

No order had been given to evacuate the plaza, and it seemed as though all the Federal generals pointed the finger at each other for the disorderly re-treat that soon turned into a rout. Munguía blamed General Bravo for having abandoned the plaza in an automobile headed for Matamoros and Argumedo for fleeing down the Coyote road. Since Argumedo commanded the greatest number of troops, his departure had preordained the fall of the plaza, at least according to Munguía, although nothing could have been further from the truth, since Argumedo commanded maybe 20 percent of the troops present at most. For his part, General Anaya said in his report that he had spent the two-hour lull in the fighting during the evening unsuccessfully trying to find Munguía, looking for him in the San Carlos Hotel and at Headquarters. When the final Constitutionalist push came he rushed back toward Las Fábricas Canyon, his section of the line, but could not even reach La Unión because his men were falling back through the train station. So he sent one of Argumedo's men to order the guns there withdrawn while he returned back into the city to begin rounding up groups of men. Anaya's story gave him cover for abandoning his position, all the while making it seem as if Munguía had been the shirker. All told, the Federals managed to round up seventeen hundred soldiers from the Division of the Nazas (it should be noted that the praetorian Anaya had less than one-fourth of these with him when he caught up to the rest of the troops at San Rafael) and linked up with General Trucy Aubert at Tizoc Station on October 6.[25]

The total tally of booty collected by the Constitutionalists included eleven cannons, in addition to "El Niño" mounted on an armored car (although Federal sources suggest that this gun had been with Ocaranza's scout train), 297 75-mm. and 36 80-mm. artillery shells, 299 Mauser rifles, 492,800 cartridges, five machine guns, 39 locomotives, and countless empty rolling stock. Villa's light losses as reported approached the ridiculous: seventeen dead, including one jefe and three officers, and forty-two wounded. Aside from the Avilés phase, the Federals lost another estimated 232 dead, of which Villa says most were Colorados; countless wounded; and an additional 109 prisoners, who were shot according to the Benito Juárez Law.[26]

ANALYSIS

Torreón fell due to numerous failures committed by the Federal leadership, chief being a lack of both cleared and interlocking fields of fire with a wire to maintain the attackers at a distance and under fire and sound defensive works. These simple yet effective measures might have raised morale among the defenders, rendered their arms and ammunition more effective, evened the discrepancy in troop strength, and perhaps permitted defensive maneuvers. But Munguía committed many more errors than these; he also piecemealed his artillery to various locations instead of massing them, placed them too far forward where they continually risked or experienced capture, and employed them in nineteenth-century-style point-and-shoot direct fire missions (such as at Huarache Canyon). For his part, Munguía blamed the loss of Torreón on his lack of artillery ammunition vis-à-vis the numerical superiority of the enemy (although if he had massed his guns, they would have had access to all the shells and three hundred would not have survived capture); the demoralizing effect of Alvírez's defeat being exaggerated (?!) by rumors; and the flight of Spaniards, panic-stricken by news of their compatriots being shot on area haciendas by revolutionaries, which in turn dragged the Federal soldiers in train. He also claimed that by engaging the Constitutionalists, Alvírez had exceeded his authority since he had only been sent to observe the revolutionary advance. However, the similarity between Munguía's actions in July and Alvírez's in the September battle seems too coincidental not to have been part of the overall plan. Or, could Alvírez have misunderstood his orders to observe and report? Probably not, since General Rubio Navarrete blamed the massacre at Avilés on Huerta's command that Munguía take the fight to the enemy, and Alvírez definitely carried out that directive. General Rubio also alleged that General Bravo had not retired because of ill health, but rather had been fired for not actively campaigning prior to the Battle of First Torreón, which might also explain the lack of defensive fortifications given the interim president's expectations for an offensive posture.[27] Had Herrera been able to cut off the Federal retreat to the north and east, the Federals would have had two disasters to lament.[28] For his incompetence, the hapless Munguía faced a court martial upon the battle's conclusion.

THE DIPLOMATIC FRONT

At the beginning of October, Huerta's regime suffered yet another setback in addition to the loss of Torreón. Since the Citadel cuartelazo, President Woodrow Wilson had been urging European countries to deny diplomatic recognition to Huerta's regime; Wilson also suggested that the general hold elections and not postulate himself as a candidate. As both these measures failed, Wilson addressed the U.S. Congress on August 27, 1913, to announce an arms embargo on Huerta's regime and ask that all U.S. citizens leave Mexico. Previously, the United States had officially banned the sale of arms only to the Constitutionalists, while Huerta was permitted to buy all that he could afford, but now all sides found themselves barred from the U.S. arms market. The revolutionaries, however, still had limited and sporadic access to suppliers in the United States via their underground contacts. Throughout September, Huerta had given signs of yielding to Wilson's position, but on October 10, he dismissed the national legislature in what has been called his "second coup," and the embargo entered into full force.[29]

Also in October, the Interim Constitutional President of the Mexican United States, Victoriano Huerta's official title, raised the authorized size of the permanent army to 150,000 men and increased the size of the "*Plana Mayor*" (the college, or corpus, of generals). With immediate effect the generalship would be divided into regulars (*permanentes*) and Auxiliaries at a ratio of three to one Permanents to Auxiliaries; the new regime still restricted the rank of general of division to Permanents while permitting Auxiliaries to receive promotion to the rank of brigadier and general of brigade. The authorized number totaled 140 generals, not including those retired:

14 Generals of Division, active or on commission
6 Generals of Division, passive, awaiting assignment
45 Generals of Brigade, Permanent
15 Generals of Brigade, Auxiliary
45 Brigadiers, Permanent
15 Brigadiers, Auxiliary[30]

Forming a Division on the Go

Villa entered Torreón amidst much fanfare an hour after the final push had begun and headed straight for the Hotel Salvador, where he established his headquarters and went about attending to the needs of the poor, making sure the hospitals had what they needed, and overseeing reprisals against those Mexicans and Spaniards who had denounced local Maderistas to the Huertistas. He also tended to reorganizing his division to accommodate both its losses and the flood of new recruits, equipping it and furnishing it with uniforms. Martiniano Servín took command of the artillery, and the men began receiving regular pay, since after Villa levied a "loan" of 300,000 pesos on the local bankers and entrusted those funds to the care of one well-versed in financial matters, a compadre of Emilio Madero by the name of Lázaro de la Garza, there was now money to pay his men.[31] Prior to this the Constitutionalist soldiers had gone seven or eight months without any pay, maintaining themselves as best they could on beef and flour tortillas, and for long stretches on meat alone, in frugal amounts. "Raggedy, shoeless, eating a piece of raw meat, you would see them in the field, possessed of an uncommon joy and good humor," in the words of Major Ontiveros, happily singing their sentimental songs, which extolled the deeds of their famously tragic leaders, in the evenings. Without funds ammunition had also been hard to come by since the revolutionaries could not readily buy it in the United States and therefore often had to supply themselves with what they took from the Federals. Additionally, the vigilance exercised by the United States authorities subjected cross-border trafficking to thousands of contretemps since, when it was not confiscated by the Americans, the ammunition sometimes fell into the enemy's hands once in national territory.[32]

After eight days of rest and recuperation General Villa ordered all the brigades to prepare to march. It had been learned that a powerful Federal column was marching down from Chihuahua to the south, and so he was anxious to return north and clear the Federal Division of the North from the state, once and for all. Villa still had not decided whether to make a feint on Chihuahua City in favor of taking Ciudad Juárez by surprise, or immediately proceed to taking the state capital by storm. Before leaving he appointed Calixto Contreras the Jefe de las Armas of Torreón and ordered General José Isabel Robles with his brigade to cover the eastern approaches to the city, should the Federals attempt to retake it. The first trains started to leave with the brigade staffs and infantry, followed by the cavalry marching mounted. Villa took all the trains in his possession save one, which he left to Contreras. The forces that he took back north consisted of the following brigades: the Villa Brigade temporarily commanded by Colonel Toribio Ortega, General Urbina's Morelos Brigade, General Eugenio Aguirre Benavides' Zaragoza Brigade, Maclovio Herrera's Benito Juárez Brigade, and the men of Domingo Yuriar, a total of four thousand men.[33]

The cavalry crossed the immense desert that extends from Torreón to Jiménez in six days, experiencing vicissitudes beyond description. Riding through dry territory without water for the horses, many could not bear the privations and fell out in the desert. The people suffered greatly without food or anywhere to acquire it on the entire trek; some regiments had to kill mules and horses just to have some meat. Upon arriving in Jiménez, finally, they learned that Federal General Francisco Castro had already reached Camargo where he commanded a column of two thousand Federals and Colorados, with advance forces in Díaz Station.[34]

CASTRO'S COLUMN

After Federal General Salvador R. Mercado found out that Villa had departed in mid-September for La Laguna he sent Brigadier Castro, commander of the 23rd Infantry, to give chase with a one-thousand-man column that included Colorados from General Antonio Rojas' Guerrero Regiment and Blas Orpinel's Brigade. Another Colorado, Marcelo Caraveo, also received orders from division headquarters to join Castro's column from his position at Salas Station on the Kansas City-Mexico & Orient Railroad. Marching in the direction of Satevó, Caraveo's brigade was supposed to head for Santa Cruz de Rosales where it would link up with Castro coming down the railroad.

Once joined, the Caraveo Brigade would take up the vanguard as the Federals continued southward toward Camargo, where Villa had left Colonel Rosalío Hernández behind in order to secure his rear as he marched off to Torreón with the rest of the forces.[35]

Caraveo reached Santa Cruz de Rosales on September 24 in the evening, and three days later Castro's column, now nineteen hundred men strong, started south with Caraveo in the vanguard. On September 29 the Federal advance forces reached La Cruz on the Central Railroad, sixteen kilometers north of Camargo, where Caraveo fought the lead elements of Hernández's Leales de Camargo Brigade. Caraveo only had 350 men because Castro had divided his 800-man brigade into two columns and sent the greater number under Lieutenant Colonel Andrés Luján off-road over the hills toward Camargo. Caraveo fought for eight hours waiting for the main body of troops to reach his position and reinforce him, but finally he had to yield and retreat against superior opposing numbers. Caraveo lost two officers, eight men, and thirty-eight horses killed, and one jefe and seven men wounded in the action.[36]

The following day the main body of Federals and Colorados arrived and forced Hernández's men to retreat back to Camargo. As soon as he learned of the Federals coming his way, Hernández had appealed for help from fellow Constitutionalist General Orestes Pereyra, who happened to be in Parral and who subsequently forwarded some reinforcements. After the Federals reorganized they caught up to Hernández at Camargo on October 3, again with Caraveo's brigade in the vanguard coming from the north and Castro with the main body attacking from the east. The Federals began to bombard the town, landing four blasts in downtown and forcing the Constitutionalists to abandon the city as the only viable means of sparing it from a terrible cannonade. Some Constitutionalists headed west for Satevó and Naica, probably the men belonging to General Manuel Chao, Colonel Trinidad Rodríguez, and Pereyra, but Hernández and his men made for some ranches located to the northeast of town where they ran straight into the main body of Castro's column before again breaking contact and fleeing.[37]

Blas Orpinel's Colorados gave chase to those Constitutionalists retreating to the west, and Caraveo's brigade went after Hernández's men. One night, not too long thereafter, Hernández allowed his camp at Hacienda de La Mora to be surprised by the Federals at midnight. In the shock of the initial encounter and the confusion of darkness military order devolved into *sálvese quien pueda* ("every man for himself"). The Federals smashed and dispersed his brigade after four and a half hours of combat, but only reported killing eight Constitutionalists, including one officer. Since Hernández's brigade alone stood between the Federal Division of the North and Villa in Torreón, there can be no doubt that Hernández had been the one who informed Villa of the large column of Federals commanded by Castro moving southward.[38]

Villa halted his northward progress at Jiménez to begin instilling some regimentation in his command, creating various staff responsibilities and putting qualified people in charge of the newly created portfolios, including the creation of a provost marshal.[39] He also adopted the Federal Army General Ordinances and tasked Juan N. Medina, the newly-appointed chief of staff for the Division of the North, with implementing them. Many of the revolutionaries, having a natural distaste for all things Federal, including Medina's instruction, did not appreciate the new order. More significantly, adoption of the ordinances entailed strict adherence to pay grades, something that did not sit at all well with the freebooter Tomás Urbina. While in Jiménez, Villa also received news that the Lagunera bankers had refused to deliver the loan he had imposed on them, causing him to return there and settle that matter. After a four-day stay in Jiménez, Villa's division again started north. The commanding general decided to leave Urbina behind in charge of the Jiménez garrison, either because he had proved too recalcitrant toward the new ordinances, because Colonel Medina feared that so close to the U.S. border Urbina's presence might give rise to the kinds of outrages characteristic of the sacking of Durango, or possibly because he was ill. At any rate, he did not participate in the campaign, and Colonel Faustino Borunda assumed tactical command of the Morelos Brigade for the time being with Urbina's blessing, since Villa had adroitly couched his decision as a request for Urbina to remain behind and cover his old compadre's back.[40]

As the Constitutionalists mobilized for Camargo, the Huertista column inside the town fell back to Chihuahua City, permitting Villa's division to freely enter. Colorado General Caraveo now provided the extreme rearguard of Castro's retreating column, with orders not to present battle and to continue pulling back toward Chihuahua City but maintain contact with the Constitutionalists.[41]

During the stay at Camargo Villa again attended to organizing for the advance on Chihuahua. In the course of administrative and command duties, he had the unfortunate occasion of having to order General Domingo Benjamín Yuriar executed, either for drunken insubordination, because he resisted the imposition of army ordinances, or because he had shot a soldier inside a house of ill-repute under questionable circumstances and then went to his brigade headquarters and defiantly armed all his people. According to this latter version of events, Villa had to send a force sufficient enough to subdue the general and then ordered him quickly shot, with

Yuriar courageously giving the commands to the firing squad that resulted in his own execution. In taking such an obdurate position against Yuriar's insubordination, Villa may have been trying to impress upon Colonel Chao, who earlier had refused to report to Camargo with all his people to participate in the Torreón campaign, just how firmly he dealt with insubordination. The day after Yuriar's execution Villa again sent for Chao to report with his men to Camargo, an order that, this time, was obeyed forthwith. Villa then removed Chao from his command, his men passing to Colonel Sóstenes Garza, and put Chao in charge of the division's artillery. Unfortunately for Chao's new command, the night before the division left Camargo the two artillery officers captured at Avilés deserted to rejoin their Federal brethren.[42]

Battle of Chihuahua City

On the twenty-sixth Villa again got underway with his division, composed of those men that he had brought from Gómez Palacio and augmented by Chao's and Colonel Rosalío Hernández's Leales de Camargo Brigade, headed for Chihuahua City. The state capital presented quite a challenge, as Colonel Medina pointed out to General Villa: unlike Torreón with its key positions that, once taken, preordained the fall of the plaza, Chihuahua possessed no such commanding geographic features. That meant that the Constitutionalist Division of the North would have to surround the city and place it under siege, and Villa knew he had neither sufficient quantities of men nor ammunition to invest the plaza. Nevertheless, Villa resolved to take the city on the strength of his recent victories and the effect that they might have on enemy morale, ignoring another unpleasant reality about the Chihuahua garrison. As opposed to Torreón, which had been defended by three-fourths Federals and one-fourth irregulars, the forces defending Chihuahua consisted mainly of irregulars under such famous Colorados as Marcelo Caraveo, José Inés Salazar, Antonio Rojas, and Pascual Orozco, Jr., himself.[43]

Exhibiting a perverse pride in his fellow Chihuahuans, Constitutionalist Major Ontiveros distinguished these Colorados from others in one key aspect:

> [T]hose unfortunate deluded defenders of an evil cause, were not the pusillanimous hordes of a Cheché Campos, of an Emilio Campa or a Benjamín Argumedo, who fled at the first shots or enclosed

themselves in plazas with their Federal accomplices; no, you have to do complete justice saying the truth. The Colorados of Chihuahua gave signs of a courage at all costs, always going out in pursuit of us, so say the battles of Saucillo, San Andrés, Ranchería, Díaz, [and the upcoming battles at] Tierra Blanca, and Ojinaga, in which they fought like the valiant.[44]

Discounting the ferocity of Campos and Argumedo would seem unwarranted and inaccurate, but Ontiveros' comments go to the state of mind of the men in Villa's division and therefore deserve mention.

NOVEMBER 4

Villa's Division of the North made one final stopover in Ortiz Station where its leaders sent a challenge to the Federals. A young teacher from the Escuela Oficial de Meoqui delivered a sealed envelope signed by Francisco Villa, Manuel Chao, Maclovio Herrera, Tomás Urbina, Juan N. Medina, Trinidad Rodríguez, Rosalío Hernández, Eugenio Aguirre Benavides, and Samuel Navarro to Federal General Mercado requesting that he either abandon Chihuahua City or designate a location to fight in the open to decide the fate of Chihuahua in order to avoid the bloodshed of any innocents. Mercado refused to respond, telling the local press that he did not answer to bandits.[45] Mercado then made his rounds to visit the various defensive sectors and drafted orders preventing anyone from leaving Chihuahua, meaning those who happened to be inside the city from surrounding towns were stuck for the duration. The whole day passed without the Federal advance positions in Colonia Dale reporting any sightings of the Constitutionalists, who had established their camp down Mápula way. But just after midnight the Constitutionalists made a reconnaissance of the Federal positions and engaged in an exchange of gunfire that lasted about forty minutes, after which the revolutionaries withdrew.[46]

NOVEMBER 5

On Wednesday the Constitutionalists began moving up for battle. From his position located outside the perimeter Federal Major Enrique Sáenz D. leading a few men from the Eduardo Armendáriz Guerrilla observed the Constitutionalist vanguard taking up positions in the hills to the southeast of the city and at Rancho de Ávalos, which was on the outskirts of Chihuahua City and near the railroad where Villa set up his headquarters. After exchanging some shots Major Sáenz retreated back inside the city without being pursued, which led General Mercado to the conclusion that the Constitutionalists would be attacking that night.[47]

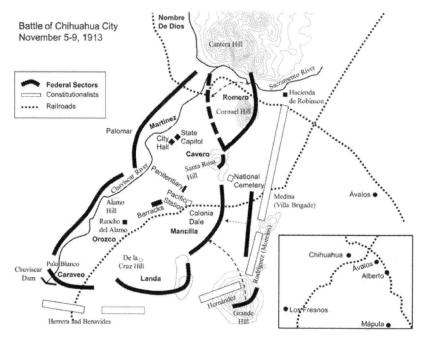

Map 1.17

Approximately six to eight thousand Federals defended the city across seven sectors of defense. Federal General Cayetano Romero in the prolongation of Juárez Avenue commanded the sector comprising Hacienda de Robinson, the pass formed by the Coronel Hill and that of Cantera Hill, and the observatory on Coronel Hill, occupied by part of Colonel Luis Guevara's 44th Auxiliary Infantry Battalion. Because of the steep gradient, this latter hill did not have any artillery placed on it. The Federals did build somewhat of a redoubt on Santa Rosa Hill occupied by Colonel Carlos S. Orozco's 6th Infantry Battalion, which provided support for the artillery located on that hill and down below between Coronel and Santa Rosa hills. General Jesús Mancilla commanded the Colonia Dale sector with the 33rd Auxiliary Battalion, Brigadier Severo López's 4th Cavalry Regiment—stationed on Grande Hill in order to take by flank any attack on Colonia Dale—and General Antonio Rojas' Guerrero Regiment, along with some smaller Guerrillas.[48]

Tactical Command	Major Unit organic to	G	J	O	T	Total
Orozco, Carlos S. (Colonel)	6th Infantry Battalion					350
Pulido, Enrique (LTC)	15th Infantry Battalion					350
Parra, Alfonso (LTC)	23rd Infantry Battalion					350
Mancilla, Jesús (Brigadier)	33rd Auxiliary Infantry Battalion	1				350
Guevara, Luis (Colonel)	44th Auxiliary Infantry Battalion					200
López, Severo (Brigadier)	4th Cavalry Regiment	1				300
Landa, Manuel (Brigadier)	7th Cavalry Regiment	1				300
Villalobos, Pedro (LTC)	25th Auxiliary Cavalry Regiment					70
Orozco, Jovito M. (Major)	Gendarmes of the Army					100
Hernández, Federico (Colonel)	Sixteen 75-mm. and eight 70-mm. Guns					150
Martínez Acosta, Felipe (2nd CPT)	Six Machine Guns					50
					Regulars	2,570
Orozco, Pascual (Brigadier)	Orozco Brigade	1				600
Caraveo, Marcelo (Brigadier)	Caraveo Brigade	1				800
Orpinel, Blas (Brigadier)	Orpinel Brigade	1				400
Salazar, José Inés (Brigadier)	Salazar Brigade	1				400
Rojas, Antonio (Brigadier)	Guerrero Regiment	1		25	200	226
Enciso, Luis (Colonel)	Sonora Regiment		1	8	180	189
Terrazas, Alberto (Colonel)	Hidalgo Regiment		1	4	180	185
Freyre, Ventura (1st CPT)	Antillón Regiment			9	150	159
Sánchez, Javier (1st CPT)	Rincón Gallardo Regiment				150	150
Cuilty, Enrique L. (Colonel)	Melchor Ocampo Regiment		1		100	101
Robinson, Reyes (Major)	Batopilas Corps		1	13	100	114
	5th and 10th Scout Corps					100
Cordero, Gilberto (Major)	Cordero Irregular Cavalry Corps		1	4	50	55
Vargas, Teófilo (Major)	Vargas Guerrilla		1	5	50	56
Culebro, Virgilio (1st CPT)	Culebro Guerrilla			9	60	69
Rascón, Platón (Major)	Rascón Guerrilla		1	3	40	44
Ortiz, Juan (Major)	Ortiz Guerrilla		1	2	40	43
Barrenada, Félix (Cmdte)	Barrenada Guerrilla		1	5	44	50
García, Blas (Major)	García Guerrilla		1	2	20	23
Caballero y Barrios, Juan (LTC)	National Guard		1	6	50	57
					Irregulars	3,821
					TOTAL FEDERALS	6,391

Table 1.10 Battle of Chihuahua City Federal Estimated Troop Strength[49]

General Manuel Landa's 7th Cavalry Regiment and two machine guns comprised the De la Cruz Hill sector forces. In Palo Blanco, General Marcelo Caraveo held command with two 70-mm. mountain guns (probably handled by Irregular Lieutenant Felipe Falcón), and a battery of four Madsen and Rexers, joined by Major Reyes Robinson's Batopilas Corps and Colonel Lázaro Alanís' Guerrilla. The wife of the latter commander, Carmen S. de Alanís, fought side-by-side with her husband throughout the battle. The Federals gave paramount importance to this position, since it supplied the city with water, and it wound up taking the brunt of successive Constitutionalist assaults. General Pascual Orozco, commanding the Alamo Sector just north of Palo Blanco, provided backup to Caraveo with General Blas Orpinel's troops, those from the 44th Auxiliary Infantry Battalion, his own eponymous brigade, and two machine guns.[50]

General Emiliano Martínez commanded the combined forces of General José Inés Salazar and Colonel Alberto Terrazas in the Palomar Sector, comprising the area between Nombre de Dios and the Quinta Carolina, far north. This sector remained devoid of any field fortifications with the irregulars relying only on the riverbank for cover and the protection of two machine guns. The Guerrillas of Eduardo Campuzano and Lizandro Gutiérrez guarded the passes at Mina Prieta and Mono. Besides these troops around the perimeter, inside the city were infantry from the 15th and 23rd Battalions and numerous Irregular corps, among them the Civiles de Chihuahua Corps commanded by Engineer José Sáenz Botello, the Esteban Coronado Corps, mounted and dismounted police commanded by Major Rodolfo Urdapilleta, and some Federal reserve corps.[51]

In General Mercado's opinion, the Federal artillery under the direction of Artillery Commander Colonel Federico Hernández and seconded by Major Julio Cavero on Santa Rosa Hill, who commanded the four 70-mm. mountain guns there, played a key role in the battle. To the north, between Santa Rosa and Coronel hills, Hernández had another eight 75-mm. Saint Chamond Mondragóns commanded by First Captain Manuel Gaspar Ruiz and supported by the 6th Infantry, as previously stated. Captain Alfonso Moreno in Colonia Dale and Major José María Villa on De la Cruz Hill, each with two Schneider Canet 75-mm. pieces, covered the south and southeast, while Second Captain Felipe Martínez Acosta commanded two mountain guns on Alamo Hill protected by Blas Orpinel's irregulars to support Orozco's position, and by extension Caraveo's, to the southwest. In the relatively quiet north, Major Manuel García de León and Captain Roberto Bernal in Nombre de Dios Avenue and Captain Luis Sánchez Hidalgo in the Romero sector commanded four 75-mm. Schneider-Canets.[52] At least one Constitutionalist agreed with Mercado's assessment that the Federals had four perfectly emplaced batteries of artillery capable of covering the city in every direction from magnificent positions, principal among them being De la Cruz Hill, owing to its central location and commanding heights: "the position was simply inexpungible."[53]

November 6

Given his extensive knowledge of the city, Villa formulated his plan of attack, ordering Maclovio Herrera to assault through the dam of the Chuvíscar River with his own Benito Juárez Brigade and Aguirre Benavides' brigade, southwest of the city. South of the city, Hernández's Leales de Camargo Brigade and those from Urbina's Morelos Brigade who had made the trip north, temporarily under the command of José Rodríguez, would attack between the

dam and Grande Hill, while to the extreme right, east of the city, the Villa
Brigade under the tactical command of Colonel Juan N. Medina was to attack between the Grande and Coronel hills. Colonel Chao remained situated
behind the Villa Brigade, in the center directing the artillery, and about one
hundred meters behind that was Villa's battlefield command center.[54]

At 5:30 p.m. the Constitutionalists began to take up position along an
immense firing line, and then began advancing on the city. As night began
to fall the shooting started. Shortly after 8 p.m. rockets from Santa Rosa,
De la Cruz, and Alamo hills filled the air announcing "enemy to the front."
Throughout the many days of battle the Federals fired off different colored
rockets across the sky as means of communications among the defenders. A
half-hour later, more or less, about two thousand revolutionaries fell furiously upon the eastern defenses in the pale moonlight, dislodging General
Antonio Rojas and other Federals from their positions between Coronel Hill
and Grande Hill, and forcing them to withdraw into the safety of Colonia
Dale. General López with the 4th Regiment fought in the Grande Hill pass
until pulled by Mercado due to the impossibility of holding out any longer.
General Mancillas with the 33rd Battalion and 4th Regiment somewhat contained the revolutionary advance, which almost got past the Federals, but
battery-powered electrified fences contained the Constitutionalists, whose
first men were "fulminated" upon trying to cut the lethal obstacle. By ten
o'clock at night Villa's men had taken both Grande and Coronel hills from
the Federals and all along the line to the Chuvíscar dam and threatened to
penetrate Colonia Dale.[55]

General Pascual Orozco, who was with part of his brigade at Rancho del
Alamo, rushed to the endangered east side accompanied by his staff and followed by three hundred infantrymen from his brigade's 1st and 3rd battalions
and another three hundred or so cavalry. General José Inés Salazar's mounted
forces also rushed to the east at the same time as Orozco. The government
forces under General Mancilla reformed, aided by Colonel Carlos S. Orozco's
6th Battalion and the constant protection of shots fired from Captain Ruiz's
batteries and the guns on Santa Rosa Hill, forcing the Constitutionalists to
retreat just as Federal reinforcements arrived to solidify the lines. After the
immediate danger had passed, some of Salazar's men remained behind in
Colonia Dale. General Orozco also left his 1st Battalion there, with jefes
Colonel José Delgado and Lieutenant Colonel Mariano Montero Villar,
while he returned with the rest of his troops to Rancho del Alamo. Upon arriving back at his sector headquarters around 11 p.m., Orozco learned that,
simultaneous to the assault against Colonia Dale, the Constitutionalists had
undertaken an attack against General Caraveo in the Palo Blanco sector, even

though minutes before they had telephoned Caraveo to say they would not attack him because they respected him too much.[56]

In effect, the revolutionary attack in the Palo Blanco sector had been so violent that the Batopilas Corps yielded the field. Some of their numbers retreated all the way to Rancho del Alamo where they reported that they had run out of ammunition and that General Caraveo had been overrun and was fleeing through the arroyos over there. Upon learning that Caraveo's position had been compromised, Orozco ordered Major José Hernández and Lieutenant Colonel José Aréchiga to take their cavalry and go to lend support. He also immediately communicated the news of these developments to division headquarters, which sent ammunition in an automobile to Caraveo posthaste: those of Caraveo's men who had remained behind to hold the line, among them Major Eleuterio Franco, had to use their gunstocks like clubs against their Constitutionalist foes in hand-to-hand combat. General Salazar also took two hundred men to reinforce Caraveo.[57]

As the attack against Caraveo took place, another group of Constitutionalists entered through the river to the Federal positions of the Chuvíscar dam where Colonels José Flores Alatorre and Evaristo Pérez, and Major Moisés Navarro and their people waited to receive them, backed up by General Blas Orpinel and the Federal artillery on Alamo Hill. Orozco took the rest of his forces, with the exception of a token force left with First Captain Jesús Casavantes, who manned the telephone of his headquarters at the ranch, and raced off to the Chuvíscar dam (on Caraveo's right); that attack took less than a half-hour to turn back. By midnight the defenders were engaged in combat along an extension of greater than eight kilometers, from Hacienda de Robinson to the Chuvíscar Dam, with Caraveo fighting into the next morning. The noise produced by the artillery fire, rifles, and detonations of dynamite bombs that the revolutionaries hurled with slings, was frightfully deafening, somewhat like the roar of an enormous volcanic eruption. Whenever the fighting grew especially intense the Federals would flash electrical spotlights on the area to reveal the Constitutionalist positions. The howls and yells of men heard a short distance away from the place of combat dominated the rifle fire, making the spectacle of death and desolation developing around the city even more horrible and imposing.[58]

During the night, the revolutionaries took possession of the walled National Cemetery on the east side. General Rojas went out to dislodge them, succeeding in this mission after heated fighting in which the revolutionaries suffered some losses. These casualties were mostly inflicted by a mine the Federals set off to blow the cemetery walls, which buried some in the rubble, and the artillery that also knocked down some walls.[59]

NOVEMBER 7

After the violence of the previous night, the day dawned relatively tranquil. The Villa and Morelos brigades occupied the ground from Coronel Hill to part of Grande Hill, with Colonel Hernández's on Grande Hill, opposite the Pacific Railroad station, and General Herrera's at the Chuvíscar Dam. But shortly after daybreak the government forces discovered the positions that the revolutionaries had occupied during the night and the Federal artillery from Santa Rosa hammered the Villistas on Grande and Coronel hills. The Constitutionalists answered with their own artillery, throwing some shells over the center of the city close to the Porfirio Díaz Hospital that caused relatively little damage. Nevertheless, the public remained indoors to avoid the artillery falling around the city.[60] Then, sometime around 11:00 a.m. Maclovio Herrera got enveloped and almost cut off by Orozco, Caraveo, and Salazar's irregulars when he rushed forward across flat terrain to save some of his men. Villa had to send some men from Aguirre Benavides' Zaragoza Brigade to rescue Herrera, causing Villa to complain that Herrera's imprudence had thrown his disposition into disarray.[61]

General Caraveo continued fighting during the whole day. He took back the positions given up earlier by the retreating Batopilas Corps and pursued the Constitutionalists to the hills to the northwest, thus avenging the death of Lieutenant Colonel Andrés Luján, one of Caraveo's most beloved subalterns who had died in the fighting the night before. Under the direction of Lieutenant Colonel Lauro F. Cejudo, the large gun "El Rorro" loaded on a railroad platform car hooked up to an armored locomotive provided cover for Caraveo's men in their maneuvers. Some artillery shells fired by the revolutionaries almost took out "El Rorro," putting four of the piece's gunners out of action with two dead (one from a direct hit in the chest) and two wounded. Only the expertise of Federal Captain Moisés Fraire kept the big gun in action.[62]

The afternoon turned relatively calm with the Villa and Hernández's brigades submitting "no news" reports but still with some shooting between the two sides, especially in Colonia Dale and places occupied by General Caraveo. Neither side could gain an advantage. The foreign consuls inside the city tried to broker an armistice, which Mercado again declined since he did not deal with "bandoleros." The fact that Federal soldiers arrived from Ciudad Juárez around nightfall with plenty of rifle and artillery ammunition may also have factored into Mercado's obdurateness.[63]

As the shooting had ceased to be heavy after the earliest part of the day, the Federals believed that the revolutionaries would not renew their attacks until the early morning hours of November 8, after the moon's light had occluded. But it was not to be, since at 8:30 p.m. the Constitutionalists set up three machine guns opposite the positions on Colonia Dale and opened fire. Aided by spotlights on Santa Rosa Hill, the Federal artillery located the machine guns and consecutively fired some six cannon shots, sufficient to quell the machine-gun fire. When the Federal soldiers approached to reconnoiter the field they found the cadavers of several Japanese, and they supposed them to have been the ones operating the now-destroyed machine guns. Since the attack on Colonia Dale was not nearly as intense as the night before, the Federals supposed that the sole purpose of that demonstration had been to draw attention to that side of the city as the Constitutionalists organized on the south side to attack the dam. They were right. At about 10 p.m. an estimated two thousand Constitutionalists attacked, throwing hand bombs that fell far from the positions of Orozco's men, who had been there since the night before. Orozco's Colorados returned fire protected by accurate artillery fire from the Federal guns on Alamo and De la Cruz hills, which were commanded by Captain Martínez Acosta and Major Villa, respectively.[64]

Promptly informed by a Captain Escobedo of the Constitutionalists' estimated numbers and determined fighting, Major Víctor Cabrero, in charge of Orozco's headquarters at Rancho del Alamo, communicated the situation directly to division headquarters, which was established on the rooftop of the offices of the jefe político. General Mercado immediately sent 100 men of the 15th Battalion commanded by a Major T. González, but just as they were arriving at Rancho del Alamo the Colorado bugles sounded *diana*, announcing success in repulsing the revolutionaries after two hours of fighting. González and his men reported to Orozco finding him on the firing line at the dam with General Félix Terrazas by his side. In this fight Captain José Encarnación Pérez died and six Colorado irregulars were wounded; the Constitutionalists retreated leaving some of their dead behind.[65]

November 8

After the attack on the dam, Orozco had his principal jefes review their troops and then ordered Colonel Alfonso Castañeda, his chief of staff, to lead all the mounted men he could muster in pursuit of the revolutionaries. They caught up to them in the early morning hours of November 8 at a place called Ojo de Buey, where they again beat the Constitutionalists, although they lamented the loss of Major Moisés Navarro in the effort. A relative calm reigned after that push until 4:20 a.m. when a large band of Constitutionalists resolutely attacked the artillery on De la Cruz Hill, approaching the foot of the hill and opening up with intense rifle fire on the Federal position and on the left flank of the camp at Rancho del Alamo. The Federals responded with machine-gun and artillery fire, sweeping the Constitutionalists from the field in less than fifteen minutes; they left behind many of their own dead and about fifteen Federal corpses.[66] Those Constitutionalists most likely belonged to Rosalío Hernández, whose men twice penetrated up to the first buildings of the Pacific train station. On one such occasion they emplaced a machine gun and opened fire on a military train forcing it to back up before the Federals turned Hernández's men back.[67]

After the attempt on De la Cruz Hill the combatants maintained their original positions with the revolutionaries in the area hills extending from Rancho de Ávalos to Las Escobas. From five in the morning of this day only a few shots rang out so General Mercado decided to order a counterattack. He had General Salazar and his men reinforced by Lieutenant Colonel Carlos Martínez's Guerrilla and the two commands were then to flank the Constitutionalist positions on the north side that they had captured on the first day of combat. Salazar obeyed with precision, exiting the city in the direction of Hacienda de Robinson as General Rojas and the 23rd Battalion undertook a frontal assault against the revolutionaries, both columns supported by artillery fire from Santa Rosa Hill. The move caught General Villa's attention, and he sent people to block its path.[68]

Salazar and Rojas' combined movement took a few hours to develop and lasted all morning long. It began with the advance forces of each side engaging and then grew in intensity as the day advanced, but did not become generalized until around 4 p.m. when the Federal guns on Santa Rosa Hill began to vomit shells in an overwhelming quantity, seeming like a volcano of iron and steel. The Federal artillery frequently and frightfully directed fragmentation shots against Coronel and Grande hills, a shower of shrapnel falling on the Constitutionalist forces where Colonel Medina was located. Federal soldiers, meanwhile, fired volleys as quickly as possible. Salazar pushed the revolutionaries back to the front of the Ávalos Foundry and General Rojas and the 23rd Battalion simultaneously charged in the center with a fury that forced the Constitutionalists back toward the southeast foot of Grande Hill where the Colorados believed Villa's headquarters to be. Salazar's men almost came to the point of taking Trinidad Rodríguez and Hipólito Villa prisoner. The first managed to escape, but his adjutant, who was shot, did not. Colorado Captain Manuel Armendáriz chased Hipólito, nearing to within twenty meters of him and shooting, but he could not get a better shot or any closer because his horse was wounded.[69]

At one point in the fighting an artillery shell fired from Santa Rosa Hill exploded very close to Villa mortally wounding Lieutenant Colonel Doctor Samuel Navarro, Chief of the Medical Service. The shell's fuse had nailed him in the chest, and when they picked him up from the ground he was already in his death agony. Someone tried to reassure him that it was not that bad a wound, and the doctor coolly answered, "Don't believe it, the wound is very serious, I know it, but I am a man and die doing my duty." Afterward, he clasped his hands and said, "I only have five minutes left; tell a medical assistant to give me a shot of morphine, I am suffering a lot." A few minutes later he breathed his last. Just moments before Villa had been talking to the doctor, who was attending to a wounded soldier. He had only stepped a few paces away to receive a battlefield report from Enrique Santos Coy sent by Colonel Medina when the deadly shell landed. It would have killed the commanding general and also Colonel Toribio Ortega, had he not joined Villa and Santos Coy to listen in.[70]

Navarro had been a leading revolutionary figure for the State of Chihuahua after the murder of Governor Abraham González, serving as vice-president of the Constitutionalist Junta in El Paso, in which capacity he had signed the Monclova Accords for the state. But this role did not satisfy his desire for action, so he abdicated those duties in order to take a more active part and headed for Ascensión where he joined Villa's brigade as the chief of its medical service. Now he had given the ultimate sacrifice for the movement; all mourned his loss.[71]

Villa then ordered Colonel Juan N. Medina to attack Santa Rosa Hill, and gathering up forces from various brigades, Medina delivered the assault. But the Federal artillery barrage and rifle fire quashed the effort. Major Eduardo Marín was mortally wounded and died shortly thereafter; Major Manuel Madinaveytia, previously wounded by a shell fragment, was removed to the hospital at Camargo.[72]

As Salazar and Rojas were effecting their maneuvers, Generals Caraveo and Orozco also went into action, dislodging the revolutionaries to their front so that they would not be able to undertake another attack, since the Colorados, and especially Caraveo's men, were exhausted from fighting ever since the battle's first moments. After the day's heavy fighting the Constitutionalists did not execute any major attack during the night, but a group of about 100 did manage to penetrate as far as the houses near the penitentiary before the Federal Army Gendarmes pushed them back toward Grande Hill in a matter of minutes.[73]

NOVEMBER 9

By Sunday the Constitutionalist "siege" seemed to be lifting. In the morning the Federal artillery again began bombarding the Constitutionalist forward positions to the east until they noticed them abandoned. The electric trolleys that for three days had only been ferrying troops day and night now began accepting civilian passengers again. Street traffic started to return to normal, but still, there was combat. Emboldened by their victory the Federals decided to give pursuit after the Constitutionalists and left their defenses to attack them on open ground. The Federals from the Colonia Dale sector completely dislodged the Constitutionalists from their remaining positions and forced them to withdraw to Alberto Station and their awaiting trains. One of Federal Captain Ruiz's guns providing cover fire for the maneuver exploded (perhaps from overuse), and the heavy combat that took place at the station forced the Federals to return to the city and their defenses. Likewise, Orozco's cavalry chased the Constitutionalists from the dam into the hills. Caraveo sallied out as far as Rancho de Fresno (about twenty kilometers to the southwest from the plaza of Chihuahua) where he exchanged fire with the Constitutionalists and dispersed the numerous groups that he was pursuing, forcing them to leave some war materiel behind, including a machine gun, an ammunition car, and other booty.[74]

Next, the Federal and Colorado cavalry led by Colorado General Marcelo Caraveo turned to the east. The combat became especially heated around 3 p.m. as they maneuvered against the Constitutionalist left flank. Because of the intensity of the Federal shelling and rifle fire, at first none of the Constitutionalists noticed as upwards of some two thousand horsemen rolled up Maclovio Herrera's left flank. Pushed back to the southwest side of Grande Hill, Herrera and his men made a stand and after being reinforced managed to turn back two follow-on charges. Soon Caraveo became outnumbered and compromised, but the Colorado commander fought on with his customary fearlessness. Caraveo's third charge finally started to break through, owing mainly to the Constitutionalists' lack of ammunition. Some men only had a few rounds left and others were completely out. As some of the Constitutionalists began to fall back, the Huertistas redoubled their efforts; they turned the defeat into a rout as Caraveo received reinforcements. General Herrera, mindful of the artillery in his care, faced the charging Colorados. With a rifle in hand, he forced a few of his men to hold their ground until the pieces could be removed. His people then retreated back to their camp where the pack train was located, somewhere between Ensenada and Mápula Station (seventeen kilometers to the southeast of the plaza of Chihuahua). The fight there lasted about another two hours; in this combat the young Major Arturo L. Quevedo (from Salazar's forces) was wounded, and he died the next day.[75]

General Villa observed the rout at the dam and, upon receiving reports from all the brigades that they were running low on ammunition, ordered all the forces to abandon their positions and join Herrera's men near Mápula Station. He was expecting the arrival of another thousand men of Contreras' brigade from Torreón, Major Manuel Ochoa from Camargo, and also General Robles' men. But only Ochoa's had arrived thus far, so Villa countermanded the orders to Robles while he considered his options.[76]

NOVEMBER 10

At 6 a.m. Generals Orozco and Caraveo left their camps under orders to inspect the hills to the northeast and pursue the revolutionaries, should they locate them. At the same time a column of three arms made up of the 23rd Battalion, a section of artillery commanded by Captain Alfonso Moreno, and cavalry commanded by Generals Landa, Salazar, and Rojas headed south. This force located the Constitutionalist advance positions at Rancho de Ávalos around 9 a.m. and, having made contact, returned to the plaza. Inside the city General Mercado ordered the musicians of the Federal Division of the North to go throughout the plaza blowing calls and playing music at 8 a.m. to announce that the government forces had won the battle. According to the official count 746 corpses were burned in the aftermath since it was not possible to bury them all. Booty captured by the Federals consisted of two guns, a tricolor flag belonging to Urbina's Morelos Brigade, two machine guns, rifles, some 15,000 rounds, several saddled horses, close to two hundred head of cattle, and sixty prisoners, who were executed by firing squad.[77] Villa lost hundreds, maybe as many as eight hundred, in the failed attack, while the Federal casualties consisted of four jefes, ten officers, and 130 men, among both killed and wounded.[78] Yet the action around the state capital still had not come to a close.

A couple of days later a loud alarm sounded alerting the Constitutionalists to a column of Colorados coming to attack the camp. Constitutionalist Colonels Ortega and Medina got the men moving and occupied some hills near Mápula. Villa stepped down from the railcar where he was eating breakfast and, jumping on his horse, went to the place of combat. The Constitutionalists scrounged up about 18,000 cartridges from Contreras' recently arrived men and the sick and wounded in the camp and gave them to Herrera's brigade to use in repelling the attack. The combat lasted about three hours. The Colorados did not want to give up on the possibility of exacting revenge, and it was only when Villa personally rallied his men that they forced the government's forces to flee the field and return to Chihuahua City. The Constitutionalists for their part embarked on fifteen trains that they brought with them and withdrew to Charco, leaving an observation force in Mápula.[79]

ANALYSIS

General Sánchez Lamego made three "observations" in Villa's failure to capture the capital city: 1) the Federal dispositions were sufficiently rational, since although the perimeter was long, the defensive organization was greatly facilitated by taking advantage of two existing obstacles: the line of hills that delimit the east and course of the Chuvíscar River to the west, and the number of Federals was also sufficient to cover that perimeter with an appropriate density; 2) Caraveo's advance position in the Chuvíscar River "was a forced solution" since it was of vital importance for the defense; and 3) the interval comprising the distance between Grande and Alamo hills, the principal sector chosen by General Villa for attack (perhaps because at first blush it seemed the easiest route) in the course of the operation became the most difficult because once the revolutionaries entered they became exposed on both flanks to the defenders on Alamo and Grande hills—although General Sánchez Lamego makes it clear that the Federals did not intentionally employ interlocking fields of enfilading fire, since these principals would only truly come into practice on the killing fields of the Great War.[80]

Of these, only the second is truly an observation and the first and third appear to be flawed analysis. First, the Federal perimeter, while indeed long, did not benefit from "an appropriate density," but rather from the proper use of interior lines to rush forces from one place to another under greater threat, as well as the well-timed execution of counterattacks. Still, none of these would have been possible without the Colorados, who manned the most vulnerable and vital points, consistently exploited the interior lines, and executed the counterattacks, which certainly validated Colonel Medina's earlier warnings to Villa.[81] The general's third observation likewise does not appear to hold water, since the Federals abandoned Grande Hill almost at the outset of the battle, and Hernández's men were able to penetrate deep into the city along a southeast-northwest axis, although they were unable to hold their positions inside the city. Finally, to say that interlocking fields of enfilading fire only came into practice during the Great War may be true, but the concept had been a part of Federal Army tactical doctrine for decades and the best of commanders employed the tactic throughout the Mexican Revolution. Moreover, Mercado's defenses did show signs of some sophistication.

The Federal maneuver regulations contained specific prescriptions for the defense of a plaza, which can present unique challenges not encountered in open field combat, most notably in the areas of communications. It can be quite difficult relaying orders to various commands when they are holed up in various houses and separated by numerous street blocks, which was why regulations warned commanders that they needed to pay particular attention to making sure that word could be spread efficiently in the event of an evacuation. In the defense of Chihuahua, the Federals had a system of communicating by telephones, runners, and rockets, but in the defense of Torreón no such provisions were made. This resulted in an improvised retreat from the latter town and led to tremendous losses in troops killed and dispersed. Additionally, the civilian population of Chihuahua City, especially the Falomirs and Creels, and Federal civilian employees aided the Federals during the battle with electric trolleys to move troops with all dispatch to various hotspots during the battle, autos and coaches for transporting ammunition and removing the wounded and dead to the aid stations and hospitals, and searchlights supplied by the power company.[82]

For their part, the Constitutionalists listed several other reasons for their failure to take Chihuahua City. Chief among them, in the minds of the Constitutionalists, was the defection of artillery Captain Torres back to his Federal brethren. When Villa's division arrived in Jiménez the Federals inside Chihuahua City believed the Constitutionalist division to number at least 10,000 men with all the artillery from Torreón and a fair amount of artillery shells. Once Torres got to Chihuahua City he gave a very thorough report to the Federal defenders, informing them that Villa was bringing less than half of what they had believed at only four thousand men; that each man had less than two hundred rounds a piece, without any reserve depot; and that the captured artillery had been disabled, with very few shells left, and was operated by inept gunners. So informed, the defenders quickly regained their morale and determination to resist and prevail. Additionally, the defenders inside the city had significantly more men, great artillery with copious ammunition, and excellent defensive positions with interior and concealed lines of communication, not to mention the benefit that comes with fighting on the defensive and the tremendous and continuous casualties that they inflicted upon the attacking force.[83]

Despite the best efforts of Colonel Martiniano Servín, Villa's artillery never really came into play for a few reasons. First, it lack sufficient ammunition and properly trained crews, and second, whenever it displaced and went into battery it no sooner had begun to fire than the dominating Federal artillery directed counterbattery fire on it. In order to save the pieces Servín had to pull them back to a safe location.[84]

After this drubbing, Villa's next move demonstrated a stealth and finesse uncommon to the caudillo accustomed to bold, direct action.

Battle of Ciudad Juárez

From his camp in Charco, Villa planned his next moves. He decided to send General Chao with all the trains, the infantry, the women, and the wounded south to Camargo, while he took the cavalry north through Villa Aldama, avoiding Chihuahua City, in the hopes of hijacking a train for use in attacking Ciudad Juárez. Such trickery seemed out of character coming from the straight-shooting Villa, but once his chief lieutenants finished "dying of laughter," as Villa remembered it, they approved his plan. He began his displacement during the night, and by dawn on November 13 he was at the copper foundry near Terrazas Station. Villa sent a telegram to General Francisco Castro in Ciudad Juárez pretending to be Mercado. In it, he said that he had just repulsed the Constitutionalist attack and was sending men to reinforce the Juárez plaza now that he did not need them. Around 5 p.m. a train loaded with coal traveling south arrived and Villa's men captured it. The general gleefully remarked, "Now you have the train that I described when I indicated that we were going to take Ciudad Juárez."[85]

It took hours after they captured the train to find a telegrapher, but the next morning Villa told him to telegraph exactly what he said, making sure to use all the right passwords, and warning him that Villa's own telegrapher (possibly Manuel Banda) was looking on, and if he made one false move he would be shot. Then Villa sent the message in the name of the captured train's engineer, E. Velázquez, claiming that his train had derailed and that the rails and telegraph to the south had been destroyed and requesting that Ciudad Juárez send further orders and another engine to hoist his back on track. A few minutes later Ciudad Juárez responded saying that there were no more engines and to look for something in the foundry to help him lift his derailed locomotive and then ask for orders after he had done it. Villa used the next two hours to have his men unload the coal, and then two thousand men of Herrera, Villa, and Urbina's brigades, along with scouts and the division staff climbed aboard. Around 8 a.m. Villa gave orders to General Rosalío Hernández and Colonels Toribio Ortega, Julián Granados, and Fidel Ávila to follow along the rails with their commands and the division's horses heading north. In the rearguard, Martiniano Servín used mules taken from the haciendas of the Terrazas to pull the artillery trains and carts loaded with supplies. Villa then telegraphed Ciudad Juárez to report that he had put the train back on the tracks, but he repeated that there was no telegraph or uninterrupted railway to the south and that he spotted a dust cloud that looked like the approach of revolutionaries. He needed orders. The response instructed him to "start back and at each station request orders." The Federals never suspected that the train had become a Trojan horse.[86]

Meanwhile, Villa's turn north had not fooled the Federals in Chihuahua City. General Marcelo Caraveo's brigade of eight hundred Colorados left Chihuahua City on November 13, racing on horseback to try to reach Villa's rearguard; General José Inés Salazar followed close behind with another one thousand men also giving chase.[87] In addition, after the Caraveo and Salazar columns had departed Chihuahua City, Mercado sent a repair train commanded by General Mancilla and accompanied by a "strong column" of infantry with eight cannons and ten machine guns to work on the railroad and telegraphs. Other trains followed loaded with the Colorados of Generals Rojas and Orpinel. Due to his seniority, General Salazar had overall command of the combined forces.[88]

During that first night a column of irregulars commanded by Salazar and Caraveo arrived where Ortega's men had been only a short while before, prior to moving off into the hills adjacent to the rails. Noticing how close the Constitutionalists' campfires were, and guessing that the next day they would continue on toward the north, Caraveo went on ahead while Salazar remained behind to attack them from the rear.[89]

The next day, as Ortega's Constitutionalists came down from the sierra and five kilometers west of the Central Railroad opposite Arados Station (near Ojo de Laguna), Salazar's Colorados suddenly attacked, taking the Constitutionalists by surprise. But Ortega's men responded with energy to repel the "the mine picker from Arizona," as Ortega's men called Salazar, and they forced the Colorados to flee after a fierce struggle. While Salazar retreated, Caraveo opened fire from the north, and the Constitutionalists turned their full attentions on his Colorados, eventually forcing them to retreat after six hours of combat, although Caraveo claimed victory in the action. Colonel Ortega especially distinguished himself by pursuing the Orozquistas with sword in hand at the front of his soldiers, allegedly running through any Colorados whom he caught up to with the white arm, although Caraveo reported losing only seven enlisted and one officer, First Captain Francisco Ramírez. Back at Arados Station Caraveo detached two hundred men to chase after the Constitutionalists, most of whom had already reached Gallegos Station; the rest of his exhausted men and horses took a much-needed rest.[90]

Villa's trains continued northward stopping at El Sauz, Laguna, Moctezuma, and Samalayuca Stations, taking due precautions and telegraphing Ciudad Juárez with updates as instructed. In Samalayuca Villa dictated orders for the assault on the plaza. The jefes were not to allow any troops to sleep. A soldier stood next to the train engineer with a dagger in hand, and in a loud voice so that they all could hear, Villa gave instructions to kill the engineer if he did not bring the trains all the way into the plaza. The railroader was only too happy to comply. As soon as the troops had unloaded within the city, Fierro was to take the train back south to collect the artillery.[91]

Villa's "Federal" train slipped into Ciudad Juárez at 2:30 a.m. on November 15 virtually unnoticed, since hardly anyone was in the station at that time of night; Federal General Castro was asleep at his home and the other jefes and officers were partying. The Constitutionalists detrained, organized in a line of shooters, and quietly swept through the city headed for the Federal barracks as the unsuspecting city continued in its slumber.[92] José Rodríguez with Urbinas' Morelos Brigade received the task of attacking the Orozquista barracks, which he later learned were in different locations scattered from Zaragoza Street to the hippodrome on the city's southeast side. Herrera and his Benito Juárez Brigade departed to the left of the train against the 15th Battalion barracks on the west side. And in the center, that is, straight ahead, Villa ordered First Captain Enrique Santos Coy to take the "Jefatura de Armas" headquarters of the plaza and occupy the international bridges. Villa made the train station (or customs house) his command post and ordered Juan N. Medina to take some men of the Guide Corps, secure the banks, and "intervene" the gambling houses and saloons, well known for the large amounts of money that circulated there, placing Carlos Jáuregui in charge.[93]

Suddenly, hundreds of voices went up cheering "¡Viva Villa!" to the sound of detonations. The Federal officers first thought that the 15th had staged a cuartelazo, but then quickly realized their error when they saw armed revolutionaries in the streets. Some Federal officers tried to put up a resistance, but others, including General Castro, fled across the border and into the United States once they saw that the majority of the city was already in Constitutionalist hands. Although Castro had no way of knowing it, Villa had already ordered that Castro's life should be spared were he to fall into Constitutionalist hands in gratitude for helping to save his life when Huerta tried to have him executed the year before. The barracks of the 15th put up the most resistance. The soldiers inside wanted to give up but an officer stood in the doorway with pistol in hand and threatened to shoot anyone who tried to surrender. Meanwhile, Constitutionalists occupied the rooftops across from the barracks and began to pour in fire. The Federal Captain ordered some men to go outside and start shooting, but as soon as anyone stepped outside they were instantly shot dead. Then he ordered a machine gun emplaced in the doorway, but soon the whole crew lay dead. After an hour of fighting the Constitutionalists stormed the barracks and it finally surrendered. They immediately executed the Federal captain. Several more officers soon shared his fate including the "three times a traitor" Captain Torres who had deserted from Camargo, and in the opinion of some Constitutionalists, very nearly single-handedly brought about the defeat at Chihuahua City. Upon recognizing him they shot him posthaste.[94]

At midnight, within two hours of entering the plaza, all the objectives had been taken and the Federals beaten, except for a few holdouts in the jail. Some of the Colorados who had escaped Ciudad Juárez in the night returned and made a feeble attempt to attack the plaza around 5 p.m., but the Villistas easily repulsed them. General Caraveo gave a different version of events, saying that this handful of Colorados had actually barricaded itself inside the bullring and continued to fight all night long and into the next day until realizing the hopelessness of their situation. They decided to surrender to Villa, who personally gave them assurances that their lives would be respected, only to have them executed forthwith. The losses to the Constitutionalists during the attack amounted to some wounded and a few killed balanced against two cannons and an equal number of machine guns captured.[95]

Immediately after entering the city, Colonel Rodolfo Fierro, a railroader in civilian life, left with two platform trains and another full of supplies to locate and retrieve the division's artillery. Villa set about buying ammunition to sufficiently supply his division, placing large orders in the United States, and likewise purchasing large quantities of uniforms to clothe his men.[96]

Upon learning of the capitulation of Ciudad Juárez, Caraveo decided to hold up and await the main Federal column under General Salazar, proceeding by train from Chihuahua City with another 2,400 men. General Mercado now found his Federal Division of the North blockaded from both the exterior and the rest of the country by Contreras' Constitutionalists at Torreón in the south and Villa in the north, so he ordered General Salazar to join Caraveo with a force composed mainly of Colorado irregulars to try to defeat Villa. Villa likewise ordered all available forces to converge north for a showdown for control of the state.[97]

Battle of Tierra Blanca

Villa's occupation of Ciudad Juárez allowed him to establish rail and telegraph communications through the United States to the First Chief in Sonora, from whom he requested funds, reinforcements, and ammunition; Carranza sent the first in the amount of ₱300,000, but no reinforcements. Regardless, Ciudad Juárez with its customs receipts, gambling houses, and saloons were profitable enterprises for the sustenance of Villa's army, and he was determined to defend it at all costs. So, when Villa found out about the approaching Federal column on November 20, he immediately sent Rodolfo Fierro with Martín López and a crane to tear up the track and slow its advance. Next, he issued orders for November 22 to have all the troops form up in front of the train station in Ciudad Juárez and pass in review, a ritual understood by all as a preparation for battle. Once formed, however, Villa did not inspect the troops, but rather called the key commanders forward to receive their orders. Within minutes the division started to march out toward Mesa Station, located some sixteen kilometers south of Ciudad Juárez, and far enough from El Paso, Texas, that stray bullets from the battle would not provoke an international incident. Villa also chose that location for combat because of the terrain there: between Mesa and Tierra Blanca stations, thirty kilometers south of Ciudad Juárez, the ground is flat and sandy, which would make it difficult for an opposing force to maneuver. Also, everyone knew that the division was short on ammunition, so in the case of defeat Villa and his generals would have a much easier time reaching the agreed upon rally point in the sierras—escaping into the United States, like Federals do, was not an option. In the meantime, Adrian Aguirre Benavides, Villa's secretary, phoned Ernesto Madero in New York to wire $10,000 to help fix the shortage of funds. Villa entrusted this money to Colonel Medina, who remained behind with some men of the Guides Corps to keep order in the city and to ferry food and ammunition to the front as might be needed.[98]

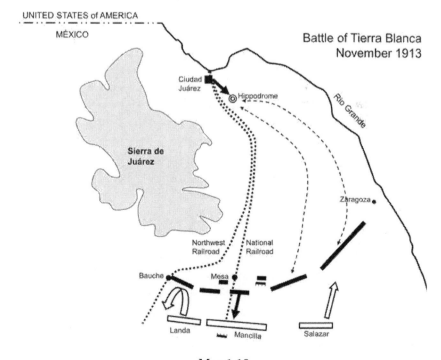

Map 1.18

After seeing to all the necessary preparations Villa marched south to Mesa Station, aligning his 6,200 troops (the Constitutionalists had recruited more men in Ciudad Juárez) perpendicular to the rail line in a slight concave angling to the north over a front of more than ten kilometers and on solid footing, leaving the sandy terrain for the Huertista cavalry and artillery to negotiate. The Constitutionalist front stretched from near the Rio Grande on the left to the water tanks at Bauche, Chihuahua, eighteen kilometers southwest of Ciudad Juárez on the Northwest Railroad.[99] The Morelos Brigade under the temporary command of José Rodríguez took up position on the left, that is, to the east, accompanied by five hundred men from Hernández's Leales de Camargo Brigade. Villa placed his artillery in the center, apparently on the firing line, under ex-Federal Martiniano Servín with the Villa Brigade under Toribio Ortega on Servín's right. Herrera's Benito Juárez Brigade and Aguirre Benavides' Zaragoza Brigade formed the right wing, accompanied by some elements of the Morelos Brigade. Villa placed his reserve under the command of Manuel Madinaveytia and Porfirio Talamantes, located so as to give the appearance of filling in the gaps in his front line. This disposition had the added benefit of locating Villa between the Federals and the nearest large water source, Ciudad Juárez and the Rio Grande. All Villa's men were dismounted with the horses placed in the care of Hernández's men, with one man holding ten horses each.[100]

Salazar had some one thousand infantrymen from the 15th, 23rd, and 33rd Battalions, brigaded under Brigadier Jesús Mancilla; approximately nine hundred riders of the 4th and 7th Regiments and the Melchor Ocampo and Hidalgo Irregular Corps, formed in a cavalry brigade under Brigadier Manuel Landa; and four Saint Chamond Mondragón 75-mm. field guns, four 70-mm. mountain cannons, and two machine guns. On the eve of battle Salazar and Caraveo learned that Huerta had promoted both of them to the rank of general of brigade in the Federal Army on November 11, in recognition of their performance during the defense of Chihuahua City.[101]

November 23-24

Close to 6 p.m. the lights of the Federals' trains announced their arrival on the battlefield. Villa had planned to advance his whole line to within two kilometers of the enemy trains at midnight, but beginning around 10 p.m. on the night of November 23, the Federals and Constitutionalists began exchanging fire intermittently up and down the line, so Villa decided to stay put. Then at 5 a.m., General Landa's cavalry attacked the Morelos and Zaragoza brigades on Villa's right, experiencing some success in the attempt to turn the Constitutionalist flank. An officer sent by Herrera arrived to report the dire situation to General Villa. At that point, he decided to proceed with his original plans, and his center made a push toward the Federal trains, which were protected by enemy infantry. Some units, especially a squadron from the reserve under Porfirio Talamantes, got very close to the lead train, where the intrepid Talamantes lost his life. As his own forces drew close to the lead Federal train, judging that he had sufficiently relieved pressure on his own right flank, Villa withdrew his center while taking deadly fire from the Federal right. He hoped to draw the Federals out of their natural cover and into pursuit, but the Federals rejected the temptation. Instead the Federal artillery units tried to advance throwing shrapnel non-stop; every four or five minutes, detonations could be heard. The explosion of shells that fell on the Constitutionalist camp produced some casualties. In response Villa ordered his artillery chief, Lieutenant Colonel Martiniano Servín, to force the Federal artillery back. His guns responded intermittently, with an artillery duel ensuing.[102]

When Servín had managed to push back the Federal artillery a sufficient distance, Villa sent Fidel Ávila with four hundred horsemen from the Villa Brigade to reinforce Herrera and Aguirre Benavides on his right; they forced the Federals back to their trains in disorder around 11 a.m., thus frustrating Landa's attempt to take possession of the water tanks at Bauche Station. About this time Salazar pressed forward on Villa's left, attacking the Leales de Camargo and Morelos Brigades, pushing them all the way back to the hippodrome of Ciudad Juárez before the Constitutionalist reserves in Ciudad Juárez counterattacked, and cutting off and annihilating those Federal units who could not keep up with the main body in retreat. For some only a dust cloud arising from the direction of Zaragoza provided the concealment that saved them.[103]

During the battle Juan Medina sent trains with water, bread, and fodder to resupply Villa. Automobiles rushed ammunition and even machine guns to the firing line. Orderlies and medicines for Villa's wounded arrived in private automobiles from Ciudad Juárez and El Paso. After his wounded had received first aid, Villa ordered them put on trains and sent back to Ciudad Juárez.[104]

NOVEMBER 25

The next morning, action again became generalized. It had grown especially heated on the Constitutionalist left when Villa ordered José Rodríguez forward. The two opposing forces tried to force the decision, with the Federals trying to advance and the Constitutionalists trying to hold them back. The Federals, confident in their presumed advantage of men and firepower, ordered the artillery to displace and move forward as the train loaded with the large caliber gun "El Rorro" did the same. The Constitutionalists received a small reinforcement from the González Ortega Regiment commanded by Major Crispín Juárez, the 2nd Squadron commanded by Major Benito Artalejo, as well as automobiles carrying ammunition sent by Colonel Medina. But then Rodríguez was wounded and his whole line faltered when a Federal counterattack again pushed those brigades back to the Juárez hippodrome. Villa knew he had to act.[105]

In response Villa sent Toribio Ortega, Fidel Ávila, and other officers to take their troops to reinforce and save his left wing, and then he issued instructions for a general cavalry charge to be effected upon the signal of two cannon shots. He waited for the right moment. About two hours later the Federals decided to unload their artillery from the train in order to advance with the infantry, who began to leave the protection of the sand dunes and move forward. Villa gave the signal and the cavalry rushed forward causing the Federals to break and run, leaving behind their artillery in the sand. The Constitutionalists fell upon the fleeing Federals, finishing them off with pistols and killing a great many. Some Federals tried hopelessly to hide themselves in the sand, while others played dead, tossed their weapons and threw themselves face down in surrender, or were shot dead. As the sun was going down the Villistas reached the Federal trains, when Rodolfo Fierro, commander of Villa's Guide Corps, performed an act worthy of a Hollywood movie. Racing on horseback to a Federal train full of enemy soldiers in retreat, the former railroad man managed to reach the lead train (that is, the one closest to the Constitutionalists), ignoring a torrent of bullets, and grab the brake lever, stopping it dead in its tracks. The Constitutionalists pounced upon the train and its hapless passengers. The pursuit devolved into carnage as hundreds of Colorados fell victim to the Constitutionalist rifle fire, with nightfall being the only protection that could save "Huerta's mercenaries" from complete annihilation.[106] Salazar lost probably fifteen hundred men among killed and wounded, and all his artillery. Casualties on the Constitutionalist side were likely very many, too.[107]

Ordinary citizens opened up their homes to wounded soldiers as makeshift aid stations and businesses on both sides of the border rushed them food and blankets, while nurses went to the battlefield carrying medicines. U.S. citizens as well as the customs administrator, Zachary Cobb, and a bakery in El Paso helped Villa and his Constitutionalists "a lot." The situation took on all of the proportions of an international relief effort.[108] Some thought the assistance extended even further. Federal General Guillermo Rubio Navarrete alleged that a railroad official with the unmistakably Anglo surname of Melville was behind sending the train that snuck Villa's men into Ciudad

Juárez in the first place. Moreover, the Americans bought the plaza from the Federal commander, General Francisco Castro, for ₱50,000 and "supplied" (it is never clear whether conspiracy theorists mean to give for free, or to sell, when they use this word) Villa with ammunition during the Battle of Tierra Blanca.[109]

Following in this same vein, General Mercado's report of the battle is possibly the most fantastical, risible, and demonstrably false battlefield account ever filed with the Secretary of War. It exposes the boundless energy with which Federals sought to incriminate the American bogeyman in order deflect blame for their own incompetence:

> The railway reconstructed [all the way] to Tierra Blanca, and when the column already had all its elements [collected], I undertook the advance toward [Ciudad] Juárez fighting with the enemy and making him back up to just before Mesa Station with great losses for him, but when I was just about to proceed to the decisive action, the enemy was reinforced with people coming from Sonora comprised of workers commanded by General Ángeles; bringing cannons with mounted Texans and with them American filibusters with all their elements, they established a very extensive line of combat, each rider carrying another man to the group. The enemy opened his artillery fire, a great distance [away] with eighty [millimeter] cannons, making sufficient damage to our troops, since all their shots were well-directed, ours not being able to reach them, the combat became generalized and after some hours of fighting the enemy hurled themselves at our infantry which held its positions until a portion of the forces of the Orozco Brigade turned tail introducing panic with this among the rest who did the same with the result that they lost a [Schneider] Canet that was mounted on a platform and that when the [train] engine pulling the platform that it was on tried to retreat, it was dead [that is, out of steam]. As the enemy continued advancing and our troops in retreat proceeded to the embarking of the cannons, which they achieved, but the enemy was already boarding the trains and because they could not back up because their engines were dead, said cannons remained in control of the enemy, without breechblocks.[110]

One is severely taxed in knowing where to begin with deconstructing the prevarications crammed into Mercado's official report. The Federals had at least two 80-mm. guns ("El Rorro" and "El Chavalito") to the Constitutionalists' possible one ("El Niño" captured at Torreón), and General Felipe Ángeles was months from making his appearance in Chihuahua. Delivering infantry into combat on the back of horses was a signature Villista tactic, and there are no other reports of American filibusters and mounted Texan gunners suddenly appearing on the battlefield like so many howling banshees, aside from Mercado's accusations. The story of "dead" engines does not square with the fact that many Federals escaped by rail, and the mention of removing breech-blocks of guns that fell into the Constitutionalists' hands sounds more like so much face-saving than reality. Finally, no one except Mercado suggests that he was within hundreds of kilometers of the battle, but he probably did not want to explain why he had placed Salazar, an irregular general with no formal training and a failed record as a battlefield commander, in charge of all the Federal division's maneuver forces.

Following his defeat, General Salazar started his return trip to Chihuahua City, leaving Caraveo to cover his retreat and burn all the railroad bridges in his wake. Villa thought Caraveo had been present at Tierra Blanca fighting alongside Landa, but in actuality he had remained to the rear, leapfrogged by Salazar who raced ahead to try to recapture Ciudad Juárez. Caraveo only arrived in time to cover the Federals' retreat and save them from utter annihilation. The Federals considered making another attempt to take Ciudad Juárez from their rally point at Villa Ahumada, but in the midst of a fog, quite unusual for that area (even though *ahumada* ironically translates as "smoking"), a train collision occurred in the early morning hours sewing much destruction and death and further demoralizing the Colorados and Federals. Both trains were traveling at full steam without their lights on, and the crash was catastrophic. The dead and wounded were left there as those who somehow came out unharmed walked back to Chihuahua City to inform Mercado of the disaster. Salazar reached Chihuahua with most of his remaining forces the following day, quickly spreading the word of the Federal defeat.[111]

After the disaster of Tierra Blanca the praetorians and Colorados held a council of war to decide on a plan of action. Straightaway Mercado resolved to abandon the city. Federal General of Division José Refugio Velasco, the new commander of the Division of the Nazas who had been appointed in October with the primary mission of retaking Torreón and bridging the territorial gap between the North and Bravo divisions would not accomplish his mission for another two weeks. Mercado could not know that, and at any rate could not wait. He had to reestablish communications with Mexico City in order to receive badly needed funds for his division, and if he could not do it through Torreón, then he would need to access the border. Ojinaga with its tiny Constitutionalist garrison seemed to provide the solution, but the Colorados remembered the torturous journey and disastrous battle there the year before and instead preferred to defend Chihuahua City once again, preserving the possibility of withdrawing to their *patria chica* in Guerrero City as a last resort. Many of the Guerrilla units did not wait for Mercado's next move and simply abandoned Chihuahua City for the western part of the state to fight the few Constitutionalists there, disowning Mercado but still swearing allegiance to the national government. General Caraveo, for one, thought that the Federals had enough men, arms, and ammunition to stay and fight, and he said so, causing Mercado to threaten Caraveo with a firing squad for insubordination. Quickly surveying the Colorados surrounding him, the general thought the better of it and changed from his "Prussian tone and attitude," in the words of Caraveo, to praising the Irregulars and their good relations with the Federal regulars. Nevertheless, despite his generals' implorations to stay and fight and promises by local businesses to finance the defense of the plaza with up to three million pesos, Mercado rejected all offers and pleas and stubbornly ordered his division to Ojinaga; he may also have burned war materiel and 200,000 cartridges. This was not the same man who exhibited such calm under fire at the Battle of First Rellano.[112]

For his part, Mercado says that he tried to get payroll for the troops (not to mention fodder for the horses), which amounted to a little more than ₱600,000 per month. After settling October's arrears he only had ₱100,000 for November, but the state government and the local offices of the federal government had run out of funds. The commanding general then had recourse to the Chamber of Commerce, which in conjunction with the Banco Refraccionario issued vouchers in twenty and fifty centavos and one peso denominations. But the total value of this issue was quite reduced so he went to the city's business interests, first with supplications and later with threats, thus obtaining very small quantities of money that still did not improve the situation. Finally, in accord with the business community, he ordered bearer scrip in the amount of fifty centavos notes to be signed by the Head of Treasury and General Mercado himself in order for businesses to later cash them with the General Treasury of the Federation in return for letters of exchange. This was a practice that went back to the colonial period in order to span the delivery of payroll, but often it expanded the money supply and sparked inflation, with deleterious effects on the local economy. In this instance, however, the General Treasury refused to cancel the Army's scrip debt with the unfortunate result that in the morning many businesses remained closed so as to avoid accepting the scrip. Lacking pay and with the Constitutionalists advancing from the north, the irregular forces began sacking not only businesses but also private residences, mainly because they believed that Mercado had the money but simply refused to hand it over. Mercado says that at this point he managed to restore a tenuous order, but the irregulars told him that without pay they would not fight and began deserting in droves. So then, Mercado told the irregulars that he would go out to face the enemy, and assembled his forces on the outskirts of town. With the soldiers outside of the city, the townsfolk began rioting, and so his only option was to hurriedly embark his men on trains and head for Ojinaga, the closest city from which he could communicate with Mexico City and receive orders, "since my situation had reached the ultimate extreme and only through the energy that had been wrought had the Division been conserved."[113]

Regarding ammunition, Mercado said that he had exhausted all his .30-30 Winchester carbine (used by irregulars) and 70-mm. mountain gun ammunition, meaning that those guns and eighteen hundred carbines, not to mention their handlers, had been rendered useless. Additionally, his 75-mm. cannon shells were very scarce, all of which made him abandon the state capital. This lends credence to the rumor that Mercado had destroyed 200,000 cartridges, perhaps his .30-30 ammunition, to neutralize the threat of the Colorados. For all the reasons he had enumerated, and to save what assets the Federal Division of the North still possessed, Mercado abandoned the city. He left behind two hundred regulars to keep order at the behest of the business class, who promised to vouch for their safety, as well as the safety of his wounded still in the hospitals, and to pay their wages; and to his credit, when Villa entered town he respected their lives.[114]

The Federal Division of the North abandoned the state capital in three columns over three days. General Manuel Landa's cavalry brigade left on November 27, camping in Villa Aldama for three days until continuing on. Next the Colorado cavalry left by train, leapfrogging Landa's brigade to reach San Sóstenes Station, 150 kilometers north of Chihuahua City. On the third day the Federal infantry, artillery, and impedimenta left. Many of the irregulars deserted, refusing to continue obeying Mercado, whom they considered inept and cowardly, an opinion shared by the leading citizens who had offered to advance Mercado the money for defense of the city and now followed the Federals to Ojinaga. Due to a lack of money to pay their wages, the railroad personnel also gave Mercado trouble, "killing" some engines and seeking the first opportunity to abandon their positions, be it before the trains reached Laguna Station or San Sóstenes Station. Because of the panic, desolation, and suffering of the flight, the column and its civilian tagalongs became known as the "caravan of death." Mercado himself left with the last few men on November 30, but his fuel ran out the next day, and the march had to be continued cross-country. The regulars finally entered Ojinaga on December

13, preceded by Generals Caraveo and Salazar's brigades on December 8 and General Orozco's on December 9, the same day that Federal General José Refugio Velasco's Division of the Nazas retook Torreón.[115] Had Mercado's division gone south his men would have had a better chance of survival, since there was nothing but four hundred dismounted Constitutionalists in Camargo, poorly armed and worse for ammunition, standing in the way of them reaching Torreón.[116]

Villa marched down to Chihuahua City and took command of the government, immediately proceeding to confiscate the properties of the Terrazas, Creel, Luján, and other families that had contributed to sustaining the Usurper's government. He also put new bills issued by the General Treasury of the State into circulation, repaired the rails and resumed passenger service to operate every three days, opened the schools in the district, and "dedicated all his attention to the people, leaving military business to his Chief of Staff, Lieutenant Colonel Manuel Madinaveytia." At this time he also learned of the recapture of Torreón by Federal General Velasco, who had sent Contreras and Robles fleeing into Durango and General Natera escaping under a Federal cannonade to the north.[117] Villa would later give Natera the opportunity to lead the final effort to finish off the Federal Division of the North in Ojinaga.

ANALYSIS

The surprise attack on Ciudad Juárez has long been considered one of the most audacious and ingenuous acts of war carried out by General Villa, although Colonel Juan N. Medina may have been the one who, possibly, thought it up rather than Villa.[118] Mercado, ever ready to suggest treachery, reported that the Superintendent of the National Railroad sent a train with twelve empty railcars and ten gondolas of coal from Ciudad Juárez to Chihuahua and "either by coincidence or malice" the Constitutionalists captured and embarked troops on it and returned to Ciudad Juárez. Worse still, Castro had seven hundred troops, two cannons, and two machine guns and yet allowed the Constitutionalists to take the plaza "without any difficulty, since not only had the necessary measures to avoid a surprise not been taken, but what is more the cannons were inside of the barracks, with the result that these were lost and the jefes, officers, and troops for the most part fell prisoner, [with] the jefes and officers who could not escape being shot."[119]

General Castro, in turn, blamed the loss of Ciudad Juárez on General Mercado, who

> ...out of foolish zeal for popularity or prestige succeeded in distancing me from Chihuahua [City] and when he appointed me Jefe de

las Armas in Ciudad Juárez he took from me all the elements for the
defense of the plaza leaving me only a few irregulars, in the majority
disarmed, the plaza remaining exposed to a coup de main, which
I had the honor of communicating [previously]...by telegraph and
which ultimately occurred.[120]

Accordingly, Castro reported that he had tried to get Mercado to duly garrison Ciudad Juárez, defended by then-Jefe de las Armas Colonel Juan N.
Vázquez, since this was the "key to the State of Chihuahua," but the commanding general declined saying; "No, let Juanito there defend it if he can or
evacuate, in the end we will easily retake the plaza." Then, after Castro took
over as commander of the plaza, Mercado took away the 15th Battalion, half
the complement of the artillery section, and much of his ammunition, offering to replace those assets with the 23rd, which never happened. Also, when
the manager of the National Railroad approached Castro for permission to
send a train loaded with coal in gondolas to Chihuahua City, Castro relayed
the request to Mercado, sure that he would deny it. But instead Mercado
agreed to allow it, and therefore he and not Castro was responsible for Villa's
surprise attack.[121]

Castro also blamed Mercado for the loss at the Battle of Tierra Blanca,
saying the division commander lied when he said that he sent a column
of 5,000 men to retake Ciudad Juárez, since the column had only 3,000
or so men (actually more like 2,500). Mercado was also the one who told
Caraveo to hold up at Villa Ahumada, because he feared that Villa would
evade Salazar's column and effect another coup de main—this time against
Chihuahua City. Castro complained that one single airplane could have
served this oversight purpose, and by preventing Caraveo from joining the
battle Mercado removed a healthy number of mounted troops, precisely what
the Federals were lacking at the Battle of Tierra Blanca.[122]

For his part, Villa always considered the Battle of Tierra Blanca his greatest victory, although he never seems to have internalized the fact that this had
been largely a defensive battle. Had he realized the benefits of assuming a tactically defensive posture combined with a well-timed counterattack, it might
have saved him from later defeat. Villa's detractors, on the other hand, gave
credit for the victory to the charge delivered by General Maclovio Herrera.[123]

* * *

The Constitutionalists' inability to gain access to a regular flow of arms
and ammunition became the greatest contributing factor in the slow

pace of military operations in Chihuahua. Villa's men had been hard pressed for arms and ammunition because of the U.S. embargo, and had to rely overwhelmingly on battlefield salvage—what they could take from the Federals. The booty from Torreón was well received, but after battling for Chihuahua City, Villa was again short of ammunition. Once he had taken Ciudad Juárez, Villa was in a good position to begin placing orders with U.S. firms, but he still had to contend with the embargo and a shortage of ammunition at Tierra Blanca. For Villa and his Constitutionalists, the United States posed the single largest obstacle to annihilating the Federals, with the lack of artillery coming in a distant second place. But General Rubio Navarrete saw events from a different perspective.

The professionals of the Federal Army could not bring themselves to admit that they could be defeated by upstart revolutionaries, such as Villa, who employed stealth, cunning, surprise, and sheer force to win victories. Instead, Rubio blamed the loss of Ciudad Juárez, the beginning of the end of the Federal Division of the North, on treachery and the United States. He averred that an American railroad official arranged to bring Villa's men into Ciudad Juárez after the United States had bought the plaza from Federal General Francisco Castro. Additionally, Rubio claimed that the United States not only failed to properly enforce its embargo against the revolutionaries, but it directly "supplied" them with the war materiel used in Villa's victory in the Battle of Tierra Blanca; all this without a shred of evidence. Even more outlandish accusations came from the commander of the Federal Division of the North, Salvador Mercado, who blamed the loss at Tierra Blanca on Texan gunners with larger caliber guns that forced the smaller Federal guns out of range so that American filibusters could overwhelm the Federal lines.

Somehow, these and other Federal generals seemed incapable of recognizing the tremendous advantage the Federal Army had enjoyed from the very beginning of Huerta's inauguration and right up through the summer of 1913, with legal access to the United States' arms markets and huge stockpiles of large caliber cannons and machine guns in the armories of Mexico City and Veracruz. The tendency of the Federal generals to downplay their own artillery power was especially curious since both the Federals and the Constitutionalists credited the guns for the Federal victory at Chihuahua City in November, where the equivalent of five batteries of artillery with sufficient ammunition executing indirect fire missions played not only a vital but an unusual role. Unusual because no other example of such massed Federal Army firepower exists in the annals of the Mexican Revolution, an exception which owed more to an improper allocation of these assets than a lack of guns, since the Federals possessed them by the score. Much more typical were battles, such as Second Torreón, where the Federals had only one or two batteries that commanders apportioned to various columns and placed on the firing line in direct fire missions, subject to capture, with the result that they had a negligible effect on the outcome of battle and ultimately fell into enemy hands.

The Federal victory at Chihuahua City also differed from the disaster at Torreón in two more key respects. First, the Federal forces in Chihuahua consisted largely of irregulars, as opposed to the trounced Division of the Nazas that consisted largely of the units of the line. Second, even though Federal Army doctrine placed an emphasis on communications in the defense of plazas precisely because of the unique challenges that urban dispositions offered, Munguía at Torreón failed to take proper measures, with the result that his command suffered casualties on the order of fifty percent, mostly among the lead elements at Avilés and subsequently upon retreat. Alternatively, Mercado in the defense of Chihuahua City used phones and rockets for efficient and timely communication of battlefield developments. And for the second time it would appear that a scout plane had figured prominently in a Federal battlefield defeat: Obregón's at Santa María and Mercado's failure to use one at Tierra Blanca.

The scope, scale, and level of sophistication of operations increasingly demanded that the practitioners of warfare be, if not educated in doctrine, then at least attuned to sensible protocols. Nowhere was the increased sophistication more visible than in the area of military economy, where Federals, operating far from Mexico City, and the Constitutionalists in Chihuahua and Durango, functioning under the aegis of an impecunious First Chieftaincy, had to attend to the matters of cash flow. The commercial class and banks in major cities in many cases provided the necessary funds; for example, the wire transfer in the amount of $10,000 from Ernesto Madero to Ciudad Juárez for materiel and bank loans in Torreón for the Constitutionalist payroll. Indeed, the importance attached to wealth gave added awareness to military objectives already significant for geographically strategic and political reasons: Torreón for its bountiful cotton harvest and Ciudad Juárez for its lucrative vice business, customs receipts, and access to the transfer of funds, however small, from the First Chief.

If Federal General Mercado is to be believed, then the ultimate loss of Chihuahua stemmed not from battlefield defeat, per se, but rather from having to abandon Chihuahua City because he did not have enough money for payroll and sustenance. The money from Mexico City had been exhausted, vouchers proved too little, and the Treasury's refusal to accept scrip from businesses caused them to shut down in order to avoid accepting more of the worthless paper and upset commerce in the process. Without payroll or food, Mercado's Colorado mercenaries had begun rebelling and sacking businesses and residences and then deserting. To restore order and hold his command together he had to exit the plaza, separating his soldiers from the civilian population and the objects of their ire and desire. It would appear that Villa later provided some temporary relief to the population by putting new bills issued by the General Treasury into circulation.

There can be no doubt that, from its very inception in September, Villa's Division of the North was off to a fast start down the road to professionalization, beginning with the incorporation of Federal artillery officers captured at Avilés bringing their technical skills and the men receiving their first pay; followed by the creation of a staff with qualified officers, a provost marshal, and adoption of the Federal Army ordinances and pay schedule; and finally the institution of regimentation and discipline, as exemplified by the shooting of Yuriar and getting Chao to report with his men. The capture of Torreón, a vibrant agro-industrial center and regional crossroads, demonstrated the ability of the revolutionaries to defeat army regulars in a pitched battle and the progress made after more than six months of preparations and operations. Over the next eight months, Villa's forces would take part in the most epic battles of the Huertista era, and for good reason.

Operations in the Division of the North's area brought together all the major Mexican military and paramilitary institutions in one theater: military colonies, Guerrillas, Rural Police Corps, state Auxiliaries, and the nation's regular army. It was a conflict of ironies. Pancho Villa's brigades formed of paramilitaries and irregulars sought to emulate the very Federal Army they were attempting to destroy by adopting their regulations and acquiring their combat doctrine; Villa needed the services of the turncoats at Torreón (and later the Federal deserters at Ojinaga, as will be seen in Chapter 9) in order to be able to prosecute warfare at the highest levels of combined arms battles. Conversely, the Federals, decrepit in their old age and decadent from decades in garrison, had to rely on the youthful vigor and enthusiasm of their irregular allies to experience any measure of success and mobility in the field. In La Laguna, Munguía had to rely on Argumedo to retake San Pedro de las Colonias, operating in dangerous territory far from a major population center. After the fall of Torreón, Caraveo's Colorados had to be in vanguard during Federal movement south, and then cover Castro's rear during the withdrawal back to Chihuahua City. Colorados proved to be the dominant factor in the Federal victory at Chihuahua City, holding the most important parts of the line, exploiting interior lines to reinforce sectors under heavy attack, and executing counterattacks. Colorados also led the chase northward after

Villa, with the irregular Salazar in command over officers of the line, such as Landa and Mancilla, which could not have sat well with those generals. Still, one cannot help but observe that in the colossal defeat at Torreón the Federal Division of the Nazas was mainly comprised of units of the line, in contrast to the Federal Division of the North, which contained a sizeable contingent of Colorado irregulars supported by artillery. Federal generals, especially General Mercado, resented having to rely on the initiative and martial spirit of their allies to execute mounted operations. They also found a convenient scapegoat in the Colorados, with Munguía alleging that Argumedo's flight marked the beginning of the end of the battle for Torreón and Mercado saying virtually the same about Orozco's Colorados during the Battle of Tierra Blanca, claiming that they retreated at a critical moment and precipitated a collapse of the Federal line. More importantly, General Mercado blamed the rioting and disobedient Colorados for the loss of Chihuahua City and, ultimately, the entire state.

However, the Colorados increasingly had little tolerance for the "Prussian tone and attitude," as Caraveo put it, of the regular army, and one begins to sense a shift in martial traditions away from the Federal Army's eighteenth century European culture. As the military historian Max Boot said, "*to fight like Europeans you had to become 'European.'* [emphasis in original] You had to adopt at least some of the dynamism, intellectual curiosity, rationalism, and efficiency that has defined the West since the advent of the Gunpowder Age."[124] Yet the Mexican Revolution provoked a rediscovery of the traditional Mexican Ways of War based on regional defense models—whether hidalgos leading Indian retainers in Sonora, the military colonies of Chihuahua, or the Suriano guerrillas under Zapata—and it even gave birth to the new phenomenon of agro-industrial elites mobilizing itinerant boomtown Lagueneros, almost all producing superior battlefield results in comparison to the faux European army bequeathed by Santa Anna, the "Napoleon of the West." As the Constitutionalists continued to beat the Federals in battle after battle it became more and more fashionable and accurate to say that the revolutionaries fighting *a la Mexicana* were beating the regulars trained, organized, and disciplined *a lo Europeo*.[125] Popular culture was being altered by a newfound trust in the moral superiority of citizen-soldiers and the Mexican Way of War. In this sentiment one glimpses the genesis of one of the Revolution's most enduring traditions—*Mexicanidad*—a pride in all things Mexican and a rejection of foreign prescriptions for warfare, and so much more.

Seven

The Tamaulipas Campaign: October–November, 1913

González Abandons Coahuila and Isolates Laredo—Villarreal's Column—Carranza's Column—González's Column—Lucio Blanco and Crises in Command—Villa del Carmen—Salinas Victoria— Rubio Recalled—Topo Chico—Monterrey—Blanco Recalled—Jesús Agustín Castro—Cesáreo Castro's Column—Montemorelos—Taxes in Linares—Federal Base of Operations in Monterrey and Laredo— Hualahuises—Garza Valdez—Peña Abandons the Pursuit—A Mission for the Blanco Brigade—Ciudad Victoria—Herradura, Joya Verde, and Huizachal—Rubio's Replacements Column—José Isabel Robles and Juan E. Gómez Threaten Monterrey—Santa Engracia—Jesús Agustín Castro Disarmed

Objective Monterrey

With his maneuver forces about to be forced out of Coahuila by Federal General Maass at the beginning of October, General Pablo González gathered his troops in Allende and prepared to invade Nuevo León State, isolate Monterrey from all lines of communication, and attack it. The Constitutionalists formed two columns and got underway. The first and largest was led by General Pablo González with the forces of Villarreal and Murguía, which had been augmented by the various commands (Dolores Torres, Ildefonso M. Castro, Enrique Navarro, Reynaldo Garza) that had been collected from Coahuila, while other minor commands remained behind to continue harassing the Federals. This column headed southward taking a course for Rosales, Hacienda de Guadalupe, Juárez, and Alamo Nuevo. The other invasion column was commanded by Jesús Carranza with the forces of Alfredo Ricaut, Francisco Sánchez Herrera, Rafael E. Múzquiz, and Pedro Villaseñor, who commanded the railroaders.[1] Carranza's column split off from the larger group at Guadalupe in order to take up the track between Lampazos and Nuevo Laredo and isolate the latter as an entrepôt for the Federals. Federal General Joaquín Maass reported as much to General Guillermo Rubio Navarrete, but the latter believed that Carranza was headed east from Guadalupe to Lampazos or Hidalgo, or some point in between, with the purpose of escaping the reach of Maass' men in Allende and Peyote (Villa Unión), failing to consider that the Constitutionalist general's displacement might be offensive in nature.[2]

Carranza's column experienced some skirmishes along the railroad at Camarón and Huizachito in the completion of its mission and then reunited with the main invasion force in Alamo Nuevo. At that point General González, ordered three columns formed: one under his own command (the corps of Francisco Murguía, Alfredo Ricaut, Benjamín Garza, Bruno Neira, and his personal escort commanded by Francisco Urquizo with Alfredo Flores Alatorre, Carlos and Arcadio Osuna, and José E. Santos as his chief of staff), one under Jesús Carranza (leaders Indalecio Riojas, Pedro Treviño Orozco, Florencio Morales Carranza, and Víctor Villarreal), and another under Colonel Villarreal (subalterns Jesús Ramírez Quintanilla, Julio Soto, Faustino García, Ildefonso Castro, and Severo de la Garza). Villarreal's column departed first, followed by González's; Carranza remained a short while longer in Alamo before departing in order to finish collecting the Constitutionalist stragglers from around Coahuila.[3]

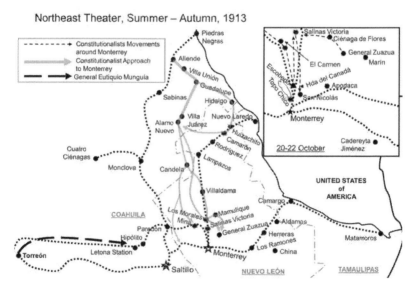

Map 1.19

VILLARREAL

Villarreal headed south in the direction of Valladares (about six kilometers northeast of Candela), crossed over into Nuevo León through Gomas Canyon, and then started tearing up track near the bridge at Los Morales Station when, on October 15, his column fought a three-hour engagement. In effect, Federal Irregular Lieutenant Colonel Ismael Tamez with sixty-six men and two officers on a cargo train traveling south from Villaldama spotted the large group of Constitutionalists and began shooting up Villarreal's column, which was on the road running parallel to the rails. Initially, a long wire fence trapped the Constitutionalists, but then Constitutionalist Captain Severo de la Garza derailed the train at kilometer 1067, and during the subsequent combat the Constitutionalists captured the train. However, while the Constitutionalists were still fighting Tamez's Federals, a Federal scout train proceeding from Villaldama arrived on the scene and ran into the derailed one, telescoping and forcing the Constitutionalists to abandon the first train and begin withdrawing from the area. Since the scout train's engine remained operable, it started to backtrack. More reinforcements came from Federal Lieutenant Colonel Enrique Luebbert in Salinas Victoria. Once informed of the derailed train and combat by the commander at Puerto Morales, Luebbert had ordered one hundred men commanded by First Captain Juan Morray to rush to Tamez's aid; the captain arrived at the place of the accident and assisted in definitively repulsing Villarreal's Constitutionalists. Because of the darkness Tamez could not scout the direction of the Constitutionalist retreat and offered the useless opinion that they had divided into two groups with one marching to the east and the other to the west. In reality, Villarreal's column left for Hacienda Mamulique and then Ciénaga de Flores and General Zuazua. The reported result of combat for the Federal Auxiliary brigade was three men and one officer killed, two dispersed, and four wounded; from the 6th Regiment one corporal wounded who died afterward; and the 39th Irregular Infantry Corps had one wounded soldier, even though the Constitutionalists claimed that they had killed the greater part of the *mochos*. There was no word on the Constitutionalist casualties.[4]

CARRANZA

Carranza left El Alamo in a formation of march to avoid any surprise because his column was passing through Candela, very close to the National Railroad, and the *pelones* had strong contingents in Rodríguez, Lampazos, and other points. Indalecio Riojas and Rafael E. Múzquiz were in the vanguard, Lieutenant Colonel Francisco Sánchez Herrera in the rearguard, and the impedimenta to the rear of the main body. Carranza's column had been the last to abandon Coahuila, and in the early morning hours of October 19 the Federals coming from Lampazos surprised him in his camp between Candela and Valladares. Not wanting to lose any time in catching up to the other two columns, Carranza left Sánchez Herrera in the rearguard to fend off the Federals while he made haste following along the railroad that the Villarreal and González columns had been so careful to avoid. At Morales Station Carranza engaged a Federal detachment overseeing repairs to the bridge there and, after a two-hour firefight on October 19, pushed those Federals down into Salinas Victoria where Lieutenant Colonel Tamez awaited with a command of some three hundred Federals, mostly belonging to the Quiroga Brigade. After spending the night encamped about ten kilometers north of Salinas Victoria, Carranza passed through Ciénaga de Flores and then to the town of General Zuazua, successfully avoiding the Federals in Salinas Victoria.[5]

González

General González left the day after Villarreal with the largest column, consisting of Murguía and Ricaut's commands. Taking a course for Candela and passing through La Carroza Pass, he headed for the International Railroad to destroy communications between Saltillo and Monterrey from the west. At this point, González had to be concerned with a threat from the west, since Villa's victory at Torreón had forced Federal General Munguía's entire Division of the Nazas eastward to Letona Station, only 167 kilometers west of Monterrey. Captain Espiridión Cuéllar took a small force and blew up twenty-two bridges to the south of Paredón to impede communications between Saltillo and Monterrey. On October 16 Colonel Murguía attacked a short Federal garrison at Mina, Nuevo León, (only about twenty kilometers from Los Morales as the crow flies) and collected arms, ammunition, and some horses as his men began to lift the rails; Murguía suffered a head wound in the action. After a light rest, the column moved to San Nicolás Hidalgo (eight kilometers southeast of Mina) where it passed the evening, just north of the main objective.[6]

Blanco

At this crucial juncture the Constitutionalists in the Northeast began to experience crises in command. The First Chief had appointed General Lucio Blanco to the position of Jefe de las Armas for the states of Nuevo León and Tamaulipas, but General Jesús Agustín Castro, who had refused to participate in the taking of Matamoros back in May because he doubted the probability of success, refused to recognize Blanco as his boss. Castro had gone to Matamoros to get arms and ammunition from Blanco, who was in control of customs and had been collecting money from the exporting of enormous quantities of cattle, but Blanco kept putting him off because he wanted Castro's 21st Brigade to submit to his orders; Castro was operating in Blanco's area of operations, after all. Fed up, and possibly under authorization from Jesús Carranza, in August Castro marched his brigade off to Ciudad Camargo, where Blanco had a garrison of about fifty men under Captain Felipe Múzquiz. Informed of Castro's presence in Camargo, Blanco demanded that Castro abandon the plaza, but the latter refused to obey Blanco's order until he had received the shipment of arms that he was awaiting from the United States. This was not the first time that Castro had availed himself of the riches of northern Tamaulipas, and the response was swift. Blanco sent Colonel Andrés Saucedo with six hundred men under orders signed by his chief of staff, Major Francisco J. Múgica, to arrest Castro, summarily execute his chief lieutenants Blas Corral and Tomás Chapa, and disarm the rest of his men. Fortunately for the Constitutionalist movement cooler heads prevailed on the scene in Camargo, and the approaching Federals, who just so happened to be kicking Jesús Carranza out of Piedras Negras around this same time, saw to Castro's expeditious exit from the area.[78]

With Jesús Carranza and Pablo González pushed out of Coahuila by the Federals and into Blanco's area of operations, another dustup occurred. General Blanco refused to recognize González as his superior, although, ironically, he did recognize Don Jesús, González's subordinate, as his boss. Blanco's case certainly had merit. On the one hand, he had captured and held one of the two most important entrepôts of supplies from the United States for the revolution at the time (along with Nogales in northern Sonora), and he had held northern Tamaulipas continuously since June, whereas González had been forced to abandon his own area of operations. He also had 4,000 "well-armed and disciplined" men operating in his zone, compared to González's 2,000 to 2,500 men, although many of Blanco's men belonged to other generals who reported up through him as zone commander. On the other hand, González outranked Blanco, had been appointed commander of the Division of the Northeast (with the Blanco Brigade a member unit), and had been actively campaigning against the Federal Division of the Bravo while Blanco remained safely ensconced in Matamoros.[9]

When the First Chief ordered Blanco to cooperate with González in the upcoming attack on Monterrey, Blanco resisted. The First Chief pleaded with Blanco to see the importance of marching at the head of his forces to participate in such an important undertaking as the conquest of the most important city in the Northeast, but Blanco refused, offering innumerable excuses for why he could not obey orders. Carranza even sent Licenciado Jesús Acuña to try to reason with him, to no avail. Finally, the First Chief ordered Blanco to turn over his troops to Colonel Saucedo and report to Sonora for a new position.[10] Confirmation that Blanco's recall arose from strictly military considerations comes from a letter written by a go-between for the First Chief informing González, confidentially, that Blanco "is being disgusted" by Don Venustiano's order to put himself under the command of González. Perhaps to soften the indelicacy of these words, the letter continued: "I do not know if you know, General, that General Blanco lately has shown a bit of disgust with the First Chief in virtue of the latter wanting the column of said general to come out of inactivity that up to now it has maintained, and for other reasons that are not to be enumerated here ... Such disgust is the reason that General Blanco went to Sonora to confer with the Supreme Chief of the Revolution and...notwithstanding the conference, General Blanco continues disgusted..."[11]

Still and all, many contemporaries believed, and biased historians who support redistributive policies persist in alleging, that the conservative Carranza recalled the *agrarista* (a supporter of land reform) Blanco to Sonora for carrying out the first redistribution of lands to campesinos during the revolution.[12] Aside from the foregoing proof, which is incontrovertible, this seems improbable for several reasons. First, none of the first-hand accounts in the archives mention the land redistribution scheme as a reason for Blanco's firing. Second, the main instigator and architect of the redistribution program had been Blanco's Chief of Staff, Múgica, whose radicalism would later receive notoriety during Lázaro Cárdenas' presidency. Yet Múgica continued on station in the Northeast and would later assume several important positions in public administration and dealing with labor over the next two years under Carranza. Third, almost two full months had passed since Blanco's staff had orchestrated the parceling out of Hacienda *Los Borregos*.[13] Finally, although Carranza did chastise Blanco for acting outside his remit and intruding on matters properly the incumbency of the First Chief in redistributing the land, Carranza *constantly* had to do the same with other generals. Gross disobedience to orders, and not indiscretion in policy matters, was the only reason he removed generals from command; something much more egregious than politics was at play in Blanco's sacking, and that was his purely selfish obstructionism in the development of sound military operations.

Battle of Monterrey

Villa del Carmen

While the First Chief dealt with Blanco, González continued his operations against Monterrey, trying to isolate the capital city's garrison from its supply lines and rolling up the outlying commands. On October 20 González's column started moving toward Villa Escobedo (near Topo Chico) when Federal Irregular General Miguel Quiroga's *pelones* rode out and attacked it near Villa del Carmen (about seven kilometers southwest of Salinas Victoria). Lieutenant Carlos Aguirre of the 1st Infantry Battalion, commanding a security detail of fifty men that was guarding a repair train doing some work close to nearby Chipinque Station, abandoned his primary mission to protect the train and went to join the battle in support of General Quiroga as soon as he heard the shooting. As the fight reached its full pitch, Quiroga's mounted irregulars noticed that they were about to be enveloped by the Constitutionalists and fled the field in disorder back to Monterrey, leaving Aguirre and his men to their fate. The Federal infantry was cut off and captured. Some of the dispersed irregulars passed by the repair train and reported what had happened; as the last of them passed, the train also started making its way back to Monterrey. The Constitutionalists found forty dead Federals and seventy saddled horses, captured numerous prisoners, and burned the bridges around Villa Escobedo. Then González sent word to Carranza and Villarreal to hurry to Salinas Victoria.[14]

Salinas Victoria

Early on October 20 Federal Major Luis G. Hernández left Monterrey headed north escorting a repair train with 194 men of the 29th Infantry Regiment. They had fixed three bridges and two sections of rail when the repair train ran into a derailed cargo train blocking the path, making it necessary to construct a detour. At that point another train approached from the north with Federal General Guillermo Rubio Navarrete aboard, who ordered Hernández to back up to Salinas Victoria station in order to allow his train to pass.[15]

As Hernández's repair train entered Salinas Victoria he heard a large firefight to the west of town. As soon as the train stopped Irregular Lieutenant Colonel Ismael Tamez approached to inform General Rubio that his corps was engaged in combat. As Hernández disembarked his men he saw an extensive line of shooters and asked Tamez whose men those were, but the irregular could not say whether they were his own or the Constitutionalists. The two wasted about fifteen minutes arguing the question when from the other direction a group of about ten riders approached at a full gallop to say that the revolutionaries had beaten them, forcing them to disperse just as the Constitutionalists began victoriously sounding the plaza's bells. Pablo González's column had killed the Jefe de las Armas, Federal Lieutenant Colonel Rodolfo Gómez, captured Federal Captain Rodolfo Tamez, a sub-lieutenant, and about thirty men and some ammunition, and the battle appeared to be over. But it was not.[16]

Straightaway General Rubio ordered Hernández to divide his command into two parts; the major took command of one and the general the other and they went off to face the Constitutionalists. Soon fighting was taking place in every direction. In fierce combat the Federals managed to push the Constitutionalists back to a distance of about one kilometer outside of the town. General Rubio ordered the men to cease fire and return to town, but around nightfall the noise of approaching horses' hooves could be heard and the Federals allowed the animals to come closer, the officers giving strict orders to their men to hold their fire because they might be reinforcements. When close enough the Federals asked, "who goes there?" Upon receiving the answer, "Carranza," they repeated the question. After receiving the same answer General Rubio ordered his Federals to open fire, forcing the Constitutionalists to flee, leaving some casualties behind, as well as some booty. General Rubio telegraphed Lampazos and requested reinforcements, appointed Hernández as Jefe de las Armas of the town, and then continued his trajectory toward Monterrey.[17]

General Rubio, commander of the Nuevo Laredo-Monterrey line, had been wanting to lead the effort to attack General Blanco in Matamoros and retake the vital port of entry for months. At the beginning of October the operation had been approved, but the fall of Torreón to Pancho Villa had caused the operation to be postponed. Now, with General González's Constitutionalists converging upon Monterrey, Rubio ordered his forces to concentrate in Salinas Victoria while he went to Monterrey to personally confer with the garrison commander about the city's defense. However, for exercising initiative, Rubio Navarrete was disciplined and recalled to Mexico City to explain his behavior to Huerta, who suspected that perhaps Rubio was preparing his own attempt on Monterrey. Rumor had it that the Federals were so worried about the loyalty of their own that they sometimes gave officers sealed orders to be opened only after they had gotten underway and had reached a certain point en route to their objectives. Rubio would never get to lead his Matamoros operation and would not be present for the Battle of Monterrey.[18]

All through the night of the twentieth and twenty-first the Federals only reported intermittent shots fired, which Hernández ordered his men not to return. At about 5 a.m. a train arrived from Lampazos commanded by Federal

Major Francisco Puga with about one hundred sappers and a machine gun section. At daybreak Hernández ordered Colonel Tamez to take about forty of his riders and go clean up the battlefield from the day before. But, either because his men were too demoralized from the earlier fight or because Tamez lacked the requisite energy and motivation, it did not happen, with the result that soon the Constitutionalists showed up to do it themselves. Hernández could not let that happen in plain view, and since he did not have any cavalry, he had to attack the Constitutionalists with 150 infantrymen, which he divided into three even groups between the center, left, and right, with the left and center each having one machine gun. He had to leave the rest of his men behind to guard the one train, since the other one under the direction of First Captain Pedro López Linares had traveled about three kilometers to the south with orders to reestablish telegraphic communications. Very quickly, the fighting became extremely intense.[19]

González's Constitutionalists attacked with machine guns served by Gloria, Díaz Couder, and Alberto Salinas, and their one cannon, "El Rorro" also went into action. After about seven hours of combat the Federals forced the Constitutionalists back toward the sierra, leaving close to one hundred casualties behind, allegedly. Hernández proceeded to clean up the battlefield when Major Puga, in charge of the right, showed up to say that he was completely out of ammunition, and another officer sent by Second Captain Cristóbal Arellano, in command of the left, reported the same. As he had no ammunition reserves, Hernández told Arellano, who was dangerously extended on the left, to fall back to his own position on a small hill west of town where Hernández had a machine gun emplaced to cover Arellano's egress. A half hour later he ordered Puga to do the same, fall back on Hernández's position, at which point Hernández would withdraw with his fifty men while Puga remained behind to provide cover. That is when all hell broke loose.[20]

The Constitutionalists, taking notice of Hernández's compromised disposition, fell upon the Federals' shortened front with all fury using their superior numbers in an enveloping maneuver. Immediately Hernández sent a detachment of twenty men from the 29th Infantry to occupy the tower of the church to cover his men's retreat as they raced back into the town. Constitutionalist Francisco Murguía's men captured a fort to the north of the town, and Captain Carlos Osuna leading González's escort took another one on the southwest side of the town (where Osuna's brother Arcadio was killed) inflicting great casualties on the Federals, when all of a sudden a dust cloud appeared coming from the direction of Ciénaga de Flores—it was Colonel Villarreal arriving after a forced march from General Zuazua. The Federals started to beat a retreat. Puga's men arrived at the train station first, now engaging Villarreal and Carranza's cavalry arriving from the north to attack the train station. Major Hernández got there a little while later, not finding "even one soldier of Lieutenant Colonel Tamez's force in their position." They were all hiding, forcing Hernández to pull his pistol to try to instill some discipline with threats and ordering all the Federals to board the trains.[21]

Hernández did not know whether to go north or south to safety, but finally told the train engineer to head for Monterrey. They traveled over bridges in flames with mounted Constitutionalists in close pursuit firing on the fleeing train as the Federals aboard returned fire. About five kilometers south of town, the Federals ran into the train commanded by Captain López, which had stopped to repair a bridge and was now holding up the convoy. At this point a considerable number of Constitutionalists caught up to them and the Federals deployed on line to keep the Constitutionalists a safe distance from the repair crews which, given the Federals' advantageous terrain, they did without much effort. After finishing the work, the Federal convoy continued on to Leal where it again had to stop to repair several bridges and the Constitutionalists again appeared. Shooting erupted from the Constitutionalist side, but not so much from the Federals. At some point Captain Arellano informed Major Hernández that there was not one cartridge left, and so the major ordered them to fix bayonets in preparation for close quarters combat, but the Constitutionalists never charged them. After repairing eleven more bridges the Federals entered Monterrey. The Constitutionalists recovered from the Federals 168 Mausers, 125 saddled horses, a little ammunition, and some dynamite. They also captured and shot Captain Rodolfo Tamez, whom they were prone to spare, but he proved so verbally abusive that he earned for himself a summary judgment and execution. González ordered the dynamiters to prepare bombs, and the Chief of Electricians, Second Captain Luis Galindo, received orders to cut the telephones and telegraphs and blow up the railroad six kilometers south of Salinas Victoria to prevent any surprises.[22]

By staying clear of the Rio Grande and the railroads until they were in position to begin destroying them, González's Constitutionalists had concealed their movement southward and managed to cut off Monterrey by rail, sufficiently avoiding detection until the latest possible moments. But they had expended so much ammunition in the effort that by now most units averaged only forty-five cartridges per man, and some only had about half that amount.[23]

TOPO CHICO

The Constitutionalists were now poised to attack Monterrey proper. The commanding feature on the approach from the north was a sizable hill called Topo Chico, located to the west of the satellite town of San Nicolás de los

Garza. Beyond that lay the city proper and the seat of government, nestled against the oft-dry Santa Catarina River and Loma Larga Hill that follow a general east-west course on the city's south side. The large Cuauhtémoc brewery, glassworks, and train stations were located on the north side of town, while Latin America's first steel mill dominated the landscape on the east side. Obispado Hill, which had figured so prominently in the U.S. Army attack on Monterrey about sixty-five years earlier, retained its tactical importance, overlooking the plaza from the west.

The morning of October 22 got off to a very early start with the sound of "boots and saddles" as the forces of Carranza and Villarreal in the vanguard took a course for San Nicolás, arriving around 11 a.m. From the town they could see Federals to the west on top of Topo Chico and on the hills between Topo Chico and Hacienda del Canadá.[24] The Federal general in charge of the defense of Monterrey, Brigadier Adolfo Iberri, had ordered a column of 350 men commanded by Irregular Brigadier Miguel Quiroga and Colonel Manuel Rojas with about 100 men of the 1st Infantry Battalion, 30 from the 20th Infantry, some 150 from Quiroga's Auxiliaries de Nuevo León Brigade, 60 from the 17th Cavalry Regiment, and two 80-mm. guns, light type, belonging to the 2nd Artillery Regiment to reconnoiter the Constitutionalist positions and if possible to defeat them, but without straying too far from the plaza—orders that sounded remarkably similar to those given to General Alvírez before the "disaster of Avilés."[25]

The Irregular Quiroga held command, seconded by Permanent Colonel Manuel Rojas, even though most of the 350 Federals belonged to units of the line. The commanders placed their two 80-mm. artillery pieces on the southeast side of the crest of Topo Chico supported by the 17th Cavalry Regiment and Quiroga's Auxiliaries, with elements of the 1st and 20th Infantry Battalions ahead and to the right on the hills between Topo Chico and Hacienda del Canadá. Their headquarters was about one kilometer west of where the railroad split with one track going to Nuevo Laredo and the other to Paredón—too far north to expect any support from the main force in Monterrey.[26]

Surveying the situation, General Pablo González ordered an assault on Topo Chico Hill. The Federals opened with a thunderous barrage of timed shells, but this did not intimidate or harm the dragoons of Murguía and Villarreal, who hid in the brush. Around noon the Constitutionalists began returning rifle fire, in the slow cadence of veterans, while the Federals, in contrast, seemed to be firing as quickly as possible in a frantic attempt to finish off the Constitutionalist threat. Villarreal and Murguía's men started advancing dismounted, leaving their horses a little way off, while Ricaut's regiment remained in the fields of

Hacienda del Canadá in reserve, since it had the least amount of ammunition. The Constitutionalists dislodged the Federal infantry from its initial positions on the rolling hills, forcing them to seek the railroad embankment for cover. But as night began to close in, the squadrons of Captain Benjamín Garza, Gaspar Cantú, and others scaled Topo Chico. Quiroga's irregulars, demoralized from the earlier defeat at Villa del Carmen, broke and ran, abandoning the artillery to the Constitutionalists. Federal Lieutenant Raúl Romero disabled the guns by removing the breechblocks, but closely pursued by mounted Constitutionalists, who killed the gunners and captured the guns, he had to ditch the heavy mechanisms. At the same time, around 5 p.m., Carranza's cavalry charged the infantry arrayed along the rail line to Paredón, and a short while later the Federals fled in disorder back to Monterrey.[27]

Brigadier Iberri blamed the defeat at Topo Chico on the broken terrain and the lack of expertise of both jefes, Quiroga and Rojas, who had advanced farther from the plaza than "prudence and good judgment advise," considering the elements in their care. By "elements" Iberri meant not just the men, but also the artillery pieces. However, two lone artillery pieces, given the state of the art of warfare in 1913, were less than useless, and to send them outside of the perimeter on an expedition amounted to little more than the Federal commanding general offering them up to the Constitutionalist cause. Moreover, at fifteen dead, numerous wounded, and about fifty missing, the cost of keeping up the appearance of an offensive posture for Iberri's superiors in Mexico City, assuming that that was indeed the purpose behind such a senseless mission, had been high.[28]

For his actions at Topo Chico Villarreal received a promotion to brigadier, and González promoted both Benjamín Garza and Gaspar Cantú, who had lost a few men taking the guns, to the rank of major. Ammunition had been spent, but two 80-mm. Mondragón's had been recovered in perfect order, although the Constitutionalists did not find one of the breechblocks that Romero was forced to discard; these were the Division of the Northeast's first real pieces. All the others cannons constructed in Piedras Negras had broken down except for the tiny "El Rorro." In this battle Carlos Osuna lost another brother killed in action, Lieutenant Cristóbal Osuna.[29]

MONTERREY PROPER OCTOBER 23-24

As his men went into camp after finishing up at Topo Chico, General Pablo González, accompanied by his leading generals and some staff officers, rode into San Nicolás de los Garza where he made a phone call to the government in Monterrey to ask General Iberri to exit the city proper for a fight on open ground in order to spare the plaza the ravages of war. Iberri refused. The battle was set for October 23, but the Constitutionalists had no hopes of winning with their pressing dearth of ammunition; rather, they could only hope to capture much-needed battlefield booty. Moreover, they only had three machine guns and three artillery pieces: the two 80-mm. guns captured the day before, one without a breechblock, and "El Rorro," which inspired more amusement than fear in the enemy. The plan of attack called for Carranza to attack the Cuauhtémoc brewery and watch over the line to the west all the way to the Obispado; Murguía would attack the Great Foundry and exercise oversight as far as San Luisito; and General González with his escort commanded by the valiant Carlos Osuna would go with Villarreal's column to attack in the center between the Gulf Railroad station and the brewery. The men and ammunition that González had requested of General Blanco from Matamoros still had not arrived, so the Constitutionalists would have to attack without them.[30]

Tactical Command	Major Unit organic to	G	J	O	T	Total
Puga, Francisco de P. (Major)	1st Sapper Battalion		1	5	109	115
Aguilar, Francisco (LTC)	2nd Sapper Battalion		1		16	17
Rojas, Manuel (Colonel)	1st Infantry Battalion		2	8	180	190
Hernández, Luis G. (Major)	29 Infantry Regiment		1	6	180	187
Doria, Alberto C. (Colonel)	37th Auxiliary Infantry Battalion		1	4	46	51
Castro, Plácido (1st CPT)	39th Auxiliary Infantry Battalion			8	98	106
Alvarez, Manuel G. (LT)	47th Auxiliary Infantry Battalion			3	59	62
Luebbert, Enrique (LTC)	6th Cavalry Regiment		1	8	110	119
Miranda, Enrique (Major)	8th Cavalry Regiment		1	12	181	194
Quintana, Teodoro (Colonel)	12th Cavalry Regiment		3	6	30	39
Olvera, Ricardo (1st CPT)	15th Cavalry Regiment			4	41	45
Pélla, Alejandro (1st CPT)	17th Cavalry Regiment			5	20	25
Mancilla, Jesús (1st CPT)	21st Auxiliary Cavalry Regiment			3	25	28
González, Eulalio (Major)	27th Auxiliary Cavalry Regiment		1	1	23	25
Quiroga, Miguel (Brigadier)	Quiroga Irregular Brigade	1	2	10	91	104
García Quiroga, Simón (LTC)	García Quiroga Irregular Squadron		1	7	61	69
De los Santos, Pablo (Colonel)	Alvarez del Castillo Irregular Squadron		1	2	21	24
Alvarez del Castillo, Zacarías (Cmdte)	De los Santos Irregular Squadron		1	8	53	62
	González Irregular Squadron		1	3	146	150
	Ortiz Bravo Scout Corps			2	22	24
Velázquez, Miguel (1st CPT)	2nd Artillery Regiment					
	(two 75-mm. Mondragóns, three Machine-gun Sections)			3	23	26
	Military Hospital			3	25	28
		1	18	111	1,560	1,690

Table 1.11 Battle of First Monterrey Federal Troop Strength

In Monterrey, about seventeen hundred Federals from a hodgepodge of units awaited the revolutionaries. Due to the large size of the town and the insufficiency of his force, the garrison commander, Federal General Adolfo Iberri, blocked off and barricaded a reduced part of the town for defense that included the most populous area: M. M. del Llano Street on the north side, commanded by Colonel Teodoro Quintana; Arista and Dr. Coss streets to the east, entrusted to Major Norberto Ayala of the 1st Infantry Battalion; the north side of the Santa Catarina River on the south side of town, under Major Luis G. Hernández; and Major Enrique Miranda in Cuauhtémoc Street on the west side. The

Federals "garrisoned" several structures, such as the statehouse, the barracks on Union Street, and the penitentiary, and by necessity Iberri maintained a short reserve with a machine gun loaded aboard a car to be able to respond quickly to any hot spots. Outside the perimeter, the Federals occupied the brewery, the slagheap of Foundry No. 3, and other tactical positions, with a small support force on Obispado Hill to provide oversight protection for the artillery located in the plaza of 5 de Mayo. Finally, because the Constitutionalists had cut Iberri's lines of communication northward to his commander, General Téllez of the Division of the Bravo, Iberri appealed directly to Mexico City for reinforcements.[31] The Secretary of War now ordered Rubio's brigade, under its acting commander Federal Colonel Jacinto Guerra, to move to Monterrey and transfer its headquarters there from Lampazos. Huerta also ordered General of Division José Refugio Velasco, the new commander of the Division of the Nazas, to send six hundred men from Saltillo as reinforcements.[32]

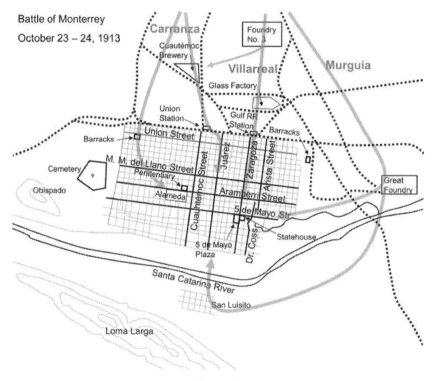

Map 1.20

Minutes before six in the morning, Villarreal began to attack the slagheaps of the Foundry. About ten minutes afterward General Carranza charged the brewery, while Murguía had to make a circular movement to attack his objective, the Great Foundry, not opening fire until about 6:30.[33] There are no reliable numbers given for these columns, but they could have ranged from three to six hundred men each since future-general Manuel W. González, who fought in the battle, estimated the whole Constitutionalist assault force to be less than one thousand men, while Juan Barragán put González's total force with principal leaders Villarreal, Carranza, and Murguía at an unbelievable twenty-five hundred.[34] Within a half-hour, the Constitutionalist column in the center had conquered the slagheaps, pushing the Federals back to the glass factory, and then Poncho Vázquez and another squadron effected an enveloping maneuver, ordered by headquarters, on the brewery. Upon sensing the movement by the two squadrons, the defenders of the brewery withdrew hastily to the Union Station and the barracks on the west side. But the two columns of Villarreal and Carranza advanced so rapidly that the Federals did not even have time to take possession of those last two points, such that by around 10 a.m., the Constitutionalists had taken control of the station, the infantry barracks, and the Gulf Railroad station, and Colonel Alfredo Ricaut's regiment had accomplished its mission of subduing the Terminal barracks and the entire Union Street. On the southeast side Colonel Murguía reported that he had occupied the Great Foundry in fighting and penetrated the city's perimeter, and he thought that by now his men controlled the San Luisito Barrio.[35]

General González set up his headquarters in the Gulf Railroad station, and then informed his subalterns that the Federal barracks had been captured, resulting in the acquisition of arms and ammunition that would be used to resupply the troops trying to occupy the eastern and southern parts of the city. He also ordered anything that could be used to bear the copious booty (which also included cloth, clothing, and medical supplies) to be brought in and hauled off everything of military value to San Francisco de Apodaca where he established his field hospital. He placed Carranza in charge of the rearguard, personally took charge of the right wing, and ordered the center and right (west) resupplied.[36] Colonel Murguía forced the Federals to cut and run from their trenches along the Santa Catarina, and then crossed over from the south to occupy the barracks in the immediate vicinity, also collecting a vast amount of materiel.[37] Lieutenant Colonel Francisco Sánchez Herrera led the charge against the penitentiary, as Captains Ildefonso M. Castro, Aureliano Esquivel, Julio Soto, and Major Fortunato Maycotte advanced clearing the Federals from the Alameda. Villarreal's column in the center, to which Ricaut belonged, made progress through Juárez and Zaragoza streets and the adjacent parallel streets to reach M. M. del Llano, fighting those Federals holed up in the statehouse, as well as the skirmishers on Aramberri Street, and Iberri's guns at the corner of Zaragoza and 5 de Mayo. Machine gun and small arms fire channeled down the main thoroughfares turned them into rivers of lead. Major Bruno Gloria was mortally wounded in an alley off Puebla Street and died before he could make it to the hospital. Captain Daniel Díaz Couder took over command of the machine guns. Murguía took La Luz barrio, and soon the Constitutionalists possessed the whole city except for Obispado Hill, the penitentiary, the statehouse, and adjacent streets.[38]

When fighting resumed early the next morning of October 24, the battle intensified and soon fighting became generalized in all sectors. Colonel Murguía in the eastern sector pressed toward the statehouse, defended by the most ardent Huertistas of the Social Defense, while cannons firing from the corner of Zaragoza and 5 de Mayo kept them at bay. Around 9 a.m., Second Captain Francisco Aponte, on machine guns, was advancing through tragic Puebla Street when he fell with two bullets to the head, prompting his brother, in grief and rage, to pick up the machine gun, dislodge the pelones, and then occupy General Jerónimo Treviño's house. The bodies of both Major Bruno Gloria and Aponte were sent to Apodaca and buried. Then, a legendary and rather humorous story took place: Lieutenant Colonel Sánchez Herrera sent a runner to inform González of his progress, including the taking of the penitentiary, and urgently requested "El Rorro." Eager to follow up on that development, González, who was still directing the battle from the Gulf train station, dispatched Major Carlos Prieto with the little cannon. The very reserved and serious Prieto returned an hour later and stood at attention before González and in his notoriously deadpan style, tinged with disgust, reported: "My General, I got to where Lieutenant Colonel Sánchez Herrera and his people were—the lieutenant colonel says that the Penitentiary is taken; this is lacking in veracity. *He* [emphasis original] is 'taken,' and his force too. Lieutenant Colonel Sánchez Herrera wanted me to raise the cannon up to the roof of a house to attack the Penitentiary, but I declared to him that it would be easier to lower the roof and put it under the cannon." To which González, also a man of few words, responded, "Very well major, return to your post." The nearby officers exploded with a guffaw and the story became regular campfire fare for the Division of the Northeast. This incident prompted González to order an inspection of all the sectors.[39]

A little before noon, General Villarreal arrived at headquarters to report that Lieutenant Colonel José E. Santos was bringing in retired Federal General Jerónimo Treviño, who had been taken from his house, mostly for his own protection, since with all the fighting there was a danger that some revolutionary might harm him. Santos brought the general on foot and without escort through Guerrero Street as the old man protested from the middle of the street that the revolutionaries were not making cavalry charges. Santos grabbed his arm and pulled him onto the sidewalk since Huertista projectiles were landing in the area, explaining, "Come onto the sidewalk, my General, because they'll kill you." General Treviño continued unabated, "No, in my time we went in with saber in hand through the bullets, not like you, who are afraid." To which Santos replied, "Yes, but in your time they shot tallow plugs and now they shoot steel bullets." Once in the company of González, Treviño again posed the question of why he did not charge the Federals, to which González responded that he did not want to sacrifice his men before the Federals behind fortifications with machine guns the way that Rurales were sacrificed by the infamous Huerta at the Citadel.[40]

In the heat of battle, the Constitutionalists playfully pressed an errant musician into service, forcing him to play "La Cucaracha" and "La Valentina," among other favorites. But they took the festivities too far. Returns from the inspection of the various sectors ordered by González revealed that by 3:00 p.m., 90 percent of his troops were intoxicated after having raided the cantinas and liquor stores. Perhaps they were following the conventional wisdom that drinking mescal in a fight tempered the nerves, lifted the spirits, and chased the thirst away, whereas drinking water induced exsanguination upon being wounded. The commanding general grew righteously and visibly disgusted. The inebriation of so many Constitutionalists caused them to take unnecessary risks and make bold attempts, resulting in high casualties that could no longer be maintained. More than one hundred wounded Constitutionalists already had been sent back to the field hospital at San Nicolás and Apodaca, and there were more dead from the Huertista machine guns in the various sectors than could be counted.[41]

Then 350 Federal irregulars commanded by Colonel Genaro B. Trías, the lead forces of a rumored 4,000-man Federal combined arms column led by Generals Eduardo Ocaranza, Luis G. Anaya, and Ricardo Peña that was coming to reinforce the Federals, began arriving through the southwest side of the city. Calculating that his own reinforcements from the Blanco Brigade would not arrive any time soon, González had to quit the battle. José E. Santos went to tell Carlos Prieto to cease fire and hitch up his mules to withdraw his pieces and be ready to receive orders. Various staff officers raced off through the lead-filled streets in the twilight to tell the sector chiefs to report to the Gulf station as Federal reinforcements began to enter into action. But González lacked an officer to deliver instructions to Murguía, so the indomitable female Constitutionalist known only by the name of "Belén" grabbed the letter, put it into her blouse, and took off at a full gallop hanging from the rear of the saddle (as they say the Apaches used to do) through the fields of fire to applause and a rousing chorus of "vivas."[42]

Once gathered, González and his subalterns agreed to withdraw since night had fallen, the shooting had attenuated, and the drunkenness of the Constitutionalists apparently was on the increase. González gave orders to retreat and indicated where to stay the night and the direction of travel to follow. The firing became sporadic until all of sudden there was a large explosion followed by intense shooting that continued for a long time. The Constitutionalists had blown the occupied Federal barracks, along with all the artillery shells they couldn't carry and the ammunition for the calibers that did not match their rifles. All manner of vehicles carried the wounded to San Nicolás, Apodaca, Los Ramones, and thence Matamoros, under the direction of General Carranza. After all the troops and the headquarters were away, around 9:30 p.m., González left the station, continuing to San Nicolás and Apodaca.[43] The pelones did not pursue, and stories of alleged cavalry charges executed by Federal General Ricardo Peña, who led a group of cavalrymen that reinforced the Monterrey garrison and compelled the Constitutionalists to quit the attack, are just that—stories.[44]

AFTERMATH

Immediately after Brigadier Lucio Blanco got on the train to leave for Sonora, his replacement in Matamoros, Constitutionalist General Jesús Dávila Sánchez, gave orders for the brigade to load up on trains and depart immediately in order to cooperate with González in the attack on Monterrey. But Dávila Sánchez ran into a column of Constitutionalists at Los Aldamas carrying wounded from the Salinas Victoria battle and the Federal artillery captured from Topo Chico. There he learned that González had quit Monterrey, and so Dávila Sánchez's column returned to Matamoros.[45] Although none of the Constitutionalist chroniclers come right out and say so, the intransigent Blanco, by refusing to participate in the battle, had cost the Division of the Northeast the glory and benefit of capturing the nation's leading industrial city. Military considerations took precedence over politics in Blanco's reassignment, and by the end of November Blanco had gotten over his "disgust" and recovered his bellicosity, requesting permission from the First Chief to arm a force and go on expedition through Jalisco and other states in the center.[46]

Similarly, Blanco's personal enemy, General Jesús Agustín Castro, did not take part in the attack on Monterrey. On October 21 Castro marched with his brigade from Ciudad Guerrero toward Sabinas Hidalgo (a mere sixty kilometers away) where, five days later and in cooperation with General Teodoro Elizondo, his brigade attacked a garrison of 230 volunteers, defeating them and capturing their weapons and horses while only suffering one killed and Colonel Navarrete wounded. Then, "upon hearing of the rumored attack on the city of Monterrey, and considering it of great importance, I advanced with the greatest speed," Castro stated without sarcasm. He moved down from Sabinas Hidalgo to Monterrey on November 2, well over a week after the assault on the city proper, and reached as far as Ciénaga de Flores the next day to cooperate in the attack on Monterrey. However, as he states, "I arrived late, having to withdraw to the outskirts of said city and continue looking for [friendly] forces on the way that would permit me to get the armament [that he had spent so many months diligently accumulating while on the border] to safety." That took him back north to Mamulique Hill, in the opposite direction of the rest of the division moving southward to Ciudad Victoria. After three days of idleness spent eating unsalted meat and tortillas that his soldiers made for themselves, the 21st Brigade finally began heading southward to catch up to González and the rest of the division.[47]

Castro's narrative makes it sound as if he took the initiative to go and participate in the Battle of Monterrey upon hearing rumors of the attack, but elsewhere in the brigade's official history it says that Jesús Carranza ordered Castro to go and participate in the battle, and those orders would not have come a week after the battle had ended. Castro's story also conflicts with the brigade's official history regarding what he did in Ciénaga de Flores, saying that Castro sent a messenger to Monterrey who returned with the news that the Constitutionalists had broken contact and that he did not venture any farther south, not that he reached the outskirts of, much less penetrated, the city limits of Monterrey. Nothing in Jesús Agustín Castro's narrative about his actions in the days surrounding the Battle of First Monterrey makes sense, except when considered within the context of his penchant for accumulating promotions and materiel while remaining as far away as possible from hard fighting.

A little after 8 a.m. on October 25, the day after the battle, a messenger sent by Constitutionalist Colonel Cesáreo Castro arrived announcing that Castro, with key subordinate Major Alejo G. González, was coming through Marín from Matamoros with 300 mounted effectives to join Pablo González, and he was bringing a telegram from the First Chief for him. The telegram announced his September 27, 1913 promotion to general of brigade and his appointment to Chief of Operations of the States of Coahuila, Nuevo León, and Tamaulipas and Commander of the Army Corps of the Northeast (although it often continued to be called a "Division" in official correspondence and on letterhead).[48] González now set his sights on conquering Tamaulipas State with the remaining booty from Monterrey: more than a thousand Mauser rifles and carbines; fourteen machine guns; 400,000 rounds of ammunition for Mausers and .30-30s; many good horses taken from the brewery; a large amount of clothing, medicines, and supplies; plus the two cannons taken from Quiroga at Topo Chico and artillery shells.[49]

Federal reports put Constitutionalist dead at seventy, but that is only what they recovered; there were many more. The Federals suffered eighty-six killed, Brigadier Quiroga among them, and 105 wounded. The customary promotions for a successful defense also followed for Iberri, Colonel Teodoro Quintana, and others. The Federal victory could be attributed to the judicious selection of a reduced defensive perimeter appropriate in length to the number of soldiers, the placing of advanced positions that (while they allowed significant commands to be beaten in detail) also consumed a good deal of the aggressors' ammunition, and the failure by the Constitutionalists to focus their main effort on one point of the Federal defense—not to mention the intoxication of the attackers. On the other hand, Federal irregulars had revealed their lack of reliability and expertise at Topo Chico, although one notices that conspicuously the first reinforcements to arrive were mounted irregulars, for which the regular Peña got all the fabricated credit. Irregulars would again factor in the Tamaulipas campaign.[50]

Fighting in Tamaulipas had fallen off to almost nil after the June capture of Matamoros. Blanco had remained contentedly in the port city, and even though some Federals thought that the town could and should have been retaken, Huerta seemed to have been happy to leave him there, and with good reason according to the regime's opposition: having a Constitutionalist stronghold in the Northeast heightened the atmosphere of crisis and justified the delay of elections.[51] In reality, a different, military reason came to bear.

Huerta had feared an invasion by the United States almost from the outset of his administration, when he received the unsettling news that Washington had moved six thousand soldiers into Texas.[52] Since the beginning of June, the Constitutionalists in "Heroic" Matamoros had effectively blocked that point of invasion historically used by the gringos, and in a bizarre manner permitted him to economize his own forces. The "Interim Constitutional President of the Mexican United States," therefore ordered Téllez to keep the two brigades of his Division of the Bravo tied to the Saltillo-Piedras Negras and Monterrey-Nuevo Laredo axes, protecting those two remaining invasion routes while also virtually denying those units the ability to campaign against the Constitutionalists. Téllez relayed those orders to his brigade commanders, but did not explain the reasoning behind them, which explains why General Rubio thought nothing of leaving Lampazos to reinforce Monterrey earlier, and why Huerta had reacted so violently. As events would later prove, Huerta's fears of a Yankee invasion were not just the result of an overactive imagination.[53]

Objective Ciudad Victoria

General González, however, was not content to remain in Matamoros and play into Huerta's hands, as had Blanco. He had bigger plans for Tamaulipas, and his promotion to command of the Northeast gave him official sanction to execute them. Leaving Apodaca on October 25 the Constitutionalists headed toward Marín. The following day González attached Ricaut's regiment and Murguía's brigade to Cesáreo Castro's fresh forces, with Major Arturo Lazo de la Vega as Castro's chief of staff, and sent them southward to spearhead the march against Tamaulipas' capital, Ciudad Victoria, while the other commands headed for Los Ramones to rest and recuperate and ship the remainder of the wounded to the hospital in Matamoros (See Battle of Ciudad Victoria map for preparatory troop movements). Castro took Cadereyta Jiménez (henceforth simply "Cadereyta") on October 28 after a short firefight and began taking up track on both the north and south sides of the town. The following day, Castro headed in the general direction of General Terán and Montemorelos, moving through San Juan without encountering any opposing forces and spending the night at Terán Station, thirty kilometers southeast of San Juan.[54]

In the morning of October 30, around 7 a.m., Castro's column attacked the town of General Terán as two hundred or so government volunteers and Rurales of the 10th Scout Corps commanded by Huertista First Officer Febronio Salazar came out to battle the Constitutionalists. After about three hours of combat Castro's force succeeded in trouncing the Huertistas, sending Salazar fleeing with his remaining Rurales and volunteers to Linares and then later to Ciudad Victoria. The Constitutionalists pressed on without bothering to stop in General Terán to arrive in Montemorelos, where they ran into stiff resistance.[55]

MONTEMORELOS

A little before noon the Constitutionalists arrived just outside Montemorelos and Colonel Castro ordered Colonel Ricaut to send part of his men along a small ridge that extended to the east of the road to Montemorelos and dislodge the enemy, if there were any, in order to keep the Constitutionalists from taking any fire on that flank. Ricaut called on Lieutenant Colonel Fortunato Zuazua to go take the hill with one hundred men. But Zuazua responded that he did not feel like fighting. Since all Constitutionalists at this point still considered themselves volunteers, Ricaut really had no recourse against Zuazua, whom it should be noted was notoriously brave and a personal friend of Ricaut. Therefore, the colonel left Zuazua in command of the regiment and personally accomplished the mission. Fifteen minutes later Zuazua showed up and said that now he felt like fighting, although it was clear by then that there were no Federals on the ridge, and Ricaut returned to the rest of his command.[56]

Shortly thereafter the shooting started, and Major Alejo González advanced against the Federals in the station as Captains Miguel González and Crispín Treviño marched toward the bridge. Facing them were thirty-eight Federals of the 8th Cavalry Regiment under Captain Jesús M. Sevilla and another fifty of the 39th Auxiliary Cavalry Regiment commanded by Captain Luciano Reyes, who in spite of their small numbers put up quite a tenacious fight. After several hours of heated combat, train whistles sounded at about 3:30 announcing the arrival of Federal reinforcements from Monterrey, and a Constitutionalist soldier reported that Captain Miguel González had been killed. Zuazua reinforced those attacking the station, but demoralization became pronounced among the Constitutionalists; their fire decreased and soldiers began leaving the firing line.[57] Colonel Castro then went to Ricaut and told him that without another push, the battle would be lost, but there were no reinforcements to be had. Ricaut went before the stragglers, gave them a quick speech colored with curse words, and then taking out a flag yelled, "Whoever is a man, follow me!" and charged off toward the firing line without looking back. As though one body, all the dispirited and lightly wounded men and officers, raced off toward the fighting. With this push the newly arrived Federals were repulsed and their train later captured. They abandoned it to the Constitutionalists who entered the town that by now was only defended by senior commanders and a few remaining Huertistas, who exited the town under cover of night. On October 31, the Constitutionalists took possession of the town.[58]

After cleaning up the battlefield and reorganizing, Castro and his men exited the plaza to make room for the main body of Constitutionalists, who had been following along under the command of General González at a distance. Shortly after arriving, those follow-on soldiers proceeded to sack the town and even burn some buildings. González clearly had a discipline problem, and this time he ordered the guilty arrested and saber whipped.

Afterward, the column continued the march in a persistent drizzle, camping in some hills where the officers occupied small leaky jacals with fires in the center, and drank mescal obtained in Montemorelos.[59]

Upon arriving in Hualahuises Cesáreo Castro learned that General González had promoted him to the rank of brigadier for the victory at Montemorelos, to which he responded very calmly, "The truth is that the one who really should be promoted here is Ricaut, because he is the one who took Montemorelos..." But Colonel Murguía did not recognize the injustice in Castro's promotion and instead used it to make the argument that he too deserved to be promoted to general. Either persuaded by Murguía's objections, or simply not wanting to debate the issue, General Jesús Carranza got González to promote Murguía to general, too, thus doubling the injustice. In order to ease any possible tensions on that score, General Carranza took Colonel Ricaut, his nephew, aside and encouraged him to hang in there, "Tú te aguantas." At any rate, the reassurance had been somewhat unnecessary since Ricaut, like many revolutionaries at that time, had not been yet gripped by the ambitions of career officers and went along humbly and tranquilly fulfilling his duties.[60]

LINARES

In Hualahuises González decided to change up the order of march. He left Castro's column to cover the rearguard against any pursuing Federals and placed Villarreal's brigade in the vanguard. Villarreal occupied Linares without incident. It was the first place to receive the Constitutionalists with a showering of flowers. Villarreal had warned his men beforehand of severe punishment for anyone who might commit any outrages and recommended that any other commanders coming to Linares issue identical admonitions and, if possible, to simply spend the night in Hualahuises. Villarreal's brigade found some arms and ammunition and many new khaki uniforms; they immediately began to collect war taxes from government employees and businessmen before continuing on. Castro took Villarreal's advice and remained in Hualahuises for the night, but the main body continued to follow. Pablo González entered Linares on November 1 to establish temporary headquarters and began planning his campaign for central and southern Tamaulipas.[61]

In order to attack Ciudad Victoria, González began massing men in the area. His men consisted of those he had brought from Coahuila (the Carranza, Villarreal, and Murguía Brigades), plus the men of Cesáreo Castro, Luis Caballero, and Jesús Agustín Castro. He left the men of the Blanco Brigade at the orders of Dávila Sánchez to guard northern Tamaulipas and, along with Ernesto Santos Coy and Francisco Coss, tie down the Federal garrison in Monterrey. Around this time González received a report from Lieutenant Colonel Francisco Artigas in Los Aldamas that a strong Federal column was in Los Ramones advancing on Matamoros and repairing the rails, while another strong column had left Laredo headed for the same destination. As the movements appeared coordinated, Artigas thought it prudent to report to all in the radius of action. The Constitutionalists had people from Los Herreras to Los Aldamas with reinforcements on the way, and Castro was still in Hualahuises as the Constitutionalist rearguard to protect against any Federal columns from Monterrey.[62]

Confident in the countermeasures against the Federals in Monterrey and Laredo, the Constitutionalist main body left Linares very early in the morning on November 3 headed for Villagrán, some forty-eight kilometers to the south. Federals in their path fled to the safety of Ciudad Victoria, but that plaza's commander, Federal General Juan de Dios Arzamendi, ordered them back north when he learned that a Federal relief column under General Ricardo Peña had departed Monterrey, belatedly, traveling southward to lend aid to the Montemorelos garrison. Arzamendi placed Colonel Romualdo B. Sánchez in charge of the Federals who had retreated before González's advance, and ordered him return northward and link up with Peña's one thousand horsemen marching southward, with the unhappy result for the Federals that the Constitutionalists defeated both in detail.[63]

HUALAHUISES, NOVEMBER 3

Peña's brigade consisted mainly of Rurales from the newly re-designated 1st, 3rd, 7th, and 14th "Scout Corps" traveling overland to Hualahuises, which does not lie on the rail line, while the rest of his men had taken a train to Linares. While only General González and his escort and staff were in the latter town and preparing to depart, some of Peña's Rurales arrived. After a twenty-minute skirmish in which one of González's assistants was killed, the Federals fled the town and the Constitutionalist headquarters departed without further incident. The rest of Peña's Federals made contact with Castro's column a few kilometers south of Hualahuises.[64]

Castro left Hualahuises at 6 a.m. bound for Linares per instructions received from González, when his rearmost troopers reported Federal cavalry approaching from the direction of Montemorelos. A little while later gunfire was heard in that direction, prompting Castro to turn around and present battle in order to protect the main column, which had already gotten underway. By 8 a.m. he had occupied a chain of hills situated to the right of the railroad at the entrance to Linares while another one hundred men aided by a detachment from General Villarreal's brigade took possession of the station and another group defended the right embankment of the railroad. The attacking Federal dragoons allowed themselves to get caught between two wire fences that formed a lane, hemming them in as Castro's Constitutionalists occupying the commanding heights poured in murderous fire that forced the Huertistas to dismount. Then a force of about four hundred Federals and volunteers commanded by General Peña tried three times to flank Castro's left but encountered such stiff resistance that they had to withdraw to the road. There Castro tried to take the initiative to attack the enemy from both his flanks, but he could not because Major Juan Castro was on the opposite side of the road from the main Constitutionalist force and cut off without any way to communicate orders to him.[65]

During the fierce firefight, the Constitutionalists captured the enemy's horses when suddenly an assistant sent by General González arrived and ordered General Castro's men to break contact and withdraw, notwithstanding their superior tactical position, because he wanted to economize ammunition for the upcoming attack on Ciudad Victoria. The Federals succeeded in taking advantage of the cover of a ravine to enter the city around 1 p.m., after about five hours of fighting, so Castro had to gather his forces and withdraw in perfect order, since his mission to protect the retreat of the main column had been accomplished. Unfortunately, the retreat could not be communicated to the two squadrons under the command of Major Castro, who remained cut off and unable to receive orders or help, which meant that the major had to fight his way out in close quarters combat. Castro succeeded in escaping but was seriously wounded; three days later this signer of the Plan de Guadalupe died from his wounds. The Constitutionalists also lost some dispersed from Major Castro's command, two dead, and six wounded. For unknown reasons General Peña did not pursue the Constitutionalists, but instead remained in Linares.[66]

GARZA VALDEZ, NOVEMBER 4

Castro was still performing the service of extreme rearguard when he arrived at Garza Valdez Station with his column around noon on November 4 where he received orders from General González to detach a force of two to three hundred men to march along the railroad toward Ciudad Victoria, destroying the rails and telegraph. To complete this mission he sent Lieutenant Colonel Porfirio González and his men accompanied by those of Major Máximo González, in total 250 men, to carry out the order immediately. Moments later Castro continued the march covering the rearguard of the main body. Soon isolated shots rang out, and when General Castro inquired, Colonel Ricaut replied that the noise was soldiers shooting pigs for food. Thereafter each time a shot was heard, without fail Castro said, "one more!" After the head of the column (including most generals but not the impedimenta) crossed the rail at Garza Valdez and traveled about maybe two kilometers, a shot was heard and Castro said, "one more!" once again, but Ricaut retorted, "No!...that [train] whistle..." Then, there was a volley and a short while later copious shooting to the rear. The Constitutionalist buglers blew "halt" and Castro sent scouts to investigate, receiving news a few moments later that a Federal force composed of infantry and cavalry, numbering four hundred men, more or less, was attacking the force that he had left in Garza Valdez. It was Colonel Romualdo B. Sánchez's Federals whom General Arzamendi had sent back to the north from Ciudad Victoria.[67]

In effect, Sánchez earlier had headed north with two hundred Rurales and then collected the Federal garrison at Santa Engracia. Another eleven kilometers farther north at La Cruz Station, he met up with another eighty-four Rurales coming from Villagrán and Hidalgo, so that by the time he reached Garza Valdez his force totaled almost 450 men of the 37th and 47th Auxiliary Infantry; the 6th, 8th, 17th, and 27th (Auxiliary) Cavalry; the 10th Scout Corps; the Sottil Irregular Corps; and the García Quiroga Irregular Squadron. The destruction of the rails forced the Federal convoy to stop and present battle, and because of his inexperience, Lieutenant Colonel Porfirio González also gave the command to dismount. But González's two hundred Constitutionalists, observing that they were outnumbered and scattered on both sides of the rail, instead headed for the sierra, all with the exception of Natividad Contreras and the escort of twenty or thirty men firing in retreat.[68]

Castro responded swiftly to contain the Federal advance, but found himself in a narrow depression enclosed by a thicket that made any dispositions difficult. With a good part of his force distracted in the transportation and custody of the wounded and the horses, he hurried to send a dispatch to General González requesting help, which contradicted the dispatch sent by his chief of staff to González at the outset of the engagement announcing his confidence in their ability to prevail. As no report of gunfire was heard to the south where Lieutenant Colonel Zuazua had gone, Colonel Ricaut sent staff officer Manuel W. González to order Zuazua to engage Sánchez's Federals, and thus give them the impression that they were being flanked. Engineer-Colonel Ezequiel Pérez accompanied "W" to carry out the commission, and as they crossed the road, a wide-open breech in the Constitutionalist line crisscrossed by copious Federal gunfire, "W" dismounted and crossed using his horse as a shield, then remounted to continue on, but Pérez did not. He was hit in the heart and killed; the bullet cut a half moon in the strap of his field glasses that he had draped diagonally across his chest. It was a sad twist of fate that Pérez died from one of the first shots fired in the first combat in which he found himself on this campaign.[69]

Zuazua initiated his attack, and a little later Castro divided his remaining force into three groups and simultaneously attacked the Federals now in possession of the very same station that Lieutenant Colonel Porfirio González had abandoned a little earlier in order to rejoin the main body of the Constitutionalists (without any consideration for the men under his command, now dispersed). Castro's column hit the center and both flanks of the Federals, roundly defeating them. They killed many and sent the rest escaping on foot along the railway toward Linares, with the Constitutionalists declining to give pursuit. Castro also sent Major Pedro Vázquez to cut off the military train in case it tried to retreat, which Vázquez achieved by destroying a bridge. This had the dual effect of turning back a second train that was coming up the line from C. Victoria to aid the first and which, if it had arrived timely, would have occasioned a true calamity for Constitutionalists. Moreover, if the Constitutionalists had not prevailed, then their impedimenta would have fallen into enemy hands because of Porfirio González's incompetence. For his performance in the field Castro requested that General González confirm the promotion of Major Vázquez to lieutenant colonel.[70]

In the early morning hours of the following day, and after careful reconnaissance with the assistance of General Villarreal, Castro's men took possession of the train that the Federals had abandoned during the night. They found merchandise, foodstuffs, and ammunition in considerable quantities in the train, which was composed of one passenger car, three freight cars, nine boxcars and a caboose. The railroaders used the train to tear up track to the north and south and then derailed it in the station. The Constitutionalists took one prisoner and found five dead Federals on the tracks along with the corpse of Constitutionalist Second Captain Gorgonio Cantú and four more troops belonging to Lieutenant Colonel Porfirio González, who were also found on the tracks. By the time of the attack on Ciudad Victoria, Porfirio González and the rest of his 1st Carabineros de Nuevo León Regiment was operating in China, Nuevo León, either banished or dispersed to that location in the north.[71]

After a forced march, likewise continuing northward, Sánchez reached Peña's column at Linares, and the two Federal commands made their way to

Monterrey a few days later.[72] Peña had received orders to suspend the pursuit and report back to Saltillo because his brigade belonged to General Velasco's Division of the Nazas, and Tamaulipas State was not in that division's area of operations. Federal General Rubio later recalled that the Federal high command had recalled Peña's column because Pancho Villa had just taken Ciudad Juárez, and therefore General Mercado's Federal Division of the North, which had been cut off to the south since the fall of Torreón in October, now found its communications to the north likewise cut. Velasco needed all his men to recapture Torreón and reestablish lines to Chihuahua immediately. However this is an ahistorical recollection of events since Pancho Villa did not take Ciudad Juárez, by surprise, until almost a week after Peña had been ordered to return to Monterrey. Nonetheless, Velasco still needed the entirety of forces at his command to participate in the recapture of Torreón, which remained quite a high priority not only because it offered hope and aid to Mercado's Chihuahua City garrison, but because it also provided a buffer for Saltillo and Monterrey from Villa's increasingly powerful Constitutionalist Division of the North.[73]

The evening of the fight at Garza Valdez the Constitutionalists went into camp at a place called Magueyes, some twenty kilometers southeast of Garza Valdez Station. From there General González ordered Castro with other detachments from General Carranza's brigade to continue along the railroad and clear the way to Ciudad Victoria, while González with the main body left the rails and continued to the center of the state to link up with Colonel Luis Caballero in Santander Jiménez. General Castro's force proceeded along the railway, skirmished with the Federals at Carrizos, and then advanced to Tinajas. Without anything more to eat than a bit of piloncillo and some wild chiles called "piquines del cerro," they bedded down near La Cruz, occupied by some Federals. In the morning they attacked the pelones, dislodging them only with great effort on November 6.[74]

By that time González had left for San Carlos (twenty-five kilometers northeast of Magueyes). He reached Santander Jiménez on November 9, and Colonel Caballero joined the main column, although he probably only had 250 men with him. The next day Caballero received a promotion to general. González's column continued toward the state capital, arriving next at Padilla on November 10. The commanding general established his headquarters there. Employing scouts familiar with the road provided by Caballero, González sent advance forces to Güemez on the road to Ciudad Victoria. That same day the commanding general received notice that General Jesús Agustín Castro with maybe four hundred men was coming from Los Herreras. They would arrive the following morning, after having passed through China, where Lieutenant Colonel Porfirio González complained that they had stolen all his warehoused corn; Colonel Teodoro Elizondo with another possible 250 men was also on the way from Nuevo León state. That still left some two thousand Constitutionalists in the northern part of Tamaulipas and Nuevo León, most of whom had belonged to Blanco's old brigade commanded by General Dávila Sánchez; they had been holding the Federals in Monterrey in check.[75]

In order to remedy the malaise prevalent among the Blanco Brigade over the loss of its commander and to get things going again in the Northeast, the First Chief formulated a set of initiatives. He ordered Pablo González to have his own men replace Blanco's in the many garrisons where they were quartered and for Blanco's men to mass and begin campaigning immediately; General Jesús Dávila Sánchez was to take all the booty and artillery captured from Monterrey and concentrate the ex-Blanco forces under his direct command in Matamoros unless and until countermanded by General González, and General Caballero should be appointed Military Governor and Commander of Tamaulipas, in substitution of Blanco, as soon as possible (which would take place immediately upon the capture of the state capital, Ciudad Victoria). For the time being, Blanco chose to remain in Sonora, which did not cause any immediate turmoil.[76] In fulfillment of these directives, González ordered General Jesús Carranza to take his brigade to Matamoros to assume command of the sector and reorder the customs duties in that port of entry and Reynosa so that their funds might proceed to the immediate purchase of arms and ammunition for the forces of the Northeast. He also ordered him to take charge of Blanco's old brigade and send a Blanco favorite, Colonel Andrés "La Muerte" Saucedo, with his regiment to occupy Sabinas Hidalgo, Lampazos, and Villaldama in order to keep Téllez in Nuevo Laredo incommunicado with Monterrey. The positioning of Saucedo constituted a preliminary movement for the upcoming campaign to capture Nuevo Laredo. The remainder of the Northeast's Constitutionalists concentrated around General González, headed south toward the state capital of Tamaulipas.[77]

Following orders received from General González, General Cesáreo Castro called in his pickets and once again got underway from La Cruz Station on November 11.[78] Federals numbering no less than 200 in a military train had been approaching Santa Engracia and then pulling back almost daily, so Castro's Constitutionalists blew the bridge there. Castro also reported to General González, erroneously, that Federal General Antonio Rábago with about five hundred men had left Ciudad Victoria for an unknown destination that might be Matamoros. Although he was wrong, this did not strike anyone as strange owing to Ciudad Victoria's naturally weak tactical position and taking into consideration that the majority of the Constitutionalists in the state by now had gathered in the southern part. Castro urged that the garrison in Matamoros send scouts southward to investigate.[79]

Castro then left La Cruz Station for Hacienda Corpus where he established his headquarters and awaited further orders from González. Castro had a man named Anselmo "El Borrado" Ruiz, a frank and loyal rancher who commanded the Ropers Corps (*"Cuerpo de Reateros"*) that rounded up the necessary cattle for butchering and feeding his 1,000-plus man force, scout pasture land for the horses to rest and feed. Castro remained at Hacienda Corpus for several days while González's troops likewise remained a spell in Padilla.[80]

Determined not to let the opportunity of the upcoming battle slip away as the promise offered by Monterrey had, González issued a broadside for his commanders to read to the men. In part, it stated:

> Listen attentively to the following: In Monterrey on the first day of combat we took control of almost the whole city, but by the night of the first day and all of the second we had upon us an enemy more formidable than the Huertista legions: the inebriation of our soldiers. You must not forget this fact: the greater part of our wounded soldiers in the aforementioned act of war were found in a complete state of drunkenness, as were those many who remained inside the city after the retreat from Monterrey and were taken prisoner and shot. The same is also true with respect to some who were in Linares and almost all those who perished in Garza Valdéz [sic].
>
> For your own well-being and above all the good of the noble cause that we defend, I exhort you not to drink liquor in Ciudad Victoria, keeping in mind that THE CONSTITUTIONALIST WHO GETS DRUNK IN BATTLE causes us greater harm than the enemy. That the soldier who gets drunk to create an artificial courage degrades himself AND WITH THIS ONE ACT PROVES HIS COWARDICE. The jefes and officers have the indispensable obligation of severely punishing those who get intoxicated. Also I am disposed to use an iron hand in teaching a lesson to those who dedicate themselves to pillage or any other act of vandalism.[81]

Meanwhile, inside the capital city the extreme ignorance, unjustifiable optimism, delusion, or outright denial among the Federals as the Constitutionalists converged upon that point was astounding. Federal General Higinio Aguilar, a prolific letter writer and egregious misspeller, penned a letter to the Secretary of War, General Aurelio Blanquet, on November 14 professing at that late date that, "I am of the persuasion that this plaza will not be attacked," and bemoaning that "as no beating has been undertaken against the enemy, he takes advantage to assault and rob small populations, burning farms and committing all manner of vandalism." He finished with a small hint that perhaps he could do better than his higher-ups, disclosing: "Very confidentially, permit me to manifest to you that if after the defeat of Monterrey...a tenacious pursuit had been undertaken, [then] banditry in this state would end without great difficulty, in virtue of the fact that the groups are easy to beat and exterminate."[82]

The next day Aguilar sent another letter, this time to Huerta, repeating some of what he had told Blanquet and advocating that he be allowed to go on the offense:

> I should inform you that attending to a disposition from Citizen Jefe de las Armas of this plaza I came here with my forces on 3rd of this month, to prevent a possible assault by those defeated at Monterrey. Nothing notable has occurred up to today, since the bandits have been disseminated to several defenseless towns, robbing as they are used to doing. If a tenacious pursuit of these gangs were undertaken, the revolution in this state would soon be put out, and so I permit myself to confidentially propose to you, as I also do to the Señor Minister of War, that it is precisely the opportune moment after the defeat of Monterrey and [the other] that has just been given to them [down] Xicoténcatl [far southern Tamaulipas] way, where 50,000 rounds and other war materiel were collected from them, with which they will be impeded from forming large concentrations [of men] and this zone would be liberated from the depredations that they commit. Of my forces I have two detachments on the railway and yesterday one of them dispersed a group that was attempting to burn a bridge. I remain here with few troops, since it has been impossible to increase them. I remain awaiting orders from Division, and I lament having left my watch in the zone from [Santander] Jiménez to Marina, where I had succeeded in making the region calm and that abandoned today, is at the mercy of bandits.[83]

The octogenarian Aguilar was about to get the surprise of his very long life.

On November 14 González established his headquarters in Güemez, planning to initiate the definitive preparations for the attack from there; Generals J. Agustín Castro and Teodoro Elizondo proceeding from Nuevo León also finally reached him there. The next morning González called in all his key commanders and, after agreeing on the date, time, and plan of attack, gave each written orders. He ordered Drs. Suárez Gómez and Gilberto de la Fuente back to Santander Jiménez, to set up a field hospital in order to receive wounded after first aid had been administered in the field, organizing ambulances with available forces. Then González began mobilizing his forces in an appropriate disposition to effect the attack at the first hours of the following day. Brigadier J. Agustín Castro was in Santa Gertrudis, and Brigadiers Antonio I. Villarreal, Francisco Murguía, Luis Caballero, and Colonel Teodoro Elizondo were in Güemez, ready to undertake the march, but first González wanted Cesáreo Castro to push the Federals out of Santa Engracia so that their presence there would not complicate the assault on Ciudad Victoria.[84]

General Castro returned to his brigade, still encamped at Hacienda Corpus, and advanced to the bridge near Hacienda Santa Engracia on November 15 to engage about fifty men of Federal General Higinio Aguilar's Brigade under the command of Colonel José de J. Argüello around 4 p.m. First Zuazua entered the fray, then Alejo González, followed by Jesús Novoa; finally, Alejo González succeeded in outflanking the overwhelmingly outnumbered Huertistas and sent them flying back to the bridge at Caballeros Station where they joined Lieutenant Colonel Jesús M. Ramírez with his "regiment" of about fifty men, also from Aguilar's "brigade."[85]

After destroying some of the railway ahead of Santa Engracia, Castro's column continued to Hacienda de la Diana to spend the night. The Constitutionalists then received a resupply of ammunition so that they had 150 rounds per soldier for the upcoming battle, more than ever before, and the string of recent victories had them in good spirits. To complete his preparations González sent a team from Caballero's force to situate itself far south between Osorio and González stations, and interrupt the rail lines and telegraph to Tampico and Xicoténcatl. The main column with General González was now positioned about twelve kilometers northeast of Ciudad Victoria and poised to attack the plaza and take control of the state from the Huertista governor, Federal General Rábago, whom they knew well. González's Auxiliaries of Coahuila had fought under Rábago in the Orozquista campaign, and they thought that the Federal general had treated them poorly; for example, he had given an ill González nothing better than a cattle car for comfort in the cold February weather on the way to Meoqui. Shortly thereafter, during the Citadel cuartelazo, González and his men had separated from Rábago's command and returned to Coahuila. The night before the assault on Ciudad Victoria, González called old Rábago to taunt his former commander, and after hanging up, ordered the lines of communication cut. The assault was scheduled to begin at 5 a.m. on November 16.[86]

Battle of Ciudad Victoria

Inside Ciudad Victoria, Federal General of Brigade Antonio Rábago held the title of military governor of the state of Tamaulipas. As Jefe de las Armas, Brigadier Juan de Dios Arzamendi had immediate tactical command of the Huertista forces, which were composed of almost one thousand officers and men representing a plethora of units. In addition, Arzamendi had about five hundred local Social Defense forces (probably draftees), although they proved less than useless since most deserted at the start of the battle, while others joined the Constitutionalists. Additionally, although Arzamendi was only forty-five years old, he had been in ill health for some time.[87]

Tactical Command In Victoria	Major Unit organic to	G	J	O	T	Total
Maciel, J. Trinidad (LT)	1st Infantry Battalion			2	61	63
Farfán, Aurelio V. (1st CPT)	20th Infantry Battalion			3	117	120
	37th Auxiliary Infantry Battalion				29	29
	47th Auxiliary Infantry Battalion				10	10
Reyes, Luciano (2nd CPT)	39th Irregular Infantry Corps			1	10	11
	6th Cavalry Regiment				8	8
García, Martín (LT)	8th Cavalry Regiment			1	14	15
	12th Cavalry Regiment				4	4
Martínez, Rosalino (2nd CPT)	17th Cavalry Regiment			1	28	29
Torres, Nabor M. (Major)	28th Auxiliary Cavalry Regiment	1	9	77		87
Riestra, Juan (2nd Officer)	10th Scout Corps			1	16	17
López, Gabino A. (LT)	Sotti Irregular Corps				3	3
Zúñiga, Eliézer (LTC)	Zúñiga Squadron		1		37	38
	Leales de Llera					50
Hernández, Enrique (LT)	Two 80-mm. Mondragóns			1	21	22
	Unassigned/in Depot		3	1	10	14
Aguilar, Higinio (Brigadier)	Aguilar Brigade	1	5	27	47	80
		1	10	47	492	600
In Caballeros (13 kms.) and la Presa (32 kms.)						
Argüello, José de J. (Colonel)	Aguilar Brigade		2	27	83	112
Military train service between Victoria and Caballeros						
Urquiza, Rafael (LTC)	28th Auxiliary Cavalry Regiment	1	3	104		108
Arroyave, Felipe (2nd Officer)	10th Scout Corps		2	40		42
Military train service between Victoria and Tampico						
Castro, Benjamín (1st CPT)	1st Infantry Battalion		2	80		82
		0	3	34	307	344
	TOTAL AREA FEDERALS	1	13	81	799	944

Table 1.12 Battle of Ciudad Victoria Federal Troop Strength

Arzamendi's disposition had Aguilar covering the northern sector from the railroad to Ramírez Heights in the east with his "brigade" that did not even top two hundred men; Lieutenant Colonel Ramón H. Hinojosa occupied the eastern sector at Hacienda de las Vírgenes, Ramírez Heights, and the cemetery with ninety men from the 6th and 17th Cavalry and the 1st Infantry. General Arzamendi established his command post at the Sanctuary (or chapel) of Guadalupe with the artillery and about 120 men of the 20th Battalion and he arranged for various "support points" at the intersection of the railroad and the road to Jaumave, on the southwest corner of town, with an advance detachment further southwest at Hacienda de Tamatán (three kilometers to the southwest of town). They were all under the command of Irregular Lieutenant Colonel Eliézer Zúñiga. Finally, there was a scout train with two hundred men commanded by Lieutenant Colonel Rafael Urquiza of the 28th Auxiliary Cavalry, who with the forty Rurales of 10th Scout Corps had responsibility for covering the rails and the station on the west side. This did not leave many regulars or Auxiliaries in reserve, and since he did not trust the men of the Social Defense, Arzamendi interspersed them among his regulars and Auxiliaries. Arzamendi had ordered improvements made of adobe and earth on his east flank at Ramírez and Las Vírgenes heights around the cemetery, Molino de Terán (which was in a field of agave, or "*henequenal*"), and the support positions around the Sanctuary of Guadalupe, which the general intended to serve as the garrison's redoubt. Finally, the Federals had opened up three lines of defense that offered limited targets to the Constitutionalists but provided covered firing positions to the Federals, which compelled the attacking forces to dismount and tie up their horses in secure locations almost immediately upon coming into view of the plaza.[88] The Sierra Madres due west of town, the Ramírez Heights to the east, and an extended hill south of town called El Muerto Heights offered some tactical advantage to the defenders.[89]

The Federals believed the Constitutionalists to have 5,000 troops, but they probably had about half that number, while the Constitutionalists calculated the Federals inside the city at about 3,000 men from the three combat arms, when in fact they had less than half those numbers, many belonging to the Social Defense.[90]

Battle of Ciudad Victoria, November 16-18, 1913

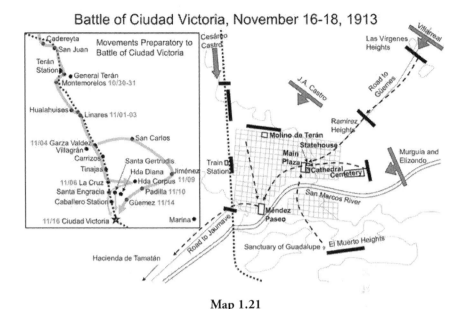

Map 1.21

NOVEMBER 16

González's plan of attack called for General Cesáreo Castro to attack from the west-southwest through Tamatán and the rail station; General Jesús Agustín Castro would attack from the station to the heights at Las Vírgenes, with the object of hitting the Federals at the agave field near the Molino de Terán; and General Antonio I. Villarreal, accompanied by division headquarters, would strike at the heights of Las Vírgenes between J. A. Castro's sector and Luis Caballero's men, who were arrayed to the left of headquarters and held in reserve. General Murguía and Colonel Elizondo attacked the cemetery and the fortifications near the Sanctuary of Guadalupe. Since all the forces were camped about three kilometers from the plaza except Don Cesáreo Castro's men at Hacienda de la Diana, the main force waited for Don Cesáreo to initiate the attack.[91]

Cesáreo Castro

At 1 a.m. Don Cesáreo left Santa Engracia Station marching along the rail line toward Ciudad Victoria with the objective of converging on time for the attack. At 5:30 a.m. his advanced troops made first contact with a much smaller Huertista force dug in behind fortifications near the iron bridge at Caballeros Station. Taking possession of the small heights that surrounded the station, completely covered by a thicket, the Constitutionalists first started taking feeble fire that increased in intensity as the main body of Castro's forces arrived. All at once Castro found himself attacked in the center and the two flanks and forced to deploy a good portion of his men in order to repulse the Federals, since his brigade found itself ambushed along the river that turns to the left of the position that his men were occupying.[92]

By 7 a.m. the Constitutionalists had succeeded in locating the fire coming from the railroad, the bridge, and the train station at Caballeros, which "to tell the truth was defended with bravura," according to Don Cesáreo. Once some of his men had occupied the bridge, others were again dislodged, withdrawing in order, although with many wounded. At one point the Federals repulsed Major Jesús Elizondo's men. They got between them and their horses tied up in the riverbed until Fortunato Zuazua's men flanked them on foot through the chaparral east of the rail station and forced the Huertistas to flee Caballeros back to the city.[93]

Around 8 a.m. the Huertistas, whom Don Cesáreo estimated at three hundred men, succeeded in embarking on two military trains whose withdrawal was impossible to cut off. The Constitutionalists took some prisoners, including two second captains whom they executed, and for the next forty-five minutes they conducted a desperate pursuit of the dispersed Federals who were fleeing while shooting, only to once again find themselves ambushed in the thick chaparral of the hills by an estimated 100 men. Cleaning up the battlefield and taking roll revealed four killed, among them a second captain from Lieutenant Colonel F. Sánchez Herrera's unit, and twenty-eight wounded among officers and men, including First Captain Pedro López. The Huertistas left on the field seventeen dead, among them regular Lieutenant Colonel Jesús M. Ramírez the jefe of the enemy force, one first captain, two second captains (the ones executed), two lieutenants, and a second sergeant. Castro also reported recovering twenty-one Mauser infantry rifles, and in close combat his men captured a tricolor flag and one bugle, as well as some saddled horses.[94]

After performing first aid on his wounded and getting vehicles to carry them, Castro again got underway, coming into view of the city around 3:30 in the afternoon. He found it impossible, however, no matter how much he tried, to make communication with General J. A. Castro until 7 p.m. when he arrived at that general's camp and thence sent González the official notice and explanation for his delay. Thus, Cesáreo Castro's men did not take part in the assault against the city proper on the first day of the battle.[95]

J. Agustín Castro

Castro's brigade left Santa Gertrudis in the early morning hours to arrive at the edge of the city around seven-thirty in the morning. The Federal artillery opened fire from the south side as soon as the revolutionaries came into sight, forcing the Constitutionalist dragoons to dismount at a distance and attack on foot. The Constitutionalists returned rifle fire in all sectors, followed a little while later by their artillery located on the north side. Castro's orders were to enter through the station and the streets that lead to the railway, because the Federals were reinforcing that direction, and try to use dynamite in the attack. Without waiting for Don Cesáreo's brigade on his right to join the fight he initiated combat at eight o'clock. Scouting the Federal positions, he dictated his disposition to his people, whom he entrusted to the immediate command of Colonel Miguel M. Navarrete, to make their way into the city guiding on Molino de Terán. Little by little the Federals yielded ground to the Constitutionalists; by noon almost the whole first line of defense was in Constitutionalist control. Castro's men succeeded in advancing between 8th and 15th streets as far as Matamoros Street, entering the train station and plaza de armas, when at mid-day Castro became aware of an apparent cessation of fire by the Constitutionalists on his left. This caused him to send a message to González to ask why. Most likely, the cessation occurred just as Villarreal's brigade had conquered Las Vírgenes heights, sending the Huertistas in flight.[96]

In the northern sector, however, Castro's men could not hold onto the barracks in the plaza de las armas due to the lack of opportune reinforcements. These would have permitted them to dig in and take the plaza, according to Castro (although General Villarreal later reported that Major Julio Soto from his forces and some of General Caballero's men had participated in the capture of the abandoned barracks, which provided the Constitutionalists with sufficient arms and ammunition to continue the combat). The Federals began concentrating fire on Castro's people from the cemetery, the chapel, and the heights of a fortress situated near the railway that had not been noticed upon the original reconnaissance—in other words, from the sectors assigned to Murguía and Don Cesáreo. Under such circumstances Castro's men had to exit the barracks and pull back some one hundred meters and again take cover, but not without first pilfering some horses and arms.[97]

By one o'clock the Federal artillery in the fort at the Sanctuary had begun to throw shrapnel at the Constitutionalist lines without inflicting much damage. On the other hand, the rifle and machine-gun fire did produce many casualties, to such a degree that the ambulances did not suffice and González' headquarters escort had to help in conducting the wounded.[98] The fighting in all the sectors was "formidable," and in the words of Constitutionalist staff officer Manuel W. González:

> there were moments when one could not talk except by yelling, because the noise of the cannonade was deafening, and the staff that came and went to the Headquarters requesting ammunition and carrying orders to the sectors was losing horses [shot out from under them] or themselves falling wounded with frightening frequency, and one could not cross uncovered spaces because death was almost assured.[99]

The main obstacle for Castro's men was the Molina de Terán, the mill located in an agave patch that the Federals had improved with a fortification to the front. The Federals occupied the rooftop, intermediate floors, and the bottom floor of the mill, and to the front a line of marksmen hidden prone in the cornfield poured in copious fire. Castro quickly had twenty-five wounded, whom he could not replace because the totality of his force had been otherwise occupied. The Constitutionalists had assaulted the enemy fortification five times and had been repulsed in each effort losing several killed and many wounded.[100]

But Castro also had other problems: the Federals were deployed over the railway down to the station where trains moved north and south with machine guns firing very copiously on his men. All morning long his men battled to clear the Huertistas along the railway from the station to some five kilometers to the north—and they were forced to do so without being able to learn the position of Don Cesáreo, at least as late as 4:50 p.m., the time of his report. He appealed for any information that González might have about Don Cesáreo's whereabouts, but González hardly knew anything more than J. A. Castro did, and it seems quite unconscionable that Don Cesáreo did not have the presence of mind to send a staff officer to either of his fellow generals to report his difficulties in advancing to his assigned sector. J. A. Castro had three hundred men pinned down inside of the city, forced to hold their positions because of the danger that turning tail and fleeing would occasion them. However, J. A. Castro suggested to González that with a cannon or perhaps by employing dynamite under the concealment of night, he might be able to destroy the "tall house" located behind the fortification at Molina de Terán that was inflicting so much damage on his brigade and then advance easily with the rest of his people who held the edge of town.[101]

When Don Cesáreo finally arrived at the camp of J. A. Castro in the evening of the first day of combat the two commanders decided to combine the efforts of their brigades the following morning, with General J. A. Castro putting carbines and ammunition for one hundred or so men at Don Cesáreo's disposal to arm some men who had just joined his brigade, perhaps defectors from Ciudad Victoria's Social Defense. General González also informed J. A. Castro that he was sending him machine guns and a cannon, but admonished him not to call off the attack to wait for them to arrive. By not having attacked earlier in morning at the appointed hour, J. A. Castro had allowed the Federals to reinforce the sector attended by González and threaten to beat the Constitutionalists in detail: the ammunition in González's sector was running low, and if he had to break contact then the Federals to his front would be able to redeploy and greatly reinforce the defenders on the station side, that is, in Castro's sector. The promised cannon arrived promptly and after the third shot on the Federal position the firing decreased a bit, which permitted Castro's men to hold their ground through the night.[102]

Antonio I. Villarreal

General Villarreal had been best positioned to initiate the attack on the city since his brigade was encamped a mere three kilometers northeast of the plaza the day before the battle, meaning he was only about one kilometer from his objective of Las Vírgenes heights. At 6 a.m. Villarreal ordered Lieutenant Colonel Reynaldo de la Garza, Major Enrique Navarro, and First Captain Baltazar C. Chapa to advance against Las Vírgenes heights where the Federals had magnificent positions and a barracks properly supported by trenches of earth and adobe. The Constitutionalists found the going tough in spite of the limited numbers of Federals opposing them because they had no cover of any nature for protection. Instead, Villarreal counted on the artillery commanded by Second Captain Manuel Pérez Treviño and the first company of machine gunners commanded by First Captain Daniel Díaz Couder to vigorously assault the seemingly impregnable forts erected on the heights. Additionally, the "boldness and constancy of the jefes and officers who expertly dictated orders of advance," according to Villarreal, dislodged the Federals from the barracks of the 17th Regiment, situated to the east of the fortifications on the heights; they left behind fifty horses with saddles, arms, ammunition, and other war materiel after putting up a stubborn fight. The Constitutionalists next defended the barracks from three successive counterattacks by the *mochos* who endeavored to retake the real estate. During one of those three assaults First Captain Cástulo Gómez, a close collaborator of Villarreal since 1906, had been killed leading his men in combat, much to the general's anguish. Ultimately the Federals had to flee from their remaining positions, abandoning the forts on Las Vírgenes heights when confronted with—in the words of General González, "a brilliant infantry charge that forced the enemy to retreat wildly toward another fortification constructed on the same heights [near the cemetery] that extended its radius of defense to the neighboring cornfield that was only a highway's width away from where our valiant soldiers fighting with grandiose enthusiasm were making deadly fire." Lieutenant Colonel de la Garza and Major Navarro undertook the pursuit, while the Captains Chapa and Faustino García took possession of the heights. Villarreal established his headquarters there at ten in the morning.[103] As previously mentioned, that was probably when Castro noticed the decrease in shooting on his left.

Subsequently, Colonel Atilano Barrera and his soldiers reinforced the squadrons commanded by Lieutenant Colonel de la Garza and Major Navarro to attack the Federal position near the cemetery, and Villarreal ordered the infantry ground assault protected by the cavalry of Captain Mateo Flores. Still, Villarreal found the Federals in the fort there inexpungable and therefore opted for having Captains Chapa, García, and Telles assault the position during the night while making use of dynamite, but that effort also failed.[104]

Francisco Murguía

General Francisco Murguía charged the east side with the cemetery and Sanctuary of Guadalupe as his objectives, the latter point having expertly designed and diligently supplied artillery fortresses. At one point the men from Murguía, Villarreal, and Elizondo's commands briefly took control of the cemetery before being forced back by Federal artillery from the Sanctuary of Guadalupe. General Murguía fought constantly throughout the day, maintaining his position but he was unable to capture and hold any ground. Colonel Elizondo and General Caballero placed their columns in reserve, sending men to reinforce other commands as ordered by González, who established his headquarters about five hundred meters from the Federal positions on the north side of the city. From there he had the satisfaction of personally directing the shots of the Constitutionalist artillery.[105]

The Constitutionalist guns were busy and well-aimed, but González wanted to answer the fire from the Sanctuary, and so he put to use an old cannon that Teodoro Elizondo's brigade had found in Ciudad Mier (hereafter simply "Mier") that probably dated from the French Intervention. This old cannon was "aimed" by raising it to the proper elevation using forked mesquite sticks of various heights; upon firing the first lucky shot, the ball landed right on the gate of the Sanctuary, rolling up Federal officers and men, but also spraying the Constitutionalists on the firing line with embers and covering them in smoke as the Constitutionalist gunners ran for their lives out of the path of the recoiling heap. Subsequent shots from the antique were not so lucky, and each shot destroyed the mesquite forks, so a large supply of these aiming sticks had to be kept on hand. The whole first day the Constitutionalists could not advance farther than the first line of defense taken from the Federals because shrapnel that fell like hail inhibited their progress.[106] As night fell the shooting began to trail off, with an errant shot going off every now and then accompanied by yells of "alert!" while the officers continually inspected the lines. By the end of the first day of fighting Villarreal had pushed the Federals from Hacienda de las Vírgenes to Ramírez Heights, J. A. Castro had bottled up Aguilar at Molino de Terán, and Cesáreo Castro stood ready to take the train station.[107]

NOVEMBER 17

In the earliest moments of daybreak the Federals' artillery again thundered and their infantry tried in vain to retake the ground lost the previous day.[108] From Matamoros, Jesús Carranza sent cars filled with ammunition and other supplies to General González in order to bring the attack and capture of the state capital to fruition.[109]

The Castros

Don Cesáreo's men reinforced the line of fire from the day before, and as General J. A. Castro's men had not been able to take the white house surrounded and perfectly protected by trenches that constituted the fort of the Molino de Terán, Don Cesáreo ordered Lieutenant Colonel Alejo González to attack it. Without reducing the white house the Constitutionalists could not advance against the train station because such a fort to their rear would be too compromising.[110] Alejo González's attack on the white house at the henequenal and Molino de Terán failed just as J. A. Castro's had the day before because the Federals had a clear field of fire and plenty of firepower. Fighting continued throughout the day of the seventeenth with constant attacks and counterattacks. Don Cesáreo requested more Mauser ammunition, and the machine gun previously sent by González went into action, which allowed the Constitutionalists to obtain fire superiority and permitted their people to move forward slowly but surely. Upon arriving at a relatively short distance from the Federals' field works the attackers could employ dynamite, and Don Cesáreo ordered Colonel Fortunato Zuazua from his brigade to assault the house. As Zuazua's men laid down covering fire, the officer who handled the machine gun directed his shots with calm accuracy and valor, almost fearless in the face of the Federals' rifle fire, and advanced his weapon, while Captain Juan Foster, Jefe of Dynamiters and a "Mexicanized" gringo in Don Cesáreo's command, charged the trenches like a "warrior of legend" (in the words of "W" González) with a knapsack full of hand bombs. Others who also had bombs followed him. Upon reaching the trenches they lobbed in the explosives, sowing terror in the Federals who began to dislodge from the fortress and trenches. After a terrific fight the defenders retreated through the back of the building to the train station where some reformed their lines while others fled into the sierra. Already in the late afternoon hours victory seemed to incline decidedly in favor of the Constitutionalists.[111]

General Higinio Aguilar's Federals took refuge in the train station and General J. A. Castro had all intentions of clearing them from there, but he wanted to give his men a little rest from the combat that they had been sustaining for over twenty-four hours. Additionally, he could not immediately assault the position because he could not be assured of the position of the Constitutionalist forces attacking in that direction. Therefore he sent a communication to General González requesting the name of the jefe and his position of the forces on that side. Castro wanted the unknown commander to contact Colonel Navarrete, who was directing the attack for Castro's 21st Brigade, in order to coordinate their efforts. The Constitutionalists battled the Federals there all night with light intervals in which Aguilar's men attempted to exfiltrate, being thwarted in those efforts several times. Upon daybreak the next day, however, it was noticed that Aguilar and his men had finally succeeded in abandoning the train station. His forces retreated to Hacienda de Tamatán, in the direction of Jaumave, where they put up a brief resistance before continuing in retreat.[112]

The East

First Captain David G. Berlanga and Second Captain Camerino Arciniega with soldiers from several squadrons under General Villarreal's command attacked the fortifications near the cemetery. In the afternoon they succeeded in dislodging the Federals who, in effecting their retreat, made an enveloping movement against Villarreal's headquarters; the maneuver was repulsed, most likely by General Caballero.[113] Caballero's men, Lieutenant Colonel Emiliano P. Nafarrate, Agapito Lastra, Raúl Gárate (and possibly César López de Lara and his brother Anacarsis), fought on the sector bordering Villarreal, where the Federals still endeavored to retake the heights of Las Vírgenes. They were supported by fire from the Sanctuary, which was answered in turn by the guns captured in Topo Chico handled by Major Carlos Prieto and First Captain Manuel Pérez Treviño, and "El Rorro" handled by Second Captain Alberto Salinas Carranza and Lieutenant Luis Herrera; the Constitutionalist guns fired sparingly under orders from González not to waste ammunition.[114] On the southeast side of town the Constitutionalist officers achieved their objective around 5 p.m., defeating elements of the 17th Cavalry and 1st Infantry under Federal Lieutenant Colonel Isaac Castro. The Federals had launched several failed counterattacks during the day before having to yield the remaining forts and give the order to regroup in the heart of the city.[115]

November 18

As night fell on the second day of fighting, the Federals had lost their main points of resistance and now were inside the city with little hope of prevailing. After seeing how few troops obeyed his orders to concentrate toward the center of town, General Rábago assayed his greatly depleted force and knew he had lost the plaza. So in front of the statehouse the Huertista general set fire to a great quantity of arms and any supplies his men could not carry, gathered everyone on the Méndez Paseo, disabled the artillery by removing and hiding the breechblocks, and abandoned the plaza at 2 a.m. in one column headed to the southwest over the Jaumave road. Constitutionalist Major Ildefonso Castro's force collaborated with General Murguía's column in assaulting the Federal fort near the Sanctuary and succeeded in dislodging the enemy in the early morning hours, recovering one hundred 80-mm. shells, four cannons, and other war materiel. Captains Flores and Telles took possession of the enemy fortification near the cemetery under the protection of the Constitutionalist artillery commanded by Second Captain Pérez Treviño with the company of machine gunners commanded by First Captain Díaz Couder, sowing demoralization among the Huertista troops. J. A. Castro's people moved in and took possession of the train station and the barracks of the 28th. The ringing of the bells by those Constitutionalists who had entered downtown announced their victory. González ordered Murguía and Villarreal to pursue the Federals as the other brigades entered the city, taking possession by 8 a.m. Four or five *marijuanero* pelones barricaded behind doors of the buildings on the street leading downtown continued to put up a resistance, in spite of all requests to surrender, until they were all dead.[116]

Upon entering the city, the Constitutionalists were able to salvage much of the materiel that the Federals had tried to burn. They found about forty dead in the hallways of the statehouse, as well as some of the dead Federal officers placed in coffins, whom González ordered buried along with about another two hundred dead Federals found in the fortifications surrounding the plaza. The commanding general also ordered Captain Luis Galindo to re-establish communications between Ciudad Victoria and Matamoros that had been cut somewhere between Victoria and Santander Jiménez, and ordered the streets cleaned in preparation for General Caballero to take his post as Governor and Military Commander of the State of Tamaulipas.[117]

In this feat of arms, González estimated having inflicted more than three hundred casualties, between dead and wounded, upon the Federals. His men also recovered four cannons, two machine guns, some 150,000 rifle cartridges, two hundred saddled horses, and the archives of Rábago, Aguilar, and Arzamendi. For their part the Constitutionalists reported thirty-eight dead and 103 wounded.[118] However, the figures reported by González appear low since J. A. Castro reported forty wounded, more or less seriously, from the two days of combat, and possibly more because he could not call roll. Don Cesáreo reported twenty-eight wounded at Caballeros Station alone, and Villarreal suffered about sixty casualties among dead and wounded.[119]

J. A. Castro presented an entire laundry list of individuals for special recommendation, including Colonel Miguel M. Navarrete; Lieutenant Colonels Blas Corral and Juan Jiménez Mendez; First Captains Pedro Viña, Martín de la Peña, Luis Mireles, Lucas de la Garza, and Enrique Barrera; Second Captains Pablo Villanueva, Abraham Martínez, and Julio Viña; Lieutenants José Rangel, Juan Acuña, Juan F. Luna, and Tomás Varela; and Sub-lieutenants Emilio Villarreal and Manuel Córdoba of his own brigade. He also recognized Lieutenant Colonel Alejo González, Major Julio Soto, and Captain Juan Foster of Don Cesáreo's brigade and Sub-lieutenant Alonso R. Velazco and private José María Torres of Caballero's Brigade.[120] Villarreal gave a simple but telling boast: "The Jefes, officers, and soldiers of my column performed their duty like good Mexicans."[121]

Herradura, Joya Verde, and Huizachal

General Villarreal organized the pursuit together with General Murguía and succeeded in reaching the Federals at a point called "La Herradura," fourteen kilometers southwest of Ciudad Victoria where combat was again joined. The Constitutionalists captured two machine guns and other war materiel and continued to pursue the Federals. They caught up to them at several more points along the road to Tula, the last time being at Rancho la Joya Verde, some forty kilometers from Ciudad Victoria. At that point the Constitutionalists surrounded the rearguard commanded by a sub-lieutenant with about fifty men of the 28th Auxiliary Cavalry, forcing them to flee into the hills to avoid complete annihilation. During the pursuit the Constitutionalists captured Rexers, other weapons, ammunition, horses, plus about eighty prisoners, among them some jefes and officers whom they executed.[122]

Separately, General Cesáreo Castro also gave chase to the Federals with only two hundred men from his command. He engaged them in a brief fire-fight at five in the morning of November 19 near El Huizachal, forty-six kilometers from Ciudad Victoria, and again in combat that lasted about an hour just a few hundred meters west of Joya Verde. Don Cesáreo calculated the total opposing force to number about three hundred men among je-fes, officers, and soldiers. According to his report, Federal General Rábago, who had previously been thrown from his horse and found himself on foot, knocked a sub-lieutenant off his horse at the first sight of the revolutionaries and hopping on it fled the Constitutionalist cavalry yelling, "every man for himself," (literally, "*sálvese quien pueda*") as he rode past the head of his ragtag column. Gripped by panic, Rábago's men fled in complete disorder while shooting their weapons in order to shamefully disband into the sierra, leaving behind their impedimenta. Many of the Huertistas, among them Federals, volunteers, and some individuals of the Social Defense, did not even put up a fight and before escaping or attempting to do so, tossed their weapons. The Constitutionalists quickly scooped them up, along with some thirty-three prisoners. Among the latter were three forced conscripts from the Monterrey Penitentiary who swore that they had been forced to take up the carbine, and accordingly had not fired a single shot. The Federals suffered six casualties, including a first captain and sub-lieutenant of the artillery and four non-commissioned officers, balanced against the Constitutionalists losses of two killed and one wounded.[123]

Castro's men spent the next five hours covering the sierra in order to col-lect "an infinity" of families who had fled Ciudad Victoria because of General Antonio Rábago's threat to burn down the whole city before permitting a single Constitutionalist soldier to step foot inside the plaza. Other civilians, many of the women wearing high heels, had escaped with their families out of fear of the revolutionaries. The Constitutionalists had to explain to them that they were not bandits, as the Federals had stated, and brought them down from the hills. Many of the Constitutionalists soldiers, moved to compassion, dismounted and placed the women on their horses. Taking the reins, they led about forty families back to town. Another fifty families were dying of hunger and fatigue, so at one of the ranches along the way Castro gave orders to butcher some cattle and furnished them with food. Old men, women, and children heaped gratitude upon the Constitutionalist soldiers for their conduct, "who I can guarantee you did not need superior notification to operate in the indicated manner," according to General Castro. The prisoners, with the exception of jefes and officers, also received attention that they did not expect, and several of them also expressed their thanks. Castro's men recovered sixty Mauser rifles, two .30-30 carbines, three thousand cartridges, and two firing pins belonging to the breechblocks of the cannons taken from the Federals the previous day in Ciudad Victoria.[124]

Some Federals later brushed aside the military significance of the Constitutionalist victory at Ciudad Victoria maintaining that it had been lightly defended by a token garrison. Federal General Higinio Aguilar, a shameless self-promoter who suffered from delusions of grandeur, cited General Arzamendi's unsuitability for command as the main reason for the defeat at Ciudad Victoria. Aside from this political excuse, the reasons for the Federal defeat sounded a familiar refrain: too few men for too large a perimeter against a sizeable enemy force close to its own supply lines to the United States, a lack of ammunition, and too many irregulars who refused to fight and in the worst of cases even joined the enemy.[125] Untrained and unmotivated conscripts and irregular forces continued to be the leading systemic vulnerability for the Federals.

Battle of Santa Engracia

At 10 p.m. on November 18, a military train bringing eight hundred raw recruits and General Guillermo Rubio Navarrete from Mexico City arrived in Monterrey. Before leaving the capital to retake command of his brigade, Huerta had ordered Rubio to escort the contingent of recruits. Secretary of War Blanquet had opposed them leaving the capital, not only because those recruits still had not received any training, but because they lacked the necessary complement of non-commissioned officers and officers. Still Huerta insisted. So, Blanquet arranged for some park rangers and excess officers from the Master School of Fencing and artillery department to help care for the recruits during the march, but he enjoined Rubio to instruct General Joaquín Téllez, Commanding General of the Division of the Bravo, that the forces that he was conducting should be distributed between those already trained in the Division of the Bravo and that in no way were they to be used in expeditions of importance, because they had limited military value. He recommended that those troops only be used to garrison cities and towns not in danger of being attacked.[126]

Téllez was waiting on the platform at the station to stop him from disembarking his charges when Rubio's train arrived. He gave Rubio a recapitulation of the situation of the zone: the Constitutionalists repulsed in the attack on Monterrey had retreated via the Gulf Railroad, through Cadereyta, Montemorelos, and Linares in the direction of Ciudad Victoria and Tampico; the Peña and Ocaranza Brigades had given chase, but subsequently had been withdrawn; the revolutionaries were massing to destroy all the Federal garrisons from Monterrey to Tampico, which had neither the time nor orders to mass for operations; General Rábago in Ciudad Victoria commanded the largest Federal force in that direction, but there had been no news of him and many feared that Victoria might have already fallen. If so, and in the case that Rábago had retreated southward endeavoring to gain the San Luis-Tampico Rail line via Jaumave, Tula (with Federal garrisons of approximately sixty and three hundred men, respectively), and Cerritos (without a garrison), then the revolutionaries might follow and threaten this line, including the vital and virtually ungarrisoned port of Tampico.[127]

ROBLES AND GÓMEZ

At the same time, the Constitutionalists that Villa had left behind in Torreón when he returned to Chihuahua had become emboldened and sought to attack and capture both Saltillo and Monterrey. On November 12, Constitutionalist Generals José Isabel Robles and Juan E. Gómez left Marte Station and headed for Monterrey, arriving at Señor Richardson's Hacienda Seguín after seven hours of travel. The Constitutionalists set camp and detached pickets for the necessary and good custody of the entrances and exits of the mountainous terrain, and thus reinforced the garrison of Parras and, by extension, the important plaza of Torreón. At that point the commanders held a council of war and resolved to make a determined advance with their combined forces against Hacienda Guadalupe, approximately twenty kilometers away, where the Federals were encamped. They were assured by the terrain and their numbers of the probability of rolling up the opposition and continuing to the town of General Cepeda, which they expected to reach by November 18 or 19 in cooperation with General Eulalio Gutiérrez, who awaited their advance. With more than three thousand effectives, including those of General Eulalio Gutiérrez, their ultimate goal was the taking of the plazas of Monterrey and Saltillo.[128]

As a practical matter and out of military protocol (Monterrey and Saltillo were in González's area of operations), Robles and Gómez reached out to the Division of the Northeast to assist in the planned operation. They informed González, Blanco (obviously unaware that Blanco had been called to Sinaloa), and Jesús Carranza of their movements thus far and asked them to bring together the necessary materiel and resources to prosecute the campaign, confident that with efficacious cooperation from their fellow revolutionaries the conquest of the referenced plazas would be not only possible but virtually guaranteed. Robles and Gómez did not believe a simultaneous siege of both state capitals to be "difficult" but still thought it would be better to besiege one or the other city, and they deferred to the Division of the Northeast's intelligence regarding the defenses of the two plazas in deciding which to besiege first. Nevertheless, they offered their opinion that the advantages to attacking the plaza of Saltillo were beyond improvement, all the while recognizing that the Federal detachments operating outside of the city once defeated would fall back and increase the number of effectives in the plaza, making the operation more difficult. Therefore, they proposed that the Division of the Northeast not attack Monterrey from the north but rather lay siege to it from the Saltillo side with part of its forces and situate the rest immediate to the railway that connected the two plazas and thus impede all aid to Saltillo. They urged the Division of the Northeast to decide with the greatest brevity as they prepared to advance on the preliminary objective of General Cepeda, a small town located on the road to Saltillo.[129]

González was already in the midst of a campaign to conquer Tamaulipas and could not respond to the proposal. A few days later Federal General José Refugio Velasco's Division of the Nazas began marching against Torreón and Robles had to appeal to General Calixto Contreras for reinforcements. As Contreras' men did not arrive in time, Robles had to yield to the Federals advancing westward in overwhelming numbers.[130]

Robles' coordination with General Eulalio Gutiérrez, who operated out of northern San Luis Potosí, his attempts at combined operations with the Division of the Northeast to conquer the state capitals of Saltillo and Monterrey, his letterhead boasting "Robles Brigade, Division of the Laguna," as well as the fact that he did not consult with General Villa about these efforts, all point to the conclusion that Robles did not consider his brigade as belonging to the Constitutionalist Division of the North, which is particularly noteworthy given the schism that would begin in only six months.

Back in Monterrey, Téllez ordered Rubio to proceed by train to Linares to collect two hundred fifty infantrymen of the 29th and 5th Battalions commanded by Lieutenant Colonel Manuel Arroyo Limón, who belonged to Rubio's brigade, and then continue to Garza Valdez, the functioning extent of the Gulf Railroad, since to the south of this point the railway had been destroyed by the revolutionaries. In Garza Valdez, Romualdo B. Sánchez with five hundred mounted men would meet the column. Rubio was to disembark the recruits, send back the trains to fetch the rest of his brigade in Lampazos, and continue south to collect any dispersed Federals, guard the railroad, and reinforce Ciudad Victoria, if it had not already fallen. In the case that Ciudad Victoria had been lost to the Constitutionalists, then Rubio was to unite with Rábago in his retreat northward, or draw the attention of those Constitutionalists pursuing Rábago if that Federal commander headed south; only if Rábago's command had been annihilated was Rubio to return to Monterrey. In reply, General Rubio produced a letter from the Minister of War expressly prohibiting the replacements under his care from being employed in important operations.[131]

General Téllez confirmed that he understood as much, and so he augmented Rubio's force with 150 Sappers under Major Francisco Puga, two sections of machine guns, and a section of field artillery commanded by Captain Carlos Rodríguez Malpica. He also reassured Rubio that the rest of his brigade was ready to embark. As soon as his brigade caught up to him he would have a capable assembled fighting force as he moved farther south. Rubio fully trusted that his brigade could be removed from northern Nuevo León, where it was performing the important mission of guarding the railroad to the border, since the railroads that ran from Saltillo and Monterrey to the border were generally free of revolutionaries. Additionally, General Velasco's Division of the Nazas in Saltillo that was preparing for its march on Torreón provided more than enough protection to contain any threat from Robles and Gómez, or anyone else, to the west.[132]

November 19

Rubio arrived in Garza Valdez the next day and by 9 a.m. had disembarked the troops and returned the trains to Monterrey and Lampazos to bring back the rest of his brigade. But instead of the five hundred mounted soldiers Téllez had promised would meet him, Sánchez only had one hundred eighty men with a mere twenty-five of those mounted. The Federal column still had no news of General Rábago and the Ciudad Victoria garrison, but available information indicated that the railway only required light repairs all the way to La Cruz. From that point farther south, however, the destruction of the bridge over the Purificación River made travel difficult. Rubio had with him approximately 1,450 men who were mostly raw recruits, two 75-mm. Saint Chamond cannons, two sections of machine guns, and about 150 rounds per man, but no money or medical service. With cars and wagons to carry the baggage, ammunition, and those who might later become exhausted by the journey, the column of recruits and stragglers undertook the march on foot toward Carrizos, twenty-five kilometers away, and then continued the following day to Tinajas, another forty-three kilometers distant.[133]

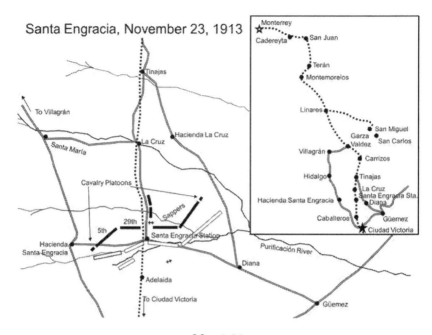

Map 1.22

The Federals did not quit the day's march until ten o'clock at night. On this first day of marching they had experienced a great number of exhausted men and heat casualties as a consequence of the excessive temperatures, the absolute lack of water, and the newness of the personnel who composed the column. Beyond Tinajas the downed and destroyed telegraph line made communications with headquarters difficult. Nonetheless, using various modes of communication, Rubio related to division headquarters that he had learned from some dispersed Federals of General Rábago's flight from Victoria in the direction of Jaumave and the pursuit by revolutionaries. The retreat of Rábago's Federals had been made difficult by the large number of civilians accompanying them from Victoria, their immense impedimenta, and a lack of ammunition. Apprised of the number and general locations of revolutionaries who might oppose him, and with Rábago headed in the opposite direction, General Rubio began to worry that he might find himself outnumbered in a fight. Monterrey answered, "this headquarters in no way changes your dispositions…" Once again Rubio requested that headquarters forward his brigade and the next morning continued marching toward La Cruz.[134]

NOVEMBER 20

The following day's march came to a halt in La Cruz where the Federals made contact with some fifty revolutionaries who fled at the approach of the column. The Federals settled into the town, occupying the hacienda, train station, and a ranch by the same name as the town. They spent the entire next day, the twenty-first, reconnoitering the La Cruz River and vicinity, as well as acquiring reports about the Constitutionalists and preparing to ford the river, which could not be effected without difficulty: an officer and two infantrymen had already been dragged away by the current. General Rubio reorganized his forces, which after collecting detachments and stragglers now totaled 1,800 men, two field guns, and four machine guns. His own situation was growing increasingly precarious. His column was now 270 kilometers from the next closest Federal force and only the twenty-five cavalrymen that he had left in Garza Valdez to assist with the disembarkation of his brigade, whom he expected to be on the way, secured his lines of communications.[135]

NOVEMBER 22

This far south, without his brigade, and maintaining only intermittent communications with division, Rubio reasoned that he had three courses of action: first, to immediately go back the way he had come; second, to undertake a flanking march protected by the Purificación River in order to retreat via Santa María, Hidalgo, and Villagrán to Garza Valdez; and third, to continue forward toward Victoria. The first solution he deemed unacceptable, since the troops' excellent morale would suffer if they were to retreat after such a vigorous advance in search of the enemy. And if they did have to fight after such "an unjustified retreat," they might become suddenly aware of their patent inferiority against an enemy with numerous and excellent cavalry and refuse to fight, making it impossible for General Rubio "to save even one soldier since we were so far away from any aid, without communications, and against an enemy three times greater in number and of an excellent morale after its success in Ciudad Victoria."[136]

The second solution also proved unacceptable; although it had the advantage of passing through towns with resources, it offered no promise of avoiding combat—especially since in the evening of November 22, Rubio received reports that an enemy column of about 1,500 men had passed the left bank of the Purificación River. He could not confirm this report because of his shortage of cavalry, but it seemed reliable because of a great dust cloud to the east of La Cruz moving to the north. Given the foregoing, Rubio decided to ford the Purificación River to take advantage of the element of surprise against the Constitutionalists, who probably would not have time to concentrate their forces. If he could beat them, then he could always undertake his withdrawal, and if not, then any defeat would be a disaster due to his lack of cavalry, shortage of ammunition, and the length of his impedimenta.[137]

The Constitutionalists knew about the approach of General Rubio's combined arms column trying to reinforce Ciudad Victoria since, according to reports that they had, the Federals still did not know that the state capital had fallen and therefore would keep moving to the south. Accordingly, on November 22 General Pablo González sent General Villarreal with Murguía, Cesáreo Castro, J. A. Castro, and Teodoro Elizondo's brigades, along with all of Major Carlos Prieto's artillery, and Díaz Couder's machine guns, to intercept Rubio's Federals. The Constitutionalists, except for General Cesáreo Castro, advanced toward Santa Engracia to await the Federals, who likewise encamped for the evening and prepared to present battle the following morning in the light of day. Cesáreo Castro's brigade undertook a flanking mission to destroy the railroad to General Rubio's rear and cut off any Federal retreat: that was the column that the Federals had spotted to the east moving north and raising a dust cloud in the evening.[138]

NOVEMBER 23

Two thousand Constitutionalists deployed around Santa Engracia to face the Federals, who forded the river at 10 a.m. to make contact. Federal scouts reported spotting a group of about 400 Constitutionalists judged to be the Constitutionalist vanguard two thousand meters from kilometer 276 on the railway. The Federal vanguard advanced immediately, while to the east of the railway and on the north bank of the Gayabas Arroyo their artillery section went into battery so that its fire could protect the advance of the infantry deploying from the west side of the railway. Constitutionalist cavalry, most likely the reconnaissance of Santa Engracia that Murguía had ordered at 7 a.m., resolutely attacked the Federal vanguard, which deployed under the protection of the Cajón River perpendicular to the direction of march. That marked the opening of the battle, but as late as 11 a.m. Murguía still had not been able to establish communications with Villarreal or any of the other Constitutionalist commanders. The Federals repulsed said attack and immediately Major Puga with the sappers and a Lieutenant (probably Luis G.) Fuentes' two machine guns deployed opposite the Constitutionalist right in order to cut off a Constitutionalist retreat toward Güemez, where the Constitutionalists had their headquarters established. At the same time Lieutenant Colonel Limón with the infantrymen from the 5th and 29th Battalions and Lieutenant Lira's two machine guns took up position against the Constitutionalist left. Lieutenant Colonel Calero assumed tactical command of the rest of the brigade.[139]

In their battle disposition the Federals attempted no maneuvers, but rather relied on their artillery. Typical of the battles of the revolution, both sides commented on the ineffectiveness of each other's artillery, with the Constitutionalists even taking delight in the Federals' cannon fire, playing "toro, toro," and yelling "here comes another cow" with each projectile fired. About mid-day the Federal shelling increased in intensity, and the Federal infantry formed up in a firing line two kilometers wide and began to move forward at the quickstep without shooting until at a distance of 500 to 600 meters from the enemy when they opened fire. The battle became generalized and vicious as the Federals entered into open ground and managed to dislodge the Constitutionalists from their first positions and pressed forward toward Santa Engracia Station where the entrenched Constitutionalists then held their positions. By now Villarreal's brigade had joined Murguía in the center and Caballero's and J. A. Castro's held the flanks; they were supported by four cannons, two of which were the 80-mm. Light Type De Bange systems that had fallen into their hands at Topo Chico, and a mortar.[140]

The Constitutionalist dragoons counterattacked, but due to the efforts of Lieutenant Colonel Limón, the Federals succeeded in dislodging the Constitutionalist left and forcing those revolutionaries to pull back to the south and west. Meanwhile on the left wing the valiant Captain of Sappers Cristóbal Arellano fell dead, which caused the extreme Federal left to falter a bit before returning to its original position upon being opportunely reinforced by a section of railroaders. Following the contour of the terrain and juxtaposed to the Constitutionalists' dispositions, the Federal right threatened the Constitutionalist left with envelopment in a disposition known as a "defensive hammer," while the Federal left supported itself on the Purificación River, whose banks strengthened with field fortifications provided protection against the possible return of the enemy forces that had passed on the left edge of the river earlier. Colonel Romualdo B. Sánchez's Sottil Irregular Corps provided the maneuver group while the recruits were held in reserve and used as ammunition bearers for resupply.[141]

After the battle had begun, Rubio received a message from Téllez that sounded downright apoplectic. The Secretary of War had taken away 500 men from his division and therefore Rubio should not count on "a single round, nor one [more] soldier" (meaning his own Rubio Brigade would not be joining him), communications south of Saltillo had been cut, and there were revolutionaries to the west of Monterrey, most likely referring to General Francisco Coss. Additionally, Rubio's presence had forced the Constitutionalists to suspend their pursuit of Rábago, who had reported in safe, so his mission had been accomplished, and he should now think about the safety of the column. Given Rubio's earlier reports Téllez feared that the latter would be cut off and destroyed, and so he commanded him to withdraw as soon as possible. However, as Rubio wisely noted: "It was not possible to obey this order, because I feared that this maneuver, extremely difficult for even veteran troops, would be disastrous for novice recruits who made up my column…retreating from combat, pursued by the enemy very superior in number and perfectly mounted, one of whose groups had been situated at my rearguard."[142]

The tenacity, or sheer desperation, of the fight put up by the Federals eventually forced the Constitutionalists to abandon their positions on the river, which Lieutenant Colonel Limón crossed. He pursued them for four kilometers and occupied Santa Engracia Station very close to five o'clock in the afternoon, but was not able to pursue beyond that point due to a lack of cavalry. By 6 p.m. the fighting attenuated, and Villarreal told Major Prieto to withdraw his guns, a command that he could not obey because four of his mules had been killed. It was getting late, and the Constitutionalist lines had already begun to pull back. This left the artillery exposed to capture in the river, where they were set up in battery. Lieutenant Colonel José E. Santos, Villarreal's Chief of Staff, and Majors Celso Téllez and Rafael Cadena went to see what was happening with Prieto and the artillery; they found Prieto staring at his dead mules. Santos told Téllez and Cadena to use ropes and their saddle horns to pull out the guns, as Federal shells continued to fall. Prieto objected, going into a discourse about how to properly haul the pieces, to which Santos replied, "While Prieto explains how to scientifically haul a cannon, each one of you rope it and let's get it up by the saddle horn." And so they lifted it out of the gulley and inside friendly lines as the engineer Prieto continued his lecture.[143]

The Federals remained in possession of the battlefield as the Constitutionalists withdrew in the direction of Güemez. The forces of General Cesáreo Castro that had passed the river got lost and did not take part in the battle, and the rest of the Constitutionalists did not fully commit to combat because they had waited in vain for Castro's brigade to join the battle. The Constitutionalists left behind about twenty dead, seventeen prisoners, sixty horses, and some arms and objects that they abandoned in their flight; the Federals lamented Captain Cristóbal Arellano and a handful of enlisted dead and twenty-four wounded. During the battle they consumed ninety-four shrapnel shells and eight impact shells for the 75-mm. Saint Chamond Mondragóns, and 80,000 7-mm. Mauser rifle and carbine rounds. Rubio's column spent the night camped between Adelaida Station and Hacienda Santa Engracia since it was not possible to pursue the enemy because of a heavy downpour, not to mention a lack of mounted personnel.[144]

November 24

The day after the battle, Rubio's Federals captured several carloads of provisions in Adelaida Station and they took a day of rest, scouting in the direction of Victoria and Güemez before undertaking the march to Santa Engracia, which it occupied without resistance since there was no indication of the enemy in the area. A telegram from headquarters sent two days earlier to Garza Valdez, which was as far as the telegraph reached south, arrived by mounted courier informing that trains with payroll and ammunition had left Monterrey headed for Garza Valdez to collect Rubio's column, but they were without escort because of a lack of troops. This telegram precipitated Rubio's return since he knew the trains would be exposed to attack by the column that had passed the left of the Purificación River days earlier; up to this point he had still held out hopes that his brigade would join him, irrespective of the message from Téllez the day before.[145]

At 7 p.m. Villarreal's brigade joined Murguía's and reported that the Federals had abandoned Santa Engracia Station headed for the hacienda of the same name. Villarreal immediately ordered Colonel Emiliano P. Nafarrate to detach a scouting detail of fifteen men to follow after the Federals, and J. A. Castro's 21st also received orders to give pursuit. The Constitutionalists still did not know Rubio's intentions, guessing that in order to avoid attack on his rearguard he was heading to the foothills to screen his movement toward Ciudad Victoria, or more probably, that he was returning to Linares. Villarreal exercised an abundance of caution, even going so far as to worry about his own ammunition resupply. He informed General González that he was leaving an escort in Caballeros and suggested that it would be a good idea to send a message ahead of those bringing the ammunition so they would not be caught by surprise.[146]

November 25-29

General Cesáreo Castro also seemed to lack any initiative, remaining at Hacienda El Carmen Renovado, just east of Adelaida Station, with scouts all along the railway to La Cruz, La Cruz Station, Santa Engracia Station, and Hacienda de la Diana, endeavoring to establish communications with Generals Villarreal, J. A. Castro, and Murguía in order to make a coordinated effort against Rubio.[147] As of November 26 Villarreal stated that he hoped to reach Hidalgo before going into camp for the evening. He expected to catch up the next day to the Federals, who moved along slowly encumbered by a great number of families riding in carriages fleeing the revolutionaries over roads in awful conditions and could only cover about twenty or twenty-five kilometers per day. The ammunition that Villarreal had requested had not reached him yet, but he still hoped to come to agreement with the other brigades in the area and deliver a coordinated attack against Rubio.[148] But it was not to be.

Villarreal's intelligence had been flawed, since General Rubio marched over four straight days of unmolested egress from the region via the main highway, traveling along muddied roads and fording swollen rivers caused by rains through Santa María (thirty-five kilometers), Hidalgo (twenty-two kilometers), and Villagrán (thirty-nine kilometers) to Garza Valdez (sixteen kilometers), meaning he had been averaging almost thirty kilometers a day.[149] During this time the Federal column cleared the Monterrey-Victoria line; they collected another three hundred Rurales of Tamaulipas commanded by Comandantes Taylor and Martínez along the way, who greatly improved Rubio's situation since they knew the region. The day before his arrival to Garza Valdez the Federal general wired ahead to notify division headquarters, reminding them not to forget loading ramps for the trains.[150]

On November 29 Rubio's troops paraded in Monterrey. After gathering up all the Federal detachments and dispersed who had found themselves isolated in the area and joined the column during its march, Rubio's original 800-man trainload of recruits had grown to over 2,158 men ready for combat. He had always remained ready to continue south, but Téllez forced him to return to Monterrey. The order never made sense to Rubio, since there were already three thousand Federals in that city, not to mention Rubio's Brigade in Lampazos, and no revolutionaries to speak of in the area surrounding Monterrey. Apparently Rubio either did not know, or forgot, that the Division of the Nazas only began operations on November 23 to retake Torreón, with advance Federal forces only as far west as Brisa Station on the Central Railroad, Guadalupe on the Coahuila-Pacific, and General Ocaranza's brigade in nearby General Terán. Robles so resisted the Federals' progress that it took Velasco fifteen days to cover the 322 kilometers to Torreón. Had it not been for Robles, lightly defended Matamoros might have been retaken with a coup de main by Federal General Gustavo Guardiola y Aguirre in Nuevo Laredo and/or Jacinto Guerra, temporarily in command of the Rubio Brigade. At any rate, Téllez's order to Rubio effectively cleared the state of Tamaulipas of all Federals except those in Nuevo Laredo in the far north and Tampico in the far south. When Huerta read the exchange of communications between the two Federal generals, he relieved Téllez, told him to turn over command to General Joaquín Maass, and ultimately sent him to babysit besieged Guaymas, Sonora. He had always conceived of General Rubio as "brave" and Téllez as "incompetent and decrepit"; it was only due to the accident of seniority that Téllez held command over Rubio.[151]

Rubio also received recognition from Secretary of War Blanquet, notably taking into consideration the circumstances in which the column in his command had operated:

> over broken terrain and lacking in resources that together with the numerous enemy located there was making the maneuver of your forces carried out very difficult, this secretariat estimates that it was developed correctly, being lamented that because of force majeure it was not possible to send you reinforcements conveniently and opportunely to take advantage of the success obtained for the immediate recapture of the plaza of Ciudad Victoria. Which I communicate to you for your information and satisfaction, in the knowledge that orders are being drafted so that the line [grade] officers who distinguished themselves in those feats of arms might be promoted to next immediate rank, provided that they have been in their current rank for six months, the same not being done for the field [grade] officers, since they were just recently promoted.[152]

General Guillermo Rubio Navarrete was one of the best that the Federal Army had to offer, but the Secretary of War underutilized his abilities.

The importance of the Santa Engracia campaign does not spring from its scale, but rather because it points out both the misallocation of Federal soldiers for developing sound operations and that the Federals had not received orders to mass for operations in Tamaulipas. Almost as importantly, it reflects the interdependence of actions, considerations, and decisions theater-wide reflective of the emerging sophistication and complexity of operations. Finally, it also provides one example of the tenacity of a few Federal officers in extremely unfavorable circumstances, and points up the incompetence of revolutionaries in the Northeast, as General Rubio summarized:

> The mission that was entrusted to the column was completed thanks to the shortcomings of enemy command. In effect, a column of infantry with ammunition for only one day of combat and distanced 270 kilometers from its base of operations and without communications, could and should have been enveloped by the enemy three

times superior in number, composed for the most part of mounted troops, knowledgeable of the region and with enough effectives not only to defeat my column, but to continue without any harm from the latter to the pursuit of General Rábago. The trains for embarkation were protected for two days in Garza Valdés [sic] by only twenty-five cavalrymen, the only ones in my column. My column, that of General Rábago, and the trains, were saved thanks to the unsettling of the enemy command as a consequence of the Battle of Santa Engracia, since it distanced it [the enemy] from the region during its [Rábago's] retreat.[153]

With only six months or so experience in independently developing operations, González and his generals still had a way to go in their education. Nevertheless, after Rubio had departed the area, the Constitutionalists withdrew to Ciudad Victoria, and Teodoro Elizondo, inexplicably, received a promotion to general.[154]

J. A. Castro did not fare so well. Initially after the Battle of Ciudad Victoria, General Pablo González had ordered Castro south to partake in the upcoming operation against Tampico, not only to comply with higher orders from the First Chief but also because he wanted Castro to secure his rearguard against any threat from the south. But as Castro was getting ready to march on Tampico, he received counter orders to go fight at Santa Engracia. When Castro returned to Victoria afterward, González again ordered him to participate in the operation of Tampico, but (apparently to keep the inveterate malingerer Castro from acting on his express desire to separate from the Division of the Northeast and go operate independently in the Center) González also ordered him to turn over all his materiel to General Caballero, effectively disarming the 21st Brigade. Castro relinquished all the materiel he had in his cargo, what he had collected from the Federals in Ciudad Victoria, the spare weapons in his possession from the numerous casualties that he had suffered in the Battle of Ciudad Victoria, his surplus, and anything else that he had planned to use to arm the two hundred men that his agents had just recruited from south of Ciudad Victoria. Castro's men, who had always lacked sufficient clothing and arms, once again were bereft of materiel to campaign. After three days in Victoria the 21st received orders to march on Tampico.[155] They would get their arms back upon their arrival at the objective.

*　　*　　*

The Americans impacted military operations in the Northeast during the fall of 1913 in matters both small and great. On a tactical level we are introduced to an active American participant in the personage of "Juan" Foster, a naturalized Mexican citizen. Although Americans no doubt took part in the fighting, they were few and far between, and the Constitutionalists had no problem in owning up to those gringos fighting in their ranks, regardless of the attempts by Federals to make political hay from such participation. The Constitutionalists experienced a much greater, and adverse, effect from American involvement in the form of the arms embargo, which compelled the Constitutionalists to attack hardened targets, such as Monterrey and Ciudad Victoria, in order to get battlefield salvage from the Federals, essentially trading lives for war materiel. While the Federals had state of the art cannons, copious machine guns, and access to the international financial and arms markets (the United States excepted), the Constitutionalists had to use homemade and outdated guns, such as the one found by Elizondo's men in Mier, and resort to imposing war taxes upon local commerce and governments, as happened in Linares, resulting in a potential deterioration in relations with the local populace.

On an operational level, the Federals felt the weight of U.S. foreign policy in the numerous American soldiers gathering in Texas. Huerta had to assign heavy columns to block possible invasion routes through Piedras Negras and Nuevo Laredo, although Blanco's forces in Matamoros may have played into Huerta's strategy to economize his forces and block the third route into Mexico's Northeast. If Blanco had remained in charge of Constitutionalist operations in Tamaulipas, his probable continued complacency would most likely have vindicated Huerta's strategy. However, the Federals in Tamaulipas had never received orders to mass for operations, essentially signaling an acceptance of Blanco's virtual cease-fire and leaving Ciudad Victoria and Tampico vulnerable once Pablo González began his drive southward, which allowed him to put his Constitutionalists in an advantageous position, with superior numbers and their supply lines close by. In response, the Federals had to scramble to try to save the region, first sending the only available troops from the Division of the Nazas under Peña and later Rubio's column of raw recruits just arriving to the Division of the Bravo, which had to limit its pursuit owing to the approach from the west by Robles and Gómez and other Constitutionalist forces in the Saltillo-Monterrey area. In short, the Tamaulipas campaign reflected the interdependence of actions, considerations, and decisions reflective of the emerging sophistication and complexity of operations not just theater-wide in the Northeast, but also among various theaters, such as the North, Center, and Northeast, as well as internationally. General González was the first Constitutionalist to demonstrate that the revolutionaries could formulate a campaign against professional soldiers over hundreds of kilometers and multiple axes of advance and still prevail.

The Federals, meanwhile, continued to conduct warfare in different theaters in a manner that tellingly mirrored one another on a tactical and strategic level. At Topo Chico, Iberri sent out Brigadier Quiroga with a mission and outcome eerily similar to Alvírez's at Second Torreón, doling out artillery to a small and vulnerable column that could not help but experience defeat in the field, virtually offering up the field pieces as a gift to the Constitutionalists. On a grander scale, Federal strategy looked very similar—exposing smaller commands to opposing forces that outnumbered and easily overwhelmed them, turning them into so much sacrifice placed upon the altar of the fatherland. Federal strategy will be discussed in detail in Chapter 9.

As the Federal Army continued to mobilize, and the Constitutionalist Army made the transition from an all-volunteer force toward regularization, common deficiencies in terms of training, loyalty, ambition, and discipline had an impact on operations. Nowhere is the lack of training more evident than with Rubio's column of raw recruits: they had not even handled a weapon before and did not have sufficient officers or non-commissioned officers to lead them. Yet the Constitutionalists' inability to cut off and destroy the Federals at Santa Engracia demonstrated that the brigade commanders of the Division of the Northeast, and especially Villarreal, still had a way to go in their professional development, while also revealing the excellent leadership qualities of General Rubio. Nonetheless, the Federal Army persisted in a dearth of qualified commanders, especially at command levels where inexperienced irregulars sometimes performed worse than their citizen-soldier counterparts in the Constitutionalist Army. For example, González and his subalterns defeated the Irregular Brigadier Quiroga and his column made up largely of Federal regulars, mostly because of Quiroga's faulty disposition, but also because of a lack of discipline among his irregulars. Untrained, untested, and unmotivated conscripts and irregular forces continued to be the leading systemic vulnerability for the Federals, as witnessed in the Battle of Ciudad Victoria.

In contrast, the disciplinary problems among the Constitutionalists had less to do with a sense of purpose and combat experience and more with behavioral defects, especially with regards to drinking during the battle of Monterrey and the subsequent sacking of Montemorelos. Additionally, Fortunato Zuazua's refusal to enter into combat provides an unusual testimony; Manuel W. González, the staff officer who disclosed the episode, also affirmed that at that point in time the Constitutionalists did not have, nor even profess to have, regular discipline. It also reminds us that though many regular officers are fond of saying that they would never give a subordinate a mission that they themselves would not carry out, only in a volunteer army can that claim be tested, as witnessed by Zuazua's commander, Colonel Ricaut, having to complete the mission that Zuazua declined to accept.

Personnel issues reached to the highest levels in both the Federal and the Constitutionalist armies during the fall campaign in the Northeast and resulted in several brigade commanders being disciplined. Huerta recalled Rubio over suspicions about his loyalty when he exercised the initiative to move south and try to save Monterrey in contravention of orders given to his division commander, Téllez. On the other side, Blanco's inactivity and refusal to heed orders to participate in the Monterrey campaign obeyed his personal ambitions, not ideological differences with the First Chief over land redistribution, and certainly not Blanco's attention to military exigencies. Similarly, Jesús Agustín Castro's brigade had to be disarmed after the Battle of Ciudad Victoria, because Castro persisted in trying to set his own agenda instead of indicating a willingness to participate in the upcoming operations of the Division of the Northeast. Humble and patient officers like Cesáreo Castro and Ricaut, who responded magnanimously to the promotions at Montemorelos and would retire later to private life and die peacefully, were in the minority to the more ambitious, like Murguía and Blanco, who tended to die a violent death, either in combat or in the periodic uprisings and purges of the 1920s. The problems created by the latter two, and other unruly generals would persist and become an acute problem for the Division of the Northeast during the winter of 1914, retarding operations.

Eight

Baja California—Garbanzos and Empalme— Riveros, Iturbe, and
San Blas—A Failed Federal Amphibious Pincer—Hill's Column—
Carranza's Speech—Obregón's Promotion—Felipe Ángeles
Arrives—Los Mochis—Sinaloa de Leyva—Battle of Culiacán—
Gustavo Garmendia—El Potrero—Siege of Mazatlán—The
Constitutionalist Year-End Strategy—Blanco Brigade Obstinacy—
Tampico—Federico Montes—Francisco Múgica's Failed Mission—
Nuevo Laredo—Operating in the Northeast

Sonora

During the last half of July 1913, General Obregón concerned himself with purely political matters surrounding the return of Governor
Maytorena to Mexican soil and the turmoil that his presence caused the
Constitutionalist Army. Eventually, and grudgingly, he accepted the legality
of Maytorena's claim to office. Returning to military matters Obregón dealt
with operations into Sinaloa hampered by the awful state of the rails and a
dearth of rolling stock belonging to the Kansas City-Mexico & Orient line.
He also ordered a short expedition on August 18 of about forty men and
officers under Colonel Luis S. Hernández to invade Baja California to try
to spread the revolution. This expedition virtually disintegrated in its trajectory due to inhospitable terrain and stiff Huertista opposition, with only

Hernández, his Lieutenant Colonel Melchor T. Vela, and a handful of soldiers making it back alive to Sonora.[1]

THE FEDERAL COUNTERATTACK

Federal General Pedro Ojeda also took a month off from military operations after the last significant combat in July in order to recuperate inside Guaymas before deciding to attack the Constitutionalists. He had heard that they were laying railroad tracks to link Tres Gitos Station to Cruz de Piedra and bypass Empalme, where they were subject to fire from the Federal gunboats and artillery in and around Guaymas. "Also, it seems it was one of the objectives of the enemy to ensure the transport of garbanzo harvests from the Yaqui and Mayo [Valleys] to Nogales and thus obtain a good quantity of money," in the words of General Ojeda. In order to push back the siege lines, take possession of Empalme, cut off the revolutionaries in the north from those to the south, and deny access to the garbanzo harvest in the Yaqui and Mayo river valleys to the Constitutionalists, Federal General Ojeda developed a plan of attack for his division. In order to carry it off, he had 3,600 men at his disposal, including about 1,500 men in the 1st Infantry Brigade, an artillery brigade composed of sixteen field guns and four machine guns, and the 3rd Infantry Brigade, which consisted of another 1,500 men. The plan was simple enough. General Luis Medina Barrón leading the 1st Infantry Brigade would demonstrate against La Calera and El Prieto Hills on the Constitutionalist right wing with the ultimate objective being to take Batamotal Pass, through which the railroad leads from Empalme to the north. Meanwhile, General Ojeda would load up the 3rd Infantry Brigade on trains and direct an assault in depth against the town of Empalme proper and the hills to the north of the town.[2]

At 5:30 a.m. on August 24, General Ojeda's men loaded into railcars and traveled across the Lagoon of El Ranchero to Empalme where the 10th Battalion immediately disembarked under fire and attacked the Constitutionalists arrayed along the embankment, pushing them back through the town in the direction of La Bomba as Constitutionalists poured in fire on the 10th from the hills to the north that dominate Empalme. The 14th Battalion came up to occupy the ground already conquered by the 10th, allowing the latter battalion, reinforced by the 28th Battalion and under covering fire from a section of 70-mm. Mondragón mountain guns and a battery of Madsen and Rexer machine guns, to turn its attention to the hills.[3]

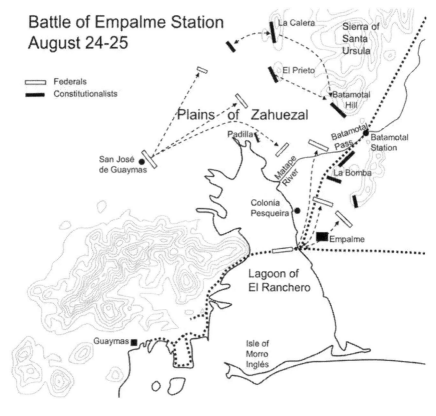

Battle of Empalme Station
August 24-25

☐ Federals
▬ Constitutionalists

La Calera

Sierra of
Santa
Ursula

El Prieto

Batamotal
Hill

Plains of Zahuezal

Padilla

Batamotal
Pass

Batamotal
Station

San José
de Guaymas

Matape River

La Bomba

Colonia
Pesqueira

Empalme

Lagoon of
El Ranchero

Guaymas

Isle of
Morro
Inglés

Map 1.23

As General Ojeda attacked Empalme from the west, General Medina
Barrón led his troops in the feint against the Constitutionalist right wing.
Federal First Captain Francisco Padilla's battery began laying down prepa-
ratory fire against the crests of La Calera and El Prieto, twice displacing for
maximum effectiveness, while the battery commanded by First Captain
Moisés Ramos remained in protective oversight. At the appointed hour
Medina Barrón's men departed San José de Guaymas and attacked along
a broad front extending from the hills north of Empalme to Batamotal
Pass and to the western side of the Sierra of Santa Ursula between Tres
Gitos and Peña Volada canyons, and most especially El Prieto Hill where
the Constitutionalists were dug in. As the Constitutionalists occupying
the forward slopes of La Calera and Presidio hills attempted to outflank
Medina Barrón's left and make for San José de Guaymas to cut him off,

Medina Barrón had to send a small cavalry force under Major Rafael A. Toledo supported by one hundred infantrymen of the 27th Battalion under Lieutenant Colonel Gilberto Rojas to hold them back. At the same time, he sent a smattering of commands that totaled about 250 men from four different units in the vanguard against the Constitutionalist positions covering a front extending from Colonia Pesqueira to the houses of Batamotal Station. Under the cover of artillery fire, Medina Barrón's Federals succeeded in finally taking El Prieto and repulsing all attempts to outflank him, but at the end of the first day of combat the Constitutionalists still held the hills of Batamotal and La Bomba.[4]

In the morning of August 25 First Captain Ramos' battery was taken back to Guaymas and brought up to Empalme by rail as Captain Padilla moved into Ramos' position on the northern edge of the Lagoon of El Ranchero to support the assault against Batamotal and La Bomba hills. After the artillery preparation, the 28th and Sierra Juárez Auxiliary battalions scaled the hills to the north of Empalme in an assault, taking them by 5:30 p.m., while the 14th continued fighting the Constitutionalists occupying La Bomba, dislodging them from there upon nightfall. The 27th and 28th Battalions, with a detachment from the 50th Infantry, also assaulted the western side of Batamotal under the protection of fire coming from Padilla's artillery, succeeding in taking the hill as the Federal cavalry continued to patrol to the north of San José de Guaymas, protecting the Federal left, while gunboat artillery covered the right, even turning back a Constitutionalist train coming up from the south. The effect of a successful battle against the Constitutionalists had a positive effect on moral for the Federal soldiers, but it would not last long.[5]

While the Federals continued to hold the ground around Empalme, several encounters with the Constitutionalists continued to take place in the vicinity throughout September and October without the Constitutionalists succeeding in taking the point back, but also without Ojeda being able to break out. Toward the end of December Ojeda began to report a swift drop-off in morale, mainly due to the lack of pay, and some of the irregulars and even Permanent officers began to desert, something that Ojeda blamed on "provincialism" and family ties.[6]

Sinaloa

After losing Empalme, and the stalemate that ensued, the Constitutionalist leadership in the Northwest turned its attention from Sonora to northern Sinaloa and the Topolobampo-San Blas-El Fuerte stretch of the Kansas City-Mexico & Orient Railroad, which ran parallel to the state line. San Blas was the Constitutionalist nerve center in Sinaloa, where Governor Felipe Riveros and General Ramón F. Iturbe had established the state government and the Sinaloa Brigade's headquarters, respectively. Riveros had originally recognized Huerta, but the dictator threw him in jail anyway. Upon his subsequent release the governor denounced Huerta's government and escaped to reach Sinaloa in July where, as the constitutionally elected Governor of Sinaloa, he succeeding in gaining approval from the First Chief to join the Constitutionalist movement. Iturbe, similarly, had only recently returned from the United States in June, interrupting his engineering studies to take command of the revolutionary forces in Sinaloa. During the months of July and August the Constitutionalists battled Colonel Miguel Rodríguez's Federals in and around the plaza of Sinaloa de Leyva, the Federal Division of the Yaqui's far northern position in the state, with little consequence. At the end of August, however, Federal General Reynaldo Díaz of the 2nd Brigade, Division of the Yaqui (and military governor of Sinaloa state with headquarters in Mazatlán), ordered a pincer movement against the Constitutionalists in the north.[7] For the time being, Iturbe would have to confront the Federals without Obregón, who was still attending to logistical matters.[8]

THE FEDERAL AMPHIBIOUS PINCER

Federal Lieutenant Colonel Teodoro Valdivieso boarded the *Tampico* gunboat in Mazatlán with 300 men from the 10th Cavalry Regiment, 8th Infantry Battalion, and some volunteer corps and set sail for Topolobampo, Sinaloa, with plans to move inland by rail to San Blas; he would be supported by Colonel Miguel Rodríguez's larger command advancing simultaneously from Sinaloa de Leyva. Colonel Valdivieso's force arrived in Topolobampo on August 27 without incident, but the next day his column encountered stiff opposition. General Iturbe personally directed the effort to drive the Federals back into the sea, but after two days of fighting he could not dislodge Valdivieso and had to withdraw to Los Mochis taking with him some sixty-six Federal volunteers who had defected to the Constitutionalist Army. Nevertheless, the Federal offensive stalled because Colonel Valdivieso received a mortal wound in the fighting of August 29, was evacuated with the wounded to Mazatlán on September 2, and died a few weeks later.[9]

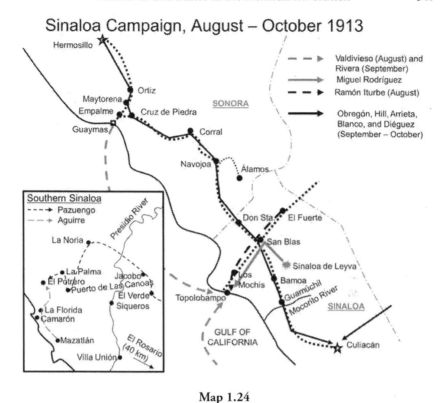

Map 1.24

Colonel Rodríguez's command fared no better. He departed Sinaloa de Leyva the same day that Valdivieso landed in Topolobampo traveling north at the head of two columns: the first under his own direction composed of about 260 men from the 8th Infantry Battalion and 10th Rural Corps taking the direct road, and the other by rail under Major Antonio Olague with about 250 men also from the 8th Infantry and 10th Rurales, Voluntarios de Sinaloa, a section of machine guns, and artillery. Rodríguez reached the San Blas rail station where he engaged the advance Constitutionalist force, easily pushing them back, but when he sent a messenger to learn the whereabouts of Major Olague, he received the disturbing news that Olague had been killed and his demoralized troops had scattered despite the best efforts of the major's subalterns to rally them. The remnants of Olague's command returned to Sinaloa de Leyva, while Rodríguez continued on to Topolobampo, linking up with Valdivieso's command at the beginning of September without encountering any more Constitutionalists along the way.[10]

CONSTITUTIONALIST OFFENSIVE IN SINALOA

Not yet disposed to yield the line, the Division of the Yaqui's commander, Ojeda, sent another Federal amphibious column commanded by Colonel Heriberto Rivera to sail from Guaymas to Topolobampo and complete Valdivieso's mission to destroy the Constitutionalists in San Blas. Rivera brought about 350 men, including a section of 80-mm. guns, to join General Miguel Rodríguez, who had been recently promoted for his actions defending Sinaloa de Leyva back in August. For his part, Obregón had also decided to move into Sinaloa with hopes of taking some of the Federal-held ports there that had been serving as supply bases for the besieged Federal garrison of Guaymas, intending to convert them to Constitutionalist use and be in a position to import supplies from California. When he learned of Rivera's mission and received reports from one of Carranza's assistants, Alfredo Breceda, of the First Chief's eminent arrival in northern Sinaloa, Obregón immediately ordered a column of six hundred men commanded by Colonel Benjamín G. Hill to march south from Sonora and reinforce the plaza of San Blas.[11]

Hill got underway at the beginning of September with Obregón traveling along so he could meet with the First Chief. Delayed by rainy weather, they did not arrive in San Blas until September 13. The next day Obregón left for El Fuerte where, along with General Iturbe, Colonel Hill, and Sr. Adolfo de la Huerta of Sonora, he met Carranza and his staff. After spending several days in San Blas, Carranza's staff and 150-man escort departed for Hermosillo on September 17, accompanied by Obregón the entire way. At the time most of the Sonoran troops were still in and around Maytorena Station, well-positioned to ensure the First Chief's safety as he passed by Guaymas. Upon his arrival in the Sonoran capital, Governor Maytorena gave the First Chief the keys to the city. In turn, Carranza delivered a speech from the balcony of the statehouse on September 24 where for the first time he mentioned the need for a new Constitution, offered a glimpse into what would become known as the Carranza Doctrine, proposed an overhaul of the banking system, and conferred upon Obregón the title of Commander of the Army Corps of the Northwest with responsibility for operations in Sonora, Sinaloa, Chihuahua, Durango, and Baja California. The crowd received the announcement with proud applause, but Pancho Villa, who was just now beginning to campaign in Chihuahua, reacted quite the opposite upon learning that he had just been made a subordinate of Obregón's.[12]

A few days later General Felipe Ángeles, who had been on commission in Europe for the Federal Army, finally decided to join the revolution and reported to Carranza in Sonora to join the Constitutionalist Army. Around this same time, between the twenty-second and twenty-fifth of September, Colonel Hill victoriously led his column in combat against Colonel Heriberto Rivera's Federals at Los Mochis, dislodging them, capturing their two field pieces, and forcing them back to Topolobampo where Colonel José María R. Cabanillas with about 300 men belonging to Iturbe's forces also attacked them. Immediately thereafter, General Rodríguez embarked all his Federals on the *Morelos* and head for Mazatlán, either due to Rivera's defeat, or because General Reynaldo Díaz had become concerned about the growing presence of revolutionaries between Mazatlán and Culiacán, where Constitutionalist Colonel Juan Carrasco and others operated. The evacuation of Topolobampo, however, left Sinaloa de Leyva as the forward-most plaza and, since a mere four hundred Federals defended it, vulnerable. On October 5 after three days of heavy fighting, General Hill (just promoted for Los Mochis) and Colonels Macario Gaxiola, José Cabanillas and Claro G. Molina captured Sinaloa de Leyva. Obregón met Ángeles briefly and then returned to Sinaloa to participate in operations to capture Culiacán, the next major objective, bringing with him Manuel M. Diéguez's column and one hundred men of the 4th Battalion of Sonora.[13]

Obregón's trains reached Bamoa on October 24. Traveling to the nearby plaza of Sinaloa he met up with Hill and Iturbe and assumed command of the combined forces of Sonora and Sinaloa states, with Iturbe serving as his second-in-command. The column then proceeded southwards, but upon reaching Guamúchil, where the Federals had burned the large bridge over the Mocorito River, Obregón received a telegram from Carranza notifying him of Ángeles' appointment to Secretary of War, effectively making the ex-Federal his boss. He caught a train back to Hermosillo to personally present his objections. Ostensibly, Obregón and his chief lieutenants in the Army Corps of the Northwest doubted Ángeles' revolutionary élan. Diéguez and Hill had even gone so far as to present their resignations. Obregón insisted that there was nothing personal in his protest, and as proof he pointed out that he had remained subordinate to Governor Maytorena upon the latter's return from self-exile because he was the constitutionally-elected governor, even though he considered Maytorena a coward. Carranza listened and then assured Obregón that Ángeles' role would be limited, and all orders would emanate from the First Chieftaincy. Satisfied with the First Chief's reassurances, the caudillo of Huatabampo promised to assuage his own underlings' fears and left to direct the operations against Culiacán.[14]

BATTLE OF CULIACÁN, NOVEMBER 12-14

Obregón arrived back in Sinaloa and ordered Diéguez's column to continue south along the rails. He sent the Sinaloa regiments and Hill's column south separately as well. The going was slow because of the condition of the rails, burned bridges, and the necessary reconnaissance missions. Constitutionalist General Mariano Arrieta had also crossed over from Durango State with his men to participate in the taking of Culiacán, coming in close proximity to the plaza where Obregón ordered him to await further instructions. On November 4, General José de la Luz Blanco in charge of the 3rd Regiment of Sinaloa took Navolato after two hours of combat, killing eleven Federals and taking twenty-three prisoners, and then proceeded to repair the rails toward the port of Altata in order for the Constitutionalists to receive supplies. Two days later Obregón arrived at Palmito, one kilometer distant from Culiacán, and ordered Lieutenant Colonel Antonio A. Guerrero and Second Captain Aarón Sáenz of his staff to reconnoiter the Federal dispositions for the defense. General Arrieta appeared at Obregón's headquarters and reported that his men on the east side of the plaza were ready to attack and then returned to his command with 31,000 rounds of sorely needed ammunition.[15]

Tactical Command	Major Unit organic to	J	O	T	Total
Federals:					
Argüelles, Casto (LTC)	8th Infantry Regiment	1	8	377	386
Chávez, Antonio (1st CPT)	10th Cavalry Regiment		2	117	119
Del Villar, Manuel (LTC)	12th Infantry Battalion	1	6	178	185
Rivera, Heriberto (Colonel)	53rd Auxiliary Infantry Battalion	1	6	151	158
Ramírez Alcérreca, Manuel (1st CPT)	4th Artillery Regiment		2	43	45
Mendoza, Faustino (LT)	5th Artillery Regiment		1	19	20
Villaseñor, Cástulo (1st CPT)	"General Rosales" Company		1	45	46
Cárdenas, Cipriano (Corporal)	Voluntarios de Cosalá		3	16	19
Alonso, Cipriano (First Officer)	Guerrilla Alonso		2	31	33
Mendoza, Francisco (1st CPT)	Guerrilla Mendoza		3	71	74
			14	164	178
					1,263
Constitutionalists (estimated):					
Center					
Gaxiola, Macario (Colonel)	1st Regiment of Sinaloa				300
Meztas, Manuel (Colonel)	2nd Regiment of Sinaloa				300
Blanco, José de la Luz (Brigadier)	3rd Regiment of Sinaloa				300
Manzo, Francisco R. (Major)	4th Battalion of Sonora				100
Arrieta, Mariano (Brigadier)					800
Hill, Benjamín (Brigadier)					600
Diéguez, Manuel (Brigadier)					600
					3,000

Table 1.13 Battle of Culiacán Troop Strengths

Obregón established his headquarters only one thousand meters from the main Federal fortifications and about three kilometers away from the Federal artillery. He located an elevation that dominated the town and the chapel of Guadalupe, the most prominent feature on the Federals' main battle line, to emplace his artillery and arrayed Diéguez's men from north to south overlooking the plaza. On November 7 Obregón continued to consult his principal subalterns and order more reconnaissance of the Federal works, but in the evening of the following day he drafted his final orders in the presence of Governor/General Felipe Riveros; Generals Iturbe, Diéguez, and Hill; and Colonels Claro G. Molina, Macario Gaxiola (1st Regiment of Sinaloa), and Manuel Meztas (2nd Regiment of Sinaloa). At 4 a.m. on November 10 General Arrieta would attack from the east with his Duranguenses, less three hundred men whom he detailed to Diéguez's column; General Hill was to advance against the Federals on a line along the Southern Pacific Railroad that ran the length of the west side of the plaza. Diéguez's infantry would deliver the main assault against the Heights of Culiacán shortly after daybreak and subsequent to a Constitutionalist artillery barrage directed at the chapel of Guadalupe. Colonel Gaxiola, commanding dismounted dragoons from the 1st, 2nd, and 3rd Regiments of Sinaloa, would prepare to support Diéguez by attacking the Occidental Railroad on the southwest side of the plaza with the intention of interrupting Federal traffic between the city proper and the chapel of Guadalupe on the hills to the south; General Blanco would remain in reserve with mounted elements of the 1st, 2nd, and 3rd Regiments of Sinaloa. Two 70-mm. mountain guns and two 75-mm. field guns remained near Palmito Station to support the assault. Obregón probably had about 3,000 men total under his command.[16]

Brigadier Miguel Rodríguez commanded the Federals defending the state capital of Sinaloa, mostly regulars numbering roughly thirteen hundred men of the three combat arms from the 8th Infantry Regiment, 12th Infantry Battalion, 53rd Auxiliary Infantry Battalion, 10th Cavalry Regiment, and 4th and 5th Artillery Regiments, along with about another 125 irregulars belonging to various Guerrillas. He organized his defense into four sectors covering the cardinal directions: the first sector to the east under Lieutenant Colonel Casto Argüelles and men from the 8th Infantry Regiment; the second sector at the command of Lieutenant Colonel Manuel del Villar defending the north with the 12th Infantry; and the third, western sector under Colonel Heriberto Rivera with the 53rd Auxiliary and an extra company. Each sector consisted of about two to three hundred men. In the fourth sector, to the south, Second Captain Crispiano Anzaldo with about one hundred volunteers and soldiers from 8th Regiment occupied a series of seven fortifications on the heights of Culiacán to provide protection for the artillery pieces, which remained far enough behind the line of defense to prevent their easy capture. Rodríguez held the remainder of his troops in reserve and ready to respond to any point of vulnerability along his seven-kilometer-long perimeter. He faced an opposing force approximately twice as numerous as his own.[17]

The day before the planned attack two events took place that postponed the battle. First, on the morning of November 9 around 9:30 a.m. a Federal patrol of about 150 men probing through the dense thicket got lost and ran across a Constitutionalist position and opened fire in close, at times hand-to-hand, combat. Upon breaking contact to try to return to the plaza they happened upon two of Obregón's cannons without infantry support and succeeded in removing the breechblocks of the guns. The Federals then tried to do the same to two more pieces located nearby, but had to retreat due to the prompt arrival of Constitutionalists under Colonel Meztas. Obregón had been close enough to observe the incident and even took a bullet to the leg, which did not cause much damage since, he surmised, it was a ricochet. In response to this breach in security, Obregón ordered the commander of the 4th Infantry Battalion of Sonora, Lieutenant Colonel Francisco Manzo, to form a firing line in front of the houses of Palmito, thus extending Hill's right to tie off with Meztas and Gaxiola's men, when he received the second bit of bad news. The Federal gunboat *Morelos* had been spotted near Altata trying to unload reinforcements to come to the aid of the besieged capital city, forcing Obregón to call off the impending attack as he sent Blanco to hinder, but not engage, the Federal advance.[18]

The Federals at Altata consisted of a portion of the 2nd Sapper Battalion commanded by Major Agustín Mora arriving aboard the *Morelos*. Mora was joined by about one hundred Federals from the 8th Infantry Regiment who had been in Altata on an earlier mission to "regularize" rail traffic along the coast, but they had been forced to cross the bay to the Peninsula of Redo after General Blanco attacked Navolato back on November 4. With a few blasts from the *Morelos'* cannons Mora landed a detachment to make a reconnaissance, but finding no Constitutionalists he had his men load back onto the gunboat and made his way down to Boca del Río at the mouth of the Culiacán River as Blanco and his men continued to repair the bridge at Limoncito in order to bring in much needed supplies. On November 12 Mora again landed a small party, this time with a machine gun, to get news—any news—of the Culiacán garrison. Constitutionalist captains Candelario Ortiz and Tiburcio Morales with about eighty dragoons from Blanco's command engaged the

Federals and forced them back on board. On November 13 the *Morelos* set sail for Mazatlán.[19]

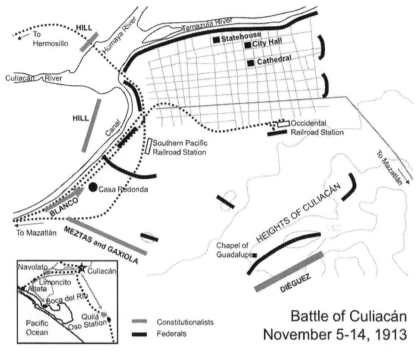

Map 1.25

As Blanco attended to the Federals at Altata, Obregón ordered General Arrieta to leave five hundred of his men on the east side of Culiacán and report with the rest of his men to Palmito to replace Blanco. At 5 a.m. on November 12, the Constitutionalists finally attacked Culiacán. Blanco's men arrived aboard a military train, and Obregón ordered them to advance still aboard the train until reaching the section house covered by Meztas' men where they were to detrain. Because of a lack of water for steam, the train could not pull back after delivering the troops railborne until 11 a.m., all the while taking copious fire and incurring some casualties among those aboard. The Constitutionalist artillery provided some protective fire, and all sectors realized some success in taking control of the trenches before them: Gaxiola and Meztas occupied the Casa Redonda fort on the west side of the town and to their left Lieutenant Colonel Félix's men took their positions at La Bomba, on the railway, as Lieutenant Colonel Antúnez dislodged the Federals from the side of the canal and at La Ladrillera, occupying that ground. The Constitutionalists did not having any luck dislodging the opposing force on the bridge side of the line. On the Constitutionalist right, General Diéguez ordered the 4th Battalion of Sonora to attack the Federal fort in front of the chapel and the 5th to take the main fort, also near the chapel, where Lieutenant Colonel Gustavo Garmendia lost his life.[20]

Garmendia was an ex-Federal and alumnus of the Colegio Militar who graduated as a Technical of artillery. He had joined the revolution in November after deserting from the Federal Army and making his way to Sonora via Cuba and the southern United States. An honorable officer and no praetorian, he had risked his life personally defending Madero during the palace coup in February. While leading the 5th Battalion assaulting the Federals defending the Chapel sector, Garmendia ordered his men to deploy and advance when a soft-nosed bullet ripped open the femoral artery in his left thigh. He had already lost too much blood before a tourniquet was applied to his leg, and he expired before he could be taken to the aid station, facing death with a stoicism that impressed all who witnessed it.[21]

In the afternoon the Constitutionalist artillery displaced from the Palmito section house to where Hill's men were, and began blowing holes in the armored railcars that the Federals had placed on the Southern Pacific line and intermittently firing on the enemy positions at the chapel. Garmendia's 5th took the main fort, but at around 4 p.m. numerous Federals launched a surprise counterattack, retaking the position. Apparently, the Constitutionalists had gone for water and food leaving the fort somewhat short of defenders. Nevertheless, the interim commander of the 5th, Major Esteban B. Calderón, fought tenaciously and was even wounded in an eye before having to retreat. The 4th continued battling fiercely to dislodge the Federals from the fort to their front. Diéguez sent the Voluntarios de Cananea Corps to reinforce them, but in the afternoon they had to withdraw to their camp due to a lack of ammunition. The Federals counterattacked several times during the night, especially against Gaxiola, Meztas, and Blanco, who had taken the positions running from the chapel to the Casa Redonda and the railroad, and Félix and Antúnez of Hill's command, who were occupying the line from the Casa Redonda up to La Bomba and the canal. The Constitutionalists on the west and southwest side refused to yield one inch. Also during the night, Diéguez's men from Cananea, employing dynamite as bombs, conquered the fort that the 4th had been assaulting earlier while being shelled by the Federal artillery emplaced at the chapel and taking rifle fire as well.[22]

On November 13 the Constitutionalists and Federals continued to direct artillery fire at each other, and that night the 5th Battalion finally recaptured the fort that it had previously held. Colonel Laveaga's men then took the place of Antúnez's men to give them a rest, while Arrieta's men reinforced the center, thus providing protection to the Constitutionalists in and around the Casa Redonda. The Federal attacks during the night became very pronounced, with intermittent periods of extremely heavy rifle and machine gun fire until around 2 a.m. on November 14, when the Federals began to abandon the plaza to the southeast. The Constitutionalists moved in and occupied the empty Federal positions and then began entering the plaza, with men from Blanco's command arriving first. Obregón ordered Blanco's cavalry to Limoncito to the west, where they had their horses, to keep any Federals from trying to board the *Morelos* and escape by sea, and he sent a message to General Juan Carrasco, who was besieging Mazatlán, to be on the lookout for any Federals from the Culiacán garrison coming his way. Diéguez also boarded trains with one thousand infantrymen to pursue the Federals by rail to the south, and Arrieta's dragoons chased after the retreating Federals along the highway.[23]

Diéguez caught up to the retreating Federals at Quilá where the railroad passes over the San Lorenzo River and entered into combat, but when the Federals disengaged he could not continue the pursuit because his men were too exhausted, so his infantry remained at Oso Station. Neither could Arrieta, whose horses were too worn out, continue on past Quilá. Blanco, however, caught the Federals at San Dimas, ninety kilometers south of Quilá and four kilometers from Las Barras on the coast, on November 20 where he fought for a brief two hours, but inexplicably made no further efforts over the next two days to prevent the Federals from embarking on ships that had been sent to collect them and escaping. The Federals could not make it all the way to Mazatlán by land and had to exfiltrate by sea because that port city was under attack by Constitutionalist Colonel Juan Carrasco, following orders that he had received from Obregón. After the last Federal had loaded onto the ships, Blanco returned to Culiacán. Obregón was upset: he had been unable to locate Blanco for three days after the battle, since he only showed up at Quilá on the seventeenth, and then watched for two days as the Federals embarked and departed from San Dimas. Although it may be mere speculation, it is possible that Blanco, who had campaigned with Obregón under General Agustín Sanginés the previous year when Blanco was a general and Obregón a lieutenant colonel, resented now having to take orders from Obregón. Shortly thereafter Blanco was sent to the United States "on commission" and did not again take an active military role in the revolution. Obregón reported Federal casualties at 150 dead and 100 prisoners and listed his own at one jefe, five officers, and thirty men killed, with two jefes, four officers, and seventy-five men wounded.[24]

SOUTHERN SINALOA

At the beginning of October 1913 Colonel Carrasco had established his headquarters at Rancho del Potrero (fifteen kilometers north of Mazatlán) in order to keep the Federals bottled up in Mazatlán with the exception of a small corridor to Siqueros. In the words of Colonel Matías Pazuengo, who belonged to Domingo Arrieta's brigade and had crossed over from neighboring Durango State into Sinaloa in order to operate with Carrasco, "This jefe, who in the whole state has distinguished himself by his military talent and courage was able to completely defeat the enemy four times and force the few who were in Siqueros to concentrate in Mazatlán." In the same time frame, Colonel Rafael Buelna defeated the Federals in El Rosario and forced the remainder back to Acaponeta in the Territory of Tepic.[25] The Federals could not suffer the defeats inflicted by General Carrasco and so Federal General Alberto T. Rasgado, who had replaced Brigadier Reynaldo Díaz as the commander of Federal forces in Mazatlán, decided to send out a column of eight hundred men under the command of Brigadier Abraham R. Aguirre to attack Carrasco's headquarters at El Potrero. The Federals trusted fully in the possibilities of success, since they had quite a few Huertista volunteers with them who led the vanguard while Miguel Rodríguez was in the rear with his Federals and two artillery pieces.[26]

Aguirre's column departed Mazatlán at 6 a.m. on October 22 headed north along the coast road in order to hide its movements and maintained a dilatory rate of advance, reaching only as far as La Florida by the following night after engaging in a short skirmish with a Constitutionalist scout patrol at kilometer 756 of the Southern Pacific Railroad. At 5 a.m. on October 24 the Federals again got underway headed toward Puerto de las Canoas. After a few kilometers they happened upon a road that led directly to El Potrero, which they took. By eleven o'clock they had reached a hamlet called Conchi where Aguirre had his men stop so he could plan his attack on El Potrero: he ordered Colonel Francisco Reynosa to take his 34th Auxiliary Infantry Battalion and those of the 2nd Sapper Battalion, a total of about five hundred men supported by the column's two mountain guns, to attack Huarache Hill, which was defended by some six hundred Constitutionalists, while Aguirre remained with the rest of the column in Conchi.[27]

Reynosa sent in the 1st Company of Sappers to attack the hill, but he could not dislodge the Constitutionalists, so he threw the 2nd Company into the fight and succeeded in pushing Carrasco's men off the hill. Simultaneously, Reynosa sent the 3rd Company of Sappers against the other dominant terrain feature, Potrero Hill, which he likewise had to reinforce with the 4th Company. Just as Carrasco was about to yield the field, Colonel Pazuengo arrived with his Constitutionalists. In effect, upon learning of the mobilization of the Federals, Pazuengo had gotten his seven hundred men, fully armed and mounted, to take a course for Situala, El Verde, Jacobo, Puerto de la Canoas, La Noria, and La Palma, arriving to link up with Carrasco as he was battling the Federals. The two colonels agreed to make an end-around to the west and hit the Federal rearguard, composed of one hundred infantrymen from the 34th Battalion and eighty cavalrymen of the 10th Regiment commanded by Major Emilio Querol y Gómez.[28]

The Constitutionalists began their movement through the mountains on the coast. Around 4 p.m., more or less, they were able to reach about one hundred meters from the Federal rear and then opened up with punishing fire. Facing such an overwhelming force, Major Querol's command fled after less than an hour and a half of combat, leaving behind one of the mountain guns with ammunition and tack for the livestock—because the artillery's infantry support from the 8th Regiment did not do its job—not to mention their dead and wounded and some weapons scattered in the mountains that they had neglected to collect in their precipitous flight. Faced with this defeat, Brigadier Aguirre gathered all his troops in Conchi and started his return trip to Mazatlán, with Querol again commanding the rearguard. About two hours later the Constitutionalists decided to see if it was possible to cut off the Federal retreat at a place called Camarón, but Pazuengo's men were too exhausted from fighting and marching and did not arrive in time.[29] At least that was Pazuengo's version of events.

Aguirre contradicted what Pazuengo said, maintaining that the Constitutionalists did catch up to and again attack the rearguard, whereupon they captured the Federals' other mountain gun before Aguirre mounted a spirited counterattack that succeeded in recovering the piece. Aguirre's testimony, however, seems very suspect on several accounts, especially his claim that he fought against 3,500 revolutionaries and inflicted 235 casualties upon them in nine hours of combat while only firing off 5,000 rifle rounds and 43 artillery shells and losing 18 killed, 13 wounded, and 43 dispersed in the attack.[30]

In the morning the Constitutionalists followed after the Federals finding carbines and ammunition in the place where the Huertistas had camped during the night. By the following day they were back in El Potrero, where they agreed that Pazuengo would establish his headquarters in Villa Unión and Juan Carrasco would locate his at El Venadillo, a mere four kilometers north of Mazatlán, because Buelna had already mentioned his intentions to head south to campaign in Tepic. That meant that Pazuengo and Carrasco would have to take over covering the points that kept the Federals bottled up in Mazatlán.[31]

From November to January in 1914 the opposing forces remained in these positions with the Federals only occasionally sallying forth to skirmish with the advance Constitutionalist positions around the port. The Constitutionalists reciprocated by attacking the railroad station and exchanging gunfire with the Federals who were dug in at Loma Atravesada and at the Casa Redonda. Around this time the First Chief promoted Carrasco to the rank of brigadier, effective October 26, for his part in the combat at El Potrero, and conferred the same rank upon Buelna, who had left to campaign in Tepic.[32] With the whole of the state of Sinaloa in Constitutionalist hands except for Mazatlán, Obregón went back to Hermosillo to begin preparing for his upcoming western campaign against Mexico City. He had logistical matters that needed tending.[33]

In his memoirs Obregón complained that the procurement of ammunition from the United States "had been made extremely difficult, due to the strict vigilance that the American guards exercised over the international line to halt the passage of war materiel to the Mexican side." In addition, the Federals in Guaymas continued sallying in the direction of Hermosillo, resulting in frequent clashes, and they blocked the rail line to the south at Empalme station. While the Constitutionalists had sufficient rolling stock north of Empalme, they were short of it to the south, meaning they had difficulty transporting assets southward for operations into Sinaloa and beyond. So, they continued to besiege Mazatlán and Tepic and proposed building a bypass of fourteen kilometers from Maytorena Station to Cruz de Piedra station in order to transfer rolling stock south, but they lacked the materials for this endeavor. Then, J. Lorenzo Gutiérrez, Obregón's chief of military trains, proposed moving trains southward by disassembling track from up north and then laying it down in sections, moving the trains forward, and then taking up the track to the rear of the convoy to again place it in the front, reusing the same track to hopscotch southward. All this took time, especially as the Federals tried to disrupt their progress with constant attacks.[34] For the next six months Pancho Villa's Division of the North and Pablo González's Division of the Northeast would take the Constitutionalist fight to the Federals.

The Northeast

THE YEAR-END STRATEGY

After the Battle of Santa Engracia the Constitutionalists started planning a series of troop movements in service to a greater strategy, which may have explained the incoherent and feckless pursuit of Federal General Guillermo Rubio Navarrete's column. In a letter to Pablo González at the end of November, the First Chief related the most recent victories obtained by Constitutionalists in Chihuahua and Sinaloa, opining that Villa's victory in Ciudad Juárez would bring about the fall of Chihuahua inside of ten days, more or less. For that reason, and since the Constitutionalists already held Torreón, he envisioned the upcoming campaign heading toward Saltillo and Monterrey before advancing farther south. Carranza intended for the greater part of the forces of Chihuahua and Durango to march toward those plazas while those at González's disposal, and others, focused on the center of San Luis Potosí in order to impede Federal reinforcements from coming to the North. At the same time the First Chief prepared appropriate orders for the forces of the South, especially those of Puebla and Michoacán, to threaten Mexico City. Meanwhile, he gave González a free hand to move his forces and engage the Federals wherever he thought most convenient, supposing that González might choose to attack the railway between Tampico and San Luis Potosí since it was closest.[35]

Carranza was only half correct in thinking that González had Tampico on his mind. González wanted to consolidate his position in Tamaulipas, which meant conquering the two remaining major ports of entry at the polar opposite ends of the state: Nuevo Laredo and Tampico. As he developed his plans for the upcoming campaign, González also renamed the various brigades in his Army Corps of the Northeast on November 25, assigning division numbers to them: 1st Division, General Villarreal; 2nd Division, Murguía; 3rd Division, Teodoro Elizondo; 4th Division, Cesáreo Castro; 5th Division, Caballero; 6th Division, Carrera Torres; 7th Division, Francisco Coss (soon to be notified of his promotion to general); and the 8th Division, J. Agustín Castro. In practice these designations did not take root until late in the spring of 1914: González's army corps continued to be called a division, commanders still referred to their divisions as brigades in official reports, and J. A. Castro continued to refer to his division as the 21st for years.[36]

While Caballero's 5th Brigade remained occupying Ciudad Victoria and other plazas in the center of Tamaulipas, González ordered Cesáreo Castro's 4th Brigade (except for Ricaut's Regiment), Teodoro Elizondo's 3rd Brigade, and an independent column under Colonel Pablo A. de la Garza and Lieutenant Colonel Carlos Osuna to move back north. Elizondo had instructions to occupy Dr. González, Los Ramones, and Pesquería with his brigade, taking charge of that sector, and not to advance beyond Cadereyta but rather to send small detachments to approach and threaten Monterrey, while Castro's brigade continued farther north in order to garrison Guerrero, Camargo, and Mier so that the forces presently occupying those plazas might concentrate in Matamoros. To effect this new distribution of forces, Castro and Elizondo left Hualahuises, Montemorelos, and General Terán under Colonel Pablo A. de la Garza's control and continued on to his assigned towns. Ricaut's regiment went to Matamoros and reported to Jesús Carranza, who was defending the vital city with only one squadron under First Captain Tirso González. González's squadron belonged to Ricaut's regiment but was temporarily attached to T. Elizondo's brigade, so it made sense for Ricaut to reclaim his squadron and at the same time reinforce Matamoros.[37]

General González also sent orders to Coss' 7th Brigade at its base of operations in the Sierra de Arteaga, east of Saltillo, and to Colonels Eulalio and Luis Gutiérrez, who had their headquarters in Concepción del Oro and Vanegas in northern Zacatecas and San Luis Potosí, to step up their activities against the communications infrastructure between San Luis and Saltillo. He also ordered the Gutiérrezes to "control" the population centers of Galeana and Dr. Arroyo, and asked that Coss and Gutiérrez send envoys in order to be able to relay future orders.[38] González was starting to put a network in place that would permit coordination of movements inside his extended area of operations and thus establish command and control.

As part of this effort, González ordered a crew to repair the telephone and telegraph lines to Jaumave and Tula and sent a courier to General Alberto Carrera Torres on November 24 ordering him to report to Ciudad Victoria to receive further orders. Carrera Torres had not participated in the taking of the state capital in any way, and his pitifully outfitted brigade did not even pursue the remaining Federal garrison as Rábago and his men passed through his domains. González wanted to ensure that Carrera Torres' brigade took a more active part in the capture of Tampico. Carrera Torres arrived in Ciudad Victoria on December 3 and then returned to Tula with orders to advance with his brigade to Ciudad del Maíz and Valles along the railroad between San Luis Potosí and the Port of Tampico in order to interrupt communications and keep Federal General Ignacio Morelos Zaragoza, who garrisoned the port, from being reinforced. General Villarreal commanded a column consisting of his own 1st Brigade and those of Murguía's 2nd and J. Agustín Castro's 8th that, maintaining contact and working in concert with Carrera Torres' 6th, would attack Tampico.[39]

After briefing Carrera Torres, Pablo González left Ciudad Victoria to establish his headquarters in Matamoros, traveling through Hacienda Dolores, Padilla, San Fernando, and Santander Jiménez, where he collected the field hospital of Dr. Ricardo Suárez Gamboa and the wounded. The hospital in Matamoros would tend to hundreds of wounded Constitutionalists until April 1914, when it would be transferred to Monterrey. González arrived in Matamoros with the Medical service as General Jesús Carranza, staff, commanders, and civilians turned out to greet the commanding general, who embraced his old friend Don Jesús. González was led to his lodgings, and he ordered a telegraph set up in the house where he had his headquarters. From there, the commander of the Army Corps of the Northeast could support and supply the entire revolutionary effort in the Northeast and maintain contact with commands from Altamira to Ciudad del Maíz, Cerritos, and Vanegas in San Luis Potosí; Dr. Arroyo, Galeana, and Montemorelos in Nuevo León; Concepción del Oro, Zacatecas, and along the border, except for Nuevo Laredo, which the Federals still possessed.[40]

Presently González put himself into contact with Brownsville businessmen—the Walker Brothers, Thomas Moore, and Macedonio J. García—ordering them to acquire and warehouse one million rounds of .30-30 ammunition and one half-million rounds of 7-mm.; two thousand uniforms, pairs of shoes, and underwear; an equal number of straps, saddles, and blankets, and a sufficient quantity of fine khaki for five hundred jefes and officers' uniforms, all of which was to be immediately paid for using funds from customs duties. The arms and ammunition could not legally cross the border into Matamoros because of the U.S.-imposed arms embargo, but the clothes and equipment passed to the Army Corps of the Northeast, whose officers now dressed handsomely. González then turned around and ordered another three million more rounds of the two rifle calibers, twenty-five machine guns, four 65-mm. cannons with 3,000 shells, one quick-fire five barrel gun with 3,500 rounds, and 5,000 complete uniforms for the enlisted, most urgently attending to the equipping of 1,000 men for the attack on Laredo.[41]

Aside from tending to matters of supply, the upcoming operation against Nuevo Laredo and continuing issues with General Blanco's old command seem to have been the main reason for his return to Matamoros, since General Jesús Carranza could easily have tended to the task of buying war materiel, and at least as late as December 8, González still intended to go to

Tampico and take charge of the upcoming battle set for December 15. But on November 22, Jesús Carranza had reported to González that he still had not taken possession of Matamoros' garrison, nor Blanco's men, and Colonel Andrés Saucedo, who had assumed command of the Blanco Brigade, had not departed for Nuevo León, nor would he for a couple more weeks.[42]

Therefore, General González had seen fit to go to Matamoros and give Colonel Saucedo definitive orders:

> According to the instructions, which via this letter I confirm through Sr. General Don Jesús Carranza, [you will] march with the Brigade that belonged to Sr. General Lucio Blanco and Colonel Jesús Garza's regiment following the designated itinerary, that is, passing through Dr. González you will arrive at Ciénaga de Flores, hitting or not Marín and the intermediate pueblos; but ordering the telephone communications that exist between these pueblos and Monterrey destroyed. From Ciénaga de Flores you will approach the railway of the National Railroad destroying it as far as Salinas [Victoria]. After having arrived at Salinas you will countermarch to Ciénaga de Flores in a circle … Leaving a small garrison in Ciénaga de Flores you will continue your march through the Cuesta de Mamulique and attack the plazas of Sabinas Hidalgo, Villaldama, Bustamante, and Lampazos, and according to the information that you acquire if you think that you can successfully attack the Laredo plaza you will execute that operation, otherwise you will establish your Headquarters in any of the points mentioned that you may have taken, giving account to this Headquarters in order to draft orders for a combined movement of forces through there for an attack on that latter stated plaza [Laredo]. Upon taking Bustamante you will order the reliable destruction of the bridge of Guadalupe and you personally will be convinced that said destruction has taken place. In your march please dedicate a detachment from the brigade to go destroying the railroad, telephone, and telegraphic means of communications. Generals Cesáreo Castro and Teodoro Elizondo are already marching up the Gulf railway, bound for Monterrey, being [presently] located in these moments between Garza Valdés [sic] and Linares, with instructions to establish their headquarters in Montemorelos. With the movement of these Jefes and your aforementioned countermarch, a great part of the garrisons that the enemy has in the pueblos on the railways of the National to the north will fall back on Monterrey thus facilitating the taking of said plazas [assigned to you].[43]

These written orders followed verbal instructions, as González summarized in a letter to the First Chief on December 8, first raising the possibility of Saucedo attacking Nuevo Laredo, should he find the plaza in a weakened state, in cooperation with the forces of Ernesto Santos Coy and Jesús Dávila Sánchez, who were operating over the line.[44]

All these movements—the 1st, 2nd, 6th, and 8th brigades toward Tampico; the 3rd and 4th brigades, the Blanco Brigade, and other minor commands against the Monterrey-Nuevo Laredo axis; and the 5th and 7th in garrison duties and harassing operations—obeyed the logic of a larger strategy that González revealed in the circular addressed to various Jefes of the South of the Republic that he had drafted on orders from the First Chief.[45]

That circular, dated December 6, enjoined the southern jefes—the valiant and honorable General Emiliano Zapata of the State of Morelos; Gertrudis Sánchez and José Rentería Luviano from Michoacán; and Colonel Vicente Segura from Hidalgo—to effect a simultaneous and coordinated threat on Mexico City at the end of December. This was intended to stop any Huertistas from leaving for the North, or in the best of conditions to get the greatest number of Huertista troops to rush to defend the nation's capital, with the only prescription being that the operation happen at the end of the month without fail, since it formed a very important part of the general campaign plan. At the same time that this was to occur in the South, González planned for his Constitutionalists operating in southern Tamaulipas to attack and take Tampico, assigning December 15 as the day of the assault. Then, in combination with those from Zacatecas, they were to attack the city of San Luis Potosí to serve as a screen for the principal operation to take Saltillo and Monterrey, which was to be carried out by the forces of Sonora, Sinaloa, Chihuahua, and Durango that would concentrate in Torreón and then converge on the plazas previously cited, thus achieving absolute domination of the North of the Republic.[46]

Although González, and even the First Chief, did not command the allegiance of many Surianos, the Constitutionalist depot in Matamoros provided ammunition, arms, clothes, and equipment, not just for the Army Corps of the Northeast but also for the upcoming expeditions of Cándido Aguilar to Veracruz; Vicente Segura, who marched off to Huejutla, Hidalgo; Macario Hernández; and even the Zapatista Gildardo Magaña, who obtained arms, money, and ammunition from the plaza to go make revolution in Morelos.[47] Therefore, the Constitutionalists could at least appeal to all revolutionaries in a common effort. But Carranza and González had gotten a bit ahead of themselves in trying to lock up the North for the Constitutionalists by the end of the year. Federal general Velasco's occupation of Torreón on December

9 foiled the grander strategy, and over the next couple of days the attack on Tampico likewise failed.

BATTLE OF TAMPICO

González assigned Generals Antonio I. Villarreal, J. Agustín Castro, and Francisco Murguía to try to take the vital oil field terminus and port of Tampico down south while he marched north with a small escort to Matamoros to begin his operations against Nuevo Laredo. Disgust with one of their own, General Alberto Carrera Torres, prevailed in the ranks of those Constitutionalists assigned to take Tampico. Carrera Torres had failed to take part in the attack on Ciudad Victoria, even though the city was squarely in his area of operations, and then, he allowed Federal Generals Rábago and Juan de Dios Arzamendi to flee right through Jaumave and Tula, Carrera Torres' "domain," and pick up the railroad to safety. Indeed, for weeks thereafter the Federals continued to maintain a garrison in Tula. Only after two and a half days of combat that began on December 1, and which resulted in a victory for the Federals, did Arzamendi order Lieutenant Colonel Rafael Urquiza and his Federals to abandon Tula on December 5 and join the main column in Cerritos, mostly because Urquiza had run out of ammunition.[48]

Tampico should have been easy pickings for the estimated 2,000 Constitutionalists counted among the combined brigades of Villarreal, Castro, and Murguía, as they were fighting against a garrison of only about 350 men from the 7th and 19th Infantry Regiments, the 7th Scout Corps, and about 100 irregulars under the command of the unimpressive Federal Brigadier Ignacio Morelos Zaragoza. However, Murguía's strength report after the Battle of Ciudad Victoria counted less than 500 men, so the presumed 2,000 Constitutionalist strength may have been an overestimate. Yet, despite the presumed difference in numbers, the Federals had been able to reinforce General Morelos by rerouting the six hundred Federals of the Ciudad Victoria garrison under General Arzamendi from their original destination of Monterrey; Arzamendi arrived at Tampico on December 10, doubling the number of defenders to more than one thousand men just as the Constitutionalists attacked the city.[49] Once again Carrera Torres had failed his fellow Constitutionalists.

Supported by the port's artillery and the accurate fire of the Federal Navy gunboat *Bravo*, the Federals managed to hold out against the Constitutionalists for two days. On December 12 Federal Colonel Ignacio M. Corona, jefe of the San Luis Potosí-Tampico rail line, sent more ammunition to the Tampico garrison, and the Federal Navy gunboat *Veracruz* arrived with another 650 or so men of the 21st Infantry Regiment and 19th Auxiliary Cavalry Regiment.

Reinforced and with additional firepower from the *Veracruz*, the Federals counterattacked the next day and pushed the Constitutionalists back to Altamira (twenty kilometers north of Tampico), where the two forces continued to battle each other. The Federals suffered forty dead and seventy-three wounded and reported the Constitutionalist casualties at an incredible 150 dead and 300 wounded. Slightly more than the Federal casualties would seem a more reasonable figure, since Castro's 21st Brigade alone suffered only thirteen killed and thirty-one wounded. The Federals prevailed owing to their overwhelming fire superiority, the timely arrival of reinforcements, the natural defensive position of the port (surrounded by swamps such as it was), and the inadvisability of a Constitutionalist attack that did not concentrate its efforts on one single weak part of the line but instead attacked along a broad front in insufficient numbers because of a self-professed lack of unity of command.[50]

A few days later General González ordered Caballero's 5th Brigade, which had been reinforced, to relieve Generals Murguía and Villarreal in front of Tampico so that they could take their brigades to Matamoros to refit and reorganize.[51] Caballero's men would be there for almost six months.

BATTLE OF NUEVO LAREDO

The attack on Nuevo Laredo at the opposite end of the state, six hundred kilometers from Tampico, fared no better for the Constitutionalists.

General González took direct charge of the operation and, for the most part, he employed men previously commanded by General Lucio Blanco in the effort. On December 12 Colonel Andrés Saucedo's column approached Salinas Victoria, to the northwest of Monterrey, where a Federal force of some six hundred dragoons commanded by a Colonel Castro and one hundred Federal infantrymen under Major José Aristi abandoned the plaza and took up position on the hills outside the plaza. Surprisingly, the cavalry departed leaving the Federal infantry behind to, perforce, cover their retreat and in the process allowing a military train with two locomotives to fall into the hands of the Constitutionalists. Afterward, Saucedo reported to González that the Federals had fifteen hundred men in Monterrey and recommended that the commanding general have the jefe de las armas in Mier repair the Cerralvo telegraph and order the advance of Jesús Dávila Sánchez's forces onward to Laredo or some nearby point. Then he used the trains captured in Salinas Victoria to tear up the railroad track in the area and, having thus carried off the feint against Monterrey, turned north.[52] From Salinas Victoria Colonel Saucedo took a northeasterly tack to Cuesta de Mamulique where he reached the highway and continued north to Sabinas Hidalgo, which his men occupied without a fight. After taking up residence for three days, Saucedo's column began moving north again to reach the hamlet of Las Tortillas. Lieutenant Colonel Francisco J. Múgica and his regiment covered the column's rear and watched out for any Federals coming up from the south.[53]

On December 21 General Cesáreo Castro started to gather his forces in Cerralvo. Earlier Cesáreo Castro's men had occupied Dr. González, Ciénaga de Flores, General Zuazua, and Los Ramones after some minor skirmishes. The planned attack on Laredo called for General Elizondo's men to garrison these towns as Castro massed his forces and marched along the banks of the Rio Grande from San Ignacio to Camargo, establishing his headquarters in Mier and relieving the detachments of the units there to retire to headquarters in Matamoros. One must keep in mind that although the Division of the Northeast had numerous effectives, with such an enormous amount of territory to garrison, it had difficulty gathering even a mere one thousand men to attack Nuevo Laredo. González urged Saucedo to finish up operations against the Federals in Lampazos and Villaldama, attacking them if he thought that he could prevail, and if not to try to cut off the Federals located in Lampazos from Nuevo Laredo and advance toward the border destroying the means of communication in order to be in the vicinity of Laredo by Friday December 26 without fail. He also informed Saucedo that he had given orders to Dávila Sánchez and Santos Coy to leave for Laredo and planned to follow two days later with the purpose being to attack the town by the next Saturday or Sunday at the latest.[54]

All of these movements, for some unknown reason, wound up being delayed, possibly because González was busy hoping, wishing, praying and trying to get the Customs Chief of Brownsville, Frank Rabb, to permit the ammunition, machine guns, and cannons stockpiled in that city to pass over the border. Rabb refused, so González had to rely on efforts to smuggle whatever he could, but these supplies were so meager that each soldier only had 125 rounds. Lieutenant Colonel Carlos Prieto, Chief of Heavy Artillery, had a mere five shells and no machine guns because they were all at Tampico, except those which they were about receive from First Captain Federico Montes.[55]

Captain Montes' Defection

On December 23, Colonel Saucedo received the happy news that Federal Captain Federico Montes wanted to defect to the Constitutionalists with his men and materiel. In turn, Saucedo sent a telegraph to Matamoros that Major José Cabrera in Sabinas Hidalgo was reporting: "First Cap. Federico Montes, of the Federal Army, with 80 men, 14 machine guns, and 150 saddled horses, coming from Monterrey saying that he comes to join the Revolution - I await orders - Respectfully.--Col A. Saucedo." Montes had been part of Madero's staff and had behaved admirably during The Tragic Ten Days, trying to protect the President at great personal risk until forced to yield; ever since he had sought the opportunity to join the Constitutionalists, but he had been under constant surveillance by the Huertistas.[56]

This news came as no surprise to headquarters because Montes had already been in touch with General González, who ordered him to report to Saucedo at Las Tortillas and there await further orders. Montes, who could not count on his fellow officers to desert to the enemy, took First Sergeant Victoriano Sarmiento, a former Maderista captain who had been drafted into the Federal Army under the leva, into his confidence and informed him of his plans. The night of December 20, 1913, he gave all of his officers, except for the two lieutenants whom he thought would follow him into the Constitutionalist camp, an assignment for the following day to make topographic maps of the Obispado. Very early the next morning Montes ordered his bugler to blow "boots and saddles" and then departed from his lodgings in the San Luisito barrio of Monterrey with his force, announcing to his superiors that he was leaving for Topo Chico on a field training exercise. With the exception of the two lieutenants whom he suspected of having revolutionary leanings, Montes only had enlisted men with him because his other officers were busy mapping the Obispado. Upon reaching Topo Chico, Montes wrote a letter to General Téllez announcing his defection that Sarmiento dropped in the mailbox. From there he went to Salinas Victoria to get information from the Huertista municipal president as to the whereabouts of Constitutionalists, telling the local official that he wanted to go out and fight them, although in reality he intended to join them. Unfamiliar with the terrain, he headed toward Mamulique. Halting at nightfall he called the two lieutenants, Anastasio Salgado (a future Zapatista general) and Carlos Huerta, and informed them of his intentions to join the Constitutionalists. Neither of the two wanted to back his move, so Montes addressed the rest of his men with his proposition. All of them wanted to defect, except Sergeant Juan Velázquez; so Montes allowed the three men to return mounted and armed even though the enlisted men wanted to kill them.[57]

Montes and his troops continued on, running into five revolutionaries coming from Coahuila who were alarmed by the soldiers in Federal garb. The Constitutionalists challenged them with "who goes there," to which Montes replied "Carranza." Montes then sent these five revolutionaries with a letter to Major José Cabrera to report that he and his men were waiting to be brought in. Cabrera went out to meet Montes with a large force. Upon approaching Cabrera deployed into two wings as a precaution, but after conferring with the young captain they convinced themselves of Montes' sincerity and returned to the plaza with the group of new Constitutionalists. However, they still had misgivings because Montes also brought with him a Federal column in close pursuit commanded by General Teodoro Quintana with some six hundred men, in round figures, from the 1st Infantry Regiment; the 39th Irregular Infantry Corps; the 6th, 8th and 12th Cavalry Regiments; and the Zuazua Irregular Corps. Lieutenant Colonel Abelardo Menchaca and Major Rafael de la Torre vetted Montes, and remained very suspicious, but after receiving Pablo González's instructions to admit the ex-Federals into their ranks, not to mention their subsequent performance in the upcoming Battle of Nuevo Laredo, they came to fully trust in Montes and his men.[58]

On December 29, González left for Ciudad Guerrero to establish his headquarters, sending Castro's brigade, which now totaled about 850 men, along with another 250 mounted soldiers commanded by Generals Jesús Dávila Sánchez and Santos Coy on to San Ignacio. Colonel Saucedo (accompanied by Lieutenant Colonel Francisco Múgica) and Captain Montes reported to Guerrero and received orders to make sure that Quintana in no way reached Nuevo Laredo to reinforce the Federals.[59]

The Federals now knew that the Constitutionalists aimed to attack Laredo, not Monterrey, and with an added sense of urgency precipitated by the addition of Montes and his guns to the enemy, rushed to aid their comrades inside the border town. Saucedo detached Lieutenant Colonel Francisco J. Múgica with five hundred men to destroy the rail bridge at Rodríguez, due west of Las Tortillas and defended only by about fifty Huertistas commanded by Major Juan Zuazua, in order to prevent Quintana's Federals from reaching Laredo. But Zuazua sensed Múgica's approach. The wily rancher outmaneuvered Múgica and managed to trick the Constitutionalists on the right and left wing trying to effect a pincer movement into firing upon each other during a nighttime firefight. In the resulting confusion the Constitutionalists dispersed without accomplishing the mission to blow the bridge, with dire consequences for the upcoming battle. González hurried his men forward to be in position for battle on New Year's Day and arrived at Sánchez Station on the last day of 1913 where he watched helplessly as Quintana's column rolled past them out of rifle range and into Laredo, augmenting the Federal garrison under the command of Colonel Gustavo Guardiola y Aguirre.[60]

Colonel Guardiola had divided the defenses into three sectors: west, south, and east. Soldiers of the 9th Infantry Regiment covered the west, and in the south and east were elements from the 1st Infantry Regiment, 42nd Auxiliary Infantry Battalion, and 6th Cavalry Regiment, with only a few cavalrymen in reserve. He located his two guns on the north side of the city. When Quintana, the senior officer, arrived on the scene, he left Guardiola's disposition unmodified and placed his own column in reserve and awaited the Constitutionalist attack. Sánchez Lamego calculated the strength of Guardiola's garrison at six hundred men from the 1st and 9th Infantry Regiments; 42nd Auxiliary Infantry Battalion; 6th and 12th Cavalry Regiments; 8th Scout Corps; 5th Artillery Regiment; and the Machine Gun Regiment.[61] Guardiola had dug trenches and employed railcars around the city to provide cover for riflemen and placed a machine gun every one hundred meters. The Constitutionalists had only about two thousand men at most and two field guns with hardly any ammunition, and they had to attack across open ground under murderous fire, although thanks to Captain Montes they now had fourteen machine guns and Rexers.[62]

January 1

Obeying their orders received on December 29, Generals Dávila Sánchez and Santos Coy had moved up their column to encamp a distance of about sixteen kilometers from Nuevo Laredo in order to be in position for the assault. After all their men had moved into position at the appropriate distance the two commanders accompanied the Zaragoza Regiment commanded by Colonel Gonzalo Novoa, with another fifty soldiers commanded by Colonel Fortunato Maycotte attached, in attacking the east side of the town at 4 a.m. on the dot. They immediately took copious rifle and machine-gun fire from the defenders over a space of more than two hours without being able to locate the Federal positions until daybreak because of the darkness. In this attack the commanders lost several soldiers killed and both were wounded, not too seriously but still enough to be evacuated from the field of battle. Thus, Dávila Sánchez and Santos Coy were taken to La Puerta where it had been agreed to establish headquarters. Shortly after arriving they were joined by Colonels Novoa and Maycotte who stated that, without support on the western and southern part of the city, it was physically impossible to sustain the positions that had been captured since, seeing that the Constitutionalists were only attacking in their sector, the Federals had concentrated in the greater part there. In view of the foregoing and seeing the necessity of protecting and saving the forces already committed, Dávila Sánchez and Santos Coy ordered forward the Rifleros de la Sierra Regiment commanded by C. Colonel Guadalupe Dávila, which had been held reserve. With these reinforcements the Constitutionalists on the east side successfully occupied good positions and maintained them during the whole first day, but they did so without being able to advance very far because of the Federals' overwhelming numbers and sound disposition of forces.[63]

At 5 a.m. General Castro ordered his first column composed of 300 men commanded by Colonel Alejo G. González to attack against the center of the plaza from the south. The Constitutionalists advanced without shooting until fire from the defenders finally forced them to return aimed fire on the Huertista redoubts. The combat in the center continued in a measured fashion until 7 a.m. when headquarters ordered Castro to throw all his men into the fight. Colonel Francisco Sánchez Herrera then entered into combat with his troops mixing into the existing firing line. In effect the battle lasted in that manner for about three hours while the Huertistas held back the Constitutionalist assault. Likewise Castro's men stopped the opposing force from exiting their firing positions, taking from them one Colt machine gun and its tripod and the second tripod of another Colt, since the reaction to the advancing Federal gun crews was so rapid that they only had time to set up one machine gun and lay down the tripod for the second when the Constitutionalists rushed them (most likely using the tactic of charging the guns mounted and lassoing the equipment). In that episode the attackers suffered several wounded and some horses killed, while the Federals lost the aforementioned equipment and the commanding Federal captain was wounded. His rank was revealed by the hat that he had to abandon when his men carried him away. The most regrettable loss for Castro was Major Salvador F. Treviño, brother of Jacinto B. Treviño, who was hit in the spine by a bullet and died a couple of hours later, and two other officers and some non-commissioned officers who were wounded. Castro's men held their positions, continually fighting for the rest of the day.[64]

Colonel Saucedo's men spent the night in Sánchez Station, sixteen kilometers to the southwest of Laredo, and did not get underway until 7 a.m. They blamed their tardiness on an inability to get food and staying up all night making preparations. The Blanco Brigade arrived on the field of combat realizing that the attack was already underway as they heard cannon fire upon approaching the plaza. Reaching the heights to the west of town they ran into General Castro and his staff who urged Saucedo to enter into combat with all his men as soon as possible, stressing the committed and precarious situation of the other forces. The Blanco Brigade then entered into combat somewhere between 9:00 or 10:00 a.m., depending on sources. Saucedo led the attack in the center of his men and managed to get within three hundred meters of the Federal lines before being forced back by withering enemy artillery fire; Lieutenant Colonel Abelardo Menchaca was wounded by a fragment to the foot during the attack.[65]

Captain Montes placed his machine guns in battery opposite the Federal trenches on the first line of fire. The Federals then began training their fire against Montes, and he ordered his men to abandon their machine guns, but to do so leaving them loaded and ready to fire. When the Huertistas saw Montes' men flee they abandoned their trenches to collect the weapons, and then Montes commanded his crews to return to their weapons and open fire, which resulted in numerous Federal casualties. The Constitutionalist machine guns continued to rattle away with such intensity and fury that at one point they quieted an enemy battery, but the crews lost Juan C. Gamboa, who fell a few meters from his position, gut shot, and died in Montes' and Victoriano Sarmiento's arms. They buried him under a tree and years later, upon passing the tree, Montes could not help but shed a tear remembering his dear friend.[66]

The battle raged all day long and the wounded started to pile up. Doctors Ricardo Suárez Gamboa, Daniel Ríos Zertuche, Gilberto de la Fuente, and Ignacio Sánchez Neira attended to the wounded Constitutionalists in the field hospital set up at Rancho El Espejo; a little after noon the Red Cross showed up with ambulances opposite the ranch on the U.S. side and offered help, which González accepted for his most serious wounded. Druggists, citizens, and local merchants contributed to the hospital and provided drugs, while other merchants sent money for food.[67]

At some point the Federal artillery succeeded in locating the Constitutionalist headquarters and began to bombard it with such intensity, dropping perhaps sixty shells, that González and staff had to flee amid explosions and spewing earth that covered the group. Then, the Federals shifted their fire in an unsuccessful attempt to hit the Red Cross ambulances. Fighting continued throughout the day and after it grew dark fifty Constitutionalist marksmen protected by the shadows advanced to surprise and kill some opposing machine gunners until the Federals counterattacked, driving them back. After nightfall González sent some men to Laredo to try to buy some ammunition, which was running low, as the battle raged until 9 p.m.[68]

January 2

Beginning at 4 a.m. General Castro ordered all his men to renew the attack, including the regiments of Colonels Alejo González and Sánchez Herrera, as well as Porfirio G. González's, which had been commanded by Lieutenant Colonel Santos Treviño. They made two unsuccessful assaults, and upon returning a third time, were again repulsed. Castro's men had to fall back and take shelter in a nearby arroyo where they were able to repulse the cavalry charges that the Federals subsequently delivered.[69] In other sectors the Constitutionalists economized their shooting, concentrating on picking off the enemy with aimed shots while Montes' machine guns continued firing until the barrels turned red hot.[70]

Around 12:30 p.m. González found out that it was impossible to transport the ammunition across the river in view of the American soldiers guarding the border. He also learned that Federal Colonel Luis Alberto Guajardo had left Piedras Negras with a column of cavalry to reinforce Nuevo Laredo. González commissioned two civilians to pass over to Palafox (a good forty-five kilometers north) opposite Hidalgo, Coahuila, and phone Laredo if Guajardo passed, with the message then to be brought across the border to his headquarters.[71]

At approximately 3 p.m. Castro commanded Lieutenant Colonel Pedro Vázquez and Major Fortino García Campos to relieve Colonels Sánchez Herrera and Alejo G. González, who had been on the firing line since the day before. But an hour and a half later he had to order Vázquez and García to quickly return to his aid since a strong column of Federal cavalry and infantry supported by artillery fire had rolled up the men of deceased Lieutenant Colonel Santos Treviño's command, which was outnumbered and running short of ammunition, and threatened to overrun Castro's camp. With the rapid reinforcement of the two jefes, who arrived in a timely fashion, Castro was able to mount a competent counterattack that almost came to hand-to-hand combat, driving back the Huertistas to the center of their positions. The fleeing Huertistas left behind sixty dead and wounded, according to Castro's estimate. Some did not stop until they reached the United States where the U.S. Army took them into custody, allegedly. Castro's brigade lost First Captain Encarnación Larralde and one soldier killed, and several others who could not be identified.[72]

At about the same time as the Huertista counterattack against Castro occurred, Federal infantry and cavalry traveling along the shores of the river surprised the Constitutionalists in the eastern sector. They forced the Constitutionalists back, until they recovered and counterattacked, retaking their original positions and forcing the Federals back to their own lines. In this clash Dávila Sánchez and Santos Coy lost the valiant First Captains Eugenio Velásquez, Francisco Moreno, and Margarito Leos and Lieutenant Telegrapher Expedito Rangel, all killed.[73]

Upon nightfall after that second day of combat, all Constitutionalist jefes reported being short of ammunition, and the call came from Laredo that Guajardo had reached Hidalgo with about six hundred cavalrymen. González gave the order to withdraw. All were to leave campfires burning and, except for Saucedo, follow along the river to San Ignacio while Saucedo was to remain in Las Tortillas to give the impression of a coming renewed attack.[74]

Upon receiving the order to retreat Castro made preparations to begin slowly pulling his men back around 7 p.m., sending a mounted force to the line of fire so that those dismounted could pull back and collect their horses. In this manner Castro's command, completely mounted, made an orderly retreat at 8 p.m. headed in the direction that had been indicated by headquarters and leaving only twenty men behind as a rearguard. The eastern sector did the same at about 8:15 p.m. protected by twenty of Colonel Maycotte's men; they managed to withdraw without losing a single soldier even though, unaware of the retreat, the Federals kept up a slow cadence of fire until almost midnight.[75]

The Constitutionalist retreat turned out as inept as the attack itself, as the vanguard under Major José T. Cantú got lost in the darkness. At daybreak the Constitutionalists were again standing before Laredo, but they had made it there without catching the notice of the Federals. In the daylight they made their way back to Matamoros without being pursued by the Federals.[76] The Constitutionalists sent the lightly wounded to Ciudad Guerrero and buried their dead in the field. From Guerrero, Pablo González continued to Matamoros and Castro garrisoned San Ignacio, Mier, and Guerrero. Villarreal and Murguía, underway from Tampico, received orders to camp near Matamoros and report with their staffs to the plaza.[77]

Analysis

The reasons for González's defeat were obvious, as General Castro recognized: superior Federal firepower, the Huertistas' inexpungable trenches, and the open terrain that his men had to cross.[78] But González attached greater weight for the loss to the way his troops entered piecemeal into combat. Even though "each one of the Jefes received instructions in writing on the way and hour that the attack should be effected on the plaza," only Generals Santos Coy and Dávila Sánchez began at "the hour fixed for the general attack." General Cesáreo Castro entered into combat two hours after them and the forces of Colonel Saucedo a full six hours behind schedule, "which made the attack more difficult not having been made simultaneously as had been agreed."[79]

Reading González's explanation leads one to believe that all sectors were to attack simultaneously, but General Castro's report, written two days after the action, calls the concerted effort into question. In his report Castro apologized to González for disobeying orders and entering into combat at 5 a.m., when he had been instructed to maneuver into position and only remain at the ready and allow the battle to develop on the flanks (most likely out of considerations for international diplomacy since the shots directed at Nuevo Laredo from due south put its sister city on the U.S. side in harm's way).

However, since Saucedo did not join the battle at the appointed hour Castro felt obliged to enter into combat in order to take the pressure off of Generals Dávila Sánchez and Santos Coy, whose position quickly became both compromised and untenable without assistance.[80] Whatever might be the case, it would appear that Colonel Andrés Saucedo and the Blanco Brigade once again had been wholly derelict in their duty. Their performance must have reminded all of the doomed attack on Monterrey in October when the Blanco Brigade, likewise, failed to join the battle in a timely fashion, resulting in defeat.

But from González's perspective the Blanco Brigade's performance also had proved wanting in allowing Federal General Quintana to reinforce Nuevo Laredo without informing headquarters of this fact, as the commanding general penciled in at the bottom of a copy of Saucedo's December 10 written campaign orders in his typical flair for understatement: "did not exactly execute as ordered. Quintana and Zuazua entered the plaza without Headquarter's knowledge."[81] Years later the then-general Juan Barragán, Saucedo's chief of staff at the time of the battle, contested this assertion by averring that he personally sent word of Quintana's arrival to General Pablo González, who ignored Saucedo's pleadings to postpone the attack. Either way, Lieutenant Colonel Francisco J. Múgica, much more accomplished as a leftist ideologue than a soldier, bore the ultimate culpability for the failed campaign because he incompetently allowed a much-inferior force to keep him from his mission of blowing the bridge at Rodríguez. For the Blanco Brigade's combined shortcomings Colonel Saucedo would have to face a court martial.[82]

According to Barragán, General González lost a staggering one thousand men among killed, wounded, and missing, but since other sources consistently put the Constitutionalist total attack force at not much more than that number, and since General Barragán's troop and casualty estimates were often egregiously off the mark, one must conclude that his figures are a politically motivated attempt to disparage González and redeem the memory of his former friend and commander, Colonel Saucedo. Castro's brigade lost a total of thirty-two killed and forty-seven wounded, around a ten percent casualty rate. Sánchez Herrera's Libres del Norte Regiment lost fifteen killed and twenty-seven wounded, Porfirio G. González's Carabineros de Nuevo León Regiment suffered eight killed and three wounded, and Alejo G. González's Regionales de Coahuila Regiment counted nine dead and seventeen wounded, including Major Treviño among the former.[83] The eastern sector over the two days of combat lost three first captains, a lieutenant, two sub-lieutenants, and twenty-four soldiers, and also thirty-five wounded, including two officers and five non-commissioned officers.[84] González reported to the First Chief a total of about fifty killed and seventy wounded, including Generals Santos Coy and Dávila Sánchez, which was surely understated since it left virtually no room for the casualties suffered by the Blanco Brigade, but it was surely a much more reasonable figure than Barragán's. According to Leonor Villegas de Magnón, the president of the Laredo White Cross, her organization collected 150 wounded Constitutionalists from the battlefield that it brought over to the United States for treatment, of whom only six later died. The Federal's losses are unknown, although they lost First Captain of Artillery José Reyes Macías on the first day, and observers from the American side informed González that the Federals had a greater number of casualties than the Constitutionalists.[85] In a later admission to the First Chief, González qualified "this combat [as] being one of the most tenacious in which I have taken part."[86]

The American Angle

Within a week of the battle, González sent a letter to the First Chief that contained some rather curious statements:

> As I told you in my message yesterday, the attack against Laredo was not only for the purpose of taking the plaza but also to bring the neighboring nation up to date on our manner of combat and the elements that we have. The fight was bloody during the two days of the assault [with] two machine guns and twelve "Rexer" rifles functioning [as] directed by Major Federico Montes, whose work greatly called the attention of the American military authorities who observed the different phases of the battle with the greatest interest. The comportment of both the American people and authorities during the Laredo attack left nothing to be desired [and] overflowed in enthusiasm to help us, not only with wounded but in the provision [illegible] of foodstuffs and war [materiel] that with every opportunity they helped to cross.[87]

González's statements appear to run counter to those made by Manuel W. González, who wrote that "a cordon of American troops watching the roads" made it impossible to cross "even one single cartridge" during the battle.[88] And it seems wholly counter to the practice by U.S. authorities during other battles on the border that endangered American towns to add fuel to the fire and allow the attacking force to cross ammunition in order to turn around and immediately fire it back toward U.S. territory. On the other hand, González may have been referring to local authorities, who would have included many pro-Constitutionalist partisan members. Furthermore, González may have been referencing non-lethal war materiel (lanterns, canteens, flashlights, and the like), although in the past even that had been closely watched by U.S. federal authorities. Finally, the phrase "every opportunity" calls into question just how much war materiel might have gotten across. Invoices related to the battle later paid to a Leocadio L. Fierros totaled $1,221.66, including $135.00 in automobile expenses.[89] Juan N. Vela also requested reimbursement for a payment he made to Sr. Fierros on an invoice for ammunition of $427.00 related to the Laredo attack.[90] The amount of ammunition at the prevailing price levels (12,000 rounds at $35/1,000, or ten cartridges per man) could easily have crossed the border amidst a greater humanitarian relief effort, but it would hardly have been consequential.

González's other comment that the battle served to display Constitutionalist might before the American military also seems strange, unless the Constitutionalists wanted to impress upon the U.S. government their strength, and therefore legitimacy, as a way to gain official recognition—or at least to have the arms embargo lifted. In this, González's efforts may have borne some fruit. A few days after the battle Captain Federico Montes and Juan Barragán passed over the border and went up to Laredo, Texas. Several U.S. Army officers noticed them eating dinner in a restaurant, and recognizing Montes from the battle, they went in to personally congratulate his conduct on the battlefield. Others on the street stopped ever-so-briefly to tap the window of the restaurant in staccato, simulating Montes' machine guns, before continuing on their way—"A manifestation of the strangeness of our [American] cousins," in the words of Barragán.[91] Still, admiration extended only so far, and did not stop the American authorities from incarcerating the wounded Constitutionalists in Fort McIntosh.[92] But in one month's time the arms embargo would be lifted.

PABLO GONZÁLEZ

González's widely-held reputation as the worst of Carranza's three army corps commanders ("the general who never won a battle") on the surface appears quite well-deserved. By the end of 1913, he still had not won a major battle, except for Ciudad Victoria, and his troops at Nuevo Laredo stood on the eve not only of the New Year but also of a colossal defeat. But in several regards, this judgment lacks an appreciation for his particular circumstances. Throughout the 1913 Constitutionalist campaign against Huerta, each of Carranza's theater commanders operated independently, developing a strategy unique to their own area of operations until such time as a national strategy could come into play. General Obregón had secured his area of operations first, by the end of June, yet the Northwest presented the simplest prospective regional strategy of all three. He only had to worry about one state, Sonora, since the Federals in Sinaloa presented no real threat, and he operated along one, two-legged, campaign axis: Guaymas-Hermosillo-Nogales and Nogales-Naco-Agua Prieta. Villa, similarly, operated in the strategic context of a single axis: Ciudad Juárez-Chihuahua City-Torreón, which ran through one state, Chihuahua, and part of another, the northeastern corner of Durango. General González, by contrast, had responsibility for a four-state area—Coahuila, Nuevo León, Tamaulipas, and San Luis Potosí—with multiple axes of operations: Torreón-Saltillo-Monterrey, San Luis Potosí-Saltillo-Piedras Negras, Monterrey-Nuevo Laredo, Monterrey-Ciudad Victoria-Tampico, San Luis Potosí- Tampico, and Matamoros-Nuevo Laredo.

Furthermore, Obregón operated in the state most isolated by distance and geography from Mexico City. Columns leaving the metropolis to operate in that remote region had to travel first by rail to the coast, and then sail to Guaymas. Villa's command also remained remote, since from June 1913 until the demise of Huerta's regime, and long before he began his campaigning in earnest, the railway between Torreón and Zacatecas remained closed to rail traffic for the Federals. All Federals traveling to fight Villa in Chihuahua had to pass through San Luis Potosí, Saltillo, and then to Torreón, in other words, through González's area of operations. And while Obregón only had to contend with one Federal division, the "Yaqui," and Villa only had to fight the Federal Division of the North and Division of the Nazas, Pablo González had to fight the Division of the Bravo and negotiate the Division of the Nazas and Division of the Center as well. Moreover, the state legislature had settled the crucial question of unity of command in Sonora from the outset, in March. Carranza made Villa the senior Constitutionalist in his area of operations in May. But unity of command had not been settled in the Northeast until the end of October, when it was declared by the First Chief from the opposite end of the country. And as will be seen, with such headstrong subordinates, the Blanco Brigade precedent, the vast territory covered by the Army Corps of the Northeast (which made it hard to bring new commands, such as that of Alberto Carrera Torres, into the orbit of headquarters), and given Tamaulipas state's role as a staging area for developing Constitutionalist commands in the Center and South, González's personnel headaches would only grow in the new year.

Finally, the Mexican Federal Army, much as the U.S. Federal Army in the Civil War—and with good reason—harbored a bias for operations in the east. The eastern ports of Matamoros, Tampico, and Veracruz dwarfed the western ports in importance as entrepôts for supplies from the United States and Europe. The nation's major energy sources, both oil in the Huasteca and coal in Coahuila, resided in the Division of the Northeast's area of operations, as did its most important transportation grid of roads and rails, hence the numerous axes of operations.[93] All these geographic considerations contributed to making the Northeast the industrial base for the Mexican nation, and gave yet another reason for attaching preeminent military importance to the region. And this area just so happened to be home to the leader of the revolutionary movement, a prime political factor. To operate in this region would require the greatest of military minds, perhaps a Frederick the Great, who could maneuver against multiple enemies and multiple lines of attack, only over a much greater expanse of territory. General Pablo González was no Frederick the Great, and he was not even the best Mexican general. That honor, by historical consensus, has been reserved for General Álvaro Obregón.

*   *   *

Although rumors of intrigue among Federal officers persisted, those who proved disloyal, in general, broke with Huertismo openly and categorically, as in the cases of officers such as Garmendia and Montes. Both had defended President Madero during the palace coup, with Garmendia and Montes personally shooting dead Lieutenant Colonel Teodoro Jiménez Riveroll and Major Rafael Izquierdo, respectively, and they remained in the Federal Army only until the first opportunity to defect to the Constitutionalists had arrived. For Garmendia this came in November and for Montes at the end of December. Garmendia died assaulting Culiacán, while Montes went on to have a long and distinguished career.

For the Constitutionalists, the main impediment to developing sound operations had to deal not with an officer corps plagued by suspicions and actual treachery, but rather nascent careerism and petty jealousies. For instance, Obregón became frustrated with the performance of José de la Luz Blanco who, most likely upset over having been leapfrogged in rank and position by Obregón, went into exile after the Battle of Culiacán. Similarly, González continued to have to deal with disobedience in the ranks of Lucio Blanco's former command. At the highest levels, two high profile appointments by the First Chief presaged continuing and future discord. Ángeles' designation as Secretary (subsequently knocked down to Under Secretary) of War provoked a minor rebellion among the leading officers of the Army Corps of the Northwest, and Obregón's promotion to commander of the Army Corps of Northwest created a latent predicament for Villa, who was by then growing in prominence, prestige, and power. In-fighting and politicking would increasingly have an effect on operations as the war continued to increase in scope, scale, and sophistication, requiring inter-theater cooperation, or at the very least a recognition that the results of operations in one theater had an impact on another, most especially between Villa and González's area of operations.

Already in November 1913, Carranza revealed a national strategy where the forces of Chihuahua and Durango would threaten the state capitals of Saltillo and Monterrey from the west as the Division of the Northeast held the Federals at bay from the south, aided by the Surianos pressuring Mexico City. This year-end strategy demonstrated that Carranza intended all along for Villa to head east on campaign, a crucial point of contention that in the spring will lead to Villa's first episode of disobedience—and the beginning of the Constitutionalist schism.

As the scope and scale of operations expanded, logistics and financing likewise grew in importance. In his Hermosillo speech, the First Chief first broached the subject of banking and currency reforms, which will be discussed in detail in chapter 14. Federal General Ojeda also realized the linkage between finances and operations when he developed his plan to attack Empalme (which relied on support from the gunboats of the Federal Navy), and deny the Constitutionalist Army profits from the garbanzo harvest. In response to this economic and logistical setback, Sonora's citizen-soldiers improvised an innovative solution, moving rolling stock south of Maytorena Station by hopscotching railroad tracks. Additionally, Obregón intended to resupply his columns by sea at Topolobampo, although he could not realistically hope to do so until the Constitutionalists possessed mastery of the seas, which the Federals held. As more territory came under Constitutionalist control their radius of operations expanded, and their lines of communication stretched farther, logistics and finances would take on an even greater dimension for the Constitutionalist Army.

The complexity of warfare also continued to grow on an operational, or intra-theater level. In Sinaloa the Federals developed an amphibious and land-based pincer movement against Constitutionalist headquarters in San Blas. That effort failed miserably, and when Constitutionalists under Juan Carrasco threatened Mazatlán, the Federal leadership had to make hard decisions about the allocation of assets, ultimately deciding to abandon Topolobampo to protect Mazatlán and in the process virtually sacrificing Sinaloa de Leyva and its garrison to the numerically superior Constitutionalists.

In the Northeast, González had to contend with numerous axes of advance over vast territory and in competition for significant economic prizes, in what can only be described as the most complex and intense of all the Constitutionalist theaters. In December González moved brigades into place to attack Tampico and Nuevo Laredo, two plazas separated by six hundred kilometers at polar ends of the state of Tamaulipas, but the failings of Alberto Carrera Torres' brigade and the Blanco Brigade, respectively, allowed both plazas to be reinforced by the Federals at the last moment, and the attacks failed in short order. On a tactical level, the Nuevo Laredo debacle testified to a need for skill and finesse in the preparation and execution of combat beyond mere brute force. As the revolution continued to progress, commanders on all sides continued to learn by doing, each promotion inked with the blood of subordinates.

By the winter of 1914 the Constitutionalists essentially suspended their military operations, preoccupied with consolidating their successes, attending to matters of public administration in those areas now under their control, recruiting and reorganizing, and trying to procure materiel to be able to continue the fight. The United States arms and ammunition blockade against the Constitutionalist war effort at this point in time took on an increasing degree of effectiveness in hindering Constitutionalist progress simply because the growing war machine required ever greater resources. Denying González the right to import arms and ammunition that the Constitutionalist Army owned in warehouses on the U.S. side of the border played a key role in the timing and outcome of the Battle of Nuevo Laredo, and it caused Obregón to suspend his campaign during the late fall and winter of 1913-1914.

For the time being, Obregón continued to recruit, train, and reorganize. All the First Chief could do on the diplomatic front was to give a preliminary glimpse of the "Carranza Doctrine," a theory of non-interventionism by all nations in the affairs of other states, and fundamentally a rehash of Benito Juárez's philosophy, *"El respeto al derecho ajeno es la paz,"* which he did not fully articulate until the end of 1915.

Glossary

ABC	Argentina, Brazil, and Chile
Agrarista	A supporter of land reform
Auxiliaries	Auxiliary soldiers admitted to service according to the decree of December 4, 1856
Bailarinas	Constitutionalist slang for machine guns
Bajío, El	A region north of Mexico City that comprises the states of Aguascalientes, Querétaro, Guanajuato, and part of Jalisco
Blue Jackets	U.S. Navy sailors
Border brokers	Those civilian brokers and agents in Sonora who used their personal and business networks to manage the finances and purchasing function of Sonora's Constitutionalists
Broncos	Yaquis who refused to accommodate Mexican authority
Cabecilla	Rebel chieftain/ringleader
Cacique	Extra-official political boss, also an Indian chief
Capitalino	Of or relating to Mexico City
Carraclanes	Villa's name for Carrancistas
Caudillo	A strongman who combines political with military power
Centaur	Half-human, half-horse creatures in Greek mythology; a moniker adopted by Villistas to describe themselves and their leader, the Centaur of the North, for their ability to ride as though one with the horse
Chichimeca	Mexica name for the indigenous tribes of the North, which translates as "sons of dogs"; see Mecos
Ciudadela, La	The Citadel in Mexico City
Cóconas	Constitutionalist slang for machine guns
Colegio Militar	Colegio Militar de Chapultepec, the national military academy
Colina/cerro/cuesta	Translated as hill
Comisario	The magistrate responsible for enforcing law and order in an unincorporated locale

Compadrazgo	Close friendship, usually involving shared godparent status
Conventionist	A supporter of the Convention of Aguascalientes after November 10, 1914
Cuartelazo	A barracks uprising
Cuerpo de Ejército	Literally, "army corps," a unit composed of multiple maneuver divisions
Diana	A bugle call used for reveille, but also can signal "mission accomplished," or that a particular objective has been achieved during combat
Divisionary	General of Division, the highest ranking general
Don de Mando	The military's fictional monopoly on the "gift of command"
Don Venus	Villa's name for Venustiano Carranza
EME, EMG	Army General Staff, "Estado Mayor Especial," or "Estado Mayor General"
Empresario	Businessman
Escalafón	A seniority listing of Federal Army officers by department, rank, and date of promotion
Felicistas	Supporters of Don Félix Díaz
Filibuster	A person engaging in unauthorized warfare against a foreign country
First Chief	Leader of the Constitutionalist Army: Venustiano Carranza
Fiscal Gendarmes	Armed customs agents who belonged to the Treasury (*Hacienda*) Department
Fuego segador	Grazing fire
Grand Chichimec	The vast area to the north of the Valley of Mexico named after the Mexica word for its inhabitants, "Chichimeca"
Guerrilla	A type of paramilitary unit organized under the May 25, 1862 law, *cap.*
Güero	A fair-haired, lighter-complected person
Haberes	Soldier's pay consisting of wages and per diem
Hacendado	Landowners in general, but chiefly the owner of a hacienda

Hacienda	A large estate sometimes with the economic diversity and institutions of a small town; also, the Ministry of Finance
Huertistas	Supporters of Interim Constitutional President of the Mexican United States, Victoriano Huerta
Intervene	To seize income producing property and manage it for revolutionary purpose
Jacal	A thatched wattle-and-daub hut
Jarocho	A native of Veracruz State
Jefatura político	Offices of the jefe político
Jefatura de armas	Command center of the jefe de las armas
Jefe	Generally, a chief or leader; specifically, field-grade officers
Jefe político	A local magistrate with near-dictatorial power appointed by the federal and sometimes state government
Jefe del detall	Adjutant; administrative chief of a Rural Police Corps equivalent to army major, usually associated with training duties
Juárez Law	Benito Juárez's Law of January 25, 1862, that fixed the immediate penalty of death upon all those caught collaborating with the enemy
Juchiteco	Indigene from Oaxaca State
Laguneros	People from the Laguna region, centered on the twin cities of Torreón, Coahuila and Gómez Palacio, Durango
League	Measure of approximately 4.2 kilometers
Leva	Forced military enlistment
Liberals	Members of PLM
Licenciado	Lic., licentiate (typically a lawyer)
Line of Foragers	Term for an open order line of cavalry
Line of Shooters	Term for the firing line of an infantry unit deployed under the ternary system
Loberos	Foxholes, primary fighting position
Loma	Translated as "eminence," "elevation," or "heights" when plural
Magonistas	Liberals

Manso	A "tame" Yaqui
Máquina loca	A runaway train usually loaded with dynamite and launched at an enemy, literally "crazy engine"
Martillo defensivo	A disposition with a wing in a concave position to the center of the line
Martillo offensivo,	"Hammer strike" maneuver, that swings out and hits the opponents flank martillazo on a near perpendicular line
Mecos	Abbreviation of *Chichimecas*, "sons of dogs," derogatory name for Norteño Constitutionalists; see Grand Chichimec
Mexicanidad	Mexicanness
Militarism	The exaltation of a military ethos, often perpetuated by soldiers, in finding solutions to national problems on an applied or practical level, typically incompatible with liberal democracy, and often with market economics
Military Economy	On a micro level it is the allocation of limited resources to achieve a military objective, that is, the balancing of principles of mass and economy of force; on a macro level it refers to the sum total of goods and services produced for, consumed by, or under the control of, the defense establishment
Mixed section	Another name for a combined-arms column
Mixed train	A train with both freight and passenger railcars
Mochos	Specifically a reference to those soldiers who wore a truncated shako that looked like a cut-back version of the taller style, but more generally, any Federal soldier
Monte	Mount
Nacionales	National Guardsmen
Neutrality Laws	International law that prevents a neutral nation from offering assistance to belligerents, either the principal hostile powers or their allies

Norteño	Northern/Northerner
Oficial ("officer")	Generally, an officer; specifically, a line-grade officer
Pelones/Pelados	Federal Army soldiers, whose close-cropped hair gave them the appearance of penitentiary inmates
Permanents	Army officers with a regular commission
Plana Mayor	The college of generals
PLM	Partido Liberal Mexicano (Liberals)
Porfiristas	Supporters of Porfirio Díaz
Practicals	Those officers who had come up through the ranks
Praetorianism	Abusive political influence exercised by a military group
Pronunciados	Rebels
Pronunciamiento	Declaration of rebellion
Puerto	Port or mountain pass
Regiomontanos	A native of Monterrey, Nuevo León
RMA	A revolution in military affairs
Rurales	Mexico's national Rural Police Corps
Sábanas	Villista paper money, so called because of their large size, lit. "sheets"
Scout Corps	The new designation for Rural Police corps after their transfer from Interior to War
Serranos	Mountain folk
Soldaderas	Women who accompany soldiers in the field, generally for logistical support but also as combatants at times
Stars and Bars	Insignia of field- and line-grade officers, respectively
Supreme Powers	The federal level legislature, executive, and judiciary; also the old guard units organized for their defense
Surianos	Chiefly Mexican word for "Southerners"
Tacos	Slang for leggings
Tacticals	Those officers who graduated the Colegio Militar's three year curriculum and went into the combat arms
Technicals	Those officers who graduated from the Colegio Militar under the extended ("*fac-*

	ultativos") 7- or 8-year program for artillery, engineers, or the general staff
Terrenos baldíos	Spanish for "idle" or "uncultivated" lands; an official designation for unsurveyed lands that permitted land survey companies and speculators to legally gain title to unclaimed lands that too often became an instrument for separating the politically-disenfranchised from their patrimony
Theoreticians	Those officers who studied the military arts and sciences, mainly of the EME
Three arms	Infantry, cavalry, and artillery
Three Ms	Money, Men, and Materiel
Three Ps	Position, Promotion, and Pension
Vainillales	Vanilla-producing lands
Vazquista	Supporter of Emilio Vázquez Gómez
Vecinos	Generally, neighbors; specifically, citizens
Viejas	See Soldaderas
White arm	Weapons with a blade, such as sabers and bayonets

Timeline

1910

November 20 (Mexico) official start date for the Mexican Revolution as set by Francisco I. Madero

1912

December 18 (Jalisco) Cándido Aguilar's 38th Rural Police Corps recaptures Huejuquilla from Colorados Benjamín Argumedo and Cheché Campos

1913

February 18 (Mexico City) Federal General Victoriano Huerta and his fellow praetorians remove President Francisco Madero and his Vice President José María Pino Suárez from office and advise the nation of his assumption of power; (Coahuila) the state government authorizes Governor Venustiano Carranza to borrow funds; (Durango) Manuel Chao declares revolution against Huerta

February 19 (Coahuila) the state government supports Carranza's stance refusing to recognize Huerta, and grants the governor special powers to organize armed forces and encourages other states to follow suit

February 22 (Mexico City) President Madero and Vice President Pino Suárez are murdered by praetorians; (Chihuahua) the Federal Army arrests Governor Abraham González for the "crime" of authorizing the state's auxiliaries to buy arms and ammunition

February 23 (Coahuila) in the first military act under Governor Venustiano Carranza, Jacinto B. Treviño and Miguel M. Acosta commandeer a passenger train on its way to Saltillo and return it to Ramos Arizpe for service in the new army; (Sonora) Federal General Miguel Gil intercepts and impounds in Empalme Station a remittance of war materiel for use against the rebellious Yaquis, providing the Sonoran legislature a legal basis to revolt under the allegation that the federal government had violated the state's sovereignty; Aniceto Campos in Fronteras is first to rebel, disarming the local garrison

February 23 (Chihuahua) Colonel Chao attacks and takes Santa Bárbara as Captain José Rodríguez joins the anti-Huerta movement in Guerrero District

February 26 (Sonora) Governor José María Maytorena requests a leave of absence, turns over office to Interim Governor Ignacio Pesqueira, and abandons the country

March 4 (Sonora) the Sonoran state legislature votes to withhold recognition of Huerta's government

March 5 (Chihuahua) Colonel Chao attacks Parral

March 6 (Sonora) Colonel Álvaro Obregón loads his battalion on trains and heads north to clear the border of Federal Army units as Colonel Ramón V. Sosa goes south toward Guaymas to recruit, organize, and destroy the rails between Ortiz and Empalme; Federal Colonel Emilio Kosterlitzky urges General Pedro Ojeda to concentrate his forces in Nogales to defend the border town; (Coahuila) Colonel Roberto Rivas attacks San Pedro de las Colonias

March 7 (Chihuahua) Federal Army praetorians murder Governor González

March 8 (Chihuahua) Villa crosses border with eight supporters to begin campaigning against Huerta's government

March 13 (Sonora) Obregón captures Nogales

March 15 (Sonora) Ojeda defeats Colonel Plutarco Elías Calles at La Morita

March 20 (Sonora) After two days of combat, Colonel Benjamín Hill turns back Federal Colonel Eleazar Muñoz at La Dura and La Concentración; (Chihuahua) Colonel Chao and the Herrera brothers (Luis and Maclovio) take Santa Bárbara

March 22 (Chihuahua) Colonel Toribio Ortega occupies Ojinaga after the Federals flee

March 23 (Coahuila) Governor Carranza's attack on Saltillo fails; (Chihuahua) Federals retake Santa Bárbara

March 25 (Mexico City) the 2nd Carabineros de Coahuila Corps jumps its barracks in Mexico City and journeys south to operate with Genevevo de la O's Zapatistas, thus encouraging other Rural Police and Auxiliary corps to join the revolution against Huerta

March 26 (Coahuila) Governor Carranza assumes the title of First Chief after penning the Plan de Guadalupe, which serves as the organic charter of the Constitutionalist Army upon being endorsed by a group of militia officers; (Sonora) Cananea falls to Colonel Obregón after three days of combat

March 28 (Sonora) Ojeda defeats Calles at San José Canyon; (Nuevo León) Jesús Carranza attacks and takes Lampazos; (Durango) Calixto Contreras and Orestes Pereyra defeat the praetorian General Luis Anaya at San Gabriel Station

March 29 (Mexico) Comandante Jesús Agustín Castro leaves Tlalnepantla to confer with the First Chief

March 30 (Mexico) Miguel Navarrete leads the 21st Rural Police Corps north to Tamaulipas; (Durango) Colonel Tomás Urbina defeats the Federal garrison and captures Mapimí

April 1 (Mexico City) Huerta announces that 84 former insurgent leaders with 6,000 troops, mostly Colorados, will fight for his regime, and he "suppresses" military zones in order to organize the units in those geographical entities into operational divisions

April 2 (Chihuahua) Colonels Hernández and Herrera defeat Federals at Conchos Station

April 10 (Chihuahua) Villa attacks a passenger train and captures silver bars worth $75,000 to finance his upcoming campaign; (Zacatecas) Second Officer Pánfilo Natera of the 26th Rural Police Corps takes up arms against Huerta

April 11 (Coahuila) Jesús Agustín Castro departs Baján to find his command in Tamaulipas

April 13 (Sonora) Obregón defeats General Ojeda and captures Naco; (Chihuahua) Colonel Urbina attacks Jiménez, taking it the next day after Federals had reinforced it

April 17 (Sonora) Colonel Hill captures Alamos

April 18 (Sonora) Federal General Gil defeats Colonel Sosa at San Germán; (Coahuila) representatives of the states of Sonora, Coahuila, and the revolutionary junta of Chihuahua sign the Monclova Accord to endorse the Plan de Guadalupe

April 20 (Coahuila) The First Chief offers to recognize the rank of all Federals, except for certain praetorians, who defect to the Constitutionalist Army within thirty days

April 22 (Tamaulipas) Navarrete leads the 21st Rural Corps in a failed attack to capture Ciudad Victoria; (Mexico City) Medina Barrón's column leaves Mexico City to reinforce the Federal Division of the Yaqui

April 23 (Chihuahua) Colonels Chao, Herrera, and Rodríguez capture Camargo, destroying the garrison; (Durango) the Arrietas and Pazuengos with Contreras and Pereyra attack Durango City, having to retreat after three days when Campos' Colorados hit the Constitutionalists from the rear

April 24 (Sonora) Federals defeat the Constitutionalists of Rodríguez and Hill at Lencho Station in the southern part of the state

April 26 (Coahuila) The First Chief authorizes the first issuance of Constitutionalist money, five million pesos

May 1 (Mexico City) Huerta increases soldiers' pay and publishes decree number 436, making the School of the Soldier "rudimentary"; (Sonora) Federal Brigadier Luis Medina Barrón arrives in the port of Guaymas with reinforcements for the Division of the Yaqui

May 3 (Nuevo León) General Jesús Carranza destroys the Federal garrison at Villaldama resulting in General Trucy Aubert's sacking

May 4 (Tamaulipas) General Jesús Agustín Castro reunites with his 21st Rural Police Corps and declines to participate in the attack on Matamoros

May 6 (Chihuahua) Federal General Salvador Mercado abandons Parral

May 8 (Nuevo León) Federal generals Joaquín Téllez and Fernando González arrive to assume command of Trucy Aubert's old brigade and the Division of the Bravo, respectively; (Zacatecas) Constitutionalist General Natera takes Fresnillo

May 10 (Coahuila) The First Chief decrees indemnification of foreign-owned property and requires his officers to respect said property

May 11 (Sonora) Colonel Obregón defeats Federal Brigadier Luis Medina Barrón in the Battle of Santa Rosa

May 13 (Sonora) Federal General Pedro Ojeda arrives in Guaymas to take over command of the Division of the Yaqui

May 15 (Mexico City) Huerta institutes a system of military trains to protect the rail system

May 22 (Sonora) Federal Colonel Jesús P. Díaz abandons Torín for Empalme, leaving the southern part of the state, including the wealthy Yaqui Valley, to the Constitutionalists

May 26 (Chihuahua) Francisco Villa accepts a general's commission from Carranza, catapulting him in rank over the numerous colonels who had been operating in state for months

May 30 (Chihuahua) Villa directs his first battle as a Constitutionalist commander in a victory over the Federals at Conchos Station; (Mexico City) Huerta signs Decree 438, raising the army to a permanent level of 80,000 men

May 31 (Chihuahua) General Mercado assumes command of the Federal Division of the North

June 1 (Mexico City) Decree 437 signed by Huerta abrogates the law of May 28, 1869, which had instituted the lottery and volunteer system of recruitment, in favor of a Law of Obligatory Military Service

June 3 (Tamaulipas) Colonel Lucio Blanco attacks and takes the plaza of Matamoros

June 5 (Chihuahua) Villa abandons Camargo and begins moving toward the state's northwest in order to recruit among the military colonies, organize, and receive war materiel from Sonora and the United States

June 6 (Zacatecas) Natera's Constitutionalists capture the state capital

June 13 (Mexico City) Huerta and his general hold a council of war to agree a plan to address the loss of Matamoros and Zacatecas, and General Manuel Mondragón resigns as Secretary of War to be replaced by General Aurelio Blanquet

June 15 (Mexico City) Generals Joaquín Maass and Guillermo Rubio Navarrete depart the nation's capital over two days to open the Federal campaign in the Northeast

June 16 (Zacatecas) Federal General José Delgado retakes the state capital

June 18 (Durango) the Federals lose the state capital and with it essentially the whole of the state

June 25 (Sonora) Federal General Ojeda realizes that he cannot beat Obregón at San Alejandro and begins his retreat, suffering a debilitating defeat at Santa María

June 27 (Sonora) the Constitutionalists invest the port of Guaymas

July 1 (Coahuila) General Orozco's column of Colorados departs Torreón headed for Chihuahua

July 2 (Coahuila) General Rubio's Federals run Colonel Jesús Carranza out of Candela

July 3 (Mexico City) Huerta signs decree 442, which terminates the Escuela Nacional de Aspirantes and creates the new rank of "cadet" to fill out the officer corps, abolishes the Colegio Militar to replace it with the Preparatory Military School, and creates the Professional Military School for Technicals and the Superior Military School for post-graduate study

July 4 (Coahuila) the First Chief decrees the creation of seven Constitutionalist army corps—the Northwest: Sonora, Chihuahua, Durango, Sinaloa, Baja California; the Northeast: Coahuila, Nueva León, Tamaulipas; the East: Puebla, Tlaxcala, Veracruz; the West: Jalisco, Colima, Michoacán, Tepic; the Central: Zacatecas, Aguascalientes, San Luis Potosí, Guanajuato, Querétaro, Hidalgo, and México; the South: Morelos, Guerrero, Oaxaca; the Southeast: Yucatán, Campeche, Tabasco, and Chiapas

July 8 (Coahuila) Colonels Pablo González and Carranza retake Candela, and then have to abandon it immediately

July 10 (Coahuila) Federal General Joaquín Maass takes Monclova

July 11 (Sonora) another 1,136 Federals disembark in Guaymas with twelve artillery pieces and a great amount of ammunition; (Coahuila) Federal General Felipe Alvírez arrives in Torreón from Mexico City with his Sapper Battalion and Duranguense volunteers to form a column to retake Durango City

July 12 (Chihuahua) General Orozco's column of Colorados defeats Maclovio Herrera and Trinidad Rodríguez at Díaz Station

July 14 (Chihuahua) General Orozco's column of Colorados defeats Rodríguez, Herrera, Chao, and Hernández at Camargo; (Sonora) Pedro Ojeda promoted to general of division for the successful defense of Guaymas

July 15 (Coahuila) the First Chief leaves Cuatro Ciénagas for Torreón to direct the assault on that plaza, beginning an odyssey that will take him away from Coahuila for almost a year; (Mexico City) Huerta abrogates Madero's Decree 429 of May 4, 1912, once again outlawing the importation of arms, ammunition, or any related materiel, as well as dynamite, caps, or any other explosives for industrial use without the express permission from the Secretary of War

July 22 (Coahuila) the Constitutionalists initiate an assault on Torreón; (Chihuahua) General Orozco's column of Colorados arrives in Chihuahua City

July 30 (Coahuila) the Constitutionalists quit the attack on Torreón in failure, and Cándido Aguilar departs for the Huasteca

July 31 (Mexico City) Huerta signs decree 445, which transfers the Rural Police Corps from the Secretary of the Interior to War and renames them "Scout Corps"

August 5 (Chihuahua) during his southward trajectory to link up with General Villa, Toribio Ortega attacks a Federal train returning from the border with provisions for Chihuahua City at Ranchería Station

August 15 (Mexico City) the Rural Police Corps are moved to War and cease to exist as an institution

August 16 (Coahuila) González's Constitutionalists defeated in the Battle of Las Hermanas

August 18 (Sonora) the state legislature ratifies the Monclova Accords and Obregón sends a doomed expedition to invade Baja California; (Chihuahua) Toribio Ortega links up with General Villa at San Buenaventura

August 25 (Mexico City) per Decree number 449 the Permanent and Auxiliary infantry units are re-designated "regiments," and with the cavalry set on a war footing

August 26 (Chihuahua) Villa defeats Colorado General Félix Terrazas at San Andrés

August 27 (Washington) President Wilson addresses Congress and asks that all U.S. citizens leave Mexico as he imposes an arms embargo on Huerta's regime; (Sinaloa) Federal Lieutenant Colonel Teodoro Valdivieso lands in Topolobampo as one part of the pincer to attack San Blas, an operation that ends in failure

August 29 (Mexico City) General Felipe Ángeles released from Federal custody and exiled to Europe

August 30 (Tamaulipas) General Lucio Blanco carries out famous distribution of lands belonging to Hacienda Los Borregos, owned by Félix Díaz

September 1 (Sinaloa) Major Antonio Olague's Federals of the land-based pincer operation on San Blas return to Sinaloa de Leyva

September 2 (Sinaloa) Colonel Miguel Rodríguez's Federals of the land-based pincer operation on San Blas arrive in Topolobampo and evacuate with the wounded to Mazatlán; (San Luis Potosí) General Cándido Aguilar arrives at Rancho Tepemiche and begins organizing the 1st Division of the East

September 14 (Sinaloa) in El Fuerte Obregón meets the First Chief, who has arrived from Durango

September 24 (Sonora) the First Chief receives the keys to the city of Hermosillo and delivers a landmark speech from the balcony of the statehouse

September 27 (Sonora) the First Chief promotes Pablo González to general of brigade

September 29 (Durango) at Hacienda La Loma Villa's Division of the North comes into existence and the Battle of Second Torreón begins, resulting in the "*desastre de Avilés*" on this first day of combat

October 1 (Coahuila) Villa captures Torreón

October 5 (Sonora) General Hill and Colonels Macario Gaxiola, José Cabanillas, and Claro G. Molina capture Sinaloa de Leyva

October 7 (Coahuila) the Federals finally march into Piedras Negras, previously vacated by the Constitutionalists

October 10 (Mexico City) Huerta dismisses the Congress in what has been called his "second coup"

October 24 (Mexico City) Huerta signs Decree number 454 raising the permanent army to 150,000 men, and Decree number 455 increases

authorized number of generals to 140; (Nuevo León) the Battle of First
Monterrey ends in a Federal victory; (Tamaulipas) Lucio Blanco turns
over command to General Jesús Dávila Sánchez, who immediately gives
orders to mobilize and go to the aid of González attacking Monterrey,
only to learn along the way that the battle has ended in defeat for the
Constitutionalists

November 3 (Nuevo León) Cesáreo Castro's Constitutionalists defeat General
Ricardo Peña's Federal pursuit column at Hualahuises

November 9 (Chihuahua) after five days of combat Villa's Division of the
North calls off its siege of the capital city

November 14 (Sinaloa) Obregón's Army Corps of the Northwest wins the
Battle of Culiacán, which gives the Constitutionalists control of the entire state except for Mazatlán

November 15 (Chihuahua) Villa's Division of the North uses a Trojan horse
stratagem to slip into Ciudad Juárez during the night and capture the
vital entrepôt; (Coahuila) Constitutionalist generals José Isabel Robles
and Juan E. Gómez propose a combined operation to capture Saltillo or
Monterrey with González's Division of the Northeast

November 18 (Tamaulipas) González's Division of the Northeast captures
Ciudad Victoria, virtually securing control of the entire state with the
exception of Nuevo Laredo and Tampico at the polar ends of the state

November 23 (Tamaulipas) González's Division of the Northeast turns back
General Rubio Navarrete's pursuit column at Santa Engracia

November 25 (Chihuahua) Villa's Division of the North defeats a Federal
combined-arms column of Federals and Colorados at Tierra Blanca, pre-
cipitating the Federal loss of the state; (Tamaulipas) González's Division
of the Northeast officially raised to the designation of the Army Corps
of the Northeast

November 27 (Sonora) the First Chief predicts that the Federals will evacuate
Chihuahua City and proposes his first national strategy that calls for Villa
to attack Saltillo and Monterrey while González invades San Luis Potosí
to block Federal reinforcements as the Zapatista converge on Mexico
City, all to take place at the end of December

November 30 (Chihuahua) Mercado evacuates Chihuahua City

December 13 (Chihuahua) the last of the Federal Division of the North
arrives at Ojinaga; (Coahuila) Federal General José Refugio Velasco's
Division of the Nazas retakes Torreón from General Calixto Contreras,
foiling the First Chief's strategy; (San Luis Potosí) Federals repulse the
Constitutionalist attack on Tampico

December 23 (Nuevo León) Colonel Andrés Saucedo receives news that Federal Captain Federico Montes wants to defect to the Constitutionalists with his men and machine guns

1914

January 1 (Tamaulipas) the attack opens on Nuevo Laredo; (Chihuahua) Constitutionalists arrive to lay siege to Ojinaga

January 4 (Chihuahua) Constitutionalists deliver first assault on Ojinaga; (Tamaulipas) Jesús Agustín Castro arrives in Matamoros to answer to charges of "usurpation of office"

January 7 (Tamaulipas) González proposes to the First Chief that as soon as Villa takes Ojinaga he should help the Division of the Northeast attack Monterrey

January 9 (Mexico City) Secretary of War authorizes Federal division commanders to impose forced loans

January 10 (Chihuahua) Villa's Constitutionalists take Ojinaga

January 11 (San Luis Potosí) Eulalio Gutiérrez's Constitutionalists attack Matehuala and Ignacio Corona's Federals push the Cedillos out of Alaquines and Ciudad del Maíz the next day

January 12 (Tamaulipas) González submits his proposal to Villa for their two divisions to take Monterrey

January 14 (Coahuila) González orders Fernando Peraldí, Esteban Falcón, Sebastián Carranza, Samuel Vázquez, Fortunato Zuazua, and Ildefonso Vázquez to form one column and begin attacking the Federal garrisons; (Sonora) the First Chief informs González that Villa will take Torreón first, and then cooperate to take Monterrey and Saltillo; (San Luis Potosí) General Francisco Romero appointed to command the Federal Division of the Potosí

January 15 (Chihuahua) Villa declines González's strategy proposal and announces his intention to take Torreón first and then cooperate to take Monterrey; (Mexico City) General of Brigade Eduardo Camargo files his strategy proposal

January 17 (Chihuahua) Villa invites Carranza to Chihuahua to help settle the state's affairs while he marches off to battle

January 22 (Tamaulipas) Jesús Agustín Castro acquitted of the charge of usurpation of office; (Sonora) the First Chief promotes Cándido Aguilar to general of brigade and gives him command of Army Corps of the East

January 28 (San Luis Potosí) Colonel Miguel Navarrete attacks Tablas Station while General Alberto Carrera Torres attacks San Bartolo Station

January 30 (Nuevo León) Federals launch offensive to recapture Matamoros as Brigadier Ignacio Muñoz takes Cadereyta

January 31 (Tamaulipas) González issues orders to Francisco Murguía, Cesáreo Castro, and Francisco Coss to destroy rails and position their brigades to attack Monterrey

February 1 (Nuevo León) Federal Brigadier Muñoz forces Antonio I. Villarreal's 1st Brigade out of Los Ramones

February 3 (Washington) President Wilson removes the arms embargo against the Constitutionalist Army

February 6 (Tamaulipas) González applies to have U.S. authorities release war materiel previously impounded under the March 14, 1912 proclamation and gives a February 15 deadline for all small unit commanders to join a major unit and begin campaigning, or face execution under the Juárez Law

February 9 (Chihuahua) Federal Secretary of War divides Chihuahua into three zones and assigns command to Colorados for the purpose of organizing guerrilla warfare

February 10 (Nuevo León) Constitutionalist General Teodoro Elizondo unsuccessfully tries to retake Cadereyta

February 12 (Sinaloa) the First Chief issues decree number 18 to authorize the printing of a tranche of thirty million pesos to take advantage of the lifting of the arms embargo by the United States; (San Luis Potosí) Navarrete's 8th Brigade attacks Espinazo del Diablo Station

February 13 (Nuevo León) Federal Irregular Colonel Pablo de los Santos departs Cadereyta and attacks Elizondo in Dr. González resulting in the capture of the town

February 17 (San Luis Potosí) Navarrete's 8th Brigade battles Colonel Pablo Quintana's Huertistas at Hacienda La Boquilla

February 18 (Sonora) the First Chief issues Circular Number 8 that details those banks to be liquidated for failure to resume operations in the states occupied by Constitutionalists

February 22 (Nuevo León) Muñoz's Federals renew offensive pushing Elizondo out of Papagallos and Villarreal out of Los Ramones

February 24 (Nuevo León) Constitutionalist General Cesáreo's 4th Brigade unsuccessfully tries to take Lampazos as Murguía's 2nd Brigade annihilates the Federal garrison at Rodríguez Station

February 25 (Nuevo León) Elizondo and Villarreal counterattack and put an end to Muñoz's campaign to capture Matamoros

February 26 (Sonora) the First Chief departs Hermosillo for Chihuahua; (San Luis Potosí) General Carrera Torres' 6th Brigade annihilates Colonel Pablo Quintana's irregular column at Pozo de Acuña

February 28 (Sinaloa) the Federal vessel *Tampico* defects to the Constitutionalists

March 4 (Sonora) the First Chief authorizes printing of ₱200,000 worth of bills in small denominations

March 10 (Coahuila) Generals Murguía and Castro attack Monclova and fail to take it after two days of fighting

March 13 (Chihuahua) Toribio Ortega's González Ortega Brigade embarks on trains and heads for the staging area at Yermo Station to join the other brigades that had left a few days earlier

March 15 (Tamaulipas) Federal Brigadier Gustavo Guardiola y Aguirre's column departs Nuevo Laredo to attack Matamoros; (Coahuila) Federal Lieutenant Colonel Juan Felipe Rico again defeats generals Murguía and Castro, this time at San Buenaventura

March 21 (Mexico City) Federal General Javier de Moure's column departs for the North to participate in taking of Matamoros; (Nuevo León) Villarreal departs Los Ramones and Rancho del Peine to stop Guardiola's advance on Matamoros as Colonel Pablo de la Garza leaves Montemorelos to put pressure on Monterrey

March 23 (Tamaulipas) Villarreal defeats Guardiola at Ciudad Guerrero and Guardiola is recalled to stand trial for his failure; (Chihuahua) Villa's Division of the North opens the attack on Gómez Palacio-Torreón; (Nuevo León) the deadline for Murguía and Castro to arrive at their positions for the attack on Monterrey expires; (Coahuila) Murguía arrives at Ocampo and Castro fights Federals at Espinazo Station

March 24 (Nuevo León) Colonel de la Garza takes Villa Santiago; (Coahuila) General Francisco Coss defeats a Federal column in Villa de Arteaga

March 25 (Nuevo León) Federals departing Cadereyta and Monterrey retake Villa Santiago and push Colonel de la Garza back to Allende

March 26 (Nuevo León) the Federal pincer to retake Villa Santiago leaves Cadereyta with a short garrison, and General Elizondo moves in and occupies the town after a brief firefight; (San Luis Potosí) General Miguel Navarrete ordered to take the 8th Brigade north to participate in attack on Monterrey; (Durango) the Constitutionalist Division of the North moves in to occupy Gómez Palacio after more than three days of combat

March 27 (Nuevo León) Federals attacking from Monterrey force Elizondo out of Cadereyta and he withdraws to Allende

March 28 (Chihuahua) the First Chief arrives at Ciudad Juárez

March 29 (Coahuila) Federal General Javier de Moure's column arrives in
La Laguna after the failed campaign to recapture Matamoros; (San Luis
Potosí) Colonel Blas Corral of the 8th Brigade captures the town of
Alaquines, coming to dominate the eastern part of the San Luis Potosí-
Tampico rail line

March 31 (San Luis Potosí) Elements of the 8th Brigade begin departing
Ciudad del Maíz to participate in the campaign for Tampico

April 2 (Coahuila) Torreón falls to Villa's victorious Division of the North;
(Tamaulipas) González leaves Matamoros to begin the Monterrey campaign

April 4 (Tamaulipas) The Constitutionalist White Cross gets the remaining
Constitutionalists detained by U.S. authorities after the Battle of Nuevo
Laredo released from custody; (Mexico City) Huerta creates the new rank
of General of Army

April 5 (Coahuila) Federal Lieutenant Colonel Rico pushes Murguía into
western part of the state; (Tamaulipas) Constitutionalist General Luis
Caballero begins demonstrating against Tampico as General Aguilar's
Constitutionalist Division of the East leaves Xicoténcatl to begin the
Veracruz campaign

April 12 (Tamaulipas) General Luis Caballero halts attack on Tampico; (San
Luis Potosí) General Aguilar's Constitutionalists attack and take Ciudad
Valles

April 13 (Coahuila) Villa's Division of the North destroys the numerous
Federal columns and divisions at San Pedro de las Colonias

April 14 (Sonora) Obregón orders his Army Corps of the Northwest to depart Navojoa for Culiacán, resuming his western campaign

April 15 (Nuevo León) Elizondo's 3rd Brigade of the Division of the Northeast
takes Cadereyta

April 16 (Nuevo León) Villarreal's 1st Brigade and Castro's 4th Brigade of the
Division of the Northeast take Salinas Victoria

April 18 (San Luis Potosí) At San Mateo Navarrete's 8th Brigade encounters
General Corona trying to return to his headquarters in Cárdenas Station
and forces the Federals back to Valles

April 20 (Coahuila) Federals defeated at San Pedro de las Colonias abandon
Hipólito Station in an attempt to reach Saltillo; (Nuevo León) González's
Division of the Northeast begins the assault on Monterrey proper

April 21 (Veracruz) U.S. Navy and Marines invade Veracruz

April 22 (Tamaulipas) Federal General Teodoro Quintana torches Nuevo
Laredo and then abandons the border town; (Hidalgo) Aguilar's
Constitutionalist Division of the East takes Huejutla

April 23 (Washington) President Wilson resumes the arms embargo against the Constitutionalists; (Texas) the reinforced U.S. 5th Brigade gets orders to depart for Veracruz and sets sail from Galveston the next day with General Frederick Funston, as General Tasker Bliss in in San Antonio urges the United States to occupy border towns on the Mexican side immediately; (Coahuila) Federals defeated at San Pedro de las Colonias begin filtering into Saltillo

April 24 (Nuevo León) Federal General Wilfrido Massieu abandons Monterrey to González's Division of the Northeast; (Tamaulipas) General Luis Caballero renews attack on Tampico; (San Luis Potosí) General Carrera Torres destroys the column of Federal General Juan de Dios Arzamendi at La Herradura

April 26 (Coahuila) General Murguía defeats Huertista General Luis Alberto Guajardo in Allende, variously killing, dispersing, and incorporating portions of Guajardo's command; (San Luis Potosí) General Miguel M. Navarrete leads attack on Rodríguez Station and is killed

April 27 (Veracruz) Aguilar's Division of the East induces the seven hundred Federals garrisoning Tantoyuca to flee for Tampico, reinforcing the garrison defending the port

April 28 (Nuevo León) Castro's 4th Brigade leaves the Monterrey area for Altamira to join in the attack on Tampico

April 30 (Coahuila) Federal General Wilfrido Massieu's Monterrey garrison reaches Saltillo; (San Luis Potosí) Colonel Manuel Lárraga receives orders to move from Tancanhuitz to El Ébano in order to block any Federals trying to retreat from Tampico

May 2 (Veracruz) General Funston establishes a military government in the port of Veracruz

May 3 (San Luis Potosí) General Alberto Carrera Torres' 6th Division destroys Federal Alberto T. Rasgado's column, forcing the Federals to yield the western portion of the San Luis Potosí-Tampico rail line

May 5 (Tepic) Federal General Juan Solares surrenders the plaza of Acaponeta to the Constitutionalists

May 11 (Veracruz) General Aguilar's Division of the East opens formal battle against the Federals occupying the chokepoint at Tamiahua; (Coahuila) the first of Villa's Division of the North depart Porvenir on course for Saltillo

May 13 (Tamaulipas) González's Army Corps of the Northeast defeats General Ignacio Morelos Zaragoza's Federals and captures the port of Tampico

May 16 (San Luis Potosí) Colonel Lárraga's lead elements arrive at El Ébano to block the Federals in their egress from Tampico; (Tepic) General Manuel

M. Diéguez defeats General Domingo Servín's Federals defending the territorial capital, but Servín's column manages to escape; (Sinaloa) General Obregón decides to leave Mazatlán under siege and continue the campaign heading southward, urged onward by the First Chief who is beginning to suspect the conduct of Villa and Ángeles

May 17 (Coahuila) Villa's Division of the North destroys the Federals assembling at Paredón

May 19 (Mexico City) Huerta grants all the civilian employees of the War Ministry uniforms and military rank based on their pay level

May 20 (Coahuila) the Federals abandon Saltillo, shamefully setting fire to the casino and Banco de Coahuila

May 21 (Tamaulipas) González outlaws the exportation of cattle under penalty of up to five years of prison

June 7 (Coahuila) the First Chief arrives in Saltillo; (San Luis Potosí) around this time Federal General Maass' column was arriving in the state capital from Saltillo

June 10 (Mexico City) General Morelos Zaragoza's Tampico garrison arrives in the nation's capital; (Sonora) Colonel Calles takes his 3rd Infantry Battalion of Sonora north to Nogales to avoid a confrontation with Governor Maytorena's supporters and begins recruiting for an upcoming conflict

June 11 (Zacatecas) Generals Natera and Arrieta open a formal attack on Zacatecas; (Coahuila) the First Chief orders Villa to send 3,000 men and artillery to reinforce Natera and Arrieta

June 13 (Coahuila) after days of refusing to send forces and materiel to Natera and Arrieta in the attack on Zacatecas, General Villa instead resigns his command, but his subordinates refuse to replace him and instead resolve to go to Zacatecas together as a division

June 14 (Zacatecas) the attack on Zacatecas fails when Colorado General Benjamín Argumedo reinforces the plaza, and Medina Barrón receives a promotion to divisionary

June 15 (Coahuila) brigades of the Division of the North begin departing Torreón to participate in the Battle of Zacatecas

June 18 (Zacatecas) lead forces of the Division of the North begin arriving at Calera Station and reconnoitering Zacatecas; (San Luis Potosí) General Antonio Olea departs the state capital with assets belonging to the Federal Army Corps of the Potosí to reinforce the defenders of Zacatecas

June 20 (Zacatecas) preliminary fighting begins around Zacatecas; (Aguascalientes) Orozco arrives at Soledad and refuses to advance any farther toward Zacatecas; (Chihuahua) Villista military authorities in

Ciudad Juárez arrest the Treasurer General of the Constitutionalist Army, send him to prison in Chihuahua City, and confiscate all the assets of the offices of the First Chieftaincy still in the city

June 21 (Zacatecas) Federal Colonel Alberto García Tello reaches Palmira with a Federal column and advances no farther

June 23 (Zacatecas) the Constitutionalists defeat Federal General Medina Barrón's Federals and take the plaza of Zacatecas by fire and sword

June 25 (Zacatecas) generals of the Division of the North begin responding receptively to the Army Corps of the Northeast's offer to broker a rapprochement between Villa and the First Chief

June 26 (Zacatecas) the Division of the North begins moving southward toward Mexico City; (Jalisco) Obregón's advanced cavalry first encounters the Federals at Hacienda El Refugio, some twenty-five kilometers ahead of the camp at Ahualulco

June 27 (Zacatecas) the Division of the North reverses course and begins the movement back north

June 29 (Jalisco) Obregón receives a promotion to general of division, catapulting him in rank over Villa

July 4 (Coahuila) representatives of the Division of the North and Army Corps of the Northeast meet in Torreón to arrange the reconciliation of Carranza and Villa; (San Luis Potosí) General Jesús Carranza arrives in Cerritos to organize for the attack on the state capital

July 6 (Jalisco) The Battle of Orendáin begins

July 8 (Coahuila) Torreón Accords are finalized and General Francisco Murguía mobilizes his forces from Saltillo to Charcas, San Luis Potosí, while Villa tells Obregón that he cannot continue southward for another month because he lacks the materiel; (Jalisco) Obregón's Army Corps of the Northwest occupies Guadalajara

July 12 (San Luis Potosí) General J. Agustín Castro's 21st Brigade, 2nd Division of the Center, begins leaving Valles toward the state capital

July 15 (Mexico City) Huerta resigns and goes into exile; the new Interim President of the Republic, Francisco Carbajal, and Minister of War, General José Refugio Velasco, order Federal forces to evacuate the states of San Luis Potosí, Aguascalientes, and Querétaro

July 16 (Chihuahua) General Toribio Ortega dies of typhoid fever

July 17 (San Luis Potosí) the Federal Army Corps of the Potosí evacuates the state capital bound for Querétaro; (Sonora) Téllez's Division of the Yaqui abandons Guaymas

July 18 (San Luis Potosí) General Eulalio Gutiérrez's brigade of the 2nd Division of the Center occupies the state capital

July 20 (Colima) General Juan Cabral's forces take up position outside Manzanillo ultimately compelling General Téllez's Federal Division of the Yaqui to put to sea for Salina Cruz

July 22 (San Luis Potosí) the mounted divisions of the Army Corps of the Northeast begin arriving in the state capital as General Carrera Torres engages the Federal rearguard on the Villa de Pozos road; (Mexico) Federals are pursuing the "rebels" belonging to Colorado Generals Antonio Rojas and José Flores Alatorre

July 27 (San Luis Potosí) the Constitutionalist Army Corps of the Northeast begins its drive on Mexico City

July 29 (Querétaro) Murguía captures the state capital; (Guanajuato) Carrera Torres takes the state capital experiencing only light resistance, General Rafael Cepeda recovers trains abandoned by the Federals in Empalme González, and Obregón's lead cavalry commanded by General Sosa and Colonel Acosta attack and take Irapuato after a brief fight

July 31 (Guanajuato) General Sosa and Colonel Acosta destroy General Rómulo Cuéllar's Federal Division of the Center at Hacienda Temascalco as Obregón arrives in Irapuato

August 1 (Querétaro) Commanders and staffs of the Constitutionalist Army Corps of the Northwest and Army Corps of the Northeast link up in the state capital; (Guanajuato) Generals Pascual Orozco, Francisco Cárdenas, and José Pérez Castro attack and sack León

August 3 (Guanajuato) Carrera Torres defeats Orozco and Cárdenas near León; Orozco heads north for the United States and exile, while Cárdenas flees to Central America

August 6 (Mexico City) Federal General José Refugio Velasco receives the report commissioned to study the defense of the nation's capital

August 7 (Mexico) General Murguía captures the state capital, Toluca

August 8 (Hidalgo) General Jacinto B. Treviño captures the state capital, Pachuca; (Sonora) Governor Maytorena orders General Salvador Alvarado arrested; (Mexico City) the Treasury issues the "de Carbajal" scrip, which commerce rejects

August 9 (Sinaloa) Constitutionalists take the port of Mazatlán, evacuated by the Federals; (Sonora) Constitutionalist Lieutenant Colonel Ramón Gómez and his men from Alamos take possession of Navojoa and declare Maytorena to be their only chief; (Mexico) General Obregón arrives in Teoloyucan, and the First Chief joins him two days later

August 12 (Mexico City) President Carvajal abandons the office of the federal executive, leaving Velasco to negotiate the army's surrender

August 13 (Mexico) the Federal Army surrenders under the Second Act of the Treaties of Teoloyucan

August 15 (Mexico City) the Yaquis, Mayos, Pimas, and other Indians of the Constitutionalist Army Corps of the Northwest triumphantly entered Mexico City, exacting the Revenge of the Grand Chichimec upon the imperialist descendants of the Mexica

August 20 (Tlaxcala) General González moves his headquarters to Apizaco to begin mustering the Federal Army out of service

August 24 (Chihuahua) General Obregón arrives in the state capital to broker a truce between Colonel Calles and Governor Maytorena

August 25 (Veracruz) General Aguilar enters the state capital, Jalapa

August 29 (Sonora) The Nogales Accord is signed

August 30 (Sonora) The Nogales Accord becomes void when Obregón fires Maytorena as Military Commander of the State

September 1 (Yucatán) General Carrera Torres' brigade arrives in Progreso to muster out the ex-Federals in Yucatán and Quintana Roo states

September 3 (Chihuahua) Villa and Obregón sign another set of accords that replaces Maytorena as Governor and State Military Commander of Sonora with General Juan G. Cabral and requires Carranza to assume the title of Interim President of the Republic

September 6 (Oaxaca) the mustering out of 3,943 ex-Federals in the Isthmus of Tehuantepec is concluded

September 8 (Chihuahua) Villa requests that General Hill withdraw his forces from northern Sonora to Casas Grandes; (Washington) the United States lifts the embargo against "arms and munitions of war going into Mexico"; (Chiapas) J. Agustín Castro receives the appointment to governor and military commander of Chiapas State

September 13 (Mexico City) Obregón leaves to return north to again confer with Villa regarding Sonora

September 19 (Chihuahua) Obregón appoints General Hill as the new interim civil and military governor of Sonora after Maytorena refuses to receive Cabral

September 23 (Chihuahua) Obregón returns to neutral ground and Villa breaks definitively with the First Chief; (San Luis Potosí) the First Chief instructs Eulalio Gutiérrez to begin destroying the Central Railroad between Torreón and Zacatecas

September 25 (Sonora) Maytorena's troops depart Nogales and march on Naco, attacking Lieutenant Colonel Arnulfo R. Gómez at Martínez Station

Endnotes

Preface

[1] See, for example, Alan Knight, *La Revolución Mexicana del Porfirato al Neuvo Régimen Constitucional*, 2 vols. (México: Editorial Grijalbo, S. A. de C. V., 1996), vol. 1: *Porfiristas, Liberales y Campesinos*, p. 802, where the difference is noted and a few examples cited.

Introduction

[1] Max Boot, *War Made New: Technology, Warfare, and the Course of History, 1500 to Today* (New York, NY: Gotham Books, 2006), pp. 8, 83-84, 88, 114, Boot admits that after the Thirty Year's War the prosecution of warfare "became more limited" but not less frequent, and "turning 'the scum of the earth' (as the Duke of Wellington affectionately described his men) into effective soldiers required iron discipline" such that Lieutenant Colonel Jean Martinet's surname found its way into the lexicon, but Boot disavows the RMA of mass armies to suggest that Napoleon's innovations were merely "incremental expansions of what the áncien regimes had already been doing...[bringing] the old style of war to its ruthless zenith." Boot does concede, however, that "Scholars may quibble about exactly how many revolutions have occurred or when they started and ended," and in fact many still consider the advent of mass armies to be just such an RMA.

[2] Ignacio Muñoz, *Verdad y Mito de la Revolución Mexicana (Relatada por un Protagonista): Gestación, Estallido y Consecuencias*, 4 vols. (México: Ediciones Populares, S.A. México, 1961), 2: 161.

[3] Muñoz, *Verdad y Mito*, 2: 144, elsewhere Muñoz boasted that Agustín "El Cubano" Valdés was of elevated stature and "correct features, energetic nose, and curly hair; sported a carefully cut beard, and dressed impeccably. Well it is that all [Federal] generals of that time could boast of a similar quality."

[4] Ibid., 2: 161.

[5] Ibid., 3: 95.

[6] Ibid., 2: 172.

[7] Ibid., 2: 162-163.

[8] Alfredo Aragón, *El Desarme del Ejército Federal por la Revolución de 1913* (Paris: Soc. an. des Imprimeries Wellhoff et Roche, 1915), p. 54.

[9] Miguel A. Sánchez Lamego, *Historia Militar de la Revolución Constitucionalista*, 5 vols. (México: Talleres Gráficas de la Nación, 1956-1960), 1: 157. Barragán, *Revolución Constitucionalista*, 1: 187-188.

[10] AHSDN XI/481.5/96.656, May 23, 1914, from General A. Blanquet to the state governors, the rank scale to which he refers in his letter is not present in the files.

[11] Carl von Clausewitz, *On War*, Edited with an Introduction by Anatol Rapoport. First published 1832. This translation published by Routledge & Kegan Paul Ltd 1908. (New York: Penguin Putnam Inc., 1982), p. 311, "Artillery and prisoners are therefore at all times regarded as the true trophies of victory, as well as its measure."

[12] Peter H. Wilson, "Defining Military Culture," *The Journal of Military History*, Volume 72, No. 1 (Jan., 2008), pp. 22-5, discusses the Weberian concept of the state's monopoly on violence via the Army and challenges to the monopoly by various paramilitaries, some legal.

[13] Juan Barragán Rodríguez, *Historia del Ejercito y de la Revolución Constitucionalista*, 2 vols. (México: Instituto de Estudios Históricos de la Revolución Mexicana, 1985), 1: 24, 65, 153, 156, 169, 229, 327.

[14] Ibid., 1: 114.

[15] Barragán, *Revolución Constitucionalista*, 1: 70, 182, 355, 567; Carranza even tried to save the life of General Mier at Orendáin, but Mier died in battle—such was Carranza's respect for "veterans of the second war of independence" against the French. Guzmán, *Memorias*, p. 284.

[16] Barragán, *Revolución Constitucionalista*, 1: 569. Martín Luis Guzmán, *Memorias de Pancho Villa* (México: Compañía General de Ediciones, S. A.), 1951, pp. 271, 299, 417, Villa refused Eugenio Aguirre Benavides' request for Alessio Robles' to serve in his cavalry brigade.

[17] Barragán, *Revolución Constitucionalista*, 1: 411, 685.

[18] I. Thord-Gray, *Gringo Rebel: Mexico 1913-1914* (Coral Gables: University of Miami Press, 1960), pp. 108-109. Presumably the increased lack of prestige of the infantry required an inducement for men to switch that the more incapable were eager to accept.

[19] Alberto Calzadíaz, *Hechos Reales de la Revolución*, 8 vols. (México: Editorial Patria, S.A., 1959-65), 1: 171; Barragán, *Revolución Constitucionalista*, 1: 185, 577.

[20] Barragán, *Revolución Constitucionalista*, 1: 119, 201, Constitutionalists made dynamite "cannon" in the guayule factory in Cedral, San Luis Potosí, composed of tubes of plate metal mounted on wheels and two 80-mm. and one small 70-mm. guns constructed in the workshops of the railroad at Piedras Negras.

[21] Barragán, *Revolución Constitucionalista*, 1: 69-70, 128, 172.

[22] See, for example, BLAC-CPGMR, Film 20,898, Reel 48, message from Captain Ismael Rueda to Pablo González dated April 23, 1914, and earlier notes dated April 21, and April 22, 1914, showing disparity of .30-30 rounds to Mauser in shipments.

[23] Calzadíaz, *Hechos Reales*, 1: 109. Guzmán, *Memorias*, p. 66.

[24] Calzadíaz, *Hechos Reales*, 1: 91.

[25] Barragán, *Revolución Constitucionalista*, 1: 239-240. Guzmán, *Memorias*, pp. 187-189.

[26] Barragán, *Revolución Constitucionalista*, 1: 89, 118 (Barragán's quote), 165. Álvaro Obregón, *Ocho Mil Kilómetros en Campaña*, (México: Fondo de Cultura Económica, 1959), p. 56, Constitutionalist Benjamín Hill forced the irregulars who surrendered at Alamos, Sonora, in April, 1913, to pony up fines, since most of them came from well-to-do families. Calzadíaz, *Hechos Reales*, 1: 106, Orozquista Antonio Rojas took Sahuaripa, Sonora, capturing Rosario García, from whom he extracted a rather large ransom before setting him free with the promise to withdraw from the region.

[27] Calzadíaz, *Hechos Reales*, 1: 140, for the Villista method. For the Federal regulations see Estados Unidos Mexicanos-Secretaría de Estado y del Despacho de Guerra y Marina, *Reglamento para El Ejercicio y Maniobras de la Caballería*, 2 vols. (México: Librería de la Vda. De Ch. Bouret, 1921), 2: 187-188.

[28] Calzadíaz, *Hechos Reales*, 1: 93, 215, contains references to Villa's lack of technical knowledge in fighting *a lo Europeo* who destroyed the crème de la crème of the Federal Army attacking and destroying them *a la Mexicana*, and the quote attributed to Federal General Gustavo Salas.

[29] All the major goals, objectives, accomplishments, and results associated with the revolution save one have failed or are failing. Anti-clericalism failed first under the weight of rebellion, and because it is simply un-Mexican and repugnant to the international community. Agrarian engineering (ejidos, cooperatives, military colonies) failed on a micro level for the same reason that socialism always fails (politics, mismanagement, individualism, and its inability to satisfy the need for self-actualization), and on a macro level because of enormous urbanization in the twentieth century and modernization of the economy. Likewise, state capitalism came undone in the 1980s and 1990s as a result of the debt and currency crises, and because the parastatals simply cost too much (that is, they lost money), with only the iconic energy sector surviving due to the serendipitous discovery of the Cantarell field in the 1970s and the high political cost attached to privatization—but even that is under pressure to open up due to the exigencies of technology and financing, given the precipitous decline of the Cantarell. The end of militarism is the only outcome of enduring and unmistakable benefit (anti-reelectionism still exists, but is of questionable benefit).

[30] Aside from the dislocation caused by foreign capital that modernized the economy and drove Mexicans to revolution, Marxists are most concerned with the Convention-Constitutionalist Schism that occurred in the 1914-15 time frame, which is covered in the third volume of this trilogy; they begin making their case, however, with events as early as the October 1913 sacking of Lucio Blanco, which is why I dedicate so much attention to that event in this book.

[31] Barragán, *Revolución Constitucionalista*, 1: 213, reinforces the point that a lack of specific proposals in the Plan de Guadalupe allowed the greatest number of forces to unite under Carranza to overthrow Huerta.

[32] AHSDN XI/481.5/95.29, January 15, 1914 and AHSDN XI/481.5/95.43, January 23, 1914, are Federal General of Brigade, Enrique Paz's plan to defeat Constitutionalists and finish the "the obstinate rebelliousness of the northern border." Lon Tinkle, *13 Days to Glory: The Siege of the Alamo*, (College Station: Texas A&M Press, 1985), p. 107, characterizes Santa Anna's Army that marched into Texas in 1836, and typifies the metropolis' conception of an army. Amparo Rubio de De Ita (compil.), *La Revolución Triunfante: Memorias del General de División Guillermo Rubio Navarrete*, (México: Libros en Red, 2006), pp. 53, 63. Federico Cervantes, *Francisco Villa y la Revolución*, (México: Ediciones Alonso, 1960), p. 125.

Chapter 1

[1] Obregón, *Campaña*, pp. 31-35. Rubio, *La Revolución Triunfante*, p. 44, Rubio Navarrete bemoans Obregón's superior strategic position and numbers. Rómulo Velasco Ceballos, La Infamia Yanqui (México: Edición Privada, 1914), pp. 33-4, 39. Héctor Aguilar Camín, *La Frontera Nómada: Sonora y la Revolución Mexicana*, (México: León y Cal Editores, S.A. de C.V., 1999), pp. 373-4, 392-3.

[2] Obregón, *Campaña*, pp. 36-7. Ceballos, *La Infamia Yanqui*, p. 9. Sánchez Lamego, *Constitucionalista*, 1: 109-10.

[3] Obregón, *Campaña*, pp. 36-37. Sánchez Lamego, *Constitucionalista*, 1: 109-110. AREM 830/1/4-5, n.d., report by Ángel Aguilar signed by Kosterlitzky and Reyes.

[4] Obregón, *Campaña*, pp. 36-8. AREM 830/1/4-5, n.d., report by Ángel Aguilar signed by Kosterlitzky and Reyes. AREM 830/1/17, newspaper clipping, "Battle of Nogales," *The Border Vidette* (Nogales, AZ), March 15, 1913. Sánchez Lamego, *Constitucionalista*, 1: 109-10, 112. Cornelius C. Smith, Jr., *Emilio Kosterlitzky: Eagle of Sonora and the Southwest Border*, (Glendale, CA: The Arthur H. Clark Company, 1970), p. 209.

[5] Smith, *Emilio Kosterlitzky*, pp. 197-203, contains Kosterlitzky's report dated March 19, 1913, which is a very detailed blow-by-blow, hill-by-hill recapitulation of the action, but much too detailed to include in the narrative because the "battle" really did not amount to much tactically, although it was of immense strategic importance. Sánchez Lamego, *Constitucionalista*, 1: 111.

[6] Obregón, *Campaña*, pp. 36-8. Sánchez Lamego, *Constitucionalista*, 1: 109-10, 112.

[7] Obregón, *Campaña*, pp. 37-8. AREM 830/1/4-5, n.d., report by Ángel Aguilar signed by Kosterlitzky and Reyes. Sánchez Lamego, *Constitucionalista*, 1: 112-3.

[8] AREM 830/1/6-7, n.d., report by Ángel Aguilar signed by Kosterlitzky and Reyes. Ceballos, *La Infamia Yanqui*, p. 41. Smith, *Emilio Kosterlitzky*, pp. 183, 201 (Kosterlitzky's report contains incident of Constitutionalists captured by U.S. Army).

[9] Obregón, *Campaña*, pp. 38-9. Sánchez Lamego, *Constitucionalista*, 1: 113-4.

[10] AREM 830/1/7-8, n.d., report by Ángel Aguilar signed by Kosterlitzky and Reyes. AREM 830/1/17, "Battle of Nogales." Smith, *Emilio Kosterlitzky*, p. 185. Most likely, this was when Reyes' horse was killed.

[11] AREM 830/1/8-9, n.d., report by Ángel Aguilar signed by Kosterlitzky and Reyes. Obregón, *Campaña*, pp. 38-9. AREM 830/1/17, "Battle of Nogales," confirms that Major Tate demanded that Kosterlitzky give the order to cease fire. Sánchez Lamego, *Constitucionalista*, 1: 113-4.

[12] AREM 830/1/17, "Battle of Nogales."

[13] AREM 830/1/8-9, n.d., report by Ángel Aguilar (quote) signed by Kosterlitzky and Reyes. Smith, *Emilio Kosterlitzky*, pp. 179-81, contains a map of how the Federals exited the town.

[14] Obregón, *Campaña*, p. 39. AREM 830/1/17, "Battle of Nogales."

[15] Obregón, *Campaña*, pp. 38-9. AREM 830/1/17, "Battle of Nogales." Smith, *Emilio Kosterlitzky*, pp. 179-82, p. 179 contains a map of how the Federals exited the town. Sánchez Lamego, *Constitucionalista*, 1: 113-4.

[16] Obregón, *Campaña*, p. 39. Sánchez Lamego, *Constitucionalista*, 1: 115. Smith, *Emilio Kosterlitzky*, pp. 191-5.

[17] Ceballos, *La Infamia Yanqui*, pp. 69-71.

[18] Ibid., p. 72.

[19] Ibid., pp. 43-44. Sánchez Lamego, *Constitucionalista*, 1: 115-6, Sánchez Lamego attempted to pull together a schedule of Ojeda's force, since there is nothing definitive in the archives; his number of 550 men matches Ceballos' before any defections, but since Ceballos conferred directly with Ojeda, his number of 450 will be used. Sánchez Lamego did allow that some of Escandón's "Cuerpo Auxiliar Federal de Agua Prieta" defected to join Calles. Smith, *Emilio Kosterlitzky*, p. 195.

[20] Ceballos, *La Infamia Yanqui*, p. 44, it is not clear if the Federal "deserters" to the Constitutionalists in Agua Prieta and the "Voluntarios del Norte" federal auxiliaries were one and the same. Smith, *Emilio Kosterlitzky*, p. 195.

[21] Ceballos, *La Infamia Yanqui*, pp. 44-5. Sánchez Lamego, *Constitucionalista*, 1: 115, says that Ojeda arrived on March 12, but he could not have learned of the Federal loss of Nogales until the night of March 13.

[22] Aguilar Camín, *Frontera Nómada*, pp. 117-8, 240-8, 373, 392-3. Sánchez Lamego, *Constitucionalista*, 1: 117.

[23] Obregón, *Campaña*, pp. 40-1.

[24] Ceballos, *La Infamia Yanqui*, pp. 44-5. Sánchez Lamego, *Constitucionalista*, 1: 116-7.

[25] Ceballos, *La Infamia Yanqui*, p. 45. Sánchez Lamego, *Constitucionalista*, 1: 117.

[26] Ibid.

[27] Ceballos, *La Infamia Yanqui*, pp. 45-6. Sánchez Lamego, *Constitucionalista*, 1: 117.
[28] Ceballos, *La Infamia Yanqui*, pp. 46-7. Sánchez Lamego, *Constitucionalista*, 1: 117-8.
[29] Ceballos, *La Infamia Yanqui*, p. 47. Sánchez Lamego, *Constitucionalista*, 1: 118.
[30] Obregón, *Campaña*, p. 41. Sánchez Lamego, *Constitucionalista*, 1: 119-20.
[31] Ceballos, *La Infamia Yanqui*, p. 49.
[32] Obregón, *Campaña*, p. 41. Sánchez Lamego, *Constitucionalista*, 1: 119-20.
[33] Ceballos, *La Infamia Yanqui*, p. 38.
[34] Obregón, *Campaña*, pp. 41-2. Sánchez Lamego, *Constitucionalista*, 1: 120-2.
[35] Obregón, *Campaña*, pp. 41-2. Ceballos, *La Infamia Yanqui*, pp. 49-50. Sánchez Lamego, *Constitucionalista*, 1: 120-2.
[36] Obregón, *Campaña*, p. 42. Ceballos, *La Infamia Yanqui*, p. 50.
[37] Ceballos, *La Infamia Yanqui*, pp. 51-2.
[38] Obregón, *Campaña*, pp. 42-4.
[39] Obregón, *Campaña*, pp. 42-4. Ceballos, *La Infamia Yanqui*, pp. 54-5.
[40] Ceballos, *La Infamia Yanqui*, pp. 55-6.
[41] Obregón, *Campaña*, pp. 44-5. Ceballos, *La Infamia Yanqui*, p. 56. Sánchez Lamego, *Constitucionalista*, 1: 125-6.
[42] Obregón, *Campaña*, pp. 44-5. Ceballos, *La Infamia Yanqui*, pp. 56-7. Sánchez Lamego, *Constitucionalista*, 1: 125-6.
[43] Ceballos, *La Infamia Yanqui*, pp. 58-9.
[44] Ibid., p. 57.
[45] Ibid., pp. 57-8.
[46] Ibid., pp. 50-2.
[47] Ibid., pp. 63-4.
[48] Obregón, *Campaña*, pp. 47-8. Ceballos, *La Infamia Yanqui*, p. 64. Sánchez Lamego, *Constitucionalista*, 1: 127-9.
[49] Obregón, *Campaña*, pp. 47-8. Sánchez Lamego, *Constitucionalista*, 1: 127-9.
[50] Ceballos, *La Infamia Yanqui*, p. 65.
[51] Ibid.
[52] Ibid., p. 66.
[53] Ibid.
[54] Ibid., p. 67.
[55] Ibid., p. 77.
[56] Ibid., p. 78.
[57] Obregón, *Campaña*, p. 47, Obregón's motto was "Respect for the vanquished is the dignity of victory," and he recoiled at the "inconceivable luxury of cruelty and barbarism" practiced by Ojeda who had handkerchiefs tied around the civilians' necks, and then inserting a sticks began twisting them until the victims slowly strangled to death.

[58] Ibid., pp. 47-8.

[59] Ceballos, *La Infamia Yanqui*, p. 79.

[60] Ibid., pp. 78-9. Sánchez Lamego, *Constitucionalista*, 1: 130-1.

[61] Obregón, *Campaña*, pp. 49-50. Sánchez Lamego, *Constitucionalista*, 1: 131-2.

[62] Ceballos, *La Infamia Yanqui*, p. 79.

[63] Ibid., pp. 79-80.

[64] Ibid., pp. 80-1.

[65] Ibid., pp. 81-2. Sánchez Lamego, *Constitucionalista*, 1: 133-4.

[66] Obregón, *Campaña*, p. 50. Ceballos, *La Infamia Yanqui*, pp. 82-3.

[67] Obregón, *Campaña*, p. 50. Ceballos, *La Infamia Yanqui*, pp. 84-5.

[68] Ceballos, *La Infamia Yanqui*, p. 83.

[69] Ibid., pp. 83-4.

[70] Ibid., p. 85. For origin of "meco" see: Arturo Langle, *Vocabulario, Apodos, Seudónimos, Sobrenombres Y Hemerografía de la Revolución*, (México: Universidad Nacional Autónima de México, Instituto de Investigaciones Históricas, 1966), p. 54; some recent scholars have tried to rescue the word "Chichimeca" from its derogatory connotation in order to exculpate the Mexica of any prejudice, but there can be no doubt that it had just such a negative connotation in Federal usage.

[71] Ceballos, *La Infamia Yanqui*, p. 86.

[72] Obregón, *Campaña*, pp. 50-1.

[73] Ibid., p. 51. Sánchez Lamego, *Constitucionalista*, 1: 134-5.

[74] Obregón, *Campaña*, pp. 51-2. Sánchez Lamego, *Constitucionalista*, 1: 131-5.

[75] Obregón, *Campaña*, p. 52. Sánchez Lamego, *Constitucionalista*, 1: 135-6.

[76] Obregón, *Campaña*, p. 52.

[77] Ceballos, *La Infamia Yanqui*, pp. 86-7.

[78] Obregón, *Campaña*, pp. 52-3. Ibid., pp. 87-8. Sánchez Lamego, *Constitucionalista*, 1: 135-6.

[79] Obregón, *Campaña*, pp. 52-3. Sánchez Lamego, *Constitucionalista*, 1: 135-6.

[80] Ceballos, *La Infamia Yanqui*, pp. 88-9.

[81] Obregón, *Campaña*, pp. 53-4. Sánchez Lamego, *Constitucionalista*, 1: 135-8.

[82] Ceballos, *La Infamia Yanqui*, pp. 89-90.

[83] Ibid., p. 90.

[84] Obregón, *Campaña*, pp. 53-4. Ibid., p. 91. Sánchez Lamego, *Constitucionalista*, 1: 137-8.

[85] Ceballos, *La Infamia Yanqui*, pp. 91-5.

[86] Obregón, *Campaña*, pp. 53-4. Sánchez Lamego, *Constitucionalista*, 1: 137-8.

[87] Sánchez Lamego, *Constitucionalista*, 1: 141-2.

[88] Ceballos, *La Infamia Yanqui*, pp. 100-1, 127-8. Ibid., 1: 143.

[89] Ceballos, *La Infamia Yanqui*, p. 101. Sánchez Lamego, *Constitucionalista*, 1: 143-4.

[90] Ceballos, *La Infamia Yanqui*, p. 102. Sánchez Lamego, *Constitucionalista*, 1: 144.

[91] Ceballos, *La Infamia Yanqui*, pp. 102-4. Sánchez Lamego, *Constitucionalista*, 1: 144-5.

[92] Ceballos, *La Infamia Yanqui*, pp. 101-5. Sánchez Lamego, *Constitucionalista*, 1: 145.

[93] Ceballos, *La Infamia Yanqui*, pp. 104-5.

[94] Obregón, *Campaña*, pp. 55-6 contains Hill's report. Sánchez Lamego, *Constitucionalista*, 1: 145.

[95] Ceballos, *La Infamia Yanqui*, p. 100.

[96] Obregón, *Campaña*, p. 55, Hill's report. Sánchez Lamego, *Constitucionalista*, 1: 146.

[97] Obregón, *Campaña*, p. 55, Hill's report. Sánchez Lamego, *Constitucionalista*, 1: 146-7.

[98] Ceballos, *La Infamia Yanqui*, p. 10.

[99] Obregón, *Campaña*, pp. 54-5. Sánchez Lamego, *Constitucionalista*, 1: 153-4.

[100] Ceballos, *La Infamia Yanqui*, p. 10. Sánchez Lamego, *Constitucionalista*, 1: 150.

[101] Ceballos, *La Infamia Yanqui*, pp. 118-9. Sánchez Lamego, *Constitucionalista*, 1: 151.

[102] Sánchez Lamego, *Constitucionalista*, 1: 150-1.

[103] Ceballos, *La Infamia Yanqui*, p. 115.

[104] Ibid., p. 116.

[105] Ceballos, *La Infamia Yanqui*, pp. 116, 118-9. Sánchez Lamego, *Constitucionalista*, 1: 142, 151-3.

[106] Ceballos, *La Infamia Yanqui*, p. 119. Sánchez Lamego, *Constitucionalista*, 1: 152-3.

[107] Ceballos, *La Infamia Yanqui*, pp. 118-20.

[108] Obregón, *Campaña*, pp. 54-5.

[109] Sánchez Lamego, *Constitucionalista*, 1: 147-8.

[110] Ceballos, *La Infamia Yanqui*, pp. 127-8.

[111] Ibid., pp. 128-30. Sánchez Lamego, *Constitucionalista*, 1: 148.

[112] Ceballos, *La Infamia Yanqui*, pp. 131-3.

[113] Sánchez Lamego, *Constitucionalista*, 1: 148-9.

[114] Ceballos, *La Infamia Yanqui*, pp. 130-4. Sánchez Lamego, *Constitucionalista*, 1: 149.

[115] Ceballos, *La Infamia Yanqui*, pp. 39-40.

[116] Ibid., pp. 113-4, 117-8, 123-5.

Chapter 2

[1] CEHM-GRN 2.54.02, manuscript that is essentially a Federal Army postmortem.

[2] Ibid.

[3] Rubio, *La Revolución Triunfante*, p. 59.

[4] Barragán, *Revolución Constitucionalista*, 1: 114. Miguel A. Sánchez Lamego, *Generales de la Revolución*, 2 vols. (México: Biblioteca del Instituto Nacional de Estudios Históricos de la Revolución Mexicana, 1979, 1981), 1: 16. Justo Manzur Ocaña, *La Revolución Permanente: Vida y Obra de Cándido Aguilar* (México: B. Costa-Amic Editor, 1972), pp. 55-6.

[5] Barragán, *Revolución Constitucionalista*, 1: 114-5. Sánchez Lamego, *Generales de la Revolución*, 1: 17. Manzur Ocaña, *Cándido Aguilar*, pp. 59-60, 69.

[6] Francisco L. Urquizo, *Memorias de Campaña*, (México: Fondo de Cultura Económica, S. A. de C. V., [1971], 1985), p. 38.

[7] Manuel W. González, *Con Carranza Episodios de la Revolución Constitucionalista, 1913-1914*, 2 vols. (México: Instituto Nacional de Estudios Históricas de la Revolución Mexicana, 1933), 1: 84.

[8] Urquizo, *Origen*, p. 19.

[9] González, *Con Carranza*, 1: 52.

[10] Urquizo, *Origen*, pp. 16-17.

[11] Ibid., p. 17.

[12] Jacinto B. Treviño, *Memorias (de) Jacinto B. Treviño* (México: Editorial Orion, 1961), pp. 37-9. Aragón, *El Desarme del Ejército Federal*, pp. 66, 68.

[13] Treviño, *Memorias*, p. 37.

[14] Alberto J. Pani, *Apuntes Autobiográficos*, 2 vols. (México: Senado de la República, 1945 [2003]), 1: 170.

[15] Barragán, *Revolución Constitucionalista*, 1: 116-21. Sánchez Lamego, *Constitucionalista*, 1: 261-2, 276, 278; Sánchez Lamego and others credited the uprising of the 2nd Regiment of Carabineers of Coahuila with encouraging others to rebel in Guerrero and Mexico states; its commander, Gregorio Osuna, remained loyal to Huerta until the end, being appointed to the position of Jefe de Armas, southern district of Baja California per the January 31, 1914 Federal Army Escalafón, p. 196. Javier Echeverría Adame Marquina, "¡Viva Carranza!: Mis Recuerdos de la Revolución," *El Legionario* 49, 5 (March, 1955): p. 21.

[16] Barragán, *Revolución Constitucionalista*, 1: 120.

[17] J. M. Marquez, *El Veintiuno: Hombres de la Revolución y Sus Hechos: Apuntes Sobre el General de División Jesús Agustín Castro, Jefe de la División "Veintiuno," 1a del Cuerpo de Ejército del Sureste, y demás Ciudádanos que lo han acompañado desde 1910* (México, 1916), p. 36.

[18] Ibid.

[19] Ibid., p. 37. Ricardo L. Vázquez, *Poncho Vázquez*, (México: Ediciones Botas, 1940), pp. 115-6.

[20] Marquez, *El Veintiuno*, p. 37.

[21] Ibid. Barragán, *Revolución Constitucionalista*, 1: 121-2. Sánchez Lamego, *Constitucionalista*, 1: 66, Sánchez Lamego believed that Pérez Gil was sent to chase Blanco, but his men were long gone, and most likely the marauders that General Mier referred to were Castro and his escort.

[22] Barragán, *Revolución Constitucionalista*, 1: 121-2, Blanco occupied Coss on April 13 and China the next day.

[23] Marquez, *El Veintiuno*, pp. 38, 40

²⁴ Ibid., p. 40.

²⁵ Ibid.

²⁶ Ibid., p. 41, says the river crossed was the Amasazintla, but this must have been a different name for the Moctezuma.

²⁷ Ibid., pp. 41-2, On April 8, the 21st left for Tres Lagunas, Charco, Rayón, Barbecho, Hacienda de Asunción, Rascón Station, the Rascón Sugar Mill, and Salto de Agua where they took part in a dance on April 13. The next day, the two hundred Constitutionalists left for Tamaulipas State passing through Papagallos to arrive at Ocampo where they stayed there until April 16 and then departed for Ciudad Chamal, then, skirted Xicoténcatl to arrive at Llera. The column left Llera for Forlón passing through the haciendas of San Rafael, La Purísima, San Antonio, Reforma, and Clementina.

²⁸ Ibid., p. 42.

²⁹ Ibid., pp. 42-3.

³⁰ Ibid., p. 43.

³¹ Ibid.

³² Ibid., p. 44. Barragán, *Revolución Constitucionalista*, 1: 122.

³³ Marquez, *El Veintiuno*, p. 44: After a brief skirmish in Güemez, Hernández's men headed for San Carlos; spent the night (April 23) about a half league from the hacienda (Corpus) in a reed bed; then (April 24) went to Hacienda del Carmen, Camacho, and Magueyes; continuing on (April 25) to El Refugio, Carrillos, and Gávia; arriving at San Carlos (April 26). They headed for San Juan, China, because they had no food, and continued on to Hediondilla to spend the night. By the time they reached Burgos they learned that Blanco had gone to San Fernando, and so after a brief rest they turned around and on April 27 reached Cruillas, and the following day in the early morning hours passed thru Laguna, Perico, Santa Rita, and Misión. In La Ceja they ran into one of Blanco's scout parties and with joy they joined the main group at Santander Jiménez.

³⁴ Barragán, *Revolución Constitucionalista*, 1: 122. Ibid., p. 38, 44-5. After being surprised at Cerralvo, Jesús Agustín Castro caught up to the escort and spent the night at General Treviño (a town, not a person) and in the early hours of April 25 they left for Dr. Coss (a town, not a person) arriving on the morning of 26. That day they spent in General Bravo (a town, not a person) and the following day they continued the march through China, going into camp at Rancho de La Guitarra; on the twenty-eighth they continued through La Reforma, Tanque de Flores, and then on May 1 arrived at Cruillas, Tamps., having rejoined his corps on May 4 at Hacienda Encinal. Captains Navarrete and Nafarrate spent the night of April 22 in Alberca retreating to the north and arriving April 23 at Generala, (24) at Magueyes, San Carlos (25), San Nicolás (27), Cruillas (28), then headed between Cruillas and Santander Jiménez arriving on April 30.

[35] Marquez, *El Veintiuno*, pp. 45-6.

[36] Barragán, *Revolución Constitucionalista*, 1: 122.

[37] Ibid., 1: 116-7. González, *Con Carranza*, 1: 10, Carranza attacked and took Lampazos.

[38] Sánchez Lamego, *Constitucionalista*, 1: 59-62; the Constitutionalists probably had about five hundred men.

[39] Ibid., 1: 63-5. Apparently the forces that attacked Nuevo Laredo were 150 men belonging to Ramírez Quintanilla, Pablo Santos, and Juan Manuel Lozano who also attacked and took Mier on April 21.

[40] Ibid., 1: 69-72. AHSDN XI/481.5/95.02, March 13, 1913, contains makeup of Medina Barrón's column of 3rd and 8th Rural Corps as well as some from the Auxiliary Corps of Guanajuato.

[41] Sánchez Lamego, *Constitucionalista*, 1: 72-3.

[42] Ibid., 1: 65-9.

[43] Ibid., 1: 73-4.

[44] AHSDN XI/481.5/88.129-130, Decree 435, April 1, 1913.

[45] AHSDN XI/481.5/88.176, Decree 433, April 24, 1913.

[46] AHSDN XI/481.5/88.185, Decree 434, April 28, 1913, effective May 1. AHSDN XI/481.5/88.262, Decree 436, May 1, 1913.

[47] AHSDN XI/481.5/88.265-266.

[48] Urquizo, *Origen*, pp. 19-20.

[49] Aragón, *El Desarme del Ejército Federal*, p. 54.

[50] Ibid., pp. 58, 60, 64.

[51] Barragán, *Revolución Constitucionalista*, 1: 182-185 (quote). Treviño, *Memorias*, p. 37.

[52] Rubio, *La Revolución Triunfante*, p. 82. In a letter to Arizona Governor George Hunt, Carranza defended the January 25, 1862 law on the basis of the Federal Army's attack "trying to subvert forever our political institutions," Cervantes, *Francisco Villa*, pp. 68-70.

[53] AHSDN XI/481.5/88.292 (Decree 438, May 30, 1913), 299-300 (Acuerdo No. 130549, June 3, 1913).

[54] Urquizo, *Origen*, p. 19.

[55] AHSDN XI/481.5/88.281, May 15, 1913, memo from "President" Huerta to Secretary of War, establishing military train system. AHSDN XI/481.5/88.741, December 23, 1913, Jesús Acuña asked American consul in Saltillo for protection for his wife who might be made to ride a military train, "as has been the case with others [sic] Consitutionalists [sic] families." CEHM-MWG 1.9.1194.1, n.d., notes given to Manuel W. González for his book regarding family members of General Coss who were forced daily to ride the trains traveling between Saltillo and San Luis Potosí.

[56] Francisco de P. Ontiveros, *Toribio Ortega y la Revolución en la Región de Ojinaga*, (Chihuahua: Gobierno de Chihuahua, 2003 [1914]), pp. 10, 134.

[57] Ibid., p. 72

[58] Ibid., p. 134.

[59] Ibid., p. 71.

[60] Ibid., p. 133.

[61] Francisco Villa, *Pancho Villa: Retrato autobiográfico, 1894-1914,* eds. Guadalupe and Rosa Helia Villa. (México: Santillana Ediciones Generales, S.A. de C.V.: Universidad Nacional Autónoma de México, 2003), pp. 531-3. Guzmán, *Memorias*, pp. 185-8.

[62] Villa, *Pancho Villa*, pp. 534-5. Guzmán, *Memorias*, pp. 193-4.

[63] Villa, *Pancho Villa*, pp. 535-6. Ontiveros, *Toribio Ortega*, pp. 77-8. Cervantes, *Francisco Villa*, pp. 50-1. Friedrich Katz, *Pancho Villa*, 2 vols. (México: Ediciones Era, S. A. de C. V., 1998), 1: 241-5.

[64] Villa, *Pancho Villa*, pp. 535-6.

[65] Ontiveros, *Toribio Ortega*, p. 78. Katz, *Pancho Villa*, 1: 244.

[66] Villa, *Pancho Villa*, pp. 535-6. Guzmán, *Memorias*, p. 196. Sánchez Lamego, *Constitucionalista*, 1: 215-16. Paco Ignacio Taibo, II, *Pancho Villa: Una Biografía Narrativa* (México: Editorial Planeta Mexicana, 2006), p. 181, says that Villa stayed two weeks in Bachíniva negotiating with Wells Fargo to monetize the silver, selling it back to the company at a steep discount, but only returning ninety-three bars, saying his men had stolen the other twenty-eight, leaving one unaccounted for.

[67] Calzadíaz, *Hecho Reales*, 1: 22-4, 116, quotes on p. 22; Baca and Luján were natives of Namiquipa, while Terrazas came from Cruces.

[68] Calzadíaz, *Hecho Reales*, 1: 102-4, Villa appointed Colonel Telesforo Terrazas as administrator of the Santa Clara hacienda, while Belisario Ruiz, Julián Pérez and Belisario Chávez took charge of the haciendas of la Quemada and Rubio.

[69] Daniel Nugent, *Spent Cartridges of Revolution: An Anthropological History of Namiquipa, Chihuahua* (Chicago: The University of Chicago Press, 1993), pp. 5, 44, 46-7, 55.

[70] Mark Wasserman, *Capitalistas, Caciques y Revolución: La Familia Terrazas de Chihuahua, 1854-1911*, transl. Beatriz Guiza from the 1984 edition by The University of North Carolina Press, 1984, (México: Editorial Grijalbo, S.A., 1987), pp. 293-5.

[71] Nugent, *Spent Cartridges*, p. 68.

[72] Katz, *Pancho Villa*, 1: 79: "An advantage of those old military colonies was that they were much closer to the urban middle class than the pueblos of the other parts of Mexico. The military colonies and the urban middle class also had a similar social origin." Nugent, *Spent Cartridges*, p. 77.

[73] Sánchez Lamego, *Constitucionalista*, 1: 203.

[74] Ibid., 1: 203-4.

[75] Ontiveros, *Toribio Ortega*, p. 75, lists Carreón's first name as Francisco. Sánchez Lamego, *Constitucionalista*, 1: 210.

[76] Ontiveros, *Toribio Ortega*, pp. 74-5. Sánchez Lamego, *Constitucionalista*, 1: 205-6, 208.

[77] Ontiveros, *Toribio Ortega*, pp. 75-6.

[78] Ibid., p. 76.

[79] Ibid., p. 78.

[80] Ibid., p. 79, mistakenly gives Ramírez's name and rank as Colonel Adolfo Rivera. Lamego, *Constitucionalista*, 1: 206-8; on p. 223, he says that Emilio P. Campa (not Campos) pushed Urbina out of Mapimí, but this is an obvious error.

[81] Ontiveros, *Toribio Ortega*, p. 79.

[82] Ibid., pp. 79-80. Sánchez Lamego, *Constitucionalista*, 1: 207-8.

[83] Ontiveros, *Toribio Ortega*, p. 80. Sánchez Lamego, *Constitucionalista*, 1: 208-9.

[84] Sánchez Lamego, *Constitucionalista*, 1: 209.

[85] Ontiveros, *Toribio Ortega*, p. 80. Ibid., 1: 209-10.

[86] Sánchez Lamego, *Constitucionalista*, 1: 210-211.

[87] Ibid., 1: 211.

[88] Ontiveros, *Toribio Ortega*, pp. 80-1, says that Herrera captured two Rexers, which are very similar to Madsens, but they must have been captured later, because Herrera had not yet taken the church, which is where the Federals had placed the machine guns. Sánchez Lamego, *Constitucionalista*, 1: 211.

[89] Ontiveros, *Toribio Ortega*, p. 81, Ontiveros characterized Carbajal. Sánchez Lamego, *Constitucionalista*, 1: 211-212.

[90] Ontiveros, *Toribio Ortega*, pp. 81-82, gives Cirilo Ortiz as the name of the Federal major who escaped. Sánchez Lamego, *Constitucionalista*, 1: 212.

[91] Sánchez Lamego, *Constitucionalista*, 1: 209-12. Although Urbina's men probably took part in the battle, Ontiveros did not mention it.

[92] Ibid.

[93] Ontiveros, *Toribio Ortega*, p. 82. Sánchez Lamego, *Constitucionalista*, 1: 212-3.

[94] Ontiveros, *Toribio Ortega*, p. 83. Sánchez Lamego, *Constitucionalista*, 1: 212, 216. Taibo, *Una Biografía Narrativa*, p. 182.

[95] Sánchez Lamego, *Constitucionalista*, 1: 215-216. Barragán, *Revolución Constitucionalista*, 1: 240. Cervantes, *Francisco Villa*, p. 56. Katz, *Pancho Villa*, 1: 244-248, Katz states that none of the Constitutionalist commanders wanted to subordinate themselves to Villa, much less to each other, but he does not seem to recognize that Carranza made him higher ranking than Hernández, Urbina, Herrera, Ortega, and Chao, none of them generals at the time, and rather unconvincingly attributes Villa's growing popularity to his ascendancy over the others; Chao and the Herreras especially disliked having to subordinate themselves to Villa.

[96] Ontiveros, *Toribio Ortega*, p. 84.

[97] Ibid. Cervantes, *Francisco Villa*, pp. 51-52.

[98] Ontiveros, *Toribio Ortega*, pp. 84-5. Cervantes, *Francisco Villa*, p. 52, Lieutenant Colonel Benito Navarro, who took part in the action, provided the information about the battle to Cervantes; Navarro's brothers were the famous Doctor Samuel Navarro and Saúl Navarro. General Sánchez Lamego does not mention the battles at Saucillo and Conchos stations.

[99] Matías Pazuengo, *Historia de la Revolución en Durango: de Junio de 1910 a Octubre de 1914*, (Cuernavaca, Mor.: Tip. Del Gobierno del Estado, 1915), pp. 21-2, 30-1.

[100] Ibid., pp. 33-4.

[101] Ibid., pp. 34-5.

[102] Ibid., p. 36.

[103] Ibid., p. 1. Sánchez Lamego, *Generales de la Revolución*, 2: 31.

[104] E. Brondo Whitt, *La División del Norte* (Chihuahua: Ayuntamiento de Chihuahua, 1984 [1940]), p. 44, describes Contreras. Pazuengo, *Historia de la Revolución en Durango*, pp. 6-7.

[105] Pazuengo, *Historia de la Revolución en Durango*, p. 7.

[106] Ibid., pp. 7-9. The Maderistas comandantes served in General Emilio Madero's 2nd Division of the North, which covered the states of Durango, Coahuila, and Chihuahua.; Mariano Arrieta, of the same rank, was appointed inspector of all the Rural Police of the state of Durango. AGN-CR 135.488.14, "1912 Estado de Fuerzas-Cuerpos Rurales," December 15, 1912. Sánchez Lamego, *Constitucionalista*, 1: 239.

[107] Sánchez Lamego, *Constitucionalista*, 1: 22, 206, 221-228. Severiano Ceniceros in Cuencamé; Orestes Pereyra and his son, Orestes, Jr., both of the 22nd Rural Corps in Nazas; and Calixto Contreras in Ocuila rebelled at the beginning of March.

[108] Pazuengo, *Historia de la Revolución en Durango*, pp. 36-7. Sánchez Lamego, *Constitucionalista*, 1: 224-5. Barragán, *Revolución Constitucionalista*, 1: 156-7.

[109] Sánchez Lamego, *Constitucionalista*, 1: 225-6.

[110] Ibid., 1: 227-8.

[111] Pazuengo, *Historia de la Revolución en Durango*, p. 37. Sánchez Lamego, *Constitucionalista*, 1: 228-9.

[112] Sánchez Lamego, *Constitucionalista*, 1: 229-30.

[113] Pazuengo, *Historia de la Revolución en Durango*, p. 37. Barragán, *Revolución Constitucionalista*, 1: 156-7. Ibid., 1: 230-1.

[114] Sánchez Lamego, *Constitucionalista*, 1: 231-2.

[115] Ibid., 1: 231-5.

[116] Pazuengo, *Historia de la Revolución en Durango*, pp. 37-39. Ibid., 1: 234.

[117] Sánchez Lamego, *Constitucionalista*, 1: 235.

[118] Ibid., 1: 235-6.

[119] Pazuengo, *Historia de la Revolución en Durango*, pp. 39-41.

[120] Sánchez Lamego, *Constitucionalista*, 1: 236.

[121] Pazuengo, *Historia de la Revolución en Durango*, pp. 41-2.

[122] Ibid., p. 42. Sánchez Lamego, *Constitucionalista*, 1: 236. Katz, *Pancho Villa*, 1: 301, discusses Contreras' failings as a military commander; even though he was one of the revolutionary generals with prior military experience, his political skills far outstripped his military abilities.

[123] Pazuengo, *Historia de la Revolución en Durango*, pp. 43-4. Sánchez Lamego, *Constitucionalista*, 1: 236-7.

[124] Pazuengo, *Historia de la Revolución en Durango*, p. 47, Contreras also had defeated in that area an Orozquista General Luis Caro. Sánchez Lamego, *Constitucionalista*, 1: 237-8.

[125] Sánchez Lamego, *Constitucionalista*, 1: 238-9.

[126] Ibid., 1: 238-42.

[127] Tinkle, *13 Days to Glory*, p. 107.

Chapter 3

[1] Obregón, *Campaña*, p. 56. Ceballos, *La Infamia Yanqui*, p. 136, and Rubio, *La Revolución Triunfante*, p. 67, said that 1,000 of the Federal reinforcements were raw recruits. Sánchez Lamego, *Constitucionalista*, 1: 154-6.

[2] Ceballos, *La Infamia Yanqui*, pp. 136-7.

[3] Ibid., pp. 18, 137: "And it is not to be supposed that these Yaquis of the irregular forces to which we are referring were the whole tribe, and that, consequently, could be annihilated at the least sign of rebellion, no: it was a small part who had been attracted by promises almost celestial, augmented with others who were forced to come from the South of the Republic; from Territory Quintana Roo; the main group does not want the smallest dealings with the white [man]; he wants his savage liberty."

[4] Obregón, *Campaña*, p. 56.

[5] Sánchez Lamego, *Constitucionalista*, 1: 156.

[6] Ceballos, *La Infamia Yanqui*, p. 137. Obregón, *Campaña*, pp. 56-7. In addition to the 27th, it would appear that General Gil left behind many but not all of Colonel Manuel F. Santibáñez's estimated 300 infantrymen of the 14th Infantry Battalion in Empalme.

[7] Ceballos, *La Infamia Yanqui*, pp. 137-8. Obregón, *Campaña*, pp. 56-7.

[8] Obregón, *Campaña*, p. 57-8. Sánchez Lamego, *Constitucionalista*, 1: 156-7, Sánchez Lamego also lists 300 men of the Sierra Juárez Auxiliary Battalion under Colonel Pedro León (with two machine guns), but Ceballos says these were not present until the Battle of Santa María.

[9] Ibid.

[10] Ceballos, *La Infamia Yanqui*, p. 138. Sánchez Lamego, *Constitucionalista*, 1: 157.

[11] Ceballos, *La Infamia Yanqui*, pp. 147, 163-165. Sánchez Lamego, *Constitucionalista*, 1: 155. Francisco P. Troncoso, *Las Guerras con las Tribus Yaqui y Mayo* (México: Instituto Nacional Indigenista, 1977 [1905]), pp. 23-24. The Yaquis and Mayos are related with only slight variations in their languages and customs; the first tribe put an estimated 3,000 warriors in the field in the rebellion of 1875 and latter tribe mobilized 2,000 in the rebellion of 1882, meaning that their tribes could have numbered as many as 30,000 and 20,000, respectively. However, after twenty years of fighting and suffering the ravages of small pox their populations may have been reduced by as much as half by 1901. Therefore, one has to question the difference between the *batallas* and *combates* waged by Medina Barrón during his campaigns in the first decade of the century as reported in his service record.

[12] Obregón, *Campaña*, p. 57. Ceballos, *La Infamia Yanqui*, p. 138. Sánchez Lamego, *Constitucionalista*, 1: 157-8.

[13] Obregón, *Campaña*, pp. 58-9.

[14] Ibid., p. 59. Ceballos, *La Infamia Yanqui*, p. 138.

[15] Ceballos, *La Infamia Yanqui*, p. 139.

[16] Obregón, *Campaña*, pp. 59-60.

[17] Ibid., p. 60. Ceballos, *La Infamia Yanqui*, pp. 146-7, 152-3, contains the conspiracy theory behind Bule's death: General Luis Medina Barrón spent his first youth in constant combats with the Yaquis, and after many years with a benign, astute, and also steady firmness succeeded in gaining the good will of some Yaqui leaders and even got some to swear obedience and submit to the Federal government, among them Luis Bule, the bravest and most prestigious of the tribe. Bule and Medina Barrón became loyal and close friends and later they entered into *compadrazgo* and the closest bonds. When Bule agreed to join the Constitutionalists he swore that he would not fight against Medina Barrón. So, when the general arrived he sent a letter to Bule before beginning the march, reminding the Yaqui of what he had sworn in Pitahaya and Bule's many promises. When the letter arrived, some revolutionaries close to Obregón snatched it from his hands, accusing him of betrayal. But Bule accurately remarked that he could not help what people wrote to him. Then, noticing some men making suspicious moves he withdrew to his own people as soon as possible. As day broke the word began to spread among the revolutionaries that Luis Bule and his closest and bravest lieutenants had been killed during the night by Constitutionalist jefes who were afraid of the sway that Medina Barrón held over the Yaqui chief, according to rumors. "This point goes a long to explain the fact that that same second night of combat, a group of like eight hundred Indians, headed by the also famous leader Cibaloame [sic], after the death of Bule, calmly organized themselves and in the view of the rest of the force took a course for wherever they wanted, separating from the rebellion [sic]." Obregón met them and asked under whose orders they were withdrawing, "On these orders" they said beating their cartridge belts.

Thus, the promise that Bule made to Comandante Luis Medina Barrón in Pitahaya got him killed.

[18] Obregón, *Campaña*, p. 60. Ceballos, *La Infamia Yanqui*, p. 139.

[19] Ceballos, *La Infamia Yanqui*, pp. 139-40.

[20] Ibid., p. 140; nowhere else in the literature is there mention of a "25th" Battalion or Corps in the area, so this may be an error on Ceballos' part.

[21] Obregón, *Campaña*, p. 60.

[22] Ibid. Ceballos, *La Infamia Yanqui*, pp. 140-1. Sánchez Lamego, *Constitucionalista*, 1: 160-1.

[23] Ceballos, *La Infamia Yanqui*, p. 141. Sánchez Lamego, *Constitucionalista*, 1: 161.

[24] Ceballos, *La Infamia Yanqui*, p. 142.

[25] Ibid.

[26] Ibid., p. 143.

[27] Ibid., p. 144.

[28] Ibid.

[29] Obregón, *Campaña*, p. 60.

[30] Ibid., pp. 60-1.

[31] Ceballos, *La Infamia Yanqui*, p. 145.

[32] Ibid.

[33] Ibid., p. 146.

[34] Obregón, *Campaña*, p. 61. Ibid., pp. 147-8.

[35] Obregón, *Campaña*, p. 61 Ceballos, *La Infamia Yanqui*, pp. 148-9.

[36] Ceballos, *La Infamia Yanqui*, pp. 148-9.

[37] Ibid., pp. 149-50.

[38] Ibid., p. 150.

[39] Ibid., p. 151.

[40] Obregón, *Campaña*, p. 61.

[41] Ceballos, *La Infamia Yanqui*, pp. 148-9, 151-2.

[42] Ibid., p. 153.

[43] Ibid., p. 154.

[44] Obregón, *Campaña*, pp. 61-2.

[45] Ceballos, *La Infamia Yanqui*, p. 155.

[46] Ibid.

[47] Obregón, *Campaña*, p. 62. Ibid., pp. 155-6.

[48] Obregón, *Campaña*, pp. 60-1. Sánchez Lamego, *Constitucionalista*, 1: 161-3; Sánchez Lamego could not find a Federal account of the battle, so for now Obregón's version of events prevails, p. 158.

[49] Ceballos, *La Infamia Yanqui*, p. 156. Rubio, *La Revolución Triunfante*, p. 67, General Guillermo Rubio Navarrete characterized the battle's outcome as "indecisive."

[50] Ceballos, *La Infamia Yanqui*, pp. 156-7. Sánchez Lamego, *Constitucionalista*, 1: 155.

[51] Ceballos, *La Infamia Yanqui*, pp. 157-8.

[52] Obregón, *Campaña*, p. 63.

[53] Ibid., p. 64. Aguilar Camín, *Frontera Nómada*, pp.458-9.

[54] Sánchez Lamego, *Constitucionalista*, 1: 165.

[55] Ceballos, *La Infamia Yanqui*, p. 159.

[56] Ibid., pp. 159-60.

[57] Obregón, *Campaña*, p. 64. Sánchez Lamego, *Constitucionalista*, 1: 165-6.

[58] Ceballos, *La Infamia Yanqui*, p. 161.

[59] Ibid. Sánchez Lamego, *Constitucionalista*, 1: 164.

[60] Obregón, *Campaña*, p. 64. Ceballos, *La Infamia Yanqui*, pp. 167-8, says Ojeda only left five hundred men in the port to protect it against the Constitutionalists to the south toward Cruz de Piedra. Sánchez Lamego, *Constitucionalista*, 1: 167-70.

[61] Obregón, *Campaña*, pp. 64. Sánchez Lamego, *Constitucionalista*, 1: 170-2.

[62] Ceballos, *La Infamia Yanqui*, p. 167.

[63] Ibid., pp. 167-8.

[64] Obregón, *Campaña*, pp. 64-5.

[65] Ceballos, *La Infamia Yanqui*, pp. 168-9.

[66] Obregón, *Campaña*, p. 65. Ibid., p. 168. Sánchez Lamego, *Constitucionalista*, 1: 173-4; a complete Federal recount of the march and battle are not extant.

[67] Obregón, *Campaña*, p. 66. Sánchez Lamego, *Constitucionalista*, 1: 174-6.

[68] Sánchez Lamego, *Constitucionalista*, 1: 175-6.

[69] Obregón, *Campaña*, p. 65. Ceballos, *La Infamia Yanqui*, pp. 168-70.

[70] Ceballos, *La Infamia Yanqui*, pp. 170-1.

[71] Obregón, *Campaña*, p. 66. Sánchez Lamego, *Constitucionalista*, 1: 174-6.

[72] Obregón, *Campaña*, pp. 66-7.

[73] Ceballos, *La Infamia Yanqui*, pp. 171-2. Sánchez Lamego, *Constitucionalista*, 1: 178-9, says that Lieutenant Colonel Juan N. de la Vega's 8th Rural Corps provided the mounted escort.

[74] Ceballos, *La Infamia Yanqui*, pp. 171-2. Sánchez Lamego, *Constitucionalista*, 1: 178-9.

[75] Obregón, *Campaña*, pp. 66-7. Sánchez Lamego, *Constitucionalista*, 1: 177-8.

[76] Ceballos, *La Infamia Yanqui*, p. 172. Sánchez Lamego, *Constitucionalista*, 1: 179.

[77] Ceballos, *La Infamia Yanqui*, pp. 172-3.

[78] Ibid., p. 173.

[79] Ibid., pp. 173-4. Sánchez Lamego, *Constitucionalista*, 1: 179.

[80] Ibid.

[81] Ceballos, *La Infamia Yanqui*, pp. 174-5.

[82] Ibid., p. 175.

[83] Obregón, *Campaña*, p. 67.

[84] Ceballos, *La Infamia Yanqui*, pp. 175-6.

[85] Ibid., pp. 176-7. Sánchez Lamego, *Constitucionalista*, 1: 180.

[86] Ceballos, *La Infamia Yanqui*, pp. 177-8.

[87] Ibid., pp. 176-7.

[88] Obregón, *Campaña*, p. 67.

[89] Ceballos, *La Infamia Yanqui*, p. 181.

[90] Ibid.

[91] Sánchez Lamego, *Constitucionalista*, 1: 180.

[92] Ceballos, *La Infamia Yanqui*, pp. 181-182. Ibid.

[93] Obregón, *Campaña*, p. 67. Ceballos, *La Infamia Yanqui*, p. 183.

[94] Obregón, *Campaña*, pp. 67-8. Sánchez Lamego, *Constitucionalista*, 1: 181.

[95] Obregón, *Campaña*, p. 68. Ceballos, *La Infamia Yanqui*, p. 183. Sánchez Lamego, *Constitucionalista*, 1: 181.

[96] Ceballos, *La Infamia Yanqui*, p. 185.

[97] Sánchez Lamego, *Constitucionalista*, 1: 182.

[98] Ceballos, *La Infamia Yanqui*, pp. 185-6. Sánchez Lamego, *Constitucionalista*, 1: 182.

[99] Obregón, *Campaña*, p. 68. Sánchez Lamego, *Constitucionalista*, 1: 181.

[100] Ceballos, *La Infamia Yanqui*, p. 187.

[101] Ibid.

[102] Ibid., p. 186.

[103] Ibid., p. 187. Sánchez Lamego, *Constitucionalista*, 1: 182.

[104] Ceballos, *La Infamia Yanqui*, pp. 187-8.

[105] Ibid., p. 188.

[106] Ibid., pp. 188-90.

[107] Obregón, *Campaña*, p. 68.

[108] Ibid., pp. 68-9.

[109] Ibid., p. 69.

[110] Ibid. Ceballos, *La Infamia Yanqui*, p. 190.

[111] Ceballos, *La Infamia Yanqui*, pp. 190-1.

[112] Ibid., p. 191.

[113] Ibid., pp. 191-2.

[114] Ibid., p. 192. Sánchez Lamego, *Constitucionalista*, 1: 184-5.

[115] Ceballos, *La Infamia Yanqui*, p. 192.

[116] Obregón, *Campaña*, p. 70.

[117] Ceballos, *La Infamia Yanqui*, pp. 192-3.

[118] Obregón, *Campaña*, pp. 70-1. Ibid., pp. 193-4. Sánchez Lamego, *Constitucionalista*, 1: 186. *Crónica Ilustrada Revolución Mexicana*, 6 vols. (México: Publex, S. A., 1966-1972), 3: 251, per Engineer and Colonel Eduardo Treviño, who joined the Constitutionalists in 1913 and became head of the Military Shops of the Army Corps

of the Northwest. He quit his lucrative job (an American-educated engineer he was the only Mexican in the company paid in dollars) with the Cananea mining company to join the army and help repair the breech blocks; afterward his boss, Juan Cabral, went back on campaign and then-First Captain Treviño went to Chihuahua to offer his services to Villa, but he just looked up and down at the young officer and said, "I don't want Obregón's spies here. I'll give you twenty-four hours to get out of my domains; if you don't do it, I'll order you 'thundered.'"

[119] Ceballos, *La Infamia Yanqui*, p. 171. Sánchez Lamego, *Constitucionalista*, 1: 176, citing Ojeda.

[120] See NewspaperArchive.com: *The Galveston Daily News*, July 15, 1913, p. 2; and, *The Reno Evening Gazette*, July 9, 1913, p. 2.

[121] Obregón, *Campaña*, pp. 73-4.

[122] José María Maytorena, *Algunas Verdades Sobre el General Álvaro Obregón*, (Los Angeles, CA: 1919), pp. 68-9.

[123] Ceballos, *La Infamia Yanqui*, pp. 197-8.

[124] Obregón, *Campaña*, pp. 71-3.

[125] Ibid., p. 74.

[126] Ibid., pp. 74-5. Ceballos, *La Infamia Yanqui*, p. 198.

[127] Obregón, *Campaña*, pp. 74-5.

[128] Ibid., pp. 76-7. Treviño, *Memorias*, pp. 47-8, regarding Mori and his broncos.

[129] Obregón, *Campaña*, pp. 73, 76-8. Ceballos, *La Infamia Yanqui*, pp. 204-5.

[130] Miguel Alessio Robles, *Obregón como Militar*, (México: Editorial Cultura, 1935), p. 65.

[131] Ceballos, *La Infamia Yanqui*, pp. 205-6. Sánchez Lamego, *Constitucionalista*, 3: 266, Ojeda's promotion date was July 14, 1913.

[132] Ceballos, *La Infamia Yanqui*, pp. 2, 111-13, 124, 178-80.

[133] Ibid., pp. 100, 195-7, 203-5.

Chapter 4

[1] Barragán, *Revolución Constitucionalista*, 1: 154-5. Sánchez Lamego, *Constitucionalista*, 1: 248-53.

[2] Barragán, *Revolución Constitucionalista*, 1: 154, Barragán said that the Federals had fifteen hundred men from three units, the 31st Regiment, 44th Rural Corps and 21st Infantry Battalion, which would have meant that the units would have to be full strength or oversized. Sánchez Lamego, *Constitucionalista*, 1: 253-5.

[3] Sánchez Lamego, *Constitucionalista*, 1: 255-6.

[4] Barragán, *Revolución Constitucionalista*, 1: 154-5.

[5] Ibid., 1: 122-3. Sánchez Lamego, *Constitucionalista*, 1: 91.

[6] Sánchez Lamego, *Constitucionalista*, 1: 91-3.

[7] Barragán, *Revolución Constitucionalista*, 1: 126-8, 631-7 (Blanco's Report). Ibid., 1: 94.

[8] Barragán, *Revolución Constitucionalista*, 1: 126-8, 631-7. Sánchez Lamego, *Constitucionalista*, 1: 95.

[9] Barragán, *Revolución Constitucionalista*, 1: 128, 635-7. Treviño, *Memorias*, pp. 37-8. Sánchez Lamego, *Constitucionalista*, 1: 94-5.

[10] Rubio, *La Revolución Triunfante*, pp. 55, 59. Sánchez Lamego, *Constitucionalista*, 1: 95-6.

[11] Barragán, *Revolución Constitucionalista*, 1: 128, 635-7. AREM 718/1/21, June 10, 1913, Antonio Lozana to "Relaciones," regarding an alleged attack by 2,000 revolutionaries on Laredo, and Jesús Carranza in Candela-Lampazos. AREM 718/1/140, June 10, 1913, from R. I. Bravo, Eagle Pass, to Mexican consul, Laredo (quote). See also dated in late May and early June: AREM 718/1/77-9, 111, 114, 159, 163.

[12] Barragán, *Revolución Constitucionalista*, 1: 155, 189. Sánchez Lamego, *Constitucionalista*, 1: 256-9, Sánchez Lamego says that Emilio Campa's men engaged Natera's before occupying Zacatecas, and that (quite improbably) the council of war intended for Rubio Navarrete to follow the route Monterrey-Villaldama-Bustamante-Monclova, the last leg being overland away from the rail and ignoring the key Constitutionalist depot of Matamoros. Barragán, however, says that the council of war took place on June 17, an obvious error since he agrees that Delgado entered Zacatecas on June 16 after fighting the Constitutionalists in Guadalupe the day before.

[13] Pazuengo, *Historia de la Revolución en Durango*, pp. 45-6.

[14] Ibid., pp. 46-47.

[15] Ibid., p. 48.

[16] Ibid., pp. 44-5. Barragán, *Revolución Constitucionalista*, 1: 157.

[17] Pazuengo, *Historia de la Revolución en Durango*, p. 49.

[18] Ibid., p. 51

[19] Ibid., p. 44. Sánchez Lamego, *Constitucionalista*, 1: 242-4.

[20] Pazuengo, *Historia de la Revolución en Durango*, p. 50. Sánchez Lamego, *Constitucionalista*, 1: 244.

[21] Pazuengo, *Historia de la Revolución en Durango*, pp. 51-2. Barragán, *Revolución Constitucionalista*, 1: 158. Sánchez Lamego, *Constitucionalista*, 1: 244-5.

[22] Pazuengo, *Historia de la Revolución en Durango*, pp. 52-3. Sánchez Lamego, *Constitucionalista*, 1: 244-5.

[23] Pazuengo, *Historia de la Revolución en Durango*, p. 53. Sánchez Lamego, *Constitucionalista*, 1: 245

[24] Pazuengo, *Historia de la Revolución en Durango*, p. 56. Sánchez Lamego, *Constitucionalista*, 1: 245.

[25] Pazuengo, *Historia de la Revolución en Durango*, p. 57.

[26] Ibid., pp. 56-7.

[27] Sánchez Lamego, *Constitucionalista*, 1: 245-6.

[28] Pazuengo, *Historia de la Revolución en Durango*, pp. 69-70. Justino N. Palomares and Francisco Múzquiz, *Las Campañas del Norte (Sangre Y Héroes)* (México: Andrés Botas Editor, 1914), p. 13 (quote), Palomares and Múzquiz were editors of the Torreón daily, *La Lucha*. Silvestre Dorador, *Mi Prisión: La Defensa Social y la Verdad del Caso* (México: Departamento de Tallares Gráficos de la Secretaría de Fomento, 1916), p. 207. Ibid., 1: 245.

[29] Pazuengo, *Historia de la Revolución en Durango*, p. 58. Barragán, *Revolución Constitucionalista*, 1: 159-60, contains details of the sacking.

[30] Pazuengo, *Historia de la Revolución en Durango*, pp. 58-9.

[31] Ibid., pp. 59-60.

[32] Sánchez Lamego, *Constitucionalista*, 1: 245-6.

[33] Pazuengo, *Historia de la Revolución en Durango*, pp. 62-3.

[34] Cervantes, *Francisco Villa*, pp. 52-3. Barragán, *Revolución Constitucionalista*, 1: 242, Villa went to Ascención and "communicating with Señor Carranza and the Jefes of Sonora so that they might supply him with ammunition to be able to begin the siege of Ciudad Juárez. Sánchez Lamego, *Constitucionalista*, 1: 216, 218; Mercado assumed his new command on May31. Katz, *Pancho Villa*, 1: 244-245. Taibo, *Una Biografía Narrativa*, p. 182, reasons Rábago got fired.

[35] Cervantes, *Francisco Villa*, p. 53.

[36] Barragán, *Revolución Constitucionalista*, 1: 241-2 contains Villa's report. Ontiveros, *Toribio Ortega*, p. 91. Cervantes, *Francisco Villa*, p. 53. "Old man" quote from Sánchez Lamego, *Constitucionalista*, 1: 216-7, says that Mancilla was coming from Chihuahua City, but this does not match what Ontiveros and Cervantes wrote, and does not make sense given how the battle developed.

[37] Ontiveros, *Toribio Ortega*, p. 95.

[38] Ibid., pp. 95-6. Sánchez Lamego, *Constitucionalista*, 1: 218-9.

[39] Ontiveros, *Toribio Ortega*, p. 95.

[40] Sánchez Lamego, *Constitucionalista*, 1: 218.

[41] Ibid.

[42] Cervantes, *Francisco Villa*, pp. 53-4.

[43] Calzadíaz, *Hecho Reales*, 1: 116.

[44] Villa, *Pancho Villa*, p. 537. United States Congress, Senate Committee on Foreign Relations, *Revolutions in Mexico: hearing before a subcommittee of the Committee on Foreign Relations, United States Senate, sixty-second Congress, second session, pursuant to S. Res. 335, a resolution authorizing the Committee on Foreign Relations to investigate whether any interests in the United States have been or are now engaged in inciting rebellion in Cuba and Mexico* (Washington, D.C.: Government Printing Office, 1913), pp. 577-578, Walter A. M. Roxby's testimony; the San Pedro Ranch, about ninety-seven kilometers west of Casas Grandes and seventy-two kilometers southwest of Ascensión, had been raided by Colorado Colonel Jerónimo Ascárate with about

200 men, Jesús Terrazas with about 200, and a man called Fabian Enrique who had about eighty. Calzadíaz, *Hecho Reales*, 1: 116-117, mentions contact with Columbus businessman Samuel Ravel.

[45] Villa, *Pancho Villa*, p. 536. Ontiveros, *Toribio Ortega*, pp. 91-2. Barragán, *Revolución Constitucionalista*, 1: 242. Cervantes, *Francisco Villa*, p. 54.

[46] Villa, *Pancho Villa*, p. 536. Ontiveros, *Toribio Ortega*, p. 92. Cervantes, *Francisco Villa*, p. 54. Barragán, *Revolución Constitucionalista*, 1: 242.

[47] Villa, *Pancho Villa*, p. 536. Ontiveros, *Toribio Ortega*, pp. 92-3. Cervantes, *Francisco Villa*, p. 54. Barragán, *Revolución Constitucionalista*, 1: 242. There are several discrepancies in reports, with Cervantes saying that Villa took 107 prisoners, while he lost five killed and seventeen wounded of his own; Barragán says that in his official report to the First Chief, Villa reported taking ninety-five prisoners and finding only twelve dead; and Barragán says the battle took place on June 18, not June 20, and at Nuevo Casas Grandes Station. Sánchez Lamego, *Constitucionalista*, 1: 217. Villa said that Azcárate died in this fight, while Sánchez Lamego said Azcárate arrived in Ciudad Juárez on June 25 with the remaining two hundred Colorados; the January 31, 1914 Escalafón listed both Irregular Major Jerónimo R. Azcárate and his first captain son, Jerónimo Jr., meaning that both had survived the 1913 battle, pp. 233, 236.

[48] Villa, *Pancho Villa*, p. 537. Cervantes, *Francisco Villa*, p. 54. Calzadíaz, *Hecho Reales*, 1: 117-8.

[49] Sánchez Lamego, *Constitucionalista*, 1: 216.

[50] Ontiveros, *Toribio Ortega*, pp. 93-94. Cervantes, *Francisco Villa*, p. 54. See NewspaperArchive.com, *The Galveston Daily News*, July 15, 1913, p. 2: "Villa is reported to have sent 500 of his command back to Casas Grandes, 130 miles south of [Ciudad] Juarez, where on Saturday his rebel [sic] garrison was reported attacked by Independents under Maximo Castillo, supposed to be operating for the federal government."

[51] Katz, *Pancho Villa*, 1: 309. Sánchez Lamego, *Constitucionalista*, 1: 217; Sánchez Lamego says that Villa appointed Medina his Chief of Staff, but per Guzman, *Memorias*, p. 202, that honor fell to José Eleuterio Hermosillo.

[52] Villa, *Pancho Villa*, p. 441. Guzmán, *Memorias*, pp. 97, 198-202: first quote on p. 198 and the second one on p. 199.

[53] Barragán, *Revolución Constitucionalista*, 1: 240. Guzmán, *Memorias*, pp. 199-201, quote on page 201.

[54] Ontiveros, *Toribio Ortega*, pp. 86-7.

[55] Ibid., p. 87. Sánchez Lamego, *Constitucionalista*, 1: 213-4, the revolutionaries collected six pesos per head of cattle exported into the United States through Ojinaga, which Toribio Ortega's revolutionaries had occupied without a fight on March 22.

[56] Ontiveros, *Toribio Ortega*, p. 87.

[57] Ibid., pp. 87-8.

[58] Ibid., p. 88.

[59] Ibid., p. 93.

[60] Sánchez Lamego, *Constitucionalista*, 1: 369-70. Paul J. Vanderwood, "Response to Revolt: The Counter-Guerrilla Strategy of Porfirio Díaz," *The Hispanic American Historical Review* 56, 4 (November, 1976), p. 558, gives a 10:1 ratio of government forces to revolutionaries necessary to put down an insurrection.

[61] Sánchez Lamego, *Constitucionalista*, 1: 374-5, 379.

[62] Rubio, *La Revolución Triunfante*, p. 63.Aragón, *El Desarme del Ejército Federal*, pp. 54, 56, quote about the malfeasance by Federal cavalry officers comes from Aragón.

[63] Juan Manuel Torrea, *Decena Trágica* (México: Academia Nacional de Historia y Geografía, 1963), pp. 12-13.

[64] Barragán, *Revolución Constitucionalista*, 1: 244, Barragán betrays his origins as an auxiliary officer turned professional by the Revolution.

[65] Marcelo Caraveo, *Crónica de la Revolución (1910-1929)* (México: Editorial Trillas, 1992), pp. 77, 85 (quote).

[66] Sánchez Lamego, *Constitucionalista*, 1: 377. Calzadíaz, *Hecho Reales*, 1:193.

Chapter 5

[1] Michael C. Meyer, *Huerta: A Political Portrait* (Lincoln: University of Nebraska Press, 1972), p. 5.

[2] AHSDN XI/481.5/88.326-8, Decree 442, July 3, 1913. AHSDN XI/481.5/88.351-4, July 21, 1913.

[3] AHSDN XI/481.5/88.326-8.

[4] Ibid. Muñoz, *Verdad y Mito*, 2: 160, Muñoz said that in his unit in the Spring of 1914 all "the officers, muchachos of the Colegio with great ambitions, had barely reached 23 years, many being between sixteen and twenty."

[5] Adrián Cravioto Leyzaola, *Historia Documental del Heróico Colegio Militar A Través de la Historia de México*, 3 vols. (México: Costa-Amic Editores, S. A., 2000 [1982]), 2: 491.

[6] AHSDN XI/481.5/88.367, Decree 445, July 31, 1913.

[7] AHSDN XI/481.5/88.442-443, Decree 449, August 25, 1913, Reorganization Decree. Secretaría de Guerra y Marina, *Reglamento de Maniobras de Infantería* (México: Imprenta y Fototipia de la Secretaría de Industria y Comercio, 1914), p. VI.

[8] AHSDN XI/481.5/88.443-4, Decree 449, August 25, 1913.

[9] AHSDN XI/481.5/88.365, Decree 446, July 30, 1913. AHSDN XI/481.5/88.330, Decree 439, July 3, 1913. AHSDN XI/481.5/88.494-5, Decree 452, September 17, 1913.

[10] AHSDN XI/481.5/88.336, Decree 440, July 6, 1913.

[11] Sánchez Lamego, *Constitucionalista*, 1: 98, 142, for characterizations of discipline levels.

[12] Ibid., 1: 68-69; 3: 13-14, 18. Generals Maass and Rubio's columns departed Mexico City June 15 and 16, 1913.

[13] Ibid., 3: 25-26; Rubio stepped off on June 26. CEHM-GRN 2.55.03, see transcribed telegram from Huerta to Rubio, June 22, 1913.

[14] CEHM-GRN 2.55.03, see transcribed telegram from Huerta to Rubio, 24-Jun-13, and from Rubio to Minister of War, over the next two days.

[15] González, *Con Carranza*, 1: 10, 13-14.

[16] Sánchez Lamego, *Constitucionalista*, 3: 26-9. Rubio, *La Revolución Triunfante*, pp. 60-1.

[17] González, *Con Carranza*, 1: 15-16. Sánchez Lamego, *Constitucionalista*, 3: 26-9.

[18] CEHM-GRN 2.55.03, July 03, 1913, see transcribed telegram from Rubio to Minister of War.

[19] Sánchez Lamego, *Constitucionalista*, 3: 26-9. Rubio, *La Revolución Triunfante*, pp. 60-1.

[20] González, *Con Carranza*, 1: 17, 20 (quote).

[21] Barragán, *Revolución Constitucionalista*, 1: 190, 192, General Barragán reports that even at this early date the revolutionaries were making the transformation into soldiers, performing the "services of campaign," a reference to the proscriptions regarding such basics as marching, camping, field works, security, the basics of combined arms combat, etc.; see the razor-thin booklet: Secretaría de Guerra y Marina, *Reglamento para el Servicio de la Artillería de Campaña*, (México: Talleres del Departamento de Estado Mayor, 1908)—not to be confused with the more comprehensive Regulations and Maneuvers manual—and Secretaría de Guerra y Marina, *Instrucción Práctica para el Servicio de la Infantería en Campaña*, (México: Imprenta del Gobierno en el Ex-Arzobispado, 1898). Sánchez Lamego, *Constitucionalista*, 3: 29-30. Treviño, *Memorias*, p. 41. González, *Con Carranza*, 1: 20. Aragón, *El Desarme del Ejército Federal*, p. 72.

[22] González, *Con Carranza*, 1: 21-4, 26. Treviño, *Memorias*, p. 40. Aragón, *El Desarme del Ejército Federal*, p. 72. Ricardo L. Vázquez, *Poncho Vázquez* (México: Ediciones Botas, 1940) p. 121, contains story as related by José López Zuazua, who participated in the battle. The latter two sources mention the 11 p.m. firefight, while the first two maintain that absolute surprise was obtained.

[23] Treviño, *Memorias*, pp. 40-1. Barragán, *Revolución Constitucionalista*, 1: 194.

[24] González, *Con Carranza*, 1: 28.

[25] Ibid. Aragón, *El Desarme del Ejército Federal*, pp. 72, 74, 76. Sánchez Lamego, *Constitucionalista*, 3: 26, 30.

[26] Treviño, *Memorias*, pp. 40-1. CEHM-GRN 2.64.02, November 19, 1943, is copy of a letter from General Rubio Navarrete to a magazine correcting some errors of fact in an article. Barragán, *Revolución Constitucionalista*, 1: 192, 194-5. González, *Con Carranza*, 1: 28-9, 33. Aragón, *El Desarme del Ejército Federal*, pp. 74, 76, 78. Sánchez Lamego, *Constitucionalista*, 3: 32-3.

[27] Treviño, *Memorias*, pp. 40-1, Treviño says that the Federal 9th's commander, José Alessio Robles, fled the field in a most cowardly fashion with a minor wound to his leg, abandoning his troops to get help from Rubio Navarrete; Treviño had a blood feud with Alessio Robles that lasted into the 1920's when they had a shoot-out on the streets of Mexico City and Treviño's assistant shot Alessio Robles dead. CEHM-GRN 2.64.02. Barragán, *Revolución Constitucionalista*, 1: 192, 194-195. González, *Con Carranza*, 1: 28-9. Aragón, *El Desarme del Ejército Federal*, pp. 76, 78. Vázquez, *Poncho Vázquez*, pp. 121-3, per José López Zuazua, the priest manned one of the machine guns in the church belfry. Sánchez Lamego, *Constitucionalista*, 3: 32-3.

[28] González, *Con Carranza*, 1: 155.

[29] Aragón, *El Desarme del Ejército Federal*, pp. 76, 78.

[30] González, *Con Carranza*, 1: 30.

[31] CEHM-GRN 2.64.02.

[32] Barragán, *Revolución Constitucionalista*, 1: 196. Sánchez Lamego, *Constitucionalista*, 3: 33-5.

[33] Ibid.

[34] González, *Con Carranza*, 1: 37-8, says that González took the men of Murguía and Sánchez Herrera, but since sappers are organized along the same lines as infantry, it makes more sense that he would have those with him along with the other dismounted troops. Barragán, *Revolución Constitucionalista*, 1: 196-7. Sánchez Lamego, *Constitucionalista*, 3: 35, 38.

[35] González, *Con Carranza*, 1: 38. Barragán, *Revolución Constitucionalista*, 1: 197. Sánchez Lamego, *Constitucionalista*, 3: 35-40.

[36] González, *Con Carranza*, 1: 35-36, 38, 40. Sánchez Lamego, *Constitucionalista*, 3: 36. Treviño, *Memorias*, p. 42 on the "pitchfork."

[37] González, *Con Carranza*, 1: 41-2. Barragán, *Revolución Constitucionalista*, 1: 197-8. Sánchez Lamego, *Constitucionalista*, 3: 35-40.

[38] Barragán, *Revolución Constitucionalista*, 1: 197-8. Sánchez Lamego, *Constitucionalista*, 3: 36.

[39] Barragán, *Revolución Constitucionalista*, 1: 190, Barragán's opinion.

[40] CEHM-GRN 2.64.02.

[41] AREM 847/6/60, July 31, 1913, Arturo M. Elías, Inspector of Consuls, to Secretary of Foreign Affairs on the encounter at Nadadores. González, *Con Carranza*, 1: 50-51. Vázquez, *Poncho Vázquez*, p. 58, Domingo González, brother of Pablo González established a business in Morelos, a business that he lost precisely because of the Revolution, since the Federals sacked it when they learned that he was the brother of one of those fighting them. Jack London, *México Intervenido: Reportajes desde Veracruz y Tampico, 1914*, Translated by Elisa Ramírez Casteñeda, (México: Ediciones Toledo, 1990), p. 108, A Constitutionalist major that London met in Tampico in June 1914

"had spent four years on campaign. He had fought for Madero; he was now fighting for...Carranza. Two of his brothers had died. All his property had been razed."

[42] Barragán, *Revolución Constitucionalista*, 1: 206-7.

[43] González, *Con Carranza*, 1: 56, "W" claimed that González won the Revolution by tying up the Federals in the Northeast.

[44] Barragán, *Revolución Constitucionalista*, 1: 206-7.

[45] Pazuengo, *Historia de la Revolución en Durango*, pp. 65-6, reported numbers are not as reliable as those from strength reports and payroll records.

[46] Ibid., pp. 70-1. Sánchez Lamego, *Constitucionalista*, 3: 60-1.

[47] Sánchez Lamego, *Constitucionalista*, 3: 62.

[48] Manzur Ocaña, *Cándido Aguilar*, p. 73, from Aguilar's report of January 5, 1914. Ibid., 3: 55-6, contains details of the July 14 action. Sánchez Lamego, *Generales de la Revolución*, 1: 17.

[49] Barragán, *Revolución Constitucionalista*, 1: 207. Sánchez Lamego, *Constitucionalista*, 3: 61-3. Palomares and Múzquiz, *Las Campañas del Norte*, p. 13, put the Constitutionalist strength at 5,438 men.

[50] Pazuengo, *Historia de la Revolución en Durango*, p. 66.

[51] Sánchez Lamego, *Constitucionalista*, 3: 57-9. Palomares and Múzquiz, *Las Campañas del Norte*, p. 14, Palomares and Múzquiz say that the initial engagement took place on July 18 and 19; they report that at daybreak on that first day, Munguía's column left Torreón and caught sight of the Constitutionalist advance forces, exchanged some small arms fire, and then deployed for battle. On the right margin of the San Carlos Arroyo and in some nearby ditches the infantry of the 12th, 18th, and 23rd Battalion took up position; on the small rises to the east of Avilés, Munguía placed the cavalry of the 5th and 32nd Regiments commanded by Lieutenant Colonel Antonio Gallardo, and the artillery went into battery over the line of the Central Railroad, with the famous "El Niño" cannon on a rail platform supported by the armored car commanded by Second Captain Blas Macías.

[52] Sánchez Lamego, *Constitucionalista*, 3: 59-60. Palomares and Múzquiz, *Las Campañas del Norte*, pp. 14-15, says that lacking sufficient cavalry and running short of ammunition, they received orders to fall back on Torreón during the night, although this sounds more like a cover story that the Federals probably fed to the two reporters.

[53] Pazuengo, *Historia de la Revolución en Durango*, p. 66. Palomares and Múzquiz, *Las Campañas del Norte*, p. 16.

[54] Pazuengo, *Historia de la Revolución en Durango*, pp. 66-7.

[55] Palomares and Múzquiz, *Las Campañas del Norte*, pp. 16-18.

[56] Sánchez Lamego, *Constitucionalista*, 3: 63-4. Ibid., p. 18.

[57] Sánchez Lamego, *Constitucionalista*, 3: 65-6. Caraveo, *Crónica*, p. 77, describes Argumedo in battle.

[58] Sánchez Lamego, *Constitucionalista*, 3: 66-7.

[59] Ibid., 3: 67-8.

[60] Ibid., 3: 63-5, 67-8. Palomares and Múzquiz, *Las Campañas del Norte*, pp. 18-19, offers a slightly different Federal disposition with a bit more detail: General Bravo ordered the most important defensive points reinforced, sending part of the men from Avilés to Cerro de la Cruz where he had a battery of 75-mm. guns and Rexers commanded by Major Arellano; a group composed of the 18th Infantry and 32nd Cavalry commanded by Lieutenant Colonel Antonio Gallardo was situated in Huarache Canyon; the Cazadores del Nazas (only about 100 men, Sánchez Lamego said that this corps consisted of officers and men who had been tried and convicted, possibly those who had belonged to Campos' command) commanded by its organizer, Major Luciano Enríquez occupied the Casa Redonda to the south of town; with part of the 9th Battalion, Sub-lieutenant Luis Villanueva took up position in the old furniture factory La Vencedora to the southeast of the city; and the rest of Munguía's column was on La Fe and La Union hills, La Alianza barracks, and the National Railroad station, with Munguía commanding the west and southwest sectors. The men's spirits, in spite of the defeats already suffered, were excellent.

[61] Palomares and Múzquiz, *Las Campañas del Norte*, pp. 19-20.

[62] Sánchez Lamego, *Constitucionalista*, 3: 68-70. Ibid., p. 20.

[63] Sánchez Lamego, *Constitucionalista*, 3: 70. Palomares and Múzquiz, *Las Campañas del Norte*, p. 20.

[64] Sánchez Lamego, *Constitucionalista*, 3: 70. Palomares and Múzquiz, *Las Campañas del Norte*, p. 21.

[65] Palomares and Múzquiz, *Las Campañas del Norte*, pp. 21, 23.

[66] Sánchez Lamego, *Constitucionalista*, 3: 70. Ibid., pp. 20-1.

[67] Sánchez Lamego, *Constitucionalista*, 3: 70-1. Palomares and Múzquiz, *Las Campañas del Norte*, p. 21.

[68] Palomares and Múzquiz, *Las Campañas del Norte*, p. 22, also mentions a small firefight in the morning of the twenty-fourth on the northwest side where Sixto Ugalde led a small of Constitutionalists in trying to penetrate the Chinese orchards before some of Colonel Reyna's men turned them back; Ugalde sat out the revolution against Huerta in a Torreón jail, but that may have been after this battle.

[69] Sánchez Lamego, *Constitucionalista*, 3: 71.

[70] Ibid., 3: 72; 4: 67.

[71] Ibid., 3: 72, Federal reports only mention an attack on cemetery that lasted three hours. Palomares and Múzquiz, *Las Campañas del Norte*, pp. 22-3.

[72] Sánchez Lamego, *Constitucionalista*, 3: 72; 4: 67.

[73] Ibid., 3: 73. Palomares and Múzquiz, *Las Campañas del Norte*, pp. 23-4.

[74] Palomares and Múzquiz, *Las Campañas del Norte*, p. 24.

[75] Sánchez Lamego, *Constitucionalista*, 3: 73. Ibid., p. 26.

[76] Sánchez Lamego, *Constitucionalista*, 3: 73.

[77] Palomares and Múzquiz, *Las Campañas del Norte*, pp. 23, 26, says that this action took place on the twenty-fifth because the Constitutionalists had been on Metalúrgica Hill and digging in since the twenty-fourth. Most likely, the Constitutionalists had been there since the twenty-fourth, but Bravo only felt capable of dislodging them on the twenty-ninth, or he wanted to protect the provisions entering on the east side of town.

[78] Pazuengo, *Historia de la Revolución en Durango*, p. 72. Manzur Ocaña, *Cándido Aguilar*, pp. 73-4, from Aguilar's report of January 5, 1914. Sánchez Lamego, *Generales de la Revolución*, 1: 17.

[79] Pazuengo, *Historia de la Revolución en Durango*, p. 72.

[80] Ibid., p. 74.

[81] Ibid., pp. 74-5. Palomares and Múzquiz, *Las Campañas del Norte*, pp. 25-6. Sánchez Lamego, *Constitucionalista*, 3: 73-4.

[82] Pazuengo, *Historia de la Revolución en Durango*, pp. 74-5. Sánchez Lamego, *Constitucionalista*, 3: 73-4, 86.

[83] Pazuengo, *Historia de la Revolución en Durango*, p. 73. Palomares and Múzquiz, *Las Campañas del Norte*, pp. 11-12. Miguel S. Ramos, *Un Soldado: José Refugio Velasco* (México: Ediciones Oasis, S.A., 1960), pp. 121-2. Instituto Nacional de Estudios Históricos de la Revolución Mexicana, *Diccionario Histórico y Biográfico de la Revolución Mexicana*, 8 vols. (México: Instituto Nacional de Estudios Históricos de la Revolución Mexicana, 1991), 2: 878.

[84] Pazuengo, *Historia de la Revolución en Durango*, p. 73. Shortly before dying, Campos admitted to burning 144 haciendas, José Juan Tablada, *Historia de la Campaña de la Divisón del Norte*, (México: Imprenta del Gobierno Mexicano, 1913), p. 38.

[85] Pazuengo, *Historia de la Revolución en Durango*, pp. 73-4.

[86] Ibid., pp. 67-8.

[87] Sánchez Lamego, *Constitucionalista*, 3: 75-6.

[88] Palomares and Múzquiz, *Las Campañas del Norte*, p. 27. Ibid., 3: 85.

[89] Sánchez Lamego, *Constitucionalista*, 3: 76.

[90] Pazuengo, *Historia de la Revolución en Durango*, p. 69.

[91] Barragán, *Revolución Constitucionalista*, 1: 150-1, 209-12. Sánchez Lamego, *Constitucionalista*, 3: 76.

[92] González, *Con Carranza*, 1: 50-1.

[93] Ibid., 1: 52-3, 56.

[94] Barragán, *Revolución Constitucionalista*, 1: 199-201. Urquizo, *Memorias*, pp. 60-8. Sánchez Lamego, *Constitucionalista*, 3: 41-2.

[95] CEHM-GRN 1.6.2, n.d., General Téllez to Rubio Navarrete, probably sometime in June 1913.

[96] CEHM-GRN 1.30.18, July 24, 1913, General Rubio Navarrete to the President and his ministers of War, Communications, Interior, Foreign Relations, Justice, and Public Instruction, regarding reestablishment of rail lines between Monterrey and Laredo. See other numerous citations: CEHM-GRN 1.29.10, n.d.; CEHM-GRN 1.30.21, July 26, 1913; CEHM-GRN 1.30.26, August 2, 1913; CEHM-GRN 1.30.41, September, 1913; CEHM-GRN 1.31.20, September 8, 1913. CEHM-GRN 2.38.02, December 11, 1913, Senate ratifies Rubio's promotion to General of Brigade.

[97] CEHM-GRN 2.64.02, November 19, 1943, is copy of a letter from General Rubio Navarrete to a magazine correcting some errors of fact in an article. Sánchez Lamego, *Constitucionalista*, 3: 50, Federal General Fernando González made an application for his own removal from command of the Division of the Bravo; his name does not even appear in the January 1914 Escalafón.

[98] CEHM-GRN 1.31.26, September 21, 1913, operation proposed by General Rubio to Téllez.

[99] CEHM-GRN 1.31.28, September 26, 1913, General Rubio to Huerta. See also CEHM-GRN 1.31.29, September 26, 1913, where General Rubio implores Colonel Manuel Corral in the War Ministry to use his influence with Huerta to get him reassigned.

[99] CEHM-GRN 1.31.28, 26.

[100] González, *Con Carranza*, 1: 56, 61.

[101] Ibid., 1: 59-60.

[102] AHSDN XI/481.5/88.345-6, July 15, 1913, abrogation of Decree 429.

[103] González, *Con Carranza*, 1: 63-4. Barragán, *Revolución Constitucionalista*, 1: 199-201. Sánchez Lamego, *Constitucionalista*, 3: 41-4: no documentation exists in the Defense archives concerning activities of Rubio Navarrete and Maass' columns on the last days of their operation, including the battle of Hermanas.

[104] Barragán, *Revolución Constitucionalista*, 1: 201-203. Urquizo, *Memorias*, pp. 70-3.

[105] Barragán, *Revolución Constitucionalista*, 1: 203-204. Sánchez Lamego, *Constitucionalista*, 3: 42. González, *Con Carranza*, 1: 64-6.

[106] Barragán, *Revolución Constitucionalista*, 1: 204.

[107] Ibid. González, *Con Carranza*, 1: 66.

[108] AHSDN XI/481.5/88.426, August 23, 1913, letter from General Blanquet to Secretary of Foreign Relations regarding General Téllez's campaign objective; Téllez was commander of the Division of the Bravo, technically Maass' and Rubio Navarrete's boss.

[109] CEHM-GRN 1.29.22, n.d., Federal General Téllez to General Guillermo Rubio Navarrete.

[110] CEHM-GRN 1.30.06, n.d., Federal General Guillermo Rubio Navarrete to General Téllez.

[111] González, *Con Carranza*, 1: 67-8.

[112] González, *Con Carranza*, 1: 70. Vázquez, *Poncho Vázquez*, pp. 125-6.

[113] Barragán, *Revolución Constitucionalista*, 1: 206-7, 248-50. Sánchez Lamego, *Constitucionalista*, 3: 41, 45, 48, 50-1. Colonel Murguía's forces set up their new base at Santa Gertrudis (ten kilometers) north of San Buenaventura and destroyed the track between Gloria and Baján stations, to Maass' rear. CEHM-GRN 1.31.15, September 8, 1913, report from Téllez to Rubio that Maass had just defeated González in San Buenaventura, sending some north through Abasolo while others passed from the North to the east, without more specifics.

[114] González, *Con Carranza*, 1: 70-1.

[115] Ibid., 1: 71-4. Sánchez Lamego, *Constitucionalista*, 3: 43.

[116] González, *Con Carranza*, 1: 74.

[117] Barragán, *Revolución Constitucionalista*, 1: 249-50.

[118] CEHM-MWG 1.6.762.1-2, October 6, 1913, copies of the telegram and letter received from the First Chief in Hermosillo dated October 6, 1913 appointing General of Brigade Pablo González to command the Army Corps of the Northeast.

[119] Meyer, *Huerta*, pp. 97-8. Google "Huerta hugging Orozco" to see the infamous photograph.

[120] Sánchez Lamego, *Constitucionalista*, 3: 80-1; 4: 82 (Orozco's report). Barragán, *Revolución Constitucionalista*, 1: 244-5, Barragán insulted the Federals for their lack of offensive nature, admitting that they were good at defending plazas, although this actually was not true.

[121] Ontiveros, *Toribio Ortega*, pp. 96-7. Sánchez Lamego, *Constitucionalista*, 3: 81, Sánchez Lamego says that the combat at kilometer 1364 became quite heated and Orozco had to send in the rest of his cavalry. With the arrival of General Argumedo's infantry the Colorados won the day, although Orozco's report does not mention any such drama, nor the presence of Argumedo; 4: 82 (Orozco's report).

[122] Sánchez Lamego, *Constitucionalista*, 4: 82-3 (Orozco's report). Ontiveros, *Toribio Ortega*, p. 97.

[123] Sánchez Lamego, *Constitucionalista*, 4: 83 (Orozco's report).

[124] Ibid.

[125] Ontiveros, *Toribio Ortega*, pp. 97-8. Ibid., 4: 83-4 (Orozco's report).

[126] Ontiveros, *Toribio Ortega*, pp. 97-8. Sánchez Lamego, *Constitucionalista*, 4: 84 (Orozco's report). Caraveo, *Crónica*, p. 78, said that "the fight was waged on the streets of the city."

[127] Caraveo, *Crónica*, p. 78. Sánchez Lamego, *Constitucionalista*, 3: 79-80, 82.

[128] Rubio, *La Revolución Triunfante*, p. 115.

[129] Ontiveros, *Toribio Ortega*, p. 99, Ontiveros said that Villa decided to postpone the attack on Ciudad Juárez for various reasons, but did not elaborate. Cervantes, *Francisco Villa*, p. 54. Sánchez Lamego, *Constitucionalista*, 1: 219.

[130] Ontiveros, *Toribio Ortega*, pp. 99-100. Caraveo, *Crónica*, p. 78, Mancillas' mission. Sánchez Lamego, *Constitucionalista*, 3: 82.

[131] Ontiveros, *Toribio Ortega*, p. 100. Sánchez Lamego, *Constitucionalista*, 3: 82, differs from Ontiveros by saying that the Federal force only consisted of Mancilla's 33rd Battalion, and it was being beaten until the arrival of Lieutenant Colonel Enrique Pulido of the 15th Battalion with 100 men from his battalion and a machine gun along with 200 Colorados from the "Caraveo" Brigade and one hundred more of the "Salazar" Brigade.

[132] Ontiveros, *Toribio Ortega*, pp. 100-101.

[133] Ibid., p. 101.

[134] Ibid., pp. 101-2.

[135] Ibid., pp. 102-103. Cervantes, *Francisco Villa*, p. 55.

[136] Ontiveros, *Toribio Ortega*, pp. 104-5. Barragán, *Revolución Constitucionalista*, 1: 684. Cervantes, *Francisco Villa*, p. 55.

[137] Barragán, *Revolución Constitucionalista*, 1: 243, 684-6, these pages contain Villa's battle report; note his misapplication of the word "strategic." Caraveo, *Crónica*, p. 78, placed the number of Terrazas' men at 600. Rubio, *La Revolución Triunfante*, p. 115, Rubio Navarrete put Terrazas' force at 400 instead of the 982 men quoted in Villa's report, which seems low given that the Constitutionalists recovered 421 rifles.

[138] Ontiveros, *Toribio Ortega*, pp. 104-5. Barragán, *Revolución Constitucionalista*, 1: 684.

[139] Ontiveros, *Toribio Ortega*, p. 105. Barragán, *Revolución Constitucionalista*, 1: 684.

[140] Ontiveros, *Toribio Ortega*, pp. 105-6. Barragán, *Revolución Constitucionalista*, 1: 243, 684-6.

[141] Ontiveros, *Toribio Ortega*, p. 106.

[142] Caraveo, *Crónica*, p. 78.

[143] Barragán, *Revolución Constitucionalista*, 1: 243, 684-6. Ontiveros, *Toribio Ortega*, pp. 105-6. Guzmán, *Memorias*, p. 203.

[144] Barragán, *Revolución Constitucionalista*, 1: 685-6. Ontiveros, *Toribio Ortega*, p. 107. Guzmán, *Memorias*, pp. 204-6: says that Fidel Ávila escorted the Villista wounded to Agua Prieta, but Ontiveros says that it was Acosta. Since Ávila does not appear on the list of officers who took part in the Battle of San Andrés, and surely he would not have been overlooked, we must assume that Guzmán made a mistake.

[145] Ontiveros, *Toribio Ortega*, p. 107, says that Ávila only brought back 60,000 rounds, but Granados and Carranza may have also brought some ammunition. Cervantes, *Francisco Villa*, p. 57. Guzmán, *Memorias*, p. 205.

[146] Ontiveros, *Toribio Ortega*, p. 107. Barragán, *Revolución Constitucionalista*, 1: 243-4.

[147] Ontiveros, *Toribio Ortega*, p. 107. Cervantes, *Francisco Villa*, pp. 57-8.

Chapter 6

[1] Guzmán, *Memorias*, pp. 205-6, 252. Cervantes, *Francisco Villa*, pp. 58-9. Pazuengo, *Historia de la Revolución en Durango*, p. 72, says that Urbina gave Carranza one thousand pesos in gold coins.

[2] Ontiveros, *Toribio Ortega*, pp. 107-8.

[3] William K. Meyers, *Forge of Progress, Crucible of Revolt: The Origins of the Mexican Revolution in La Comarca Lagunera, 1880-1911*, (Albuquerque: University of New Mexico Press, 1994), pp. 28, 32, 34, 78, 145.

[4] Ibid., pp. 4, 7, 33, 116-7, 119, 121, 125, 128, 136-7, 139, 187, 230.

[5] AHSDN XI/481.5/88.445, August 26, 1913, orders for Colonel Delgadillo. CEHM-HS 1.1.30.1 Cándido Aguilar's Report. Sánchez Lamego, *Constitucionalista*, 3: 84-6.

[6] Sánchez Lamego, *Constitucionalista*, 3: 86-7.

[7] Calzadíaz, *Hecho Reales*, 1:129-30, Major Julio Piña formed a cavalry squadron in the two day September 20-21 time frame, and a week later had enough to make a regiment from recruits at Hacienda Santa Teresa, which was in the vicinity of Torreón.

[8] Guzmán, *Memorias*, pp. 206-7. Calzadíaz, *Hecho Reales*, 1:129-30. Cervantes, *Francisco Villa*, pp. 58-9. Sánchez Lamego, *Constitucionalista*, 3: 86-7.

[9] Ontiveros, *Toribio Ortega*, p. 108. Cervantes, *Francisco Villa*, pp. 58-9.

[10] Guzmán, *Memorias*, pp. 206-7. Sánchez Lamego, *Constitucionalista*, 3: 65, 86-8.

[11] Guzmán, *Memorias*, pp. 206-7. Sánchez Lamego, *Constitucionalista*, 3: 86-7.

[12] Guzmán, *Memorias*, pp. 207-8.

[13] Ontiveros, *Toribio Ortega*, p. 108. Ibid., pp. 206-8. Sánchez Lamego, *Constitucionalista*, 3: 65, 84-8.

[14] Ontiveros, *Toribio Ortega*, pp. 108-9.

[15] Ibid., p. 109.

[16] AJBT 1/1/14-16, October 6, 1913, official battle report by Villa. Barragán, *Revolución Constitucionalista*, 1: 689-90 (also contains Villa's report). Ibid. Pazuengo, *Historia de la Revolución en Durango*, p. 71. Guzmán, *Memorias*, pp. 208-9.

[17] Pazuengo, *Historia de la Revolución en Durango*, p. 71. Barragán, *Revolución Constitucionalista*, 1: 264. Calzadíaz, *Hecho Reales*, 1:134. Ontiveros, *Toribio Ortega*, pp. 109-10, 121. Sánchez Lamego, *Constitucionalista*, 3: 88-90.

[18] Sánchez Lamego, *Constitucionalista*, 4: 103-4, Anaya's report.

[19] Ibid, 3: 90-1; 4: 103-8, the official Federal battle report.

[20] Ibid., 3: 90-1.

[21] Guzmán, *Memorias*, pp. 210-11. Ontiveros, *Toribio Ortega*, p. 110, said combat began at noon. Ibid. There is some discrepancy here about Campa's Colorados, whom Munguía says covered the San Antonio Cut, while the Constitutionalist version holds that Campa was pushed back to La Pila Hill. If true, Campa most likely proceeded to the relative safety of the San Antonio Cut. Calzadíaz, *Hecho Reales*, 1: 136-7, 140.

[22] Ontiveros, *Toribio_Ortega*, p. 110. Guzmán, *Memorias*, p. 211. Sánchez Lamego, *Constitucionalista*, 3: 91-2; 4: 94-5.

[23] Sánchez Lamego, *Constitucionalista*, 3: 92-3; 4: 96-7, Munguía's report. Ontiveros, *Toribio Ortega*, p. 110.

[24] Ontiveros, *Toribio Ortega*, p. 110. Guzmán, *Memorias*, pp. 211-2. Sánchez Lamego, *Constitucionalista*, 3: 92-4. Benavides, *Las Grandes Batallas*, pp. 30-1.

[25] Sánchez Lamego, *Constitucionalista*, 3: 93-4; 4: 97-8 (from Munguía's report), 105-6 (from Anaya's report).

[26] Barragán, *Revolución Constitucionalista*, 1: 691, Villa's report.

[27] Rubio, *La Revolución Triunfante*, p. 116; General Munguía had sent Alvírez to engage Villa instead of remaining inside Torreón, and Alvírez had been annihilated in the process. Pazuengo, *Historia de la Revolución en Durango*, p. 71, also repeated the belief that "One day General Alvírez resolved to advance against Durango with just six hundred men, against the opinion of General Bravo who saw in this an act of imprudence."

[28] Sánchez Lamego, *Constitucionalista*, 3: 88, 94-5.

[29] Friedrich Katz, *La Guerra Secreta en México: Europa, Estados Unidos, y la Revolución Mexicana*. (México: Ediciones Era, 1981), pp. 184, 195-6, 214, 216, 270-1. Meyer, *Huerta*, pp. 146-54.

[30] AHSDN XI/481.5/88.522, Decree 453 signed October 15, 1913. AHSDN XI/481.5/88.545, Decree 454: raised permanent army to 150,000 men, October 24, 1913. AHSDN XI/481.5/88.547-548, Decree 455: increased Plana Mayor, October 24, 1913. NARA-USDS 812.20.

[31] Ontiveros, *Toribio Ortega*, p. 111. Guzmán, *Memorias*, p. 214.

[32] Ontiveros, *Toribio Ortega*, pp. 134-5. London, *México Intervenido*, p. 108, the Constitutionalist major of London's acquaintance "was a veteran, with four years at war. It had been a long struggle, days and weeks of hunger, times that just thinking of a tortilla made them languish in nostalgia. [Eating only] a simple piece of meat, without condiment, cooked directly on the fire could get old after a month."

[33] Ibid., p. 111. Guzmán, *Memorias*, pp. 215-6. Calzadíaz, *Hecho Reales*, 1:143-4.

[34] Ontiveros, *Toribio Ortega*, p. 111.

[35] Sánchez Lamego, *Constitucionalista*, 3: 223-4; 4: 274-5 (Caraveo's report). Ibid., p. 112.

[36] Sánchez Lamego, *Constitucionalista*, 3: 224; 4: 275 (Caraveo's report). Ontiveros, *Toribio Ortega*, p. 112.

[37] Ibid.

[38] Sánchez Lamego, *Constitucionalista*, 3: 225; 4: 275 (Caraveo's report), 280 (Mercado's report). Ontiveros, *Toribio Ortega*, p. 112-3.

[39] Ontiveros, *Toribio Ortega*, p. 113.

[40] Ibid., p. 115, claims Urbina was ill. Guzmán, *Memorias*, pp. 216-9. Calzadíaz, *Hecho Reales*, 1:146-7.

[41] Sánchez Lamego, *Constitucionalista*, 4: 275 (Caraveo's report). Ontiveros, *Toribio Ortega*, p. 113. See Caraveo, *Crónica*, pp. 79-80, regarding orders to retreat without battle.

[42] Ontiveros, *Toribio Ortega*, p. 113, Yuriar in the brothel version. Guzmán, *Memorias*, pp. 205, 220, Yuriar insubordinate. Calzadíaz, *Hecho Reales*, 1:144-6, Yuriar for resisting the ordinances and as an example to Chao. Katz, *Pancho Villa*, 1: 344, says only that Villa shot Yuriar for drunken insubordination for refusing to enter into combat, but mentions Chao almost being shot for "disloyalty" in the sentence immediately following. Katz offers these two examples as exceptions to the rule that "Villa never ordered any of his leading officers executed," an erroneous statement.

[43] Guzmán, *Memorias*, pp. 218-23. Calzadíaz, *Hecho_Reales*, 1:147. Benavides, *Las Grandes Batallas*, p. 47.

[44] Ontiveros, *Toribio Ortega*, p. 134.

[45] José Reyes Estrada, *Sangre y Metralla: Cinco Días de Lucha a las Puertas de Chihuahua*, (Chihuahua?: El Libro Rojo, 1913), p. 3. Reyes' pamphlet, like Ontiveros' book, says that the fighting took place from November 5 to November 10 and contains more detail than Mercado's report or Guzman's book. Hence, Reyes and Ontiveros' accounts received greater weight in the narrative.

[46] Ibid., pp. 3-4.

[47] Ibid., p. 5. Calzadíaz, *Hecho Reales*, 1:147.

[48] Reyes, *Sangre y Metralla*, p. 4. Benavides, *Las Grandes Batallas*, p. 51, Mercado's report. Sánchez Lamego, *Constitucionalista*, 3: 228-31.

[49] Other units mentioned in the historical record of unknown strength that do not appear in the estimated troop strength table include: the Civiles de Chihuahua Corps commanded by José Sáenz Botello; Lázaro Alanís' Guerrilla, Enrique Sáenz D.'s Eduardo Armendariz Guerrilla, and the Esteban Coronado Irregular Corps.

[50] Reyes, *Sangre y Metralla*, p. 4. Sánchez Lamego, *Constitucionalista*, 3: 228-31.

[51] Reyes, *Sangre y Metralla*, pp. 4-5. Sánchez Lamego, *Constitucionalista*, 3: 228-32.

[52] Benavides, *Las Grandes Batallas*, pp. 49-52, Mercado's report. Reyes, *Sangre y Metralla*, pp. 4-5, Reyes mentions a Major Paliza who commanded the guns on Alamo, but neither the 1910 nor the 1914 Federal Army Escalafón contains any artillery officer with that surname. Sánchez Lamego, *Constitucionalista*, 3: 228-32.

[53] Ontiveros, *Toribio Ortega*, p. 114.

[54] Guzmán, *Memorias*, pp. 222-3. Calzadíaz, *Hecho Reales*, 1:147-8. Caraveo, *Crónica*, pp. 79-80, does not necessarily confirm the disposition of Villa's various commands, but does confirm three main columns that he numbered about 7,000 in total.

[55] Reyes, *Sangre y Metralla*, pp. 5-6. Ontiveros, *Toribio Ortega*, pp. 114, 116. Benavides, *Las Grandes Batallas*, p. 50, Mercado's report. Guzmán, *Memorias*, pp. 223-224.

[56] Reyes, *Sangre y Metralla*, pp. 6-7.

[57] Ibid. Caraveo, *Crónica*, p. 81, confirms that fighting around Chuvíscar dam at times became so fierce that Caraveo's men engaged in hand-to-hand combat.

[58] Reyes, *Sangre y Metralla*, p. 7. Ontiveros, *Toribio Ortega*, p. 116.

[59] Reyes, *Sangre y Metralla*, p. 9.

[60] Ibid., pp. 8-9. Ontiveros, *Toribio Ortega*, p. 114. Guzmán, *Memorias*, p. 224.

[61] Benavides, *Las Grandes Batallas*, p. 48. Guzmán, *Memorias*, p. 224. Calzadíaz, *Hecho Reales*, 1:149-50.

[62] Reyes, *Sangre y Metralla*, pp. 8-9.

[63] Ibid., pp. 9-10, 12. Ontiveros, *Toribio Ortega*, p. 114. Guzmán, *Memorias*, p. 225.

[64] Reyes, *Sangre y Metralla*, p. 10.

[65] Ibid., pp. 10-11.

[66] Ibid., pp. 11-12.

[67] Ontiveros, *Toribio Ortega*, p. 115.

[68] Reyes, *Sangre y Metralla*, pp. 12-13. Ibid., pp. 114-15.

[69] Reyes, *Sangre y Metralla*, p. 13. Ontiveros, *Toribio Ortega*, p. 114.

[70] Ontiveros, *Toribio Ortega*, p. 115. Guzmán, *Memorias*, p. 225. Benavides, *Las Grandes Batallas*, p. 49. Cervantes, *Francisco Villa*, pp. 63-4. Calzadíaz, *Hecho Reales*, 1: 151, contains the names of others killed and wounded in the explosion.

[71] Ontiveros, *Toribio Ortega*, p. 115.

[72] Ibid., p. 116.

[73] Reyes, *Sangre y Metralla*, pp. 13-14.

[74] Ibid., pp. 14-15. Sánchez Lamego, *Constitucionalista*, 3: 233.

[75] Ontiveros, *Toribio Ortega*, p. 116. Reyes, *Sangre y Metralla*, pp. 15, 17. Guzmán, *Memorias*, pp. 224-5.

[76] Ontiveros, *Toribio Ortega*, pp. 116-17.

[77] Reyes, *Sangre y Metralla*, pp. 16-18. Benavides, *Las Grandes Batallas*, p. 52, Mercado's report.

[78] Benavides, *Las Grandes Batallas*, pp. 49-50.

[79] Ontiveros, *Toribio Ortega*, p. 117. Reyes, *Sangre y Metralla*, p. 16.

[80] Sánchez Lamego, *Constitucionalista*, 3: 233-4.

[81] Benavides, *Las Grandes Batallas*, p. 51, Mercado's report credited General Salazar, who responded to Mercado's requests to reinforce various points during the battle with "the great part of the success of operations." See Guzmán, *Memorias*, p. 218, where Medina warns Villa about three-fourths of Chihuahua City's defenders being Colorados.

[82] Benavides, *Las Grandes Batallas*, pp. 51-2, Mercado's report.

[83] Ontiveros, *Toribio Ortega*, pp. 117-18.

[84] Ibid., p. 115.

[85] Ibid., pp. 117, 119. Villa, *Pancho Villa*, p. 538. Juvenal (pseudonym for Enrique Pérez Rul), *Quien es Francisco Villa?* (Dallas: Impr. Poliglota, 1916), p. 65. Caraveo, *Crónica*, p. 81. Guzmán, *Memorias*, pp. 226-7.

[86] Villa, *Pancho Villa*, pp. 538-40. Ontiveros, *Toribio Ortega*, p. 120. Cervantes, *Francisco Villa*, p. 64. Guzmán, *Memorias*, pp. 227-8.

[87] Caraveo, *Crónica*, p. 81, says the action with Villa's rearguard took place at Arados Station (Ojo de Agua) and that the Villistas initiated the action. Sánchez Lamego, *Constitucionalista*, 3: 241-2; 4: 277 (Caraveo's report), 295, General Mercado's report to the Secretary of War.

[88] Sánchez Lamego, *Historia Constitucionalista*, 4: 295, General Mercado's report to the Secretary of War.

[89] Ontiveros, *Toribio Ortega*, p. 119.

[90] Caraveo, *Crónica*, p. 81, says the action with Villa's rearguard took place at Ojo de Agua, and that the Villistas initiated the action. Sánchez Lamego, *Historia Constitucionalista*, 3: 241-2; 4: 277 (Caraveo's report). Ontiveros, *Toribio Ortega*, pp. 119-20.

[91] Villa, *Pancho Villa*, p. 540.

[92] Ontiveros, *Toribio Ortega*, p. 120.

[93] Cervantes, *Francisco Villa*, pp. 64-5. Guzmán, *Memorias*, pp. 229-32, 238. Calzadíaz, *Hechos Reales*, 1: 153, 155.

[94] Ontiveros, *Toribio Ortega*, pp. 120-1. Guzmán, *Memorias*, p. 230. Luis and Adrian Aguirre Benavides, *Las Grandes Batallas de la División del Norte al Mando de Pancho Villa*, (México: Editorial Diana, S.A., 1964), p. 29, says the artillerist and future historian Elías Torres was among the Federal artillery officers captured, but Ontiveros, *Toribio Ortega*, pp. 109-10, 121, says that Federal artillery Captain Elías Torres captured at Second Torreón returned the favor of being spared by betraying Villa and that "Captain Torres" was killed after being recaptured in Ciudad Juárez. In his book on Villa, Elías L. Torres, *20 Vibrantes Episodios de la Vida de Villa: fragmentos de la vida revolucionaria del general Francisco Villa* (México: Editorial Sayrols, S. A., 1934), pp. 7-16, Torres does not use the first person in the part that covers Villa's Chihuahua campaign (which he surely would have done had he been present), and in the introduction he says that he was neither a supporter nor enemy of Villa and had never served under him, but did visit him at Canutillo to gather notes, so it seems more likely that Elías Torres the engineer and historian was not the same as Elías Torres the artillery officer, and the Benavides brothers were mistaken.

[95] Ontiveros, *Toribio Ortega*, p. 121. Caraveo, *Crónica*, p. 81, gives the name of the Colorado commander as Colonel Enrique Portillo, doubtfully the same as the Constitutionalist officer wounded at Torreón. Guzmán, *Memorias*, p. 231.

[96] Villa, *Pancho Villa*, p. 540. Ontiveros, *Toribio Ortega*, p. 121.

[97] Barragán, *Revolución Constitucionalista*, 1: 269. Guzmán, *Memorias*, pp. 236-7, 254. Calzadíaz, *Hecho Reales*, 1: 157.

[98] Ontiveros, *Toribio Ortega*, pp. 122-3. Barragán, *Revolución Constitucionalista*, 1: 269. Benavides, *Las Grandes Batallas*, p. 71. Cervantes, *Francisco Villa*, pp. 670-671. Guzmán, *Memorias*, pp. 231-2, 236-7, 238, 240-1, 384. Calzadíaz, *Hechos Reales*, 1: 153, 155.

[99] Barragán, *Revolución Constitucionalista*, 1: 270; Calles reported the front as twelve miles (nineteen kilometers) long. Guzmán, *Memorias*, pp. 240-5.

[100] Guzmán, *Memorias*, pp. 243-5. Benavides, *Las Grandes Batallas*, p. 72.

[101] Sánchez Lamego, *Historia Constitucionalista*, 3: 241-2.

[102] Ontiveros, *Toribio Ortega*, pp. 122-3. Benavides, *Las Grandes Batallas*, p. 72. Guzmán, *Memorias*, pp. 245-6.

[103] Guzmán, *Memorias*, pp. 246-7.

[104] Ibid., p. 247.

[105] Ontiveros, *Toribio Ortega*, p. 123. Ibid., pp. 246-8.

[106] Ontiveros, *Toribio Ortega*, p. 123, Ontiveros used the phrase, "Huerta's mercenaries." Guzmán, *Memorias*, pp. 248-50. Calzadíaz, *Hecho Reales*, 1: 159.

[107] Ontiveros, *Toribio Ortega*, pp. 123-4.

[108] Guzmán, *Memorias*, p. 247.

[109] Rubio, *La Revolución Triunfante*, pp. 117-21.

[110] Sánchez Lamego, *Historia Constitucionalista*, 4: 295-6, General Mercado's report to the Secretary of War.

[111] Caraveo, *Crónica*, pp. 81-2, Caraveo always maintained in his memoirs and official reports that he had not fought at Tierra Blanca, but had only arrived in time to cover the Federal retreat and save them from utter destruction. Villa, for his part, thought Caraveo had been present with Landa's men during the battle. Ontiveros, *Toribio Ortega*, pp. 123-4, says the train crash happened at Ranchería Station. Sánchez Lamego, *Constitucionalista*, 3: 246-8.

[112] AHSDN XI/481.5/31.06, January 6, 1914, Velasco's orders to link operations between North and Bravo divisions. AHSDN XI/481.5/70.12, January 10, 1914, Secretary of War and Navy memo that cites letter from José Reyes Estrada to the Secretary of Foreign Relations suggesting that Mercado's conduct should be investigated. Caraveo, *Crónica*, p. 82, "Prussian" quote. Sánchez Lamego, *Constitucionalista*, 3: 205-11, 213-17, 246-8; 4: 298-304, report from Consul General Arturo M. Elías contains the most detailed and credible description of Mercado's cowardice and ineptitude.

[113] Sánchez Lamego, *Historia Constitucionalista*, 4: 296-7, General Mercado's report to the Secretary of War.

[114] Ibid., 4: 297.

[115] Ibid. Rubio, *La Revolución Triunfante*, p. 117, the Creel commercial house had been loaning funds for the Federal payroll for six months, but on the eve of battle for the capital, the Creels had refused to front any more money, per General Rubio Navarrete. Sánchez Lamego, *Historia Constitucionalista*, 3: 248-250. The consummate coward, Mercado ordered prisoners in the penitentiary shot before leaving the city. Cervantes, *Francisco Villa*, p. 71, contains "caravan of death" quote.

[116] Ontiveros, *Toribio Ortega*, pp. 125-6.

[117] Ibid., pp. 126-127.

[118] Sánchez Lamego, *Historia Constitucionalista*, 4: 285, affidavit from General Salvador Mercado to the Secretary of War, written on Juan N. Medina's behalf for his personnel file.

[119] Ibid., 4: 294-295.

[120] Ibid., 4: 309, Castro's clarifications sent to the Secretary of War at the urgings of S. Diebolte, Inspector of Consulates.

[121] Ibid.

[122] Ibid., 4: 309-310.

[123] Barragán, *Revolución Constitucionalista*, 1: 269-70, 272. Luis F. Bustamante, La Defensa de "El Ébano": Los Libertarios (Tampico, Tamps.: Imprenta "El Constitucional," 1915), p. 220, "It was not Villa, but the natural strategic [sic] talent of Maclovio Herrera that won that battle."

[124] Boot, *War Made New*, p. 101.

[125] Ramos, *Un Soldado*, p. 15, Ramos affirms that "The military culture of the officers who came out of the H. Colegio Militar was European."

Chapter 7

[1] González, *Con Carranza*, 1: 77.

[2] CEHM-GRN 1.32.04, October 1913, General Téllez reporting Maass' information to General Rubio. González, *Con Carranza*, 1: 92, 96. Barragán, *Revolución Constitucionalista*, 1: 249-50.

[3] González, *Con Carranza*, 1: 77, 91-2, 94. Dates are somewhat in question, as González says that the Constitutionalists departed Rosales on October 15 and arrived in Alamo Nuevo on October 17. González left for Candela the following day and Carranza followed on October 18 or 19. But this timeline seems too late for González and Villarreal. Barragán, *Revolución Constitucionalista*, 1: 250, says Villarreal left Juárez on October 6 and González the following day, which seems more accurate.

[4] CEHM-GRN 2.35.03, October 16, 1913, from Lieutenant Colonel Enrique Luebbert to General Rubio. González, *Con Carranza*, 1: 95-6. Barragán, *Revolución Constitucionalista*, 1: 250, Barragán says that Villarreal's Constitutionalists killed seventy Federals in the Los Morales melee, but Tamez only had about seventy men,

and the Federal report only listed a handful of killed, wounded, and missing, per Luebbert's report to General Rubio.

[5] González, *Con Carranza*, 1: 92, 96. Sánchez Lamego, *Constitucionalista*, 3: 120-1.

[6] González, *Con Carranza*, 1: 96. Barragán, *Revolución Constitucionalista*, 1: 250. Sánchez Lamego, *Constitucionalista*, 3: 87, 93; Ocaranza and his brigade had remained stuck here with the relief column of Trucy Aubert during the battle for Torreón—General Munguía arrived at this same location with the remnants (1,700 of all arms) of the garrison on October 6, the same day González began his campaign for Monterrey.

[7] Barragán, *Revolución Constitucionalista*, 1: 251-3. Marquez, *El Veintiuno*, pp. 12, 47.

[8] Marquez, *El Veintiuno*, p. 56, In Ciudad Guerrero, Tamps., in July Castro had been able to equip and clothe his 450 men.

[9] Barragán, *Revolución Constitucionalista*, 1: 254-6. Besides Blanco's direct command of some 2,000 "well-armed and disciplined men," in the words of Barragán, he adds those of Generals Santos Coy, Dávila Sánchez, and Coss to reach the 4,000 mark. Add in González's 2,000 plus those of Luis Caballero, Teodoro Elizondo, Jesús Agustín Castro, Cesáreo Castro, Porfirio González, and others and the total Constitutionalist effectives operating in Nuevo León and Tamaulipas probably still did not sum up to 8,000 men, the figure that Barragán quoted.

[10] Ibid., 1: 253-6. Jorge Useta, *Impresiones de Guerra: Breve relato de los acontecimientos políticos Mexicanos comprendidos entre el mes de agosto y el noviembre de 1914* (Laredo, TX: Edición del Autor, 1915), pp. 14-18, the journalist Useta, who worked for *El Progreso* in Laredo, Texas, offered the worst impressions of Blanco, saying that after he conquered Matamoros he lost all interest in military activity, pilfered the public coffers in order to live extravagantly, suffered from delusions of grandeur, and so the First Chief had to send Lic. Jesús Acuña to recall Blanco to Sonora.

[11] CEHM-MWG 1.6.785.1, November 6, 1913, from E. Meade Fierro in Matamoros to Pablo González in the field.

[12] Although this line of thought is inaccurate, it is also ubiquitous. For a contemporary example see, Guzmán, *Memorias*, p. 644, where Villa, obviously ignorant of the issues, expresses his distaste for Carranza's transfer of Blanco as a result of the distribution of land in Tamaulipas. For a perpetuation of this error, see Silvia González Marín, *Heriberto Jara, luchador obrero en la Revolución Mexicana* (México: El Día en libros, 1984), pp. 146-7, which states that Carranza found out about the redistribution while traveling and sent Blanco a letter reproaching him for arrogating functions that properly belong to the First Chief (which was true); Carranza let the distribution stand, but began to take away Blanco's forces and sent him to Obregón in the Northwest over the matter (which was false; it was not this matter that got Blanco fired). Finally, to see an attempt by an avowed leftist to draw even further implications from this classical misunderstanding of events, and grounded in

an ignorance of the military dimensions of the Mexican Revolution, in general, see Hart, *Revolutionary Mexico*, p. 281.

[13] Barragán, *Revolución Constitucionalista*, 1: 173-4, "the first distribution of lands carried out by the Revolution…[in August, 1913 under] General Lucio Blanco, stimulated…particularly through the efforts to realize this work by his Chief of Staff, Francisco J. Múgico."

[14] González, *Con Carranza*, 1: 95-6. Barragán, *Revolución Constitucionalista*, 1: 256. Sánchez Lamego, *Constitucionalista*, 3: 121-2. *Crónica Ilustrada*, 2: 28, "Pelados."

[15] Sánchez Lamego, *Constitucionalista*, 3: 122; 4: 136-7.

[16] Ibid., 3: 122, 124; 4: 137. Barragán, *Revolución Constitucionalista*, 1: 256.

[17] Sánchez Lamego, *Constitucionalista*, 3: 122; 4: 137.

[18] CEHM-GRN 1.32.02, October, 1913, from General Téllez to General Rubio on the Matamoros operation. CEHM-MWG 1.9.1205.1, January 31, 1914, Emilio Salinas from Laredo, Texas to Pablo González reporting what had been heard from Federal officers in the Nuevo Laredo garrison about sealed orders. Barragán, *Revolución Constitucionalista*, 1: 256, Barragán personally confirmed with General Rubio, years later, that he was on his way to Mexico City and did not attend to the defense of Monterrey. Rubio, *La Revolución Triunfante*, pp. 107, 109-10, regarding Rubio Navarrete's plans and censure.

[19] Sánchez Lamego, *Constitucionalista*, 3: 124; 4: 137-8.

[20] Ibid., 3: 122; 4: 138-9. González, *Con Carranza*, 1: 98.

[21] Sánchez Lamego, *Constitucionalista*, 4: 139. González, *Con Carranza*, 1: 98. Barragán, *Revolución Constitucionalista*, 1: 257.

[22] Sánchez Lamego, *Constitucionalista*, 4: 139-40. González, *Con Carranza*, 1: 98-100, says that the Constitutionalists executed a "Major Ismael Tamez," but "Colonel Ismael Tamés" is listed in the January 31, 1914 Escalafón, p. 196, as Chief of 4th Irregular Cavalry Corps, so González must have referred to Captain Rodolfo Tamez, whom all sources agree that the Constitutionalists captured. Barragán, *Revolución Constitucionalista*, 1: 256-7.

[23] González, *Con Carranza*, 1: 100.

[24] Ibid., 1: 101. Sánchez Lamego, *Constitucionalista*, 3: 127.

[25] Sánchez Lamego, *Constitucionalista*, 3: 128; 4: 141-2 (pp. 140-9 contains Iberri's report).

[26] Ibid., 3: 127-8, it appears that Sánchez Lamego thought those present were saying that the Federals occupied Hacienda Canadá, but the mistake was his.

[27] González, *Con Carranza*, 1: 101. Ibid., 3: 128-9 (contains Francisco Urquizo's recollection); 4: 142.

[28] Sánchez Lamego, *Constitucionalista*, 3: 129-30; 4: 142.

[29] González, *Con Carranza*, 1: 101-2.

[30] Ibid., 1: 102-4.

³¹ Ibid., 1: 104. Sánchez Lamego, *Constitucionalista*, 3: 131-4. It is possible that Lieutenant Colonel Enrique Gorostieta had command of the machine guns.

³² Sánchez Lamego, *Constitucionalista*, 3: 134.

³³ González, *Con Carranza*, 1: 104.

³⁴ Ibid. Barragán, *Revolución Constitucionalista*, 1: 255; Barragán had a knack for consistently overestimating the size of forces, both Constitutionalist and Federal.

³⁵ González, *Con Carranza*, 1: 104-6.

³⁶ Ibid., 1: 105-6.

³⁷ Barragán, *Revolución Constitucionalista*, 1: 257.

³⁸ González, *Con Carranza*, 1: 108-9.

³⁹ Ibid., 1: 108, 111-3.

⁴⁰ Ibid., 1: 114.

⁴¹ Ibid., 1: 108-9, 112-14, 116-17. Urquizo, *Memorias*, p. 116, like "W," Urquizo confirms the drunkenness of Constitutionalists.

⁴² González, *Con Carranza*, 1: 115. Urquizo, *Memorias*, p. 116, also lists the Constitutionalist idea of not keeping plazas at the time as a reason for the retreat. Sánchez Lamego, *Constitucionalista*, 3: 136-8.

⁴³ González, *Con Carranza*, 1: 115-16.

⁴⁴ Barragán, *Revolución Constitucionalista*, 1: 258, According to the Federal version of events, Ocaranza got held up by the condition of the rails and had to send the cavalry ahead overland under General Ricardo Peña, who allegedly drove off the Constitutionalists with a bold mounted charge. Barragán denies that Peña's celebrated cavalry charge ever took place and says that no one has ever been able to figure out where the story of Peña's fabled charge originated, Barragán, *Revolución Constitucionalista*, 1: 258. "W" González also denies Peña's famous cavalry charge ever took place, and says the Federals did not even give pursuit, Ibid., 1: 115-17.

⁴⁵ Barragán, *Revolución Constitucionalista*, 1: 256, 259; Barragán was among those who loaded up on the trains to head for Monterrey after Blanco had left the scene. Andrés Saucedo received tactical command of Blanco's brigade, while General Jesús Dávila Sánchez became the new zone commander.

⁴⁶ CEHM-MWG 1.7.846.1, November 27, 1913, from Venustiano Carranza in Hermosillo to Pablo González in Brownsville.

⁴⁷ Marquez, *El Veintiuno*, pp. 47-8, 56-7.

⁴⁸ González, *Con Carranza*, 1: 116-17. Barragán, *Revolución Constitucionalista*, 1: 260; says Castro's brigade joined with González's column at San Francisco de Apodaca on 26 October. Sánchez Lamego, *Constitucionalista*, 3: 119, date of González's promotion.

⁴⁹ González, *Con Carranza*, 1: 116-7. Barragán, *Revolución Constitucionalista*, 1: 258.

⁵⁰ Sánchez Lamego, *Constitucionalista*, 3: 138-139, contains General Sánchez Lamego's analysis.

[51] Rubio, *La Revolución Triunfante*, pp. 55.

[52] AHSDN XI/481.5/88.34, April 4, 1913, Undersecretary of Foreign Relations, Carlos Pereyra, informs Secretary of War of a February 28, 1913 report from the Texas City consul about 6,000 American soldiers who will be "the first to advance," if necessary.

[53] Rubio, *La Revolución Triunfante*, pp. 109-10, Rubio only learned of the reasoning behind his orders not to abandon the rail lines much later. Meyer, *Huerta*, pp. 146-54.

[54] González, *Con Carranza*, 1: 116, 119. Sánchez Lamego, *Constitucionalista*, 3: 140.

[55] González, *Con Carranza*, 1: 120. Sánchez Lamego, *Constitucionalista*, 3: 141.

[56] González, *Con Carranza*, 1: 120-1.

[57] Ibid., 1: 121-2. Sánchez Lamego, *Constitucionalista*, 3: 141-2.

[58] González, *Con Carranza*, 1: 122.

[59] Ibid., 1: 122-3.

[60] Ibid., 1: 124.

[61] CEHM-MWG 1.6.779.1, November 2, 1913, Villareal to González. Ibid., 1: 124-5. Barragán, *Revolución Constitucionalista*, 1: 260.

[62] CEHM-MWG 1.6.780.1, November 3, 1913, from Artigas in Los Aldamas to González. Barragán, *Revolución Constitucionalista*, 1: 289. Sánchez Lamego, *Constitucionalista*, 3: 143.

[63] González, *Con Carranza*, 1: 127. Sánchez Lamego, *Constitucionalista*, 3: 143-5.

[64] González, *Con Carranza*, 1: 127-8. Sánchez Lamego, *Constitucionalista*, 3: 143-4.

[65] CEHM-MWG 1.6.781.1, November 3, 1913, Castro's report to González. González, *Con Carranza*, 1: 127.

[66] CEHM-MWG 1.6.781.1, November 3, 1913, Castro's report to González. González, *Con Carranza*, 1: 127-8, 130. Sánchez Lamego, *Constitucionalista*, 3: 144.

[67] CEHM-MWG 1.6.784.1, November 4, 1913, Castro's report to González. CEHM-MWG 1.6.782.1, November 4, 1913, Chief of Staff Major A. de la Vega, confirms orders with Pablo González to cut railroad. González, *Con Carranza*, 1: 128-9. Sánchez Lamego, *Constitucionalista*, 3: 144.

[68] CEHM-MWG 1.6.784.1. González, *Con Carranza*, 1: 130. Sánchez Lamego, *Constitucionalista*, 3: 144-5.

[69] CEHM-MWG 1.6.784.1. CEHM-MWG 1.6.783.1, November 4, 1913, Chief of Staff Major Arturo de la Vega, reports Castro's brigade being attacked upon leaving the Santa Rosalía Hacienda by a Federal force arriving by train, unsure of their numbers, but confident in his ability to beat them. González, *Con Carranza*, 1: 129-30.

[70] CEHM-MWG 1.6.784.1. González, *Con Carranza*, 1: 130.

[71] Ibid. CEHM-MWG 1.7.812.1, 2, November 16, 1913, reports on skirmishes involving Lieutenant Colonel Porfirio González's men in China, among other minor movements.

[72] González, *Con Carranza*, 1: 128-9. Sánchez Lamego, *Constitucionalista*, 3: 143-6. The combined Federal commands reached Monterrey on November 7.

[73] CEHM-GRN 2.62.02, April 11, 1930, letter from General Rubio to the editor of *El Universal*, rebutting an article by General Juan Barragán. Sánchez Lamego, *Constitucionalista*, 4: 155, Arzamendi's report where he mentions Peña's orders to return to Monterrey. Rubio, *La Revolución Triunfante*, p. 111.

[74] CEHM-MWG 1.7.826.1, November 19, 1913 from Pablo González to C. Undersecretary of War and Navy, Hermosillo, Sonora. González, *Con Carranza*, 1: 130-1. Sánchez Lamego, *Constitucionalista*, 3: 147-8.

[75] CEHM-MWG 1.7.826.1, November 19, 1913 from Pablo González to C. Undersecretary of War and Navy, Hermosillo, Sonora, arrived at Santander Jiménez on November 9. CEHM-MWG 1.6.801.1, November 14, 1913; and CEHM-MWG 1.6.808.1, November 15, 1913, Francisco J. Múgica to Pablo González regarding stolen corn. González, *Con Carranza*, 1: 132. Sánchez Lamego, *Constitucionalista*, 3: 147-8.

[76] CEHM-MWG 1.6.785.1, November 6, 1913, and CEHM-MWG 1.6.795.1, November 12, 1913, from E. Meade Fierro in Matamoros to Pablo González in the field. CEHM-MWG 1.7.820.1, November 18, 1913, General Luis Caballero's appointment to Military Chief and Governor of Tamaulipas.

[77] González, *Con Carranza*, 1: 134. Sánchez Lamego, *Constitucionalista*, 3: 147-8.

[78] CEHM-MWG 1.6.794.1, November 11, 1913, Castro responding to González's orders to resume advance on Ciudad Victoria.

[79] CEHM-MWG 1.6.797.1, November 13, 1913, Cesáreo Castro to Pablo González.

[80] González, *Con Carranza*, 1: 133-4.

[81] CEHM-MWG 1.6.798.1, November 14, 1913, González to his comrades in arms.

[82] CEHM-MWG 1.6.802.1, November 14, 1913, General Higinio Aguilar to Aurelio Blanquet.

[83] CEHM-MWG 1.6.809.1, November 15, 1913, General Higinio Aguilar to Victoriano Huerta.

[84] CEHM-MWG 1.7.826.1. González, *Con Carranza*, 1: 134, 137-8.

[85] González, *Con Carranza*, 1: 138. Sánchez Lamego, *Constitucionalista*, 3: 151-3.

[86] González, *Con Carranza*, 1: 138-9.

[87] Barragán, *Revolución Constitucionalista*, 1: 290. Sánchez Lamego, *Constitucionalista*, 3: 150-1. CEHM-MWG 1.6.800.1, November 14, 1913, from Arzamendi (?) to Division Chief (Téllez) giving total troops available, which tops the 700 that he reported to War.

[88] González, *Con Carranza*, 1: 142. Sánchez Lamego, *Constitucionalista*, 3: 150-2.

[89] Sánchez Lamego, *Constitucionalista*, 3: 148.

[90] González, *Con Carranza*, 1: 142. Sánchez Lamego, *Constitucionalista*, 3: 153.

[91] González, *Con Carranza*, 1: 141-2.

[92] CEHM-MWG 1.7.816.1, November 17, 1913, from General Cesario Castro and Lazo de la Vega on the outskirts of C. Victoria to Pablo González. González says that Castro spent the night at Hacienda de la Diana, but Castro's report stated he departed from his encampment at Santa Engracia, González, *Con Carranza*, 1: 142.

[93] Ibid.

[94] CEHM-MWG 1.7.816.1.

[95] Ibid.

[96] CEHM-MWG 1.7.811.1, November 16, 1913, J. Agustín Castro to González. CEHM-MWG 1.7.824.1, November 18, 1913, General J. A. Castro from Headquarters in Victoria to C. General in Chief of the Division of the Northeast, Pablo González. CEHM-MWG 1.7.826.1; says General J. Agustin Castro attacked through the cemetery. González, *Con Carranza*, 1: 142-3. Marquez, *El Veintiuno*, p. 48. Sánchez Lamego, *Constitucionalista*, 3: 154.

[97] CEHM-MWG 1.7.824.1. CEHM-MWG 1.7.834.1, November 21, 1913, Antonio I. Villarreal in Ciudad Victoria to General of Brigade, Jefe of the Division of the Northeast Pablo González.

[98] González, *Con Carranza*, 1: 143-4.

[99] Ibid., 1: 143.

[100] CEHM-MWG 1.7.813.1, November 16, 1913, J. Agustín Castro from the edge of Victoria to General Pablo González. CEHM-MWG 1.7.824.1.

[101] Ibid.

[102] CEHM-MWG 1.7.824.1. Marquez, *El Veintiuno*, pp. 48, 56-7.

[103] CEHM-MWG 1.7.826.1. CEHM-MWG 1.7.834.1. González, *Con Carranza*, 1: 146.

[104] CEHM-MWG 1.7.826.1. CEHM-MWG 1.7.834.1.

[105] CEHM-MWG 1.7.826.1.

[106] González, *Con Carranza*, 1: 144-5.

[107] Barragán, *Revolución Constitucionalista*, 1: 697-8. González, *Con Carranza*, pp. 141-51. Sánchez Lamego, *Constitucionalista*, 3: 154-5.

[108] González, *Con Carranza*, 1: 147.

[109] CEHM-MWG 1.7.818.1; CEHM-MWG 1.7.819.1, November 17, 1913, Carranza to González.

[110] González, *Con Carranza*, 1: 146.

[111] CEHM-MWG 1.7.814.1, November 17, 1913, J. Agustín Castro from Camp in Victoria to General Pablo González. CEHM-MWG 1.7.817.1, November 17, 1913, General Cesarío [in early reports, Don Cesáreo signed his name "Cesarío"] Castro from camp on the outskirts of C. Victoria to Pablo González regarding the shortage of Mauser ammunition. CEHM-MWG 1.7.824.1. CEHM-MWG 1.7.826.1. González, *Con Carranza*, 1: 150. Marquez, *El Veintiuno*, p. 48, Jesús Agustín Castro stated that when he saw that no progress had been made by noon, he ordered

Navarrete to take Molina de Terán at all costs, which he did after three hours of heated combat, since the mill was the key to the city's defense. Given J. Agustín Castro's character and that of Don Cesáreo, the latter's account is considered more accurate, although based on his performance in other battles there is no doubt that Navarrete conducted himself honorably in this engagement.

[112] CEHM-MWG 1.7.814.1. CEHM-MWG 1.7.815.1, November 17, 1913, J. Agustín Castro from the edge of Victoria to General Pablo González. Sánchez Lamego, *Constitucionalista*, 3: 155-6.

[113] CEHM-MWG 1.7.834.1.

[114] González, *Con Carranza*, 1: 148.

[115] Sánchez Lamego, *Constitucionalista*, 3: 155-6.

[116] CEHM-MWG 1.7.824.1: Castro claimed that his men recovered four cannons with their breechblocks removed, eighty-eight unfired shells and some empty shell casings, as well as about forty new Mauser rifles and some 8-mm. ammunition, but since the Constitutionalists only captured four cannons in total, Villarreal gave the credit to Murguía's men, and Castro's boastfulness, his report is suspect. CEHM-MWG 1.7.834.1. González, *Con Carranza*, 1: 150. Sánchez Lamego, *Constitucionalista*, 3: 155-6.

[117] González, *Con Carranza*, 1: 151-2.

[118] CEHM-MWG 1.7.826.1. Sánchez Lamego, *Constitucionalista*, 3: 157. Sánchez Lamego states that the Constitutionalists must have been mistaken about capturing four guns when the Federal artillery officer mentioned only commanded two guns, but generals Castro, Villarreal, and González all cited four cannons captured.

[119] CEHM-MWG 1.7.816.1. CEHM-MWG 1.7.824.1. CEHM-MWG 1.7.834.1.

[120] CEHM-MWG 1.7.824.1.

[121] CEHM-MWG 1.7.834.1.

[122] CEHM-MWG 1.7.826.1. CEHM-MWG 1.7.834.1. Sánchez Lamego, *Constitucionalista*, 3: 157-8.

[123] CEHM-MWG 1.7.832.1, November 20, 1913, from General Cesario Castro to Pablo González.

[124] CEHM-MWG 1.7.832.1. González, *Con Carranza*, 1: 151.

[125] Sánchez Lamego, *Constitucionalista*, 3: 159.

[126] CEHM-GRN 2.64.02, November 19, 1943, is copy of a letter from General Rubio Navarrete to a magazine correcting some errors of fact in an article. CEHM-GRN 2.36.02, typewritten manuscript of November events.

[127] CEHM-GRN 2.36.02. CEHM-MWG 1.6.800.1, November 14, 1913, Tula, Jaumave, and Tampico garrison strengths.

[128] CEHM-MWG 1.6.803.1, November 15, 1913, campaign suggestions from Constitutionalist Generals J[osé] Isabel Robles and Juan E. Gómez at the "Seguín Military Camp" to Lucio Blanco, Pablo González, and Jesús Carranza, "wherever you may be."

[129] Ibid.

[130] Ontiveros, *Toribio Ortega*, p. 119.

[131] CEHM-GRN 2.36.02. CEHM-GRN 1.7.1, page 2 of a written manuscript. CEHM-GRN 2.64.02.

[132] CEHM-GRN 2.36.02. CEHM-GRN 1.7.1. CEHM-GRN 2.64.02. CEHM-GRN 2.39.01 Report of Santa Engracia has the feel of an official document, but not the look, since there is no date, letterhead, or rubric.

[133] CEHM-GRN 2.39.01. CEHM-GRN 2.36.02. CEHM-GRN 2.39.02, manuscript and notes by Rubio.

[134] CEHM-GRN 2.36.02. CEHM-GRN 2.39.01. CEHM-GRN 2.39.02. CEHM-GRN 2.42.01, January 26, 1914, Rubio's report with map.

[135] CEHM-GRN 2.36.02. CEHM-GRN 1.32.20, November 20, 1913, from Téllez in Monterrey to Rubio, received in La Cruz Tamaulipas. CEHM-GRN 2.39.01. CEHM-GRN 2.39.02.

[136] CEHM-GRN 2.36.02.

[137] CEHM-GRN 2.39.01.

[138] González, *Con Carranza*, 1: 155-6.

[139] CEHM-GRN 2.39.01. CEHM-GRN 2.42.01. CEHM-MWG 1.7.836.1, November 23, 1913, from General F. Murguía Santa Elena to General in Chief P. González. Ibid., 1: 156. Rubio, *La Revolución Triunfante*, pp. 112-13.

[140] CEHM-GRN 2.39.01. González, *Con Carranza*, 1: 156. Barragán, *Revolución Constitucionalista*, 1: 292. The sources do not say which flank Caballero and Castro occupied, respectively.

[141] CEHM-GRN 2.36.02, contains "martillo defensive" statement. CEHM-GRN 2.39.01.

[142] CEHM-GRN 2.36.02. CEHM-GRN 2.64.02. CEHM-GRN 1.32.20.

[143] CEHM-GRN 2.39.01. González, *Con Carranza*, 1: 156-8.

[144] CEHM-GRN 2.36.02. CEHM-GRN 2.39.01. CEHM-GRN 2.39.02. González, *Con Carranza*, 1: 156-8. Marquez, *El Veintiuno*, p. 51, J. Agustín Castro's 21st Brigade had to retreat toward Güemez when Villarreal started to withdraw his men, neither side having gained the advantage per Castro. Barragán, *Revolución Constitucionalista*, 1: 292.

[145] CEHM-GRN 2.62.01 1913, November 22, 1913, Notice of C. Victoria's capture by González sent by Rubio to Téllez on Letterhead of José y Jacobo Martínez Hacienda de Santa Engracia y Anexas, Tamaulipas says, "Generals Rábago, Arzamendi, and Aguilar evacuated the plaza with greater part of the garrison, after two days of combat through Jaumave and Tula. Rebels [sic] occupy Victoria and Caballeros having headquarters in Güemes [sic]; another group marches bound for the north through La Cruz. The reinforcements that I await of my troops from Lampazos can come through road Hidalgo, Santa Maríz, Santa Engracia. The enemy in yesterday's

combat had many losses but we have not fought but a third or at least a half of the enemy forces. The terrain is wooded and cavalry is indispensable for me to scout since the force from Romualdo Sanchez is on foot. The railway has [a] few breaks [and] it would be easy to fix, at least to La Cruz. The enemy had begun an advance against my column but it was repulsed...I need artillery ammunition. I have 25 wounded that I urgently need to evacuate." González, *Con Carranza*, 1: 158, González said that Rubio's Federals left behind impedimenta such as a great number of rifles, war munitions, and hats, as well as many dead, losing perhaps one thousand men in the operation, none of which sounds believable.

[146] CEHM-MWG 1.7.837.1, November 24, 1913, from General Caballero to Pablo González, relaying message from General Antonio I. Villarreal. Marquez, *El Veintiuno*, p. 51.

[147] CEHM-MWG 1.7.840.1, November 25, 1913, from General Cesáreo Castro at El Carmen Renovada Hacienda to C. Pablo González, Gen. in Chief of the Division of the Northeast, Güemez Tamps. CEHM-MWG 1.7.841.1, November 25, 1913, from General Cesáreo Castro at El Carmen Renovada Hacienda to Generals Villarreal, Castro, Murguía, and Elizondo.

[148] CEHM-MWG 1.7.840.1. CEHM-MWG 1.7.844.1, November 27, 1913, from General Caballero to Pablo González, relaying November 26 message from General Antonio I. Villarreal in Santa María Hacienda; General Cesáreo Castro in C. Victoria on November 27 told Caballero that by the night of November 26 General Villarreal should have been in possession of the ammunition.

[149] CEHM-GRN 2.39.02.

[150] CEHM-GRN 2.36.02. CEHM-GRN 1.32.31, November 25, 1913, from Rubio in Villagrán to Téllez in Monterrey.

[151] Rubio, *La Revolución Triunfante*, pp. 113-14. The Escalafón dated January 31, 1914 lists Téllez as "available in Monterrey" for duty, p. 17. See Victoriano Huerta, *Memorias de Victoriano Huerta* (México: Ediciones "Vértice," 1957), pp. 18-19. Rubio claimed that his brigade included 1,000 infantrymen, six hundred cavalry-men, one field and one mountain gun battery, a mounted squadron of machine guns, and four sections of machine guns, 2,000 men total: CEHM-GRN 1.7.1; CEHM-GRN 2.62.02, April 11, 1930, letter from General Rubio to the editor of *El Universal*, rebutting an article by General Juan Barragán. CEHM-GRN 2.36.02. Sánchez Lamego, *Constitucionalista*, 3: 214-21, chronicles Velasco's operations to re-take Torreón.

[152] CEHM-GRN 2.36.02.

[153] Ibid.

[154] González, *Con Carranza*, 1: 158.

[155] Marquez, *El Veintiuno*, pp. 51-2, 57.

Chapter 8

[1] Obregón, *Campaña*, pp. 80-1.

[2] Sánchez Lamego, *Constitucionalista*, 3: 266-9, August 25, 1913; see also Ojeda and Medina Barrón's reports, 4:320-5 (quote on 321).

[3] Ibid., 4: 321.

[4] Ibid., 4: 321-5.

[5] Ibid., 4: 322.

[6] Ibid., 3: 270-271.

[7] Obregón, *Campaña*, p. 79. Ibid., 3: 276-282.

[8] Obregón, *Campaña*, pp. 80-1.

[9] Sánchez Lamego, *Constitucionalista*, 3: 282-3.

[10] Ibid., 3: 283-285, Olague's command returned to Sinaloa on September 1 and Rodríguez reached Topolobampo the next day.

[11] Obregón, *Campaña*, pp. 81-2. Ibid., 3: 285-6.

[12] Obregón, *Campaña*, pp. 82-3. Barragán, *Revolución Constitucionalista*, 1: 186-7, 212-13, per Carranza's July 4, 1913 decree there would be seven Constitutionalist army corps—the Northwest: Sonora, Chihuahua, Durango, Sinaloa, Baja California; the Northeast: Coahuila, Nueva León, Tamaulipas; the East: Puebla, Tlaxcala, Vera Cruz; the West: Jalisco, Colima, Michoacán, Tepic; the Central: Zacatecas, Aguascalientes, San Luis Potosí, Guanajuato, Querétaro, Hidalgo, and México; the South: Morelos, Guerrero, Oaxaca; and the Southeast: Yucatán, Campeche, Tabasco, and Chiapas. Treviño, *Memorias*, p. 47, the bulk of the army was still at Maytorena Station. Antonio Manero, *La Reforma Bancaria en la Revolución Constitucionalista* (México: Biblioteca del Instituto Nacional de Estudios Históricos de la Revolución Mexicana, 1958), p. 67. González, *Heriberto Jara*, pp. 147-8, the Carranza Doctrine may have been expressed in a different speech, on September 27.

[13] Obregón, *Campaña*, pp. 83-4. Sánchez Lamego, *Constitucionalista*, 3: 285-91, the plaza of Sinaloa was defended by approximately four hundred Federals under First Captain Manuel from the 8th Infantry Battalion, 4th Artillery Regiment, 10th Scout Corps, and other irregulars including the Volunteer Corps of Sinaloa.

[14] Obregón, *Campaña*, pp. 84-6.

[15] Ibid., pp. 86-8, 95. Sánchez Lamego, *Constitucionalista*, 3: 300; Sánchez Lamego agrees with Federal Army reports that maintain the General Blanco mentioned by Obregón was in fact General José de la Luz Blanco, and not Lucio Blanco. However, the biographer of the latter maintained that the general in charge of the 3rd Regiment of Sinaloa was Lucio Blanco: Armando de María y Campos, *La Vida del General Lucio Blanco* (México: Instituto Nacional de Estudios Históricos de la Revolución Mexicana, 1963), p. 82. As Obregón does not give the first name of "General Blanco," one cannot be sure which Blanco this was, although a general of Lucio Blanco's stature would

have commanded more than a regiment, and he only departed from Matamoros in the last week of October and did not get over being "disgusted" until the end of November, when he requested permission to go on campaign in Jalisco: CEHM-MWG 1.7.846.1, November 27, 1913, from Venustiano Carranza in Hermosillo to Pablo González in Brownsville. See also Useta, *Impresiones de Guerra*, p. 17, who says that Blanco found himself waking up in Hermosillo one morning and spent the next several months organizing a regiment of cavalry.

[16] Obregón, *Campaña*, pp. 86, 88-90. Important jefes Francisco R. Manzo, Gustavo Garmendia, Carlos Félix, Antonio A. Guerrero, Antonio Norzagaray, Juan José Ríos, Esteban B. Calderón, Camilo Gastélum, Juan Mérigo and Pablo Quiroga also attended. Sánchez Lamego, *Constitucionalista*, 3: 302-3.

[17] Sánchez Lamego, *Constitucionalista*, 3: 304-5.

[18] Obregón, *Campaña*, pp. 91-2.

[19] Ibid., p. 92. Sánchez Lamego, *Constitucionalista*, 3: 301.

[20] Obregón, *Campaña*, pp. 92-4.

[21] Ibid., p. 94. Treviño, *Memorias*, pp. 51-3: says that a shell exploded and a fragment ripped open the femoral artery in his left thigh. At the conclusion of the battle the lieutenant colonel was found with a thick blood trail leading from the point of impact to the final position where he had dragged himself and bled out. Since Obregón was actually there, his version of the story, as given in the main text above, should be accepted as more factual.

[22] Obregón, *Campaña*, p. 94.

[23] Ibid., pp. 95-7.

[24] Ibid., pp. 96, 98-100, 105, on the latter page, Obregón introduces "Lucio Blanco," who left for Culiacán to begin organizing the army corps' cavalry, further suggesting that the other Blanco was José de la Luz Blanco. José de la Luz Blanco joined Obregón's command in 1913 and inexplicably left for the United States after the Battle of Culiacán on a mission that effectively amounted to exile: INEHRM, *Diccionario Histórico*, 2: 284.

[25] Pazuengo, *Historia de la Revolución en Durango*, p. 81, during October Carrasco reported four encounters with Federal detachments in Batar and the port of Mazatlán..

[26] Ibid., pp. 81-2, mistakenly says that General Miguel Rodríguez led the Federal column. Sánchez Lamego, *Constitucionalista*, 3: 292-3.

[27] Sánchez Lamego, *Constitucionalista*, 3: 294.

[28] Pazuengo, *Historia de la Revolución en Durango*, p. 82, Pazuengo says that the battle took place on the morning of October 25. Sánchez Lamego, *Constitucionalista*, 3: 294-5.

[29] Pazuengo, *Historia de la Revolución en Durango*, pp. 82-3. Sánchez Lamego, *Constitucionalista*, 3: 295.

[30] Sánchez Lamego, *Constitucionalista*, 3: 295.

[31] Pazuengo, *Historia de la Revolución en Durango*, p. 84.

[32] Ibid., pp. 84-5. Sánchez Lamego, *Constitucionalista*, 3: 295.

[33] Obregón, *Campaña*, p. 100.

[34] Ibid., pp. 99-102, quote is Obregón's.

[35] CEHM-MWG 1.7.846.1, November 27, 1913, from Venustiano Carranza in Hermosillo to Pablo González.

[36] González, *Con Carranza*, 1: 159-60.

[37] CEHM-MWG 1.7.866.1, December 6, 1913, from Pablo González in Brownsville to Venustiano Carranza in Hermosillo. González, *Con Carranza*, 1: 158-9, 170-1, González gave Castro and Elizondo their orders on November 25.

[38] González, *Con Carranza*, 1: 160.

[39] Ibid., 1: 158, 160, 162-3.

[40] Ibid., 1: 164, 166-7, 169-70, "W" González stated that Pablo González arrived at Matamoros on December 12, but this seems too late, and a December 8 letter from González to the First Chief from Matamoros with González's professed wishes to lead the Tampico battle suggests that "W" erred in his recall.

[41] Ibid., 1: 170.

[42] Ibid., 1: 153.

[43] CEHM-MWG 1.7.850.1, December 10, 1913, orders from Pablo González to Colonel Andrés Saucedo, leading the Blanco Brigade.

[44] CEHM-MWG 1.7.866.1.

[45] Ibid.

[46] CEHM-MWG 1.7.858.1, December 6, 1913, Campaign Plan Circular from Pablo González in Brownsville to be addressed to Southern Caudillos.

[47] González, *Con Carranza*, 1: 162, 164, apparently Miguel Zapata, a Constitutionalist who was serving as an escort for Colonel Vicente Segura, abandoned him and took the shipment of arms and ammunition that he had purchased with his own money in the United States.

[48] González, *Con Carranza*, p. 158. Sánchez Lamego, *Constitucionalista*, 3: 168. From December 21 to 23 Carrera Torres fought the Federals, who had reoccupied the plaza, at Tula, Beatriz Rojas, *La Pequeña Guerra: Los Carrera Torres y los Cedillo* (Zamora, Mich.: El Colegio de Michoacán, 1983), pp. 37-8.

[49] Sánchez Lamego, *Constitucionalista*, 3: 163-70. CEHM-MWG 1.7.829.1, November 20, 1913, Murguía's strength report.

[50] González, *Con Carranza*, p. 170, mentions that Villarreal reported capturing Altamira on 14 December, but says nothing more of the Battle of Tampico. Marquez, *El Veintiuno*, pp. 11-12, 54, the Battle of Tampico was suspended because of a "lack of elements," mostly meaning ammunition, and because the Constitutionalist generals did not operate in agreement. Castro's brigade was engaged in the fighting around Doña Cecilia (today Villa Madero). Sánchez Lamego, *Constitucionalista*, 3: 163-71.

Vázquez, *Poncho Vázquez*, p. 129, Villarreal's brigade covered the northern sector from Escuela del Norte to Arbol Grande.

[51] González, *Con Carranza*, 1: 178.

[52] CEHM-MWG 1.7.872.1, December 12, 1913, report from Colonel Andrés Saucedo of the Blanco Brigade in San Fernando to Pablo González. Barragán, *Revolución Constitucionalista*, 1: 293-4.

[53] Barragán, *Revolución Constitucionalista*, 1: 294.

[54] CEHM-MWG 1.7.887.1, December 21, 1913, orders from Pablo González and Chief of Staff Alberto Fuentes D[ávila] to Sr. Col. Andres Saucedo in Sabinas Hidalgo. González, *Con Carranza*, 1: 170-1.

[55] González, *Con Carranza*, 1: 177-8.

[56] Ibid., 1: 172, reproduces Saucedo's telegram. Barragán, *Revolución Constitucionalista*, 1: 58-62, 294-6: Telegram to First Chief from Pablo González reproduced on pages 295-6 says Montes brought 80 artillerymen, two machine guns, twelve Rexers, 130 horses, 50,000 rounds, and 80 Mausers; CEHM-MWG 1.7.892.1, December 23, 1913, to the C. Jefe of Arms in Sabinas Hidalgo, N.L. [Saucedo], from Federico Montes, Ex-member of Staff of Sr. Madero, Camp in El Encino, N.L. See also CEHM-GRN 1.32.14, November 17, 1913, Lieutenant Colonel José Rebollo reports to General Salvador Herrera y Cairo, Department of Artillery, Mexico, that Lieutenant Atanasio Salgado is in the Madsen Fusilier Squadron commanded by Montes.

[57] González, *Con Carranza*, 1: 172-3.

[58] Ibid., 1: 173-4. Sánchez Lamego, *Constitucionalista*, 3: 178-9.

[59] González, *Con Carranza*, 1: 178.

[60] Barragán, *Revolución Constitucionalista*, 1: 298-9.

[61] Sánchez Lamego, *Constitucionalista*, 3: 178-9.

[62] González, *Con Carranza*, 1: 179.

[63] CEHM-MWG 1.7.908.1, January 5, 1914, from Brigadiers Jesús Dávila Sánchez and Ernesto Santos Coy, "Expeditionary Column of the Center," in Matamoros to General Pablo González.

[64] Barragán, *Revolución Constitucionalista*, 1: 300, 700-1, General Castro's report.

[65] Barragán, *Revolución Constitucionalista*, 1: 299-300, the recollection of Barragán, who was Saucedo's Chief of Staff at the time.

[66] González, *Con Carranza*, 1: 179-80. *Crónica Ilustrada*, 3: 139, recollection of future General Juan F. Azcárate.

[67] González, *Con Carranza*, 1: 180.

[68] Ibid., 1: 180. Barragán, *Revolución Constitucionalista*, 1: 300.

[69] Barragán, *Revolución Constitucionalista*, 1: 701, General Castro's report.

[70] González, *Con Carranza*, 1: 180.

[71] Ibid., 1: 180-1.

[72] Barragán, *Revolución Constitucionalista*, 1: 701-2, General Castro's report.

[73] CEHM-MWG 1.7.908.1. González, *Con Carranza*, 1: 180-1.

[74] González, *Con Carranza*, 1: 181.

[75] CEHM-MWG 1.7.908.1. Barragán, *Revolución Constitucionalista*, 1: 702, General Castro's report.

[76] Barragán, *Revolución Constitucionalista*, 1: 301.

[77] González, *Con Carranza*, 1: 181.

[78] CEHM-MWG 1.7.908.1.

[79] CEHM-MWG 1.7.918.1, January 7, 1914, from General Pablo González in Matamoros to Venustiano Carranza in Nogales, Sonora.

[80] Barragán, *Revolución Constitucionalista*, 1: 702-703, General Castro's report.

[81] CEHM-MWG 1.7.850.1, December 10, 1913, quote penciled in at the bottom of the file copy of the orders from Pablo González to Colonel Andrés Saucedo for the Blanco Brigade.

[82] Barragán, *Revolución Constitucionalista*, 1: 298-9. González, *Con Carranza*, 1: 179-80.

[83] Barragán, *Revolución Constitucionalista*, 1: 301, 702 (General Castro's report).

[84] CEHM-MWG 1.7.908.1.

[85] CEHM-MWG 1.7.918.1. UH-LVM 3.3.4 Manuscript of the Cruz Blanca; of the 150 wounded Constitutionalists taken from the battlefield to Laredo for medical attention, only six died.

[86] AHSDN XI/481.5/88.748, January 7, 1914, telegram from General Pablo González to V. Carranza (quote).

[87] CEHM-MWG 1.7.918.1, this—the only—mention of materiel aid from the U.S. to the Constitutionalists, while perplexing, must be mentioned and dispelled in order to avoid allegations of cherry-picking facts, a favored ploy in Leftist historiography.

[88] González, *Con Carranza*, 1: 180-1.

[89] CEHM-MWG 1.9.1224.1, January 31, 1914, from General Pablo González in Matamoros to Sr. D. Melquiades García Laredo, Texas. CEHM-MWG 1.9.1258.1, February 3, 1914, from Constitutionalist Colonel Emilio Salinas in Laredo, Texas to Pablo González in Matamoros. Subcommittee on Foreign Relations, *Revolutions in Mexico*, Felix Sommerfeld, a Maderista agent in El Paso testified that he had to get permission from U.S. authorities to import non-lethal war materiel such as that listed in parentheses, p. 391.

[90] CEHM-MWG 1.10.1330.1, February 8, 1914, from Juan N. Vela in Laredo, Texas to Pablo González in Matamoros; the individuals involved in these transfers as Constitutionalist agents and providers of services seemed tied to *El Radical*, the independent daily: L.L. Fierros, President; Juan N. Vela, Manager, and Manuel García Vigil, Director.

[91] Barragán, *Revolución Constitucionalista*, 1: 305, quote is Barragán's own.

[92] UH-LVM 3.3.4 Manuscript of the Cruz Blanca, many wounded Constitutionalists who recovered crossed back into Mexico to rejoin the Constitutionalist Army, evading the American authorities, who had the remaining 35 wounded soldiers incarcerated at Fort McIntosh. The White Cross got them released on April 3, 1914.

[93] Sánchez Lamego, *Constitucionalista*, 3: 130-1, 165.

Index